Medicine and the Law in the Middle Ages

Medieval Law and Its Practice

Edited by

John Hudson (St. Andrews)

Edited by

Paul Brand (*All Souls College, Oxford*)
Emanuele Conte (*Università Roma Tre / EHESS, Paris*)
Dirk Heirbaut (*University of Ghent*)
Richard Helmholz (*University of Chicago*)
Caroline Humfress (*Birkbeck, London*)
Magnus Ryan (*Peterhouse, Cambridge*)
Robin Chapman Stacey (*University of Washington*)

VOLUME 17

The titles published in this series are listed at *brill.com/mlip*

Medicine and the Law
in the Middle Ages

Edited by

Wendy J. Turner & Sara M. Butler

BRILL

LEIDEN | BOSTON

Cover illustration: Wound man. WMS 49, folio 35 recto, ink and watercolor, between 1420–30.
Courtesy of the Wellcome Trust Library, London.

Library of Congress Cataloging-in-Publication Data
Medicine and the law in the Middle Ages / edited by Wendy J. Turner & Sara M. Butler.
     pages cm. — (Medieval law and its practice, ISSN 1873-8176 ; volume 17)
   Includes bibliographical references and index.
   ISBN 978-90-04-26906-4 (hardback : alk. paper) — ISBN 978-90-04-26911-8 (e-book) 1. Medical
jurisprudence—History. 2. Medical laws and legislation. 3. Medicine, Medieval—History. I. Turner, Wendy J.
(Wendy Jo), 1961- editor of compilation. II. Butler, Sara M. (Sara Margaret) editor of compilation.
   RA1021.M43 2014
   614′.1—dc23

                                                                                    2013049495

This publication has been typeset in the multilingual 'Brill' typeface. With over 5,100 characters covering
Latin, IPA, Greek, and Cyrillic, this typeface is especially suitable for use in the humanities.
For more information, please see brill.com/brill-typeface.

ISSN 1873-8176
ISBN 978-90-04-26906-4 (hardback)
ISBN 978-90-04-26911-8 (e-book)

In memory of our friend and fellow scholar
Shona Kelly Wray
1963–2012

∴

Contents

Medicine and the Law in Hagiography   267

Acknowledgements

In April of 2011, we, Sara Butler and Wendy Turner, attended the Medieval Academy of America conference in Arizona where we talked for days about connections between law and medicine. It became apparent that more work was needed in this area. Not only was medicine as a field becoming more legal in its presentation toward the end of the Middle Ages, but also more juries were hearing testimony from medical experts on wounds, the post mortem condition of bodies, and other medical matters. Those conference exchanges laid the base for this project.

As with every major work, we are indebted to our families. Wendy wishes to thank her husband, Nathan Yanasak, for his many wondrous dinners and for his patience. Sara extends her gratitude to her husband, Mark LaBine, whose single parenting without complaint during research trips was invaluable.

This book would not be the same without the contributions by Wray. We are indebted to her sister, Maggi, in particular for allowing us access to Shona's notes on her planned essay for this volume. Shona will be missed greatly

Our many thanks to Brill's wonderful staff and editors, most especially Marcella Mulder, as well as the anonymous reviewer of this work.

About the Authors

Sara M. Butler
is an Associate Professor of History at Loyola University New Orleans. She is the author of two books: *The Language of Abuse: Marital Violence in Later Medieval England* (2007), and *Divorce in Medieval England: From One to Two Persons in Law* (2013). She is also the 2007 winner of the Sutherland Prize (the American Society for Legal History's award for the Best Article in English Legal History) for her paper, "Degrees of Culpability: Suicide Verdicts, Mercy, and the Jury in Medieval England," *Journal of Medieval and Early Modern Studies* 36.2 (2006): 263–90.

Joanna Carraway Vitiello
is an Associate Professor of Medieval History at Rockhurst University in Kansas City, Missouri. She completed her doctorate at the Centre for Medieval Studies at the University of Toronto, and her research investigates issues pertaining to law and legal procedure in late medieval Italy. Her current work focuses on archival studies of judicial records from Bologna and Reggio Emilia.

Jean Dangler
is an Associate Professor of Spanish and Medieval Iberian Studies at Tulane University. She is the author of *Mediating Fictions: Literature, Women Healers, and the Go-Between in Medieval and Early Modern Iberia* (2001) and *Making Difference in Medieval and Early Modern Iberia* (2005). Her current book project, *Edging Toward Iberia*, proposes updated frameworks and theoretical paradigms for comprehensive research on medieval Iberia. She is also working on a series of articles on the dream space and the body in late medieval Catalan literature such as the *Spill*.

Carmel Ferragud
is a Professor at the University of Valencia (Spain), where he has worked since September, 2012. Before then, he was a Professor at the University Miguel Hernández de Elche (2010–2012). He has a PhD in Geography and History from the University of Valencia (2002), where his thesis was on medical practitioners of the Crown of Aragon in the fourteenth century. His publications include *Medicina i promoció social a la Baixa Edat Mitjana (Corona d'Aragó, 1350–1410)* (2005), and *La cura dels animals: menescals i menescalia a la València medieval* (2009).

Fiona Harris-Stoertz

is an Associate Professor of History at Trent University (Canada). She is the author of several articles and book chapters on gender, childbirth, childhood, and adolescence during the High Middle Ages, and recently published an article on "Pregnancy and Childbirth in Twelfth- and Thirteenth-Century French and English Law" (2012). Harris-Stoertz is currently working on a monograph on high medieval pregnancy and childbirth.

Máire Johnson

is currently finishing her first book, *Human yet Holy: Heroic Sanctity in the Lives of Irish Saints*. She holds a doctorate from the University of Toronto's Centre for Medieval Studies and teaches classes in western civilization, medieval society, and early modern England both online and in person for multiple institutions. Her upcoming projects include work on verbal assault, criminal justice, and capital punishment in saints' *Lives* and the laws of early Ireland.

Hiram Kümper

is at the University of Bielefeld. He is the co-editor with Vladimir Simic of *Practicing New Editions. Transformation and Transfer of the Early Modern Book, ca. 1450–1800* (2011). Kümper is also the author of several articles and book chapters, including "Old Europe—(Post-)Modernity in Search for Common Cultural Roots," in Katharina Kunter, ed., *Inventing Europe. The Power of Faith, Vision and Belonging in European Unification* (2011).

Iona McCleery

is a Lecturer in Medieval History at the University of Leeds. She focuses on the history of medicine in late medieval Portugal, but her wider interests include the history of food, daily life and the cult of the saints. She has published on royal health, illness in chronicles and healing miracles. She runs *You Are What You Ate*, a Wellcome-Trust funded project that uses historical food to get modern people thinking about diet (www.leeds.ac.uk/youarewhatyouate).

Han Nijdam

is the Coordinator for the Old Frisian and the Frisian Language Database at the Fryske Akademy (Netherlands, also known as the "Frisian Academy"). His main areas of research are Old Frisian law, legal anthropology, cognitive sciences and its implications for the humanities. He has published on Old Frisian compensation tariffs, embodied honor, revenge and feud, from a comparative and cognitive perspective.

Kira Robison
is a Visiting Assistant Professor in medieval history at the University of
Alabama in Huntsville. Her research topics are varied, but revolve mainly
around medical pedagogy at the University of Bologna and the civic context
of the students and professors of medicine.

Donna Trembinski
is an Associate Professor of Medieval History at St Francis Xavier University in
Antigonish, Nova Scotia. Her research interests lie in the intersection of
disability, medicine and religion in the thirteenth century. She has published
articles in *Franciscan Studies, Florilegium* and *Journal of Ecclesiastical History*
and is currently completing a monograph on the disabilities of St Francis
of Assisi entitled *Illness and Authority: Abilities and Disabilities in the Life of
St Francis of Assisi.*

Wendy J. Turner
is a Professor of History at Georgia Regents University. She is the author of
*Care and Custody of the Mentally Ill, Incompetent, and Disabled in Medieval
England* (2013). She is the editor of two other works, *Madness in Medieval Law
and Custom* (2010) and, with Tory Vandeventer Pearman, *The Treatment of
Disabled Persons in Medieval Europe* (2010). She is also the author of several
articles on issues touching medieval mental health and medieval alchemy.
She is currently working on new projects attempting to understand the
repercussions of trauma in society and to define disability.

Katherine D. Watson
is a Senior Lecturer in the history of medicine at Oxford Brookes University
and a Fellow of the Royal Historical Society. Her research focuses on areas
where medicine, crime and the law intersect. She is the author of *Poisoned
Lives: English Poisoners and their Victims* (2004) and *Forensic Medicine in
Western Society: A History* (2011), and the editor of *Assaulting the Past: Violence
and Civilization in Historical Context* (2007). Her most recent publication,
"Women, violent crime and criminal justice in Georgian Wales," *Continuity
and Change*, 28.2 (2013), arises from research on medico-legal practice in
England and Wales 1700–1914, funded by the Wellcome Trust.

Shona Kelly Wray
was a remarkable scholar, teacher, mother, and friend—and not necessarily
in that order.

Abbreviations

AC	*Compilatio assisiensis*
ASB, *Statuti*	Archivio di Stato di Bologna, *Statuti*
AMC	Municipal Archives of Cocentaina
ANTT	Arquivos Nacionais da Tore do Tombo, Lisbon
ASRe	Archivio di Stato di Reggio Emilia
AU	*Annals of Ulster*
BHM	*Bulletin of the History of Medicine*
BSR mss.77	*Biblioteca del Senato della Repubblica, Statuti mss. 77, 67v–68r*
CCR	Calendar of Close Rolls
CELT	Corpus of Electronic Texts
CFR	Calendar of Fine Rolls
CIM	Calendar of Inquisitions Miscellaneous
CIPM	Calendar of Inquisitions Post Mortem
CJ	Court of Justice
CPR	Calendar of Patent Rolls
CS	*Chronicon Scotorum*
CUP	Cambridge University Press
DIAS	Dublin Institute for Advanced Studies
DYNAMIS	*Acta hispanica ad medicinae scientiarumque historiam illustrandam*
FF	*Fontes Franciscani*
FS	*Franciscan Studies*
HdeA	Henry d'Avranches, *Legenda sancti Francisci versificata*
HMSO	Her Majesty's Stationery Office
JHMAS	*Journal of the History of Medicine and Allied Sciences*
JRSAI	*Journal of the Royal Society of Antiquaries of Ireland*
JS	Julian of Speyer, *Vita Sancti Francisci*
L&HR	*Law and History Review*
LTS	*Legenda trium sociorum*
MH	*Medical History*
OUP	Oxford University Press
PRO	Public Record Office, a division of TNA
PROME	Parliamentary Rolls of Medieval England
SHM	*Social History of Medicine*
TNA	The National Archives (UK)
VP	*Vita prima sancti Francisci*
VS	*Vita secunda sancti Francisci*

Medicine and Law: The Confluence of Art and Science in the Middle Ages

Wendy J. Turner and Sara M. Butler

In the thirteenth-century, the faculties of Law and of Medicine at the University of Bologna became rivals, but rivals with an unusual relationship. The Law faculty had its own college, while the Medicine faculty belonged to the College of Arts. When the School of Law settled in its own discrete area of town away from the Arts' faculties, the topography of the medieval city defined and propagated this division. By 1319, both Medicine and Law faculties had their own set of institutional rules governing all aspects of their lives, including training and salaries, teaching and curriculum, textbooks and teaching methodologies, research and intellectual scholarship, and examinations. Regulations of this genre were typical in the highly structured and hierarchical institutions that medieval universities had become. The Medicine faculty's rising social status, along with their rules of conduct quite distinct from other Arts' faculties, propelled them into a surprisingly congenial alliance with the Law faculty over the course of the next century.

A study of the lives of the faculty members of Law and Medicine was to be Shona Kelly Wray's next project.[1] She was working on an analysis of

---

1   Shona Kelly Wray's major works include: with Dennis Dutschke, "Un ritrovato laudario italiano," *Italianistica* 14 (1985): 155–183; "The Experience of the Black Death in Bologna as Revealed by the Notarial Records," *Journal of the Rocky Mountain Medieval and Renaissance Association* 14 (1993): 44–64; "*Speculum et Exemplar*: The Notaries of Bologna during the Black Death," *Quellen und Forschungen aus italienischen Archiven und Bibliotheken* 81 (2001): 200–227; "Women, Family, and Inheritance in Bologna during the Black Death," in *Love, Marriage, and Family Ties in the Middle Ages*, ed. Isabel Davis, Miriam Müller, and Sarah Rees Jones (Turnhout: Brepols, 2003), pp. 205–215; "Boccaccio and the Doctors: Medicine and Compassion in the Face of Plague," *Journal of Medieval History* 30 (2004): 301–322; "Tracking Family and Flight in Bologna during the Black Death," *Journal of Medieval Prosopography* 25 (2004): 145–160; "Instruments of Concord: Making Peace and Settling Disputes through a Notary in the City and *Contado* of Late Medieval Bologna," *Journal of Social History* 42 (2009): 733–760; *Communities and Crisis: Bologna during the Black Death* (Leiden: Brill, 2009); with Jutta G. Sperling, ed., *Across the Religious Divide: Women, Property, and Law in the Wider Mediterranean (ca. 1300–1800)* (New York and London: Routledge, 2010); "Women, Testaments, and Notarial Culture in Bologna's Contado (1348)," in *Across the Religious Divide*, pp. 81–94; with Roisin Cossar, "Wills," in *Reading Medieval Sources*, ed. Joel Rosenthal

© KONINKLIJKE BRILL NV, LEIDEN, 2014 | DOI 10.1163/9789004269118_002

the evolving relationship between these two groups of professionals in fourteenth-century Bologna as an essay for this volume. Wray was in Italy on a Villa I Tatti fellowship from the Harvard University Center for Renaissance Studies when she collapsed from an aneurism and went into cardiac arrest.[2] Her work on law and medicine in medieval Bologna remains unfinished. Yet, even the remnants of her notes and thoughts embody what we intended for this volume: a closer examination of the interaction between the disciplines and professions of law and medicine in both theory and practice. Wray's career in history exemplifies the aims of this book. Her unending curiosity and bold disregard for traditional historical boundaries prompted new ways of looking at historical questions. As Eric Dursteler remarks in his *Renaissance Quarterly* review of *Across the Religious Divide: Women, Property, and Law in the Wider Mediterranean ca. 1300–1800* (co-edited with Jutta Sperling), Wray shone the spotlight on subjects typically overlooked by others in her field. Describing it as an "important book," Dursteler writes, "While probably no topic has attracted greater attention from scholars in the past four decades, the study of gender in the Mediterranean has lagged conspicuously, particularly in comparison to the rich literature on the Atlantic world."[3] *Across the Religious Divide* has garnered much praise for breaking new ground methodologically: "until quite recently, most studies have focused either on the Braudelian question of the unity of the Mediterranean and its viability as a category of analysis, or on some localized sliver with little reference to the wider whole." *Across the Religious Divide* instead "attempts to bridge these two modes . . . by focusing on numerous local cases, but placing them in an expansive regional context."[4] Wray's eagerness to champion history heretofore neglected, and to explore new historical territory is what this book hopes to achieve in examining intersections of law and medicine.

(New York: Routledge, forthcoming). Wray was also an experienced translator: Giorgio Chittolini, "A Geography of the 'Contadi' in Communal Italy," in *Portraits of Medieval and Renaissance Living: Essays in Memory of David Herlihy*, ed. Samuel K. Cohn, Jr. and Steven A. Epstein, trans. Wray (Ann Arbor: University of Michigan Press, 1996), pp. 417–438; and Umberto Eco and Costantino Marmo, eds., *On the Medieval Theory of Signs*, trans. Wray (Amsterdam: John Benjamin, 1989).

2 For a summary of her career and achievements, see Roisin Coisar, "*In Memoriam*: Shona Kelly Wray," in *The Medieval Review* 12.06.22: https://scholarworks.iu.edu/dspace/handle/2022/3631.

3 Eric Dursteler, review of Jutta G. Sperling and Shona Kelly Wray, eds., *Across the Religious Divide: Women, Property, and Law in the Wider Mediterranean (ca. 1300–1800)*, in *Renaissance Quarterly* 63.4 (2010): 1325.

4 Dursteler, review, 1325.

A substantial portion of medieval law centered on injury or death, and the perspective of a physician could bring much to the conversation regarding intent and injury assessment through examination and testimony based on professional medical experience. At the same time, medicine was slowly evolving into a profession: medical practitioners turned to the law to discourage interlopers without (what they considered to be) appropriate training and to maintain rigorous standards in the quality of medical care. Much like the legal profession, medical practitioners hoped to see their discipline embrace science, meaning to adopt an approach that was both theoretically sound and consistent. Wray's observations on medieval Bologna underscore this aspiration.

Wray remarked that law professors (*doctores legum*) and medical professors (*doctores medicine*) stood apart from their practicing associates, the lawyer (*iurisperitus*) or judge (*iudex*) and the physician (*medicus*). In terms of their scholarship and teaching, *doctores legum* often specialized in a branch of law: they became professor of canon law (*doctor decretorum*), or professor of civil law (*doctor iuris civilis*), or professor of both (*doctor utriusque*). The study of medicine did not include such specializations in this period, though some educators boasted the title professor of physic or healing (*doctor fisice*) instead of professor of medicine (*doctor medicine*). In medieval Bologna, both professors of medicine and physicians bore the title of *magister*. Further, both professors of medicine and law served the community in their respective fields outside the university setting. Professors of law wrote deliberations (*consilia*) to aid judges in court cases; so, too, did professors of medicine when asked to consult on a case of assault or homicide. Their titles as professors at the university distinguished them from other physicians and lawyers, adding to their prestige in Bolognese society.

According to Wray, between 1319 and 1363 when the faculty of Theology established its own division within the university, interactions between the faculties of Law and Medicine went well beyond the halls of intellectual discourse. Most of these men were married with families and—in terms of wealth for dowries and marriages—professors of medicine were much closer to the social status of their colleagues on the Law faculty than they were to their counterparts in the College of Arts. Wray uncovered copious examples of how these university physicians and lawyers forged links through marriage. For example, Zanna, daughter of the esteemed physician Alberto Zancari, married a law professor; Martino di Fra Giovanni de Erri, a professor of medicine, contracted marriage with the daughter of Law Professor Giovanni Lapi. These families and others sought training in either or both of the professions for their children. Wray observed that Professor Mondino de Liuzzi took out a loan in 1345 to send his two grandsons to the university in Law and Medicine respectively.

The lives of these faculty members became socially entangled in other ways as well: serving as guardians of underage children, executors of wills, witnesses to testaments and inventories of estates, and as business partners.[5] In some cases, professors of law and medicine appear side-by-side in these roles on a testament or will. In her surviving notes relating to this project, Wray commented:

> An important figure in the professional lives of professors, especially in Law and Medicine were their *familiares*. These men travelled with law professors in their capacity as legal advisors and with jurists and medical professors as ambassadors; they show up in the witness lists of jurist *consilia* that were drawn up as notarial acts. I have found the will of the *familiaris* of eminent jurist Giovanni d'Andrea (although as testator he is not identified as *familiaris*). This man made bequests to members of the d'Andrea family, to students, and many others. He had a few law books, in pawn,[6] and had lots of dealing in cattle; perhaps he worked also in parchment production. I have identified more *familiares* of jurists associated with Giovanni d'Andrea and hope to also find their wills. *Familiares* are named only in the testaments of law and medicine, but I have found one example of a household member from the will of a widow of a Grammar professor. She left 4L to a man, named only by his first name and nickname, who was *morante cum magistro Galvano*.
>
> What to say about this? It is important to recognize that the careers of professors, especially [those in] law and medicine, were supported by the members of their households.

This excerpt opens a window into the intriguing way Wray worked through a problem, how questions percolated through her mind. In line with the findings of Nancy Siraisi and Roberto Greci, she observed that professors from either the faculty of Law or that of Medicine owned books from the opposing discipline.[7] Wray contended that, "medicine and law professors are similar

---

5   Katharine Park, *Doctors and Medicine in Early Renaissance Florence* (Princeton: Princeton University Press, 1985) on similar partnerships in Florence, see pp. 29–30.

6   It is unclear from Wray's notes whether this refers to the jurist having pawned his books to someone else for money, or to his holding books in pawn for someone else, which might indicate a lending relationship between members of the town.

7   On the library of Giovanni di Marco da Rimini, see Nancy Siraisi, *History, Medicine, and the Traditions of Renaissance Learning* (Ann Arbor, MI: University of Michigan Press, 2007), p. 14; Roberto Greci, "Tra economia e cultura: il commercio librario nel Trecento," in *Mercanti,*

in that both display great intellectual breadth in their possession of books, at least for the very successful who had many books." Nancy Siraisi, who has written the foundational research on this subject, has emphasized repeatedly that late medieval and Renaissance medical professors were interested in not only the health of the human body, but also a healthy civic life. Accordingly, they wrote on topics such as economics, ethics, even poetry.[8] Wray's research confirms this: she noted that one wealthy professor of medicine, Castellano Yngrani, owned an "entire room" of medical books, three civil law codices, and major works on notarial law.

At least in Bologna, Wray discovered that professors of law and medicine shared a similar status and wealth, in spite of the fact that Medicine faculty belonged to the Arts. The social standing of professors of medicine is such that it cannot be compared to their colleagues in the other disciplines in Art, who had far lower salaries and little opportunity to expand their work outside the classroom. Wray supplied the example of the widow of one professor of grammar who had only enough money to provide her daughter a dowry "to marry a second-hand clothes dealer (strazarolus)." In terms of status, only the professors of medicine could approach the wealth and stature of the faculty of law.

It is a shame that we have lost the voice of Shona Kelly Wray, a talented, generous, and loving colleague, mother, friend, and professor. We only have these few glimpses of what she intended for this project. Yet, it is important for us to remember the last thing she wrote for this chapter: "Historians have long emphasized the gulf between medicine and law, although art historians study-ing Bologna's famous tombs of the professors do note that the rivalry ended at death, since both law and medical professors chose burial in the Dominican church." Wray demonstrated that, at least for the fourteenth century, this gulf never really existed. Faculty members of Law and Medicine in Bologna were colleagues in every sense—they shared their professional lives, their families, their interests in scholarship, and their social status, even if they belonged to different fields, colleges, and disciplines.[9]

---

politica e cultura nella società Bolognese del basso medioevo (Bologna: CLUEB, 2004), pp. 109–170, and see also the appendix, which includes the names of professors of medicine who sold law books. See also G. Baader, "die Bibliothek des Giovanni di Marco da Rimini. Eine Quelle der medizinischen Bildung im Humanismus," Studia codicologica 124 (1977): 43–97.

8 Siraisi, History, Medicine, and the Traditions, pp. 112, 129, 148, 163, 198–201, and 207.

9 Many thanks to Roisin Cossar and Maggi Kelly who managed to retrieve Shona's notes for the chapter and gave us permission to include her work here.

Medicine and Law

Wray's work is pioneering, in large part because of her confidence and passionate sense of righteousness about the need for historians to move more easily
across disciplinary divides. Wray's research defies categorization: she was not
simply an historian of medicine and disease; she was equally dedicated to the
histories of women, law, the Mediterranean and the urban experience. Wray's
daring career contrasts the traditional reluctance of scholars to cross boundaries, especially the yawning chasm separating medical history and legal history,
two very rigidly defined fields. Both disciplines require their own unique skill
sets in terms of languages, paleography, philosophy, and mechanics; both disciplines also have produced historiographies that are often so technical and
jargon-filled, they are inaccessible to those outside the field. The inimitability
of their histories tends to be a product of elite authorship: for much of the
twentieth century, many of the leading legal historians were lawyers;[10] many
of the most well-known medical historians were physicians.[11] Given the air of
privilege that enshrouds both histories, it is not surprising that historians have
been hesitant to cross that seemingly impenetrable barrier. In many respects,
the boundary between disciplines is exposed best by the 2010 publication of
Faith Wallis's documentary text entitled *Medieval Medicine: A Reader*. Of the
107 documents included in the text, only four intersect in one way or another
with the law.[12] Yet, the benefits of interdisciplinary work are boundless. For
medical history, the source material is largely prescriptive, drawn from the
study of medical treatises, literature, and legislation. While all of this offers
profound insight into the way healthcare workers *should* practice medicine,
it tells us much less about the way they *actually* practiced it. This is especially
true of the medical treatises: even when penned by renowned surgeons or
physicians, founded on the experience garnered in the course of their medical
careers, they still belong to a very privileged, atypical group of practitioners.
The vast majority of medieval healthcare workers did not write treatises and,

---

10   In many respect, the coupling of law and legal history began with F.W. Maitland, the
      pre-eminent scholar in this field, co-author (with F. Pollock) of *The History of English Law
      before the Time of Edward I*, 2 vols. (London: C.J. Clay & Sons, 1899).

11   The history of legal medicine shows a similar crossover. The foremost authority in the
      field for English history for much of the twentieth century was Thomas R. Forbes, author
      of (among others), *Surgeons at the Bailey: English Forensic Medicine to 1878* (New Haven:
      Yale University Press, 1985). Forbes was an anatomist and endocrinologist working out of
      Yale's Medical School.

12   Faith Wallis, ed., *Medieval Medicine: A Reader* (Toronto: University of Toronto Press, 2010).

most likely, were not even literate. A study of medical practice through the eyes of the law, however, furnishes a unique opportunity to see medicine in action. Legal history also has much to gain from such a venture: while the practice of medicine became more regulated and legal in its journey towards profession-alization, at the same time, the practice of law began to exploit the expertise of physicians as witnesses in complicated cases involving poisons, illnesses, injuries, and other medical or health-related issues.

Wray's final research project emphasizes the continuity in lifestyle, priori-ties, and incentives between legal and medical specialists. This book hopes to underline those parallels and more. Silvia De Renzi remarks on the meth-odological connection allying the two disciplines. She writes that medieval "jurists and physicians had to use clues to reconstruct events that were hidden, either because they had happened in the past or because they were altogether invisible."[13] The scientific veneer of the medical profession has done much to obscure this parallel. In the twenty-first century, many people think of medi-cine as "science," and yet it remains one of the greatest of the Arts. There are no hard and fast rules in medicine. There is no master computer into which a physician can slide her/his patient to generate a definitive and comprehensive evaluation of patient health. Rather, there are indications and symptoms, clues to health or illness. Sophisticated, even daunting, technology produces some of those clues: MRIs, optical imaging, X-Rays, CT scans, endoscopies, blood and urine tests, and others. Still, a physician cannot know with complete cer-tainty what is wrong with her patient; (s)he can only make a reasonably good and educated guess. Granted, the medical profession is the first to emphasize erudition, advances in scientific theory, and technological proficiency over analysis and interpretation: as a science, medicine appears impregnable. The layperson cannot poke holes in theories that (s)he does not understand. The profession itself has cultivated this aura as a measure of self-defense: disgrun-tled patients are typically too intimidated to sue when the results are not as expected. Nevertheless, in doing so, science has denied medical practitioners recognition for talent verging on art: a keen eye and a good sense of the whole picture makes for a better physician.

In many respects, lawyers are the mirror image of physicians; they practice the art of law using methodology and exactness akin to science. On paper, law has always shared a closer affinity with science than with the arts. Law has clearly defined rules that can be tested, tried, and confirmed; granted, these rules are socially and politically constructed. Nevertheless, a law-breaker

---

13   Silvia De Renzi, "Medical Expertise, Bodies, and the Law in Early Modern Courts," *Isis* 98.2 (2007): 319.

exists well outside a legal boundary. However, in practice, it was something else entirely. Clues needed to be assembled, and they did not always present a clear analysis of the situation. Murky and muddled, judges, courts, and juries (in England, at least) had to try to make sense of imperfect evidence and give their best decision. While the law was straightforward, implementation could be messy. In law and medicine, then, art and science are blended together to create a judgment, a diagnosis of a situation, using the best reasoning lawyers and physicians could come to at any given moment.

In terms of crossing boundaries, legal medicine might be the one exception to the rule: since the field emerged, scholars have had to work comfortably in both realms in order to understand and explain the significance of their findings. Medical testimony in the courts was one of the many legal experiments implemented in the wake of the abolition of the ordeal. Without access to God's testimony, courts of law were required to look elsewhere for evidence.[14] Nonetheless, as Guido Ruggiero's 1978 study of legal medicine in Renaissance Venice reminds us, the incentives for adopting legal medicine were varied and mutually beneficial. While the state viewed medical expertise as a necessary evidentiary innovation to control levels of violence, physicians rejoiced in their involvement because it provided them an opportunity to exert their superiority in the medical hierarchy.[15] Ruggiero's study remains the landmark investigation in this field and very much acts as a call to arms for historians. Since that publication, there have been a number of remarkable forays into the realm of legal medicine. In particular, Joseph Shatzmiller's 1989 documentary collection centered on medical practitioners and their interaction with the judicial system of medieval Manosque (Provence) is fundamental in furnishing a firsthand account of the scope of activities medical practitioners might perform in service to the state, as well as the grievances patients might sue against them.[16] Michael McVaugh's 1993 investigation of the Crown of Aragon's municipally appointed physicians is the first book-length exploration of legal medicine. His research expands the parameters of the field dramatically. His vision of

14   Many legal historians have emphasized that torture was the Continent's response to the abolition of the ordeal. Richard Fraher has emphasized that this was just one solution among many. See Richard Fraher, "Conviction According to Conscience: The Medieval Jurists Debate Concerning Judicial Discretion and the Law of Proof," *L&HR* 7.1 (1989): 23–88.

15   Guido Ruggiero, "The Cooperation of Physicians and the State in the Control of Violence in Renaissance Venice," *JHMAS* 33 (1978): 156–66.

16   Joseph Shatzmiller, ed., *Médecine et Justice en Provence Médiévale. Documents de Manosque, 1262–1348* (Aix-en-Provence: Publications de l'Université de Provence, 1989).

legal medicine includes also public health measures, from leprosy examinations to municipal regulation of waste removal and water quality. McVaugh approaches the subject from a humanist perspective, exploring not only the nature of the work performed by these practitioners on behalf of the crown, but also attempting to appreciate better the people involved and the relationships between practitioners.[17] These studies, however, serve only to highlight the broad diversity across time and space in terms of forensics in practice.

The six chapters that begin this book have much to contribute to this growing field of scholarship. Han Nijdam's chapter builds on Lisi Oliver's 2011 monograph on injury tariffs in barbarian law.[18] The Germanic peoples endorsed a system of law that assigned value to individuals according to sex, age and rank in order to provide compensation in event of homicide, the central goal, of course, being to offer a legal process through which to take revenge financially, thereby curbing actual rates of violence in society. The law addressed not only homicide, but also assault, assessing compensation for each body part on a scale of functionality; for example, the thumb is worth more than the ring finger because it has a greater role to play in grasping weaponry. Nijdam applies this to the various regions of Frisia (comprising the modern-day Netherlands and parts of Germany) to examine the origins of compensation at law, how the law's focus on compensation evolved over time, and the impact of medicine and medical texts on the writing of the law. Astutely, Nijdam provides us with a useful reality check, reiterating that the commodification of the body, while seemingly barbaric, continues today in the form of organ harvesting and medical insurance claims. More important still, he explains that assault wounds not only the body, but also masculine honor. Thus, Frisian law mapped the body for compensation of injuries to body and reputation (what Nijdam refers to as "embodied honor"), helping to explain first, why the same codes address also damage to goods and lands, members of one's household and aspersions of one's character; and second, why injury tariffs place such emphasis on the visibility of physical injury. Nijdam's analysis of the Old Frisian injury tariffs highlights the modernity of their practices in law and medicine: not only were there provisions for physicians to testify as expert witnesses, but he reveals a society adept in wound treatment with a sound knowledge of human anatomy.

---

17   Michael R. McVaugh, *Medicine before the Plague: Practitioners and their Patients in the Crown of Aragon 1285–1345* (Cambridge: CUP, 1993). Along those same lines, see chapter two, *"Iudicium leprosorum*; Medical Judgment," in Luke Demaitre, *Leprosy in Premodern Medicine: A Malady of the Whole Body* (Baltimore: Johns Hopkins University Press, 2007), pp. 34–74.

18   Lisi Oliver, *The Body Legal in Barbarian Law* (Toronto: University of Toronto Press, 2011).

Nijdam's study has much to offer also outside the realms of law and medicine. The law demonstrates that the "Free Frisians" owed their freedom primarily to rhetoric: in practice, hierarchy just as rigidly divided their society as it did the rest of medieval Europe.

Much like the legal responsibilities of the expert witnesses in Nijdam's study, Fiona Harris-Stoertz examines midwives in the High Middle Ages as skilled professionals, held legally responsible for baptism and called upon as witnesses. Through an expert use of an incredible range of sources, most prominently legal sources, Harris-Stoertz takes up the challenge of finding evidence for birth attendants during the sixth to the thirteenth centuries.[19] Her essay gives the reader insight into the lives and position of midwives as medical specialists for pregnant women as well as their connection in the cultural perception of the Virgin Mary. Harris-Stoertz is able to weave together real case studies from legal sources and chronicles with examples from saints' vita, miracle collections, fictional accounts, and apocryphal and iconographic literature. She looks at the existence and importance of midwives in the High Middle Ages, who worked within a network of caregivers for pregnant women. Fiona Harris-Stoertz and Hiram Kümper together add much to our understanding of how legal texts represented medieval women.

Hiram Kümper's study of medical expertise in rape cases targets the ambiguous place of rape in the history of the law. Because Roman law employed the same terminology (*raptus*) to address sexual assault, abduction, and theft, medieval law essentially merged these categories: the medieval world inherited this perplexing fusion of terminology.[20] The result is a blurring between rape and abduction (often played out as elopement), and an emphasis on the will of the family, rather than the victim's will. To date, studies of this phenomenon are highly regional and tend to take little notice of each other. Adopting a pan-European perspective, Kümper ties all of this together and pushes back the date of transmission to the period before the rediscovery of Roman law: he reveals that this ambiguity was present already in the early Germanic law

---

19   The challenge comes from Monica H. Green, see in particular, "Bodies, Gender, Health, Disease: Recent Work on Medieval Women's Medicine," *Studies in Medieval and Reanaissance History*, 2 (2005): 1–46.

20   English historians have examined this field most closely. See Emma Hawkes, "'She was ravished against her will, what so ever she say': Female Consent in Rape and Ravishment in Late-Medieval England," *Limina* 1 (1995): 47–54; Christopher Cannon, "*Raptus* in the Chaumpaigne Release and Newly Discovered Document Concerning the Life of Geoffrey Chaucer," *Speculum* 68 (1993): 74–94; and Henry Ansgar Kelly, "Statutes of Rape and Alleged Ravishers of Wives: A Context for the Charges against Thomas Malory, Knight," *Viator* 28 (1997): 361–419.

codes. Looking specifically to how vocabulary in the law-books and treatises change over time, he tracks an important transition in the interpretation of *raptus* to assist scholars in better assessing the nature of the crime and its evolution. While rape law emerged as a legal remedy to compensate the family for the abduction of a woman against the will of her father, it eventually developed into a crime marked by sexual violence against the will of the victim herself.[21] Perhaps even more critical, while the historiography holds up "juries of matrons" as an early modern innovation, Kümper observes the presence of women as medical experts in the medieval legal forum. In this respect, his findings are truly path breaking. Not only did the courts eschew the expertise of midwives over the wisdom of "old women," they mandated physical examinations only when the victim was a virgin. Thus, when a court summoned the wise women, the crime was essentially one of child molestation, not simply rape.

Chapters by Carmel Ferragud and Joanna Carraway Vitiello share many similarities in their willingness to venture into new territory. Both chapters expand our knowledge of legal medicine geographically, by analyzing regions heretofore neglected, but also by re-envisioning the medical setting, reminding us that professional medicine was not restricted to the large urban center. Ferragud explains the highly formalized role of legal medicine in Cocentaina, a small town in southern Valencia (an unlikely place for innovation in medicine or medical practice) as a product of border traffic and intercultural influences. Having been recently reclaimed from the Muslims, the newly Christian Cocentaina was plagued with an itinerant population and a disruptive criminal element. In an effort to assert greater control over such a diverse populace (socially, politically and religiously), local government tightened the efficiency of the criminal process by experimenting with new evidentiary requirements. The introduction of medical expertise in lawsuits springing from assaults represents one of those experiments, inspired by the travels of the notary, Domingo Cepillo, who exploited his family's influence to pioneer legal practices he encountered in Rome. Local authorities refined their evidentiary requirements not only to develop a more efficient legal process, but also to discourage private feuding by persuading locals to take private grievances to court. The town's interest in medicine expanded beyond its legal uses: local

---

21 Kümper's global study provides an interesting contrast to the English situation. As Caroline Dunn has demonstrated the English continued to show concern about the abduction of women against their family's will (essentially elopement), but did so by employing conjunctive vocabulary (i.e. *rapuit et abduxit*) in order to distinguish abduction from sexual assault. See Caroline Dunn, *Stolen Women in Medieval England: Rape, Abduction, and Adultery, 1100–1500* (Cambridge: CUP, 2013).

authorities encouraged the growth of medical practice as a stabilizing and positive influence on the local population.

The sights of Italian scholars have focused primarily on the settings of Bologna and Venice; Vitiello's study of Reggio Emilia authenticates that even the smaller Italian cities shared in the practice of soliciting court testimony from medical practitioners. Reggio Emilia's experience bears many similarities to that of Cocentaina: the need for medical expertise sprang chiefly from crisis. An almost constant state of war, plague and famine led the city's authorities to offer tax concessions for resident physicians to care for a diminishing and often impoverished population. Vitiello's study enlarges our perception of the multiple ways medical professionals interacted with the state. The city's physicians not only provided medical testimony in assault and homicide cases, but they were also state employees tasked with caring for the population's medical needs, and, too, they were state informants, obligated to notify local authorities every time they treated an injury springing from a criminal assault.[22] The city's vision of medical expertise, however, contrasts starkly with the experience of Cocentaina. While legal authorities in Cocentaina relied primarily on barbers, those from the bottom of the medical hierarchy, in Reggio Emilia authorities preferred either physicians (that is, from the highest rank in the medical hierarchy), or laymen with no medical background whatsoever.[23] Much as Kümper proposes in chapter two, the medieval courts did not valorize the opinions of medical practitioners to the exclusion of all others. Quite simply, professional medicine had not yet achieved widespread recognition as the sole scientific authority on issues of health; nor had they successfully medicalized death in order to claim that only physicians can "confirm and explain death."[24] Indeed, the medieval courts placed great value also on the opinions of ordinary people, including women. While Kümper witnesses the importance of "old women" in the courtroom setting, whose experience with sex and the female body made them the acclaimed experts on virginity, Vitiello sees a distinct respect for women as experts on death (through their role in the preparation of the

---

22   Ruggiero observes similar requirements in Renaissance Venice. See Ruggiero, "Cooperation of Physicians and the State," 156–66.

23   For more on the professional pyramid in medicine, see Vivian Nutton, "Medicine in Medieval Western Europe, 1000–1500," in *The Western Medical Tradition 800 BC to AD 1800*, ed. Lawrence I. Conrad, *et al.* (Cambridge: CUP, 1995; repr. 2008), pp. 139–206.

24   Lindsay Prior, *The Social Organization of Death: Medical Discourse and Social Practices in Belfast* (New York: St Martin's, 1989), pp. 33 and 45.

corpse) and also as parents of the dead.[25] Both Kümper and Vitiello confirm that the education and experience of the professional medical cadre complemented but did not replace lay participation in the medieval courts.

Moving to an English setting, Wendy J. Turner introduces us to yet another variant of lay medical expertise: the escheator. Concerned primarily with inventorying properties owed to the king, escheators (or local authorities on their behalf) regularly examined the mental competence of heirs in order to assess their capacity to govern estates independently. Not only did the medieval English courts trust ordinary men to make judgments relating to mental capacity, the total absence of medical practitioners from the process implies that it would not have been appropriate for medical professionals to do so. While medical treatises claimed authority over the mentally ill, in English practice, mental competence existed outside a physician's jurisdiction. These ordinary citizens blur the line between layman and medical expert: escheators, sheriffs and jurors alike readily distinguished between cognitive disorders, memory dysfunction, manic episodes, and altered perception. Moreover, their vocabulary and health descriptors reveal a distinct awareness of medieval medical sources. This example illustrates the dangers of imposing artificial categories on the past: in a world in which medical practice was chiefly domestic in nature, the ordinary layman had a much better grasp of medical theory and practice than do the laity today.[26]

Much like Ferragud and Vitiello, Turner underscores the role of the state in medical matters. The crown issued legislation enforcing the guardianship of the mentally ill; its officers carried out the examinations necessary to declare mental (in)capacity; the crown appointed appropriate guardians and determined what happened to the profits of the inheritance, dictated by the onset and nature of the illness; and finally, crown representatives punished guardians who strayed in their duties. Crown intervention undeniably had its benefits: guardianship of the mentally incompetent and disabled meant

---

25   Much more research still needs to be done on the subject of ordinary women in medieval medicine, as opposed to female medical practitioners. Much of medieval medicine was domestic in nature, and yet the role of the ordinary women in medical matters is mostly undocumented. One exception to the rule is Debra Stout, "Medieval German Women and the Power of Healing," in *Women Healers and Physicians: Climbing a Long Hill*, ed. Lilian R. Furst (Lexington: University Press of Kentucky, 1997), pp. 13–42.

26   Faye Getz, *Medicine in the English Middle Ages* (Princeton: Princeton University Press, 1998), p. 5. For more on the domestic nature of medicine see Peter Dendle and Alain Touwaide, eds., *Health and Healing from the Medieval Garden* (Woodbridge: Boydell, 2008).

that those with mental health conditions had specialized laws and practices designed specifically to address this medical issue. However, guardians were not the least among those persons taking advantage of the precarious state of those with mental incapacity. Escheators and other royal officials regularly fined guardians, family members, and neighbors for "waste," if not downright theft, of a mentally incapacitated individual's property.

By the thirteenth century, courts began to call upon physicians to testify not only about medical conditions, but also against other physicians who were liable for injury or death in cases of malpractice. None of this could have taken place without the late medieval move towards the professionalization of medicine, marked by the emergence of medical licensing and examination procedures, addressed in different ways and in different settings by Kira Robison, Iona McCleery, Jean Dangler, and Sara M. Butler. These four chapters do not present a united perspective on the subject, especially as they relate to the origins of professionalization. All four concur in the contention that developing professionalization relied heavily on the cooperation of the state and the medium of state legislation to enforce the needs of the profession. They differ primarily in the *locus* of inspiration for crown regulation. McCleery credits the crown with imposing professionalization on Portugal's disparate group of medical practitioners, who, much as McVaugh discovered in his study of the crown of Aragon, "had not yet come together as a body to control and restrict their craft."[27] In her study of fifteenth-century Valencia, Dangler is largely in accord with McVaugh and McCleery. In the English context, Butler sees just the opposite occurring. While the universities relied on royal legislation to defend their interests, Butler shifts our gaze instead to the medical practitioners themselves (largely associated with the universities) and their self-awareness as a profession, one that included a coterie of surgeons in addition to physicians. In England, professionalization in medicine was largely the product of that self-awareness. Robison's examination of medical practice in Bologna proposes yet a third path to professionalization. She also sees professionalization as a product of competition between medical practitioners, although in the Bolognese setting it pitted the academic superiority of physicians against the practical expertise of surgeons and other empirics. Robison refers to this hierarchical ideal as "the text versus the knife." Robison emphasizes how the changing fortunes of the state played a critical role in the process. When the city broke free of papal power in the 1376 rebellion that established Bologna as an independent commune, control of the university itself shifted from the core of students supported by the pope, to the city government. In a desire to

---

27   McVaugh, *Medicine before the Plague*, p. 239.

remain free of papal intervention, the university threw in its lot with the city, creating an alliance that foreshadows the sixteenth-century development of the *Protomedicato* tribunal, devoted to the regulation of medicine for the protection of the public.[28] Professionalization of medicine in this context, then, was very much a joint venture that was mutually beneficial. Regional distinctions existed also in the valuation of medicine: where the Bolognese and the English both prioritized academic over practical medicine, the Portuguese medical exam, required by all medical practitioners hoping to purchase a license, demanded high standards in both. Acknowledging these discrepancies in the history of medical professionalization is critical: regional distinctions of this nature serve as a useful reminder that there is more than just one narrative.

Robison's chapter is an important complement to Wray's final work. Wray rejected historical perceptions of tension between the disciplines of medicine and law at the university in Bologna. Robison shifts the lens instead to examine conflict within the discipline of medicine itself, revolving around the background and training of practitioners, setting academic physicians against guild-trained surgeons. While recent scholarship has placed much emphasis on the equalizing influence of the medical marketplace,[29] Robison contends that, in Bologna, market competition did little to diminish those divisions. Rather, political conditions heightened the divide by establishing medical professors in a position of authority over all other medical practitioners. University physicians allied themselves with the *podestà* in a mutually beneficial relationship. In the interests of creating a monopoly on medical practice for the academics, the *podestà* supported the ideal of limiting medical practice within the city to university trained physicians. While it might be argued that the relationship between the *podestà* and the medical professors fulfilled much the same role as the sixteenth-century *Protomedicato* tribunal, Robison makes it clear that the motivations behind their actions were distinct. Where the *Protomedicato* tribunal functioned to protect the people against medical malpractice, the medieval Faculty of Medicine was far more self-interested. Their concern centered chiefly on asserting their superiority in the medical hierarchy: a concern that is mirrored in the significantly greater fines imposed on those who practiced medicine without the requisite educational background compared to those who practiced bad medicine. For their part, the *podestà* not only exploited the

---

28   See John Tate Lanning and John Jay TePaske, *The Royal* Protomedicato: *The Regulation of the Medical Profession in the Spanish Empire* (Durham, NC: Duke University Press, 1985).

29   For example, see Mark S.R. Jenner and Patrick Wallis, eds., *Medicine and the Market in England and its Colonies, c. 1450–c. 1850* (New York: Palgrave Macmillan, 2007).

services of academic physicians, but also used their newly won control of the university to oust papal authority in Bologna at every level.

McCleery, Dangler and Butler also grapple with hostilities within the medical hierarchy during the period of growing professionalization, but from different perspectives. Reminding us that medical licenses in the medieval context speak much more closely to the status of the practitioner than his competence, McCleery endeavors to unravel the origins of medical licensing in medieval Portugal. She builds on the seminal work of Luis García Ballester, Michael McVaugh, and Agustín Rubio Vela who laid the foundation for explaining the origins of licensing practices. In their study of medieval Valencia, they argued that medical professionalization was a product of state control: the crown imposed licensing on the medical profession for a multitude of reasons. The primary goal was to establish better control of medical and surgical practice; nonetheless, the crown was inspired also by a desire to assert its power, to profit from medical malpractice suits, and to Christianize medicine and thus drive Jewish medical practitioners out of business.[30] McCleery proposes a shift in perspective: while accepting the basic premise that professionalization was imposed from above during the Portuguese crown's increasing centralization of authority, she contends that the crown learned to appreciate good medical practice from the people. McCleery sees this as an instance of "governmentality from below." McCleery also avoids the traditional explanation of intercultural antagonism as the impetus for medical licensing. Rather, despite growing hostility towards practitioners of Judaism, the crown protected the interests of Jewish medical men because it understood the value of their contribution to imperial medicine. McCleery also offers some plausible arguments why Portuguese medical practitioners chose to participate in the state's licensing efforts. A number of cultural features motivated the purchase of a license. Sometimes a license represented the end of an apprenticeship: the newly independent physician proclaimed his availability by buying a license. Some medical practitioners may have believed that a license provided them with the king's protection against malpractice suits. The one major element that is missing is the patient's perspective: McCleery asks, what did a license mean to the patient? Did the license represent trust? Power? McCleery is not able to answer this for the Portuguese setting, but her study acts as an important call to arms for historians to think more closely about the impact of licensing on the consumer.

Dangler's account of medical professionalization in Valencia, as it is appears through the eyes of a highly creative and misogynistic medical practitioner,

---

30   Luis García Ballester, Michael R. McVaugh and Agustín Rubio Vela, *Medical Licensing and Learning in Fourteenth-Century Valencia: Transactions of the American Philosophical Society* (Philadelphia: American Philosophical Society, 1989), pp. 41–50.

provides a useful contrast to McCleery's study of medieval Portugal. Where McCleery dismisses the exclusionary goals of professionalization, Dangler sees them as a necessary component of the process in fifteenth-century Valencia. Indeed, Dangler contends that Jaume Roig, a royal physician and medical examiner, also author of the *Espill* (The Mirror), a book in rhymed verse recounting a man's fictional journey through life marked by his "perilous experiences with ordinary women," is very much a product of this exclusionary environment. Where McVaugh and McCleery spotlight intercultural antagonism, Dangler illuminates yet another dimension of the conflict. She sees professionalization integrally tied to hostility against women healers. The *Espill* is a work of propaganda intended to reinforce the professionalization of medicine by exposing the dangers of seeking medical assistance from a woman (whose mere loveless presence drove the protagonist's father into a consumptive frenzy, eventually killing him), thereby promoting male medical professionals as the only safe healers. Roig's goal, however, was much larger than merely defending the Christian male medical practitioner: Dangler asserts that the exclusionary goals of professionalization are a reflection of a larger social shift in which Christian masculinity is revalorized as the ideal. Roig envisioned women as a risk not only to men, but also to society as a whole: as the ultimate source of disease, women hope to subvert the patriarchy through the legal institution of marriage. In the interests of protecting one's self and upholding the social order, men must not only shun women, but also, as Roig explained, call for greater punitive measures to be imposed against women and their treacheries. Women's bodies lead them innately towards adultery: thus why should the law reward women by protecting their interests? Roig demanded a return to Biblical forms of punishment (such as stoning and decapitation) for adultery as well as the elimination of the trousseau (a remuneration for a woman who marries as a virgin) and the dowry. Reinforcing the social hierarchy in this manner, in his opinion, would create a stronger, healthier, Christian society.

Butler moves the battle for professionalization to the English context where medical professionalization paralleled many of the Continental advances. Much like what Robison finds in the Bolognese context, in England the universities also played a critical role in articulating the superiority of academically trained physicians over mere craftsmen. The one obvious distinction, however, is that in England surgery did not become a subject for study at the universities as it did in many places on the Continent.[31] Thus, while English surgeons also aspired to participate in the late medieval process of professionalization that aligned surgeons more closely with physicians, simultaneously pitting them

---

31   Michael R. McVaugh, "Surgical Education in the Middle Ages," *DYNAMIS* 20 (2000): 283–304.

against barbers, the English surgeon could not justify his authority through a university education. The next best thing was to form close links with the university environments through increased literacy and intellectual exchange with medical professors.[32] Butler hopes to offer an alternative perspective of how a surgeon might climb the ladder of professionalization. Adopting a microhistorical perspective, she assesses the legal behavior of one fifteenth-century surgeon, Nicholas Wodehill, caught in the act of self-fashioning. Resident in London during the era that witnessed the creation of the extremely short-lived joint College of Physicians and Surgeons, Wodehill had the opportunity to participate in forging a new identity both for English surgeons and for himself. Rather than book learning, however, Wodehill turned to the law as a tool in his rise to prominence. Internalizing the rhetoric of his discipline in which medical professionals established confidence in their patients by claiming to work hand-in-hand with *Christus Medicus* (Christ the Physician), Wodehill claimed that membership in his profession entitled him to the rank of gentleman. He saw the law as a means to an end as he sued his way to the upper ranks of the social hierarchy.

Both Butler's and Dangler's works remind us that the professionalization of medicine was not a battle manned entirely by medical professionals. Indeed, in the perspective of Dangler's misogynist physician, this development entailed a reinforcement of the medical hierarchy that very much reflected the ideal social hierarchy in a harmonious and righteous state. In all of this, marriage is the key. Roig saw marriage as the foundation of a necessary patriarchy tasked with suppressing the inherent evils of the "daughters of Eve," and inevitably to prevent them from participating in the medical profession for the common good of society. Both Wray and Butler also emphasize the centrality of marriage to the growing professionalization of medicine. In medieval Bologna, *doctores medicine* enhanced their professional and social status through intermarriage with *doctores legum*. Butler's earnest surgeon turns to marriage before all else in his hopes to make a place for himself among the English gentry. Thankfully, Wodehill's efforts failed: but his recognition that intermarriage with the elite brought with it professional as well as social success is a useful reminder that the professionalization of medicine was merely one facet of a much larger social transition.

The final two papers examine the intersection between law and medicine in hagiographical works. Donna Trembinski scrutinizes the *vitae* of Saint Francis

---

32   McVaugh has studied the surgical process of professionalization through the adoption of academic medicine in his *The Rational Surgery of the Middle Ages* (Florence: SISMEL, Edizioni del Galluzzo, 2006).

of Assisi in an effort to bring his ailments to the forefront of studies surrounding his retirement. Francis's life was marked by episodes of ill health: he suffered from malaria (or some comparable disease) contracted during his mission to bring peace to the Levant as well as an optical disorder that eventually caused his eyesight to fail, and during the last years of his life he was often too weak to walk without assistance. His personal suffering was the inspiration for his mystical outlook and the foundation for his spiritual authority: an impassioned advocate of *imitatio Christi*, his visible torment brought him closer to Christ and the people long before he was inflicted with the *stigmata*. Nonetheless, the church recognized that the very same physical frailty that motivated men across Europe to abandon their responsibilities and rededicate their lives to an apostolic existence also prevented Francis from participating fully as the order's leader. Trembinski contends that Francis's condition led to the codification of legislation on the need to replace ill prelates and leaders, eventually used against Francis to force him out of his position of leadership. Trembinski's work offers a significant reassessment of Francis's last years. While Francis's retirement has always been interpreted as voluntary, Trembinski argues instead that the church imposed it for the good of the order. Moreover, while tensions over corporate poverty are thought to have dominated his last years,[33] Trembinski proposes that Francis's ill health assumed equal priority. Guardians appointed by the church sought to heal Francis's afflictions; much like Christ, Francis chose instead to embrace his suffering.

Where Trembinski focuses on a saint's ill health and its impact on the church, Máire Johnson explores instead the ability of saints to inflict ill health on others in order to regulate Irish politics. Johnson considers law in the *vitae* of Irish saints and religion in Irish law texts. She finds that law, medicine, and miracles all come together in the saints' *Lives*. These holy men acted as judges, touting written law as a means to distinguish the bad from the good; similarly, they put their miracles to work to punish the guilty and reward the innocent. Medicine became the focal point in the nature of those miracles. The Irish saints inflicted severe bodily punishments on the guilty, such as paralysis or blindness; while they simultaneously cured the innocent of their ailments. Johnson's work has much in common with Nijdam's. Where the Frisians spoke of the man-price (*wergeld*), a commodification of the body that Nijdam sees is intimately related to honor, Irish law addressed the subject in a much more straightforward manner, seeing attacks on the body as an assault on one's honor-price (termed variously as *lóg n-enech, díre*, or *eneclann*). Through their

---

33   See David Burr, *The Spiritual Franciscans: From Protest to Persecution in the Century after Saint Francis* (University Park: The Pennsylvania State University Press, 2001).

miracles, the saints exacted what Johnson refers to as a "medical honor-price," saving the most humiliating retributions for those who violate the saint's land, church, or person.

Trembinski and Johnson, much like Turner, venture into the relatively nascent field of medieval disability history.[34] Trembinski's reappraisal of Francis's illnesses sheds new light on the leadership of the order and the hostilities that plagued the order in the last few years of Francis's life. Johnson reveals that Irish secular authorities long preceded the church's intolerance for physically unfit leaders. An early Irish king's health was integral to his rule: a king with a paralyzed arm or damaged hearing was no king at all. However, Johnson emphasizes that the Irish understood health in a much broader scope: a king who failed to govern his lands was equally disabled. Turner, elsewhere, discusses this issue of the health of the ruler being seen as an indicator of the health of the kingdom.[35] Here, Turner brings to bear the concept, like both Trembinski and Johnson, that the lay understanding of medicine and of how medical issues might shape a legal outcome was much broader and deeper than previously conceptualized. Further, the social understanding and cultural acceptance of medicine and medical theory influenced laws and legal practices pertaining to medical issues—especially those laws and practices impacting the disabled, ill, impaired, and incompetent.

As Butler, Dangler, McCleery, and Robison assert, there was a growing desire to professionalize, standardize, and legalize the practice of medicine. In such a discussion, John of Gaddesden (c. 1280–1349/61) wrote a scathing piece about medical "*idiota*,"[36] in which he implied that bad doctors and midwives were akin to "idiots." According to Gaddesden, these untrained and superstitious

---

34   See also: Irina Metzler, *Disability in Medieval Europe: Thinking about Physical Impairment in the High Middle Ages, c. 1100–c. 1400* (New York: Routledge, 2005); Edward Wheatley, *Stumbling Blocks before the Blind: Medieval Constructions of a Disability* (Ann Arbor, MI: University of Michigan Press, 2010); Josh Eyler, ed., *A World of Difference: Essays on Disability in the Middle Ages* (Aldershot: Ashgate, 2010); Wendy J. Turner and Tory Vandervent Pearson, eds., *The Treatment of Disabled Persons in Medieval Europe: Examining Disability in the Historical, Legal, Literary, Medical, and Religious Discourse of the Middle Ages* (Lampeter, Wales: Edwin Mellen Press, 2010); Irina Metzler, *A Social History of Disability in the Middle Ages: Cultural Considerations of Physical Impairment* (New York: Routledge, 2013).

35   "A Cure for the King means Health for the Country: The Mental and Physical Health of Henry VI," in *Madness in Medieval Law and Custom*, ed. Wendy J. Turner (Leiden and Boston: Brill, 2011), pp. 177–195.

36   Most often this word *idiota* is translated as "quack" in the context of medical works and as "idiot" in administrative or legal works.

physicians were killing rather than curing their patients.[37] Guy de Chauliac (c. 1298–1368), writing near the same time as Gaddesden, wrote that madness (including *idiotsy*) was from God and, though it seized people who were saints,[38] it was a God-sent disease mostly affecting women, idiots, and fools who were "unlike the saints.... God shall [do] to me as it pleases him; God shall take [sanity from whomever he likes]; the name of our lord be blessed. Amen."[39] Although these two physicians were writing about two different subjects, the "madness" of not legalizing the practice on the one hand and about madness as a disorder on the other, the idea that incompetence—in medicine or any other aspect of life—meant a weak individual was often equated to "female." Butler's case study of Wodehill—whose name invokes quite serendipitously the early medieval idea that sleep on a fairy hill could bring on *wodeness* or "madness" but, in all seriousness, probably had nothing to do with his name, which could also be translated as the innocuous "wooded hill"—was one of a man trying to demonstrate that his profession strengthened him, and accordingly, his position in society. Dangler's study of Roig also invoked this idea of male strength and clarity as the opposite of female weakness and "quackery." Roig openly ridiculed female physicians and the men who might seek out their care. Further, Johnson's Irish saints healed and punished quite in line with the opinions of the surgeon Guy de Chauliac. The saints' *vitae* describe how honor was revoked through ridiculous paralytic postures, disabling sinners, but also de-masculinizing them. Much like in Dangler's study of Roig's discussion of women, men who did not act like men should not remain part of the established male order. This loss of honor, prestige, and ability left these men legally weaker and physically ill or disabled. For example, in a dispute over the land of one of St Patrick's earliest converts, now an old man, St Finian launches into a war of miracles against a ruler who denied a man his plot of land. Among other curses, St Finian inflicts the king with paralysis as he wanders out to relieve himself one morning, freezing him in the most humiliating of positions, emphasizing that which identifies him as male, but at the same time de-masculinizing him through embarrassment. Finian refuses to release the

---

37   Cholmeley, *John of Gaddesden*, above, 88.

38   Guy de Chauliac, *Anatomy*, in *The Middle English Translation of Guy de Chauliac's Anatomy, with Guy's essay on the History of Medicine*, ed. Björn Wallner (Lund: CWK Gleerup, Håkan Ohlssons Bokryckeri, 1964), p. 20, line 27.

39   "[O]f wommen and of many ydeotis or foles. fle whiche remitten seke men for all man*ere* of sekenesse onliche to seyntes. foundynge ham *per*fore vp flat God zaf to me as it plesede hym; God schal take fro me when it schall like gym[;] fle name of oure loord be blessid[.] amen." Chauliac, *Anatomy*, p. 21, line 28.

ruler from his mortification until he agrees to offer the disputed plot of land
to God and begin the penitential process. In this tale, it was not so much that
the ruler was feminized, but that his virility was made an object of mockery.
The body as an object of parts and medical afflictions, at its most vulnerable in
a ruler, was part of the law giver and defender—weak or strong depending on
the wielder and his belief in God and God's messengers.

Physicians called as expert witnesses, laws governing medical conditions,
lawyers who called on their physician friends to stand for them in court, medical practitioners who exploited the law in their mission to professionalize: all
of these examples reveal that the juncture of law and medicine in the Middle
Ages was a powerful one. As these chapters contend, whether it was the court
calling on the assistance of a physician, or a physician wanting his profession to be legally regulated, the connection between law and medicine in the
Middle Ages has been understudied. We hope that this collection begins a new
discussion toward discovering the complex influences of law on medicine and
medicine on law.

Medical Matters in Law and Administration of Law

∵

CHAPTER 1

Compensating Body and Honor:
The Old Frisian Compensation Tariffs

Han Nijdam

The Old Frisian compensation tariffs (ca. 1250–1500) are a unique group of law texts. Going back to the injury tariffs found in the early medieval *Leges Barbarorum*, they meticulously inventory, measure and assess all kinds of bodily injuries and other damages resulting from conflicts. This chapter discusses these texts by looking at their cultural and anthropological roots as well as their synchronic context. What types of injuries did these tariffs list? What can we learn about their composers' medical knowledge? Finally, what did the tariffs aim to compensate and by what mechanisms?

Putting a Price on the Body and Its Parts

The first compensation tariffs can be found in the law code of the Mesopotamian king Hammurabi, dating to the eighteenth century BCE. This is the first written example of a price on human life and the body's various parts for the purposes of compensating loss, or loss of functionality as the result of an injury inflicted by someone else. Until that time, the only option for an injured person—other than to let the matter rest—was revenge: an eye for an eye, or worse. Psychologist Nico Frijda calls revenge "one of man's strongest emotions."[1] At first glance, revenge seems counterproductive: it can consume one for years on end; some people sacrifice their lives in order to take revenge; revenge often leads to a level of violence that surpasses the original act by far. Yet, Frijda also sees a productive side to revenge. He suggests the following benefits: (1) determent; (2) restoration of a loss or lack of power; (3) restoration of pride and escape from shame; (4) healing from pain; (5) bringing the scales of suffering (justice) into balance. In other words, a wronged person must be brought to a state of powerlessness, shame and hurt. Taking revenge discourages one's wrongdoer from attacking again, which (1) restores one's sense of power; (2) provides a sense of winning the upper hand; (3) restores one's pride,

---

1 Nico H. Frijda, *De wetten der emoties* (Amsterdam: Bakker, 2008), pp. 293–318.

eliminating feelings of shame at being defeated; (4) eases the emotional pain; and lastly, (5) equalizes the two parties. To these five a sixth gain can be added: (6) revenge provides a life goal. The drive to take revenge can keep a person going for years. Frijda mentions this briefly as a negative outcome of revenge, but it can also be a positive outcome, because it can literally give you something to live for.

Because the drive to take revenge is so strong, people have to be persuaded to accept compensation rather than retaliate.[2] In premodern societies, taking revenge was the more honorable option, and it took an effort to make people perceive accepting compensation as equally honorable. Even a recent cross-cultural survey demonstrated that in 95% of societies, people endorse the notion of taking a life for a life.[3] William Miller describes the situation nicely for medieval Iceland: "[t]he culture had contempt for the man too eager to give up on vengeance and too willing to settle for compensation at the same time that it honored men of peace and admitted infinite negotiability: 'everything is compensable.'"[4]

In medieval Iceland, people overeager for compensation were seen as "carrying their kin in their purse."[5] Conversely, a king might benefit from creating legislation requiring compensation, since it would diminish the amount of violence among his citizens.[6] Of course, even a society without a strong ruler does not desire on-going feuds between families or clans. Excessive levels of violence disturb a social system and threaten its survival.

Once compensation tariffs and the concept of blood money or *wergeld*— compensation for the next of kin in homicides to eliminate the need for revenge—had been invented, life itself, the human body and its various parts began to be worth money. This process of capitalization of human life has been going on ever since, and the impact of this development can hardly be underestimated. In an episode of the television show *QI*, originally broadcast on March 2011, the host Stephen Fry asked his panel: "How much are you worth?"

---

2   Han Nijdam, "Belichaamde eer, wraak en vete. Een historisch- en cognitief-antropologische benadering," *Tijdschrift voor Geschiedenis* 123 (2010): 192–207. J. van der Dennen, "Waarom wraak zoet is," http://www.nvmp.org/030304.htm. Accessed Mar. 1, 2013.

3   Steven Pinker, *The Better Angels of our Nature. Why Violence has Declined* (New York: Viking, 2011), p. 47.

4   William I. Miller, *Bloodtaking and Peacemaking. Feud, Law, and Society in Saga Iceland* (Chicago and London: University of Chicago Press, 1990), pp. 189–190.

5   Miller, *Bloodtaking and Peacemaking*, 190.

6   In his recent work *The Better Angels of our Nature*, Steven Pinker shows a long-term decline of violence because of state formation. The goal of his work is to show that contrary to what people intuitively think, humanity is now at an unprecedented low in homicide percentages.

Panelist Alan Davies immediately answered: "You mean if you sold all your bits; your kidneys, liver, *et cetera*?"[7] That was, indeed, the answer Fry was seeking. A person's worth increases enormously if you consider selling your organs and body parts on the market.

Because human life is often considered priceless, the idea of converting the body into hard cash by cutting it up into bones, organs and chunks of meat makes some people uncomfortable. In *Eye for an Eye*, William Miller puts it thus: "[t]alking about humans as money or property is not, we feel, consistent with certain pieties we have regarding the proper way to talk about the immeasurable specialness of human value."[8] On second glance, one realizes that modern society assigns a value to humans all the time. Someone might be described as a "million dollar man" based on his annual income. In honor cultures, people with honor are worth more than those without. Even between men of honor there are differences in just how honorable they are. In Anglo-Saxon England there were 200-shilling men, 600-shilling men and 1200-shilling men. These amounts referred to the *wergeld* to which they were entitled. In other words, these were the amounts necessary to prevent revenge by kinsmen in instances of homicide. Alternatively, you needed to execute three 200-shilling men to avenge properly the death of a 600-shilling man.[9]

How did the body and its parts come to be commodified? Today, bodies and body parts are worth money in the two domains that are the topic of this volume: medicine and law. Body parts, blood and even DNA have become commodities because the technological advancement of modern medicine. Surgeons can transfer organs from one body to another, making those organs valuable, especially to the person in dire need of a new heart or kidney. The scarcity of availability drives the market. Yet, the mechanisms behind compensation for injured bodies or body parts work differently. Compensation relies on law on the one hand and revenge on the other. Today, compensation for injuries still exists in various legal systems.[10] For the most part, the amounts of compensation are legislated by the state who fixes the price. In premodern societies, revenge set the price. Simply put, if you did not agree to the price a wrongdoer offered for the loss of your eye, you always had the option of

7   BBC, QI Series H, episode Humans, first broadcast Oct. 8, 2010 (http://www.bbc.co.uk/programmes/b006mlog/episodes/guide#boottsl6). Accessed Mar. 1, 2013.

8   William I. Miller, *Eye for an Eye* (Cambridge: CUP, 2006), p. 111.

9   Miller, *Eye for an Eye*, 109.

10   Ulrich Magnus, "Compensation for Personal Injuries in a Comparative Perspective," *Washburn Law Journal* 39 (2000): 347–362.

gouging out his.[11] How law valued body parts depended on a number of elements that will be addressed in this chapter.

Compensation Tariffs in Medieval Frisia

The early medieval *Leges Barbarorum*, or "Laws of the Germanic peoples," redacted during the reigns of the Merovingian and Carolingian kings, form the historical starting point.[12] Unlike in Stephen Fry's *QI* question, in these texts not every human life was valued equally. The *wergeld* varied according to rank: whether a man belonged to the nobility, or he was a freeman or slave. There were also a number of sub-categories. The *Lex Frisionum* ("Law of the Frisians"), drawn up towards the end of the eighth century, distinguishes between noblemen (*nobiles*), free men (*liberi*), half-free men (*lites*) and slaves (*servi*). The *wergeld* of a free man was the point of departure. A free man was

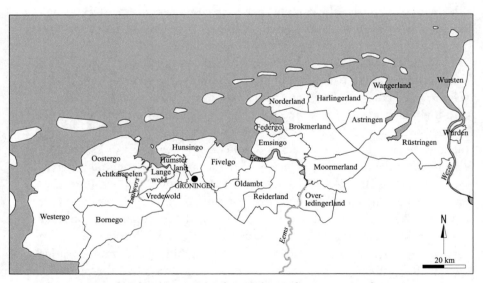

FIGURE 1   *Map of Medieval Frisia. Taken from Nijdam,* Lichaam, eer en recht, *p. 282.*

---

11   Miller, *Eye for an Eye*, pp. 48–54.
12   One of the most recent studies on this topic is Gerhard Dilcher and Eva-Marie Distler, eds., *Leges—Gentes—Regna. Zur Rolle von germanischen Rechtsgewohnheiten und lateinischer Schrifttradition bei der Ausbildung der frühmittelalterlichen Rechtskultur* (Berlin: Erich Schmidt Verlag, 2006).

worth twice as much as a *litus*. Or, put in golden *solidi* (and converted to silver shillings): the *wergeld* of a noble was 80 *solidi* (= 240 shillings); that of a free man 53 *solidi* + 1 *tremissus* (= 160 shillings); that of a *litus* 27 *solidi* minus 1 *tremissus* (= 80 shillings).[13] This yields a ratio of 3:2:1. It is noteworthy that the compensation tariffs give an undifferentiated amount of money because they viewed compensation for a freeman as the default state.

Frisia was divided into three territories according to the *Lex Frisionum*: a central part between the Rivers Vlie and Lauwers (the modern province of Friesland in the Netherlands), a Western part between the Rivers Zwin and Vlie (thus comprising the provinces of South and North Holland in the Netherlands), and an Eastern part between the Rivers Lauwers and Weser (i.e. Groningen in the Netherlands and Ostfriesland in Germany) (see Fig. 1).[14] The immensely elaborate compensation tariffs single out the *Lex Frisionum* from other *Leges Barbarorum*. The core text of the *Lex Frisionum* is followed by the additions of two "wise men," called Wlemar and Saxmund. A recent analysis by Lisi Oliver of the body legal across *Leges Barbarorum* concludes that the *Lex Frisionum* is by far the most elaborate code as far as injuries are concerned.[15] Most probably, this can be ascribed to the fact that the surviving text seems to have been a draft and not the final edited version of the "Law of the Frisians." A further telltale sign is that no medieval manuscripts containing the text have survived to this day. The first and only version stems from the integral edition of the *Leges Barbarorum* by Johannes Herold in 1557, who copied it from a manuscript which is now lost.[16]

After the eighth century, the sources fall silent. No Frisian law text was handed down for the period between the eighth and the thirteenth centuries. What happened to Frisia during the ninth to eleventh centuries is not entirely clear, due to an overall scarcity of written sources for this period. The Viking presence in the North Sea region played a significant role at this time. In part, Frisia developed into a frontier of the Carolingian empire in defense against the Vikings. The Carolingians granted a number of regions of Frisia as fiefs to

---

13   Harald Siems, *Studien zur Lex Frisionum* (Ebelsbach: Gremer, 1980); Dirk Jan Henstra, *The Evolution of the Money Standard in Medieval Frisia. A Treatise on the History of the Systems of Money of Account in the Former Frisia (c. 600–c. 1500)* (Groningen: D.J. Henstra, 2000); Kees Nieuwenhuijsen: http://www.keesn.nl/lex/lex_en_text.htm. Accessed Oct. 21, 2012.

14   There was some variation in *wergeld* among these various territories, but this chapter will not address that concern.

15   Lisi Oliver, *The Body Legal in Barbarian Law* (Toronto: University of Toronto Press, 2011).

16   Johannes Herold, ed., *Originum ac Germanicarum Antiquitatum libri* (Basel: Henricus Petri, 1557), pp. 131–148.

Viking rulers in an attempt to pacify them. Later, in the eleventh and twelfth centuries, the Saxon counts of the house of Brunswick had a claim to Frisia east of the River Lauwers, while the counts of Holland and the bishops of Utrecht simultaneously claimed the western and central regions.

From the twelfth century onward, Frisia between Vlie and Weser (i.e. the old central and eastern parts) began to deviate from its neighboring regions.[17] The various counts with a claim to Frisia did not succeed in establishing a suzerainty (German *Landesherrschaft*). Hence, the Frisians continued to rule themselves, only paying small tithes and taxes to church and worldly lord, but keeping direct control from a sovereign lord at bay. Rule by a duke or count would have meant a change in the courts of law, with the appointment of a royal judge. Very likely, too, old customary laws would have been rewritten. Instead, the various autonomous Frisian communities or *terrae* ruled themselves. Calling themselves "Free Frisians" (OFris. *fria Fresa*), the Frisian elite elected judges-administrators from among themselves (see Fig. 2). This office circulated on a yearly basis. The area west of the River Vlie developed into the county of Holland (ruled by an earl) and did not partake in the Frisian Freedom.

The "Free Frisians" and their "Frisian Freedom"—a political reality and an ideology at once—provided the incentive to codify Frisian customary laws. The Frisians saw it as their prerogative, allegedly granted by Charlemagne himself, to uphold their indigenous legal system. The earliest manuscripts date from the thirteenth century, but earlier ones must have existed. Exactly when this process began is a matter of some debate: some say already in the twelfth century, according to others not before 1200.[18] For the most part, the high medieval Frisian law manuscripts were written in the vernacular, called Old Frisian, with some texts in Low German or Latin. They derive from the entire Free Frisian area between the rivers Vlie and Weser. After 1400, a large corpus of Low German translations of Frisian law began to take shape.

The "Free Frisian" ideology covers up the social ranks in medieval Frisia like a blanket, keeping them out of clear view for modern scholars. The central

---

17   Han Nijdam, *Lichaam, eer en recht in middeleeuws Friesland. Een studie naar de Oudfriese boeteregisters* (Hilversum: Verloren, 2008), pp. 107–119; Oebele Vries, "Geschichte der Friesen im Mittelalter: West- und Ostfriesland," in *Handbuch des Friesischen. Handbook of Frisian Studies*, ed. Horst Haider Munske, *et al.* (Tübingen: Niemeyer, 2001), pp. 538–550.

18   Rolf H. Bremmer, *Hir is eskriven. Lezen en schrijven in de Friese landen rond 1300* (Hilversum: Uitgeverij Verloren, 2004); Dirk Jan Henstra, "De eerste optekening van de algemeen-Friese keuren," *It Beaken* 64 (2002): 99–128; Nijdam, *Lichaam, eer en recht*, p. 86.

FIGURE 2   *Seal with two archetypical Frisian warriors, 1338. Groninger museum, Groningen.*

myth of the Frisian Freedom recounts how Charlemagne awarded Frisians
their freedom because of Frisian heroic deeds while in service to him. This
myth justified Frisian autonomy to the outside world. At the same time, nobles
and freemen seem to conflate into one group called Free Frisians in the Old
Frisian law texts. Recent research, however, shows that nobles and freemen
remained separate ranks throughout medieval Frisia, although evidence from
contemporary sources is scarce.[19] Compensation tariffs usually do not distinguish between ranks. The compensation they give is that of a free man, to be
scaled up in the event of a nobleman.[20]

---

19   Paul Noomen, "Eigenerfd of edel? Naar aanleiding van de afkomst van de Aytta's," *It
      Beaken* 73 (2011): 257–301.
20   S. Rubin, "The *bot*, or Compensation in Anglo–Saxon Law: A Reassesment," *Journal of
      Legal History* 17.1 (1996): 144–54.

The positive outcome of the Frisian Freedom is the large corpus of indigenous law texts. Among these, compensation tariffs take a prominent position.[21]
They fill between 10% and 25% of the manuscripts that contain compilations
of law texts. In the oldest manuscripts, stemming from the thirteenth century
and from the Eastern part of Frisia (between the Rivers Lauwers and Weser),
both a *General Old East Frisian Compensation Tariff* and various regional tariffs
were redacted. The general tariff dates from at least the twelfth century, as is
apparent from the various redactions found in the thirteenth-century manuscripts. The regional tariffs are *in statu nascendi* in the thirteenth century but
have grown into mature texts in the manuscripts of the fifteenth century, both
in size and in scope. In the younger manuscripts, the old general tariff dis-
appears. Apparently, concomitant with the growing autonomy of the various
regions during the thirteenth century, each developed its own compensation
tariff for use in the regional courts of law. To offer some figures: the old general
tariff had an average of *ca.* 130 stipulations. The oldest versions of the regional
tariffs contained around 70 stipulations in average, which is less than the two
complete tariffs that survived in the *Lex Frisionum*: these each had almost 90
stipulations. The youngest Old East Frisian tariffs easily make up for this: the
first contains roughly 200 paragraphs, the second slightly more than 400, making it the largest Old Frisian tariff.

West of the River Lauwers, that is in the present-day province of Friesland
in the Netherlands (one of the few regions where the Frisian language still survives), all surviving manuscripts stem from the fifteenth century. They contain a large number of regional compensation tariffs. Most are rather small:
ca. 130 stipulations on average. One tradition, the *Bireknade Bota* or "Calculated
Compensations," expanded, probably developing into a general West Frisian
tariff, and reached a size of around 300 paragraphs.

The reason the legal genre of compensation tariffs flourished in medieval
Frisia lies in what this chapter described previously. Medieval Frisia was a feuding society, a society without a feudal overlord but with a broader powerbase,
in this case the Free Frisian elite, who ruled themselves and the rest of society
through the annual election of a judge-administrator. The Free Frisians gathered in local and supralocal courts that adjudicated lawsuits and made politics.
Only the Free Frisians had the right to attend these meetings. In a feuding society, everything revolves around status, prestige and honor. The elite had certain rights, but they had to defend them constantly from competitors in order
not to lose them. One of the ways to find a balance of power in such a society
is by feuding. Because of the high value placed on personal and familial honor,

---

21   The following overview is taken from Nijdam, *Lichaam, eer en recht*, pp. 84–105.

offences have to be retaliated. This can spiral out of control when someone is killed, because it sets in motion a process of revenge and counter revenge.[22]

The practice of compensating, rather than feuding or having to suffer court-mandated corporal punishment, was seen as a prerogative of the Free Frisians. One of the oldest law texts, *The Seventeen Statutes*, contains an explicit statement on this: "This is the sixteenth statute, that all Frisians have the right to compensate with money any breach of the peace."[23]

The Body in the Old Frisian Compensation Tariffs

Compared to the *Lex Frisionum*, the Old Frisian tariffs are more detailed and elaborate in two ways. First, they provide copious detail concerning various types of physical injuries. Second, they mention other types of damages to a person and his possessions: damages to someone's house, land and cattle, as well as the members of his household. The picture that strongly emerges from the texts is that of a freeholder managing a farm and its complete entourage. Only some stipulations indicate that the intended audience included also the nobility, such as those that say: "If someone's castle has been overtaken. . . . "[24] Table 1 gives a schematic overview of the types of stipulations found in the Old Frisian compensation tariffs.

When attention is paid to the physical body, it is interesting to see which body parts and organs are mentioned and which are not. Most tariffs treat the body and its various wounds in a head-to-toe order. This section will look at the way the body is treated in the tariffs, which body schemata can be found and in which way a functioning body was defined. The following section will look at the types of wounds, wound treatment and what kind of medical knowledge becomes apparent from the tariffs.

---

22 Christopher Boehm, "The Natural History of Blood Revenge," in *Feud in Medieval and Early Modern Europe*, ed. Jeppe Büchert Netterström and Birte Poulsen (Aarhus: Orhus University Press, 2007), pp. 189–203.

23 *Thet is thiu sextendeste kest, thet alle Fresa hira frethe mith fia bete.* Seventeen Statutes §16; Wybren Jan Buma and Wilhelm Ebel, eds., *Das Hunsingoer Recht*. Altfriesische Rechtsquellen 4 (Göttingen: Vandenhoeck & Ruprecht, 1969), p. 28.

24 *Hwasa otheren sin stenhus ofwint. Emsingo Compensation Tariff* §174; Wybren Jan Buma and Wilhelm Ebel, eds., *Das Emsiger Recht*. Altfriesische Rechtsquellen 3 (Göttingen: Vandenhoeck & Ruprecht, 1967), p. 126.

TABLE 1   *Schematic overview of the content of the Old Frisian compensation tariffs*

1) Physical injuries to the human body
2) Damaging a person
   a) Pulling, singeing or cutting someone's hair or beard (OFris. *faxfang, berdfang*)
   b) Throwing someone into the water (OFris. *wapeldepene*)
   b) Fettering someone or taking him hostage (OFris. *bende*)
   c) Robbing (OFris. *raf*)
   d) Threatening, waylaying (OFris. *quade ber, weiwendene*)
   e) Chasing someone (OFris. *gelene, jagia*)
   f) Hitting someone in a humiliating way (OFris. *dustslek, halsslek, daveddusinge*)
   g) Hitting someone so that he falls to the ground (OFris. *gersslinge, muldeslek, bekhlep, fotsperne*)
   h) Hitting someone unconscious (OFris. *soldede, dathswima*)
   i) Pouring liquid over someone, spitting, urinating, throwing mud or dirt (OFris. *swarte sweng, biarhlem, onspia, pissia, horewerp*)
   j) Tearing up someone's clothes, tearing away headdress, making someone look naked (OFris. *blezene*)
   k) Verbal injury (OFris. *unieve word*)
   l) Assaulting or raping a woman (OFris. *nedmund*)
3) Other damages
   a) Stealing soil, crops or confiscating plots of land (*londbrekma*)
   b) Illegal entry into a house (*hemsekene*)
   d) Torturing, robbing or illegally riding cattle (*sketquelene*)

Not touching upon the medical details yet, there are a number of general principles in the treatment of the body. First, visibility was important. Wounds were considered less grave, and thus demanded a lower compensation, if they could be covered up by hair or clothing. This is true for most indigenous laws of medieval Europe.[25] Second, functionality was also important. Numerous stipulations contain details on the extent to which a victim had use of a body part after the wound had healed.

---

25   Rudolf His, "Die Körperverletzungen im Strafrecht des deutschen Mittelalters," *Zeitschrift der Savigny–Stiftung für Rechtsgeschichte. Germanistische Abteilung* 41 (1920): 75–126; Oliver, *The Body Legal*.

Table 2 addresses all body parts and related terms (such as those for various body fluids) encountered in the compensation tariffs.[26]

TABLE 2   *Body Part Terms in the Old Frisian Compensation Tariffs (Old Frisian terms in italics)*

---

1. Body
corpse (*hre*)
body/life (*lif*) (also: "torso")
body/corpse (*lik*)
body (*likhama*)

2. Head
head (*haved, holla, meldke, kop*)
scalp (*swarde*)
brain (*brein*)
skull area (*breinklova*)
skull (*breinpanna*)
meningeal (*helibrede*)
face (*ondlete*) (*wlite*: only in *wlitewlemmelse*)
complexion (*bli*)
forehead / front part of the mouth (*forhaved* / *farahaved*)
natural opening in the skull (*hol*)
wrinkle (*leseke, wirsene*)
eye (*age*)
eyeball (*agappel*)
eye pupil (*sia*: alleen in *siawerdene*)
eyebrow ([*ag*]*bre*)
orbit (*aghring*)
eye socket (*kolk*)
eyelid (*aghlid*)
upper eyelid (*ura hlid*)
lower eyelid (*nithere hlid*)
eyelash (omschreven in *faxfeng on tha age*)

(*Continued*)

---

26   In fact, Table 2 provides what can be found on body parts in the entire Old Frisian corpus, since almost all terms appear in the tariffs. Those few that materialize elsewhere (there are two short Old Frisian texts, an oath formula and an embryology, which are concerned with the human body) have also been added to the list.

TABLE 2   *(Continued)*

corner of the eye (*ongneil*)
eye area (*agebred*)
nose (*nose*)
nose bone (*noseben*)
nostril (*nostern*)
mouth (*muth, mula, mund, snabba, snavel*)
lip (*were, lippa*)
upper lip (*ura were*)
lower lip (*nithere were*)
tongue (*tunge*)
eight front teeth (*achta sa hit is a fara[havede]*)
tooth root (*herna*)
tooth crown (*stapul*)
canine (*herntoth, sleitoth*)
molar (*kese, inra toth*)
tooth (*toth, tusk, tond*)
jaw / cheek (*ziake*)
jaw (*zinbakka*)
ear (*are*)
earlobe (*arlippa*)

hair and hair styles
hair (*her, fax*)
beard (*berd*)
tonsure (of a priest) (*platta*)
moustache (*kanep*)
lock of hair (*top heres*)
curls (*frisle*)

3. Torso
torso (*lif*)
side (*side*)

upper torso
neck (*hals*)
back of the neck (*hnekka*)
larynx (*strotbolla, throtbolla, halsknap*)

(Continued)

TABLE 2   *(Continued)*

---

neck sinew (*halssine*)
gullet / trachea (*wasanda*)
collarbone (*widuben*)
armpit (*axle*)
shoulder (*skuldere*)
shoulder bone (*axelben*)
shoulder blade (*herdbled*)
breast (*burst, briast, borst*)
breastbone (*burstben, borstben*)
nipple (*warte*)
back (*hreg*)
backbone / back marrow (*walduwaxe, waldsine*)
bone in the back (*hregben*)
lung (*lungen*)
lung lobe (*flard*)
rib (*rib*)
heart (*herte*)

lower torso
diaphragm (*midhrif*)
abdomen (*buk*)
stomach (*maga*)
the "small part" of the stomach (*klene thes maga*)
navel (*navla*)
navel button (*navlahring, navlathiukke*)
loins (*lenden*)
uterus (*benete burch*)
intestines (*inhrif*)
intestine (*therm*)
bowel fleece (*nette*)
liver (*livere*)
kidney (*lundlaga*)
spleen (*milte*)
coccyx (*quemben*)
venus? ([*nethere*] *swoll*)
genitals (*mecht*)
penis (*pint*)

(Continued)

TABLE 2   (*Continued*)

---

testicle (*pralling, prelling, hothe, tiling*)
vagina (*kunte*)
ability to reproduce (*tochta*)
"reproduction sinew" (*fruchtsine*)
"testicle sinew" (*skalsine*)
"make it go up sinew" (*stiapsine*)
Limbs
limb (*lith, lithmata*)

4. Arm
arm (*erm*)
bone in the upper arm (*henzeben*)
arm marrow (*ermmerg*)
armpit (*ermskethe*)
sinew in the armpit (*henzesine*)
elbow (*elboga*)
cubit (*pipe*)
humerus (*pre*)
radius (*skidel*)

5. Hand
hand (*hond*)
fist (*fest*)
palm of the hand (*hondbled*)
wrist (*hondwrist*)
finger (*finger*)
lower joint / member (*feritste lith*)
middle joint / member (*middelste lith*)
upper joint / member (*minneste lith*)
middle joint of the finger (*middelknokel*)
nail (*neil*)
thumb (*thuma, haldere*)
index finger (*skotfinger*)
middle finger (*grate finger*)
ring finger (*goldfinger*)
little finger (*liteke finger, slutere*)

(*Continued*)

TABLE 2   (*Continued*)

6. Leg
been (*ben, skunka*)
thigh (*thiach, thiachskunk*)
thigh marrow (*thiachmerg*)
knee (*kni*)
hollow of the knee (*hoxene*)
kneecap (*knibeltride*)
ankle (*ankle*)
heel (*hela*)
heel sinew (*helsine*)

7. Foot
foot (*fot*)
ankle joint (*fotwerst*)
foot sole (*ile*)
toe (*tane*)
big toe (*grate tane*)
little toe (*litike tane*)

8. Other
tear (*tar*)
mucus (*snotta*)
phlegm (*saver*)
saliva (*spedel*)
feces (*quad, threk*)
urine (*mese*)
blood (*blod*)
sweat (*swet*)
sinew (*sine*)
bone (*ben*)
bones (*benete*)
flesh (*flask*)
bone marrow (*merch*)
vein (*eddre*)
gristle (*gristel*)
breath (*ethma, omma*)

(*Continued*)

TABLE 2   *(Continued)*

---

partition (wall) (*wach*)

skin (*fel, filmene, hed*)

joint (*hwerfta, lithalet*)

edge of a wound (*ende*)

cut off piece of flesh (*lappa*)

pus (*smere*)

piece of skin between two bleeding wounds (*dom* literally "dam," *middeldom*)

unscathed piece of skin (*lond* (literally "land")

wound opening (*mutha* literally "mouth of a river")

feelings / heart / emotions (*mod*)

mind (*hei*)

mental capacity (*wit*)

thoughts (*thochta*)

anger (*hast*)

soul (*sele*)

The list of terms appears long because some of the terms are mentioned only once in one specific tariff. It includes only a few internal organs. The scarcity of stipulations concerning wounds to the internal organs speaks to what doctors were able to heal and what they considered a lost case: if someone died because of his wounds, his next of kin claimed the entire *wergeld*. A few interesting body schemata can be discerned throughout the various Old Frisian tariffs.[27] One of the most pervasive is that of the so-called "six limbs," i.e. the eyes, hands and feet. Even today, these are our most prized body parts. Small wonder, then, that half a *wergeld* was set on the loss of each. This is already the case in the *Lex Frisionum* and in a large number of the other Germanic law codes.[28] But in the Old Frisian tariffs, eyes, hands and feet were a category. The "six limbs" became a health check of sorts: the law considered a man able as long as he still had the full use of his "six limbs."

The diaphragm functioned as an imaginary horizontal axis along which the body was mirrored. One text interprets the diaphragm as the boundary between the upper torso and the lower torso. More implicitly, in all texts the arms and legs are seen as each other's mirror images (i.e. shoulder = hip; elbow = knee; wrist = ankle; hand = foot; finger = toe). This parallel led to such

---

27   For this overview see Nijdam, *Lichaam, eer en recht*, pp. 217–225 and 254–272.

28   Oliver, *The Body Legal*, pp. 247–261.

terse stipulations as: "[f]or the compensation of the toes see the compensations for the fingers," meaning that a big toe was worth the same as a thumb,
and so forth.[29] This is a near-universal phenomenon. The *Lex Frisionum*, however, still contains compensations for the various toes, which are no longer
extant in the Old Frisian tariffs because of the equation "fingers = toes."

Another measure of health was to look at the degree to which a man still
had the use of his five senses. Isidore of Seville's *Etymologiae* was an important
source for the spread of this gauge throughout medieval Europe. In Frisia, the
thirteenth-century encyclopedic works of Bartholomeus Anglicus and Vincent
of Beauvais played an important role in its dissemination.[30] That the concept
must stem from a learned work is evident from the fact that in the Old Frisian
tariffs there are Latin terms together with vernacular ones: *uisus, auditus, gus-
tus, odoratus et tactus; sione, here, smek, hrene, fele* "sight, hearing, taste, smell,
touch."[31] It is easy to see why the tariffs so readily adopted the concept of the
five senses. They were partly linked to the "six limbs" (eyes = sight, hands =
touch), but also to other vital organs such as the ears (hearing), nose (smell)
and the tongue (taste), for the loss of each of which a third part of a *wergeld*
could be claimed.

In the tariffs, the loss of the five senses is linked frequently to the so-called
eleven *wendan* (literally "things" or "movements"), which were the outcomes
of an injury to either the spine, back or lower abdomen. The *General Old East
Frisian Compensation Tariff* supplies a typical example:

> (a) The compensation for an injury to the spine is 36 shillings; if as a con-
> sequence of this his five senses have deteriorated.
> The first is, that he cannot see as well as he did.
> The second is, that he cannot hear as well as he did.
> The third, that he cannot smell as well as he did.
> The fourth, that he cannot taste as well as he did.
> The fifth, that he cannot feel as well as he did.
> The compensation for the loss of each of the senses is 36 shillings.
> (b) On top of this, that he is not able to be as good as he was in bath nor
> in bed, on horseback nor in a carriage, on the road nor on the water [i.e.

---

29   *Tha tana hagon alsa grate bote alsa tha fingra*: "For the toes, the same compensations
     can be claimed as for the fingers." *General Old East Frisian Compensation Tariff* §9n;
     Wybren Jan Buma and Wilhelm Ebel, *Das Rüstringer Recht*. Altfriesische Rechtsquellen 1
     (Göttingen: Vandenhoeck & Ruprecht, 1963), p. 74.
30   Raymond van Uytven, *De zinnelijke middeleeuwen* (Louvain: Davidsfonds, cop., 1998), p. 10.
31   *General Old East Frisian Compensation Tariff* §1r; Buma and Ebel, *Das Rüstringer Recht*, 60.

in a ship], in his house nor in church, nor is able to perform as well with his wife as he used to, nor to manage himself as well either in front of his fire or at any expedition. If this is the case, then the compensation for each of these eleven *wendan* is 12 shillings.[32]

Here, the *wendan* are seen as resulting from an injury to the spine (*walduwaxe*). In other compensation tariffs, they are named in conjunction with a paralysis of the lower abdomen (*buklamethe*) or a paralysis of the back (*beklamethe*).[33] The injury described in these phrases must have been located in the lower part of the body, causing rather severe paralysis.

Like the injury of the *walduwaxe* and the ensuing eleven *wendan*, very often the tariffs depict injuries in terms of their impact. Overall, an able body, capable of functioning within society was what people aspired to maintain or recover. The tariffs explain this in simple terms. They include little sophisticated medical knowledge, such as references to the humors.

Wounds and Medical Knowledge in the Compensation Tariffs and in Medieval Frisia

Obviously, the compensation tariffs are not medical tracts or manuals. The subject of the wounded body, however, is something the two genres have in common. As a result of the shared subject matter, references to wound treatment have seeped through into the tariffs. They include also some interesting comments on physicians, their activities and their role in court procedure.

The tariffs can be viewed as a record of violence in medieval Frisia. They register the outcomes of both unarmed and armed encounters. The evidence ranges from bruises that leave the skin intact to amputations and other severely incapacitating injuries, with a sauce of insults sprinkled over it. These insults might be verbal or physical (such as hair pulling), and can be found in other *Leges Barbarorum*. Lisi Oliver rightly observes that grabbing someone's hair was

---

32   (a) *Thera walduwaxe bote sex and thritich skillinga; therfon send him ergerad sina fif sin. / Thet forme is, thet hi sa wel sia ne mi. / Thet other is, thet hi sa wel hera ne mi. / Thet thredde, thet hi sa wel hrena ne mi. / Thet fiarde, thet hi sa wel smekka ne mi. / Thet fifte, thet hi sa wel fela ne mi. / Thera fif sinwerdena iahwelikes bote sex and thritich skillinga. / (b) Therefter, thet hi sa wel wesa ne mi an bethe ni an bedde, ni an widzia ni an weine, ni an wi ni an wetire, ni an huse ni an godis huse, ni mith sinre wiue sa wel wesa ne mi, sa hi er machte, ni bi sina fiore ni an nenere ferde hini selua sa wel bithanka, sa hi er machte, sa is thera andloua wenda iawelikes bote twilif skillinga.* General Old East Frisian Compensation Tariff §8a–b; Buma and Ebel, *Das Rüstringer Recht*, pp. 62–64.

33   Nijdam, *Lichaam, eer en recht*, pp. 265–272.

an insult in itself (and certainly so in medieval Frisia, where a Free Frisian was defined by his hairstyle), but could also be the start of a more serious quarrel.[34]

Blows (OFris. *slek*) and bruises belong to the most innocent and inexpensive (in terms of compensation) category of injuries. However, the bruises had to be visible in order for the victim to claim compensation. If the victim was able to cover his bruises with clothing or his hair, there was no room for compensation. A few tariffs specify the number of days the bruises must remain visible: 21, 42 or 63. Each time span demanded a specific compensation.

Next are bleeding wounds (OFris. *blodresene*) and simple cut wounds (OFris. *metedolch*, which literally means "a measur(abl)e wound"). The moment a cut or opening of the skin reached the size of an inch or, put in Frisian terms, the measure of the first joint of the thumb, it was categorized as a *metedolch*. The *Lex Frisionum* cites three methods of measuring wounds (including the inch), yielding a total of 15 separate sizes.[35] Conversely, the Old Frisian tariffs measures all wounds according to the *mete* "measure-unit = inch." It seems that a deliberate simplification of the system had taken place. For a sizeable wound, the tariffs ordered a measurement of the wound's length and compensation was paid out by inch (*mete*). Anything shorter than an inch was called a *blodresene*, and this also had its price. Thus, each wound was the sum of a *blodresene* and / or several *metes*.

As a unit of measurement, the inch proved to be a useful tool for Old Frisian lawmakers. Or, so it would seem judging from the tariffs, for there it is used as a tool to measure more than mere flesh wounds. For instance, in a shooting, the tariffs stipulated the measurement of the shortest distance across the body from the entrance of the arrow to the exit wound. They considered this length a *metedolch* and compensated accordingly. Some tariffs dictate compensation for three quarters of the distance. Other tariffs propose an additional compensation for an internal injury (OFris. *inreth*) as well. In a comparable fashion, the lawmakers required measurement and compensation for the circumferences of bite wounds, burns and hewn-off pieces of flesh as lengths of *metedolch*.

The trail of the *metedolch* also offers insight into medicine in practice. The tariffs operated on the general principle that surgery should be interpreted as a physician inflicting wounds upon the victim, which then must also be compensated by the perpetrator. The following stipulation illustrates this point:

---

34 Oliver, *The Body Legal*, pp. 108–111.

35 Han Nijdam, "Measuring Wounds in the *Lex Frisionum* and the Old Frisian Registers of Fines," in *Philologia Frisica Anno 1999. Lêzingen fan it fyftjinde Frysk filologekongres 8, 9 en 10 desimber 1999*, ed. Piter Boersma, *et al.* (Leeuwarden: Fryske Akademy, 2000), pp. 180–203; Han Nijdam, "Klinkende munten en klinkende botsplinters in de Oudfriese rechtsteksten: continuïteit, discontinuïteit, intertekstualiteit," *De Vrije Fries* 89 (2009): 45–66.

Concerning the head: If someone is struck on the head with a piece of wood or with a club, or shot with iron, to such a degree that the wounded man has to be incised by a physician, then the victim must receive two ounces for the incision [i.e. for the treatment]. And the wound is to be measured around along the longer side with the upper joint of the thumb, each measure unit to be compensated with 16 pennies. And the victim has to swear that he did not have the incision applied in order to get more money but only to get his health back.[36]

In the same way, the perpetrator must compensate for the incision and any needle stitches made by physicians in stitching together a wound. Likewise, the victim deserved compensation also for trepanation. The compensation tariffs mention almost no other types of wound treatment. There is one allusion to cauterization and one unique paragraph in which pus (OFris. *smere*, literally "grease") is cut from a festering wound.[37]

The tariffs identify more categories of cut wounds than the mere *metedolch*. The terms they employ are OFris. *kerf* and *skredene*, which both translate as "cut." There are various compounds with *kerf* and *skredene* as second elements. Thus, there exists e.g. OFris. *sinekerf*, "sinew cut," and *gerstelkerf*, "cartilage cut," which both point to serious wounds. On the other hand, it is unclear what the tariffs meant by *wirsenekerf*, "a cut across the wrinkles of the forehead," or *ilekerf*, "a cut across the sole of the foot." These injuries seem to be mostly aesthetic or symbolic, another useful reminder of the fact that status and honor were important elements in the tariffs.

Injuries that penetrated deep into the body were unmistakably serious. The generic term for this was OFris. *inreth*. They demanded additional compensation for the complex injury they inflicted. A deep wound might also cause a fistula (OFris. *siama*). The tariffs include several compounds with this element, such as *breinsiama*, "fistula in the brain," *lungensiama*, "fistula in the lungs," *lithsiama*, "fistula in a limb or joint," and *gristelsiama*, "fistula in the cartilage."

---

36   *Fan da haude. Huam so ma slacht iefta mit yrsen syuth iefta mit holte ieff mit stupa oen*
     syn haud, dat ma him snya schil, so aegh hi dan des snides tua einsa; so aeg ma him om toe
     metten bi da lingra igh bi des tumma knockela langh, aller meta lyc xvi penninghen. Ende
     dat mei een ede oen to bringhen, dat hy den snei naet deen habbe oem nene fyafollinghe mer
     om sine liwes sonda. Bireknade Bota §36; Nijdam, *Lichaam, eer en recht*, p. 556.

37   Among late medieval physicians there was a heated discussion on whether wounds
     should be left to fester or whether they should be disinfected. See Erwin Huizenga, *Tussen*
     autoriteit en empirie. De Middelnederlandse chirurgieën in de veertiende en vijftiende eeuw
     en hun maatschappelijke context (Hilversum: Verloren, 2003), pp. 15, 283–285.

More problematic is the OFris. *lithwei*, a term found among the few vernacular words used in the *Lex Frisionum* where it is rendered as *liduwagi*. According to Annette Niederhellmann, this term should be seen as the Frisian variant of German *Gliedwasser*: *Glied* = *lith* / *lidu* "member / joint" and *wasser* = *wagi* / *wei* "fluid," in other words: synovial fluid.[38] The relevant paragraph in the *Lex Frisionum* accords with this interpretation. It states that if someone has been struck on a joint of a finger to such a degree that fluid runs from the wound, then the vernacular refers to this as *liduwagi* (*quod liduwagi dicunt*).[39] Problems with interpreting the material arise in the Old Frisian tariffs where *lithwei* is no longer confined to the joints—there are *lithweis* mentioned on the head, under the nail, on the larynx, on the palm of the hand and even on the tongue—and there is no longer an explicit reference to "fluid." Horst Haider Munske pointed to the fact that there is also a term *sinewege* in the tariffs, which is rendered as *membrorum mobilitas* "mobility / instability of the limbs / joints" in the surviving Latin version of this text. This implies a different meaning of the OFris. element *weg-* / *wei-*, pointing more in the direction of some kind of spraining. Munske thus settles on a meaning *Gliedverrenkung* "spraining of a joint."[40] But in another Old Frisian tariff a *riucht*, "rightful, according to the law," *lithwei* is a "wound which runs across the joint / limb and measures a *mete* ("inch") on the outside."[41] This again points to a wound instead of a sprain, and on closer inspection *lithwei* still seems to refer to synovial fluid—or some other kind of fluid—emitting from a wound. The references of *lithwei* on the head and especially the tongue are odd, but also rare. Therefore, it seems safe to assume

---

38   Annette Niederhellmann, *Arzt und Heilkunde in den frühmittelalterlichen Leges. Eine wort– und sachkundige Untersuchung* (Berlin and New York: de Gruyter, 1983), pp. 196–200.

39   *Si quislibet digitus ex quatuor longioribus in superioris articuli iunctura ita percussus fuerit, ut humor ex vulnere decurrat, quod liduwagi dicunt, I solido componatur*: "If one of the four longer fingers is hit on the upper joint in such manner that fluid runs out of the wound, which the people call *liduwagi*, this is to be compensated with 1 *solidus*." *Lex Frisionum* Tit. 22 §.35; Karl A. Eckhardt, and A. Eckhardt, eds., *Lex Frisionum*. Monumenta Germaniae Historica. Fontes iuris Germanici antiqui in usum scholarum separatim editi XII (Hannover, 1982).

40   Horst Haider Munske, *Der germanische Rechtswortschatz im Bereich der Missetaten. Philologische und sprachgeografische Untersuchungen. I. Die Terminologie der älteren westgermanischen Rechtsquellen* (Berlin and New York: de Gruyter, 1973), pp. 136–137.

41   *Thet is riucht lithwey, aldeer thet dolch gheth vr thet lith ende abuta tha metha haed.* Compensation Tariff of Ferwerderadeel and Dongeradeel §72. Wybren Jan Buma and Wilhelm Ebel, eds., *Westerlauwerssches Recht I. Jus Municipale Frisonum*. Altfriesische Rechtsquellen 6. 2 vols. (Göttingen: Vandenhoeck & Ruprecht, 1977), p. 440.

continuity between the *Lex Frisionum* and the Old Frisian tariffs, with a slight
expansion of the meaning of *lithwei*, the exact details of which remain unclear.
The case of the *lithwei* provides an instructive example of the problems in trying to interpret the more obscure terms in the Old Frisian tariffs. The scribes
obviously felt little need to explain what was already clear to them. It is apparent, however, that some kind of cut is involved, which brings the synovial fluid
back into the picture and makes a sprain the less likely solution.

The discussion of bone fractures and amputations, which together con-
stitute a large part of all stipulations, is much more straightforward. The Old
Frisian term for a bone fracture is *benbreke*. Two kinds of bone injury deserve
mention here. One is where a weapon not only cuts the flesh but also the bone.
In OFris. this is called *benes biti*, literally "bone biting." It is a metaphor for the
sword biting the bone, imagery that is also found in medieval heroic poetry
and literature such as *Beowulf* and the Old Icelandic sagas. The second type of
bone injury occurs when bone fragments protrude from a wound in the skull.
If these splinters are large enough to be heard from a few steps' distance when
dropped into a shield or bowl, they demand separate compensation. This stipulation is an archaic one, found in the *Lex Frisionum* as well as in various other
Leges Barbarorum.[42] The procedure must have worked satisfactorily, since it
reappears in the Old Frisian tariffs five centuries later and remains part of the
text tradition until the end of the fifteenth century.[43]

Discussions of amputations also yield a large corpus of body part terms.
These paragraphs address all fingers, down to the smallest joint and even
down to the fingernail. And they did not stop at this: every body part one could
think of being cut off was listed: nose, ear, eyelid, penis, and so forth. While
the amputation of the hands, eyes and feet demanded half a *wergeld* each, the
loss of other important body parts, such as the nose, tongue and ears, usually
exacted a third of a *wergeld*.

This overview of wound types in the Frisian compensation tariffs is far from
complete. A whole range of finer details of wounds and their complications
has been omitted here because of space constraints. The picture that emerges,
however, is that the authors of these texts knew a lot about injuries resulting from fights and armed conflicts. Yet, in comparing the Old Frisian tariffs
with the early medieval *Leges Barbarorum* in terms of references to medical
practice and wound treatment, the younger Old Frisian texts present a bleaker
picture. There is, for instance, no mention of intestines being pushed back
into the abdomen, or of other wounds to the stomach that cannot be closed

---

42   Oliver, *The Body Legal*, pp. 74–92.
43   Nijdam, "Klinkende munten en klinkende botsplinters," 45–66.

by medical treatment—something that is found in the *Lex Frisionum*.[44] How should this be explained?

Medieval Frisia was not a backward region. Most likely, physicians' skills and medical knowledge were commensurate with neighboring areas (which still meant that doctors often were not able to cure their patients). However, because of the general scarcity of sources surviving from medieval Frisia, little or nothing can be said about it.[45] The thirteenth century chronicle from the monastery of Bloemhof (*Cronica Floridi Horti*) near the village of Wittewierum provides some valuable information. In one instance, mention is made of a contagious disease that was spreading across the country in the year 1250. The illness presented first as a poisonous blister, often located in the neck or on the shoulder. If a physician cut the blister away and then cauterized the wound, most patients would survive. Patients not treated in this way usually died within a week. In another part of the chronicle, the founder and first abbot of the monastery, Emo of Romerswerf, experienced an imbalance in the humors near the time of his demise in 1215. He underwent a round of bloodletting in order to restore the balance and cure him of his dizziness. The chronicle also contains a number of references to Hippocratic and Galenic works. Lastly, it addresses another plague in the Frisian countries in the year 1237, because of which all hospitals (*infirmitoria*) were full.[46]

Since medical knowledge was available in medieval Frisia, this cannot have been the reason why there is so little information on medical treatment in the tariffs. There are two other possible reasons. First, the absence may be explained by boundaries between genres and the specific uses of the compensation tariffs. The tariffs map the various wounds in order to claim compensation for them in a court procedure. Second, most tariffs stem from the period roughly between 1100 and 1300. The majority of the texts handed down through fifteenth-century manuscripts originated in the thirteenth century or earlier. They were updated, but not drastically reworked. In any case, their

---

44   *Lex Frisionum, Additiones Sapientum, Wlemar* 1–3. Eckhardt and Eckhardt, *Lex Frisionum*. Niederhellmann, *Arzt und Heilkunde*, pp. 75–77.

45   During the Reformation, all monasteries were closed down and their possessions were confiscated by the Protestant state toward the end of the 16th century. No monastic library and only a few fragments of monastery archives have survived. Bremmer, *Hir is eskriven*, pp. 13–17.

46   *Cronica Floridi Horti*; H.P.H. Jansen and Antheun Janse, eds., *Kroniek van het klooster Bloemhof te Wittewierum* (Hilversum: Verloren, 1991), pp. 49 (death of Emo), 289 (Hippocrates), 289 (hospitals), 309 (Galen), 378–379 (plague in 1250), 379 (Galen), 427 (Galen).

anonymous authors and copyists did not see any reason to take into account medical handbooks.

There is one exception to the rule. The *Compensation Tariff of Kampa Jeldric* (see Fig. 3) is a curious text, dating to around 1400, and lacking a counterpart in the Old Frisian tradition. The text emerged after a period of stagnation and dispute between practice-oriented surgeons and theory-oriented medics (*doctores medicinae*); rather, the fourteenth century witnessed a new development in surgical knowledge and practice, with the appearance of important works such as those of Henri de Mondeville (ca. 1260–1316) and Guy of Chauliac (ca. 1290–ca. 1368). Surgeons began to dissect corpses to learn more about human anatomy. The fourteenth century also saw the rise of surgical handbooks written in the vernacular.[47] This vernacularization may also have played a role in the reception of medical knowledge in the compensation tariffs. Whatever the reasons, the *Compensation Tariff of Kampa Jeldric* is the only compensation tariff that considers medical handbooks. Before discussing these instances, it is necessary to take a closer look at the text and at what makes it stand out. The text survives in a paper manuscript from the Fivelgo area dated around 1430. It is the longest text of its genre, counting 408 stipulations. One of its unique features is the fact that it is the only non-anonymous tariff text. The epilogue mentions the author:

> 408. Now understand this text and this noble piece of writing
> In this way all wounds to the body shall be assessed.
> And a wise man has composed this in his mind
> and had it written down here the way it came out of his mouth:
> Kampa Jeldric the counselor.
> Whoever is not able to understand this book
> will never correctly legally assess [literally "write"] a wound inflicted on a woman or a man.[48]

This text stands out not only because it reveals the identity of its author, but also because it was composed very deliberately. On closer inspection, the text

---

47   Huizenga, *Tussen autoriteit en empirie*, pp. 86–102.

48   *408. Nu understondat thisse dicht and thine ethela scrifta. Aldus scemma scriwa on alle tha lickama tha unda. And thit heth edicht en wis mon in sina sinne and heth let thet scriva ut sina munde, Kampa Jeldric thi thingmon, alhiron. Wasa thit bok nout understonda ne kan, nammer scrift hi nen unda riucht wif iefta mon.* Compensation Tariff of Kampa Jeldric, §408; Wybren Jan Buma and Wilhelm Ebel, eds., *Das Fivelgoer Recht.* Altfriesische Rechtsquellen 5 (Göttingen: Vandenhoeck & Ruprecht, 1972), p. 134.

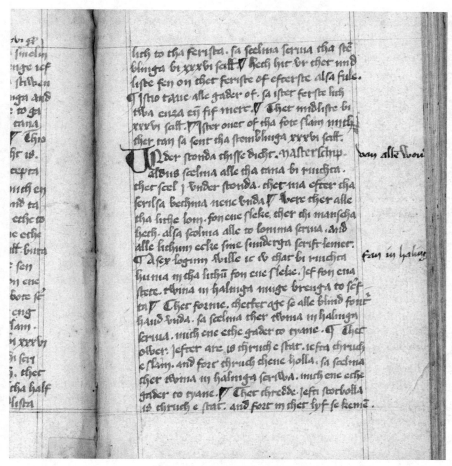

FIGURE 3   *Kampa Jeldric's treatise on Wounds, with the rubric Masterscip in red. A page from
the Codex Fivelgo (Tresoar Leeuwarden, Von Richthofen collection, hs. R4).*

falls into two parts. Running from §1 to §316, the first part is a compensation
tariff in the classical sense of the word. The second part—§317 to §408—begins
with an interlinear rubric entitled *Masterscip* "Teaching." And indeed, just like
in a teaching setting, the author (*ic*, "I") addresses his students / audience (*iu*,
"you"): "I want to tell you on which six body parts two additional legal claims
can be brought into the register when there has been a single blow or thrust
[by the assailant]."[49] After this, Kampa Jeldric continues by explaining how

49   *A sex logum wille ic iv that biriuchta, hu ma in tha lithum fon ene sleke jef fon ena stete twina
inhalinga muge brenga to scrifta. Compensation Tariff of Kampa Jeldric*, §320; Buma and
Ebel, *Das Fivelgoer Recht*, p. 118.

wounds are brought before a court of law, which type of wound can be added
to another type in order to claim a higher compensation, and which types
cannot be added up. He also reiterates the major compensations: a *wergeld* for
the loss of two eyes, two hands, two feet, etc.

The first section—the actual compensation tariff—treats the human body
from head to toes with all possible injuries and consequences. Kampa Jeldric
reworked and restructured the old *General Old East Frisian Compensation
Tariff*. He then took the side effects or disabling consequences of injuries mentioned in the tariff and applied them systematically to all applicable body
parts. This explains why Kampa Jeldric's tariff is so long. A few examples will
suffice to illustrate this point. In the *General Old East Frisian Compensation
Tariff* there is talk of a side effect called *abel and inseptha*, referring to scar
tissue that either protrudes or has sunken into the skin. The *General Old East
Frisian Compensation Tariff* mentions this side effect only three times, but
Kampa Jeldric refers to it 17 times in his text. The same applies to the terms
sinewerdene, "deterioration of the sinew," and *wlitewlemmelsa*, "disfigurement,"
which only appear once in the *General Old East Frisian Compensation Tariff*,
but 13 and 12 times respectively in Kampa Jeldric's tariff. The term *wlitewlemmelsa*, which originally meant "disfigurement to the face," is transformed in
Kampa Jeldric's hands into a generic term denoting all kinds of disfigurement
that might arise through an injury. This mechanism of generalizing terminology for side effects is apparent in at least 17 technical terms. Obviously, this
approach multiplied the number of stipulations a tariff had counted until
then. These examples also reveal that Kampa Jeldric thoroughly systematized
and restructured the compensation material.

In the process of reworking and restructuring, Kampa Jeldric likely made
use of one or more of the vernacular medical handbooks circulating at the
time. The clues are threefold. First, Kampa Jeldric discusses certain body parts
in combination with information on whether wounds to these organs will heal:
"There are six organs in the body, a wound to which shall not be written down
in the court register, because the victim will certainly die of it. These are the
intestines, the kidneys, the spleen, the liver, the heart and the gullet / trachea."[50]
The next section will take a closer look at the court register (OFris. *skrift*),
legally assessing or "writing" (OFris. *skriva*) and the official assessor or "writer"

---

50   *Sex thing senter in tha liwe, ther ma thor nout scriwa, thetter ammer muge libba, ther ther
       ene dolch one hebbe. Thet ene senta thirman anta lunglagan and thio milte and thio liwere,
       thio herte and thi wasanda. Hwasa thene breinsiama heth inda haude, sa mei hi thach libba
       and hi wert thach sere therfon ewert. Compensation Tariff of Kampa Jeldric,* §407; Buma and
       Ebel, *Das Fivelgoer Recht,* p. 134.

(OFris. *skrivere*). Important to note for now is that four of these six organs are only found here in this stipulation and nowhere else in the compensation tariffs. Moreover, a wound to the gullet or trachea (it is not entirely clear which of the two OFris. *wasande* refers to) is mentioned in some other compensation tariffs as serious (exacting a third of a *wergeld*), but not life threatening. Altogether, it is likely that Kampa Jeldric derived this stipulation from a list of curable and incurable injuries in a medical handbook.[51]

In §§389–390, Kampa Jeldric mentions gout and epilepsy as potential outcomes of an unspecified injury, and bladder stones as the possible result of an injury to the abdomen. While medical handbooks commonly address these three diseases, they do not appear in any of the other compensation tariffs. Together with the fact that the text of the second section is set in rhyme here and there, these three aspects point to the influence of some vernacular, rhymed medical handbook.[52]

Looking at the compensation tariffs from the perspective of knowledge about human anatomy, wounds and wound treatment, then, offers both a wealth of material as well as identifying limitations brought about by the genre. Standard medical knowledge was available in medieval Frisia, but it only meagerly found its way into the compensation tariffs. The unique Kampa Jeldric seems to have made use of medical handbooks, but he specifically employed it on compensation practices.

Legal Procedure and the Old Frisian Skrivere

The tariffs make little reference to physicians; rather, they usually offer neutral descriptions: "If the victim has to be incised," etc. One instance where a physician is explicitly named, is in the following stipulation: "If the skull has been thrust through or hewn through: the compensation is 1 mark and to be claimed with the help of the attestation of the physician."[53] The only times physicians are mentioned by their title (OFris. *letza* "physician") in the compensation tariffs is when they are described as expert witnesses before the court. Physicians came into contact with the law in various ways.[54] First, they had to protect

51 E. Fischer-Homberger, *Medizin vor Gericht. Gerichtsmedizin von der Renaissance bis zur Aufklärung* (Berne, Stuttgart, and Vienna: Hans Huber, 1983), pp. 31–34.

52 Huizenga, *Tussen autoriteit en empirie*, pp. 470–476.

53 *Cop truchstet ieuua truchhauuen: en marck, and mith tha leza te winnane.* Emsingo *Compensation Tariff* §E1 VII,22; Buma and Ebel, *Das Emsiger Recht*, p. 66.

54 Huizenga, *Tussen autoriteit en empirie*, pp. 206–210.

their own liability when accepting a patient. Before agreeing to treatment, physicians tried to obtain solid guarantees that they would not be subject to prosecution if their treatments failed. Second, the courts summoned physicians as experts on various occasions: to establish the cause of death, assist the executioner, or act as an expert witness. The Old Frisian compensation tariffs addressed physicians in this last function especially.

Frisian legal procedure did not deviate much from that of neighboring regions.[55] What is most critical here is the way a court of law handles injuries. Just as in Germanic times, only free men and nobles had the right to attend courts of law. They could bring a case to court and they would function as judge-administrator, presiding over the court *cum* parliament for a period of one year, after which another Free Frisian assumed the office. They would also act as warden for their wives, children, members of their household and their small retinue of warriors (not more than a handful until the end of the 15th century). There were three regular court sessions or *things* over the course of a year. Apart from the judge, few other officials were active within the court. The law speaker (OFris. *asega*) knew the law by heart and assisted the judge in reaching his verdict by providing information on law and legal procedure. In a later period, the Free Frisians formed a jury of assistant-judges. Also, there appears to have been an expert on injury compensation, the *skrivere*, which literally means "writer."

Since there was no strong central government, the two litigants were to a certain extent autonomous. The judge might exhort the community to enforce a verdict if one of the parties blatantly defied it, but this was as far as his authority reached. Besides, this year's judge might well be next year's litigant. In any case, if a claim was granted, the claimant had to see to it himself that the accused paid up.

When the plaintiff sued his case before the court, it summoned the accused to defend himself against the allegation. The law obliged the defendant to appear before the court or run the risk of being found in contempt, hunted by an *ad hoc* army of neighbors, and having his house destroyed.[56] If the defendant appeared, he would hear the charges brought up against him. In the most

---

55   See Nijdam, *Lichaam, eer en recht*, pp. 151-173; Oebele Vries, *"Her Bendix is wrbeck fonden. De altfriesische Terminologie im Bereich des Zivilrechts,"* in Oebele Vries, *De taal van recht en vrijheid. Studies over middeleeuws Friesland*, ed. Anne Popkema, Han Nijdam and Goffe Jensma (Gorredijk: Bornmeer, 2012), pp. 308–345.

56   Oebele Vries, *"Seka mit brande and mit breke.* Oudfriese terminologie met betrekking tot het rechtsinstituut 'woesting,'" in Vries, *De taal van recht*, pp. 284–307.

archaic period, he would then assert his innocence by swearing an oath. If the court deemed the case serious, the defendant might have to call in the assistance of oath-helpers. The graver the charge, the more oath-helpers he required. Oath-helpers acted as character witnesses, declaring that they knew the defendant to be an honorable man who would not tell a lie. Since a man of honor always does everything out in the open and takes responsibility for his actions, how can he do otherwise but tell the truth about his actions?[57] This legal procedure evidently leans heavily on honor and status and the delicate relationships that exist within small-scale societies. Losing the case meant also losing status and honor.

Over the course of time, however, more forms of evidence and truth finding entered Frisian procedural law.[58] This development prompted the appearance of two related concepts in the compensation tariffs. When neighbors or bystanders witnessed an injury it was called *burkuth* or *gakuth* in Old Frisian. A court official also had to inspect the injury in order to produce testimony concerning the injury if the plaintiff pled a suit in court. Testimony made it harder (if not impossible) for the defendant to deny an accusation. The claimant's strengthened position was expressed by the term *onbrinze*, which literally means that the claimant had obtained stronger rights to "bring in" his case than the defendant had to exonerate himself. In the compensation tariffs, various types of wounds are typified as *onbrinze* by their very nature.

It is instructive to look also to the court register (OFris. *skrift*), the official wound assessor (OFris. *skrivere*), and the rules and practice of legally assessing wounds (OFris. *skriva*). Regrettably, not a single medieval court register has survived. A few scanty remarks in the Old Frisian law texts attest to their existence. One stipulation in the *Statutes of the Brokmerlanders* states that cases should be written down in the register twice a year, namely on St Michael's (29 September) and on St Peter's (29 June).[59] A few passages in both the compensation tariffs as well as elsewhere in the Old Frisian law texts explicitly state that a wound had to be healed before the court could address the suit so that

---

57   Frank H. Stewart, *Honor* (Chicago: Chicago University Press, 1994).

58   M.S. van Oosten, "Inleidende beschouwingen over het oudere Friese bewijsrecht," *Tijdschrift voor Rechtsgeschiedenis* 18 (1950): 440–76; Oebele Vries, "*Toe aer heer ende aegh syoen* (Zu Ohrenhör und Augensicht) Eine altfriesische alliterierende Paarformel im Sinnbereich des Zeugenbeweises," in Vries, *De taal van recht*, pp. 371–382.

59   *Brokmonna Bref* ("Statutes of the Brokmerlanders") §115; Wybren Jan Buma and Wilhelm Ebel, eds., *Das Brokmer Recht*. Altfriesische Rechtsquellen 2 (Göttingen: Vandenhoeck & Ruprecht, 1965), p. 76.

they were aware of the consequences of the injury. If a plaintiff brought his case to court half way through the healing process, the patient might still die of his injury, in which case the defendant owed a full *wergeld*.

Not much information survives on the *skrivere* or injury assessor. The thirteenth-century *Statutes of Fivelgo* states that the person elected to the office of *skrivere* has to take an oath. Furthermore, the *skrivere* is entitled to a fourteenth part of any compensation allotted by the court.[60] Thanks to the information in the compensation tariffs, it is possible to say a tad more about the practice of assessing wounds (OFris. *skriva*, meaning "to write"). In this process, the *skrivere* identified the legally correct claim concerning an injury and recorded it in the court register, after which the plaintiff might bring his case before the court. The tariffs consistently employ the metaphor that wounds are written on the body. The following stipulation from the *Compensation Tariff of Kampa Jeldric* illustrates this point and offers an instructive example of assessment rules: "Three wrinkles cut: each 5 shillings [. . .]. The wrinkles are nowhere to be assessed ("written") except in three places: on the forehead and on the palms of the hands and on the soles of the feet. No matter how many wrinkles have been cut, no more than three should be 'written.'" This description evokes a mental image of the *skrivere* working with a drawing of a human being, not unlike the images of men in medical handbooks. There one can find the zodiac man, with all the astrological symbols to highlight the parts of the body they govern; or, the wound man, with all kinds of weapons thrust into his body and their related injuries. It is as if the *skrivere* might identify the category of wounds by writing them on the body.

The stipulation on cutting wrinkles proposes a few rules concerning the assessment: a cut through wrinkles might only be claimed if the cut wounds are on the forehead, hands or feet, and no more than three wrinkles are to be compensated. These rules are scattered throughout the corpus of tariffs— especially densely in the *Compensation Tariff of Kampa Jeldric*. They prescribe maximal amounts or maximal numbers of certain types of wounds that can be added up in an assessment. For instance, if an eye is poked out, all lesser injuries merge in the compensation of the poked-out eye (which is half a *wergeld*). Chains of claims also occur: "if you want to claim such and such a type of injury, you first have to claim such and such type." The overriding sense is that the law is an intricate game that must be mastered

---

60   *Statutes of Fivelgo* §16; Thomas S.B. Johnston, ed., *Codex Hummercensis* (*Groningen, UB, PEIP 12*). *An Old Frisian Legal Manuscript in Low Saxon Guise* (Leeuwarden: Fryske Akademy, 1998), p. 312.

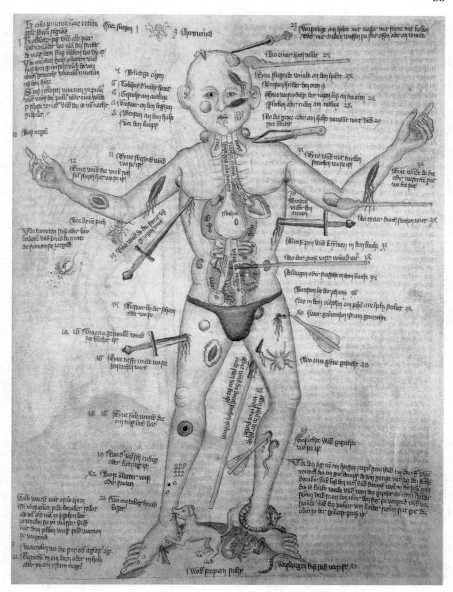

FIGURE 4   *Wound Man. Wellcome Library, Londen, ms. WMS49, f. 35.*

before the *skrivere* is able to hold office satisfactorily. Hence, Kampa Jeldric's admonition at the end of his text, cited earlier: "Whoever is not able to understand this book will never correctly legally assess [literally 'write'] a wound inflicted on a woman or a man."

Conclusion: Compensating Embodied Honor

The Frisian compensation tariffs harbor an impressive amount of anatomical knowledge and unveil just enough to infer that there was ample knowledge of wound treatment available in medieval Frisia as well. What these texts express mostly, however, is an expertise on wounds from a legal perspective and on legal assessment of wounds in order to compensate them satisfactorily. This acts as a reminder of the fact, that in the end, the compensation tariffs compensated more than just the physical body; they compensated also the lasting effects.[61] Injuries might produce nasty scars in plain sight, or the victim might not be able to behave in public as he had before. In addressing these issues, this chapter argues that it is necessary to look beyond the mere physical plane and see that the body formed the core of "embodied honor."

Several zones of the human body constituted the totality of the honor of a Free Frisian. These zones, labeled as the social body and the political body, contained elements such as: his house, lands, gold and first degree relatives (social body) and his wife, servants, cattle, silver and textiles (political body). The tariffs employ body metaphors to describe the social body. Thus, land is described as a body and *vice versa*.

Defining embodied honor in this way solves a few questions. First, it explains why the compensation tariffs treated all these elements. In short, the tariffs not only map the physical body of a Free Frisian, they more precisely map the embodied honor of a Free Frisian. Second, this view also explains exactly how compensation worked. You cannot compensate an eye with an eye if you want to refrain from revenge. In that case, you have to accept that money can somehow replace an eye. If, however, the embodied honor is viewed as the extended body of a free Frisian, then you can take a pound of his flesh and replace it for a plot of land, because they are both elements of his extended body. In the end, the sum total remains constant.

To return to the beginning of our chapter, this last point addresses how the commodification of body parts worked. Body parts were valued for their functionality, but there was also an aesthetic aspect. Remember the disfigurements (OFris. *wlitewlemmelsa*) and the scars that could not be hidden beneath hair or clothes. There was also the symbolic value of certain body parts. This chapter has already discussed the special meaning hair had; but the three middle fingers of the right hand were valued more because of the blessing that could be performed by these "against the devil."

---

61   For this paragraph see Nijdam, *Lichaam, eer en recht*, pp. 281–321.

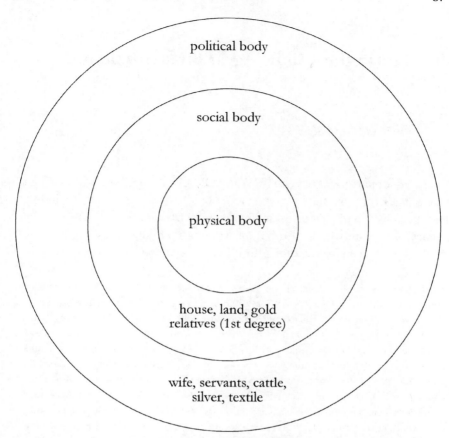

FIGURE 5   *Concentric Model of Embodied Honor. From: Nijdam,* Lichaam, eer en recht, *p. 282.*

In short then, the Old Frisian compensation tariffs are a rich source for anyone interested in revenge, honor, compensation and the way the law perceives the injured physical body in relation to embodied honor. Medieval Frisian physicians not only had to heal wounds, but played a role in healing the victim's honor as well.

CHAPTER 2

Midwives in the Middle Ages? Birth Attendants, 600–1300

Fiona Harris-Stoertz

Who cared for parturient women in Western Europe during the Early and High Middle Ages (approximately 600–1300)? For decades, historians, including most specialists in the history of medieval childbirth, confidently asserted the primacy of the midwife in the care of women in childbirth throughout the Middle Ages.[1] Recently, in a thoughtful "the emperor has no clothes" analysis,

---

1   In such claims, most authors rely on Greek, Roman, or late Antique texts or texts from the twelfth century or later. Peter Biller, "Childbirth in the Middle Ages," *History Today* 36 (1986): 42–49, provides several examples of midwives, all from the twelfth century or later. Ginger Lee Guardiola, "Within and Without: The Social and Medical Worlds of the Medieval Midwife, 1000–1500," Ph.D. Diss., University of Colorado, 2002, assumes throughout that midwives were the normal birth attendant between 1000 and 1500, but much of her evidence for the earlier period comes from medical texts, which are based on classical or Arabic sources. Muriel Joy Hughes, "Medieval Midwives," in *Women Healers in Medieval Life and Literature* (Freeport: Books for Libraries Press, 1943), pp. 100–13, spends much of the chapter discussing the twelfth-century women of Salerno, who were not necessarily midwives. Carole Rawcliffe, "Women and Medicine: The Midwife and the Nurse," in *Medicine and Society in Later Medieval England* (London: Sandpiper Books, 1999), esp. pp. 194–205, relies on late Roman and later medieval evidence. Sylvie Laurent, *Naître au moyen âge: de la conception à la naissance: la grossesse et l'accouchement (XIIe–XVe siècle)* (Paris: Léopard d'Or, 1989), pp. 172–79, likewise relies on later evidence. Shulamith Shahar, *Childhood in the Middle Ages* (London and New York: Routledge, 1990), pp. 32–52, assumes the presence of midwives, using Greek and Roman texts read in the Middle Ages and evidence from the twelfth century and beyond. R. C. Finucane, *The Rescue of the Innocents: Endangered Children in Medieval Miracles* (New York: St Martin's Press, 1997), pp. 17–42, demonstrates the presence of midwives in miracle stories from the twelfth century onwards. Renate Blumenfeld-Kosinski, *Not of Women Born: Representations of Caesarian Birth in Medieval and Renaissance Culture* (Cornell: Cornell University Press, 1990), esp. pp. 15–21, 61–74, uses Greek and Roman texts and tends to focus on the thirteenth century and beyond. Erwin H. Ackerknecht, "Midwives as Experts in Court," *Bulletin of the New York Academy of Medicine*, 52.10 (1976): 1224–28, assumes the presence of midwives throughout the Middle Ages, although he focuses on the later medieval and ancient civilizations. Edward J. Kealey, *Medieval Medicus: A Social History of Anglo-Norman Medicine* (Baltimore and London: Johns Hopkins University Press, 1981), p. 35, speaking of the Anglo-Norman period says, "Naturally there must have been innumerable midwives, but they do not appear in the records." See also p. 49 for the same assumption.

© KONINKLIJKE BRILL NV, LEIDEN, 2014 | DOI 10.1163/9789004269118_004

Monica H. Green has called this assumption into question, pointing out that little evidence of professional midwives being active before the thirteenth century can be found, and that most evidence for practicing midwives comes from the later Middle Ages, particularly the fifteenth century. Green argues that the use of professional midwives probably declined in the crises of the sixth and seventh centuries and that midwifery re-emerged as a specialized profession only in the thirteenth century, first in larger urban areas where rising population densities could support them and only slowly in smaller towns. She suggests that this re-emergence was slow and uneven and that still, by the end of the fifteenth century, many regions still did not have professional midwives.[2]

A few other authors have noted the absence of midwives in specific types of sources before 1300, thus lending support to Green's argument. Kathryn Taglia in her examination of Northern French synodal legislation found only one piece of legislation relating to midwives before 1300.[3] Likewise, in my own studies of French and English secular law *compendia* between 600 and 1300 and twelfth- and thirteenth-century chivalric literature, I found no explicit mention of midwives.[4] Recent historians touching on this subject have tended to accept Green's conclusions.[5] However, a number of historians, including many who assume the presence of midwives throughout the Middle Ages, have noted evidence of midwives in twelfth-century miracles. Thus, the idea that

---

2 Monica Green has addressed this question in a number of works. See especially Monica H. Green, "Bodies, Gender, Health, Disease: Recent Work on Medieval Women's Medicine," *Studies in Medieval and Renaissance History* 2 (2005): 15–17 (1–46); Green, *Making Women's Medicine Masculine: The Rise of Male Authority in Pre-Modern Gynaecology* (Oxford: OUP, 2008); throughout, but especially pp. 34–36 and 127–29, 134–40. On conditions in the fifteenth century, see especially Annie Saunier, "Le visiteur, les femmes et les "obstetrices" des paroisses de l'archdiaconé de Josas de 1458 à 1470," in *Santé, Médecine et Assistance au Moyen Âge* (Paris: Comité des travaux historiques et scientifiques, 1987), pp. 43–62.

3 Kathryn Taglia, "Delivering a Christian Identity: Midwives in Northern French Synodal Legislation, c. 1200–1500," in *Religion and Medicine in the Middle Ages*, ed. Peter Biller and Joseph Ziegler (York: Boydell and Brewer, 2001), pp. 77–90.

4 Fiona Harris-Stoertz, "Pregnancy and Childbirth in Chivalric Literature," *Mediaevalia: An Interdisciplinary Journal of Medieval Studies Worldwide* 29.1 (2008): 27–36, and "Pregnancy and Childbirth in Twelfth- and Thirteenth-Century French and English Law," *Journal of the History of Sexuality* 21.2 (2012): 263–81. I have since found a midwife (*ventriere*) in an early thirteenth-century romance.

5 See for example, Katherine Park, "Birth and Death," in *A Cultural History of the Human Body in the Medieval Age*, ed. Linda Kalof (Oxford and New York: Berg, 2010), p. 23, and Tiffany D. Vann Sprecher and Ruth Mazo Karras, "The Midwife and the Church: Ecclesiastical Regulation of Midwives in Brie, 1499–1504," *BHM* 85.2 (2011): 173 (171–92).

midwives re-emerged only in the thirteenth century should be re-considered carefully.[6]

Green's argument for the disappearance of midwives is based primarily on the silence of sources regarding practicing midwives between the sixth and thirteenth centuries. Thus, it largely leaves open the question of who cared for women in childbirth during this period. This essay attempts to assess the evidence for birth attendants in the regions that became France and England between the sixth and thirteenth centuries, both to test Green's hypothesis, but also to establish more clearly who the caregivers were in this period. Sources relating to the identity of birth attendants are limited, particularly for the period before 1000, so it is impossible to reach any definitive conclusions one way or the other for the period 600 to 1000. While there is little evidence of practicing midwives during this period, the concept of midwives remained part of learned Latinate culture and to some degree popular culture. The concept of midwifery was preserved in classical sources, such as medical texts, read and copied in the period, and particularly through the presence of midwives in Apocryphal accounts of the Nativity, which were popularized in sermons and public art as part of the increasingly important cult of the Virgin Mary. Thus, midwives continued to have a cultural presence, which would perhaps have encouraged their revival in the High Middle Ages; although, it may also have had a tendency to distort the sources. There is far more evidence of birth attendants for the High Middle Ages, particularly the twelfth and thirteenth centuries. In this period, it appears that parturient women were routinely attended by a sizable group of female neighbors, family members, and servants. While the birthing chamber was idealized as a woman-only space in a wide variety of literature, sometimes, particularly in the case of elites or in emergencies, men—husbands, priests, and physicians—played a role in

---

6 Biller, "Childbirth in the Middle Ages," 42–49; Shahar, *Childhood in the Middle Ages*, pp. 32–52; Finucane, *The Rescue of the Innocents*, pp. 17–42; Hilary Powell, "The 'Miracle of Childbirth': The Portrayal of Parturient Women in Medieval Miracle Narratives," *SHM* 25.4 (2012): 795–811; Carole Rawcliffe, "Women, Childbirth, and Religion in Later Medieval England," in *Women and Religion in Medieval England*, ed. Diana Wood (Oxford: OUP, 2003), pp. 91–117; Fiona Harris Stoertz, "Suffering and Survival in Medieval English Childbirth," in *Medieval Family Roles*, ed. Cathy Jorgensen Itnyre (New York: Garland Press, 1996), pp. 101–20. For an early twelfth-century Flemish case, see Fernard Vercauteren, "Les médecins dans les principautés de la Belgique et du nord de la France, du VIIIe au XIIIe siécle," *Le Moyen Age* 6 (1951): 66 (61–92). Green notes the latter case in Monica H. Green, "Documenting Medieval Women's Medical Practice," in *Practical Medicine from Salerno to the Black Death*, ed. Luis Garcia-Ballester, Roger French, Jon Arrizabalaga, and Andrew Cunningham (Cambridge: CUP, 1994), p. 338 (322–52).

caring for parturient women. In addition to these attendants, it is possible to find some evidence of midwives in the twelfth century, and considerably more in the thirteenth century. This chapter will argue that the use of midwives re-emerged in the twelfth-century and had become an accepted and even in some places institutionalized part of care for women in at least some regions of North-Western Europe by 1300, although midwives always supplemented, not replaced, other types of attendants.

Because evidence for birth attendants is scarce and scattered, this chapter draws on a wide range of sources, including histories and chronicles, ency-clopedias, saints' *vitae*, miracle collections, secular law codes, medical texts, advice manuals, fictional works, *inquisitions post-mortem*, apocryphal litera-ture, iconographic evidence, and more. Legal sources, such as the *inquisitions post-mortem* and saints' lives and miracle stories included in canonization proceedings, generated by the centralization and bureaucratization of secular and religious governments in the High Middle Ages are particularly important resources for the study of childbirth, as they reveal intimate details of everyday life, not usually available in earlier medieval sources. These are the best sources for the actual care of parturient women as they provide detailed accounts of real births, drawn from the observations of interested participants and neigh-bors. These sources are not without pitfalls. Accounts, apart from the miracle stories, usually come from male witnesses who were, in most cases, not actu-ally present at births. Moreover, the accounts as they survive have been filtered through the lenses of literate male officials and translated into Latin. Thus, we cannot be entirely certain that *obstetrices* mentioned in such sources were truly professional midwives, and not just knowledgeable neighbors. Although the fact that such terms were used in our sources indicates their cultural importance to literate, Latinate males, at the very least. While flawed in some respects, these sources provide our best means of discovering the identity of obstetrical caregivers in the High Middle Ages.

This chapter's focus on midwives should not be taken as a claim that mid-wives ever were the dominant caregiver for women during the Middle Ages or that midwifery was the only possible medical role for women. As Green has demonstrated persuasively in a number of works, women would have received obstetrical and gynecological help from a wide variety of caregivers, and women likewise served in a variety of medical roles, not just as midwives; although, historians' excessive focus on the figure of the midwife has tended to distract from these facts.[7] The findings of this chapter confirm the idea that

---

7 See especially Monica H. Green, "Gendering the History of Women's Healthcare," *Gender & History* 20.3 (Nov. 2008): 487–518, a wonderful historiography of the excessive focus

midwives were far from having a monopoly as caregivers even in childbirth, let alone the wider scope of women's healthcare. While recognizing this multiplicity of caregivers, though, given their place in the historiography of birth, it is valuable to explore what place, if any, midwives held during the Early and High Middle Ages.

There appears to be little doubt that midwives were involved in at least some births at both the end and the beginning of the Middle Ages. Midwives began being regulated and institutionalized in some regions in the fourteenth and fifteenth centuries, suggesting that they were then present in sufficient numbers to make this a meaningful course of action, although this was a process that took place at very different times in different parts of Europe.[8] Even by the

---

on midwives in histories of women's medical practice. For the variety of women's medical roles and caregivers, see Green, "Documenting Medieval Women's Medical Practice," 322–52, and also Green, "Women's Medical Practice and Health Care in Medieval Europe," in *Sisters and Workers in the Middle Ages*, ed. Judith M. Bennett, *et al.* (Chicago and London: University of Chicago Press, 1989), pp. 39–78. For an older survey of women in medicine, see Kate Campbell Hurd-Mead, *History of Women in Medicine from the Earliest Times to the Beginning of the Nineteenth Century* (Haddam: The Haddam Press, 1938).

8   Midwives began to be more closely regulated at different times in different parts of Europe. Recent scholarship has demonstrated that this process should not be seen only as "control" or marginalization, but also as a way to channel the potentially valuable labor of midwives. See for example Taglia, "Delivering a Christian Identity," pp. 77–90; Adrian Wilson, *The Making of Man-Midwifery: Childbirth in England, 1660–1770* (Cambridge, MA: Harvard University Press, 1995); Ginger L. Smoak, "Midwives as Agents of Social Control: Ecclesiastical and Municipal Regulation of Midwifery in the Late Middle Ages," *Quidditas: On-line Journal of the Rocky Mountain Medieval and Renaissance Association* 33 (2012): 79–96; Jean Donnison, *Midwives and Medical Men: A History of Inter-Professional Rivalries and Women's Rights* (London: Heinemann, 1977); Myriam Greilsammer, "The Midwife, the Priest and the Physician: The Subjugation of Midwives in the Low Countries at the End of the Middle Ages," *Journal of Medieval and Renaissance Studies* 21.2 (1991): 285–329; Richard L. Petrelli, "The Regulation of French Midwifery during the *Ancien Régime,*" *JHMAS* 26.3 (1971): 276–92; Saunier, "Le visiteur, les femmes et les "obstetrics" des paroisses de l'archdiaconé de Josas de 1458 à 1470," 43–62; Thomas G. Benedek, "The Changing Relationship between Midwives and Physicians during the Renaissance," *BHM* 51.4 (1977): 550–64; Vann Sprecher and Karras, "The Midwife and the Church," 171–92; Merry E. Wiesner, "Early Modern Midwifery: A Case Study," in *Women and Work in Preindustrial Europe*, ed. Barbara A. Hanawalt (Bloomington: Indiana University Press, 1986), pp. 94–113; John R. Guy, "The Episcopal Licensing of Physicians, Surgeons, and Midwives," *BHM* 56 (1982): 528–42; Thomas R. Forbes, "The Regulation of English Midwives in the Sixteenth and Seventeenth Centuries," *MH* 8.3 (1964): 235–44. Monica H. Green, "Gendering the History of Women's Healthcare," 487–518, points out convincingly that historians have tended to overdraw the contrasts between earlier and later periods. Women never entirely controlled childbirth and men never entirely took over.

end of the Middle Ages, not everyone would have had access to medical professionals such as midwives, whether because of availability, custom, or cost. Midwives were likewise an established part of childbirth in Greek and Roman antiquity, well attested to in the Hippocratic corpus and Soranus' *Gynecology*, although doctors, assistants, and other caregivers also certainly played a role.[9] Midwives still appear to have been significant around the fifth or sixth century, when Muscio wrote his Latin translation of Soranus' *Gynecology*. Muscio not only discusses midwives in his text, but also explicitly targets midwives as an audience, arguing that his translation is essential because most midwives do not know Greek.[10]

The Early Middle Ages, 600–1000

Green argues that midwives disappeared in the crises of the sixth and seventh centuries as urban life atrophied.[11] During that time, European populations were devastated by war and plague cycles. While cities certainly did not disappear between 600 and 1000, and there was much accommodation and assimilation between Roman and "Barbarian" cultures, the population was small and scattered in the regions that became France and England, and would have been less able to support specialists such as midwives. The presence of specialists presupposes a sufficient client base to support specialization, and specialists in general were rare during this period. Already on the decline in Western Europe before the sixth century, literacy and literary production declined still further until the ninth century when a gradual process of recovery began. In general, specific evidence about caregivers for birthing women during the Early Middle Ages is scarce. It would be untrue to say that early medieval sources, limited as they are, had no interest in birth. Chronicles mention the births of

---

9   See Christine Bonnet-Cahilhac, "Si l'enfant se trouve dans une présentation contre nature, que doit faire la sage-femme? " in *Naissance et petite enfance dans l'Antiquité*, ed. Véronique Dasen (Fribourg: Academic Press, 2004), pp. 199–208; Helen King, "Imaginary Midwives," in her *Hippocrates' Woman: Reading the Female Body in Ancient Greece* (London : Routledge, 1998), pp. 172–87; Ann Ellis Hanson, "A Division of Labor: Roles for Men in Greek and Roman Births," *Thamyris* 1.2 (1994): 157–202; V. French, "Midwives and Maternity Care in the Roman World," *Helios*, n.s. 13.2 (1986): 69–84; Rebecca Flemming, *Medicine and the Making of Roman Women: Gender, Nature, and Authority from Celsus to Galen* (Oxford: OUP, 2000).

10   Muscio, "Gynaecia," in *Sorani Gynaeciorum vetus translatio Latina*, ed. Valentin Rose (Leipzig: Teubner, 1882), p. 3 (3–128).

11   See especially Green, *Making Medicine Masculine*, pp. 34–36.

important individuals frequently, and many saints' lives dwell on the birth of saints, as it was a *topos* that signs and wonders such as bright light or visions occurred in association with such births.[12] Unfortunately, though, while the sources give us some details about pregnancy and birth, they tell us little about caregivers.[13] Although literary production increased considerably in the ninth and tenth centuries with the Carolingian and Anglo-Saxon renaissances, evidence regarding caregivers remains slim until the High Middle Ages.

Historians of early medieval women or medicine sometimes assume the presence of midwives, but most cite no concrete evidence for them.[14] Such evidence as survives suggests that women were attended by knowledgeable female members of the household, including servants, and also perhaps neighbors. This is suggested by two Anglo-Saxon saints' lives written in the eighth century. According to the *Life of St Wilfrid*, Wilfrid's mother gave birth in her house with women (*mulieres*) around her, while men stood outside.[15] St Guthlac's mother too had at least one female attendant (*mulier*) who emerged to announce Guthlac's birth.[16] That men might perhaps attend in an emergency, is suggested by the ninth century *Annals of St Bertin*, which tell us that the pregnant empress Richildis was sent to safety in the company of an abbot and a bishop, rather than stay with her husband on campaign.

---

12   On signs and wonders associated with the births of saints, see Jane Tibbetts Schulenburg, "Saints and Sex, CA. 500–1100: Striding Down the Nettled Path of Life," in *Sex in the Middle Ages: A Book of Essays*, ed. Joyce E. Salisbury (New York and London: Garland Publishing, 1991), pp. 205–07 (203–31).

13   Particularly useful studies of early medieval birth include: Sally Crawford, *Childhood in Anglo-Saxon England* (Stroud: Sutton Publishing Ltd., 1999), pp. 57–84; Valerie Garver, "Childbearing and Infancy in the Carolingian World," *Journal of the History of Sexuality* 21.2 (2012): 208–44; Valerie Garver, *Women and Aristocratic Culture in the Carolingian World* (Ithaca and London: Cornell University Press, 2009), pp. 215–22; Marilyn Deegan, "Pregnancy and Childbirth in the Anglo-Saxon Medical Texts: A Preliminary Survey," in *Medicine in Early Medieval England*, ed. Marilyn Deegan and D. G. Scragg (Manchester: Centre for Anglo-Saxon Studies, University of Manchester, 1989), pp. 17–26.

14   See for example, Lisa M. Bitel, *Women in Early Medieval Europe, 400–1100* (Cambridge: CUP, 2002), p. 234; Crawford, *Childhood in Anglo-Saxon England*, p. 61; Garver, "Childbearing and Infancy in the Carolingian World," 216 (208–44); Carol Neuman de Vegvar, "Images of Women in Anglo-Saxon Art II: Midwifery in Harley 603," *Old English Newsletter*, 25.1 (1991): 54–56.

15   Eddius Stephanus, *The Life of Bishop Wilfred*, ed. Bertram Colgrave (Cambridge: CUP, 1927), pp. 4–5: *Nam cum mater eius dolore paturientis fatigata in domo sua iaceret et mulieres circa se mansissent.*

16   Felix, *Life of Saint Guthlac*, ed. Bertram Colgrave (Cambridge: CUP, 1956), pp. 74–77.

Unfortunately, she gave birth on the road and the child died.[17] In Anglo-Saxon England, as Michael J. W. Wright has demonstrated, vernacular terms for midwife, *byrþ-þinen* and *beorþor-þinen* (both meaning childbirth attendant) did exist, but they were used only to translate the Latin word *obstetrix* from classical texts in a very few cases, and not otherwise used. Often *obstetrix* was translated only as attendant.[18] The fact that no Old English term for midwife survived into the High Middle Ages and that the Old English terms that existed were little used during the Early Middle Ages supports Green's contention that no separate professional class of midwives existed during this period. While the apparent absence of midwives may be a matter of optics—given the paucity of evidence, one cannot be certain whether there were practicing midwives—if there had been practicing midwives, one would expect some mention of them in saints' lives, law codes, chronicles, or encyclopedias, places that did address other aspects of pregnancy and birth.

While there may have been no practicing midwives during the Early Middle Ages, the idea of the midwife did not entirely disappear in literate circles, as the term survived in classical works read, copied, and translated throughout the period; although, as Wright suggests, the concept did not always survive the process of translation. Perhaps the most significant venue for the cultural survival of the concept of midwives was the stories of the Nativity associated with the increasingly popular cult of the Virgin Mary. The idea that a midwife had been among the first witnesses to Jesus' birth appears in the *Protoevangelium* or *Infancy Gospel of James*, probably written in the mid-second century in Egypt or Syria.[19] In this story, when Mary tells Joseph en route to Bethlehem that the baby will soon be born, he leaves her with his sons in a cave and goes to fetch a midwife. On his return with the un-named midwife, they see a miraculous light in the cave, which when it fades reveals the infant Jesus nursing at Mary's breast. The midwife rejoices at the miracle, recognizing that it represents the salvation of Israel, then leaves the cave and tells the story to Salome, who is not identified as a midwife in this story, Salome, disbelieving, returns to the cave with the midwife and tests Mary's virginity with her finger, whereupon

---

17   Janet L. Nelson, trans., *The Annals of St Bertin* (Manchester and New York: Manchester University Press, 1991), pp. 196, 199. We do not know whether the clerics attended the birth.

18   Michael J. W. Wright, "Anglo-Saxon Midwives," *ANQ: A Quarterly Journal of Short Articles, Notes, and Reviews* 11.1 (1998): 3–5.

19   Miri Rubin, *Mother of God: A History of the Virgin Mary* (New Haven and London: Yale University Press, 2009), p. 9.

her hand withers. The hand is restored when she touches Jesus.[20] The story is substantial, and would have been difficult to ignore, given the pervasive interest in Mary's virginity.

Although excluded from the New Testament Canon and criticized by some authorities, such as St Jerome, the *Infancy Gospel of James* was widely read in the Greek East, and spread quickly, becoming a fundamental text for the massively popular cult of the Virgin Mary.[21] Over 140 Greek manuscripts survive, in addition to Syriac, Coptic, Irish, Ethiopic, Arabic, Slavonic, and Georgian translations.[22] Thus, the work had a considerable influence on literature in the Greek East and beyond, and depictions of Salome with her withered hand became a popular subject in Byzantine art.

In the Latin West, the *Infancy Gospel of James* also received a mixed reception, but was important in establishing details of Mary's biography. However, the direct impact of the *Infancy Gospel of James* was much less in the Latin West than in the Greek East. The text was known and discussed in the West during the fourth and fifth centuries, and explicitly excluded from the New Testament canon by Pope Gelasius. Latin translations, some of them incomplete, survive from both Carolingian Francia and Anglo-Saxon England, showing that it continued to be of interest to scholars.[23] Nevertheless, the text would be superseded in the West by a Latin text that retold the story in a revised format.

The most influential infancy text read in the Latin West was the *Pseudo Matthew* or *Infancy Gospel of Matthew*, written in Latin in the sixth century by an unknown author.[24] This version is based on the *Infancy Gospel of James*, with some tidying up of details to make it correspond better to the New Testament gospels. Notably in this story, Salome is transformed into a second midwife. In

---

20   This story is readily available in many English translations. Several translations of this story and a Greek edition are available at Peter Kirby, ed., "Infancy Gospel of James," *Early Christian Writings*, (2001–2013) http://www.earlychristianwritings.com/infancyjames. html, accessed Sept. 4, 2013. In most versions ch. 18–20 focus on the midwife incident.

21   For the development of the Cult of Mary in the Roman Empire and Greek East, see Rubin, *Mother of God*, pp. 17–82.

22   Mary Clayton, *The Apocryphal Gospels of Mary in Anglo-Saxon England* (Cambridge: CUP, 2006), p. 11.

23   Clayton, *Apocryphal Gospels*, pp. 16–17; "Apocrypha about Christ and Mary," in *Sources of Anglo-Saxon Literary Culture: The Apocrypha*, ed. Frederick M. Biggs, Instrumenta Anglistica Mediaevalia 1 (Kalamazoo: Medieval Institute Publications, 2007), p. 22 (21–36).

24   See O. Cullmann, "Infancy Gospels," in *New Testament Apocrypha*, v. 1, rev. and ed. W. Schneemelcher, English trans. R. McL. Wilson (Louisville and London: Westminster John Knox Press, 1991), pp. 414–20. The prologue claims that the work was written by Matthew the Evangelist in Hebrew and translated into Latin by Jerome.

the *Infancy Gospel of Matthew* version of the story, Mary retreats alone into the cave where she gives birth to the Christ child, while Joseph goes to get two midwives, Zahel (the name varies from text to text) and Salome. On their return, Joseph advises Mary to be prudent and allow the midwives to examine her in case she is in need of their care. Zahel enters the cave first and, upon examining Mary, recognizes that she is yet a virgin, although she has brought forth a son and her breasts are filled with milk. The second *obstetrix*, Salome, disbelieving, insists on testing Mary's virginity by inserting her finger, whereupon her hand shrivels. Her hand is again cured by the touch of the Christ child.[25] The story gives the impression that midwives are a routine part of birth care, and the portrayal of Zahel at least is very positive.

The *Infancy Gospel of Matthew* proved extremely popular, with approximately 130 manuscripts still surviving. The work became more prominent in the ninth century and beyond with the Carolingian and Anglo-Saxon intellectual renaissances and increased copying of manuscripts. Several copies survive from the ninth, tenth, and eleventh centuries, and numerous copies from the twelfth and thirteenth centuries.[26] The episode of the midwives is a prominent one in the work, and thus the story ensured a place for midwives in literate and Latinate culture. The *Infancy Gospel of Matthew* also affected popular culture insofar as it was highly influential in shaping the burgeoning cult of Mary in both England and Francia. Ideas from the work were popularized through various new works on Mary, such as those by Paschasius Radbertus, abbot of Corbie in the ninth century, and sermons by influential clerics, such as Hincmar of Reims and Fulbert of Chartres.[27] The influence of the story is shown by its impact on other early medieval works on the Nativity. Midwives (*obstetrices*) appear in the tenth-century Freising Christmas play,[28] and also

---

25 Jan Gijsel, ed., *Libri de Nativitate Mariae: Pseudo-Matthaei Evangelium*, Corpus Christianorum Series Apocryphorum 9 (Turnhout: Brepols, 1997), ch. 13 (pp. 415–27).

26 Mary Clayton, *Cult of the Virgin Mary in Anglo-Saxon England* (Cambridge: CUP, 2003), p. 1. Clayton, *Apocryphal Gospels*, provides editions of Latin and Old English versions from Anglo-Saxon England; all omit the birth of Jesus and story of the midwives. The critical edition by Gijsel includes a list of surviving manuscripts.

27 Paschasius Radbertus, *De partu uirginis*, ed. E. Ann Matter, Corpus Christianorum Continuatio Mediaevalis, 56 (Turnholt: Brepols, 1985), see p. 10, note 8 for a list of mariological works. For the cult of Mary in England, see Clayton, *Cult of the Virgin*. For Francia, see Rubin, *Mother of God*, pp. 100–04.

28 Samuel B. Hemingway, ed., *English Nativity Plays* (New York: Russell and Russell, 1964), p. *xi*.

in Hrotswitha of Gandersheim's tenth-century *Historia Navitatis*.[29] In the thirteenth century, the story of the two midwives would be retold in Jacobus de Voragine's phenomenally popular *Golden Legend*, again following *Pseudo-Matthew*, as proof of Mary's virginity.[30]

As its inclusion in sermons suggests, reception of the story was not limited to literate, Latinate audiences. It had considerable impact on visual representations of the Nativity and was represented in manuscript illustrations, ivories, and frescoes and reliefs in churches. Although the New Testament nativity accounts mention no female attendants, a significant proportion of nativity scenes from the Carolingian period onwards (earlier in the Greek East) incorporate female figures bathing the Christ child or attending to Mary. While it is, of course, probable that some of these figures reflect medieval cultural assumptions that birthing women should be attended by other women—most birth scenes do include female attendants—it is likely that many were intended to be depictions of the two midwives. This is occasionally indicated by signifiers such as the unusual positioning of a female attendant's hand, alluding to Salome's injury.[31] This public depiction of the story of the midwives would

---

29   See Hrotswitha *Historia Nativitatis Laudabilisque Conversationis Intactae Dei Genitricis Quam Scriptam Reperi Sub Nomine Sancti Jacobi Fratris Domini*, ed. Migne, *Patrologia Latina*, v. 137, pp. 1074–5, ch. 89, http://www.documentacatholicaomnia.eu/04z/z_0930–1002_Hrorshitha_Gandersheimensis_Historia_Nativitatis_Sub_Nomine_Jacobo_Fratris_Domini_MLT.pdf.html, accessed Sept. 4, 2013, and also Hrotswitha, *Historia Nativitatis*, in *Hrotsvithae Opera*, ed. Paulus de Winterfeld, Monumenta Germania Scriptores rerum Germanicarum in usum scholarum separatism editi (SS rer. Germ), v. 34, line 589 ff, pp. 21–22 (pp. 5–29), accessed Sept. 4, 2013, http://www.dmgh.de/de/fs1/object/display/bsb00000736_meta:titlePage.html?sortIndex=010:070:0034:010:00:00.

30   Jacobus de Voragine, "De Nativitate domini nostri Jesu Christi," in *Legenda Aurea: Vulgo historia Lombardica dicta*, ed. Th. Graesse (Dresden and Leipzig: Libraria Arnoldiana, 1846), ch. 6, p. 42 (39–46). For the popularity of the work, see Sherry L. Reames, *The Legenda Aurea: A Reexamination of Its Paradoxical History* (Madison, WI: University of Wisconsin Press, 1985), pp. 3–5.

31   For the evolution of these figures, see: Rosalie Green, "The Missing Midwife," in *Romanesque and Gothic: Essays for George Zarnecki*, ed. Neil Stratford (Woodbridge: Boydell, 1987), pp. 103–05; Hélène Toubert, "La Vierge et les deux sages-femmes: L'iconographie entre les Evangiles apocryphes et le drame liturgique," in *Georges Duby, l'ecriture de l'histoire*, ed. Claudie Duhamel-Amado and Guy Lobrichon (Brussels : De Boeck Universite, 1996), pp. 401–23. For another example, see Rubin, *Mother of God*, p. 111. For images of birth, see L. C. MacKinney, "Childbirth in the Middle Ages as Seen in Manuscript Illustrations," *Ciba Symposium* 8.5/6 (1960): 230–36. Neuman de Vegvar, "Images of Women," 55–56, identifies all birth attendants in Anglo-Saxon depictions as midwives, although this may not have been the intent of the artist in all cases.

continue and increase during the High Middle Ages. Thus, midwives had a significant place in the literature and art of the cult of the Virgin Mary, which gave them a considerable cultural presence not only in literate and Latinate circles, but also to some degree in the wider popular culture through art and sermons.

The High Middle Ages, 1000–1300

Europe then entered the new millennium with perhaps no recent tradition of practicing midwives, but with significant cultural awareness of the idea and function of midwives as helpers in childbirth. This likely helped pave the way for the re-emergence of midwives in the more propitious climate of the High Middle Ages. The High Middle Ages were a time of growth. The population doubled or tripled by 1300. Trade and commerce, already beginning to revive in some areas at the end of the Early Middle Ages, expanded rapidly in the High Middle Ages, facilitating the spread of ideas and information as well as goods. Existing towns expanded rapidly and new towns were founded, providing a place for the development of specialized crafts and new educational institutions of various kinds. Education, literacy, and literary production all increased exponentially and the ideas of literate and Latinate culture became more widely disseminated. Interest in classical ideas, already strong in the Carolingian period, grew stronger, and in the eleventh, twelfth, and thirteenth centuries scholars sought and studied classical and Arabic texts, particularly medical and scientific works. Scholars also wrote many new works, often founded on the new learning. In the twelfth and especially the thirteenth centuries, many works were written in or translated into vernacular languages, making learned ideas available beyond those literate in Latin. Rulers, both secular and religious, built more centralized and powerful governments, supported by growing bureaucracies and law courts. These were increasingly staffed by literate men, trained in the liberal arts and sometimes law or theology at the new universities, who left copious records of their activities.

As a result of these social transformations, the number and nature of sources relating to childbirth increased tremendously during the High Middle Ages. Michael Clanchy has characterized this period as one of transition from "memory to written record," and this is evident in the number and variety of sources available.[32] Not only do traditional sources such as chronicles, histories, saints' lives, new and old medical texts, and law codes survive in abundance, but also

---

32   See Michael Clanchy, *From Memory to Written Record: England 1066 to 1307*, 2nd. ed. (Oxford: Blackwell, 1993).

a plethora of other kinds of literature, from courtly fiction to educational treatises. In the thirteenth century especially, legal records of various kinds reveal
much about everyday life. The arguments of this chapter rely especially on two
types of sources that become particularly useful in the High Middle Ages.

Miracle stories, long part of saints' *vita* on a small scale in the Early Middle
Ages, grew in importance in the tenth and eleventh centuries. In the twelfth
and thirteenth centuries they survive in numerous large detailed collections
of posthumous miracles, often with depositions from multiple witnesses.[33]
Rachel Koopmans describes this as a "miracle-collecting mania," lasting from
the late eleventh century until the mid-thirteenth century.[34] This phenomenon can be attributed in part to the growing role of miracles as "proof" of
sanctity, which culminated in the second half of the twelfth century with the
centralization of canonization processes in the hands of the Papal Curia.[35] In
the same period, birth miracles became more prominent in collections, both
because of the sheer number of records, but also because in the twelfth and
thirteenth centuries it became more common for miracles to be performed
from a distance using vows and relics, rather than at a shrine.[36] By their
nature, most birth miracles needed to be long-distance miracles, performed
at or near the birthing chamber, although mothers and other witnesses travelled to shrines to give their thanks and report details of the miracles. Birth
miracles were never particularly prominent—estimates from the High Middle
Ages range from 0.5% to 2% of all recorded miracles, but this still adds up to

---

33   R. I. Moore, "Between Sanctity and Superstition: Saints and their Miracles in the Age of
      Revolution," in *The Work of Jacques le Goff and the Challenges of Medieval History*, ed. Miri
      Rubin (Woodbridge: Boydell Press, 1997), pp. 55–67.

34   Rachel Koopmans, *Wonderful to Relate: Miracle Stories and Miracle Collecting in High
      Medieval England* (Philadelphia: University of Pennsylvania Press, 2011), p. 2. See also
      Ronald C. Finucane, *Miracles and Pilgrims: Popular Beliefs in Medieval England* (Totowa:
      Rowan and Littlefield, 1977); Pierre-André Sigal, *L'homme et le miracle dans la France médié-
      vale* (Paris: CERF, 1985); and Benedicta Ward, *Miracles and the Medieval Mind: Theory,
      Record, and Event, 1000–1215* (Philadelphia: University of Pennsylvania Press, 1982; rev. 1987).

35   For canonization, see André Vauchez, *Sainthood in the Later Middle Ages*, trans. Jean
      Birrell (Cambridge: CUP, 1997), pp. 22–84 and Eric W. Kemp, *Canonization and Authority
      in the Western Church* (New York: AMS Press, 1980).

36   Vauchez, *Sainthood*, 446–48; Pierre André Sigal, "La Grossesse, l'accouchement et
      l'attitude envers l'enfant mort-né à la fin du Moyen Âge d'après les récits de miracles,"
      in *Santé, Médecine et Assistance au Moyen Age* (Paris: Comité des travaux historiques et
      scientifiques, 1987), p. 24 (23–41). Powell, "Miracle of Childbirth," 795–811, argues for a
      change in interest and policy, suggesting that monks were deliberately choosing to tell
      more stories of birth after the mid-twelfth century.

a significant number of detailed stories about birth.[37] Such stories bring us closer to women's experiences of birth than any other source of the time, since women came to the shrines to tell their stories. While accounts were filtered through the male, Latinate gaze of monks recording the miracles, and may be distorted by both witnesses and authors to promote the merits of the saint, they do convey perspectives on birth that do not otherwise survive.[38]

Another valuable source that provides details of real births are proofs of age, part of the English *inquisitions post-mortem*. These are records of inquests into the age of heirs to lands held by the king, which determined whether an individual was old enough to inherit land.[39] Age was determined through the testimony of a jury of local men who were familiar with the age of the heir. From the reign of Edward I in the thirteenth century, there are individual depositions from jurors. Because jurors were asked to explain how they knew the age of the heir, jurors often detail their memories relating to the birth of the child, drawing on information provided by female kin, neighbors, and servants. While it may have been to the advantage of jurors to prove the heir's age, the stories, if fabricated, at the very least had to be believable to the officials recording them, and thus reflective of birth at the time. Like the miracle stories, the depositions

---

37   For a typology of childbirth miracles, see: Renate Blumenfeld-Kosinski, "Gautier de Coinci and Medieval Childbirth Miracles," in *Gautier de Coinci: Miracles, Music, and Manuscripts*, ed. Kathy M. Krause and Alison Stones (Turnhout: Brepols, 2006), pp. 198–205 (197–214). Vauchez, *Sainthood*, p. 468, finds only 1.2% of miracles in processes of canonization between 1201 and 1300 dealt with birth, including infertility cures. Finucane, *Miracles and Pilgrims*, p. 144, using English and French miracles, sets the number at 2%. Sigal, *L'homme et le miracle*, p. 265, using mostly miracles from the eleventh and twelfth centuries, finds only 0.5%.

38   Several historians have used miracles to reveal details of childbirth. See especially: Biller, "Childbirth in the Middle Ages," 42–49; Shahar, *Childhood in the Middle Ages*, pp. 32–52; Finucane, *The Rescue of the Innocents*, pp. 17–42; Hilary Powell, "Miracle of Childbirth," 795–811; Carole Rawcliffe, "Women, Childbirth, and Religion," pp. 91–117; Sigal, "La grossesse," pp. 23–41; Didier Lett, *L'enfant des miracles: Enfance et société au Moyen Âge (XIIᵉ–XIIIᵉ siècle)* (Paris: Aubier, 1997), esp. pp. 241–260; Harris Stoertz, 'Suffering and Survival," pp. 101–20; Blumenfeld-Kosinski, "Gautier de Coinci and Medieval Childbirth Miracles," pp. 197–214; Blumenfeld-Kosinski, *Not of Women Born*.

39   The English *Inquisitions Post-Mortem* are stored in the National Archives in Kew, U.K. Most have been translated and calendared in *Calendar of Inquisitions Post Mortem and Other Analogous Documents Preserved in the Public Record Office*, vols. 1–23 (London: HMSO, 1904–1955). I have cited the calendared version (CIPM) in most cases, as it is more easily accessible to most readers, but have consulted the originals at the National Archives and cite the Latin originals when the precise word choice is important. Although proofs of age are available up to the fifteenth century, I have used only those up to 1325 for this chapter.

were recorded in Latin by royal officials and are somewhat removed from the women who first shared details of the births.[40]

Birth in the High Middle Ages was idealized as an occasion attended by women only. This idea appears in a wide range of sources. Pierre de Fontaines, advisor to Louis IX, in his legal treatise written ca.1253, comments that a husband should not come near his wife during labor.[41] Likewise, the *Placitorum Abbreviatio*, a text written in England in the late thirteenth-century, states that to be considered a live birth (important in some inheritance cases), a child must be heard to cry, since women could not testify in court and men could not enter the birthing chamber.[42] The *Book on the Conditions of Women*, composed in the twelfth century and the most popular obstetrical and gynecological text of the thirteenth century, claims to be written to help women who feel too much "shame and embarrassment" to discuss diseases affecting their private parts with a physician. This address was, however, omitted in some versions, and it seems likely the book in its Latin versions at least was read predominately by men.[43] That it was considered shameful for a man to see a woman give birth or even to visit her shortly afterwards is suggested by the thirteenth-century French romance, *Silence*. When Cadar enters the birth chamber to discover the sex of his offspring, his wife, Eufemie, is embarrassed by his visit, and the author comments that Cadar's "desire to know the truth took away any feeling of shame which would have kept him from approaching a woman in childbed."[44] Likewise, Josian, in *Beues of Hamtoun*, rejects

40   For information about proofs of age, see: Sue Sheridan Walker, "Proof of Age of Feudal Heirs in Medieval England," *Mediaeval Studies* 35 (1973): 306–23; John Bedell, "Memory and Proof of Age in England 1272–1327," *Past and Present*, 162 (1999): 4–12 (3–27); and Becky R. Lee, "A Company of Women and Men: Men's Recollections of Childbirth in Medieval England," *Journal of Family History* 27.2 (2002): 92–100, and "Men's Recollections of a Women's Rite: Medieval English Men's Recollections Regarding the Rite of the Purification of Women after Childbirth," *Gender & History* 14.2 (2002): 224–41.

41   M. A. J. Marnier, ed., *Le conseil de Pierre de Fontaines, ou Traité de l'ancienne jurisprudence Française* (Paris: Joubert and Durand, 1846), p. 20.

42   Cited in Frederick Pollock and Frederic William Maitland, *The History of English Law before the Time of Edward I*, 2nd ed., (London: CUP, 1968), v. 2, p. 418.

43   Monica H. Green, ed. and trans., *The Trotula: A Medieval Compendium of Women's Medicine* (Philadelphia: University of Pennsylvania Press, 2001), pp. 70–71; Green, *Making Women's Medicine Masculine*, pp. 50–53. Green argues that this prologue was actually intended to advise male physicians how to better aid their patients.

44   Sarah Roche-Mahdi, ed. and trans., *Silence: A Thirteenth-century French Romance* (East Lansing, MI: Colleagues Press, 1992), lines 2003–2007: "Li voloirs qu'a del voir savoir/Tolt qu'il ne puet vergoigne avoir/ Qu'al lit ne voist de l'acolcie."

her husband's help in delivering twins out of a sense of shame.[45] Caesarius of Heisterbach in the early thirteenth century describes an image of St Nicholas miraculously turning to face the wall rather than witness a birth.[46]

These texts are, of course, all prescriptive in nature. Recent scholarship by authors such as Jacqueline Musacchio, Becky Lee, and Ronald Finucane suggests that while women provided most primary care for birthing women, men were very much aware of the events of the birthing chamber, and often sought to influence them in a variety of ways.[47] Green likewise has argued at length against the idea of a strict sexual division of labor in women's healthcare.[48] The evidence considered in this chapter suggests that while birth was an event attended mostly by women, men actively intervened with considerable regularity during the High Middle Ages, ideals of women's shame notwithstanding.

What is particularly striking to a modern reader is just how many people might attend a high medieval birth. While, from the twelfth century onwards the group might include one or more midwives, it usually also included many other women, and occasionally some men. Eufemie in *Silence* gave birth attended only by a cousin due to her husband's desire for secrecy, but this is portrayed as an unusual and difficult scenario: "The lady ... never had a more difficult task, for she was alone, without anyone to help her, throughout the countess's delivery."[49] Multiple caregivers were clearly preferred. In one of St Thomas Becket's miracles from the twelfth century, Aaliza of Middleton is attended by seven *obstetrices* as well as her mother.[50] "Father, friends, and family" (*patrem, amicos ac parentes*), concerned about Guibert of Nogent's

---

45   Eugen Kölbing, ed., *Romance of Beues of Hamtoun*, Early English Text Society 46 (London: Kegan Paul, Trench, Trübner & Co., 1885), pp. 171–72. See Jennifer Fellows, "Mothers in Middle English Romance," in *Women and Literature in Britain, 1150–1500*, ed. Carol M. Meale (Cambridge: CUP, 1993), p. 54 (41–60).

46   Renate Blumenfeld-Kosinski, "Gautier de Coinci and Medieval Childbirth Miracles," 206.

47   See Jacqueline Musacchio, *The Art and Ritual of Childbirth in Renaissance Italy* (New Haven: Yale University Press, 1999), *passim*; Lee, "A Company of Women and Men," 92–100; and Finucane, *The Rescue of the Innocents*, pp. 33–35. In contrast, Gail McMurray Gibson, "Scene and Obscene: Seeing and performing late Medieval Childbirth," *Journal of Medieval and Early Modern Studies* 29.1 (1999): 7–24 argues that male entrance to the birthing chamber was "strictly controlled and restricted."

48   Green, "Women's Medical Practice and Health Care in Medieval Europe," 39–78 and *Making Women's Medicine Masculine, passim*.

49   *Silence*, lines 1789–1793. "La dame ert cozine al segnor./ Onques n'ot mais traval gregnor,/ Car seule fu sans compagnesse/ Al delivrer de la contesse."

50   James Craigie Robertson, ed., *Materials for the History of Thomas Becket*, 7 vols., Rolls Series 67 (London: Longman & Co, 1875–85), v. 2, pp. 222–23.

mother's long and dangerous labor, made a vow to the Virgin Mary, suggesting that a considerable number of caregivers had gathered to support her.[51]

As might be expected, family members sometimes tried to be nearby their parturient relative during births. Aaliza's mother attended the birth in addition to the seven midwives.[52] Likewise, Robert de Everingham's sister attended his wife during the birth of their son Adam early in the reign of Edward I.[53] In a miracle of Louis of Toulouse, the parturient woman's sister was in attendance.[54] Some women arranged to stay with their natal families when their children were born. Matilda, Duchess of Saxony, stayed with her father Henry II in Normandy and England for the birth of two of her children, suggesting a desire to be with her family for the birth of children.[55] Margaret, daughter of Henry III of England and wife of Alexander III of Scotland, insisted on staying in England for the birth of her first child so that she could be with her family.[56] Such patterns were not limited to royal women. Ermentrude gave birth to Andrew de Saukevill in a chamber at her brother's house during the reign of Edward I,[57] and Isabel, mother of Anketin Salvayn, after the death of her husband, went to stay with her brother in York for the duration of her pregnancy. Her sister and sister's husband joined them immediately after the birth of the child.[58] It is noteworthy that women chose to be near male as well as female relatives when they gave birth.

According to the evidence of proofs of age, husbands virtually always remained outside the birthing chamber.[59] This study has uncovered only one thirteenth-century exception to this pattern in the proofs of age. William de Ferariis asked his wife's chamberlain to open the door of her chamber so that

51   Guibert of Nogent, *Histoire de sa vie (1053–1124)*, ed. Georges Bourgin (Paris: Alphonse Picard et fils, 1907), ch. 3 (p. 9).

52   *Materials for the History of Thomas Becket*, v. 2, pp. 222–23.

53   William Brown, ed., *Yorkshire Inquisitions of the Reigns of Henry III and Edward I*, 4 vols., Yorkshire Archaeological and Topographical Association Record Series, vols. XII, XXIII, XXXI, XXXVII (1892–1906), v. 4, p. I.

54   Cited in Finucane, *Rescue of the Innocents*, p. 35.

55   Roger de Hoveden, *Chronica*, 1181–82 and 1184, ed. William Stubbs, 4 vols. (London: HMSO, 1868–71), v. 1, pp. 270, 285.

56   John Carmi Parsons, "Mothers, Daughters, Marriage, Power," in *Medieval Queenship*, ed. John Carmi Parsons (New York: St Martin's Press, 1993), p. 70.

57   CIPM v. 3, no. 627.

58   *Yorkshire Inquisitions*, 4.L.

59   See Lee, "A Company of Women and Men," 92–100. While Lee examines a much longer time span, my own reading of proofs up to 1325 confirms this.

he could come in to speak with her while she was in labor.[60] Other sources, like Guibert, suggest that it was not unusual for husbands to enter if things were going badly. In miracle stories, there are many cases of men being at their wives' bedsides and helping them appeal to a saint, although in some cases the husbands have been called in because the woman appears to be dying.[61] According to John of Joinville, Louis IX visited his wife Marguerite of Provence who had been seriously injured giving birth and was feared to be dying, although his mother, Blanche of Castile, attempted to make him leave.[62] In courtly literature, likewise, the example of Josian notwithstanding, husbands sometimes help their wives give birth in the absence of other caregivers.[63] Other men might also attend in extraordinary circumstances. Queen Marguerite, at the end of a pregnancy, with Louis recently having been taken captive, asked an eighty-year-old knight to stay with her, holding her hand while she slept.[64]

It appears to have been customary in the High Middle Ages for a woman's friends, neighbors, and servants to attend her when she gave birth. A 1289 proof of age from Manosque in Southern France, where women were able to testify personally, reveals that women of the neighborhood habitually attended each others' births, with many present at each birth.[65] In a miracle of St Margaret of Scotland, a woman gave birth to a long dead fetus aided by devout and respectable (*deuotas ac honestas*) women.[66] Neighbors (*affines*) removed the bones of the dead child from an eleventh-century Norman woman whose uterus

---

60   CIPM v. 3, no. 149.

61   See for example, *Materials for the History of Thomas Becket*, v. 1, pp. 226–67; v. 1, pp. 345–46; and v. 2, p. 196; Finucane, *The Rescue of the Innocents*, pp. 33–35. Finucane cites one unusual case (p. 35) where a man was with his wife when she gave birth, but the attendants were outside. In this case, the husband was not particularly helpful. See also Sigal, "La Grossesse," p. 28.

62   John of Joinville, "Life of Saint Louis," in *Joinville and Villehardouin: Chronicles of the Crusades*, trans. Caroline Smith (London: Penguin, 2008), p. 297.

63   See Ferdinand Heuckenkamp, ed., *Le Chevalier du Papegau* (Halle: Max Niemeyer, 1896) p. 82, lines 13–25. Esther C. Quinn, ed., and trans., *The Penitence of Adam: A Study of the Andrius Ms* (Mississippi: University of Mississippi, 1980), p. 77.

64   Joinville, "Life of Saint Louis," pp. 243–44.

65   Joseph Shatzmiller, ed., *Médecine et Justice en Provence Médiévale: Documents de Manosque 1262–1348* (Aix-en-Provence: Publications de l'Université de Provence, 1989), pp. 66–69. For an analysis of the case, see Caley McCarthy, "Midwives, Medicine, and the Reproductive Female Body in Manosque, 1289–1500," M.A. Diss., University of Waterloo, 2011), pp. 65–69.

66   Robert Bartlett, ed. and trans., *Miracles of Saint Aebbe of Coldingham and Saint Margaret of Scotland* (Oxford: Clarendon Press, 2003), pp. 80–83.

had been miraculously opened by St Vulfran.[67] A miracle of Louis of Toulouse around 1300 also mentions a crowd of women in attendance.[68] The English proofs of age likewise reveal birth to have been a social occasion. Jurors in the proofs of age report hearing about births from their wives, mothers, neighbors, and servants who attended the births. Although the parturient women, as members of families that held land from the king, must have had considerable social status, women attending births could come from a wide range of social backgrounds. Lady Amice de Say attended the birth of William, son of John le Mareschal, during the reign of Edward I. That her role was more than social or symbolic is implied by the complaint of a juror who tried to meet with her about a piece of business but could not because she was too busy with the mother.[69] Christiana le Browystere, whose name implies a lower social rank, and Christina de la Dale (perhaps the same person) attended the mother of Thomas de Louayne, and subsequently gossiped about it to two jurors.[70] The wives of several jurors, who were not obviously of high standing, likewise attended births.[71]

Servants and members of the household played an important role in birth in the case of elite women at least. The presence of servants makes sense given the often unpleasant and messy tasks associated with birth, but servants and other women of the household would also be likely to know the parturient woman well and be able to offer support and comfort. This is suggested by Marie de France's *le Fresne*, where the mother of twin girls is assisted, comforted, and advised by members of her household.[72] The presence of servants is also demonstrated by English proofs of age. The mother of John Knot was the servant of Joan Cordeboef and attended the birth of Joan's son John early in the reign of Edward I.[73] Other families appear to have lent their servants to parturient women. Ralph de la Mare's servant (*ancilla*) attended the mother of Geoffrey de Lucy in childbirth, although it is possible that she was in the

---

67   *Miracula S. Vulfranni Episcopi*, AASS Boll., March, tome 3, p. 150 (149–65). Translated as "Pregnant Woman's Delivery of a Stillborn Baby, Normandy, Mid-eleventh Century," in *Medieval Writings on Secular Women*, trans Patricia Skinner and Elisabeth van Houts (London: Penguin, 2011), pp. 14–15.

68   Finucane, *Rescue of the Innocents*, p. 35.

69   CIPM v. 3, no. 483.

70   CIPM v. 5, no. 539.

71   See for example CIPM v. 6, no. 200; v. 6, no. 435.

72   Marie de France, "Le Fresne," in *The Lais of Marie de France*, trans. Robert Hanning and Joan Ferrante (Durham, North Carolina: The Labyrinth Press, 1978, 1982), p. 75 (73–87), lines 95ff.

73   CIPM v. 3, no. 434.

de Lucy family's service at the time.[74] In a less ambiguous case, Lady Isabel de Grey sent her maid Joan to Margaret, mother of Hugh de Plessetis, six days before the birth with instructions to stay until after the birth.[75] Did these servants have special skills or expertise expected to be helpful? Personal ties to the mother? Or, was it simply considered valuable to have extra servants present given the work associated with caring for a woman in childbirth?

Sometimes physicians and priests assisted in a professional capacity. Monica Green has demonstrated that twelfth-century Salernitan physicians had considerable practical experience in assisting with women's ailments, including gynecological problems, although they appear to have preferred to use women to perform tasks requiring physical manipulation.[76] Physicians were also consulted in cases of difficult childbirth elsewhere. William le Ken, who lived at the manor of Huntingfeld where Joan, mother of Ralph Basset, was staying near the end of her pregnancy, was sent by the lord of the manor to Norwich to fetch a doctor for her.[77] Gunnilda, in a Becket miracle, consulted a doctor about a childbirth related illness,[78] and a couple in a Louis of Toulouse miracle arranged for a surgeon to extract part of a dead fetus, although he requested that the husband or a relative be present.[79] Twelfth-century chronicles tell us that many physicians were consulted during the troubled first pregnancy of Matilda, wife of Henry I of England. Faritius, abbot of Abingdon, and his lay colleague Grimbald cared for her throughout her pregnancy. That medical care for women and a clerical vocation might not always be compatible is underlined by a chronicler's report that two bishops later argued that it was inappropriate for a man as familiar with women's urine as Faritius was to become

---

74 CIPM v. 2, no. 697; TNA: PRO C 133/52 (5).

75 CIPM v. 6, no. 124; TNA: PRO C 134/60 (9).

76 Green, *Making Women's Medicine Masculine*, pp. 39–45. While obstetrical and gynecological texts were plentiful in the High Middle Ages, there is no evidence that women owned or read the various gynecological texts in circulation. Green argues persuasively that such texts were written for literate and Latinate physicians. It is possible that women read vernacular translations, but there is no evidence that any of the surviving copies were ever owned by women. See Monica H. Green, "Books as a Source of Medical Education for Women in the Middle Ages," *Dynamis* 20 (2000): 331–369 and "The Possibilities of Literacy and the Limits of Reading: Women and the Gendering of Medical Literacy," in Monica H. Green, *Women's Healthcare in the Medieval West: Texts and Context* (Aldershot: Ashgate Variorum, 2000), section VII, pp. 1–76.

77 CIPM, v. 6, no. 335; TNA: PRO C 134/72 (1).

78 *Materials for the History of Thomas Becket*, v. 2, pp. 136–37.

79 See Finucane, *Rescue of the Innocents*, p. 32, and Green, *Making Women's Medicine Masculine*, pp. 111–12.

archbishop of Canterbury.[80] While Faritius appears to have cared for Matilda in his capacity as physician, priests too might be called upon if the situation was desperate. In a Becket miracle, a priest was summoned to give the last rites, when Alditha of Worth's life was despaired of after three days of labor.[81] In another miracle of Becket, the priest seems to have witnessed much of the crisis and even offered a medical opinion.[82] An eleventh-century English charm meant to ensure a successful birth assumes clergy might be in the birthing chamber and thus able to recite the words over the laboring mother.[83] Thus, it is clear that women and their families were willing to set aside shame and allow men to enter the birth chamber if the situation warranted it.

The Re-emergence of Midwives in the Twelfth- and Thirteenth-Centuries

Green argues that midwives only re-emerged as specialized caregivers in the thirteenth century. She notes mentions of midwives in some of the new works written in twelfth-century Salerno, such as Petrus Musandinus' *Practica*, John of St Paul's *Breviarium*, and the *Trotula* ensemble, but argues that such references do not indicate the presence of a professional class of midwives.[84] While obstetrical and gynecological medical texts offering prescriptive advice for the care of women in childbirth are relatively plentiful for the high medieval period, and sometimes mention midwives,[85] it cannot be assumed that midwives were routinely present at births. Medical texts and learned texts in

---

80   Lois L. Hunneycutt, *Matilda of Scotland: A Study in Medieval Queenship* (Woodbridge: Boydell Press, 2003), p. 74; Faye Getz, *Medicine in the English Middle Ages* (Princeton: Princeton University Press, 1998), p. 14.

81   *Materials for the History of Thomas Becket*, v. 2, pp. 48–49.

82   *Materials for the History of Thomas Becket*, v. 1, pp. 227–28.

83   Tony Hunt, *Popular Medicine in Thirteenth-Century England: Introduction and Texts* (Cambridge: D. S. Brewer, 1990), p. 90 (38).

84   Green, *Making Medicine Masculine*, pp. 42, 43. See *The Trotula*, p. 106 (118) for mention of a midwife providing physical remedies and p. 236 (note 48) for the removal of another reference to midwives.

85   For a handlist of manuscripts relating to obstetrics and gynecology, please see Monica H. Green, "Medieval Gynecological Texts: A Handlist," in *Women's Healthcare in the Medieval West: Texts and Contexts* (Aldershot: Ashgate Variorum, 2000), section VIII, pp. 1–36. The most important and popular obstetrical text, particularly in the thirteenth-century, was the so-called Trotula ensemble. Please see Green's study and edition of the text, cited above. Beyond specialist texts, most high medieval medical compendia contained advice on childbirth.

general during the High Middle Ages were significantly influenced by classical and Arabic traditions and may have had little relation to actual practices. Green points out that copies of high medieval texts sometimes omit references to midwives, including at least two eleventh-century versions of Muscio, which leave out the address to midwives,[86] and an early thirteenth-century French translation of *Conditions of Women*, which substitutes "woman with a small hand" for *obstetrix*.[87] This implies that the copyists felt the concept would not be relevant to readers.

While Green's reading of the evidence is compelling, and the scarcity of midwives in twelfth- and thirteenth-century courtly stories supports her thesis,[88] a considerable amount of evidence regarding midwives survives from the twelfth century, suggesting that midwives began to re-emerge rather earlier than Green suggests. The population was growing rapidly in the twelfth century and urban centers able to support specialists had re-emerged. Specialized crafts were developing in many fields at this time, including medicine and surgery, and medicine was emerging as a scholarly discipline supported by a university education.[89] The strong presence of midwives in both popular and literate, Latinate culture would have encouraged their re-emergence as a profession. While one does not find high medieval guilds of midwives, female guilds in general were rare, so this is not particularly surprising.

Outside of medical texts and nativity stories, the earliest evidence for midwives is found in twelfth-century saints' lives and miracle stories. The *Life of Arnulf of Soissons*, written around 1110, describes distraught midwives

---

86   Green, *Making Women's Medicine Masculine*, pp. 33–35

87   Green, "Bodies, Gender, Health, Disease: Recent Work on Medieval Women's Medicine," 16.

88   See Harris-Stoertz, "Pregnancy and Childbirth in Chivalric Literature," 27–36. I have since found a midwife (*ventriere*) in an early thirteenth-century romance. Additionally, in the *Story of Merlin* judges lock Merlin's pregnant mother, accused of fornication, in a tower with two women to help her give birth. The story describes the women as *preude femes*, a term implying qualities such as honesty, wisdom, and loyalty, and says they are the best the judges can find for this purpose, suggesting the women may have had special skills and experience. Gaston Paris and Jacob Ulrich, eds., *Merlin: Roman en prose du XIIIᵉ siècle* (Paris: Librairie de Firmin Didot et Cie, 1886), p. 18: "*deus des plus preudefemes que il porent trouver avoec li et misent.*"

89   The emergence of medicine as a scholarly discipline has been traced by numerous historians. For an excellent general study, see Nancy G. Siraisi, *Medieval and Early Renaissance Medicine* (Chicago and London: University of Chicago Press, 1990). For a recent study of the University of Paris, see Cornelius O'Boyle, *The Art of Medicine: Medical Teaching at the University of Paris 1250–1400* (Leiden: Brill, 1998). For England, see Getz, *Medicine in the English Middle Age* .

(*obstetrices*) delivering a child without eyes, later helped by Arnulf.[90] William Fitzstephen's *Life of Thomas Becket* claims a midwife was present at the saint's birth and predicted his future greatness. Becket was born in London, the biggest city in England at the time, so the claim that a midwife was present at his birth is not impossible. As one of Becket's chaplains and an intimate member of his household for many years, as well as a fellow citizen of London, William was in a position to know personal details and London customs.[91] In the early 1170s, several of Becket's miracles likewise mention one or more midwives (*obstetrices*).[92] As mentioned above, seven midwives attended Aaliza of Middleton.[93] A midwife likewise attended the birth of a stillborn child to Eva, wife of a knight.[94] In another case, the attempts of the midwives to turn a child caused the arm of the child to swell, making delivery impossible.[95] As the latter example suggests, midwives in the miracle stories, as rival healers, are sometimes portrayed as incompetents, but often they appear to be doing their best in an impossible situation. They also sometimes participate in the invocation of saints, as in the miracles of thirteenth-century Simon de Montfort, where midwives "measure" the parturient woman to Simon, a common ritual where the subject's body is measured with a thread or string, which is later used to make a candle given to the saint.[96]

This evidence can be interpreted in a number of ways. Witnesses to miracles would have given their testimony in the vernacular and saints' *vitae* were written in Latin, so, on the one hand, it is possible to argue that learned monks simply translated female neighbors attending births as *obstetrices*, following classical sources. On the other hand, given that large miracle collections were a relatively new phenomenon and sources for the Early Middle Ages are scarce, one could argue that the "reappearance" of midwives was simply the func-

90 Hariulf Aldenburgensi, *Vita S. Arnulfi Confessoris*, AASS Boll. August, tome 3 (v. 37), p. 240 (230–59). See also Vercauteren, "Les médecins dans les principautés," 66. Green, "Documenting," 338, n. 62 notes this case.

91 *Materials for the History of Thomas Becket*, v. 3, pp. 13, 3, *xiii–xvii*.

92 Several historians have used some of these miracles in discussions of midwives. Biller, "Childbirth in the Middle Ages," 42–49; Shahar, *Childhood in the Middle Ages*, pp. 32–52; Finucane, *The Rescue of the Innocents*, pp. 17–42; Powell, "The 'Miracle of Childbirth,'" 795–811; Harris-Stoertz, "Suffering and Survival," pp. 101–20.

93 *Materials for the History of Thomas Becket*, v. 2, pp. 222–23.

94 *Materials for the History of Thomas Becket*, v. 1, pp. 345–46.

95 *Materials for the History of Thomas Becket*, v. 1, pp. 227–28. For another case, see v. 1, pp. 504–05.

96 James Orchard Halliwell, ed., *The Chronicle of William de Rishanger of the Barons' War; The Miracles of Simon de Montfort*, Camden Old Series 15 (New York: Johnson Reprint Corporation, 1968, orig. 1860), p. 84.

tion of new sources being available and that practicing midwives had never truly disappeared.

The inclusion of midwives in another twelfth-century source suggests that the presence of midwives in saints' lives and miracle stories and medical texts during the twelfth century was not merely an intellectual conceit and that midwives did re-emerge, rather than simply become visible because of a change in the nature of sources. Beginning in the later twelfth century, midwives began to be included in encyclopedias. This is significant not only because it provides additional support for the evidence of twelfth-century midwives found in medical texts, saints' vita, and miracle stories, but also because midwives were absent from earlier encyclopedias. Early medieval encyclopedias, collections of important knowledge such as those by Rabanus Maurus and Isidore of Seville, although vast in size, do not mention midwives. Three of the earliest high medieval encyclopedias, written in the late twelfth and early thirteenth century do mention midwives. This is especially striking, since they used Isidore and Rabanus as models. Isidore and Rabanus would have been familiar with the concept of midwives through classical literature and stories of the Nativity, but they did not choose to include them. The fact that all three of these high medieval encyclopedists include midwives thus implies that something had changed. This, added to the weight of references to midwives in medical texts and miracle stories, suggests that the process of re-emergence began in the twelfth century, and was well-established already by the thirteenth century. Collectively, these sources suggest the emergence of a professional identity for midwives, separate from that of ordinary women attending births.

The first of the three encyclopedias, *De naturis rerum*, was written between 1187 and 1204 by Alexander Neckham, an English scholar and monk, trained in Paris. This date places it close in time to the Salernitan medical texts and Becket miracles. In a discussion of the stages of life, traditional in encyclopedias, Neckham briefly describes the difficulties and dangers of childbirth and the skill and care that needed to be exercised by midwives to ensure a successful birth.[97] Neckham presents midwives as holders of specialized skill and knowledge, who could be expected to be available to help in difficult childbirth situations such as malpresentations and retention of the afterbirth. There is no sense that they are rare or unusual, although of course this understanding of midwives could have been drawn from classical sources.

97　Alexander Neckam, *De Naturis Rerum*, ed. Thomas Wright, Rolls Series 34 (London: Longman, Green, Longman, Roberts, and Green, 1863), p. 241. R. W. Hunt, *The Schools and the Cloister: The Life and Writings of Alexander Nequam*, ed. and rev. Margaret Gibson (Oxford: Clarendon Press, 1984), p. 26.

Thomas of Cantimpré, a Dominican from the Low Countries, takes a rather different approach in his *Liber de natura rerum*, probably composed between 1228 and 1240. Following lengthy sections on the reproductive parts and conception, Thomas provides a much more substantial discussion of the midwife's work, which was (according to Green) ultimately derived from Muscio, although attributed to Cleopatra, thus lending female authority.[98] Speaking of the danger of fetal malpresentations, Thomas says experienced midwives could readily correct them, but laments that experienced midwives are rare. He then provides a detailed discussion of techniques to resolve various kinds of malpresentations and ends by suggesting that priests should secretly teach them to midwives, who will teach others, thus spreading this information and saving lives and souls. This work is difficult to interpret. Is Thomas saying that midwives are rare? Or, that midwives possessing the specialized information that he presents are rare? In fact, it is highly unlikely that midwives would be familiar with the information he presents, since most would not have had access to Latin medical works and some of the presentations he discusses would be quite unusual, not something a midwife would gain extensive experience of through regular practice. In any case, Thomas does assume midwives are present in society and can be located and taught. Thomas's work was widely read and copied, although not as extensively as the work of his contemporary, Barthomaeus Anglicus.

De proprietatibus rerum, written before 1245 by the English Franciscan Bartholomaeus Anglicus, was the most widely read of the three texts.[99] Bartholomaeus, like Neckham, places his description of a midwife in his stages of life section. His description too is based on function.

> A midwife is a woman who has the art to help a woman in childbirth so that she bears and brings forth her child with less woe and sorrow. And so the child should be born with less difficulty and sorrow, she anoints and foments the mother's uterus and helps and comforts her in that way. Also she draws the child out of the uterus and ties his navel four inches long. With water she washes away the blood of the child and rubs him with salt

98   Thomas de Cantimpre, *Liber de natura rerum*, ed. H. Boase (Berlin and New York: Walter de Gruyter, 1973), v. 1, pp. 74–76; Green, *Making Medicine Masculine*, pp. 139, 147–150.

99   For background on Bartholomaeus and Thomas, see M. C. Seymour, "Introduction," in *Bartholomaeus Anglicus and his Encyclopedia*, ed. M. C. Seymour, *et al.* (London: Variorum, 1992), pp. 1–35. Michel Salvat, "L'accouchement dans la literature scientifique medievale," in *L'enfant au Moyen Age*, Senefiance 9 (Paris: Cuerma, 1980), pp. 89–106, examines Bartholomaeus' encyclopedia as a source for the history of childbirth.

and honey to dry up the humors and to comfort his limbs and members, and swaddles him in clothes and cloths.[100]

This description is precise in detail, and not obviously derived from any classical sources, so it is tempting to assume that it is based on contemporary practice, although of course one cannot be certain

In the thirteenth century, besides encyclopedias, midwives appear in numerous sources. Not only do they continue to appear in miracle stories,[101] but also in sources generated by the centralization and bureaucratization of secular and religious government. A council in Sens, *c.* 1212–3 forbade Christian midwives (*obstetrices*) to care for Jewish women in childbirth.[102] There would seem to be little point in such legislation if midwives were not reasonably well-established as a profession. Midwives also appear in the visitation register of Eudes, Bishop of Rouen. Nichola, a nun of St-Saëns in 1259 was found to have given birth to her second child attended by two midwives from the village.[103] Midwives can also be found in some of the earliest detailed proofs of age, although they are relatively few in number. Four knights claimed that they learned of the birth of John Paynel during the reign of Henry III "from the relation of godmothers and midwives who were present when he was born, and of religious and other trustworthy persons of the neighbourhood." This piece of evidence is particularly important as it indicates that several women were present, but only some were identified as midwives. One of the jurors specifically identified his source of information as a midwife named Katherine de Novo Burgo.[104] That being said, in at least two cases the jurors identify their wives as the midwives who tended to the mothers, so it is not clear how "professional" they were.[105]

---

100   For convenience, I have based my translation mostly on John Trevisa's fourteenth-century English version presented in Bartholomaeus Anglicus, *On the Properties of Things: John Trevisa's Translation of Bartholamaeus Anglicus De Proprietatibus Rerum, a Critical Text* (Oxford: Clarendon Press, 1975), v. 1, 6.10 (p. 305), but I also consulted British Library MS Ashmole 1512 (1292). The process of anointing and fomenting (*fomentis*) the uterus probably involved putting warm wet cloths on the woman, something that modern midwives claim helps prevent tearing. The image of a woman washing the baby is a common one in birth iconography.

101   See for example, Sigal, "La grossesse," pp. 23–41, Finucane, *Rescue*, pp. 31, 35.

102   Taglia, "Delivering a Christian Identity", p. 88.

103   Jeremiah F. O'Sullivan, ed., *The Register of Eudes of Rouen*, trans. Sydney M. Brown (New York and London: Columbia University Press, 1964), p. 384.

104   CIPM v. 2, no. 553.

105   CIPM v. 5, no. 153; TNA: PRO C 134/13 (5).

Midwives also begin to appear in vernacular texts intended for lay people during the mid-thirteenth century. Aldebrandino of Siena, in a French treatise on maintaining health dedicated in 1256 to his patron Beatrice of Provence, mother-in-law of Louis IX, suggests that a skilled midwife (*sage baile*) should turn the baby should it be badly positioned and unable to come out.[106] This text echoes the *Trotula* ensemble and Thomas of Cantimpré in its focus on the role of midwives in dealing with fetal malpresentations. That at least some elites used midwives is suggested by an Anglo-Norman poem probably composed between 1240 and 1250 by Walter de Bibbesworth, a member of a minor English landed family. The stated goal of the poem is to teach essential French vocabulary to the children of Dionisie de Munchensi, wife of a prominent English landowner, to help them manage their estates when they come of age.[107] The poem is organized with French rhymes and English rubrics meant to help the reader interpret the rhymes. The first four lines of the long poem, included here in both the original languages and translation, teach the terms for giving birth and midwife (*ventrere/midwif*):[108]

> Femme ke aproche sun teins
> De enfaunter moustre seins (English rubric: to belittre, that is give birth)
> Quant se purveit de une ventrere (English rubric: midwif)
> Qui seit avisé cunseillere.[109]

---

106 Aldebrandin de Sienne, *Le Régime du Corps*, ed. Louis Landouzy and Rober Pépin (Paris: Honoré Champion, 1911), p. 73. Translated as "Lifestyle advice for all: Aldobrandino of Siena on Health throughout the Life Cycle," in *Medieval Medicine: A Reader*, trans. Faith Wallis (Toronto: University of Toronto Press, 2010), p. 495.

107 T. Wright, ed. "The Treatise of Walter de Biblesworth," in *A Volume of Vocabularies, A Library of National Antiquities* (Liverpool: Joseph Mayer, 1882), v. 1, pp. 142–74, identified this text as having been written shortly before 1300. Recent authors place the text in the mid-thirteenth century. If true, this would make it by far the earliest use of the Middle English term "midwife." See: W. Rothwell, "A Mis-Judged Author and a Mis-Used Text: Walter de Bibbesworth and His 'Tretiz,'" *The Modern Language Review*, 77.2 (1982): 282–93. Andrew Dalby, "Introduction," in *The Treatise: Le Tretiz of Walter of Bibbesworth* (Blackawton: Prospect Books, 2012), p. 15 suggests an even earlier date of 1234 or 35.

108 The precise word used varies from text to text. British Library MS Sloane 809, a text from around 1300 on a vellum scroll, is very difficult to decipher, but appears to read "mydeffis." For a study of the work as a teaching tool, see Karen K. Jambeck, "The *Tretiz* of Walter of Bibbesworth: Cultivating the Vernacular," in *Childhood in the Middle Ages and Renaissance: The Results of a Paradigm Shift in the History of Mentality*, ed. Albrecht Classen (Berlin and New York: Walter de Gruyter, 2005), pp. 159–183.

109 Walter de Bibbesworth, *Le Tretiz*, ed. William Rothwell (Aberystwyth: The Anglo-Norman Online Hub, 2009), 1 (lines 1–4), http://www.anglo-norman.net/texts/bibb-gt.pdf. Accessed Sept. 3, 2013.

A woman who is near her time shows that she is about to give birth when she sends for a midwife who will be an experienced advisor.[110]

Most of the terms taught in the poem are relatively practical ones, so the prominent place of these verses implies that midwives were well-established as birth attendants by this period.

Robert Mannyng's Middle English *Handlyng Synne*, begun in 1303, and intended to provide religious instruction for "lewed men" who could not read French or Latin, instructs priests to teach *mydyues* emergency baptism procedures and examine them to make sure that they know the appropriate words and gestures. This instruction is followed by a substantial exemplum about a *mydwyff* who caused the soul of a child to be lost through her errors in speech and action in baptizing the infant. In punishment, she was forbidden to attend births in future.[111] Use of a midwife is not portrayed in any way exotic or unusual, although this section does not appear in the Anglo-Norman poem on which the work is based.[112] The section ends with a stern warning to midwives:

Midwives, I told this for you
That if you can, learn how
To save what God bought full dear
The points of baptism I advise you to learn
A midwife is a perilous thing,
Unless she learns the points of christening...[113]

---

110   See Dalby, *The Treatise*, 38ff. for a recent translation of the poem.
111   Robert Mannyng of Brunne, *Handlyng Synne*, ed. Idelle Sullens (Binghamton: Medieval & Renaissance Texts & Studies, 1983), p. 4 (line 43) and pp. 240–41 (lines 9621–62).
112   See appendix 2 in the edition by Sullens for a chart of the stories and their sources. The portions of the Anglo-Norman original used by Robert Mannyng are edited in a facing translation: Robert of Brunne, *Handlyng Synne, A.D. 1303, with those parts of the Anglo-French Treatise on which it was founded*, ed. Frederick J. Furnivall, EETS 119 (London: Kegan Paul, Trench, Trübner, and Co, Ltd., 1901), see pp. 300–02 (lines 9587–9658) for the section on midwives. The Middle English version edited by Furnivall is a later version in a Midlands dialect, probably completed before 1400. See Raymond G. Biggar, review of Robert Mannyng of Brunne, *Handlyng Synne*, ed. Idelle Sullens, *Speculum* 62.4 (1987): 969–73, for an assessment of the manuscripts edited by both Furnivall and Sullens.
113   *Handlyng Synne*, ed. Sullens, p. 241 (lines 9657–62).
      Mydwyues, y told þys for ʒow
      Þat ʒyf ʒe kunnat, lerneþ how
      To saue þat god boghte ful dere,
      Þe poyntes of bapteme y rede ʒow lere.
      Mydwyff ys a perylus þyng
      But she kunne þe poyntes of crystenyng

The idea of emergency baptism by laypeople had been taught for at least 100 years and probably longer, but the idea that midwives were the most important group to teach is a new one that emerged around 1300, and reflects that established role that midwives appear to have achieved by this time. This idea was echoed in French legislation of the fourteenth century. A statute from a Paris synod of 1311 states, "there should be in every vill skilled midwives sworn to perform emergency baptism."[114] A Cologne council of 1310 likewise instructed midwives on emergency baptism procedures.[115] In some regions later in the fourteenth century, midwives were required to take an oath and receive a certificate of approval from the bishop's court.[116]

The role of midwives in emergency baptism underlines the increasing separation of midwives from other women who attended births. Caley McCarthy's analysis of Manosquin midwives suggests that they were "acknowledged professionals." For example, in the 1289 proof of age from Manosque in Southern France discussed above, the female witnesses were routinely asked who the *bajula que levavit eum* (midwife who lifted the child) had been, suggesting that her role was different than that of the other neighborhood women, and that officials could expect there to have been a midwife in attendance.[117] Likewise, in a miracle of Louis of Toulouse from around 1300, a midwife is clearly distinguished from the numerous other women attending the birth.[118] Midwifery as a profession begins to show up more as an identifier around the same time. For example, three Parisian *ventrières*, Michele, Emeline and Guibourc, are recorded in 1292 and 1297.[119] Midwives after 1300 were also given specialized tasks beyond childbirth. For example, in a 1314 case of battery, midwives were asked to determine whether the woman was still pregnant, implying special knowledge.[120] Similarly, the 1312 municipal accounts of Bruges record payment for two midwives (*ii vrorde wifs*) called to examine an abandoned neonate.[121]

---

114   Taglia, "Delivering a Christian Identity," p. 83.

115   Cited in Smoak, "Midwives as Agents," 82.

116   Taglia, "Delivering a Christian Identity," pp. 84–85.

117   Shatzmiller, *Médecine et Justice en Provence*, pp. 66–69. For an analysis of the cases, see McCarthy, "Midwives, Medicine, and the Reproductive Female Body," pp. 79–95.

118   Finucane, *Rescue of the Innocents*, p. 35.

119   Hughes, *Women Healers*, 110; Danielle Jacquart, *Le Milieu Medical en France du XIIe au XVe Siecle* (Geneva: Librairie Droz, 1981), p. 48.

120   Shatzmiller, *Médecine et Justice en Provence Médiévale*, p. 131; McCarthy, "Midwives, Medicine, and the Reproductive Female Body in Manosque, 1289–1500", p. 92.

121   Cited in Isaac Joseph De Meyer, *Recherches historiques sur la pratique de l'art des accouchements, a Bruges depuis le XIV Siècle jusqu'à nos jours* (Bruges: Felix de Pachtere, 1843), 9. See Greilsammer, "Midwife,"285–329, esp. 291, for the larger context.

This chapter has argued that midwives as caregivers, while they probably disappeared in practice (if not in thought) during the Early Middle Ages, re-emerged in the twelfth century and were well-established in North-Western Europe by 1300. By 1300, and probably earlier, midwives were viewed as professionals with a set of skills distinct from other women who attended birth. They were present in sufficient numbers that they could be, to some degree, held responsible for lay baptism, and could be considered essential to one's vocabulary. It is difficult to know, though, what proportion of births midwives would have attended. Probably they were not available in all regions, and factors such as cost and personal preference would have played a role in determining who had access to midwives. Moreover, it is clear from the sources that midwives always were supplemental to other types of care by kin, neighbors, and other professionals like physicians and priests. Usually, when a source notes a midwife, it mentions many other caregivers besides. Historians must resist the temptation to envision a midwife ever working singly, unsupported by others. Sources before 1300 are limited compared to the fifteenth century, but historians should be similarly be cautious about applying findings from the fifteenth century to the thirteenth. The great divide of plague cycles lay between, and the population of Europe in 1300 was at least twice as large as it would have been in 1450. This must have affected the ability of populations to support midwives and the availability of trained midwives. Ultimately, given the nature of the sources, any arguments made about birth care must remain, to some degree, speculative.

CHAPTER 3

Learned Men and Skilful Matrons: Medical Expertise and the Forensics of Rape in the Middle Ages

Hiram Kümper

Rape is a crime perpetrated by the use of one body upon another. It is fundamentally a corporeal crime. This remains true whether its motive is primarily sexual, or an exercise of power, or both. Insofar as bodies are concerned, ideas of the body, its function, and its integrity figure prominently in modern rape discourse. Bodily examination, DNA tests, and other medical expertise play a crucial role in the investigation of a crime where often there is no outwardly visual sign of loss or damage, where frequently one testimony stands against the other, and where there are often no direct witnesses. In this context, English scholars frequently cite Sir Matthew Hale (1609–1676), the "most quoted authority on the law of rape"[1] in England, who addressed it as "an accusation easily to be made and hard to be proved, and harder to be defended by the party accused, tho' never so innocent."[2] However, one sees the peculiar twist that makes Hale's apprehension differ from modern approaches to the crime: it is not so much the protection of possible rape victims but the anxiety over false accusation that he problematizes. And indeed, at the end of this chapter, one may rightfully suspect that this is a powerful concern in many medieval juridical considerations as well.

This chapter will tackle two basic questions: first, which medical ideas (in terms of gynecology, anatomy, or physiology) did medieval law connect with the crime of rape, and second, what role did medical professionals play in the theoretical conceptualization as well as the actual juridical prosecution of rape? This chapter approaches these two questions in three steps. First, it argues that only by the invention of a conception of rape that puts consent at the heart of the crime did medical expertise become theoretically relevant

---

1 Barbara Toner, *The Facts of Rape* (London: Hutchinson, 1977), p. 95.

2 Matthew Hale, *History of the Pleas of the Crown* (London: A. Strahan, 1763), v. 1, p. 635. On Hale and his influence on rape jurisdiction in England, see Gilbert Geis, "Lord Hale, Witches, and Rape," *British Journal of Law and Society* 5 (1978): 26–44.

as a means of proof. This fundamentally new conceptual framework brought about new uncertainties about the presence or absence of a consenting will. To demonstrate this fundamental difference this chapter contrasts normative texts from the early and later medieval periods, and discusses the issues of terminology that complicate investigations of medieval rape laws. Second, this chapter sketches the place of both learned and practical medical experts in medieval legal culture, highlighting their relevance to the theory and practice of rape jurisdiction. In doing so, it locates a gap between "learned men" and "skilful matrons." While the latter frequently appear in both normative texts and juridical records, the place of the former needs further study. This will be done in a third step. Ultimately, by pulling these strings together this chapter addresses whether the expertise of female practitioners was not so much a general practice in rape jurisdiction, as often suggested, but rather limited to two specific sorts of cases, namely those involving the loss of virginity and those involving children.

The "Invention" of Rape in the Twelfth Century

The term *raptus*, which still lives on in the English *rape*, derives from the verb *rapere* (to steal away something). Indeed, the earlier Roman law of *raptus* almost exclusively focused on the taking away, as in carrying off, of a woman and the harm done to her guardian. The term *stuprum*, in contrast, signified various forms of pollution through illicit sexual acts, which in single cases could also include rape.[3] The *Lex Iulia de adulteriis*, an act of Augustus that was frequently cited by the jurists of the later Middle Ages and early modern period, figures as one of the prominent loci for the compounding of rape and extramarital intercourse.[4] But only with the legislation of Justinian in the earlier sixth century was the definition of *raptus* extended to sexual crimes against unmarried women.[5] This terminology makes it hard to identify the traces of

3   Fabio Botta, *"Per vim inferre": Studi su stuprum violento e raptus nel diritto romano e bizantino* (Cagliari: Edizioni AV, 2004).
4   On its reception, see Giunio Rizelli, *Lex Iulia de adulteriis. Studi sulla disciplina di adulterium, lenocinium, stuprum* (Lecce: Edizioni del Grifo, 1997), pp. 249–261.
5   Theodor Mommsen *et al.,* eds., *Corpus Iuris Civilis* (Berlin: Weidmanns, 1877), v. 2, p. 378 (Cod. 9.8.1): "de raptu virginum."

early Roman rape laws at all; and this is why it is discussed chiefly only along with other crimes.[6]

The ambiguities of the term remain in the period of Germanic legal text (*Leges Barbarorum*).[7] These texts see rape as a social crime rather than a sexual one, with very few exceptions. This is true as early as Merovingian legal writing—as far as the *Formulae* of Marculf can be held to be representative of it—and it seems to hold true still for cases when women themselves were compensated, as is the case in one formula that Marculf transmits.[8] It is noteworthy, however, that in these early Germanic law texts women could bring their own charges to court,[9] which is not the case in most legal texts of later centuries. Yet there is virtually no mention of the female will—with few and discussable exceptions[10]—and consent is only a matter of aggravation or mitigation of the punishment or fee; it is not of constitutive quality for the crime itself.

In the thirteenth century, consent suddenly rises to the heart of normative writings about rape. In England, for instance, Henry de Bracton's *De Legibus et Consuetudinibus Angliae*, written c. 1220, states:

---

6   Theodor Mommsen, *Römisches Strafrecht* (Leipzig: Duncker&Humblot, 1899), pp. 652–66, and Olivia F. Robinson, "Unpardonable Crimes: Fourth Century Attitudes," in *Critical Studies in Ancient Law, Comparative Law and Legal History*, ed. in John W. Cairns (Oxford: OUP, 2001), pp. 117–126. Remarkably enough, Susan Deacy and Karen F. Pierce, eds., *Rape in Antiquity: Sexual Violence in the Greek and Roman World*, (London: Duckworth, 2002) provide several studies on Roman historiography and drama but not on legal history.

7   For general accounts on the subject see Suzanne F. Wemple, "Consent and Dissent to Sexual Intercourse in Germanic Societies from the Fifth to the Tenth Century," in *Consent and Coercion to Sex and Marriage in Ancient and Medieval Societies*, ed. Angeliki E. Laiou (Washington, D.C.: Dumbarton Oaks Research Library and Collection, 1993), pp. 227–43. On the various semantic problems of *raptus* and *vis* see Hans-Rudolf Hagemann, "Vom Verbrechenskatalog des altdeutschen Strafrechts," *Zeitschrift der Savigny-Stiftung für Rechtsgeschichte, Germanistische Abteilung* 91 (1974): 1–72.

8   Alice Rio, ed., *The Formularies of Angers and Marculf. Two Merovingian Legal Handbooks* (Liverpool: University of Liverpool Press, 2008), p. 305 (index, s.v. "disputes, over raptus"). The Latin text appears in MGH *Formulae*, pp. 85–6.

9   Rio, *Formularies*, pp. 69–70, no. 26.

10   Such as the *Lex Alamannorum*, ed. Karl August Eckhardt, *Die Gesetze des Karolingerreiches 714–911, vol. 2: Alemannen und Bayern* (Weimar: Böhlau, 1934), p. 41, c. 58. The sentence of c. 81 §1 (*ibid.*, 59) is open to interpretation whether the will of the woman or the will of her owner is in question here ("*Si quis cum alicuius ancilla hostiaria concupierit contra voluntatem eius, VI solidos conponat*"). I would dare to suspect: it is rather the owner's.

Man-made as well as divine laws forbid the rape of woman ... If he throws her upon the ground against her will, he forfeits the king's grace ... And if she was a whore before, she was not a whore then, since by crying out against his wicked deed she refused her consent.[11]

Key terms in this description, which remind a twenty-first-century audience of modern conceptualizations of rape, are "against her will" (*contra voluntatem*) and "she refused her consent" (*consentire noluit*).[12] Around about the same time, one of the earliest law-books in German vernacular, the *Sachsenspiegel*, written by Eike von Repgow, finds it necessary to explain: "A man may commit rape with a common woman or his concubine and therefore receive the death penalty if he sleeps with her without her consent."[13] Eike does not formally define rape (*notzog*) in his law-book. Still, he makes clear that the absence of consent constitutes rape while he explicitly grants common women and those women who had already been sexually engaged with their rapists the protection of the law against violent sexual exploitation. Other authorities were even more explicit. The law-book of Mühlhausen (Thuringia), dating to roughly the same time as Eike's *Sachsenspiegel*, provides a more elaborate depiction of what *notzog* was:

---

11 George E. Woodbine and Samuel E. Thorne, eds., *Bracton on the Laws and Customs of England* (Cambridge, MA: Belknap Press, 1968), v. 2, pp. 418–9: "*Raptus mulieris ne fiat defendit tam lex humana quam divina. ... Si autem contra voluntatem eius iactet eam ad terram, forisfaciat gratiam suam ... Et si meretrix fuerit ante, tunc non fuit meretrix, cum nequitiae eius reclamando consentire noluit.*" England is probably the single best researched area in the medieval West in terms of rape prosecution. Just recently, Caroline Dunn, "The Language of Ravishment in Medieval England," *Speculum* 86 (2011): 79–116, has reviewed the vast body of literature that has been produced on the subject since the 1980s.

12 These are crucial elements of rape legislation even today. See Vanessa Munro and Clare McGlynn, eds., *Rethinking Rape Law: International and Comparative Perspectives* (Milton Park: Routledge, 2010). Accordingly, Susan Brownmiller's study of rape in Western culture that initiated much of the historical research on the topic is entitled *Against Our Will: Men, Women, and Rape* (New York: Simon and Schuster, 1975).

13 Carl Gustav Homeyer, ed., *Des Sachsenspiegels erster Theil oder das Landrecht*, 3rd ed. (Berlin: Dümmler, 1863), p. 342 (III 46 §1): "*An varendeme wive unde an siner amien mach die man not dun unde sin lif verwerken, of he sie ane iren dank beleget.*" A slightly different English translation is provided by Maria Dobozy, ed., *The Saxon Mirror: A "Sachsenspiegel" of the Fourteenth Century* (Philadelphia: University of Pennsylvania Press, 1999), p. 127. She "modernizes" in terms of modern rape legislation when she translates "*ane iren dank*" as "against her will".

If a man lies with a woman without her consent and against her will, and if she does not want this, she shall defend herself with clamor, and afterwards she shall immediately declare it [the deed] with torn clothes and with hand-wringing and with tears and with disheveled hair. And having these four things presented everyone shall follow her to the judge, wherever she may find him.[14]

In France, where this notion arrived in normative writing only decades later, Philippe the Beaumanoir, in his *Coutumes de Beauvasis* of 1283, provides a fully-fledged definition of rape: "Rape is when someone has carnal intercourse by force with a woman against her will and when she does what she can to defend herself."[15]

These are only some examples to illustrate that consent became a crucial issue in conceptualizing rape during the thirteenth century. The fact that they all derive from normative writings, such as law-books and legal commentaries, should not be underestimated. It took considerable time, with great variation across Europe, until actual court records reflected this new consent-based idea of rape consistently.[16] Moreover, a great number of normative writings adhere to the traditional, ambivalent concept of rape and ravishment. This is true of

---

14   Herbert Meyer, ed., *Das Mühlhäuser Reichsrechtsbuch aus dem Anfang des 13. Jahrhunderts, Deutschlands ältestes Rechtsbuch: Nach den altmitteldeutschen Handschriften herausgegeben, eingeleitet und übersetzt.* 3rd ed. (Weimar: Böhlau, 1936): *"Liet ein man bi einimi wiebisnamin an urin danc undi widir urin willin is uri dan leit, so sal su sich weri mit gescrei undi sal iz danach zu hant cundigi mit zurizzinir waitz undi mit giwundin hendin undi mit weniningen oigin undi mit bustrubitemi hairi. Mit den vier sachin sal alliz diz sicreigi miti volgi biz an den richteri, sua su den vindit."*

15   Amédée M. Salmon, ed., *Coutumes de Beauvaisis: Texte critique publié avec une introduction, un glossaire et une table analytique* (Paris: A. Picard et fils, 1899), v. 1, pp. 469–70, c. 829: *"Femme eforcier si est quant aucuns prent a force carnele compaignie a feme contre la volonté de le feme, et sor ce qu'ele fet tout son poir du deffendre soi."* The English translation is taken from F.R.P. Akehurst, ed., *The Coutumes de Beauvaisis of Philippe de Beaumanoir* (Philadelphia: University of Pennsylvania Press, 1992), p. 303. Earlier French coutumes stress violence but do not mention consent—also see Annik Porteau-Bitker, "La justice laïque et le viol au Moyen Âge," *Revue historique de droit français et étranger* 66 (1988): 494–6.

16   For English common law, this is illustrated in detail by Kim M. Phillips, "Written on the Body: Reading Rape from the Twelfth to the Fifteenth Century," in *Medieval Women and the Law*, ed. Noël James Menuge (Woodbridge: Boydell, 2003), pp. 125–44.

the *Laws of Sicily*, issued in 1231 by Emperor Frederik II,[17] the Castilian *Siete Partidas*, compiled under the reign of King Alfonso X (1252–84),[18] or many of the Italian civil statutes of the thirteenth and even fourteenth centuries.[19] But still, even if initially of a more theoretical nature, the idea of consent fundamentally transformed the understanding of rape during the Middle Ages and even more so in the early modern period.

In some regions of Europe, this conceptual change slowly brought about a differentiation in terminology as well. As long as Latin prevailed in juridical writing, the term *raptus* remained one of multiple possible meanings, truly a "concept polysémique."[20] But from the thirteenth century onwards, many European vernaculars strove to differentiate between the abduction of a woman against *her kin's* will for the purpose of marriage ("abduction"), seizing a woman by force ("ravishment"), and actual sexual violence done to

---

17   Wolfgang Stürner, ed., *Monumenta Germaniae Historica: Constitutiones et acta publica imperatorum et regum...*, *Supplementum: Die Konstitutionen Friedrichs II. für das Königreich Sizilien* (Hannover: Hahn'sche Buchhandlung, 1996), p. 173, I 20: "*Si quis rapere sacratas Deo virgines aut nondum velatas occasione etiam iungendi matrimonii presumpserit, capitali sententia feriatur*" ("If anyone presumes to commit *raptus* upon nuns or novices, even for the purpose of marriage, he shall be punished by death"). Here, *raptus* clearly seems at least to involve, if not even to comprise, only abduction (this seems similar to the English "ravishment," also reproduced in Latin as "raptus."). For a learned commentary on these and other sentences on rape in the *Laws of Sicily* see Hermann Dilcher, *Die sizilische Gesetzgebung Kaiser Friedrichs des Zweiten. Quellen der Constitutionen von Melfi und ihrer Novellen* (Cologne: Böhlau, 1975), pp. 123–36.

18   See the translation provided by Robert I. Burns and Samuel Parsons Scott, eds., *Las Siete Partidas* (Philadelphia: University of Pennsylvania Press, 2001), v. 5, pp. 1425–6. In the realms of Aragon, such terminological problems do not seem to have existed. See Rebecca Lynn Winer, "Defining Rape in Medieval Perpignan: Women Plaintiffs before the Law," *Viator* 31 (2000): 168. Still, consent does not play a role in either the normative texts or the court records of the thirteenth century that Winer discusses.

19   For a general account see Trevor Dean, *Crime and Justice in Late Medieval Italy* (Cambridge: CUP, 2007), pp. 138–41, who also briefly touches the thirteenth century. More details provided by Georg Dahm, *Das Strafrecht Italiens im ausgehenden Mittelalter: Untersuchungen über die Beziehung zwischen Theorie und Praxis im Strafrecht des Spätmittelalters, namentlich im XIV. Jahrhundert* (Berlin and Leipzig: Walter de Gruyter, 1931), pp. 429–36.

20   Mireille Vincent-Cassy, "Viol des jeunes filles et propagande politique en France à la fin du Moyen Âge," in *Le corps des jeunes filles de l'antiquité a nos jours*, ed. Louise Bruit Zaidman (Paris: Perrin, 2001), pp. 117–40, at 124. This is also what Dunn, "The Language of Ravishment," demonstrates on a broad basis with Latin sources from England, c. 1150–1500.

a woman against *her* will ("rape"). German vernacular, for instance, developed most technical here, with *notzog* or *notzucht* clearly designating rape in the sense of sexual violence.[21] Old French, from the thirteenth century onwards, knows the verb *fame esforcer* along with a number of other circumscriptions, only considerably later *la viol*.[22] Still, as demonstrated above, these terms are frequently combined with the explicit designation of a dissenting will (*contre la volonté, ane iren dank, against her will*).

This is certainly not to say that this new consent-based concept of rape approved of women's choice. Still, the rapist inflicted harm not so much upon the woman and her personal integrity, but rather on her father, husband, or other kin in terms of honor, social respectability, or the chances to contract a profitable marriage for the rape victim. But from the twelfth century onwards, the crime was recognized as a sexual offence with the lack of a woman's consent as its core element. As this author has argued elsewhere that medieval canon law might be, if not the origin, than at least the prime mover of this fundamental change.[23] Nevertheless, this chapter will leave this matter aside. For what is more important to the question of medical expertise in the legal prosecution of rape is that this new consensual perspective on the constitution of the deed brought about new juridical problems. Once an inner disposition is in question—and the consenting will or its absence is truly an inner disposition—methods and instruments are needed to discern reliably such an inner state of mind. This becomes, and still is, the central problem of assessing rape in the courtroom.

Naturally, medieval practitioners in court as well as learned jurists took their time to adapt to this new problem. Hence, they started at the outward indications of the consenting will or its absence: women were required to raise a hue and cry immediately after the deed, and to come to court with bleeding wounds, torn clothes, and disheveled hair. Witnesses and oath-helpers played a crucial role, and both the victim's and the alleged perpetrator's repute provided strong indications for the evaluation of the case. In Ranulf Glanville's *Tractatus*, for example, a rape victim was supposed to show "to trustworthy

21 Its early etymology discusses Jacob Grimm, "Über die Notnunft an Frauen," *Zeitschrift für deutsches Recht- und deutsche Rechtswissenschaft* 5 (1841): 1–29.

22 Kathryn Gravdal, *Ravishing Maidens: Writing Rape in Medieval French Literature and Law* (Philadelphia: University of Pennsylvania Press, 1991), pp. 2–6.

23 Hiram Kümper, "Did Medieval Canon Law Invent Our Modern Notion of Rape? Revisiting the Idea of Consent Before and After 1200," in *Law and Marriage in Medieval and Early Modern Times*, ed. Per Andersen, Kiris Salonen, Helle Møller Sigh, and Helle Vogt (Copenhagen: DJØF, 2012), pp. 127–38.

men the injury done to her, and any effusion of blood there may be and any tearing of her clothes."[24] Late medieval law-books and legal commentaries from throughout Western Europe have similar requirements.[25] Besides these outward signs of violence, however, legal tradition paid increasing attention as well to more hidden injuries of the body, lesions of the genitals and—where the victim was held to have been a virgin before—especially of the hymen.

Rape and Medical Experts in Court

Michael McVaugh observes a "growing European readiness in the last decades of the thirteenth century to concede a separate sphere of authority to medical expertise, a readiness particularly apparent in some criminal proceedings."[26] Indeed, despite all geographical variances in intensity and pace, especially surgeons were an increasingly important expert group at medieval courts in cases of murder and assault.[27] But as far as forensic expertise on women's bodies is

---

24   George D.G. Hall, ed., *Ranulf of Glanvill, The Treatise on the Laws and Customes of the Realm of England commonly called Glanvill* (London: Clarendon, 1965), pp. 175–6, XIV 6: *"Tenetur autem mulier que tale quid patitur mox dum recens fuerit maleficium uicinam uillam adire, et ibi iniuriam sibi illatam probis hominibus ostendere et sanguinem si quis fuerit effusus et uestium scissiones."* This is later echoed by Bracton. See Woodbine and Thorne, *Bracton on the Laws and Customs of England*, v. 2, p. 416.

25   For examples, see Mariann Naessens, "Sexuality in Court: Emotional Perpetrators and Victims versus a Rational Judicial System?" in *Emotions in the Heart of the City: 14th–16th Century*, ed. Elodie Lecuppre-Desjardin and Anne-Laure Van Bruaene (Turnhout: Brepols, 2005), pp. 119–56; Patricia Orr, "Men's Theory and Women's Reality. Rape Prosecutions in the English Royal Courts of Justice, 1194–1222," in *The Rusted Hauberk. Feudal Ideas of Order and their Decline*, ed. Liam O. Purdon and Cindy L. Vitto (Gainesville: University Press of Florida, 1994), pp. 121–59; Heath Dillard, "Women in Reconquest Castile: The Fueros of Sepúlveda and Cuenca," in *Women in Medieval Society*, ed. Susan Mosher Stuard (Philadelphia: University of Pennsylvania Press, 1976), pp. 80–1; Madeline H. Caviness and Charles Nelson, "Silent Witness, Absent Women and the Law Courts in Medieval Germany," in *Fama: The Politics of Talk and Reputation in Medieval Europe*, ed. Thelma Fenster and Daniel Lord Smail (Ithaca and New York: Cornell University Press, 2003), pp. 47–72.

26   Michael R. McVaugh, *Medicine before the Plague: Practitioners and their Patients in the Crown of Aragon, 1285–1345* (Cambridge: CUP, 1993), pp. 207–8.

27   Notably early in Spain; see Don Antonio Hernández Morejón, *Historia bibliográfica de la medicina española* (London: Johnson Reprints, 1967 [1842]), v. 2, pp. 156–64. For France, see Charles Desmaze, *Histoire de la médecine légale en France d'après les lois, registres et arrêtes criminels* (Paris: Charpentier, 1880), pp. *xiii–xiv* and Robert Peter Brittain, "Origins

concerned, examinations usually seem to have been undertaken by women. In the sources, varying terms that address such experts appear, such as "upright and mature women" (*honestae mulieres et veteranae*),[28] "old women" (*vetulae*),[29] and other terms that contemporaries may not have used as rigidly as they seem to appear.[30] Hence, drawing overall conclusions, especially wide-ranging ones for the whole of medieval Europe, will always result in generalizations. Still, from at least the sixteenth century onwards, tendencies can be observed in many European regions, especially in the larger cities, to differentiate not only the male but also the female personnel of healthcare and expertise. Midwives and other women concerned mainly with obstetrics were in juxtaposition to a group of sworn women, who received their function from reputation rather than expertise.[31] One passage in the mid-twelfth century *Decretum* of Gratian, however, suggests that at least this idea, if not its institutional implementation, was already much older. He writes: "And because . . . the hand and the eye of midwives are often deceived, we wish and command that in this matter you take care to depute upright, discerning and prudent matrons to inquire whether the said girl is still a virgin."[32] Double formulas (or conjunctive

---

of Legal Medicins: The Origin of Legal Medicine in France," *Medico-Legal Journal* 34 (1966): 168–74. For Germany, see Esther Fischer-Homberger, *Medizin vor Gericht: Gerichtsmedizin von der Renaissance bis zur Aufklärung* (Berne, Stuttgart, Vienna: Hans Huber, 1983), pp. 20–5. For Italy, see Alesssandro Simili, "The Beginnings of Forensic Medicine in Bologna," in *International Symposium on Society, Medicine, and Law: Jerusalem 1972*, ed. Heinrich Karplus (Amsterdam and London: Elsevier, 1973), pp. 91–100, who also gives references from other cities in Italy. A comprehensive history of forensic medicine in the medieval and early modern period is now provided by Katherine D. Watson, *Forensic Medicine in Western Society: a History* (London: Routledge, 2011), pp. 9–45.

28   James A. Brundage, *Law, Sex, and Christian Society in Medieval Europe* (Chicago: University of Chicago Press, 1987), p. 224, citing Ivo of Chartres, *Epistula CCV* (in *Patrologia Latina*, v. 162, col. 210).

29   Jole Agrimi and Chiara Crisciani, "Medici e "vetulae" dal Duecento al Quattrocento: problemi di una ricerca" in *Cultura popolare e cultura dotta nel Seicento*, ed. Paolo Rossi (Milan: Franco Angeli, 1983), pp. 144–59.

30   Monica Green, "Women's Medical Practice and Health Care in Medieval Europe," *Signs* 14 (1989): 438–9 and 453–6.

31   For a recent summary, see Watson, *Forensic Medicine in Western Society*, pp. 46–9, as well as, for the fifteenth and sixteenth centuries, Leigh Whaley, *Women and the Practice of Medical Care in Early Modern Europe, 1400–1800* (New York: Palgrave Macmillan, 2011), pp. 91–111. A more specific institution, which shall not be discussed here, is the largely early modern "Jury of Matrons." See James C. Oldham, "On Pleading the Belly: A History of The Jury of Matrons," *Criminal Justice* 6 (1985): 1–64

32   Emil Friedberg, ed., *Corpus iuris canonici* (Leipzig: Bernhard Tauchnitz, 1839), v. 1, p. 315 (lib. II, tit. xix, c. 14): "*Et quia . . . saepe manus fallitur et oculus obstetricum, volumus*

phrasing), which frequently appear in normative texts, mirror this idea. In the early-thirteenth century *Coutumiers de Normandie*, for example, the duke's chief justice is required to have "the girl and her injuries examined by good women and trust-worthy matrons, who know how to discern the injuries of rape."[33] This statement, moreover, suggests that some kind of expert knowledge beyond the usual experience of midwives in obstetrics was required in the eye of the *coutumier* to judge cases of rape.

If, for a certain period, there had been a distinction between assisting midwives and reporting matrons as forensic experts, much of this must have been leveled to some degree by the recognizable tendencies of professionalizing the medical practice of women in the later Middle Ages. On the one hand, this was realized by legal sanctioning, when women were prohibited from practicing in certain areas of medicine. On the other hand, sometimes it was accomplished by subjecting them to the licensing of a "master in the art," as, for instance, Michael McVaugh has observed for fourteenth-century Aragon,[34] or at least to swearing an official oath, as became common for midwives and other female town officials in the fifteenth and sixteenth centuries in many parts of Europe.[35] From then on, records from England, France, and Germany employ terms such as *matrone juree*, *sworn matron*, or *gesworen fraw*. Double formulas, such as "midwives and sworn women" (*Hebammen und geschworne Weiber*) continue in use as well.[36]

Men, however, seem to have played a marginal—or, where they were present, a rather symbolic, not a practical—role in these inspections. The theoretical writings reveal this role. William of Saliceto, for instance, in his 1285 *Summa conservationis*, makes a distinction between the fields of expertise for

---

et mandamus, ut adhuc honesta matronas providas et prudentes deputare curetis ad inquirendum, utrum dicta puella virginitatis privilegio sit munita." The translation is quoted from Monica H. Green, "Documenting Medieval Women's Medical Practice," in *Practical Medicine from Salerno to the Black Death*, ed. Luis García-Ballester, Roger French, Jon Arrizabalaga, and Andrew Cunningham (Cambridge: CUP, 1994), p. 339.

33   Ernest-Joseph Tardif, ed., *Coutumiers de Normandie*, v. 1: *Le très ancien coutumier de Normandie* (Rouen: Espérance Cagniard, 1881), p. 40, c. 50 § 1: "*Si aliquis aliquam puellam rapuerit, si in villa, vel in campis, vel in nemore fuerit, oportet eam clamare si poterit, et vicinos clamorem audisse. Raptor tenebitur, capere si possint, et puella, quam citius poterit, in continenti festinare [debet] ad primam justiciam Ducis, quam invenire poterit, justiciaque faciet puellam videri et ejus lesionem per bonas mulieres et legales matronas, que hujus raptus lesionem noveri[n]t discernere*".

34   McVaugh, *Medicine before the Plague*, pp. 105–7.

35   For examples, see Thomas G. Benedek, "The Changing Relationship between Midwives and Physicians during the Renaissance," *BHM* 51 (1977): 550–64.

36   *Württembergische Medicinal-Ordnung* (s.l.: 1755), s.p. (tit. 11 §4).

the doctor (*medicus*) and the midwife (*obstetrix*) when he deals with signs of virginity. Some doctors, he reports, try to judge a girl's purity by urine probes; others believe in physical examination of the mouth of the vulva. This examination, however, ought to be carried out by a midwife who has been carefully instructed on female anatomy by the doctor, not by the doctor himself.[37] It is plausible to suspect all this mirrors a certain hesitancy of female patients about exposing their bodies to male physicians that was widely accepted in medieval societies.[38] At least, this is what the well-known female physician Jacoba Félicie argued in her trial for malpractice in Paris 1322:

> It is better and more seemly that a wise woman learned in the art should visit a sick woman and inquire into the secrets of her nature and her hidden parts, than that a man should do so, for whom it is not lawful to see and seek out the aforesaid parts, nor to feel with his hands the breasts, belly and feet, etc., of women.[39]

Whatever the reason might be, in this regard forensic examination lagged behind the general marginalization of female expertise in obstetrics that Renate Blumenfeld-Kosinski has observed from the later Middle Ages onward,[40] and that Monica Green has considerably antedated.[41] Theoretical debate and

---

37   Guilielmus de Salceto, *Liber Magistri Gulielmi Placentini de Saleceto... incipit, qui summa conservationis & curationis appellatur* (Venice: Marinus Saracenus, 1490), fo. 8v: "*Quidam vero notare super virginitatem per aspectum in ore vulve, et hoc est officium obstreticis que consueta est in hoc et docta fuit a medico secundum viam anathomie illius loci.*" On this passage and William's view of sexuality in general see Helen Rodnite Lemay, "William of Saliceto on Human Sexuality," *Viator* 12 (1981): 180.

38   Eileen Power, *Medieval Women* (Cambridge: CUP, 1975), pp. 86–8.

39   Quoted in Pearl Kibre, "The Faculty of Medicine at Paris, Charlatanism and Unlicensed Medical Practices in the Middle Ages," *BHM* 27 (1953): 8–12. A similar argument is brought forward by an anonymous fourteenth-century Englishman in the introduction for his translation of a gynecological text. See Charles Singer, "Thirteenth Century Miniatures Illustrating Medical Practice," *Proceedings of the Royal Society of Medicine* 9 (1915): 29–47, at 37 (appendix B).

40   Renate Blumenfeld-Kosinski, *Not of Women Born: Representations of Caesarean Birth in Medieval and Renaissance Culture* (Ithaca and London: Cornell University Press, 1990), pp. 91–119.

41   Monica Green, *Making Women's Medicine Masculine: The Rise of Male Authority in Pre-Modern Gynaecology* (Oxford: OUP, 2008).

its production were a male prerogative;[42] the actual examination of female bodies in forensic questions and the collection of bodily proof, however, remained a field of female practice until the Renaissance.

The evidence of actual court records supports this impression. In Germany, there are no known examples of a male physician's expertise in a rape case before the later sixteenth century, and elsewhere in Western Europe (England, France, the Iberian Peninsula) scholarly literature and printed sources provide the same picture. Even the *Constitutio Criminalis Carolina*, issued in 1532 by Emperor Charles V as the German Empire's first universal penal code, still required, in cases of alleged child murder, the examination of the suspect by female practitioners. It states: "... if a woman is suspected of such a deed she shall be examined by experienced women in her private parts insofar as to be helpful for further investigation."[43] In the following chapter, however, one catches a glimpse of the two-foldedness of medical expertise in the rationale of the *Constitutio*:

> However, when the child was murdered so recently that the mother still produces milk in her breast ... this is a strong indication for the exercise of torture against her. Still, many personal physicians believe that there might be a number of other natural causes for a woman who had not born a child to have milk in her breasts, so that they might excuse themselves referring to such cases; these women shall be examined further by the midwives.[44]

What is presented here seems to be the classic "division of labor" of medieval medical expertise in court: the production of medical knowledge was a male

---

42   This is certainly not to say that no woman participated in the medieval theoretical discourse. But there is no indication that any of those important works, such as the *Trotula*, had an impact on the conceptualization of the female body in respect to sexual violence.

43   Arno Buschmann, ed., *Textbuch zur Strafrechtsgeschichte der Neuzeit: die klassischen Gesetze* (Munich: C.H. Beck, 1998), p. 118, c. 35: "... *wo dann dieselbige Dirn ein Person ist, dazu man sich der verdachten that versehen mag, soll sie durch verstendige Frawen an heymlichen stetten, als zu weiter erfarung dienstlich ist, besichtiget werden.*"

44   Buschmann, *Textbuch*, p. 118, c. 36: "*Wo aber das Kindlein so kürtzlich ertödt worden ist, dass der Mutter die milch in den brüsten noch nicht vergangen, ... die hat dess halb ein starck vermütung, peinlicher frag halber wider sich. Nachdem aber etliche Leibärzte sagen, dass auss etlichen natürlichen ursachen etwann eine, die kein Kindt getragen, milch in brüsten haben möge, so sich ein Dirn inn diesen fellen also entschuldigt, soll desshalb durch die Hebammen sonst weiter erfarung geschehen.*"

prerogative, its practice in the case of the examination of female bodies left to female practitioners. Interdependences are certainly plausible but hard to grasp. Joan Cadden suggests that

> learned male authors sometimes mentioned women as their informants. They reported variously what midwives, Frenchwomen, Saracen women, and prostitutes said or did. Not all of these references are reliable... but they suggest the likelihood that the ideas and practices of the individuals and groups outside a small elite could have made their way into the writings of the educated.[45]

Still, most of the male expertise on the forensic dimensions of rape mirror suspicion against (rather than reliance on) the practical experience of midwives and other female practitioners. This suspicion increased throughout the early modern period. French surgeon Ambroise Paré (c. 1510–1590), whose works were rapidly translated into a number of European vernaculars, wrote:

> Midwives take pride in themselves that they... were easily able to tell a virgin from one that has been sexually ashamed and that has had sexual intercourse... and so judges and authorities often fail by believing in their expertise all too easily and hence render unjust judgments. But we have ample evidence that these impudent and outrageous shrews often fail.[46]

Despite the increasingly institutionalized education of midwives and the growing regulation of midwifery, such suspicions amass during the seventeenth century. By the end of the century, with forensic medicine newly established as a powerful voice in European rape discourse, they had already become a commonplace in the writings of the learned doctors.[47]

---

45   Joan Cadden, *Meanings of Sex Differences in the Middle Ages: Medicine, Science, and Culture* (Cambridge: CUP, 1993), p. 5.

46   Ambroise Paré, *Wund-Artzney, oder Artzney spiegell...*, trans. by Peter Uffenbach (Frankfurt: Jacob Fischer, 1635), p. 980: *"Zwar die Hebammen rühmen, dass sie... eine Jungfraw, von einer, so geschwächt und beschlaffen worden, leichtlich unterscheiden zu können... und fellen die Richter oder Oberkeiten, in dem sie ihnen allzubald gläuben und meynen, es könne solche ihre Aussage nicht fehlen, manchmal sehr unbilliche Urtheil. Denn dass diese frechte unnd unverschämpte Weiber... nichts gewisses haben können, ist.. gnugsam abzunemen."*

47   For one influential statement in this debate see Johannes Bohn, *De officio medici duplici clinici nimirum ac forensis,* 3rd ed. (Leipzig: J.F. Gleditsch, 1704), pp. 560–75, who makes the

From Natural Philosophy to Medical Thought: Rape and Conception

If until the later sixteenth century female practitioners—in the persons of mid-wives, "sworn matrons," and others—were the central personnel concerned with physical expertise in rape cases, what role then did male physicians play? Scholars of medieval medicine have well understood that "the creation of epistemologies on the female body are not limited to those who inhabit female bodies."[48] As far as rape is concerned, actually the opposite seems to be true. While practical examination remained a female prerogative, exclusively male authorities focused on theoretical issues.

One notion that many scholars associate with the Middle Ages is the idea that conception arising from a violent sexual encounter implied consent and hence legally obviated rape. More recently, Elise Bennett Histed has discussed its impact in English legal thought from the thirteenth through to the eighteenth century in detail.[49] But, even before her work, a number of scholars have repeatedly pointed to its probable origins in twelfth-century French natural philosophy.[50] Grounded in Galenic and Soranic thought, William of Conches first explicitly brought up the idea that "although raped women dislike the act in the beginning, in the end, however, from the weakness of the flesh, they like it."[51] The idea might have been transmitted to England via its reception in the

---

point that women's hesitance about exposing their bodies to male physicians had resulted in the diminished importance of midwives and sworn matrons, and hence hindered the creation of proper forensic expertise.

48 Monica Green, "Gendering the History of Women's Health Care," *Gender and History* 20 (2008): 508.

49 Elise Bennett Histed, "Medieval Rape: A Conceivable Defence," *The Cambridge Law Journal* 63 (2004): 743–69.

50 Classical references include Danielle Jacquart and Claude Thomasset, *Sexuality and Medicine in the Middle Ages*, trans. by Matthew Adamson (Princeton: Princeton University Press, 1985), pp. 63–4; Cadden, *Meanings of Sex Difference*, pp. 93–5; and also the much debated Thomas Laqueur, *Making Sex: Body and Gender from the Greeks to Freud* (Cambridge, MA: Harvard University Press, 1990), pp. 161–2. Probably the first, albeit brief, mention of the problem in modern scholarship may be credited to Paul Diepgen, *Frau und Frauenheilkunde in der Kultur des Mittelalters* (Stuttgart: Thieme, 1963), pp. 73–4, although due to a false attribution in the *Patrologia Latina*, he associates this idea with William of Congeinna (c. 1080–1154).

51 Italo Ronca and Matthew Curr, eds., William of Conches, *A Dialogue of Natural Philosophy (Dragmaticon Philosophiae)* (Notre Dame, IN: University of Notre Dame Press, 1997), p. 136, VI 8 § 6. It follows the critical edition of the Latin text: Italo Ronca, ed., William of Conches, *Dragmaticon Philosophiae (Corpus Christianorum Continuatio Mediaevalis*

so-called *Prose Salernitan Questions,* then taken up in at least three thirteenth-century English legal commentaries, namely *Fleta, Britton,* and *The Mirror of Justices.*[52] Bennett Histed and others have presented an impressive panorama of sources for the idea that pregnancy indicated actual complicity in the sexual act that allegedly had been committed violently and without the woman's consent. One fifteenth-century Inner Temple Reading, a sort of juridical training lecture at the London Inns of Courts, suggests:

> In an appeal of rape it is a good plea to abate the writ that she is pregnant by the same rape, because that proves her consent. It was said by the counsel of Bishop Nevill of York that although the body consents nevertheless the mind does not; to which the justices said that their authority extended only to the body and not the mind.[53]

Although England seems to be an exceptional case regarding the early and explicit adoption of this notion in actual juridical discourse, the idea of conception as obviating rape permeates Western European legal writing from the Renaissance onwards and has since then shown a remarkable longevity.[54] Accordingly, it is now cited as a basic element of pre-modern legal thought in scholarly literature on the various aspects of a woman's life in the medieval and early modern periods.[55]

---

152) (Turnhout: Brepols, 1997), p. 209: *"Etsi raptis in principio opus displicet, in fine tamen ex carnis fragilitate placet."* For the Renaissance's reception of William of Conches one must also consider the printed edition of the *Dragmaticon* under the title *Dialogus de substantiis physicis* (Strasbourg: Rihelius, 1567). The respective passage is at pp. 241–2.

52   Bennett Histed, "Medieval Rape," 744 provides all respective quotations.

53   S.E. Thomas and J.H. Baker, eds., *Readings and Moots at the Inns of Court in the Fifteenth Century,* v. 2 (Selden Society, v.105, 1989), p. 275.

54   There is no comprehensive study of the debate in Renaissance and early modern Europe yet. See the many citations in Paulus Zacchia, *Quaestiones medico-legales . . . Editio tertia, correctior, auctiorque, non solum variis passim locis, verum & subjunctis, quae nun recens prodeunt* (Amsterdam: Joannis Piot, 1651), pp. 145–47. On the longevity of the idea of lust as a prerequisite for conception also see Audrey Eccles, *Obstretrics and Gynaecology in Tudor and Stuart England* (London and Canberra: Croom Helm, 1982), pp. 34–5, and Leslie Tuttle, *Conceiving the Old Regime: Pronatalism and the Politics of Reproduction in Early Modern France* (Oxford: OUP, 2010), pp. 141–62, and Jennine Hurl, "'She being bigg with child is likely to miscarry.' Pregnant Victims Prosecuting Assault in Westminster, 1685–1720," *London Journal* 24 (1999): 18–33.

55   With the oft cited Laqueur (*Making Sex,* p. 161) being an important source of such wide recognition.

It cannot have been all too universally accepted (or known), though, for there are several instances of pregnant women successfully pleading rape cases in both England and elsewhere in medieval and early modern Europe.[56] If pregnancy proved consent, and consent obviated raped, how is this possible? Many of the arguments discussed by early modern medical and juridical experts derived from actual forensic experience, but the heart of this debate was embedded intrinsically in theoretical assumptions about the process of conception. The same will prove to be true when looking back at the Middle Ages. From this perspective, a certain ambivalence about the role of pregnancy in rape charges in the actual sources is much less surprising.

One should be aware that, when he brought up the idea of the female weakness of the flesh, William of Conches was by no means discussing rape; he was discussing conception.

> DUKE. I recall what you just said, that nothing is conceived without the seed of the woman, but this is not plausible. For we see that raped women, who have suffered violence despite their protest and weeping, still have conceived. From this it is apparent that they had no pleasure from such an act.

> PHILOSOPHER. Although raped women dislike the act in the beginning, in the end, however, from the weakness of the flesh, they like it. Furthermore, there are two wills in humans, the rational and the natural, which we often feel are warring with us: for often what pleases the flesh displeases the reason. Although, therefore, a raped woman does not assent with her rational will, she does have carnal pleasure.[57]

---

56   For England, see the example provided by Bennett Histed, "Medieval Rape," 755. Two more are provided by Karen Jones, *Gender and Petty Crime in Late Medieval England: The Local Courts in Kent, 1460–1560* (Woodbridge: Boydell, 2006), p. 79. For Germany, I have found a number of instances from the fifteenth century onwards (some are dubious in dating), but of which only one has been printed. See Guido Kisch, ed., *Leipziger Schöffenspruchsammlung* (Leipzig: Hirtzel, 1919), p. 135, no. 108. For France, I have found no record in the printed material that I surveyed.

57   Ronca, *Dragmaticon Philosophiae*, pp. 209–10: "*DVX: Ad memoriam uenit michi quod nuper dixisti, sine semine feminae nichil concipi: quod non est uerisimile. Videmus enim raptas, reclamantes et plorantes uiolentiam passas, concepisse. Vnde apparet illas nullam in illo opere habuisse delectationem. . . . PHILOSOPHVS: Etsi raptis in principio opus displicet, in fine tamen ex carnis fragilitate placet. Iterum sunt in homine duae uoluntates, ratiocinatiua et naturalis, quas saepe in nobis repugnare sentimus: displicet enim saepe rationi quod placet carni. Etsi igitur in rapta non est uoluntas rationis, est delectatio carnis.*"

What is being discussed here is the opposition between Aristotelian and Galenic notions of conception, with the former seeing only male seed as necessary for conception, the latter proposing the production (and orgasmic emission) of seeds by both sexes.[58] Hence, William actually replied to the Aristotelian problem that "often female conceives without the sensation of pleasure in intercourse"[59] in defense of the Galenic two-seeds-theory. There was, however, at least one authoritative opposition to this problem that entered the debate in the late thirteenth century and gained much influence in the following centuries. In his *Colliget*, which became widespread in the Latin West through its translation by Michael Scotus in the 1230s, Spanish-Arab philosopher and physician Averroës (Ibn Rušd, 1126–1198) held the Aristotelian position to be "manifest to sense and known through argument":

> After I read the books of Aristotle I asked many women about this, and they replied that many were impregnated without emitting seed: and even if intercourse did not give them pleasure. And I saw many who had been raped by males [and still] impregnated by them.[60]

For Averroës, female "seed" is auxiliary in character. He complements this position not only by his reading of Aristotle, but also by experience when he recalls the oft-quoted episode of a woman he personally knew who got pregnant by bathing (*generatio in balneo*) in water polluted with seeds from "evil men" (*homini mali*) who had ejaculated into the same water.[61] Western medieval writers, such as Giles of Rome, not only referenced Averroës as an authority on conception without female lust, but also added more arguments.[62] Albertus

---

58   Cadden (*Meanings of Sex Difference*, pp. 117–9) cautions us not to overestimate the opposition between these two positions in actual medieval medical writings.

59   Aristotle, *On the Generation of Animals*, 727b, from Jonathan Barnes, ed., *The Complete Works of Aristotle*, v. 1 (Princeton: Princeton University Press, 1984), p. 1129.

60   Averroës, *Colliget libri VII*, ed. by Hieronymus Surianus (Venice: Otinus de Luna, 1497), f. 50v (II.x): *postquam legi libros Aristoteles ego quesivi a multis mulieribus de hoc, et responderunt quod plures impregnate fuerunt absque spermatizatione, et etiam si displicuisset eis coitus. Et etiam vidi quamplures ex istis impregnatas que fuerant a masculis violate.* As cited in Peter Biller, *The Measure of Multitude: Population in Medieval Thought* (Oxford: OUP, 2000), p. 156.

61   Details provided by Maaike van der Lugt, *Le ver, le démon et la Vierge: Les théories médiévales de la génération extraordinaire. Une étude sur les rapports entre théologie, philosophie naturelle et médecine* (Paris: Les Belles Lettres, 2004), pp. 99–104.

62   M. Anthony Hewson, *Giles of Rome and the Medieval Theory of Conception: a Study of the "De formatione corporis humani in utero"* (London: The Athlone Press, 1975), pp. 87–8.

Magnus, though not as influential by far in this respect, testified that "some women say, that they were impregnated from sex in which they did not have pleasure."[63] Aristotelian positions towards the possibility of conception even under extremely displeasing circumstances then certainly were all but obsolete throughout the Middle Ages, and therefore hearing the case of a pregnant woman who claimed to have been raped was subject to positioning within the spectrum of these conflicting perceptions.

What Did Female Practitioners actually Testify in Rape Cases?

Having considered now the role of female involvement and (male) theory for the prosecution of rape cases in court, one very practical question still remains: what kind of expertise was it that female practitioners actually contributed? Did they testify on wounds of the flesh, or did they examine the victim's sexual organs? Sources reveal little, for testimonies are usually extremely short. What sources do tell, however, is that medical expertise in medieval rape cases, with notable frequency, revolved around two specific themes: defilement and pregnancy, the former outnumbering the latter by far. Consequently, this is why midwives and matrons appear most often in those court records dealing with sexual assaults on children—or, more seldom, otherwise virginal women—while documentary evidence for gynecological examinations of alleged rape victims is otherwise slim, and usually so brief that it remains hard to interpret.

   Looking at some exemplary case studies may illustrate the point. The records from fourteenth-century Catalonia, studied by Monserrat Cabré, are interesting in a variety of ways.[64] In the 1389 case of nine-year-old Cateriniqua in Zaragossa, for instance, only one of the four women who examined the child was identified as a *mardina o ama* ("midwife and wet-nurse"), while the others were referred to as "honorable women." In the other cases Cabré discusses, the records address the examining women as simply *mujeres* ("women"). The only male physician that spoke in these trials testified about the illness that detained one of the defendants from attending the court session. It is striking that all of

---

63   Hermann Stadler, ed., *Albertus Magnus. De animalibus lbri XXVI: nach der Cölner Urschrift*, v. 2 (Münster: Aschendorff, 1920), p. 1056, XV 2 § 11: "*quaedam mulieres dicunt se impraegnatas a coitu non habuerunt delectationem.*" For a comment on this passage, see Jacquart and Thomasset, *Sexuality and Medicine*, pp. 68–9.

64   This following case is reported by Monserrat Cabré, "Women or Healers? Household Practices and the Categories of Health Care in Late Medieval Iberia," *BHM* 82 (2008): 31–6.

these women testified concerning a child's virginity. For the judges, these were reliable indications that further investigation for rape was warranted.

The same problem emerges from the fourteenth- and fifteenth-century cases from Dijon and Lyon discussed by Nicole Gonthier: the court called in midwives only where the "rape" victim had been a virgin–as, for instance, in the case of ten-year-old Catherine Malonne (1418).[65] In a rape charge dating from the first quarter of the fifteenth century, a father, whose name is not given in the record, accused a certain Hans Menteler from Poznań of "bringing shame upon his child" who had been in Menteler's custody during the absence of her father. The charge was brought before the town's lay jury but

> they agreed that it was not lawful for them to see such things and to examine the maiden['s body] and therefore commissioned honorable matrons... in whom they trusted to have them examine the maiden. And the same honorable matrons testified that the maiden was hurt in her private parts ['business'], and in all of her members, and that she was bereaved of her virginity.[66]

This is also one of the very few instances where the involvement of female experts is grounded explicitly on the premise that such an investigation would be highly indecent for male practitioners.

These few examples illustrate the general impression that physical examination of rape victims was largely limited to cases when virginity was in question. In retrospect, these findings are hardly surprising. Intimate knowledge of the female anatomy was sparse among male experts (both medical and juridical), so that their understanding of the potential damage a sexual assault might inflict upon the body were very basic. It is not before the late sixteenth century that detailed testimonies of medical experts appear in the records of rape cases, thus, it is hard to tell which diagnoses from midwives, matrons, and others were actually heard in court.

---

65 Nicole Gonthier, "Les victimes de viol devant les tribunaux à la fin du Moyen Âge d'après les sources dijonnaises et lyonnaises," *Criminologie* 27. 2 (1994): 23–5.

66 Theodor Goerlitz, ed., *Magdeburger Schöffensprüche für die Hansestadt Posen und andere Städte des Warthelandes* (Stuttgart and Berlin: Kohlhammer, 1944), pp. 83–5, no. II 11, at 84: "... do wordyn sy [the lay jury] mit enander eyntrachticlichen, das yn sulche ding nicht fugete zu besehin noch czu beschawen dy mayt, und besante daorczu ander erber frawen..., den wol czu glewbin, was dy do besogen dy junge mayt. Dy selbigen erbern frawen bekanthin, das dy jugne mayt vorterbit wer an erem geschefftnisse und an allin erin gledin beschamet und berobit wer erer juncfrawlichen eren."

During the early modern period, whenever medical experts testified in rape cases, the focus remained on virginity. Detailed accounts of other injuries to the female anatomy are extremely rare, apart from the publication of some few forensic *consilia* by learned (and, of course, male) academics.[67] In one example, c. 1616, eighteen-year-old Henriette Pelliciére was examined by three midwives commissioned by the city of Paris (*matrons jurées de la ville de Paris*) with both their eyes and fingers (*au doigt et à l'oeil*). Because of her age, Henriette could well have been married already. Yet she was not, and so the women examined her for violent defloration (*avoir été forcée et déflorée*), of which they testified to have discovered reliable evidence and even gave a detailed diagnosis.[68] Still, even in the eighteenth century, with forensic medicine already a well-established institution in juridical discourse, male physicians were more than reluctant to diagnose rape once the alleged victim was neither a child nor a virgin anymore.[69]

Conclusion

This chapter hopes to have illustrated that both medical ideas and actual forensic examinations in medieval rape trials answered to a specific problem of juridical investigation that arises only after the emergence of consent as a constitutive element of the concept of rape. As long as abduction and ravishment played crucial roles in the constitution of the deed, and the actual sexual act resided as a minor detail, female integrity was considered injured even without the occurrence of corporeal harms. But with an increasing focus on pollution, both bodily and spiritually, through intercourse, new experts were needed to testify concerning what exactly had happened.

---

67 An early example is provided by Basel town physician Felix Platter (1536–1614) in his *Observationes in hominis affectibus plerique, corpori & animo, functionum læsione, dolore, aliá ve molestiâ & vitio incommodantibus* (Basel: König, 1614), p. 562.

68 Gustave-Joseph Alphonse Witowski, *Histoire des accouchements chez tous les peuples* (Paris: G. Steinheil, 1887), p. 652 prints their testimony: "... le tout veu et visité au doigt et à l'oeil, avons trouvé que la babole estoit abatue, l'arrière-fosse ouverte, l'entre-fesson ridé, le guilevart eslargi, le braquemard escrouté, la badaude relancée, le ponnant débiffé, le halleron démis, le quilbuquet fendu, le lipion recoquillé, la dame du milieu retirée, les toutons desvoyez, le lipondis pilé, les barres froissécs, l'enchenart retourné; bref, pour le fair court, qu'il y avait trace de viol ..."

69 For instance, see Johann Valentin Müller, *Entwurf der gerichtlichen Arzneiwissenschaft, nach juristischen und medicinischen Grundsätzen für Geistliche, Rechtsgelehrte und Aerzte*, v. 1 (Frankfurt: Andreae, 1798), p. 88.

Moreover, this chapter proposes that the established image of medical knowledge and the forensics of rape in the Middle Ages should be rendered more precisely in two respects: (1.) The idea of pregnancy as generally obviating rape charges should not too readily be applied to the whole medieval period. Rather, there was considerable dissent about this issue in learned discourse outside the juridical sphere that certainly would not have left the latter unaffected. Moreover, there is no indication that the whole issue played a role in actual court decisions before the early modern period. The sole fact that high medieval natural philosophy, as well as a limited number of learned legal commentaries, shared the idea of pregnancy obviating rape with the authorities of seventeenth and eighteenth centuries' legal forensics does not fill the chronological gap between the two. The underlying understanding of the role of female seed in conception may have been constantly around in the centuries in-between. Still, one should be aware that it was not as much a consolidated truism as is commonly pictured, and not everyone drew conclusions for rape charges from it. (2.) The expertise of female practitioners in rape trials seems to have been more limited than is commonly asserted. Rather than examining every alleged rape victim, their expertise seems to have been called upon mainly in respect for two kinds of ruptures: the loss of virginity and the rupture of children's genitals.

CHAPTER 4

Expert Examination of Wounds in the Criminal Court of Justice in Cocentaina (Kingdom of Valencia) during the Late Middle Ages

Carmel Ferragud[1]
Translated by Jonathan Whitehead

In the final years of the thirteenth century, at the height of the process of the "medicalization" of society, the development of civil and canon law made it possible to use doctors to provide evidence in some civil and criminal trials. The doctor, physician or surgeon, and other medical practitioners (barbers and midwives) gave evidence on the gravity of an injury or the prognosis of the victim in order to establish the innocence or guilt of an individual in such particularly complex circumstances as wounds. They also gave opinions on the causes of violent death, on pregnancies in rape victims, on the annulment of a marriage on the grounds of the husband's impotency and on a growing list of cases that gradually came into their fields of competence. Indeed, Justinian's *Corpus Iuris Civilis* (529–534), Gratian's *Decretum* (c. 1140) and the various collections of papal letters, known as the Decretals (particularly those in the compilation of Raymond of Peñafort in 1234), underlined the relevance of the expert testimonies of members of the medical profession.[2] These legislative traditions, based on Roman Law, incorporated the idea that judges could investigate crimes and reach a verdict on the basis of evidence collected and examined, including that given at trial and the conclusions offered in written submissions. Over time, some jurists came to see this expert

---

1   This research is part of the project sponsored by the Ministerio de Ciencia e Innovación, later Ministerio de Economía y Competitividad "Digital Corpus of the Medieval Science in the Crown of Aragon in Its Latin and Romance Context: Vernacular Works, Arnau de Vilanova and Vicent Ferrer (CIVERLAT)" (FFI2011-29117-C02); Prometeo Programme for research groups of excellence of the Generalitat Valenciana (ref. Prometeo 2009–122); and is the work of the research group Grup de Recerca Consolidat de la Generalitat de Catalunya (2009 SGR 1452) "La Corona catalanoaragonesa, l'Islam i el mon mediterrani."
2   Michael R. McVaugh, *Medicine before the Plague: Practitioners and their Patients in the Crown of Aragon, 1285–1345* (Cambridge: CUP, 1993), pp. 207–209. Katherine D. Watson, *Forensic Medicine in Western Society: a History* (London: Routledge, 2011), pp. 9–10.

testimony as positive.[3] Undoubtedly, the epistemological similarities between doctors and jurists and their social assimilation facilitated the participation of the former in the courts of law and the trust afforded by the latter to medical experience.[4]

Among the activities of doctors in the courts, one in particular stood out: the examination and assessment of wounds. There were two focal points for the development of the practice on mainland Europe: France and northern Italy. It subsequently spread across the rest of the continent. In France, it appears that the Bishops of Maine and Anjou had relied on the assistance of medical experts since the eleventh century, and the practice was in evidence in Paris the following century.[5] In 1260, Louis IX suppressed trial by ordeal and/ or combat and replaced them with written testimonies, which opened the way to the use of medical evidence. Successive kings then definitively established the role of surgeons, physicians and midwives in the law courts. At the same time, the procedure was also adopted in Montpellier, where there was an important faculty of medicine and a remarkable interest in surgery.[6] In this period the city belonged to the Crown of Aragon, under the rule of Jaime I, who appointed two surgeons to make expert examinations of wounds.[7] Expert reports had also been introduced in Provence in about 1258, and a study has

3 Mario Ascheri, "'*Consilium* sapientis', perizia medica e 'res iudicata': Diritto dei 'dottori' e istituzioni comunali ," in *Proceedings of the Fifth International Congress of Medieval Canon law*, ed. Stephen Kuttner and Kenneth Pennington, [*Monumenta Iuris Canonici*, ser. C, v. 6] (Vatican City: Biblioteca Apostolica Vaticana, 1980), pp. 538–548.

4 Silvia de Renzi, "Witnesses of the Body: Medico-legal Cases in Seventeenth-century Rome," *Studies in History and Philosophy of Science* 33 (2002): 223.

5 Watson, *Forensic Medicine*, pp. 32–33. The first references to surgery in Paris (1261–1270) have to do with a requirement introduced by the provost of the city, whereby surgeons would be required to testify in the courts on the wounds of their patients. Danielle Jacquart, *La médecine médiévale dans le cadre parisien. XIVe–XVe siècle* (Paris: Fayard, 1998), p. 23.

6 However, not until 1290 did Montpellier reach the height of its prestige and influence, especially as a center for the translation of medical texts from Arabic to Latin, and also with the presence of such notable teachers as Arnau de Vilanova or Bernard of Gordon. Danielle Jacquart, "Comienzos de la enseñanza médica en Montpellier: una puesta a punto," in *Granada 1492–1992. Del Reino de Granada al futuro del mundo mediterráneo*, ed. Manuel Barrios and Bernard Vincent (Granada: Universidad de Granada–Diputación Provincial de Granada, 1995), pp. 330–333.

7 María D. Cabanes, ed., *Documentos de Jaime I de Aragón. 1258–1262* (Saragossa: Anúbar, 1982), v. 4, pp. 204–205.

been made of the process until the early decades of the fourteenth century in the town of Manosque.[8]

In the case of Italy, Bologna (where there was a faculty of medicine that showed special interest in surgery) and Venice were two pioneers in the introduction of the practice in the last quarter of the thirteenth century, although there is evidence that it already existed as early as mid-century in procedures for the assessment of the seriousness of injuries received in cases of aggression.[9] The practice quickly spread towards Piedmont and Tuscany. It reached the Hispanic kingdoms towards the end of the thirteenth century. Expert reports appear in the *Fuero real* (Royal Charter) of Fernando III *el Santo* (the Holy), the *Leyes del Estilo* and the *Partidas* of Alfonso X *el Sabio* (the Wise), the *Espéculo* and some municipal legislation.[10] In the case of the Crown of Aragon, the use of doctors in the courts to give expert testimony on injuries was introduced at the end of the thirteenth century and was given the name *dessospitació*, literally "remove from suspicion" (*traure de sospita*), meaning that the victim could be pronounced "out of danger." It consisted of the testimony of a surgeon on the health of an injured party and the prognosis in relation to the potential loss of an organ, mutilation or death as a result, exclusively, of the wound.[11] In the city of Valencia, the first recorded case was not until 1321, and it was included in the Furs (territorial laws) of 1329–30.[12]

---

8   Joseph Shatzmiller, ed., *Médecine et Justice en Provence Médiévale. Documents de Manosque, 1262–1348* (Aix-en-Provence: Publications de l'Université de Provence, 1989), pp. 27–52. Shatzmiller also carried out a comparative study of the Italian cities and the case of Provence. The summary is useful despite the unequal category of the regions studied. Joseph Shatzmiller, "The Jurisprudence of the Dead Body: Medical Practition at the Service of Civic and Legal Authorities," *Micrologus* 7 (1999): 223–230.

9   Alessandro Simili, "Sui primordi e sulla procedura della medicina legale in Bologna," dins *Atti e Memorie dell'Accademia di Storia dell'Arte Sanitaria*, Serie II, Any IX (1943), pp. 41–45. Gerardo Ortalli, "La perizia medica a Bologna nei secoli XIII e XIV," *Deputazione di storia patria per la provincia di Romagna. Atti e memorie*, n.s., 17–19 (1969), pp. 223–259. Guido Ruggiero, "The Cooperation of Physicians and the State in the Control of Violence in Renaissance Venice," *JHMAS* 33 (1978): 156–166. The most extensive study for the two cities is the one by Eugenio Dall'Osso, *L'organizzazione medico-legale a Bologna e a Venezia nei secoli XII-XIV* (Cesena: Università di Bologna, 1956).

10   Anibal Ruiz Moreno, *La Medicina en la legislación medieval española* (Alcalá la Real: Formación Alcalá, 2009), pp. 193–210.

11   *Dessospitació* was first used in the Crown of Aragon in 1307. McVaugh, *Medicine before the Plague*, pp. 207–209. Francesc Cardoner, *Història de la medicina a la Corona d'Aragó (1162–1479)* (Barcelona: Scientia, 1973), pp. 104–108.

12   Mercedes Gallent, "Precedentes medievales de la medicina legal: la *dessospitació* en el Reino de Valencia," *Saitabi* 50 (2000): 11–28.

The doctor made his appearance in the law courts in Cocentaina, a small town on the southern border of Valencia, two decades earlier than in the capital. In 1304, the supreme judicial authority of the town of Cocentaina, the *justícia* (judge),[13] summoned Bernat de Cérvoles and Bernat Sesglea, presumably both barbers as the record states *qui eren e sabien de l'art de sangria* (who practiced and knew of the art of bloodletting), and the physician Pere de Soler to examine the wounds suffered by one of the town's inhabitants, Domingo Pallaruelo. The examination was carried out at the request of his assailant, Pere d'Oriola.[14] This episode is the first evidence of such an intervention in the history of the Kingdom of Valencia, founded in 1236 after King Jaime I of Aragon conquered the lands from the Muslims. What led to such a significant event in a small rural town that at the time was still part of the Crown of Aragon?

Cocentaina was a strategically important enclave on the southern border of the Kingdom of Valencia. Seized from the Muslims in 1245, it remained in royal hands until 1291 when the fief was granted to Admiral Roger de Llúria and the town lost its royal status. In the next century, ownership changed, as was usual with the small Valencian dominions, passing from one noble to another or even returning for a while to the crown.[15] During the thirteenth century, the Christian inhabitants of Cocentaina were faced with many difficulties. The first was their numerical inferiority; throughout the century the Muslim population in the area outnumbered both the Christian and, of course, the Jewish populations. Furthermore, the newcomers—often warriors rather than farmers—found it difficult to settle on the land. There were also suspicions of the indigenous population, who were involved in various rebellions, and fears of possible alliances with the Muslims of Granada. In 1304, the inhabitants of Cocentaina witnessed an attack on the city by troops of the king of Granada, which had disastrous consequences.[16] Nevertheless, it proved to be the beginning of a transformation of the town that led to significant economic growth.

It is strange that such a process, the medicalization of judicial proceedings, should have taken place in Cocentaina, where scholars have found no other

---

13   On the figure of the judge, court and competences, see Francisco Roca Traver, *El justicia de Valencia (1283–1321)* (Valencia: Ayuntamiento de Valencia, 1970). For Cocentaina, see Carmel Ferragud, *El naixement d'una vila rural valenciana. Cocentaina, 1245–1304* (Valencia: Publicacions de la Universitat de València, 1998), pp. 93–95.

14   Ferragud, *El naixement d'una vila*, pp. 101–102.

15   Luis Fullana, *Historia de la villa y condado de Cocentaina* (Valencia: Imprenta Huici, 1920), pp. 81–104.

16   Maria Teresa Ferrer i Mallol, "La incursió de l'exèrcit de Granada de 1304 pel regne de València i l'atac a Cocentaina," *Alberri* 15 (2002): 53–149.

evidence of medical activities. However, what seems clear is that the authorities were willing to take whatever measures necessary to improve social and political conditions by enhancing the administration of justice.

This chapter aims to contextualize the beginnings of the expert forensic examination of injured persons in the Kingdom of Valencia in terms of the prevailing medical and socio-economic circumstances. It shall then analyze a specific case in order to describe how such a medical procedure was carried out.

The Practice of Medicine in Cocentaina

Care Structures and Medical Practitioners

The lack of sources and the poor condition of those that are available make it difficult to carry out even an approximate census of medical practitioners in medieval Cocentaina. Although ample judicial records do, in fact, exist, there are none related to municipal organization and no notary registers, which would allow a proper estimate.[17] There are no references to medical practitioners during the thirteenth century at all. Nevertheless even in the absence of explicit reports, there is evidence to suggest that some kind of medical care did exist. On 19 August 1275, Bernat Ferrer accused Ramon Calandri of having stabbed him in the arm with a knife. The judge saw the wound and only then authorized the payment of bail for the accused. He later ordered the defendant to pay both compensation for the costs of treatment and also the court costs.[18] Indeed, the Charter of Jaime I established that a person found to have inflicted a wound should pay a fine, of which half would go to the authorities and half to the victim. He was further liable for the medical costs. Under oath the victim would inform the justice of the costs and the judge would settle the amount to be paid.[19] This description leads to the conclusion that there were people

---

17 A detailed study of medical practitioners in Cocentaina during the fourteenth century has been carried out by Carmel Ferragud, "Organització social i atenció mèdica a la Cocentaina baixmedieval: el procés a Abrahim Abengalell (1318)," *Asclepio* 57.2 (2005): 3–24, and his "La práctica de la medicina en una frontera. El establecimiento de un sistema asistencial en Alcoi y Cocentaina (Reino de Valencia) durante los siglos XIII y XIV," *Mediterranean Chronicle* 2 (2012): 117–33.

18 Ferragud, *El naixement*, p. 101, note 176. Transcript in Joan J. Ponsoda, *El català i l'aragonés en els inicis del Regne de València segons el Llibre de Cort de Justícia de Cocentaina (1269–1295)* (Alcoi: Marfil, 1996), p. 95.

19 *Aquell qui nafrarà altre, restituescha a aquell que haurà nafrat, oltra la pena que en dret és establida, tots los dans e les despeses que haurà feites en metges e en les nafres a guarir.*

in Cocentaina during the thirteenth century who charged for their medical services. Another case, in the year 1304, gave further evidence of the presence of doctors in the neighborhood. Domingo, a young apprentice to Pere d'Ivorra, had suffered such serious injuries that his life was in danger.[20] The apprenticeship contracts always included a clause by which the master was required to provide his charges with food, drink, clothing and medical care. As Ivorra refused to pay the medical bill, the doctor decided to stop treating his patient until his fees were paid. The judge ordered the sale of some of Ivorra's goods in order to pay the debt, which in fact was an insignificant amount.

The judge carried out the examination of injured parties in person by studying the wounds. Obviously, his training did not allow him to make a valid judgment on the prognosis of the injured person and he could only act according to his own lay experience. In the course of the thirteenth century, it was never considered necessary for a doctor to assess the wounds of a victim of assault or to make a prognosis It is important to bear in mind that the people who made up the municipal council and held executive posts, as well as the position of judge in Cocentaina, had no special academic training, judicial or medical. They were part of the *probi homines* or *prohoms* (good men), members of the leading families who had settled in the town after the defeat of the Moslems. They were wealthy landowners and the most prestigious members of the population. To perform their obligations they had advisors, but it seems that they had no special training either.[21] However, it is likely that the situation began to undergo a change when these citizens realized that their training was insufficient for the quantity and variety of the cases that appeared before the courts.

The first explicit reference to medical practitioners is the case mentioned above of Bernat de Cérvoles and Bernat Sesglea, the two barbers who intervened at the request of the Cocentaina judge. Given that bloodletting was the therapeutic measure most associated with barbers, the court scribe registered them accordingly.[22] It is remarkable that a figure such as the barber, so familiar in both town and country, should not appear more often in the curial records.

Enadeix lo senyor rey que les messions del nafrat sien provades per sagrament del nafrat, tatxatió del jutge denant anant. Germà Colón and Arcadi Garcia, eds., *Furs de València*, v. 4 (Barcelona: Barcino, 1983), pp. 76–77.

20   Ferragud, *El naixement*, p. 205.
21   Ferragud, *El naixement*, pp. 88–90.
22   Ferragud, "Organització social," 3–8. On barbers and their practice in Valencia, Luis García Ballester and Michael R. McVaugh, "Nota sobre el control de la actividad médica y quirúrgica de los barberos (barbers, barbitonsores) en los Furs de Valencia de 1329," in *Homenatge al doctor Sebastià Garcia Martínez* (Valencia: Conselleria de Cultura, Educació i Ciència—Universitat de València, 1988), pp. 73–88. Carmel Ferragud,

Indeed, only two other barbers in medieval Cocentaina are identifiable, a man by the name of Pere del Pont, who promised in January 1317, under the threat of a fine, to cease playing dice, and Miquel Sànxeç, who appeared as a witness while the judge interrogated an injured man in 1363 and in other cases not related to medical questions.[23] Most likely, these practitioners were present during the second half of the thirteenth century in Cocentaina, as by then the newcomers from the north (Catalonia, Aragon and Navarra) were already accustomed to medical care of this kind.[24]

One individual who played an important role in the judicial tribunal was the *metge sirurgià* (surgeon) Domingo Sanç, who, as it will become apparent, was summoned on several occasions to give expert testimony. On 19 October 1380, there is a reference to Mestre Ramon Mir, *metge de casa del senyor Rey* (the king's personal doctor), who is described as a resident of the town. Strangely, the term *físic* (physician) was applied only once, to Pere de Soler, who also took part in the expert examination of 1304 in Cocentaina, mentioned above. On the other hand, the scribes systematically used the generic term *metge* (doctor), which could be used to refer to both physicians and surgeons. Nevertheless, the term suggests that these individuals had no academic training, but had been trained instead through an open system of apprenticeship.[25] This would have been the case with the doctors Joan de Satorre, Joan de Messina, Joan Ponç and Joan Peris, all of whom appear in the records of Cocentaina during the fourteenth century. Although during the fourteenth century only a small elite enjoyed access to university education, the circulation of medical texts in the Crown of Aragon encouraged the development of a common medical culture. This generated structures of intellectual and professional promotion among all kinds of practitioners and levels of practice. Indeed, the dialogue and relations among the different types of medical practitioners, university graduates or otherwise, and of different religions was close. Furthermore, although the areas of competence of physicians and surgeons were varied, in fact they tended to overlap and often became confused.[26]

"Els barbers de la ciutat de València durant el segle XV a través dels llibres del justícia criminal," *Anuario de Estudios Medievales* 41.1 (2011): 31–57.

23   AMC, CJ, 1318, f. 182 (25-2-1318); 1363, s.f. (26-4-1363) and 1364 (30-4-1364).

24   Carmel Ferragud, *Medicina per a un nou regne* (Alzira: Bromera, 2008), pp. 67–122.

25   Garcia Ballester, *La medicina a la València medieval*, pp. 73–80. Carmel Ferragud, *Medicina i promoció social a la Baixa Edat Mitjana* (*Corona d'Aragó, 1360–1410*) (Madrid: CSIC, 2005), pp. 85–125.

26   McVaugh, *Medicine before the Plague*, pp. 38 and 108–112.

A few apothecaries are identifiable in the records, which is surprising given their role in the supply of a significant range of goods essential to daily life: food products, sweets and jams, wax and all the derivatives for lighting, medicines, etc.[27] Only three have been identified: Ramon Canet, Bernat Domínguez and Pere Polo. The last two appear in the records of 1393, which show them purchasing products from a merchant and another apothecary in the city of Valencia.[28]

By the end of the century, and as one would expect of a frontier community, there was a convergence of medical practitioners of different religions, including Jews—although they were not residents of the town—and also Muslims. Records exist of the Jewish practitioners Abrahim Abengalell (1318) and Abrahim Tahuell (1341) and the Muslim practitioners Jucef Hatep (1392) and Hamet Azeni (1397).[29]

If there are few references to medical practitioners, there is even less documentation of medical practice. However, records of the work of doctors as medical examiners are more common, undoubtedly because of the nature of the sources.

Expert Medical Reports at the Beginning of the Fourteenth Century

In 1288, the notary Domingo Cepillo was given a lifetime appointment as scribe of the court of justice of Cocentaina, and held the post until 1328,[30] with a temporary period of leave in 1303. That year, the notary decided to travel to Rome and was replaced as scribe to the court by Guerau de Torroella, another of the town's notaries. The motives for this temporary absence remain unclear. Nonetheless, we suspect that the consequences of the journey were hugely significant for the future of the administration of justice in the town. Indeed the first-ever expert medical examination in the entire Kingdom of Valencia took place in the year following his travels. It was also one of the earliest such examinations in the Crown of Aragon. It is not a coincidence that three medical practitioners were summoned to give their opinions on the health of a plaintiff so soon after Cepillo's return from abroad. Most likely, it was in Rome—although

---

27   Carles Vela, *Especiers i candelers a Barcelona a la Baixa Edat Mitjana. Testaments, família i sociabilitat* (Barcelona: Fundació Noguera, 2007), pp. 22–25.

28   AMC, CJ, 1393 (12 and 22-12-1401). In fact, it was common for apothecaries in those towns farthest from the main trade circuits to acquire their products in the cities. Ferragud, *Medicina i promoció social*, p. 437.

29   On the Jews and Moors of Cocentaina, see Carmel Ferragud, "La sociabilitat i el treball dels jueus a Cocentaina abans de la pesta negra," *Alberri* 15 (2002): 151–178, and Ferragud, "Organització social," 6.

30   Ferragud, *El naixement*, pp. 94–95.

there is no evidence to suggest that this was the aim of his journey—that he learned of expert interventions that had been customary in several Italian cities since the end of the thirteenth century. Indeed, procedures, albeit different in nature, developed simultaneously in Bologna and Venice and then spread to different cities of northern Italy.[31] Although there is no information concerning when the procedures were first used in Rome, given the importance of the city, they would soon have been incorporated into the justice system. By the thirteenth century, the presence of Italians in the Kingdom of Valencia and also in Cocentaina was a reality. Moreover, the mobility of doctors, not only locally but also abroad, was common.[32] All this leads us to believe that news of these developments had somehow reached Domingo Cepillo. Nonetheless, the question remains: who exactly was he?

The Cepillo family was one of the first to settle in the town. The first evidence of them comes from1269.[33] They were part of the local elite, the *probi homines* or *prohoms* (good men or great men), and held most posts in the municipal administration. In the second half of the thirteenth century, they already held some positions—Ramon Cepillo was a counselor in 1276—and in 1318 two of the four councilors, members of the supreme executive of the Valencian municipalities, belonged to the Cepillo family.[34] Thus, the notary Domingo Cepillo was one of the most influential figures in Cocentaina and even of the region. His office was one of the most important in both the economy and the social relations of the town, as his functions included witnessing numerous contracts between members of the population. Furthermore, he represented several individuals from different municipalities in litigation and acted as attorney in specific business and administrative proceedings.[35] Cepillo was a landowner and one of the chief traders in agricultural products in the region. In 1294, he was involved in 98 sales transactions, mostly of cereals (especially wheat), many more than any other trader found among the records.[36] He was able to make his fortune by taking advantage of the opportunities offered by an expanding market, his own privileged position within the framework of local power—although he never held an executive post—and the particular nature of his work as notary. As a member of the local oligarchy, his prestige reached

---

31 Eugenio Dall'Osso, *L'organizzazione medico-legale a Bologna e a Venezia nei secoli XII–XIV* (Cesena: Università di Bologna, 1956), pp. 69–71.

32 The death of a Lombard merchant was recorded in Cocentaina in 1275. Ferragud, *El naixement*, p. 165.

33 Ferragud, *El naixement*, p. 68.

34 Alabau, *Espai agrari i activitats comercials*, p. 9, note 9. Ferragud, *El naixement*, p. 90.

35 Ferragud, *El naixement*, pp. 103–104 and 115.

36 Ferragud, *El naixement*, pp. 160–161.

beyond the boundaries of Cocentaina. People not only requested favors, but inevitably they also accused him of the excesses and arbitrary actions common to men who hold unlimited power.[37]

It would be difficult to explain how such a sophisticated process could take place in 1304 in a small village, far from any large urban area, were it not for the personal intervention of someone of the standing of Domingo Cepillo. Whatever the exact circumstances, he must have come into contact with this procedure and done all that was in his power to apply it. In light of the facts, this is the most plausible hypothesis.

In the case of Cocentaina, in addition to this personal intervention, the introduction of expert forensic reports must also be due, in part, to the fact that it was a border town with a high level of violence, a consequence of the nature of a population constantly in movement, composed of peasants in need of land where they might settle, colonists who had failed to put down roots, peddlers moving through markets and fairs, soldiers of fortune and the usual common criminals.

Cocentaina would soon become the center of an intense market for live-stock, agricultural products, money and cloth. The credit mechanisms of the time allowed for swift and efficient exchange. The market encouraged extraor-dinary demographic mobility and provided for all those newcomers who were still unable to rely on their own production.[38] From its foundation as a Christian settlement re-conquered from Islam, the town of Cocentaina remained essen-tially agricultural throughout the second half of the thirteenth century and the whole of the fourteenth century. Although there were some commercially oriented crops such as saffron, most production was aimed at family and domestic needs. There is also evidence in trading circles of significant live-stock production. However, it is also true that a hundred years later the town's economic activities had undergone significant change. Developments in craft-work skills ensured they would continue to do so as the century progressed. Indeed, manufacturing had entered its preliminary stages and as early as the end of the thirteenth century it was possible to identify craftsmen working

---

37   Ferragud, *El naixement*, pp. 196–197.

38   In short, although the population was small, the economic role of Cocentaina was substantial and would increase even more over time. Cocentaina then can be categorized as a semi-urban nucleus, common in the Kingdom of Valencia where there were only two large cities: the capital and Xàtiva. Antoni Furió and Ferran Garcia-Oliver, "Rural Mobility in a Frontier Land (the Valencian Country, 1250–1350)," in *La mobilità sociale nel medioevo*, ed. Sandro Carocci (Rome: École française de Rome, 2010), pp. 513–554. Ferragud, *El naixement*, pp. 80–88.

with textiles, leather, wood, or metal. Even some dye workshops had appeared. At this time, many artisans and foreign traders were operating in the town and some had settled there. These activities continued to grow and at the turn of the fifteenth century there is evidence of the significant development of artisanal textile manufacturing, based on the handling, production and exchange of woolen cloth, as well as other diverse activities in related sectors such as dyeing.[39] Although it is not possible to determine exactly the role played by medicine in this process of economic growth and social development, it seems clear that the authorities were convinced of it enormous contribution.

Medicine gained a significant role in society because of its usefulness. The great intellectual rigor achieved by medicine during the 1200s and the first decades of the 1300s, the undeniable progress of surgery and, in particular, the treatment of wounds, as well as the prestige of physicians and surgeons, was sufficient argument for the authorities to judge it essential.[40] The authorities required the proper instruments to control such a heterogeneous group and consolidate a population that, at the turn of the fourteenth century, was still considered unstable. The doctor played a fundamental role in the cases of wounded victims of aggression. Through his testimony he cooperated with the courts in order to clarify guilt and helped avoid private acts of revenge that were so prevalent at the time[41] and that usually resulted in the death of one or more of the individuals involved in the dispute. Vendettas were a significant

---

39   On the agricultural landscape, see Ferragud, *El naixement*, pp. 41–48. Josep A. Alabau, *Espai agrari i activitats comercials d'una comunitat rural a inicis del XIV. Cocentaina (1314–1318)*, unpublished research (Valencia: Universitat de València, 2004), pp. 15–24 and 186–190. The handcraft phenomenon in Cocentaina has been studied in great detail in José Antonio Llibrer Escrig, *Los orígenes de la industria de la lana en la Baja Edad Media: el Comtat en el siglo XV* (Valencia: Consell Valencià de Cultura, 2007); id., "La formacion de compañías para el tintado de paños. El caso de Cocentaina en el siglo XV," *Anuario de Estudios Medievales* 41.2 (2011): 59–72; Escrig, "Industria textil y crecimiento regional: la Vall d'Albaida y el Comtat en el siglo XV" (Ph.D. Diss., Universitat de València, 2010), 2 vols. The censuses of artisans involved in the processing of wool and the manufacture of fabrics in Cocentaina have shown that many residents, including the Muslims, were employed in the trade. The earliest census dates from 1426, although from the second half of the century onwards the number of artisans increased considerably.

40   Luis García Ballester, *La búsqueda de la salud. Sanadores y enfermos en la España medieval* (Barcelona: Península, 2001), pp. 194–199. Ferragud, *Medicina i promoció social*, pp. 623–627. Michael R. McVaugh, *The Rational Surgery of the Middle Ages* (Florence: SISMEL, Edizione del Galluzzo, 2006), pp. 89–134.

41   In Venice, according to the records one of the first cities to apply medical reports in justice tribunals, it was considered that the aim of this cooperation was to maintain social peace and contribute to the successful management of business and its enormous trade empire.

factor of destabilization in medieval society.[42] Several references to the practice of *dessospitació* exist from fourteenth-century Cocentaina. From 1376 onwards, the surgeon Domingo Sanç, who is first mentioned in the records in 1363, was summoned on different occasions by the courts in order to offer expert testimony. During this procedure, Sanç would review the state of the injury and give a prognosis in the customary laconic language of such examinations. The experts do not appear to have examined pulse and urine, the two most common factors in both determining a person's health and offering a prognosis. However, they did quote pain, based on the subjective perception of the patient, and fever, a hugely important element of Galenism and considered an illness itself. Some doctors may have used variations in color, smell and consistency of feces as a diagnostic factor, as they contained the "bad humors" and indeed some Latin treatises and vernacular translations appeared to recommend such considerations. In this case, however, it is not clear whether this was taken into account beyond the simple fact that the injured party was able to defecate normally or not. In July 1380, the judge requested the doctor Domingo Sanç to examine the wounds of Ferrer Busaldó and Ramon Pasqual, and to offer a prognosis. The expert report stated the following:

> having examined the above cited wounds to the person of Ferrer Busaldó and the person of Ramon Pasqual, which they had inflicted on each other, and having seen that the wounds had now been treated, and that Ferrer Busaldó and Ramon Pasqual had neither fever nor pain, and were able to defecate properly, as healthy people, I consider that providing the wounds heal and the two men suffer no further accident they are out of danger and in no risk of death as a result of the above cited wounds.[43]

Guido Ruggiero, "The Cooperation of Physicians and the State in the Control of Violence in Renaissance Venice," *JHMAS* 33 (1978): 157.

42 Rafael Narbona, *Malhechores, violencia y justicia ciudadana en la Valencia bajomedieval (1360–1399)* (Valencia: Ayuntamiento de Valencia, 1990).

43 The practice of *dessospitació* in Cocentaina during the XIV century can be seen in detail in Ferragud, "La medicina en una frontera": *vistes e ben regonegudes les naffres e ferides desús declarades et en la persona dels desús dits en Ferrer Busaldó e en Ramon Pasqual e per cascun de aquells contra l'altre feites, et aver atrobades aquelles dites nafres ben curades e guarides, e los dits en Ferrer Busaldó e en Ramon Pasqual aver atrobats sens febra e sens dolor e que açellaven bé e menjaven bé, així com a persones sanes, per la qual cosa per les dites nafres aquells tenint bon regiment e altre mal accident a aquell no sobrevinent ésser fora de perill e dupte de mort de e per les nafres o ferides dessús dites.*

In the last decade of the century there is another significant development. In 1392 and 1397 two Muslim doctors, Jucef Hatep and Hamet Azeni, intervened in examinations using fever, excretion and the proper functioning of the body to determine the state of health of an injured party. This event is significant as the presence and prestige of Muslim doctors appeared to have declined throughout the kingdom.

In short, poorly conserved records, or even the complete lack of documents, make it difficult to observe continuity in doctors' interventions in the court of justice of Cocentaina. Nevertheless, at the beginning of the fifteenth century, the records of one particular trial provide us with the opportunity to carry out a more detailed study of what must have been a common event.

The Case of the Aggression against Llorenç de Roda

On 11 November 1405, the supreme judicial authority of Cocentaina, Judge Joan Martínez de Vera, received a report that in the course of a street fight near the Santa Maria Church, Llorenç or Llorencet Roda, a *macip* (young worker) in the workshop of the *pelaire* Llorenç Celler,[44] had been injured while on his way to visit the son of one Marrades.[45] The latter was the first suspect in the investigation. The injured man had been carried by passers-by to the nearest house, belonging to one Bernat Masana. Once there, the barber-surgeon Bernat Prats, who was attending to the patient when the judge arrived and requested he describe the injuries, treated him. The barber uncovered the wound and revealed that a sword or a sharp pointed dagger had caused it and that the victim had lost much blood.[46] Roda complained loudly and as the wound had been made from behind the barber did not dare to turn him over for fear of increasing his pain. The judge asked the victim to identify his assailant in order to proceed with his arrest. However, this was not possible and no report was made, even though it is clear that the chief suspect was one Francés Manyes.

The following morning the victim was not responding well to treatment and was transferred to the house of a wool merchant by the name of Joan Satorre.[47]

---

44   The *pelaire* was an artisan who specialized in the processing of wool, before weaving. He also cleaned it of impurities and defects once it had been turned into cloth. Over time, he became a trader who supervised and controlled the different stages of production of woolen cloth and its commercialization. Llibrer Escrig, *Los orígenes*, pp. 92–97 and 230.

45   AMC, CJ, ff. 20–30v (11-11-1405 / 11-12-1405).

46   ... *aquell hera nafrat en la cuxa dreta de part de dins e aparia ésser de colp d'espà o de coltell de punta, del qual nafra ho colp avia exida molta sanch.*

47   ... *ab la congoxa que tenia del colp o nafra no avia a bé respost.* All the *pelaires* involved in the process (Llorenç Roda, Llorenç Celler, Marrades and Joan Satorre) belonged to what must have been the first generation of wool artisans to be worthy of consideration for

This cooperation illustrates the solidarity among members of the same profession. The young Roda might not have had any close family, possibly because, like many others, he had come to Cocentaina as an apprentice. Be that as it may, it is true that at no point over the following days did his parents or close family visit the young man and throughout his recovery the Satorre household cared for him. Why he was not treated in the home of his employer, Llorenç Celler, is unclear, although it is true that the victim was no longer an apprentice and therefore his employer's obligations did not extend to feeding him, clothing him and affording health care at times of illness.[48] Whatever the circumstances, it appears that a group of wool merchants had built a firm support network, which provided cover in the event of illness or injury.

It was, therefore, in Satorre's house that the victim was once more interrogated on the identity of his assailant. This time he claimed the perpetrator was not Marrades, but rather one Francés Manyes and that more individuals had been involved. Because the judge felt the circumstances were unclear, he ensured that his notary and court scribe Joan de Pujaçons accompanied Llorenç. It then became obvious that the events must be related to one of the many violent episodes that occurred among the youth of medieval towns. Indeed, the aggression occurred at night when a group of four young men, Llorenç, Fortunyet, Francés and Marrades, were in the street, in front of the dye workshop (*tint*) of one Genís Cerdà.[49] Llorenç exchanged words with Marrades, who followed him, overtook him and verbally provoked him: "Lorenç, now is the time, if that is what your heart tells you."[50] He then threatened him with a

---

their social importance. The important studies on these artisans in Cocentaina begin in 1426, and therefore we cannot give more details.

48   Among the clauses of the Valencian apprenticeship contracts (*afermament*), it was usual for the master to undertake to provide for all the needs of the apprentice and to treat him fairly and honestly and to teach him the profession so long as remained in his house. At times he also promised to offer a small salary and work-clothes, at the end of the contract. On the other hand, the apprentice owed his master obedience and undertook not to abandon his house until the established time had elapsed. See Ricardo Sixto, *La contratación laboral en la Valencia medieval. Aprendizaje y servicio doméstico (1458–1462)* (Ph.D. Diss., Universitat de València, 1993).

49   The reference to the dye-workshop is also significant. Genís Cerdà was one of the few dyers in the Cocentaina census of 1426. It is worth noting that information we have found on many apprentices has been in connection with the conflicts and crimes in which they were involved and which compelled them to attend the court of justice. On dyeing and apprentices, see Llibrer Escrig, *Los orígenes*, pp. 102–106 and 178.

50   *Lorenç, ara és ora si lo cor t'o diu.* See note 49 above.

knife. Llorenç responded that he was willing to fight,[51] and in turn took out a long knife. Subsequently, Marrades fled the scene and the events become confused because the victim could say only that he was then attacked from behind and was therefore unable to identity his aggressor.

The interrogation then turned to the surgeon, Bernat Prats. He was asked to give his opinion on how the injury had been caused and what weapon had been used. It appeared obvious to everyone that the injury must have been caused from behind with a sword, as the weapon had entered the back of the thigh and passed completely through the leg. Consequently, the surgeon stated that the attack had indeed been made with a sword, rather than a knife or a dagger, as the entry wound was wide (the breadth of a hand) and the exit wound was narrower. The judge therefore asked the victim if Manyes or Fortunyet had been carrying a sword at the time. He replied that the former was wearing a cape and he had not seen any weapons and that the latter was carrying only a dagger. Nor had he seen that Marrades was in possession of a sword. In short, Llorenç was unable to accuse anyone and as a result, the judge decided to act *ex officio* with the advice of the councilors.

The evidence subsequently obtained by the lieutenant of the judge pointed towards Joan d'Estanya, who had been seen bearing a sword during the brawl. The Estanya family was one of the oldest in the town, had a significant sociopolitical role and influence and by the second half of the fifteenth century several family members, including two with the same name, were involved in the wool trade.[52] Some citizens informed the judge that Estanya had left the sword with which he had wounded Llorenç in the house of Andreu de Pujaçons, a local farmer. The judge visited the house of Pujaçons and questioned his wife regarding the sword that Estanya had left there. However, the woman claimed he had taken it away in the early hours of the morning. Estanya had already been taken into custody as a suspect and the judge now proceeded to the local prison to question him about the weapon. The prisoner claimed he did not own a sword, that it was his father's and that they would find it in the family home. However, at the house of the Estanya, when the judge asked Francesca, Joan's mother, for her husband's sword, she denied that it had been used, as she herself had stored it away two months before. The sword was in its sheath, covered in dust and without a trace of blood, which suggested it had indeed not been used. The judge consequently returned to the prison to demand the whereabouts of the sword that had been used the night of the aggression.

---

51   *Fer-te'n he placer.* See note 49 above.
52   Ponsoda, *El català i l'aragonés*, p. 341. Llibrer Escrig, *Los orígenes*, p. 176.

The prisoner now claimed he had borrowed the sword from Bartomeu Manyes three weeks before and that it must still be in the house unless Manyes had taken it. The weapon was at last discovered and when the judge examined it, it was clear that it had recently been sharpened. The judge continued to interrogate both Manyes and Estanya and asked who had sharpened it. Several people examined the sword and confirmed the judge's belief that it had been recently washed and sharpened and that there was a trace of blood on the point.[53]

Joan d'Estanya and Francés Manyes were held in the common prison, accused of the aggression against Llorenç Roda. On 16 November, they claimed they were innocent of the charges against them. They requested that the authorities search for Bartomeu Marrades, the real culprit, in Bocairent, a town near Cocentaina, where he had moved, and that the local judge should interrogate him.[54] They then made another crucial statement. Llorenç was no longer receiving treatment from the surgeon Bernat Prats, whom they considered highly suitable for medical practice (*lo qual és bon cerurgià*), and had now become the patient of the son of a Muslim by the name of Jucef Facén, who was not apt to be a doctor. Therefore, Joan and Francés claimed that they could not be blamed for anything that now happened to the patient. Clearly, one of the factors to be taken into account when a person was wounded was the medical care that he or she received. The assailants feared that deterioration in the patient's condition, or even his death through medical negligence, would increase the likelihood of their conviction.

Once more the judge returned to the home of Satorre, where the injured man remained, unable to move, in order to take a further statement at the request of another wool merchant by the name of Pasqual Munyoç. Llorenç now made a full and detailed statement of the events, in which he accused the four young men and claimed that their intention had been to kill him. He declared that after the confrontation with Marrades and once Marrades had fled, Joan d'Estanya attacked him from behind and thrust the sword into his leg. He admitted that until then he had chosen to say nothing, but now declared that he wished to accuse the four men who had ambushed him.

---

53   *... hera lavade e smolada de poch a ençà, e que aparia que y havia ves la punta senyal de sanch, però no hera masa bé aparexent.* See note 52 above.

54   Geographic mobility was common at this time, which made it difficult on occasion to detain and interrogate suspects of different offenses. Communication among officials of the different municipal areas was essential. However, it is clear that if they failed to act quickly, delinquents could make good their escape and thus avoid punishment.

Thus, on December 1, Bartomeu Manyes declared in writing before the judge, that he upheld his accusation against Bartomeu Marrades, inhabitant of Bocairent. However, in order to avoid any complication that might arise in the future, he demanded a forensic report: the *dessospitació*. The father of Joan d'Estanya filed an appeal according to the Charter of Valencia (*furs*) approved by King Alfons *el Benigne* (the Benign) in 1329.[55] In this charter there was a chapter entitled "Doctors" (*metges*) that established a new statute to regulate the medical profession and medical practice. Among the seven provisions was the order that any surgeon treating a patient must declare, under oath, without pecuniary reward and whenever required, whether the injured person was out of danger.[56] The laconic nature of the order is in stark contrast to the detailed clauses of the Bologna statutes that were constantly amended and modified.[57] The lack of detail can only be explained by the fact that the procedure had by now been in effect for some time and doctors were perfectly aware of the meaning of "fora de sospita" (*free of suspicion*).[58]

Consequently Estanya did no more than refer to the terms of the law: according to the fur (Charter) of King Alfons, the surgeon was obliged to state, under oath, and whenever the Court required, whether the victim, on the basis of the condition of the injury, was out of mortal danger.[59] The prisoners therefore demanded to know whether the victim was indeed out of danger, so that they might post bail and leave prison. The lieutenant of the judge subsequently complied with the requirements of the law and summoned Bernat Prats, the surgeon. In response to the question whether the patient was out of danger, Prats stated that he was not in pain, did not have a fever and was able to perform all bodily functions naturally and that therefore his condition was normal and he was in no danger of imminent death.[60]

---

55   Garcia Ballester, *La medicina a la València medieval*, pp. 53–57.

56   *Tot cirurgià qui tinga algun nafrat en poder sia tengut de dir, ab sagrament sens alcun salari, quantesque vegades request ne serà si·l nafrat es fora de sospita o no.* See note 55 above.

57   Ortalli, "La perizia medica," 224–243.

58   The same reflection has been made in the Bologna case in Dall'Osso, *L'organizzazione medico-legale*, 19. In fact, in the city of Valencia there are records of a *dessospitació* in 1321. Gallent, "Precedentes medievales," 17, note 14.

59   *... segons lo fur del rey n'Anfos deia dir ab sagrament tota vegada que request o amonestat ne serà per la cort si lo dit nafrat per raho de dita nafra és fora de perill de mort.* See note 57 above.

60   *... fon interrogat lo dit nafrat si hera fora de perill de mort o no, e lo qual axí interrogat dix que per lo sagrament que feyt havia que ell, en lo present dia, havia vist lo dit nafrat e aquell que·l havia trobat que hera sens febra e sens dolor e que fahia bé ses opperacions axí com a*

This development led to Llorenç withdrawing the charges on 3 December. According to his version of the story, on the advice of various people he decided to withdraw all his accusations and to request that the prisoners be released. He added that even if he later died from the wound, the accused should be exonerated. The judge was reluctant to accept his decision, but the victim insisted that he was acting in good faith and following the advice of his friends. Nonetheless, the judge still held the suspects in custody for another eight days until, on the recommendation of his councilors, he decided to absolve them and release them from prison.

As on so many other occasions, the full facts of the case were never uncovered and the historian might suspect that pressure had been brought to bear on the plaintiff. It is possible, that the social standing of the Estanya family swayed the result, or perhaps it was the confusion surrounding the events. Whatever the case, the culprit was not brought to justice, in spite of the best efforts of the judge who used all mechanisms available to him.

Expert Examinations through the Example of the Surgeon Bernat de Prats

The inquiries carried out by Judge Joan Martínez de Vera in the case of the assault on Llorenç Roda represent the most significant and complete trial to be found in the records of the judicial courts of Cocentaina. The range of developments as the case unfolded allows us to examine a practice that had become commonplace in Valencian municipalities since the middle of the fourteenth century, with some precedents, as in the first case of Cocentaina, considered above. Nevertheless, no case provided the depth of investigation or the same level of paperwork as that of Llorenç Roda. Indeed, the length of the process illustrates one of the reasons for introducing expert examinations; the fact that judges lacked the forensic expertise to make a judgment based correctly on the facts.[61]

The intervention of the surgeon Bernat de Prats occurred a century after the first recorded expert report. Over the course of those hundred years, much had changed in the town of Cocentaina. Once the victim of border tensions and the social pressures of an unstable population that lived in fear of attacks from Muslim troops, Cocentaina had now achieved a certain level of security and calm and a population committed to the wool textile industry. Violence had other roots although the function of the judge remained the same: to uphold

---

persona sana, e que aquell, tenint-se a bon regiment, que hera fora de perill de mort, altre mal no sobrevinent. See note 57 above.

61   Ortalli, "La perizia medica," 224 and 226.

order and to punish all criminal acts. This was the only way to guarantee the stability that would allow the townsfolk to carry out their daily tasks in peace. By now, medical and surgical knowledge had made substantial progress and the *dessospitació* was becoming more and more precise.

Although the judge had sufficient experience to determine that a sword had caused the wound, he refused to accept the fact until confirmed by the expert testimony of the surgeon. In other words, medical expertise was essential confirmation of the evidence. Indeed, so important was the surgeon's opinion, that once the cause of the wound had been clarified, the accused used his findings to argue their own innocence. When Francés Manyes protested at the judicial proceedings, his imprisonment and the calumnies against his honor, he claimed that on the night of the aggression he had only been carrying a small dagger, while the surgeon had testified that the victim had suffered a sword-wound.[62]

Prats illustrates the special authority of those learned figures with expert knowledge in the late Middle Ages. Indeed, on various occasions, the accused in this case resorted to his professional prestige in order to defend their arguments: "he practices surgery and has been examined and licensed in said practice."[63] After the charter granted by Alfons the Benign in 1329, medical practice in the Kingdom of Valencia underwent a significant transformation. Anyone wishing to practice medicine was now required to take an examination and would then be granted a license to practice in the town and the kingdom. Although many medical practitioners failed to comply with this requirement, it is important to stress that those who did abide by the law must have enjoyed a high social standing, as appears to be the case with Bernat de Prats.[64] However, in the city of Valencia, the authorities went further and sought to ensure that it should be the most prestigious representatives, those with a university education, who participated in the *dessospitacions*, in addition to any barber or surgeon who might be treating the victim. In the fifteenth century, responsibility was placed exclusively in the hands of these doctors, appointed

---

62   ... *e mostràs per relació del dit metge cirurgià que la dita nafra fòra feyta ab spà e donchs ell seria inmune e sens culpa.* See note 61 above.

63   ... *que hussa de cirurgia e examinat e licenciat en aquella.* See note 61 above.

64   Information is available on these examination tribunals in the XIV century; how they worked, who took part, and the type of practitioners who underwent the examination. Luis García Ballester, Michael R. McVaugh y Agustín Rubio Vela, *Medical Licensing and Learning in Fourteenth-Century Valencia, Transactions of the American Philosophical Society,* v. 79, pt. 6 (Philadelphia: American Philosophical Society, 1989).

by the king, and who received the title *dessospitador* (medical examiner) of all injured parties.[65]

Their prestige placed them far above those other medical practitioners disqualified by their lack of competence. Precisely one of the concerns of the two accused in custody was that Roda had replaced Prats with an unnamed Muslim doctor, referred to simply as the son of Jucef Facén.[66] From that moment on, the prisoners were concerned that should Llorenç Roda die as a result of the medical negligence of the new doctor, they might still be held to blame for his death.

There was a precedent for an accusation of malpractice against a member of a religious minority; some decades earlier, the Jewish doctor Abrahim Abengalell was accused of causing a Christian woman to miscarriage.[67] However, the context was different; the prestige of Jewish doctors was undeniable and in spite of the early pressure of the Church, suspicions against the Jewish community were rare. What is most surprising in the case of Llorenç Roda is that a Muslim doctor should replace a Christian surgeon. This would seem to indicate that the Muslim doctor was well esteemed, or that his services were more economical and the change was based on questions of cost. In any case, the example illustrates the lack of religious prejudice in the choice of doctor. Indeed, at the turn of the fifteenth century there is clear evidence of the presence of the Muslim doctor in Cocentaina, although to date no information on his practice has been uncovered. In fact, there are scarcely any references in the records to the practice of medicine by Muslim doctors in the Kingdom of Valencia. García Ballester has explained this as both the gradual abandonment of the medical profession based on rational principles and its degeneration, with some exceptions, towards other types of care more akin to folk medicine.[68] The cause was the departure into exile of the scientific-cultural and economic elite as a result of Christian conquest and the massive ruralization of the Muslim population in the inland mountainous areas of the kingdom, such as Cocentaina. Furthermore, there was growing social alienation. Once

---

65   Gallent, "Precedentes medievales", 21–25. The same title was given to the first doctors who undertook this practice in Bologna. At times they were in fact doctors hired by the municipal authorities. Dall'Osso, *L'organizzazione medico-legale*, pp. 15–16.

66   *Que en Bernat Prats, barber, metge cirurgià, tenia en cura lo dit nafrat, lo qual és bon metge, e aquell sia stat mes en poder del fill de Jucef Facén per curar aquell, qui no seria abte tant com lo dit Bernat, que protestaven que si per culpa de mal metge aquell moria que fos inputat a qui degués.* See note 65 above.

67   Ferragud, "Organitzacio social," 3–24.

68   Luis García Ballester, *Historia social de la medician en la España de los siglos XIII al XVI*, [v. I, *La minoría musulmana y morisca*] (Madrid: Akal, 1976), pp. 42–46.

the schools of medicine had declined, it became difficult to educate scientifically advanced medical practitioners among the minorities. Consequently, it is interesting that two Muslim surgeons appeared in Cocentaina at the end of the fourteenth century and that they were called upon by the judge to make an expert medical examination. While it is true that both cases involved Muslims, on one occasion another of the men examined was Christian. This shows that such a delicate intervention, which for some time in the city of Valencia had been in the hands of doctors of great prestige and preferably with university training, was entrusted to doctors who shared the same medical principles and were obviously held in high enough esteem for the judge to request their services.

Nonetheless, as mentioned above, the medical practitioners who appear in this case are Bernat Prats, *barber e metge cirurgià* (barber and surgeon), and Miquel Sànxeç. Certainly, in a large city like Valencia, a judge in a complex case might call on as many as five of the most prestigious and highly trained surgeons and physicians to give evidence.[69] However, such a small town as Cocentaina had fewer resources and the judge would have to depend on the surgeon he considered most reliable, or in this case the barber-surgeon, the most common medical practitioner of the late Middle Ages. Indeed, studies show that the number of barbers continued to grow in the Kingdom of Valencia during the fourteenth and fifteenth centuries, in relation to the total number of healers. It is also significant that their presence is recorded both in the urban and rural areas, which would suggest that they were the central figures of primary care. Their work was divided between hygiene (the washing and cutting of hair or shaving) and health and surgery of greater complexity that was strictly regulated by law. Among their most common activities was phlebotomy or bloodletting, dentistry and the treatment and suture of wounds. Their inventories list all the tools required for these practices.[70] Barbers intervened in emergencies when people arrived with different injuries at their work place or responded where necessary to calls for help from people unable to move. The barber stopped the bleeding and treated and stitched the wound. On many occasions, judicial authorities visited the barber's house where he had treated the victim of a fight or accident, in order to initiate an investigation

---

69   Carmel Ferragud, "El metge sota sospita. Actuacio mèdica en els testimonis pericials a ferits devant la cort del justícia criminal de València (1396)," *Recerques* 62 (2011): 90–94.

70   Carmel Ferragud, "Barbers and Barbershops during the Late Middle Ages in the Crown of Aragon," in *International Medieval Meeting* (Brepols, 2011). *Forthcoming.*

and interrogate witnesses.[71] The case presented here is an example of such commonplace circumstances.

Barbers were given a practical training based on the terms of the usual apprentice system, stipulated in a contract before a notary. Over a set number of years, the apprentice accompanied his master and learned the rudiments of the profession until he was ready to start work either as a paid assistant in a barbershop or as a self-employed barber. Nevertheless, work soon began on the translation of surgical texts for the benefit of individuals who could not read Latin and, lacking a detailed knowledge of the art of surgery, might commit fatal errors.[72] Gradually, barbers improved their knowledge and skill until by the last decades of the fifteenth century they were virtually indistinguishable from surgeons. Under the protection of one of the first corporations to be legally established in Valencia, barbers embarked on an unceasing process of promotion. Nonetheless, the differentials of prestige, power and wealth within the sector remained, as in any other profession.[73]

In Cocentaina it appears that the authorities elected to entrust expert examinations to a single individual, although other doctors might then carry out other specific *dessospitacions*. Bear in mind that in such a small population the number of practitioners was limited, and was even more so when they were required to undertake proper training. Prats was called upon to perform *dessospitacions* on two further occasions. The first, prior to the events described here, took place in 1401, when the judge requested that the surgeon examine a small wound that one Sancho had received on his left thumb. The second intervention took place on 15 April 1409, when the pelt-monger Bernat Pineda, brother of the tailor Joan Pineda, declared that during a street brawl a resident of Alicante by the name of Bernat Perpinyà had received an injury to his arm and that Joan Pineda had been blamed for the attack. However, the victim had since recovered, as the wound was minor, and the arm was now working again normally.[74] Bernat Pineda consequently requested that the barber-surgeon

71   Ferragud, "Els barbers," 47.
72   Lluís Cifuentes, "La literatura quirúrgica baixmedieval en romanç a la Corona d'Aragó: escola, pont i mercat," in *Literatura i cultura a la Corona d'Aragó (s. XIII–XV): actes del III Col·loqui internacional "Problemes i mètodes de literatura catalana antiga"* (Girona, 5–8 de juliol de 2000), ed. Lola Badia, Miriam Cabré and Sadurní Martí (Barcelona: Curial— Publicacions de l'Abadia de Montserrat, 2002), pp. 321–335. Id. "Vernacularization as an Intellectual and Social Bridge: the Catalan Translations of Teodorico's Chirurgia and of Arnau de Vilanova's *Regimen sanitatis*," *Early Science and Medicine* 4 (1999): 127–148.
73   Ferragud, "Barbers and Barbershops."
74   ...*com sia fort poqua sia fora de perill de mort com vaja a treballar e a fer ses fahenes temporals.* See note 73 above.

Bernat Prats, who had treated the injured man, should testify in writing that he was out of danger, to cover any future eventualities.[75]

This case shares with Llorenc Roda's the fact that the person who requests the *dessospitació* acts as representative of the man in custody accused of causing the wound. In fact, until the doctor had performed the examination and until it was clarified that the injured man was out of danger, no provision for bail (*caplleuta*) had been made.[76] The prisoner subsequently made an application to the judge.

It is not at all clear whether the surgeon charged for his services. In theory, the charter obliged surgeons who were treating a patient to testify to their health and prognosis without payment. However, this procedure changed over time as the accused themselves tended to enlist the services of a surgeon who they would then pay. Such professionals charged large sums of money and, at times, would monopolize the service through the favors of the judge. In response to such abuses the authorities of Valencia took measures, which were approved by the king in 1378.[77] However, it remained true that the limited number of medical personnel in such a small town often made it necessary to use the same expert.

Another of the important features of the *dessospitació* was that the doctor was required to testify under oath. The documents record: "And this is a fair requirement, because it is established by the law that you have sworn to upkeep, and you must avoid all falsification and libel in the written records."[78] The issue was far from trivial, as the accused's life was at stake[79] and the ethical problems involved in the procedure needed to be considered. With his testimony, it was possible for a doctor to contribute to a guilty verdict against a personal enemy. It was not unknown in the city of Valencia for the expert evidence of a doctor to be rejected on the grounds of his lack of impartiality.[80]

Another feature was that these interventions were recorded conveniently and in some detail in the minutes of the judicial court. The judge was always accompanied by the scribe who recorded with great care both the facts and

---

75   AMC, CJ, 1401, f. 71v and 1409, f. 3.

76   The procedure was identical in Bologna. Ortalli, "La perizia medica," 226–227 and 236.

77   Luis Alanyá, ed., *Aureum Opus Regalium Privilegiorum Civitatis et Regni Valentie* (Valencia, 1515–1972, edicion facsímil), pp. 348–349. Published in Gallent, "Precedentes medievales," 26–28.

78   *E axí ho requiren justantment* cum ita sit faciendum *per fur, que havets jurat tenir e servar e devets squivar de vexació e calúpnia les scriptures.*

79   Dall'Osso, *L'organizzazione medico-legale*, 19.

80   Ferragud, "El metge sota sospita", 86–87.

the words, often literally, of the interrogations.[81] In the early years, a notary
filled the post of scribe. It remains unclear whether the presence of a notary
was required as guarantee of the truth of the facts as they appeared in the
records both of private protocols and municipal documents.[82] The fact that
in Cocentaina it was common for the court scribe to be a notary was due to
the scarcity of individuals with sufficient skills. Nevertheless, that the doctor's
word was law in these cases meant that the minutes of a simple scribe were
sufficient. Consequently, in the case above, wherever he went, the judge was
always accompanied by *son scrivà* (his scribe).

Innovation on the Border

The introduction of expert medical testimony in the court of justice of
Cocentaina at the turn of the fourteenth century should be understood as part
of a double process. The first specific development was the founding and colo-
nization of the Kingdom of Valencia. The flow of migrants from different parts
of Europe, who used the town either as a stopover or as their final destination,
contributed to the introduction of innovations in a country under construction. The second process was the medicalization of late medieval society.[83] As
a result of Islamic and Jewish influence and the willingness to embrace the
achievements of science and new techniques, particularly in medicine (it is
no coincidence that Arnau de Villanova, one of the most distinguished doctors
of the late Middle Ages, was originally from Valencia), it was possible to establish in a small border town an expert judicial procedure that even the most
famous European university cities had only recently implemented. There is no
doubt that the existence of medical practitioners played an important part in
encouraging colonists to settle and also in the implementation of mechanisms
designed to improve judicial administration.

---

81   In the case of Bologna, there was close collaboration between the notary and doctor.
      To regulate the process, specific systems of ratification were introduced, but over time
      tended to disappear. In theory, for the process to be official and legal, it needed to be
      documented in writing by a notary. For the examination to be valid therefore, the
      presence of both notary and doctor was essential. By the end of the thirteenth century,
      the endorsement of the notary had disappeared. Dall'Osso, *L'organizzazione medico-
      legale*, 26–31.

82   In Bologna they soon eliminated the clause requiring a notary, as the testimony of the
      doctors was deemed sufficient and the notary was only responsible for the minutes. In
      our case, it is not clear whether the presence of the notary was compulsory. However in
      Cocentaina, by coincidence, the post of scribe of the court was held by a notary. Ortalli,
      "La perizia medica," 231.

83   Marilyn Nicoud, "Formes et enjeux d'une medicalisation médiévale: réflexions sur les
      cités italiennes (XIIIᵉ–XVᵉ siècles)," *Genéses* 82 (2011): 7–30.

CHAPTER 5

Forensic Evidence, Lay Witnesses and Medical Expertise in the Criminal Courts of Late Medieval Italy

Joanna Carraway Vitiello

In Book Four of the *Speculum Iuris*, William Durandus asks us to imagine the following case:

> Person A wounded Person B, who died after he was overcome by fever. A was accused concerning the death, but he himself asserted that B died from the fever, and many lay-witnesses (*laici testes*) were brought in to say just that: but a few physicians (*medici*) said that the wound was the cause of the fever. I say, it is better that the few physicians should be believed, since they have a better understanding of the matter.[1]

Means of introducing and using forensic evidence underwent much development in the criminal courts of late medieval Italy. The relationship between academic and practical medicine remained amorphic even to university scholars during the late Middle Ages, and ambiguity about where medical expertise could be found persisted in the arena of the courtroom. Legal medicine required the practitioner or consulting physician to determine from signs on the body either what had happened to a victim in the past or what would happen in the future in terms of the victim's recovery or likelihood of death from injuries, and so, as the passage from Durandus implies, there was a larger epistemological issue involved. Judges sought information from those most likely to interpret properly the evidence of the body, and in late medieval Italy, they

---

1　Guillelmus Durandus, *Speculum iuris* (Venice, 1576), Lib.IIII, Partic.IIII, *De homicidio*, f.491. "*De facto queritur: A. vulneravit B. qui fevre superveniente decessit: accusatur de morte: ipse vero asserit illum ex febre obiisse, et plures laici testes inducti hoc dicunt: medici vero pauciores dicunt, quod vulnus extitit causa febris. Respondo potius est credendum paucioribus medicis, quia factum melius noscunt.*" Elsewhere, Durandus wrote on the issue of proof that "*magis credendum est ei, qui de arte sua testificatur.*" Mario Ascheri, "'*Consilium sapientes*,' perizia medica et '*res iudicata*,'" pp. 533–579 in *Proceedings of the Fifth International Congress of Medieval Canon Law, Salamanca, 21–25 September 1976*, ed. Stephan Kuttner and Kenneth Pennington (Vatican City: Biblioteca Apostolica Vaticana, 1980), p. 569.

relied upon both university-trained physicians and laypeople for clarification regarding wounds, the likelihood of recovery, and causes of death. Learned physicians examined victims and wrote *consilia* at the petition of the courts, but lay knowledge was likewise invaluable and could be determinative even in the most serious of cases.[2]

The use of forensic evidence and physical examinations was not an innovation of the late medieval courts: physical examinations and even autopsy had been used in other legal arenas much earlier. The practice of autopsy and post-mortem examination may have originated in ecclesiastical canonization proceedings, which sometimes considered the condition of saints' bodies for any physical evidence of sanctity.[3] Prior to Lateran IV, trials by ordeal relied upon priests to gauge the severity of wounds or infections in order to interpret verdicts. By the thirteenth century, autopsy and dissection were used in the universities as a didactic tool, and eventually, in judicial courts as part of investigations.[4]

While there was a great deal of local variation, the use of legal medicine appeared in many different areas by the late thirteenth century. By this point, expert medical opinions were used in the criminal courts of Italy, especially in Venice and in Bologna, where doctors were dispatched to crime scenes.[5] It was also not uncommon in France, as records from Manosque indicate,[6] and there is evidence for their use in Paris by the beginning of the fourteenth century.[7] In England, the office of coroner developed by 1194. Though these coroners were not medically trained, they conducted a sort of "primitive post-

---

2   Silva de Renzi, "Medical Expertise, Bodies and the Law in Early Modern Courts," *Isis* 98.2 (2007): 318–19.

3   Katherine Park, "Holy Autopsies: Saintly Bodies and Medical Expertise, 1300–1600," in *The Body in Early Modern Italy*, ed. Julia L. Hairston and Walter Stephens (Maryland: Johns Hopkins University Press, 2010), p. 63. See also Katherine Park, "The Criminal and the Saintly Body: Autopsy and Dissection in Renaissance Italy," *Renaissance Quarterly* 47.1 (1994): 1–33.

4   Katherine Park, *The Secrets of Women: Gender, Generation, and the Origins of Human Dissection* (New York: Zone Books, 2006), pp. 52–3. For an investigation of dissection as it developed in Renaissance Venice and its use as a didactic tool, see Cynthia Klestinec, *Theaters of Anatomy: Students, Teachers and Traditions of Dissection in Renaissance Venice* (Maryland: Johns Hopkins University Press, 2011).

5   ASB, *Statuti* 1389, f.280r–v.

6   Joseph Shatzmiller, "The Jurisprudence of the Dead Body: Medical Practition at the Service of Civic and Legal Authorities," *Micrologus* 7 (1999): 223–230.

7   Katherine D. Watson, *Forensic Medicine in Western Society* (London: Routledge, 2011), pp. 33–36.

mortem examination" in places where bodies were found,[8] and as late as the nineteenth century, autopsies were regularly carried out on a table in the home of the deceased.[9] This situation, however, was very different from what was developing in some Italian cities: English coroners were not physicians, and in any case, juries, not experts, remained the ultimate arbiters of facts.[10] In late medieval Italy, however, forensic evidence was used to further the goals of inquisitorial justice to discover, control and punish crime. The discernment in hidden matters was the *raison d'être* for the inquisitorial trial procedure, which dominated late medieval Italian courts. Modes of investigation developed in this period reflected this desire, firmly rooted in the scholastic tradition, to use reason, experience and logic to unravel the truth of hidden things.

Inquisitorial justice became the norm in northern Italy during the thirteenth and fourteenth centuries slowly replacing accusatorial procedure, and this innovation gave judges the power to proceed *ex officio* and to consider new types of evidence.[11] The use of forensic evidence has been examined in some important centers of late medieval Italy, particularly Venice and Bologna, but in matters of criminal procedure, there existed a great deal of local variation, which depended on the traditions, needs and particular circumstances of communities. The following contribution examines the roles of doctors and laypeople in providing forensic evidence, drawing in part from the records of the criminal court at Reggio Emilia during the late fourteenth century.[12]

---

8   Barbara Hanawalt, "Violent Death in Fourteenth and Early Fifteenth-Century England," *Comparative Studies in Society and History* 18.3 (1976): 299.

9   Katherine Watson, *Poisoned Lives: English Poisoners and their Victims* (London: Hambledon, 2004), p. 166.

10   Watson, *Forensic Medicine in Western Society*, p. 17.

11   The idea of a full and complete shift from accusatorial to inquisitorial justice has been revised in recent scholarship. Please see especially Massimo Vallerani, "Procedura e giustizia nelle città italiane del basso medioevo (XII–XIV secolo)," in *La giustizia pubblica medievale* (Bologna: il Mulino, 2005), pp. 19–73. A new English translation of this important collection of studies is now available. See Massimo Vallerani, *Medieval Public Justice*, trans. Sarah Rubin Blanshei (Washington, D.C.: Catholic University Press, 2012). On the development of criminal justice and the political uses of inquisition in this period, see Sarah Rubin Blanshei, *Politics and Justice in Late Medieval Bologna* (Leiden: Brill, 2010).

12   The most important source for criminal justice at Reggio Emilia for the years 1371–1409 are the records of approximately 1,240 trials that survive. The registers are not concurrent and have large lacunae. Archivio di Stato di Reggio Emilia, *Giudiziario*, Libri delle denunzie e querele, delle inquisizioni, degli indizi, dei costituti, delle difese e d'altri atti criminali (hereafter ASRe, *Giudiziario*, Libri delle denunzie). In the references to these sources that follow here, the Latin spelling is not standardized, but rather appears as it does in the documents.

Judges at Reggio Emilia—a small city that, in the second half of the fourteenth century, had become part of the Visconti dominion—considered the
testimony of lay witnesses but also relied upon the expertise of the few doctors who practiced at Reggio. Like many Italian cities, the population of Reggio
Emilia had dramatically declined during the fourteenth century due to war,
plague and famine. Barnabò Visconti and his wife, the formidable Regina della
Scala, acquired the city as part of their dominions in 1371 and their observations
upon their visit a year later reveal a city in crisis. They were "deeply saddened
by the devastation of the homes... The citizens visited him [Barnabò] in the
evening, whom he kindly received; but he wondered at the paucity of men,
which he would scarcely believe, had he not made inquiries...."[13] Records of
hearth taxes for the years 1401–1409 show Reggio Emilia's population at a mere
three thousand inhabitants in the city, with a possible four and a half to five
thousand inhabitants in the district under Reggio Emilia's jurisdiction;[14] this
down from as many as 17,000 people in the city alone a century earlier.

To retain medical professionals in such an environment, the government of
Reggio made concessions. In 1372, Reggio's *podestà* asked Milan for permission
to give a public salary to a doctor to keep him in the city:

> Item, on account of the health of your citizens and of those foreigners
> living in your said city, we think it is worthwhile to provide that Magister
> Paulus, a physician, who for eight years stayed [in Reggio] with a salary
> from the aforementioned Lord Feltrino,[15] should not leave the said city,

---

13   Sagacius et Petrus de Gazata, *Chronicon Regiense,*in *Rerum Italicarum Scriptores*, o.s., v.18,
     col. 77. "[1371] *Die XXI. Octobris Dominus Barnabòs cum eius uxore venit Rhegium... valde
     condoluit de domorum vastatione, et magis eius uxor. Cives illum vespere visitarunt, quos
     benigne suscepit; sed admiratus est paucitatem hominum, quod vix credere poterat, nisi de
     paucitate perquisivisset."*
14   Andrea Gamberini, *La città assediata: poteri e identità politiche a Reggio in età viscontea*
     (Rome: Viella, 2003), 91. A hearth tax of 1315 tax suggests that the city, together with
     the region under its jurisdiction, encompassed 2,500 kilometers. See Natale Grimaldi,
     La signoria di Barnabò Visconti e Regina della Scala in Reggio, 1371–1385 (Reggio Emilia:
     Cooperativa fra lavoranti tipografi, 1921), p. 127. The city had approximately 17,000
     inhabitants in the city itself, and possibly another 25,000 in the surrounding district. See
     Gamberini, 91, note 46, citing O. Rombaldi, *Agricoltori e agricoltura nel territorio reggiano,
     1315–1450*, in Contributi-Rivista semestrale della biblioteca A. Panizzi di Reggio Emilia 1
     (1977): 8.
15   Feltrino Gonzaga, *signore* of Reggio prior to its acquisition by the Visconti in 1371.

since no other medical doctor would then be in this your city, and indeed it should not be expected at the present time that another will return.[16]

In spite of this dire prediction, within the next four years, the presence of at least three surgeons is attested in surviving records.[17] At least one of them was also receiving a public salary by 1373, and physicians were granted some tax exemptions. Physicians in Reggio also enjoyed a high social status, and municipal statutes allowed special honors at their funerals.[18] In return for their salaries, these men provided certain services to the city, including help with plague control, and they evaluated victims of violence for the criminal court.

Reggio Emilia was not alone in offering tax concessions to physicians, nor were the public duties and salaries of doctors at Reggio unusual. It was not uncommon for physicians in northern Italian cities to provide some service to the state. Guido Ruggiero equated the physicians of Venice with an incipient version of the public health officer, because, in return for a public salary, they offered free services to the public and advice to the city on plague control.[19] Physicians and medical professionals also, increasingly during the fourteenth century, aided the cities' efforts to control crime.

---

16   ASRe, *Comune*, Registri dei decreti, 1371–72, September 10, 1371. *"Item dignetur ob salute civium vestrorum et forensium habitantium et in civitate vestra prefacta providere quod Magister Paulus, Physicus, qui stetit octo annis elapsis salariatus a dicto Domino Feltrino in civitate predicta non recedat de prefacta civitate cum nullus alius medicus physicus sit in dictam vostram civitatem nec etiam expetietur de presenti aliquis reversurus."*

17   Magister Paulus, Physicus (ASRe, *Comune*, Registri dei decreti, 1371, 51v); the three surgeons are Magister Antonius de Cassinariis (ASRe, *Comune*, Registri dei decreti, December 1373); Nicoloxius Spander de Alamania, and Gabrielis de Medicis de Reggio (ASRe, *Giudiziario*, Libri delle denunzie, June 11, 1374.) The difference between physicians and surgeons was in their focus and usually their education: physicians typically attained a doctorate in internal medicine, while surgeons were concerned with external conditions. Surgery was offered at the universities and degrees could be taken in that field, but most surgeons learned their craft thorough apprenticeship. See Katharine Park, *Doctors and Medicine in Early Renaissance Florence* (Princeton: Princeton University Press, 1985), pp. 62–66.

18   ASRe, *Comune*, Statuti, 1392, 195r (compare with ASRe, *Comune*, Statuti, 1335, 99v–100r; compare also the later 1411 redaction, BSR mss. 77) *"Quod deffunctus non vestiatur nec portetur cum vultu discoperto nixi fuerit de genere potentium, vel iudex, vel medicus, vel eorum uxores et filii."*

19   Guido Ruggiero, "The Cooperation of Physicians and the State in the Control of Violence in Renaissance Venice," *JHMAS* 33 (1978): 156–66.

Medical Professionals and the Reporting of Crime

Amongst the most important public duties of medical professionals at Reggio and elsewhere was crime reporting. This requirement varied regionally, and not all city-states demanded such involvement: the late medieval Florentine statutes had no such requirement,[20] while at Venice, physicians were expected to act as informants to police powers. At Reggio Emilia, a statute requiring physicians to report injuries is lacking in the 1335 and 1392 redactions of the statutes but appears in the redaction of 1411:

> That doctors and surgeons are bound to denounce those whom they treat. Since it is in the public interest that crimes not remain unpunished, and it very often happens that many crimes are committed about which the Lord *Podestà* has no notice, it is ordained that any doctor, surgeon, and any other person who becomes involved in treating wounds, is bound and obligated under the penalty of twenty pounds *rexani* for each and every time, to denounce to the Lord *Podestà* or the Criminal Judge all those wounds or strikes which he treats on that day or on the following day that he begins treatment, if he is in the city, and if in the diocese or in the district, within five days, and that the Lord *Podestà* is obligated at the beginning of his office to warn all doctors, surgeons and apothecaries about the present statute, and to have from them an oath concerning the denunciation of those whom they treat.[21]

This statute clearly links doctors' obligations to the criminal court with the larger agenda of inquisitorial justice, which was to insure "that crimes not remain unpunished" (*ne ut maleficia non remaneant impunita*). This obviously echoes the similar maxim made famous by Innocent III's *Ut famae*, which

---

20   Park, *Doctors and Medicine in Early Renaissance Florence*, p. 96.
21   BSR mss.77, 67v–68r. "*Quod medici et barberii teneantur denunciare illos quos medicant. Quoniam rei publice interest ut malleficia non remaneant impunita et sepissime contingit quod multa malleficia committuntur de quibus Dominus Potestas nullam habeat noticiam statutum est quod quilibet medicus et barberius speciarius et quis alia persona que se impedit de medicando vulneratos teneatur et debeat sub pena librarum viginti rexanorum pro quolibet et qualibet vice denuntiare domino potestati vel iudici malleficorum omnes illos vulneratos sive percussos quos medicaverint ea die vel sequenti qua inceperint medicare si fuerint in civitate et si in episcopatu vel districtu infra quinque dies et quod dominus potestas teneatur in principio sui officii amonere omnes medicos barbarios et spiciarios de presenti statuto et eis sacramentum deffere de denunciato quoscumque medicaverint.*"

famously declared that punishing crime is in the public interest.[22] Not only does the statute require medical practitioners to report wounds, but also they must swear an oath that they will do so, demonstrating clearly the intention to use doctors as part of an effort to enforce public justice.[23] This insistence on denunciation from medical professionals echoes a municipal concern with the prosecution of crime. The obligation was not limited to the trained medical professional. The statutes require the intervention not only of doctors, but of anyone who treats wounds. Doctors, however, provided additional service to the cities as they supplied criminal judges with expert testimony and opinions.

Medical-legal *Consilia* in the Criminal Court

In addition to requiring denunciation of suspicious injuries, criminal judges also solicited learned opinions from physicians to aid in their cases. These learned opinions or *consilia*, referred to here as medical-legal *consilia*, are only one type of a genre of formal medical *consilia* that in general represent, as Jole Agrimi and Chiara Crisciani have remarked, the intersection between *magisterium* and *ministerium,* or between teaching and practice.[24] Some of the most important medical scholars of the period were also practitioners and authors

---

22   For a discussion of this maxim and its origins, see Richard Fraher, "The Theoretical Justification for the New Criminal Law of the High Middle Ages: 'Rei publicae interest, ne crimina remaneant impunita,'" *University of Illinois Law Review* (1984): 577–595, and more recently, Kenneth Pennington, "Innocent III and the *ius commune,*" in *Grundlagen des Rechts: Festschrift für Peter Landau zum 65. Geburtstag,* ed. Richard Helmholz, Paul Mikat, Jörg Müller, Michael Stolleis (Rechts- und Staatswissenschaftliche Veröffentlichungen der Görres-Gesell-schaft, NF 91; Paderborn: Verlag Ferdinand Schöningh, 2000), pp. 349–366. Pennington discusses an earlier decretal, the "*Inauditum,*" in which an incipient version of this maxim made famous in the later "*Ut famae*" was written. "*Ut famae*" has some significant differences from the earlier "*Inauditum*", including reference to the public "*crimina*" instead of the more general "*maleficia,*" which could also indicate a private wrong or a delict. It is interesting that here the author of the statute paralleled the wording of the "*Inauditum*" instead of the more famous "*Ut famae.*"

23   While the idea of public justice in medieval courts has been rightly questioned, the ideal of public justice as envisioned as early as 1215 was fundamentally important to juridical thought on criminal procedure. See Fraher, "The Theoretical Justification," 577–595. More generally, on the idea of public justice, see Massimo Vallerani, *La giustizia pubblica medievale.* On the development of criminal justice and the political uses of inquisition in this period, see Sarah Rubin Blanshei, *Politics and Justice in Late Medieval Bologna in Late Medieval Bologna* (Leiden: Brill, 2010).

24   Jole Agrimi and Chiara Crisciani, *Les 'Consilia' Médicaux,* trans. Caroline Viola (Turnhout: Brepols, 1994), p. 97.

of pragmatic *consilia*; for example, Taddeo Alderotti at Bologna, whose work engaged with some theoretical problems of natural philosophy, also authored *consilia*.[25] The ability to offer this kind of learned advice was limited to trained physicians. In the late Middle Ages, medicine was becoming increasingly professionalized, and the university statutes of Bologna explicitly forbade self-trained medical professionals to author *consilia*.[26] The ability to give *consilia* was becoming part of the definition of expertise,[27] and the medical-legal *consilium*, written at the request of the criminal court, allowed judges to draw on this expertise to aid their work.

Edgardo Ortalli, in his study of the development of Bolognese statutory law concerning medical-legal *consilia*, found the first solid indication of the use of medical-legal *consilia* in the 1288 redaction, though as he notes, the redactors of the statutes no doubt were codifying what was already a practice in criminal procedure.[28] Medical experts were selected by the *podestà* who, when the need arose, took the names of two physicians from a bag containing four names of doctors who met the requirements to serve as experts. At the beginning of the fourteenth century, he was required to do this in the presence of the *anziani* ("elders") of the commune, but by the end of the fourteenth century, that requirement disappeared, and the *podestà*, his deputy, or the criminal judge could make the selection.[29]

In practice, the same doctors' names appeared repeatedly in the pool of potential experts. In a sample of *consilia* dating between 1356 and 1360, Ortalli found the same four doctors appearing again and again.[30] Though these doctors clearly spent a good deal of their careers in the service of the court, it would be premature to see here a public office of medical examiner,[31] though

---

25   Nancy Siraisi, "Two Models of Medical Culture, Pietro d'Abano and Taddeo Alderotti," in her *Medicine and the Italian Universities, 150–1600* (Leiden: Brill, 2001), pp. 80–1.

26   Chiara Crisciani, "*Consilia*, responsi, consulti: I pareri del medico tra insegnamento e professione", in *Consilium: Teori e pratiche del consigliare nella cultura medieval*, ed. Carla Casagrande, Chiara Crisciani, and Silvana Vecchio (Florence: SISMEL, Edizione del Galluzzo, 2004), pp. 259–60.

27   Crisciani, "*Consilia, responsi, consulti*," p. 260.

28   Edgardo Ortalli, "La perizia medica a Bologna nei secoli XIII e XIV: Normative e pratica di un istituto Giudiziario," *Deputazione di storia patria per le province di Romagna: Atti e Memorie*, n.s. 17–19 (1969): 229.

29   Ortalli, "La perizia medica," 239–241.

30   Ortalli, "La perizia medica," 248.

31   Ortalli found that the *signore* of Bologna, Giovanni Visconti da Oleggio, had appointed particular physicians "*ad videndum vulneratos et mortuos tam in civitate quam in comitatu*

there was clearly a small core of physicians that the commune relied upon.[32] Of course, at Reggio Emilia, as discussed above, that core was necessarily small due to the very small number of medical professionals resident in the region.

The advice of these experts, and their "epistemologically weak but socially powerful" knowledge,[33] held strong influence in the criminal courts, and the ability to offer these opinions was a mark of status for the consulting physician. Medical-legal *consilia* have some characteristics that make them unique from other non-legal medical *consilia*. Medical *consilia* that were written for the use of doctors in treating disease described the patient, the symptoms and the disease, suggesting an appropriate regimen for the patient regarding such things as diet, exercise, rest, and prescribing medical treatments.[34] The medical-legal *consilium*, however, had an entirely different focus. Like other formal medical *consilia*, the medical-legal *consilia* aimed to "establish the truth of a situation requiring the judgment—*iudicium*—of a competent doctor."[35] However, medical-legal *consilia* were written not to prescribe care for the victim, but rather to evaluate formally the condition of the patient and to speculate on the causes of injuries, or to attempt to foresee their outcome. Medical-legal *consilia* were not concerned with cures or treatment: they addressed the needs of the criminal court, not the patient.

The use of formal medical advice in medieval Italian criminal courts has been the subject of some scholarly attention, particularly concerning evidence from Bologna and Venice, where such medical-legal *consilia* survive in

---

Bononie..." ("to see wounded and dead people, in the city as well as in the contada of Bologna.") Although the continuous appointment of the same physicians to these tasks would have undoubtedly monopolized a great deal of the doctors' career, and though this may have been the seed that would grow into a new public office, Ortalli notes that this was not yet the case. Ortalli, "La Perizia Medica," 253. After the return of the city to papal control in 1360, he found a greater variety of physicians again included in the pool of experts.

32   L. Münster, "La medicina legale in Bologna dai suoi albori alla fine del secolo XIV," *Bollettino dell'accademia medica pistoiese Filippo Pacini* 26 (1966): 271.

33   de Renzi, "Medical Expertise, Bodies and the Law," 322.

34   Crisciani, "*Consilia, responsi, consulti*," 263, and note 18. While certainly not every medical *consilium* followed this pattern, during the course of the late Middle Ages, the *consilia* acquired a more or less standard form. (Crisciani, "*Consilia, responsi, consulti*," 266.)

35   Agrimi and Crisciani, Les '*Consilia*' *Médicaux*, p. 35: "Pourtant, ce qui les distingue en premier lieu des *consilia* habituels, c'est qu'ils n'ont pas pour but de prescrire des thérapies mais d'établir la vérité sur une situation nécessitant l'avis—*iudicium*—d'un médecin compétent."

abundance.[36] In both places, doctors examined living patients to determine the extent of their injuries and their likelihood of recovery, and they also used early forensic methods to determine causes of death in murder victims, sometimes performing dissections and autopsy.[37] Medical-legal *consilia* were also part of judicial procedure in smaller towns near Bologna such as Imola and Forlì, though they grew in importance there later than in Bologna, and probably as a result of Bolognese influence.[38]

At Reggio Emilia, these *consilia* do not survive in large numbers and are only occasionally recorded in the *Libri delle denunzie*.[39] It is, therefore, difficult to know how often they were used. There was no statutory requirement at Reggio as there was at Bologna for the judge to consult with physicians. That these *consilia* were used in more cases than those in which they appear in the trial record is clear from their survival in documentary form in another *fondo*.[40] Records from Bologna and Venice would indicate that evidence from medical examinations was common practice by the fourteenth century, though its particular form and use differed regionally. At Reggio Emilia, these *consilia* were sometimes introduced during the phase of the inquisitorial criminal process that today would be recognized as the trial when witnesses testified before the judge. But they were used also during the investigative stage of the inquest, for which little documentation survives, and this may explain why they do not always appear in the trial record even when they survive in documentary form.

Formal medical-legal *consilia* submitted to the court give detailed accounts of the wounds suffered by victims, and often they offer an opinion on whether the injured parties were in danger of death. For example, in August of 1381 Johannes, son of Michiletus de Burrano, had a violent quarrel with Johanna, wife of Rubeus Signardi, during which he stabbed her six times, and she in turn struck him with a rock, though doing no serious injury. Johannes was cited but, like nearly half of the defendants in Reggio's criminal court, he failed to appear

---

36   Ruggiero, "The Cooperation of Physicians and the State"; E. Dall'Osso, *L'organizzazione medico-legale a Bologna e a Venezia nei secoli XII–XIV* (Cesena: Università di Bologna, 1956); Münster, "La medicina legale," 257–71; Ortalli, "La perizia medica."

37   Ortalli shows that medical-legal *consilia* were used in injury cases to help the judge fix a penalty appropriate to the case, and in homicide cases, physicians were necessary to determine the lethal wound. (Ortalli, "La perizia medica," 226). For autopsy and dissection, see also Shatzmiller, "The Jurisprudence of the Dead Body."

38   Ortalli, "La perizia medica," 225.

39   For example, in ASRe, *Giudizario*, Libri delle denunzie, June 11, 1374; June 2, 1389; August 20, 1389; February 4, 1393; October 8, 1393.

40   For example, in ASRe, *Giudiziario*, Atti e processi civili e criminali, October 16, 1381, and October 20, 1381.

to answer the charges against him.[41] Johanna also was charged in the same trial for the wound she gave him when she threw a rock at him, though no condemnation is recorded. Johanna was badly injured, and the opinion of a doctor was required to determine whether she was likely to die from these injuries.

The *consilium*, authored by a physician and a surgeon, was not included in the trial record, but it survives separate from the trial in documentary form:

> We, Master Ghibert de Baronzono, physician, and Gabriel de Medicis, surgeon, on account of a commission made to us by the wise and prudent Lord Bernardus de Costulla, deputy of the Lord Vicar and Criminal Judge of the Lord *Podestà* of Reggio, viewed Johanna, the wife of Rubeus Signardi de Gipso Crustini of the district of Reggio, struck on the left side and on the left arm in many places, leaving bruises but without shedding blood, and also she was struck on the left hand one time with an effusion of blood, by Johannes, son of Michiletus de Buranno, an inhabitant of the aforementioned land of Gypso, as was stated [in the charge made against him.] And since we have diligently inspected, examined, and considered these wounds, we declare and make it known that Johanna neither was nor is in danger of death on account of these wounds.
>
> I, Gibertus de Baranzono, Physician, sign here.
> I, Gabriel de Medici, Surgeon, sign here.
>
> [*In another hand*]
> 20 October, 1381.
> This document was produced before the above-written lord Bernardo, deputy, by the aforementioned Masters Gibertus, physician, and Gabriel, surgeon.[42]

---

41   On contumacy, its implications and its use as a proof, see Peter Raymond Pazzaglini, *The Criminal Ban of the Sienese Commune, 1225–1310* (Milan: Giuffrè, 1979), p. 22; Desiderio Cavalca, *Il bando nella prassi e nella dottrina giuridica medievale* (Milan: Giuffrè, 1978); Joanna Carraway, "Contumacy, Defense Strategy, and Criminal Law in Late Medieval Italy," *L&HR* 29.1 (2011): 99–132.

42   ASRe, *Giudizario*, Atti e processi, October 20, 1381. "*Nos Magistri Ghibertus de Baronzono, fisicus et Gabriel de Medicis, Ciroychus, ex commissione nobis facta per sapientem et discretum virum dominum Bernardum de Costulla, locum tenentum domini vicarii et iudicem maleficorum domini potestis Regii. Vidimus Johannam Uxorem Rubey Signardi de Gipso Crotoni districtus Regii percussem super latera sinixtra* [sic] *et super brachium sinixtrum in diversis partibus cum livido sine effuxione sanguinis et in manu sinixtra una percussione cum sanguinis effuxione per Johannum filium Michileti de Buranno habitatorem*

This document is typical of medical-legal *consilia* in that it was written at the request of the criminal judge to inventory wounds and to offer an opinion about the victim's likelihood of survival.[43]

Because both the *consilium* and the associated trial record survive, one can perhaps get a sense of where this *consilium* fit into the criminal process. The *consilium* predated the stage of the inquest that would today be considered the trial, where witnesses were called and deposed, and the notary did not record the *consilium* in the trial record, suggesting that medical-legal *consilia* were used more often than the records of the notary of the *iudex maleficorum* would indicate. The *consilium* itself was not evidence in the trial—that would have been unnecessary, as Johannes' contumacy was interpreted as an admission of guilt—but rather it was a tool for the judge to determine how to charge the suspect, who was ultimately placed under a criminal ban.

A similar use of the medical-legal *consilium* appears in a case from 1381, this time involving an armed fight between two men. On October 16, 1381, Bartolomeus and Franzischinus, both men from Cremona, had a violent quarrel, in which:

> Bartolomeus...hit and wounded the said Franzischinus with a knife which he held in his hands, [causing him] one wound in the neck with a great effusion of blood, and the aforementioned Franzischinus...hit and wounded Bartolomeus one wound above the right breast, with a great effusion of blood...[44]

---

dicte terre Gipsi ut dicitur. Et inspectis et diligenter examinatis et consideratis per nos dictis percussionibus per prenotis dicimus et firmiter indicamus dictam Johannam ob dictas percussiones non fuisse nec esse in periculo mortis. Ego Giberetus de Baranzono, Fisicus, me subscripsi; Et ego Gabriel de Medicis, Ciroychus, me subscripsi. Below and in another hand: *MCCCLXXXI die XX October. Productum fuit coram superscripto domino Bernardo locumtenento per superscriptos magistros Gibertum Fisicum et Gabriellem Ciroytum."* The trial survives in ASRe, *Giudizario*, Libri delle denunzie, August 26, 1381.

43   ASRe, *Giudizario*, Libri delle denunzie, August 26, 1381.

44   ASRe, *Giudizario*, Libri delle denunzie, October 16, 1381. "*... Quod dum predicti Bartolomeus et Franzischinus superius inquixiti simul habuissent verba predictus Bartolomeus mallo modo et ordine per eius superbiam et audaciam cum uno cultello pergomasco quem in suis tenebat manibus percusit et vulneravit dictum Franzischinum uno vulnere in gulla cum magna sanguinis effussione et predictus Franzischinus inquixitus malo modo et ordine ut super percusit et vulneravit cum uno lanzono quem habebat in suis manibus predictum Bartolomeum uno vulnere desuper mamilla dextra cum magna sanguinis effusione ..."*

Again, the medical *consilium* survives as a separate document and was not referenced in the trial record. On 15 October, the day before the men were formally charged in the inquisition, the opinion of Gabriel de Medicis was delivered to the *iudex maleficorum* concerning the wounds suffered by Bartolomeus. The document retains its seal and survives separate from the trial:

> The *consilium* of me, Gabriel de Medicis, Surgeon, concerning this matter: that I saw and treated Bartholomeus de Pisamoschis de Cremona, wounded, as it is said, by Franzischinus de Aspertis de Cremona, in the right part of the chest with one wound, with an effusion of blood, whence I say and counsel that the aforementioned Bartolomeus will be in good recovery and outside the danger of death, et cetera.

> And I, Gabriel de Medici, Surgeon, wrote this with my own hand.[45]

> [*In another hand:*]

> 1381, 15 October. The above-written *consilium* was produced before the aforementioned lord vicar and criminal judge by the said Master Gabriel, Surgeon.[46]

While the *consilium* itself is not dated, the notation above shows that it was presented to the judge on the fifteenth of October, the day before the trial began. As in the above example, the function of the *consilium* was to aid the judge in determining the severity of the charges. Bartolomeus recovered, as Gabriel predicted—he was apparently well enough to flee the area before he could be tried—and he, too, was ultimately banned for contumacy.

In a criminal justice system with a strict procedural order, medical-legal *consilia* did not have a determined procedural place at Reggio Emilia. Other

---

45   ASRe, *Giudizario*, Atti e processi, October 16, 1381. "*Conscilium mei Gabrielis de Medici Ciroytum super eo quod vidi et medicari Bartholameum de Pisamoschis de Cremona vulneratum per Francischinum de Aspertis de Cremona ut dicitur in parti destra pectoris uno vulnere cum sanguinis effuxione unde dico et consulo predictum Bartholameum fore in bona convalescacia et extra periculum mortis ex predicto vulnere et cetera. Et ego Gabriel de Medicis Ciroychus propria manu superscripsi.*"

46   ASRe, *Giudizario*, Atti e processi, October 16, 1381. "*MCCCLXXXI die 16 Octobris. Productum fuit superscriptum consilium coram praedicto Domino Vicario et Iudice maleficorum per superscriptum magistrum Gabriellem Ciroycum.*"

examples of these *consilia* show physicians appearing before the court to testify along with other witnesses, usually producing at that moment a written
consilium. Their appearance was intended to assure the judge that the victim
was expected to recover,[47] or to inform the court of any permanent effects the
victims might have sustained from their injuries. In one case, a report of a permanently debilitated hand was given to the court still later, after the accused
had already confessed, but before the parties swore their peace.[48] These *consilia*, then, could enter the trial at different stages, as early as the investigative
stage or as late as the sentencing stage.

The nature of surviving evidence makes it difficult to determine how often
medical-legal *consilia* were used in criminal cases at Reggio, and in what circumstances. Medical *consilia* unrelated to the courts, such as those intended
for education and for healing, are important sources for the exercise of the
medical profession, showing us the patients that interested doctors: most
often these patients were nobles, lawyers, notaries, and others of standing in
their communities; women and children of these classes are represented as
well.[49] But the medical-legal *consilia* often concern persons of lower classes.
The prestige for the physician or surgeon came not from the status of the
patient being treated, as Agrimi and Crisciani noted, but from his role as an
expert.[50] However, it is interesting to observe that at Reggio, of five cases with
medical-legal *consilia* mentioned in the record of the inquest—including that
of Franzischinus above—two[51] concern defendants who were later absolved
because of intervention by Regina della Scala, wife of Barnabò Visconti, who
administered Reggio Emilia from the time of its acquisition in 1371 until her
death in 1384.[52] It is possible that more material survives from cases where
political authorities took a personal interest. It is also possible that these
defendants, about whom we know nothing except the name, had political
importance and so their cases received particular attention.

At Reggio Emilia, physicians sometimes gave their *consilia* in writing and
sometimes appeared before the judge to give their findings verbally, and their
formal opinions were solicited as experts, just as the opinions of jurists were
sought in civil cases. They were not included in witness lists even when they

---

47   Examples include ASRe, *Giudizario*, Libri delle denunzie, October 8, 1393 and June 21,
      1389.
48   ASRe, *Giudizario*, Libri delle denunzie, Feb. 14, 1393.
49   Agrimi and Crisciani, *Les 'Consilia' Médicaux*, pp. 99–100.
50   Agrimi and Crisciani, *Les 'Consilia' Médicaux*, pp. 99–101.
51   Another example can be found in ASRe, *Giudizario*, Libri delle denunzie, June 11, 1374.
52   Grimaldi, *La signoria di Barnabò Visconti*, p. 86.

appeared before the judge during the trial to give their findings verbally, under-scoring the particular nature of their testimony as expert advice.

Post-mortem Examinations and Expert Opinions

In addition to giving formal learned opinions about the condition of living crime victims, physicians also participated in criminal cases by conducting autopsies and post-mortem examinations.[53] As a means of investigation in criminal proceedings, autopsy was probably first introduced in Bologna, and by the thirteenth century, Bolognese officials were ordering the examination of bodies.[54] In both Bologna and Venice in the fourteenth century, surgeons and barbers participated in post-mortem examinations of corpses that some-times involved dissection.[55] Medieval physicians examined the wounds of the dead by measuring the cuts and their depth with wax candles, their fingers, or other instruments, and sometimes by cutting away upper layers of flesh to determine the extent of damage to internal organs. Exhumation was likewise not unknown.[56] With this evidence, physicians could offer professional, expert opinions on causes of death to criminal judges.

Using medical-legal *consilia* in the criminal courts, however, opened the door to some difficult legal problems, particularly when at issue was a cause of death.[57] What if, in the case described by Durandus at the beginning of this essay, the defendant claimed that the doctors, who determined that the victim died from his wounds and not from fever, were false or had committed a fraud? Might the body, before burial, be shown to other medical experts? If these

---

53   Ortalli, "La perizia medica," 226. Ortalli shows that medical *consilia* were used in injury cases to help the judge fix a penalty appropriate to the case. He also claims that in homicide cases, physicians were necessary to determine the lethal wound. For autopsy and dissection, see Shatzmiller, "The Jurisprudence of the Dead Body," pp. 223–230.

54   Katharine Park, "Relics of a Fertile Heart: The 'Autopsy' of Clare of Montefalco," in *The Material Culture of Sex, Procreation and Marriage in Premodern Europe*, ed. Anne L. McClanan and Karen Rosoff Encarnaciòn (New York: Palgrave McMillian, 2002), p. 118.

55   Shatzmiller, "The Jurisprudence of the Dead Body," p. 229.

56   Medical opinions, whether delivered in the form of a certificate or given by a specialist during questioning, were in northern Italy and in southern France not considered testimony but were understood as expert opinions, much as legal *consilia* were admitted in the civil courts. Shatzmiller, "The Jurisprudence of the Dead Body," p. 244.

57   For a full discussion of the legal problems that the use of medical experts brought, and the subsequent discussion amongst the jurists, please see Mario Ascheri, "'Consilium sapientes,' perizia medica e 'res iudicata'."

other experts decided that the wound was not the cause of death, could the
sentence once rendered be overturned? Johannes Andreae took up exactly this
point in his *additio* to Durandus' text, as Mario Ascheri has discussed, relating
the problem of the false doctors to that of false witnesses or the introduction of
forged *instrumenta*.[58] The problem was seemingly endless, however, because
all medical experts testified to their belief and understanding of events that
could not be proven otherwise. They were not providing a full "truth," but only
their expert belief in what *must have happened* or what *will likely occur*, meaning first that their *consilia* could not be considered a full proof in the inquisitorial system, and second, that a second set of experts could be as right or wrong
as the first. Theoretically, the problem was enormous, as it had implications
also for the use of juridical *consilia sapientis*. In practice, this problem does
not appear to have been widespread in the courts at the end of the fourteenth
century.[59] However, the debate underscores the point that expert attestation
to medical fact was, like the *consilium sapientis*, solicited by the judge and for
his use to determine a right course of action, even if its admissibility as a proof
was ambiguous.

This concern with fraud clearly shaped the procedures used for medical-
legal *consilia* and post-mortem examinations. Even at Reggio, where there was
a relatively small number of medical professionals, the surviving examples of
medical-legal *consilia* often are signed by two doctors. The Bolognese statutes
required that two physicians, both over the age of thirty, who had been resident in their community for at least twenty years, should attend post-mortem
or physical examinations of crime victims, and further, they also required the
notary of the criminal judge to accompany them. The doctors were required
to report under oath to the *podestà* or one of his criminal judges how many
wounds they found, and of these how many were mortal and how many not,
and what kind of wounds they were. Their reports were to be accepted unless

---

58   "*Subdit etiam quod si iudex ad dictum medici dicentis vulnus Titii cum plures vulneraverunt
      fuisse mortalem condemnavit Titium de occiso, qui Titius dicens medicum falsum dixisse
      petit ante sepulturam peritiores medicos adhiberi. Quod factum est, et illi referent illius
      vulnus non fuisse mortale retractabitur sententia sicut dicitur de lata per testes falsos vel
      instrumenta, C. si ex falsis instrumentis l. Falsam, et l. finali ff. de re iudi. l. Divus, supra de
      exceptio. Cum venerabilis*," Johannes Andreae, *additio* ad v. Noscunt, text quoted in Ascheri,
      "Consilium sapientes*, perizia medica et *'res iudicata'*," p. 535 n.5. As Ascheri discusses, this
      problem received attention not least because of parallels to the use of juridical *consilia
      sapientis*.
59   The problem is discussed in Ascheri, "*'Consilium sapientes'*, perizia medica et *'res
      iudicata'*," pp. 539–41.

evidence could be produced to the contrary.[60] These post-mortem exams were to be performed the same day the report of a suspicious death was received, unless the injury and death occurred outside the city walls, in which case the doctors were sent to see the body of the murdered person within three days, before it was handed over for burial.[61]

In many cities, professional autopsies for the criminal court were carried out by learned physicians of some fame and note, including university professors, and again, the provision of expertise for the court could be a mark of status. The famous scholar and professor of medicine Ugo Benzi conducted autopsies while a professor of medicine at Padua. An anonymous writer, probably a notary for a criminal judge, records his participation in one such examination:

> On the eighth day of the month of February. An autopsy of a certain man from Bergamo, whom someone killed in order to rob him of his gold,[62] was made in a certain home near [the church of] St Luke in the territory of Padua by the excellent and exceptional Master Ugo of Siena, there appointed to morning lecture; and I was present, together with Magister Leonardo, appointed to lecture on surgery, and this was done in the settlement of Turicellis, and there he was buried at the same church of St Luke . . .[63]

---

60   ASB, *Statuti,* 1389 f.280r–v.

61   ASB, *Statuti,* 1389, f.280r–v.

62   The text reads literally, "who killed a certain man so that he might rob him of his gold" but this is almost certainly an error. As Lockwood suggests, the printed edition is problematic and the Latin text should probably read *"quem quidam occiderat"* for *"qui quendam occiderat"* (Lockwood, p. 188 n.59.)

63   The record of this autopsy is preserved in the anonymous printed appendix entitled *De Antidotis* of Bertapaglia's *Recollectae,* and is quoted in Dean Putnam Lockwood, *Ugo Benzi: Medieval Philosopher and Physician, 1376–1439* (Chicago: University of Chicago Press, 1951), p. 148, from the version printed in Guy de Chauliac, *Ars Chirurgica,* Venice 1546, fo. 299 verso, col. 2. *"Octava die mensis Februarii. Facta fuit anotomia* (sic) *de quodam viro Bergomensi qui quendam, ut ei subriperet aurum, occiderat, per Egregium et singularem doctorem Magistrum Ugonem de Senis ibi ordinarie ad lecturam deputatum de mane in quadam domo apud sanctum Lucam in terra Patavina: et ego huic interfui cum Magistro Leonardo deputato ad lecturam chirurgie & hoc actum in squadra de Turicellis: & inde sepultus fuit ad eandem ecclesiam sancti Lucae . . ."* As Lockwood noted, the author of the document is unknown but was likely the notary of the criminal judge. This would fit well with the picture painted in the Bolognese statutes, where two doctors and the notary were required to attend together.

In this case, two professors of medicine attended the autopsy. The post-mortem examinations themselves were conducted sometimes at the scene of a crime or in a nearby building, as above, where Ugo carried out the post-mortem in a home near the scene of the crime.

At Reggio Emilia, there is only indirect evidence of professional post-mortem examination. A physician's report on a cause of death is referenced in a document recording the torture of certain murder suspects who "came to the question" concerning the death of a man whom they hit in the back of the head with swords. The document describes the wounds inflicted on the victim, and asserts "on account of the aforementioned wounds, the said Peter was and is dead, and Magister Petrus, *medicus*, says that he is dead because of the aforesaid wounds."[64] However, there was no statutory requirement for professional post-mortem examination, and the extant records do not allow us to know how often physicians or surgeons were involved in such.

At Reggio, in cases of suspicious death, lay witnesses sometimes filled this need, as they had done a century earlier in Bologna, answering questions about the appearance of bodies and any obvious wounds they might bear. Their testimony could take the place of expert medical testimony. Instead of physicians' autopsies, the court at Reggio Emilia relied on the testimony of women who washed bodies for burial, of men who found bodies, and even of parents who demanded to see the bodies of their children, to know what killed them.

Murder Investigations and Lay Witnesses

Medieval criminal judges looked for answers wherever they believed they could best find them, and the use of lay witnesses to determine cause of death changed over time and by locale. In the thirteenth century in Bologna, determination of causes of death could involve an autopsy or professional opinion, or could be determined simply by witness testimony. For example, in the 1287 investigation of the death of Domina Belda Garisendi, a medical doctor testified that the dead woman died of apoplexy, while six women also testified that her death was natural.[65] In the same way, in 1285 when a body was discovered near the church of the Franciscan Minorites, the judge sent his own

---

64   ASRe, *Giudiziario*, Atti e processi, f.161, August 14, 1373, "... *pro quibus superscriptis feritis superscriptus Petrus mortuus fuit et est et magister Petrus Medicus dicit quod mortus est pro superscriptis feritis.*"

65   Blanshei, *Politics and Justice*, p. 340.

people to investigate the crime and interrogate witnesses, none of whom were physicians.[66]

In the fourteenth century, the use of professional medical examinations grew, and even exhumation was not unheard of. In Bologna, statutory requirements obliged judges to consult with physicians regarding issues like the mortality of wounds.[67] At Reggio Emilia, however, the testimony of these *laici testes* continued to be relied upon by the criminal judges to establish cause of death and to determine whether crimes had occurred. Two death investigations from late fourteenth-century Reggio will illustrate how lay witnesses established causes of death.

In 1382, on the Feast of the Nativity, Zanardus, a citizen of Albinea, a settlement in the district of Reggio, joined a group of men gambling in a tavern.[68] While playing with Guillelmus de Cremona, Zanardus lost 20 *solidi* that he did not have. Zanardus got up from the table, saying to Guillelmus, "The Lord Bishop will give me some money—I will go to him and bring you twenty *solidi*." He left the tavern to collect the money, but he never returned.

Almost two months later, on the fifteenth of February 1382, Boninsegna, son of Raynaldus de Zudeis, was walking from Albinea to another village when he saw in the distance a flock of crows descending from the sky. Boninsegna had seen many wild beasts dead on his walk and assumed at first that the crows had found another, but when he drew closer he perceived that the crows had found the body of a man. The unfortunate Boninsegna was "greatly disturbed, sad and afraid" at his discovery; when he drew closer and "recognized that the body or cadaver was that of a man ... at once he came to Albinea and there announced this thing to the consul of the land...."[69] The body was that of Zanardus.

Witness testimony from Zanardus's case shows how officials responded to the discovery of a corpse before the official inquest of the criminal judge began. The consul, or governor, of the town sent his own men out to examine the body and to guard it overnight, and then they carried it to the church the next day. The body was examined in the presence of the consul by many different men of the commune, none of whom were apparently medically trained.

---

66   Blanshei, *Politics and Justice*, p. 340.

67   Münster, "La medicina legale," 262.

68   ASRe, *Giudiziario*, Atti e processi, 1382, 22 February (f.427r–430r).

69   ASRe, *Giudiziario*, Atti e processi, 1382, 22 February (f.427r–430r). "... *et cum fuit ibi, cognovit quod erat corpus sive cadaver unius hominis quod videns turbatus mestus et timidus factus est et statim venit Albineam et hoc factum denunciavit consuli dicte terre...*"

On the twenty-second of that month, the criminal judge of Reggio Emilia began an inquest to determine the circumstances of Zanardus's demise.[70] The judge wanted to know whether anyone fled the commune immediately after his disappearance, and whether Zanardus had bad blood with anyone. This kind of circumstantial evidence played a major role in determining whether a death would be investigated as a murder, but the judge did not stop there. Though no professional post-mortem was apparently ordered, the judge still paid careful attention to the condition of the body and evidence surrounding it.

He questioned the man who found the body as well as locals who guarded and examined the body about the condition of the corpse. Boninsegna described his terrified run to the consul of the village to report the corpse. The judge asked Boninsegna "if he knew or had heard who killed Zanardus." No, Boninsegna responded, but all the men of the commune presumed that Zanardus had died of the cold, because he had left Albinea while he was very drunk, *opressus vino*. The judge also asked Boninsegna to make assumptions about the death of Zanardus based on his observation of the corpse: he asked whether the corpse had any wounds, and whether the clothes Zanardus was wearing were punctured in any place that would lead the witness to believe that Zanardus had met with foul play. The witness responded that he had viewed the body and that birds and animals, particular in the area of the chest, had eaten the corpse and that his clothing was not torn.[71]

The men who guarded the body and transported it to the church conducted their own manner of post-mortem examination, and the judge interrogated them as well. The witnesses agreed that there was damage to the area of the chest and the head, which they believed had been caused by birds and wild animals, and they noted that one of the dead man's ears had also been pecked away by birds. Other than those wounds, there were no punctures in the flesh, *perforati*. Just as physicians did in their reports, the men catalogued the damage to the body, finding that the head had six areas in which the flesh was eaten away. As one witness reported, "if he were wounded in another part of the head, they could not see that clearly, since the flesh was eaten away, but all that were present assumed that he had not been struck." That witness then stated the prevalent belief in the community about Zanardus's death: "that the

---

70   ASRe, *Giudiziario*, Atti e processi, February 22, 1382 (f.427r–430r).

71   ASRe, *Giudiziario*, Atti e processi, f. 427v. "*Interrogotus si vidit quod in pannis seu dicto corpore esse aliqua perforatio ex quo presumere possit quod fuerit mortus vel interfectus ab aliqua persona respondit quod no, et quod dictum corpus erat esus ab avibus et feris a forcella pectoris infra et quod ab inde super non erat perforatus nec panni perforati salvo quod una ex masillis et auriculis erat ab avibus pizate . . .*"

said Zanardus died from great cold, rather than by anything else, for this reason: since ... he was drunk when he left Albinea." The witnesses concluded, because of both physical and circumstantial evidence, that Zanardus had frozen to death while drunk. It appears that the judge accepted the findings of these lay witnesses—no record of a criminal proceeding survives.

On May 16, 1395, another body was discovered, this one also in suspicious circumstances.[72] In the Villa de Veto, in the district of Reggio Emilia, Caterina, daughter of Garofalus, was found dead in her home.[73] According to the witnesses, she clearly had been murdered, strangled with a halter. Two weeks later, on May 30, a series of witnesses were interrogated about Caterina's death. All were asked first what they generally knew about the death of Caterina. They were asked if they had seen the body, and if so, whether they could determine in what manner Caterina had died. They were also asked whether they suspected any particular person, and they were asked who had fled the territory.

The first witness was Garofalus, son of Johannetus de Veto, and the father of the victim. The judge asked him next if he suspected anyone in the death, and he responded that he suspected Antonius son of Cambonellus, of the Villa de Veto, because Antonius had often threatened Caterina, and often had beat her. The judge then asked if Garofalus thought he knew how Caterina died, to which Garofalus responded that the only possibility was that Antonius had killed her.[74] Why, the investigator inquired, was he so sure that her death was a murder?[75] "He responded that when Caterina was carried to the grave, he wished to see her nude body, and he did not find her struck or wounded in any place, but her flesh and skin was very bruised from her throat to her chest. ..."[76] The surviving records show that many of Caterina's neighbors viewed her corpse, and had opinions to offer to the judge. Beltraminus, son of Ricius, told the investigator that he also saw Caterina's body, and that: "[H]e saw a certain sign of a halter on Caterina's throat, and he heard it said that some women who dressed Caterina (for burial) found a halter on Caterina's bed."[77] The

72 ASRe, *Giudiziario*, Atti e processi, 30 May 1395.
73 ASRe, *Giudiziario*, Atti e processi, 30 May 1395.
74 *"Interrogatus si suspicatur qua mortua sit morte dicta Caterina. Respondit non suspicatur quod sit mortua alia morte nisi quod dictus eam nocaverit."*
75 *"Interrogatus quare est magis suspectionis necationis quam alterius mortis ..."*
76 ASRe, *Giudizario*, Atti e processi, May 30, 1395. *"... respondit quando dicta Caterina portabatur ad sepulcuram voluit eam videre nudam et non invenit eam percussam nec vulneratam in aliquo loco sed bene ipsam sanguinolentam inter carnem et pellem a gula usque ad pectus ipsius Caterine."*
77 ASRe, *Giudizario*, Atti e processi, May 30, 1395. *"Interrogatus si vidit dictam Caterinam, respondit quod sic. Et quod vidit quoddam signum cuiusdam capestri in gugure ipsius*

judge went on to interview some of these women. Domina Dominicha, wife of
Laurentius de Veto, told the judge that:

> [W]hen she went to see the dead woman on the following morning . . . she
> saw that it was Caterina that was dead . . . asked by what death it seemed
> that Caterina had died, she responded that she saw the marks of finger-
> nails on Caterina's throat, by which it seemed [to her] that Caterina was
> suffocated, and she saw there a certain halter in the hands of Caterina's
> mother, who said, 'With this halter, my daughter was suffocated.'[78]

Pedra, wife of Petrus de Veto, testified similarly, saying that she also saw the
signs of strangulation on Caterina's neck.

   This physical evidence alone was not all that interested the judge as he
investigated the death. He asked about common suspicions, whether anyone
had disappeared the night of the murder, and if there was a reason to suspect any particular individual. The evidence indicated murder; while the trial
record has been lost, a notation in a register of condemnations records that
Antonius was sentenced to execution in absentia.[79] His contumacy was a reasonable basis for conviction.

   As in Zanardus's case, rather than ordering an examination of the body, as
was common in other Italian cities, the judge relied on testimony of witnesses
who had viewed the body to determine the manner of her death and the nature
of her injuries. It was no small number of people that viewed the corpses;
one of the women in Caterina's case stated that she had gone to the house
where the body was discovered particularly to view the corpse. Zanardus was
inspected by at least five men, in the presence of the consul. Neither the judge
nor the consul ordered a medical expert to conduct an examination on their
behalf before the body was buried. The judge was content with the findings of
non-expert witnesses, and their observations about the state of the body, to
satisfy the question of whether murder had been committed.

Caterine et quod audivit dici a quibusdam mulieribus que induerant dictam Caterinam quod
invenerant unum capistrum a [. . .] leti ipsius Caterine."

78   ASRe, *Giudizario*, Atti e processi, May 30, 1395. ". . . *quod cum iret ad videndum dictam*
     mortuam in mane sequenti dixit quod vidit dictam Caterinam mortuam interrogotus
     qua morte videbatur dicta Caterina esse mortua respondit quod vidit duo signa duarum
     ungullarum sub guture dicte Caterine per que dicta Caterina videbatur esse suffocatai et
     quod ibi vidit quoddam capistrum in manibus matris dicte Caterine que dicebat cum isto
     capistro suffocata fuit filia mea."

79   ASRe, *Giudiziario*, Podestà, Giudici, Governatore: sentenze e condanne corporali e
     pecuniarie, reg.1 b.6 f.40r (erroneous 1394).

In Reggio it is clear that the criminal court conducted examinations about the causes of death through these *laici testes* (lay witnesses). Lay accounts of illnesses and death were fundamentally important in other circumstances, as Nancy Siraisi has pointed out: they are found in many genres including not only literary texts but also quasi-legal sources like saints' lives and canonization proceedings.[80] Certainly, laypeople frequently testified to observations of violent actions to help the judge establish the degree of violent action, for example, whether an injury was significant enough to draw blood, and if so, how much blood (the claim of an "effusion of blood" intensified the severity of a criminal charge). This kind of testimony is unremarkable: no medical expertise is required to know if a party is bleeding. The use of lay witnesses to give testimony on medical issues was common in medieval and early modern courts, as judges "would routinely seek specific expertise where general consensus placed it".[81] However, in death investigations, laypeople gave detailed and knowledgeable evidence about particular injuries and causes of death, and at Reggio, these witnesses could be central to suspicious death or murder investigations. While lay testimony to causes of death gradually gave way to expert opinion in other cities, at Reggio Emilia throughout the fourteenth century, lay witnesses continued to hold an important role even in these most serious of cases.

Conclusion

While the ability to give evidence about the body became increasingly professionalized during the fourteenth century, physicians did not displace the role of lay witnesses, and this was perhaps especially true in smaller places like Reggio that lacked a large professional class. Because evidence from the first half of the fourteenth century is lacking at Reggio, it is impossible to determine whether the city used forensic testimony more when times were more prosperous, before the depopulation that war and plague brought in the mid-fourteenth century. At the end of the century, judges still placed great credence in the observations of lay witnesses, who could be pivotal in death investigations. Expert forensic testimony developed first as a predictive, not descriptive, means of testifying to facts: medical doctors alone used their skills to predict outcomes of injuries, and over the course of the thirteenth and fourteenth

---

80   Nancy G. Siraisi, "Girolamo Cardano and the Art of Medical Narrative," *Journal of the History of Ideas* 52. 4 (1991): 582.

81   de Renzi, "Medical Expertise, Bodies and the Law in Early Modern Courts."

centuries, advising on these matters became their particular domain. But speculation about what had already happened, particularly regarding causes of death, continued to be accepted from lay witnesses.

Whether inspected by neighbors or scrutinized by physicians, expert examination of the bodies of living victims surely imposed a check on the sometimes inflammatory language of accusation, thereby assisting the judge in determining the severity of charges. Recourse to expert advice and medical-legal *consilia*, like the *consilia sapientis* of jurists on difficult legal points, may also have relieved the judge of responsibility for making determinations in unclear circumstances. Lacking an expert examination of wounds, the criminal judge was quick to use the tools at his disposal to determine causes of death in suspicious cases. No one group in the late Middle Ages could claim sole expertise in the deeply pragmatic but theoretically complex practice of discerning the secrets of the body. Testimony about the body of the crime victim, however, increasingly became the province of medical professionals, first in the case of living victims and later, in the case of the dead.

CHAPTER 6

Mental Health as a Foundation for Suit or an Excuse for Theft in Medieval English Legal Disputes

Wendy J. Turner

In the first half of the thirteenth century, in legal disputes—either concerning royal lands or in areas under common law—when a party happened to be mentally incompetent, the king or his proxy presided over the quarrel or case with mental competency, or lack thereof, in mind.[1] While the king and his representatives did not seek out mentally incompetent persons, the crown considered the care of mentally incompetent landholders to be part of royal jurisdiction; although, some lords still considered this responsibility to be part of their feudal duties with a right to income from those lands until the early fourteenth century. Late in the thirteenth century, the crown began to pay more attention to these potentially lucrative lands, claiming all mentally incompetent landholders as the prerogative of the crown. The importance of these guardianships of mentally disabled persons—as opposed to those of children for instance—was that they had the potential of lasting many years or decades.

From the mid-thirteenth century, the king controlled appointments of guardianship over mentally incapacitated individuals and their properties. In the last few years of the thirteenth century and certainly by the fourteenth century, the system for placing a mentally incapacitated landholder in

---

1   Many thanks for the generous support and access for the research of this article to Augusta State University (now Georgia Regents University), Hargrett Rare Book and Manuscript Library at the University of Georgia, The National Archive and Public Record Office, the British Library, and the Bodleian Library at Oxford University. For more information on medieval mental health issues, see: Margaret McGlynn, "Idiots, Lunatics, and the Royal Prerogative in Early Tudor England," *The Journal of Legal History* 26.1 (2005): 1–20; David Roffe and Christine Roffe, "Madness and Care in the Community: A medieval perspective," *British Medical Journal* 311. 7021 (1995): 1708–1712; Stephen Harper, *Insanity, Individuals, and Society in Late-Medieval English Literature: The Subject of Madness* (Lewiston, Queenston, Lampeter: The Edwin Mellen Press, 2003); Sylvia Huot, *Madness in Medieval French Literature: Identities Found and Lost* (Oxford: OUP, 2003); and W.J. Turner, *Care and Custody of the Mentally Ill, Incompetent, and Disabled in Medieval England*, Cursor Mundi 16 (Turnhout, Belgium: Brepols, 2013).

wardship was institutionalized via "statute."[2] Stemming from Roman law,[3] this system allowed for those persons born with their conditions to have the crown manage their properties for a fee, claiming all profit, and in exchange providing for the care of the mentally incompetent person. In the case of persons who became mentally incapacitated later in life, even as children, the crown exacted a fee for the guardian, but saved the profit for the disabled individual in the event that he or she got well. The king often placed relatives in the position of guardian, especially in cases of people who became mentally disabled as adults. This seems to be in part for the comfort of the mentally disabled individual and to wrap as much of the wealth from the land back into the family.[4]

---

2   The so-called *Prerogativa Regis* claimed custody of all mentally incapacitated landholders as the responsibility of the crown. For example, John Heton became a royal ward in 1355 "pursuant to the statute." This phrase was not uncommon in records at the end of the thirteenth century and was still in use in the mid-fourteenth century. TNA: PRO C 66/245, m 13; CPR, Edward III, 1354–1358, pp. 200–01. The *Prerogativa Regis*, though, does not read like a statute. I have argued elsewhere that this announcement—a summary of particular royal entitlements that includes mentally incapacitated landholders in chapters 11 and 12—from Parliament or Great Council probably came around the time of Henry III's death while Edward I was still out of the country. *Prerogativa Regis* in A. Luders, T.E. Tomlins, J. France, W.E. Taunton, and J. Raithby, eds., *Statutes of the Realm* (London, Dawsons of Pall, Mall, repr. 1963), v. 1. See also Turner, *Care and Custody*, ch. 2.

3   Margaret Trenchard-Smith, "Perceptions of Unreason in the Byzantine Empire to the End of the First Millennium," (Ph.D. Diss., University of California Los Angeles, 2006), p. 92; W.J. Turner, "Defining Mental Afflictions in Medieval English Administrative Records," in *Disability and Medieval Law: History, Literature, Society*, ed. Cory James Rushton (Newcastle upon Tyne, England: Cambridge Scholars Publishing, 2013); and R.H. Helmholz, *Canon Law and the Law of England* (London: The Hambledon Press, 1987), ch. 12, but especially pp. 215, 219–20. See also Henry de Bracton, *De Legibus et Consuetudinibus Angliae*, ed. George E. Woodbine,trans. Samuel E. Thorne, 4 vols., (Cambridge, MA: Belknap Press, 1968–1977), v. 2, p. 61 (f. 15); and v. 4, p. 36 (f. 323b).

4   Landholders needed the income from the land to support their families and, if a landholder was mentally incompetent from birth, it was likely that he would not produce an heir. If a family wanted a line to continue, someone else needed to procreate within the bloodline and the most likely individual was the next heir in line for the land. For more information see: W.J. Turner, "Town and Country: A Comparison of the Treatment of the Mentally Disabled in Late Medieval English Common Law and Chartered Boroughs," in *Madness in Medieval Law and Custom*, ed. Turner (Leiden and Boston: Brill, 2010), pp. 17–38; Donald W. Sutherland, "Peytevin v. La Lynde," *Law Quarterly Review* 83 (1967): 527–546; W.J. Turner, "Mental Incapacity and Financing War in Medieval England," in *The Hundred Years War, Part II: Different Vistas*, ed. Villalon & Kagay (Leiden and Boston: Brill, 2008), pp. 387–402; and C.F. Goodey, *A History of Intelligence and 'Intellectual Disability': The Shaping of Psychology in Early Modern Europe* (Farnham, Surrey & Burlington, VT: Ashgate, 2011), p. 142.

In both cases of those born with mental health incompetency and those who became mentally incapacitated, the crown profited from the fee and protected the land from abuse or degradation. Guardians were not allowed to "waste" a ward's property; nevertheless, since the crown used these guardianships at times in lieu of payments for royal debts, if the guardian did not feel he was getting his payment in full or fast enough, he might strip the property of value—illegal or not—in order to "find" the money. Other persons noticed mentally incapacitated individuals with property, especially if female, and upon their inheritance, married them, coerced them into selling their property, stole movable goods, squatted on the land, or otherwise abused the person physically or financially. Guardians were not always the good Samaritans they were intended to be, though they did keep the incapacitated individual alive and often well in order to continue to get the income from lands. Family members and neighbors could be just as bad or worse as they scrambled to figure a legal way to disinherit the local person with mental health issues. All in all, medieval English persons viewed those with intellectual disadvantage, incompetence, mental incapacity, or other mental health issues as easy prey, going around the law or using the law to appropriate, skim, or cheat these incapacitated property owners.

Wardship of Mentally Incompetent Landholders

Wardship evolved out of the theoretical justification of succession to military fiefs. Mostly the system of wardship had lords protecting and training underage heirs to feudal property. The lord was to train the heir to become a good vassal, marry him or her to a friend rather than a foe. As H.E. Bell writes:

> The heir to a tenant by knight service, even though he was of full age, only succeeded to his inheritance upon paying the lord a relief for it; if he was not of full age, the lord had the rents and profits of the land in the intervening period and the wardship of the heir's body—the right, that is, to bring him up in such a way that he would become a worthy tenant.[5]

In the case of someone with a mental health condition, who could not perform knight service and who was considered to be mentally "underage," the wardship

---

5   H.E. Bell, *An Introduction to the History and Records of the Court of Wards & Liveries* (Cambridge: CUP, 1953), p. 1.

continued throughout the heir's life unless he or she had times of lucid thought, at which times he or she could seek independence in court.[6]

Escheators, the main royal officials investigating lands and inheritances, regularly examined an heir's mental state before turning over property to him or her.[7] If the escheator had questions about the individual's mental health, he would either test the person's level of competency himself or send the individual to the king's council for examination. If the person's mental state remained in question, or it was determined to be such that the person or property could benefit from having a guardian, the escheator confiscated his or her property—even those from previous land transactions—until such time that the crown could assign a guardian to this new ward of the crown. This system of investigation and wardship continued until the late fifteenth century when first Henry VII's Council Learned in the Law, then in the first years of the sixteenth century the Court of Wards began to dominate this process.[8] In boroughs with charter from the crown to make their own laws, in the fifteenth century more wills began to state that heirs with mental health concerns ought to be bypassed.[9]

For the two-hundred-and-fifty-year period of wardship of the mentally incapacitated (c. 1250 to 1500), the crown chose guardians for those mentally incapacitated landholders that came to their condition after the age of about seven from among their family members. Those born with a mental health condition or who became mentally incapacitated so early no one was certain whether they were born with the condition or not, were place in the care of either family or others whom the crown chose, sometimes because they were owed a debt. The difference is also exaggerated depending on the size and scope of an estate. Those persons with many properties and manors in several counties invariably had several guardians, often with both family and non-family

6 Bell, *An Introduction*, pp. 1–4 and 128–9.

7 For example: Agnes Prat was "found by examination to be a fatuous idiot and not of sane mind...from the time of her birth (*fatui idiota & non sane mentis...a nativitate sue*)" in TNA: PRO C 136/40, m 4; Bartholomew Saukeville was examined and found "to exist from the time of his birth as a fatuous and idiotic person (*fatuus & idiota existit...a tempe nativitatis*)" in TNA: PRO C 134/13, m 1; and Roger Stanlake upon examination was found "not to be an idiot (*non idiota*)" in TNA: PRO C 135/235, m 13. Most of the time it was either the sheriff or the escheator who examined these individuals; though, Edward II used commissioners rather than escheators to investigate land issues other than escheated land.

8 Bell, *An Introduction*, pp. 4–5.

9 Mary Bateson, ed., *Borough Customs* (Selden Society, vols. 18, 21, 1904–6), v. 2, p. 150; and Turner, "Town and Country," pp. 17–38.

caring for landholdings, peasant occupants, buildings, official appointments to church offices, and moveable goods.

The system worked fairly well, but there was abuse. Some guardians, family members, neighbors, or others grew their wealth by exploiting the vulnerability of mentally incapacitated landholders. Guardians used the questionable state of mental incapacity to sue on behalf of a mentally incapacitated individual—feigning coercion of the ward by others—or against mentally disabled landholders—claiming wrongful land transactions by wards during mental incapacity. Some guardians tricked mentally incapacitated persons into giving away their lands and signing over documents to "prove" that the guardian was the new owner. For three centuries, people took advantage of mental incompetence as an excuse to find ways around the law or to use the law in an effort to steal from, abuse, or deceive mentally incompetent relatives, neighbors, and wards.

There are a few instances in which the king chose another heir rather than using the system of guardians. In some of those cases, there was such abuse by relatives that the king gave the property of the mentally incompetent persons to his wife or son, rather than have the abuse to the individual or property continue. In two international cases, the lands in question were in Ireland or Scotland, not England. The Irish example concerned the lands of Maurice Fitz Thomas of Ireland, who died in 1359. His eldest son, Nicholas, inherited and was found an "idiot" (*idiocie Nichi[las]*). Edward III gave Nicholas's younger brother, Maurice, the wardship, but Maurice died. Instead of another wardship, Edward next gave Nicholas's property to Gerald, the youngest brother of Nicholas, "in consideration of the probity, sense and virtues which flourish in [him, Gerald]," so long as he provided care for Nicholas, his older brother.[10] The case involving Scottish lands was quite the reverse. Ralph Lasceles "an idiot" (*ydiota*), inherited his father's property in Scotland in 1305. In this case, the king assigned William Vavassour as guardian. Both Ralph's brother and his lord tried to get around English law, since they were in Scotland, but the king used the law of England for the English family rather than the laws of Scotland.[11] In these two cases, it was the international aspect that made the change in normal procedure possible, but the same happened in wholly English cases upon rare occasion as well. For example, John Brewes, discussed in more detail below, had three guardians since he had lands in three counties Surrey, Somerset, and

---

10   TNA: PRO C 66/257, m 19; and CPR 1358–1361, p. 246 (20 July 1359).

11   PROME: "Edward I," petitions, v. 1; roll 12, (vii–225) 419 (390); and Roll 12, 427 (397). For the original see TNA: PRO C 47/22/9, no. 126. See also John Hudson, *Land, Law, and Lordship in Anglo-Norman England* (Oxford: Clarendon Press, 1994), p. 126.

Lincoln. One of his guardians stripped the lands and churches under his control of value. The crown decided that the condition of John's wife and children was so poor that John's wife should have some of the income directly, without interference from his guardians.[12]

Some individuals of low intellectual capacity were quite capable of handling some responsibilities; yet, those individuals who could not carry out the responsibilities associated with property—often including knighthood—found themselves at the mercy of the crown. The Exchequer claimed it was the crown's duty to ensure that only those persons who were truly incompetent were treated as such; to that end, a test for competence evolved out of early trials. Though not called such, the "test" covered the three basic areas of medieval competence: perception, cognition, and memory. Persons tested were asked to perform common tasks and about other things that they should know, all involving these same three measures of competence. For example, the escheator went to question Thomas Genestede in May 1342, but "did not find him in his bailiwick." The escheator "took an inquisition concerning the state of the said Thomas" from his relatives and friends while "in the neighborhood of Westgrenestede," finding Thomas of unsound mind.[13] In October the escheator returned and questioned Thomas in person, having him do several tasks, including "counting money, measuring cloth, and doing all other things."[14] The escheator now found Thomas of "good mind and sane memory."[15] Such interrogations might include asking an individual to name his parents, his age and place of birth, and where he was and why he was there.[16] Emma Beston was asked to name the days of the week, to list the names of her children and other relatives, to explain where they were and why, to explain which

---

12   TNA: PRO: C 66/268, m 20. See also *CPR*, Edward III (1361–1364), p. 416.

13   CIPM, v. 8, no. 340.

14   TNA: PRO C 135/63, m 8; and CIPM, v. 8, no. 284.

15   CIPM, v. 8, no. 284.

16   Anthony Fitzherbert in the sixteenth century writes, "And he who shall be said to be a Sot and Idiot from his birth, is such a person, who cannot accompt or number twenty pence, nor can tell who was his Father, or Mother, nor how old he is, &c. so as it may appear, that his hath no understanding of reason what shall be for his profit, or what for his loss: But if he have such understanding, that he know and understand his letters, and to read by teaching or information of another man, then is seemeth he is not a Sot, nor a natural Idiot." Quote from *The New Natura Brevium,* reprint [London: W. Lee, M. Walbank, D. Pakeman, and G. Bedell, 1652], p. 583. H.E. Bell (see note above) takes this for a medieval concept, and, though based in medieval common law, the questions were in constant flux, and although the practice was continuous, it seems to have been inconsistently applied.

was more valuable copper or silver,[17] and other questions of this type. As in the case of Thomas Grenestede, sometimes persons accused of being incompetent were unavailable for a hearing for one reason or another. In those cases, the king or his representative relied on testimony from neighbors or friends. John Lyndhirst could not be found when the escheator came to investigate his alleged incompetence. The escheator learned that the bailiff and the parson of the church took John "outside the bailiwick." According to testimony from the bailiff and the parson, John had "been an idiot from his birth, and still is."[18]

There are many examples of relatives, friends, and neighbors trying to steal property that rightfully belonged to a mentally incompetent landholder. The potential benefit must have outweighed the fines for abuse or false claims because time and again relatives exploited the same mechanisms to appropriate property illegally: misrepresenting the ownership of the property, misuse of law because of mental incapacity, squatting on the property, posing as a guardian, hiding heirs, or suing them in one way or another. They used the obliviousness of the mentally incompetent person and sometimes the temporary state of the mental illness to embezzle property, goods, and inheritances of all kinds from those who could not defend themselves.

Misuse of Law because of Mental Incapacity

The English kings and their representatives—justices, sheriffs, escheators, or commissioners—judged over the competence of heirs and other persons brought to their attention. Henry III, travelling with the royal court in the early thirteenth century, fined petitioners trying to take advantage of incapacitated relatives. For example, in 1248 two sisters along with their husbands and their nephew claimed that their brother, Roger Blik, had given away their inheritance. The dispute was that Roger had been "mentally incapacitated" (*non fuit compos mentis sue*)[19] when he gave a messuage of land to the local chaplain. As his heirs, the sisters found this loss distressing. Yet, when the jury investigated the matter, they found that Roger "was of good memory and sound mind" (*fuit bone memorie et compos mentis sue*)[20] at the time he made the gift to the chaplain; although, the record implies, Roger was not of sound mind

---

17   Emma Beston. TNA: PRO C 45/228, no. 10. See also CIM, v. 4, no. 227.

18   TNA: PRO C 135/67, m 12.1–3; CIPM v. 8, no. 404 (p. 277).

19   M.T. Clanchy, ed., *The Roll and Writ File of the Berkshire Eyre of 1248* (Selden Society v. 90, 1973), pp. 186–7, no. 440.

20   *Berkshire Eyre of 1248*, pp. 186–7, no. 440.

when his sisters' initiated their suit. The investigation, based on the testimony of neighbors, friends, and perhaps other relatives, turned up enough evidence supporting Roger's competence at the time of the legal transaction that the gift stood.[21] It seems Roger's heirs tried to reverse the gift after he became mentally incapacitated. They were found in mercy for a false claim since they grasped at properties that he had given away or sold during his lifetime.[22]

There were other ways to claim property, rather than simply asserting that an incapacitated individual made a legal transaction while out of his mind. Mental incapacity could be used as a convenient way to "forget" who owned what; either by giving it to another member of the family or selling it for a profit. In another 1248 case, for example, two half brothers came to court in dispute over the property of their mutual mother, Alice Gaudi. In the trial, the first brother, John, said that Alice had "not [been] of sound mind" (*non fuit compos mentis sue*)[23] at the time she demised lands to her other son, Reynold. In anticipation of questions of this nature, years before Reynold and his mother drew up a charter and had it enrolled. Reynold's claim that Alice enfeoffed him when she was "of sound mind and good memory" (*quando fuit compos mentis sue et bone memorie*)[24] could be verified, and he produced the charter. Persons without sound mental health could not engage in land transactions, licenses, or charters of any kind, and the enrolment could only have been made if the judge, jury, escheator, or other official found all parties to be of sound mind. Therefore, Alice had to have been sane when she gave the lands to her son Reynold, and the court agreed that he should continue to hold the land.

The same point was made earlier in 1279 in a case before the King's Bench. Prior to 1279, Richard de Umfraville quitclaimed some of his property to Gilbert de Umfraville and William of Swinburn. When Richard became mentally incapacitated in 1279, the sheriff confiscated all of his lands, even those earlier quitclaimed, into the king's hand. Gilbert and William had to plead in court to get the lands restored to them, arguing that he had earlier paid a fine "before such wise men, the justices of the bench, who well knew how to weigh up if the same Richard was in his right mind or not. [...] Gilbert asks if the country can lie against the record of the justices."[25] In other words, Gilbert wanted the court to trust the earlier justices who made the initial decision when Richard was

---

21   *Berkshire Eyre of 1248*, pp. 186–7, no. 440.
22   Hudson, *Land, Law, and Lordship*, p. 126.
23   *Berkshire Eyre of 1248*, p. 105, no. 237.
24   *Berkshire Eyre of 1248*, p. 105, no. 237.
25   G.O. Sayles, ed., *Selected Cases in the Court of King's Bench, Edward I* (Selden Society, v. 55, 1936), p. 50.

sane and perfectly capable of making such legal transactions. "If either of the parties was under age or an idiot,"[26] the court could not have allowed the transaction to be completed. Gilbert won his case and that of William. Unlike John who battled in court against his brother Reynold, these men fought against the crown. The difference is that the crown, or the sheriff as the representative for the crown, wished to disadvantage them for the sake of the crown's wealth; whereas, Reynold tried to disinherit his brother for his own ends.

Stealing Property from Mentally Disabled Persons

It was not always an inheritance of land or a land transaction that was called into question once the crown or family found one of the parties involved to be mentally incapacitated. Neighbors, friends, relatives, guardians, and the king, overtly stole lands from the mentally disabled. One startling example from 1392 involved Maud, Benet Marlecomb's daughter and heir, who was "a complete idiot, and has been since birth." The escheator found that, "[t]he said Benet died seized in his demesne."

> After his death came a certain John Preyng, who straightway caused a charter to be fraudulently drawn up, and sealed it with the dead hand of the deceased, whereby the premises were named to him and his heirs and assigns. Shortly afterwards he sold the premises to Roger Aysford and his heirs. Roger sold them to Robert Courtenay and his heirs, and Robert to John Chepman of Honyton and his heirs. John Chepman now occupies them.[27]

At a guess, John Preyng hoped that his ruse would never be discovered. The daughter and heir had a congenital condition, and once John had the false deed, she would not have understood what had happened. John immediately sold the property. The new owner, Roger Aysford, might or might not have known of the fake documentation. It is interesting that he also sold the lands and the next owner sold them again, as if all of them knew that these were properties that rightly belonged to Maud Marlecomb.

Presumably, the crown would have appointed Maud a responsible guardian to look after her welfare and protect her inheritance. Yet, even guardians at times found the temptation of an unknowing ward too great to resist A

---

26   *Court of King's Bench, Edward I*, pp. 49–50.
27   CIPM v. 17, no. 147 and TNA: PRO C 136/74, m 4.

good example of a ward whose guardian tried to steal his property is that of
John Pane, heir of Robert and Joan Pane. Like Maud, John was "an idiot from
his birth" (*idiota a nativitate sua*)[28] and, as such, was vulnerable. The crown
assigned John's wardship to Thomas Moigne, knight, in payment for a royal
debt owed to Thomas. In exchange, Thomas agreed to protect John Pane's person and property, finding "the heir fit sustenance in food and raiment and support all charges on the premises."[29] Thomas, who seems not to have found the
terms of his fee for maintaining the property satisfactory, tried to steal John's
lands using a creative legal loophole.

When Thomas Moigne first tried to take possession of the property as John's
guardian, he found others already residing on John's property. Apparently, John
had given his estate to another party,[30] leaving Thomas without the income the
crown had promised. Thomas had to wait until the court could decide whether
the new holders had come into the property before or after John became mentally incapacitated. Perhaps John had a lucid interval and had been mentally
healthy when he granted the other party his lands. Whatever the case, Thomas
had to wait—years—for the court to make a decision, and he seems to have
concocted a plan to get what he could from John and the crown. Thomas
finally gained control of the property legally as John's guardian in February of
1363, yet Thomas died later that year in the autumn[31] and that appeared to the
crown and the executors to be the end of the story. This was not the case. In the
one year Thomas had control of the lands, he had created a legal nightmare.

John's extensive estates—including the manor of Laurton by Frome
[Somerset.], the manor of Pomeknoll (or Pounknolle) [Dorset.], and the ecclesiastical office at the church at Pomeknoll—had not generated enough income
to pay the debt owed Thomas. His executors, therefore, exacted payments out
of the lands. The king sent a commission in November of the following year,
when accusations surfaced that Thomas had "wasted" John's lands. The commission found the executors had "driven out the men and tenants thereof, to
the king's damage of 40*l.* and the manifest derision of the said John and his
heirs."[32] Yet, something did not seem right as more accusations against Thomas
surfaced. The commission continued to ask questions and found that Thomas
had given Peter Whette the property in fee, "whom he afterwards caused to

28   TNA: PRO C66/265, m 25 and CPR 1361–1364, p. 171 (15 Mar. 1361).
29   TNA: PRO C66/265, m 25 and CPR 1361–1364, p. 171 (15 Mar. 1361).
30   TNA: PRO C66/265, m 31d and CPR 1361–1364, p. 206 (12 Feb. 1362).
31   TNA: PRO C66/267, m 28 and CPR 1361–1364, p. 318 (22 Feb. 1363).
32   TNA: PRO C145/188, m 12 and CIM v. 3, no. 552.

refeoff him [Thomas] thereof of the inheritance of the said idiot."[33] Thomas charged the tenants the compulsory fee of 6s. 8d. for being their "new" land-lord, as had presumably Peter Whette. Stephen Ledebury, who next held the lands, used the excuse that he had a right to the land. Stephen also "refeoffed" the property to Thomas, and Thomas charged the tenants the fee. Eventually, the crown recovered the rents and damages from the executors and trans-ferred the wardship of John Pane to John Pays.[34] Thomas Moigne tried to exact the money the crown owed him out of John's tenants and, it seems, that Thomas might also have been trying to confuse the legal status of the lands such that he would end up with the estate.[35]

Other guardians invented creative methods for stealing property from men-tally disabled wards. John Estbury tried to misappropriate the lands of his ward, Joan Wantyng. Joan's family took care of her while she was young. She was born with mental incompetency, and when her brother died, Joan, "who is of the age of twenty-one years and more,"[36] became heiress to a handsome estate.[37] In 1362, John Estbury, an escheator in Berkshire, took care of Joan and her property for a short time until the crown could appoint a more permanent guardian. It was common for a sheriff or escheator temporarily to take into the king's keeping the lands of a ward of the crown. After this initial year, the king's yeoman, Walter Wyght, took over as guardian of Joan.[38] Over the next decade, Joan became heir to other properties as her nearest relatives died off. Uncles and cousins such as John Wantyng and William Harpenden devised her lands in the counties of Berkshire and Wiltshire. At some point, William de Monte Acuto, earl of Salisbury, replaced Walter Wyght as Joan's guardian. The earl gave Joan into the care of Thomas Wynterborn.[39] The following year, John Estbury confronted Wyght, wielding a "king's license to acquire the premises from [Joan]," who had sold her properties to him. This seemed odd to everyone involved, and Joan was re-examined for competency by the royal justices, John Cavendish and Thomas Ingelby, who both agreed that she was "an idiot, [and]

---

33   TNA: PRO C145/188, m 12.

34   TNA: PRO C66/268, m 4, m 9 and CPR 1361–1364, pp. 438 and 430. See also TNA: PRO C66/271, m 17 and CPR 1364–1367, p. 111 (10 May 1365).

35   TNA: PRO C66/268, m 27d, m 9, m 4. See also CPR 1361–1364, p. 448 (1 Nov. 1363).

36   TNA: PRO C66/265, m 14 and CPR 1361–1364, p. 186 (20 March 1362).

37   TNA: PRO C 54/212, m 29; C 60/195, m 9; C 66/265, m 14; C 66/267, m 14; C 66/289, m 5; C 66/290, m 26; C 135/165, m 21b; C 136/73, m 13. See also: CCR, 1374–1377, p. 4; CFR, v. 11, p. 41; CIPM v. 11, no. 219; CIPM v. 17, no. 136; CPR 1361–1364, pp. 186, 340; CPR 1370–1374, pp. 379, 418–9.

38   TNA: PRO C66/267, m 14 and CPR 1361–1364, p. 340 (6 April 1363).

39   TNA: PRO C66/289, m 5 and CPR 1370–1374, p. 379 (14 Dec. 1373).

alienations by her made will be of no worth."[40] What was John doing back in her life over ten years later?

After a thorough investigation, the inquisition concluded that Walter Wyght, Joan's original guardian, "sold" the guardianship to John Estbury. John lied to the crown about Joan's mental health in obtaining the license: "the king being uninformed by him then of her idiocy."[41] Each time Joan inherited more property, John paid Joan's fine to turn her property over to him, his wife, and his son, as if acting on the behalf of a sane person, when in reality Joan was "incapable of managing her affairs."[42] When the last property came to her from her relative Thomas Wynterburn, she was re-examined and John's "trespass, deception and contempt" discovered. The crown found Joan a new guardian, another relative, Thomas Goioun,[43] and the king pardoned John.

Stealing Movable Goods from Mentally Disabled Persons

Rather than stealing land, some guardians, relatives, or neighbors took or sold moveable property off the lands of mentally incapacitated landholders. A few even stripped churches of everything of value. Norman Swynford, a relative by marriage to John Brewes, sold off "several ecclesiastical ornaments given by the said lords to remain there [the chapel of Lee manor] for ever, *viz.* a chalice, price 13s. 4d.; a vestment entire price 30s.; a cross of gold and silver, price 10l. There were also in the said chapel divers relics, a hand of St Stephen, and a bell called "Mungowbelle", and divers other relics"[44] from the chapel on John's estate. John had an intermittent condition, but was unaware of this theft until after the death of his mother.

Norman simply gathered up movable items and sold them off. In other cases, relatives or guardians worked hard to collect on the goods of mentally incapacitated persons by cutting trees, taking down buildings, or cashing in crops. For example, when William Staynford died, leaving his mentally incompetent brother John as heir, John Gisburn of York "straightway after the death of William cut down 100 oaks worth 100s. in the said wood."[45] Together with John Coplay of Farnehill, John Gisburn also kept all income from the

---

40   TNA: PRO C54/212, m 29 and CCR 1374–1377, p. 4 (1 Feb. 1374).

41   CPR 1370–1374, pp. 418–9.

42   CPR 1370–1374, pp. 418–419.

43   TNA: PRO C66/290, m 26 and CPR 1370–1374, p. 418–419 (26 Feb. 1374).

44   CIPM, v. 10, no. 211.

45   TNA: PRO C 145/233, no. 9b and CIM v. 4, no. 284.

property until the escheator discovered them and took John Staynford and his properties under the king's protections. The oaks were already gone, though, and not replaceable. In another example, "Geoffrey Felyngdon, chaplain of St Albans... knocked down, took and carried off from the messuage, without the king's license and to the king's annual loss of 10s, a building made for John Bertelot worth 30s."[46] John Bertelot was mentally incompetent. Either church officials were as eager to steal as other guardians or they were mistaken in thinking they had rights to property that was promised or provisionally granted. Who knows what Geoffrey was thinking? In a similar example, the "last abbot and the present one and their convent have taken the profits [from the lands of Hugh Draper, a mentally incapacitated individual] ever since their acquisition of the land and they must answer to the king therefore."[47] Clearly, this the abbot and the members of his house believed that they had some rights to these profits, yet the crown reasoned quite the opposite—all lands, profits, and goods of mentally incapacitated landlords belonged to the king.

Concealing Heirs from the Crown

Relatives and neighbors sometimes concealed heirs from royal officials, taking care of the person as an unofficial guardian and keeping the rents and profits. The concealment meant that what the king did not know, he could not act on, and, therefore, the mentally incapacitated landholder was never assigned a guardian. Sometimes the intent was relatively innocent. If a sister had cared for her mentally disabled brother since he was young, she might not have even realized that now that he was of age, she should report his status. Furthermore, letting on that there was an actionable issue would have cut her out of both her brother's life and quite possibly her livelihood. For example, Philippa, the eldest daughter of William de Hacche, held a messuage and 2 virgates of land in Idemeston and other lands of the abbot of Galstonbury; she was an *idiota*. A relative, Joan de Hacche, took care of her and the crown found that Joan "ha[d] taken the profits thereof for seven years past, without the king's license, and is of the yearly value of 6s. 8d. [p. sic]."[48] Although this may sound like Joan was trying to get away with something, it was all a mistake. Philippa was not the heir of William and Joan had her living on other properties that Joan

---

46   CIPM v. 18, no. 1186. See also CFR v. 13, p. 28 and p. 88.
47   CIM v. 7, no. 295.
48   CIM v. 2, no. 1803.

had inherited. It was cleared up with the king and escheator within months.[49] In another case, similar in that the relative might have simply been trying to care for the person and not really thinking to take profit from the crown, John Lawys cared for his relative Thomas Lawys. In 1403, William Lawys died, leaving as heir his son "Thomas... a mere idiot as it is said" (*Thomas est mere idiota ut dicunt*). Thomas should have inherited the two messuages and thirty acres of arable land and meadow in North Cowton. Yet, a relative, John Lawys, possibly a younger brother or an uncle, took the profits as if they were his lands.[50] The crown found Thomas another guardian, yet it does not seem that Thomas or his property were in any danger.[51] It may be that John simply stepped in to care for his mentally incompetent relative.

Relatives sometimes tried to bypass the wardship of the king in order to assist competent relatives in gaining an early or unlawful inheritance. John Roger is a good example of what might happen. Before John was born, around 1350 his maternal grandparents gave John's parents a gift of land in Heyngham Sibille. A restriction on the gift said that it could only pass to heirs "begotten on her [Margery], with remainder to his [James's] right heirs."[52] Margery and James had a son, John Roger, "an *idiota* from his birth," but James also had a bastard son, John Fitz James Roger. When Margery died, James gave his lands, including the gift, to his bastard son with the provision that he "should give the said idiot during his life a peck of wheat and a peck of peas weekly for his maintenance, a tunic yearly at Christmas for his clothing, two pairs of boots and two pairs of shoes, and a bed worth 2s."[53] For two years, things worked as planned. John Fitz James cared for John Roger. John Fitz James then granted the lands to Richard Huraunt who did not adhere to the agreement, although he had agreed to the terms in writing. John's half-brother, John Fitz James, abandoned him. Richard "utterly refused to fulfill the condition" for nine years, and, after he died, Richard's son held the lands for seven years, also giving nothing to John Roger.[54] Eighteen years after his father's death, the escheator learned of

---

49   CCR, 1343–1346, p. 42.
50   CIPM v. 18, no. 868; and TNA: PRO C 137/40, no. 59.
51   The guardian was Henry de Pudesay. See: CFR v. 12, pp. 210–211. Six years later Pudesay died and the wardship was back in the king's hands.
52   TNA: PRO C 145/205, m 12. See also: CIM v. 3, no. 944.
53   TNA: PRO C 145/205, m 12.
54   TNA: PRO C 145/205, m 12.

John Roger and reclaimed his property, finding him a royal guardian.[55] The loss for John Roger would have been immeasurable.

Other mentally incapacitated landholders found themselves in similar circumstances. For example, Thomas de Wetenhal, knight, stole the lands Robert Launder, a mentally incapacitated individual (*fatuus naturalis*), including "a messuage and a virgate of land in Olsthorp ... and he [Thomas] has had the issues for two years past and still detains them."[56] In 1382, Nicholas Wamford took the mentally incapacitated Hugh Groos of Crakentallan "into his keeping and has taken the profits of the lands from Hugh's entry thereon till the present day, which is 20 years, by what title the jurors do not know."[57] Hugh's "friends" convinced him to enter into his own lands, and therefore the king never knew that he was mentally incompetent.[58] Robert Oble of Pychebek, "draper," took the profits of the inheritance of Agnes Sherlok of Pychebek, an idiot from birth; Robert was caught and "must answer to the king" for the profits he took from the crown and Agnes.[59] Robert Stotevyll of Cotingham abducted John, the son of the mentally incompetent Margery Anlauby in 1279. Robert had no authority to take her son, who was also her heir, and "unjustly detains him."[60] Perhaps Robert wanted to attempt to divert the inheritance in some way. William de Beverlaco held Margery's wardship; he was supposed to protect her, her son, and her property, and failed to do so.[61]

Concealment of Incompetent Persons through Marriage

The crown penalized harshly the concealment of a mentally incapacitated landholder with fines, loss of guardianship, and loss of profits from the land. However, if the landholder was legally married, there was nothing the king could do, even if the person should not have made a marriage contract in the first place—on the grounds that competency was a prerequisite to making

---

55   "John died on 2 January, 51 Edward III. John Boket, chaplain, and John Warde of Little
       Mapeltrestede, both of full age, are his heirs." CIPM v. 15, no. 138. See also CIM v. 3, no. 944;
       Miri Rubin, *Charity and Community in Medieval Cambridge* (London & New York: CUP,
       1987); and Elaine Clark, "Social Welfare and Mutual Aid in the Medieval Countryside,"
       Journal of British Studies 33 (1994): 381–406.

56   CIPM v. 12, no. 399.

57   CIM v. 4, no. 210. See also CFR vol. 9, p. 359.

58   CIM v. 4, no. 188.

59   CIM v. 4, no. 348.

60   CIPM v. 2, no. 333.

61   CIPM v. 2, no. 728.

contracts of any kind and without competency a contact would not hold up in court—if consummated, the church would not normally grant an annulment. There are several cases of this nature, relating to female mentally incapacitated landholders. For example, Elizabeth, the daughter of William Chaumbernon, was "evilly concealed from the king, namely for 13 years by William Polglas, 22 years by John Sergeaux and 8 years by John Herle, knight."[62] Elizabeth was married at least three times to leading men of the town in an effort for these men to collect her wealth. The timing of these marriages clarifies their intentions. Elizabeth married William Polglas "within 3 days" of her father dying and John Sergeaux "within 2 days" of William dying.[63] With William she had a son, Richard, who was also "an idiot from his birth," and a daughter Margaret. In order to become heir to all of Elizabeth's "possessions," John Herle married Margaret and took Richard "out of the country into unknown parts, so that no one in Cornwall knows if he is alive."[64] Richard was reported dead in 1388.[65] John Herle was only the last of a string of men who wanted to have a hand in Elizabeth's inheritance. Neither William Polglas nor John Sergeaux should have married her; she should have had a royal guardian over her estate and person.

Emma Beston of Bishop's Lynn, mentioned above, is the focus of a quite well known case. In her deposition, she claimed that she had been married three times and yet only knew the name of one of her husbands and did not know the name of her son. The town leaders warned the man, Lawrence Elyngham, who had her in his house that the guardian was coming to take her into his care, and Lawrence hid Emma from her royal guardian, Philip Wyth. The town leaders, including the mayor, Henry Betle, refused to help the king's officials locate her, writing: "they in no wise know where the said Emma has dwelt since the receipt of the writ." In another statement, they wrote (as if in her voice) that Philip had conspired with the escheator to get her property. He is "an evil man and needy, having foolishly wasted the goods which were his, so that he became overwhelmed in poverty and debts to many men and goes about any means of gaining goods, caring not how or from whom so long as he gets them."[66] Although it took some time, eventually the king's commission

62   CIM v. 6, no. 127.
63   TNA: PRO E 149/64, m 13; C 145/255, m 22; and CIM v. 6, no. 85.
64   CIPM v. 17, no. 700.
65   CIPM v. 16, no. 608.
66   CIM, v. 4, no. 227, pp. 125–128, see p. 127.

was able to examine her, finding her "to have the face and countenance of an idiot."[67]

It was not only women property-holders with mental health difficulties to find themselves in arranged marriages, but also men. Men and women with property, even those with mental difficulties, were prized as spouses for the income from their lands and businesses. If a couple had a child, that child would be the heir to the property. And, even if that child was incompetent, it was likely that the crown would name a member of the family as guardian, a potentially lucrative position. Even though the church and the crown frowned on such marriages of the mentally incompetent, once entered and consummated, the marriage could not be broken. For example, Robert Hemnale, knight, "proposed to make an enfeoffment to exclude the king by fraud and collusion from the wardship and marriage of his heir,"[68] William, his son, a "fatuous person and natural idiot" (*fatuus et idiota naturalis*). Robert died when William was only four and the plan was never completed. "John Moriell and Hugh Lancastre, clerks, and Simon Blyaunt have taken all the issues of the manors in the meantime, by what title the jurors do not at present know."[69] Robert enfeoffed them with his lands and wrote into the agreement that when his son, William, came of age they would in turn enfeoff the properties back to William, and "so by fraud and collusion" exclude the king from William's wardship.[70]

Conclusion

Mentally incapacitated landowners became the victims of abuse from relatives, neighbors, guardians, and strangers who wanted to steal their property or goods. Some wanted other, more rational, members of the family to inherit and so concealed a mentally disabled individual's existence from the crown, or married them off to protect family rights in the property. At times, guardians figured out ways to get their mentally incompetent wards to sell them property illegally, or they moved goods off the property for cash value—cutting down woods, selling buildings, and stripping churches and houses of valuables. Others simply misused the law in order to confuse a line of descent or

---

67   CIM, v. 4, no. 227, p. 128.
68   CIPM v. 18, no. 1006; TNA: PRO C 137/45, nos. 66, 67 and E 152/393. See also CIPM v. 19, no 154.
69   CIM v. 7, no. 208; and CCR 1402–1405, pp. 79–80.
70   CIPM v. 19, no. 154.

gifts of property, leaving mentally disabled persons without their inheritance or accusing the dead of mental weakness in order to alter property rights.

Generally, the crown seems to have been on guard against such abuse, and some of these swindlers were caught. Yet, the offenders were the very men charged with protecting these individuals—guardians, escheators, and sheriffs. They were in the best position to take advantage of the situation and some were without doubt successful in their abuse of the legal system in order to profit from the inherent disadvantage of mentally incapacitated landholders.

Professionalization and Regulation of Medicine

∵

CHAPTER 7

Making Right Practice?
Regulating Surgery and Medicine in Fourteenth- and Fifteenth-Century Bologna

Kira Robison

In his surgical text from the late thirteenth century, Lanfranchi da Milano described the difference between the expert surgeon and the "average" surgeon of the city, who was a person who learned his trade solely as an apprentice without much in the way of book learning. Lanfranchi illustrated the separation between these two types of surgeons when he discussed the various times a surgeon would open the body: phlebotomy, scarification, cautery, or the application of leeches. He said, "I consider the last to be a surgical activity ... although we prideful surgeons have abandoned it to barbers and female practitioners."[1] Here Lanfranchi, who considered himself an expert surgeon, articulated a hierarchy based on typical surgical treatments where the simplest effort had been relegated to the lower echelons of practitioners.[2]

---

1   *Cyrugia Guidonis de Chauliaco, et cyrurgia Bruni, Teodorici, Rolandi, Lanfranci, Rogerii, Bertapalie* (n.p.: Noviter Impressus, 1519), fo. 168v.

2   This pattern is echoed in other texts. For example, John of Arderne tells the story of an English cleric who was seeking treatment for a sore on his chest that had been bothering him for quite some time. He made multiple attempts to find a cure: first, with a medicine woman, who gave him plasters and a potion to drink, and later with a barber, who bled him and offered him a variety of intrusive cures. However, according to the case records he finally found relief through an educated surgeon, who gave him sage advice on what not to do for his wound. This, of course, included anything the barber had suggested, which could easily bring about complications and death. Here, the educated surgeon's advice (like that of John himself) was the obvious choice, since the woman's remedies were ineffectual over the course of several years, and the barber offered cutting and burning that were invasive, painful, and potentially life-threatening. Female practitioners, usually labeled "medicine women," traditionally appear at the lowest end of this hierarchy. In medieval Bologna, there is evidence of women practitioners, who were identified in the records by the phrase *medica*, though none was acknowledged as doing surgery. References to these *medicae* disappeared from the sources by the end of the sixteenth century, when the majority of female practitioners of medicine were referred to as midwives or "supernatural" healers. See Giana Pomata, "Practicing between Earth and Heaven: Women Healers in Seventeenth-Century Bologna," *DYNAMIS* 19 (1999): 121–2.

Lanfranchi's opinion of this medical hierarchy reflected a wider attitude at work in university cities such as his adopted home of Paris, where in 1311 Philip the Fair regulated in favor of the apprenticeship of surgeons and the segregation of surgical training from the academy.[3] Outside of Paris, in places like Bologna, surgery instruction became part of the curriculum at the university, although regulation of education and practice did not appear until later in the fourteenth century, when the university physicians depended on the legal assistance of the commune in the form of the *podestà* to penalize incorrect surgical and medical practice. The result of statutory regulation of surgeons by the professors at Bologna laid the groundwork for the later medical tribunal of the *Protomedicato*, although these early efforts were presented in terms of making sure the lower levels of the hierarchy had a suitable education and practiced medicine correctly.

In the example above, the "pridefulness" of which Lanfranchi spoke played out in surgical texts as an emphasis in doing surgery well because of one's proper education. For example, Lanfranchi's teacher Guglielmo da Saliceto stated that he provided a general description of the body in his book "to the end that you will be able to operate with the knife and the cautery and to use your hands without going astray," in other words, without making a serious mistake.[4] Lanfranchi copied his master's idea and offered an intellectual basis for this plan: "Galen said that a surgeon must know anatomy lest he believe that a broad ligament be a membrane, or that a round one is a nerve, and so fall into error during his operations."[5] Here Lanfranchi emphasized both the need for a proper knowledge of the body as well as the difference between the educated surgeon and the trade apprentice: that of knowing Galen's text.

For many physician-authors, trained in a university, their own education and practice was seen as being the best and most useful, while other practitioners (even the expert surgeon) were riskier, less educated, or more dangerous to consult. Much of this prejudice was portrayed within the "higher levels" of this hierarchy, namely by the academic physician and the expert surgeon. This reflected the traditional split in formal medical education between "theoretical" and "practical" medicine, "book learning" versus hands-on practice, the text versus the knife. Theoretical medicine, as taught through the traditional

---

3 This effectively prevented surgery from being taught in the University of Paris until the late fourteenth century. Michael McVaugh, "Surgical Education in the Middle Ages," *DYNAMIS* 20 (2000): 293; Luke Demaitre, "Medical Practice and Practitioners," in *Medieval France: An Encyclopedia*, ed. William Kibler (New York: Psychology Press, 1995), p. 606.

4 Guglielmo da Saliceto, *The Surgery of William of Saliceto: Written in 1275*, trans. and ed., Paul Pifteau [French]; trans. Leonard D. Rosenman [English] (Philadelphia: Xlibris, 2002), p. 181.

5 *Cyrugia... Lanfranci*, fo. 168v.

medical texts, emphasized diagnosis and treatment of disease in humoral medicine, which involved balancing the humors or internal substances of the body through various therapeutic methods. Practical medicine was the application of surgery through manipulation, cutting, stitching, and setting of bones. For the most part, many medieval physicians who were educated in the academy, such as Turisanius in Paris or Pietro d'Abano in Padua, articulated their perceived superiority based on the notion that academy-trained physicians had theoretical knowledge granted by studying books and that practical knowledge was the purview of lesser practitioners.[6] However, for physicians who also practiced surgery, like Lanfranchi, Guy de Chauliac in Avignon, and Henri de Mondeville in Paris, right practice called for the combination of theoretical and practical medicine, since "[a *medicus*] should not just be a surgeon but a physician too, because bloodletting and purgation are necessary ... but [to be] a surgeon is also necessary because afterwards manual operation is required."[7] In other words, book learning gave a physician the proper theoretical framework in which to place his surgical training.[8]

---

6   Cornelius O'Boyle sees the charters of the thirteenth- and fourteenth-century Parisian *studium* and city as concerned not as much with this hierarchy of medieval medicine (academic doctors at the top, barber surgeons in the middle, and apothecaries, midwives, and other perceived "quacks" at the bottom), but rather with making sure that those with *no* training whatsoever were prohibited from practicing. See Cornelius O'Boyle, "Surgical Texts and Social Contexts: Physicians and Surgeons in Paris c. 1270–1430," in *Practical Medicine from Salerno to the Black Death*, ed. Luis García-Ballester, *et al.* (Cambridge: CUP, 1994), pp. 156–185. In an article from the same volume, Danielle Jacquart shows that this conceptual division of education in Paris was evidence of two things: one, the concern of the authorities for the criminality of medical malpractice and the egregious lack of reporting it, and second, ultimately to regulate the "professional competence" of surgeons, which should have lowered the number of people who died at the hands of the untrained. In Paris, the barbers had to submit to a competency examination much the same as surgeons in order to practice, as at Bologna, though the Bolognese statutes only specified surgeons. However, Jacquart pictures the governmental regulations as solely concerned with that which could potentially disrupt the public order. For her, these regulations were not evidence of a rivalry of power between the educated and uneducated practitioners in early fourteenth-century Paris, but instead were an "affirmation by each profession of its uniqueness and it right to choose its representatives." Danielle Jacquart, "Medical Practice in Paris in the First Half of the Fourteenth Century," in *Practical Medicine from Salerno*, pp. 186–211.

7   Gerard de Solo on Rhazes, in Michael McVaugh, "Surgery in the Fourteenth-century Faculty of Montpellier," in *L'Université de médecine de Montpellier et son rayonnement (XIIIe–XIe siècles)* (Turnhout: Brepols, 2004), p. 43.

8   This view is reflected across the majority of surgical texts from the second half of the thirteenth century, regardless of location of author. For Dino del Garbo's perspective (Padua and northern Italy), see Nancy G. Siraisi, "How to Write a Latin Book on Surgery: Organizing

The best evidence for physicians' ideas on medical education comes from the surgical texts themselves, but these have the same problems as many sources of the period: they are the remnants of a learned, elite group in society. Scholars have tried to tease out what the relationship of surgeons and medicine would have looked like in daily life, but the results are still influenced by medieval medical authors, the actions of the medical schools, and city regulations, since these are usually the sources that survive. Modern scholars have worked to break this idea that academically educated physicians, in spite of the source bias, had intellectual superiority over other surgeons, specialists, or apothecaries who were trained in the guild system. By introducing the idea of the "medical marketplace," scholars have intended to complicate the situation by illustrating the variety of medical help available in cities like Bologna and

Principles and Authorial Devices in Guglielmo da Saliceto and Dino del Garbo," in *Practical Medicine from Salerno*, pp. 95–7. For Guy de Chauliac (Montpellier), see O'Boyle, "Surgical Texts," 176. For Gentile da Foligno (Padua), see Roger French, *Canonical Medicine: Gentile de Foligno and Scholasticism* (Leiden: Brill, 2001), p. 28. For Henri de Mondeville (Paris), see Chiara Crisciani, "Artefici *sensati: experentia* e sensi in alchimia e cirurgia (secc. XIII–XIV)," in *Alchimia e medicina del Medioevo*, ed. Chiara Crisciani and Agostino Paravacini-Bagliani (Florence: SISMEL, Edizioni del Galluzzo, 2003), pp. 135–153. For Guglielmo da Saliceto (Bologna), see Jole Agrimi and Chiara Crisciani, "The Science and Practice of Medicine in the Thirteenth Century According to Guglielmo da Saliceto, Italian surgeon," in *Practical Medicine from Salerno*, pp. 60–87. In the most recent analysis of authors of surgeries before the mid-fourteenth century, Michael McVaugh also sees them as attempting to persuade their audiences that surgery was an important part of medicine, to show that it was an intellectual enterprise just as much as traditional "theoretical" medicine was. These authors (Teodorico Borgognoni, Bruno Longoburgo da Calabria, Guglielmo da Saliceto, Lanfranchi da Milano, and Henri de Mondeville) emphasized how a surgeon, based on this influx of new texts into the European theater (the "New Galenism"), could synthesize a regimen of treatment for ailments from which future surgeons could then hypothesize. This focus on regimen and intellect, this "rationalizing" of surgery, separated it from the traditional "artisanal" interpretation commonly attributed to the practice of surgery by contemporary practitioners and modern scholars. For this discussion of rational surgery, see Michael McVaugh, *The Rational Surgery of the Middle Ages*, Micrologus 15 (Florence: SISMEL, Edizioni del Galluzzo, 2006). By emphasizing rationality, surgery was put on par with academic medicine and physicians could acquire surgical knowledge through reason, just as they could a science, "confirming it by testing it on particular cases," as quoted by Guglielmo da Saliceto, in McVaugh, "Therapeutic Strategies: Surgery," in *Western Medical Thought from Antiquity to the Middle Ages*, ed. Mirko Grmek *et al.* (Cambridge, MA: Harvard University Press, 1998), p. 282. For New Galenism, see among many, Luis García Ballester, "The New Galen: a Challenge to Latin Galenism in thirteenth-century Montpellier," in *Text and Tradition: Studies in Ancient Medicine and its Transmission, presented to Jutta Kollesch*, ed. Klaus-Dietrich Fischer, Diethard Nickel, and Paul Potter (Leiden: Brill, 1998), pp. 55–6 and *passim*.

Paris during this period and the many options that were available to patients based on their particular circumstances. Roger French, for example, points out that guild members dominated the merchant class in urban situations and in many local governments, which made this supposed superiority more difficult to articulate in a reality outside of the medical texts. French cites the example of apothecaries who would hire trained academic physicians to visit clients in their shops. This, he says, shows a lack of a rigorous hierarchy that oppressed non-academically trained practitioners.[9]

In spite of the reality of the medical marketplace, medieval authors did not cease using this idea of hierarchical education. For example, in the fourteenth and fifteenth centuries, the physician professors in the College of Arts and Medicine at the University of Bologna were still articulating their superiority through a series of increasingly stringent regulations on the practice and teaching of medicine and surgery, not just at the academic level, but including city surgeons who were unaffiliated with the university. Bologna at this time fluctuated between independence and papal overlordship as the student

---

9 French, *Canonical Medicine*, pp. 22–3. The idea of the medical marketplace was initially described by Harold Cook regarding seventeenth-century English medicine. See Harold Cook, *The Decline of the Old Medical Regime in Stuart London* (Ithaca: Cornell University Press, 1986), and was recently re-examined in *Medicine and the Market in England and its Colonies, c.1450- c.1850*, ed. Mark S.R. Jenner and Patrick Wallis (New York: Palgrave Macmillan, 2007). For the adoption of this phrase into other areas, see Roy Porter, "The Patient's View: Doing Medical History from Below," *Theory and Society* 14 (1985): 167–74; Vivian Nutton, "Healers in the Medical Market Place: Towards a Social History of Graeco-Roman Medicine," in *Medicine in Society*, ed. Andrew Wear (Cambridge: CUP, 1992), pp. 15–58; Joseph Shatzmiller, *Jews, Medicine, and Medieval Society* (Berkeley: University of California Press, 1994), p. 5; Katharine Park, "Medicine and Society in Medieval Europe, 500–1500," in *Medicine in Society*, p. 75; idem, *Doctors and Medicine in Early Renaissance Florence* (Princeton: Princeton University Press, 1985); Nancy Siraisi, *Medieval and Early Renaissance Medicine* (Chicago: University of Chicago Press, 1990), pp. 34, 189. For Bologna more generally and the idea of "professionalism," see Siraisi, *Taddeo Alderotti and his Pupils* (Princeton: Princeton University Press, 1981); Roger French, *Medicine before Science: the Business of Medicine from the Middle Ages to the Enlightenment* (Cambridge: CUP, 2003); and Vern Bullough, *The Development of Medicine as a Profession: The Contribution of the Medieval University to Modern Medicine* (New York: Hafner Publishing Company, 1966). It has been pointed out in several cases that medical students in the *studia* had to undergo some form of "apprenticeship"; in other words, before being granted a degree, students were required to practice medicine on patients under the eye of a licensed physician, which again undermines the traditional hierarchy articulated in the sources. See for example, Luis García-Ballester, "Academicism versus Empiricism in Practical Medicine in Sixteenth–Century Spain with Regard to Morisco Practitioners," in *The Medical Renaissance of the Sixteenth Century*, ed. Andrew Wear *et al.* (Cambridge: CUP, 1985), p. 268.

privileges upheld by the papacy declined in favor of civic oversight and professorial authority. The attempts by professors to control city surgeons were
couched in terms of academic superiority and betterment of practice, reflecting this traditional hierarchy of proper education, which became the seed
for a sixteenth-century tribunal made up of physicians whose task it was to
supervise the medical care available in the city, called the *Protomedicato*.[10] The
prominence of the *Protomedicato* in early modern medical thought in Europe,
however, tends to obscure the complicated and somewhat fraught beginnings of these regulations in individual instances, such as medieval Bologna.
The contention here is that in the late fourteenth century, the professors of
medicine relied on the city and its legal and governmental assistance during
Bologna's bids for independence from the papacy to maintain professorial
authority over the education of physicians. In addition, the physicians used
this support ultimately to broaden their dominance over medical practitioners
and surgeons in the city, thus laying the groundwork for the later development
of the *Protomedicato* in Bologna.

The Medical School and the City

Before continuing on to an examination of the statutes, it is first important to
lay out some terminology for the medical school and professors in Bologna.
In modern terms, "university" and "college" suggest an institutional hierarchy
and administration that students negotiate in order to obtain an education
capped by a degree. In the Middle Ages, however, "university" referred not to
an administrative infrastructure but to the body of students itself, while the
"college" represented specifically a group of professors who had formed their
own organization in order to establish educational and examination standards
during this period. These groups together were known as a *studium generale*,
or an institution of "general study," although each discipline was autonomous.[11]

---

10   David Gentilcore, "'All that Pertains to Medicine': *Protomedici* and *Protomedicati* in Early
      Modern Italy," *MH* 38 (1994): 121–142; idem, *Healers and Healing in Early Modern Italy*
      (Manchester: Manchester University Press, 1998).

11   In Latin, the student body was called a *universitas*, the college a *collegia*. For the sake of
      clarity, I will avoid the word "university" from here on, opting instead for the Latin term
      studium and a general reference to "students" or the "student body." The *collegia* may also
      be referred to by the term "faculty," but in a broad sense as teachers at an institution
      of higher learning, not as a more modern institution as is often found in European
      universities. See Albano Sorbelli, *Storia della Università di Bologna*, 2 vols. (Bologna:
      N. Zanichelli, 1944), v. 1, pp. 170–1; Olga Weijers, *Terminologie des universités au xiiie siècle*

The student body was the core of the medieval educational structure during its development in the twelfth and thirteenth centuries. The foundation of the *studium* at Bologna was tied to the formation of the student groups, which began with the civil law students in the early twelfth century. By the thirteenth century, the reputation of teachers and the lifeblood of the *studium* was student interest, for without the students there would be no *studium* and no need for professors to teach anything. Thus, the students acted as the impetus and cohesion of the Bolognese *studium*.[12] As the core policy makers during this time, the students had the support of the papacy and not only regulated what they wanted to learn, but also decided who would teach it to them. This control over their education meant that the head of the student body, the rector, was almost all-powerful. For example, the rector of medicine and arts students claimed not only to have administrative authority over every student in the discipline, but also to have jurisdiction over all teachers.[13] The professors, ultimately, held their jobs and received payment at the behest of the students. This balance of power, however, began to change in the fourteenth century as the city took over many of the rights the students had held during the thirteenth century.

The professors at Bologna, on the other hand, were grouped by discipline into civil law, canon law, arts and medicine, and theology. The College of Arts and Medicine (CAM) was formed in 1298, and was comprised of teachers (*magistri* or *doctores*) who were either physicians (*medici*) or professors (*magistri*)

(Rome: Edizione dell'Ateneo, 1987), p. 191; and Hastings Rashdall, *The Universities of Europe in the Middle Ages* (Oxford: Clarendon Press, 1895), v. 2, *passim*. I acknowledge De Coster's point that this latter use of the term "faculty" is somewhat anachronistic to Bologna during this period. Anuschka De Coster, "Foreign and Citizen Teachers at Bologna in the Fifteenth and Sixteenth Centuries: Statutes, Statistics, and Student Teachers," in *Annali di Storia delle Università italiane* 12 (2007); [journal on-line]; available from http://www.cisui.unibo.it/annali/12/testi/19DeCostner_testo.htm. Accessed May 24, 2010, n. 2.

12   For example, in the case of Padua, a Senate decision regarding staffing the *studium* read as follows, "Students follow famous teachers and if provisions for this are not made, our *studium* will be ruined," quoted in Paul F. Grendler, *The Universities of the Italian Renaissance* (Baltimore: Johns Hopkins University Press, 2002), p. 23, n. 56. For more on the acknowledgment of a good reputation for a school, see Bullough, *Development of Medicine as a Profession*, p. 66, and Gaines Post, *Masters' Salaries and Student-Fees in Mediaeval Universities* (Cambridge, MA: Medieval Academy of America, 1932).

13   Rubric xxxxvii, *De pena doctorum non obedientium Rectori*, in *Statuti delle Università e dei collegi dello studio bolognese*, ed. Carlo Malagola (Bologna: N. Zanichelli, 1888), p. 256.

in the Arts and Medicine.[14] Beginning in 1378, the CAM defined the privileges, or special rights, granted to medical practitioners outside the *studium* and couched them in the traditional terms of superiority seen above. They, as others before them, articulated this hierarchy based on education, which identified them as academically trained physicians, followed by other medical practitioners in the city, and finally by surgeons, who were divided into properly and improperly trained—proper training, of course, being defined by the members of the college.[15]

In the statutes from 1378, the college claimed to be averting "serious dangers to good physicians" that had been generated by "ignorant doctors" (*ignaros medicos*) by prohibiting the practice of medicine in Bolognese territory by anyone who had not been trained by a physician at the academy. However, even with training, anyone caught treating a patient would be fined 50 Bolognese *lire* without the proper credentials. Additionally, they levied a 100 *lire* penalty for anyone on the faculty who practiced medicine in the city without exams, license, and approval of the college. These restrictions were rather exhaustive. They determined that no one "may dare or presume to sell, deliver, or administer" any simple or compound medicines, laxatives, opiates or other sleep aids, digestives, caustics or corrosives, numbing agents, poisons, abortifacients, "or anything else dangerous," without the consent of the physicians of the college, or training in mixing medicines from the apothecaries' guild.[16] The punishment for doing so was another fine, also of 50 *lire*.[17]

---

14   This is the first extant mention of a College, occurring in the appointment of one of the professors (the son of a city magistrate) by the city fathers to the position of a city *medicus*. Mauro Sarti and Mauro Fattorini, *De Claris Archigymnasii Bononiensis professoribus: a saeculo XI usque ad saeculum XIV* (Bologna: Ex officina regia fratrum Merlani, 1896), v. 2, pp. 232–3, no. 14. Concerning terminology that may be found in this article, a *magister* was a professor (It., *maestro*); a *medicus* was a physician, a medical doctor, either in the *studium* or the city, who was not necessarily a professor. The word *doctor* was used mostly for the law professors, but came into common parlance in the mid-thirteenth century to describe all teachers of law, medicine, or arts, Albano Sorbelli, *Storia della Università*, v. 1, p. 108. However, the term "doctor" may be used herein only in conjunction with the term "professor" to indicate teachers at the *studium*, not to indicate a physician.

15   This probably included barber surgeons, although the university statutes do not differentiate between those with the right education and those without. This is much the same as the references to Galen in Lanfranchi, Guglielmo, Henri de Mondeville, and Guy de Chauliac's surgical texts, which mention making mistakes that might result in patient pain or death.

16   1378, rb. xxi, *Statuti delle Università*, pp. 441–2.

17   Bolognese silver money was broken up into *libbra* (Lat., pounds), *solidi*, and *denari*. One *libbra* equaled 20 *solidi*, which then was worth 240 *denari*. In Italian city-states, *lire, soldi,*

The statutes concerning surgeons that followed those regarding medical practitioners specifically utilized the same language as above. The professors described their worries regarding the "inexperienced among surgeons" (*impericia cirurgicorum*) and suggested that an example be set by the members of the college on how to be a "circumspect and discreet man," and "a master worthy" of the faith of his patients, echoing the traditional view that academically trained physicians were the pinnacle of their trade and worth emulating. The surgeons of whom they approved would be put on a registry of sanctioned practitioners, which would also act as a license, allowing them to practice surgery in Bologna.[18]

Part of this professorial control over surgeons also appeared in another statute of the CAM regarding "teachers of medicine on the faculty of our college able to operate in surgery."[19] According to this regulation, which was promulgated in 1378, 1395, and 1410, they required even well-established members of the *collegia* to be added to the registry of surgeons. There was one stipulation to this that "no one, who is on the list of surgeons thus far set up, may hear or presume to cure a sick person by medicine."[20] The penalty for a surgeon caught "doing medicine" was 50 Bolognese *lire*, 10 *lire* of which would go as a reward for anyone denouncing such practitioners.[21] This statement demonstrated that, at least legally, the CAM considered surgeons unqualified to diagnose and treat an illness, even if they were members of the college. This also revealed the traditional dichotomy between medicine as theoretical and surgery as practical, in that the training of a surgeon in the manipulation, cutting, and stitching of flesh and setting of bones did not equal the training of a physician in theories of disease, techniques of diagnosis, and matters of medication and treatment.

These statutes were reiterated several more times before the sixteenth century: in 1395, 1410, and in fragments that have survived generally from the

---

and *denari* were monies of account, not coins. The gold ducat was of an almost equal weight with the florin and began to be minted in Bologna in 1379–1380, and weighed about 3.55 grams, or between 32–36 *solidi* in the late fourteenth century. For Bolognese silver, see Carlo Poni, "Local Market Rules and Practices: Three Guilds in the Same Line of Production in Early Modern Bologna," in *Domestic Strategies: Work and Family in France and Italy, 1600–1800*, ed. Stuart Woolf (Cambridge: CUP, 1991), pp. 69–101; Sarah Rubin Blanshei, *Politics and Justice in Late Medieval Bologna* (Leiden: Brill, 2010), p. ix.

18   1378, rb. xxvi, *Statuti delle Università*, p. 443; 1395, rb. xxiiii, pp. 470–1; fragment xviii, p. 491; in 1410: rubric xxvi, p. 517.

19   1378, rb. xxviiii, *Statuti delle Università*, p. 444; 1395, rubric xxvii, pp. 471–2; 1410, rubric xxviiii, p. 518.

20   Ibid.

21   1378, rb. xxviiii, *Statuti delle Università*, p. 444; 1395, rb. xviiii, p. 469.

first half of the fifteenth century. The rubrics regarding non-academic medical practitioners and surgeons were repeated in full for each full edition with little change. However, a fragment of a related regulation regarding the registry of surgeons has survived from the fifteenth century, where the professors required that anyone wanting to practice surgery in Bologna, be he citizen or foreigner, must have had four years of education by a "salaried master" (*sub magistro salario*) in surgery, or reading in a public school of surgery (*in scolis publice cirurgiam*).[22] While this was more restrictive than the rule for general medical practitioners that stipulated a proper physician needed three years of education, it shows that they still, on some level, recognized the continuance of schooling in the artisanal form, possibly through private instruction or apprenticeship in the guild of barbers.[23]

The regulations of medical practitioners and surgeons in the city set by the professors of the medical school reflected their use of the traditional, hierarchical perspective regarding medical education. This perspective, by virtue of their role at the top of the hierarchy, enabled professors to assert control over medical practice in the city through a system of fines and penalties for violation of their laws. These rules were supplied in a very narrow venue, that of the college and the *studium*, but the encroachment into city practice had wider implications for those who transgressed these rules that came from the college's reliance on the city's magistrate, or *podestà*, to enforce these regulations. This relationship between professors and the *podestà* tends to be obscured by the emergence of the *Protomedicato* tribunal in the sixteenth century.

---

22   Fragment xiii, *Statuti delle Università*, p. 490.

23   For the three-year rule, see 1378, rb. xxi, *Statuti delle Università*, p. 442; 1395, rb. xviiii, p. 469. This acknowledgement, though minor in the overall scheme of the CAM statutes in which educated physicians were the focus, reflected a much larger context of medical education in the city of Bologna that fits very well with the medical marketplace. For example, in 1214, Hugo of Lucca was hired by the city as a civic physician. In addition to his medical practice, he had a small private teaching group. According to his son Teodorico, who was a physician in his own right, Hugo taught surgery as well and it was this instruction that made up part of Teodoric's own text, the *Surgery* in 1267, Siraisi, *Taddeo Alderotti*, p. 15. Bologna also accepted training from other locations, as in the case of Enrico da Pistoia, whose surgical and medical knowledge were seen as valuable to Bologna, Guido Zaccagini, *La vita dei maestri e degli scolari nello Studio di Bologna nei secoli xiii e xiv* (Geneva: Leo S. Olschki, 1926), p. 20; appendix, pp. xv, 151–2.

Crime and Regulation

These regulations of the College of Arts and Medicine are seen to be the groundwork for a later, sixteenth-century development, the *Protomedicato*, or the tribunal that oversaw the practice of medicine in Bologna. The *Protomedicato* appeared in Sicily in 1397, in Naples and Milan under Charles V in 1523, in Rome in the late fifteenth century, and Bologna in 1517. Bologna's *Protomedicato* was under the control of the Roman committee since Bologna was under the purview of the papacy from 1512, and managed little autonomous maintenance in the sixteenth century.[24] In the early modern period, the *Protomedicato* was seen as a protector of patient rights and thus a controller of physicians and medical care in the city. Gianna Pomata defines it as, "a court whose specific jurisdiction derived from the college's public responsibility to guarantee the quality of medications (by inspecting apothecaries' shops) and the skill of healers (by examining practitioners). This task of supervising the entire medical field was warranted by a social need for the protection of the public. This need, in turn, legitimized the college doctors' dominance over all other medical practitioners."[25]

In the later Middle Ages, the social need Pomata outlined above was perhaps not as clearly articulated as it was in the sixteenth century and later. The physicians themselves described, in rather more lofty terms, the reasons for the restrictions as being based on their reputations as part of the school and as Bolognese citizens. For example, the introduction to the statutes of the CAM begins, "For the honor and reverence of the Almighty God ... and also for the magnificence and exaltation of the people and the commune of Bologna and those who love her, and for perpetual teaching..."[26] Later, when introducing their rules on inexperienced surgeons they declared, "On account of the republic and so that one's own labor may be profitable to everyone, so that the best study may thrive, and so that the students may be inspired," surgeons should

---

24   Paula Findlen, *Possessing Nature: Museums, Collecting, and Scientific Culture in Early Modern Italy* (Los Angeles: University of California Press, 1994), p. 264; David Gentilcore, *Healers and Healing*, p. 33 and *passim*.

25   See Giana Pomata, *Contracting a Cure: Patients, Healers, and the Law in Early Modern Bologna* (Baltimore: Johns Hopkins University Press, 1998), p. 13.

26   Introduction to the statutes of the College of Arts and Medicine, 1378, rb. i, *Statuti delle Università*, p. 425.

be properly educated.[27] Appropriate lecturers should be put in place "for the honor of the whole Bolognese *studium*, and for the benefit of the scholars and students in medicine, and for use and public good," where public good was one of the last considerations.[28]

Many of the rules that were in place at the institution of the formal *Protomedicato* were not yet articulated in 1378; instead, it is important to see these formative years within their own social and political context. For example, the medieval college was not a tribunal. While they had control over the stages that future physicians had to go through to prove their readiness to practice medicine and surgery, they had no juridical power themselves. Thus, the main role of the *Protomedicato* as a place where patients could bring their cases was nonexistent in the Middle Ages. How, then, did the medical professors uncover violations and enforce these restrictions on unlicensed practitioners? In the same way that other crimes were revealed, mostly through the accusatory procedure, where the individual affected or their family would bring a charge to the *podestà*. The position of *podestà* in Bologna began as a chief magistracy as early as the mid-twelfth century and by 1278, the prosecution of all crimes was under the jurisdiction of the *podestà*. Accusations brought by the victim and by others, like minor officials or the college prior, would be recorded in separate registers by Bolognese notaries, although cases might be heard by either foreign or Bolognese officials in the *podestà*'s court. In the CAM statutes for this period, the informer was referred to generically as "anyone," presumably to widen the field of available accusers beyond the victim and to increase the opportunities for violators to be caught. Once the transgressor was revealed, the professors could sue for violation of the statutes.[29]

The relationship between the medical professors and the *podestà* was outlined initially in an early rubric from the 1378 statutes of the college, where the *podestà* was bound to aid the prior, or head of the college, in extracting punishment. The offender was given a month to pay or the prior could repeat the condemnation, effectively compounding the fine.[30] The *podestà* was cited in other statutes in the same supportive role; for example, he was responsible

---

27   1378, rb. xxvi, *Statuti delle Università*, p. 443; 1395, rb. xxiiii, pp. 470–1; fragment xviii, p. 491; in 1410: rubric xxvi, p. 517.

28   1378, rb. xxvii, *Statuti delle Università*, p. 443; 1395, rb. xv, p. 471; fragment xx, p. 491; 1410, rb. xxvii, p. 517.

29   See Sarah R. Blanshei, "Criminal Justice in Medieval Perugia and Bologna," *L&HR* 1:2 (1983): 251–6, and more recently her excellent and exhaustive survey *Politics and Justice*, Appendix A and *passim*.

30   1378, rb. iii, *Statuti delle Università*, p. 430.

for collecting the fine for those surgeons caught doing medicine, as well as the 100 *lire* penalty for medical students, *medici* not employed by the *studium*, and those with less than three years of teaching experience who lectured on medicine in the evenings.[31] In 1395, he was "bound to inquire into [the violation] and to punish those at fault."[32] Those surgeons who attempted to cure through medicine and caused a person's death were brought into an inquisition by the prior, other members of the college, or officers of the city, because the *podestà* of Bologna was bound by the law "to proceed against such men."[33] The *podestà* also became involved if an unlicensed medical practitioner caused a serious accident or the death of a patient, and anyone who reported this was also given a reward of ten gold ducats.[34] It is interesting to note that the reward for reporting bad medicine was more that the reward for reporting medicine done by surgeons, suggesting that the greater concern for the physician professors was controlling the education of general medical practitioners. By 1395, the *podestà* was receiving a reward from the fines paid by violators. He was given a third of the 50 *lire* penalty paid by those seen as unqualified to lecture in surgery when they were caught; one third went to the college and the last third went to the construction of the Church of San Petronio.[35]

The splitting of the fines between the *podestà*, the college, and the city was evidence of a particular partnership between the physicians and the *podestà* (as well as his representative, the *vicarius*).[36] This partnership meant that the city had taken an interest in supporting the physicians' attempts at control of medical practice in Bologna, but the faculty were very clear that the *podestà* was not to interfere with internal collegiate business. For example, by 1410, the college felt it necessary to state that although they were often in contact with the *podestà*, he did not have the right to call any of the professors in for any

---

31   1378, rb. xxviiii, *Statuti delle Università*, p. 444; 1395, rb. xxvii, p. 471; 1410, rb. xxviiii, p. 518. On lecturing, see 1378, rb. xxvii, p. 443. Here the fine was "imposed by the *podestà* of Bologna."

32   1395, rb. xviiii, *Statuti delle Università*, p. 469.

33   1378, rb. xxviiii, *Statuti delle Università*, p. 444.

34   1378, rb. xxvii, *Statuti delle Università*, p. 443. For the relationship of gold ducats and florins in Italy and greater medieval Europe, see Peter Spufford, *Money and its Use in Medieval Europe* (Cambridge: CUP, 1989, repr. 1993), p. 291ff.; Michael Moïssey Postan, *The Cambridge Economic History of Europe: Trade and Industry in the Middle Ages* (Cambridge: CUP, 1987), pp. 837, 881. 1378, rb. xxi, *Statuti delle Università*, p. 442.

35   1395, rb. xxv, *Statuti delle Università*, p. 471; 1410, rb. xxi, p. 515, with a third still going to San Petronio. By 1410, the college's third was specified as divided between the professors medicine.

36   1378, rb. xxvii, *Statuti delle Università*, p. 443; Fragment xiiii, p. 490.

misdeeds. Rather, any medical crimes or mistakes pertaining to the physician professors would be dealt with "in-house," so to speak, and presumably passed on to the *podestà* if found egregious enough.[37] This suggests a rather jealous guardianship of their rights by the professors, which would not be unusual given the overall tone of the statutes. This was especially so regarding exams and licensing of graduating students, which they held closely monitored during the fourteenth and fifteenth centuries. This management was a holdover from the thirteenth century, when students had incredible power over teacher salaries and the professors functioned almost solely at the whim of the student body. As such, the professors kept close the one part of the process over which they had power—the examination and licensing of future physicians. This early role of the *podestà* in regulating medical crime is lost with the advent of the *Protomedicato* in the sixteenth century, as is the turbulent civic context of the city of Bologna in which the professors and *podestà* lived and worked.

The City and Professors

While the medical professors saw the *podestà* as an intermediary with the city and used his office's powers as a legitimizing force behind their regulations of medical practice, the city itself was using legislation regarding the *studium* and the appointment of medical faculty as a way to distance itself from the power of its papal overlord. Bologna had long been victim of factional strife as had many cities in medieval Northern Italy, torn between aristocratic families who supported papal rule and those who believed imperial backing was best for the city.[38] Bologna also spent quite a bit of its history as a member of the Papal

---

37   1410, rb. xxxiiii, *Statuti delle Università*, p. 520.

38   A centuries-long and bitter rivalry between the Imperial Ghibelline party and the pro-papal Guelphs engulfed Northern Italy and Lombardy from the twelfth to the fifteenth centuries. By the time of Frederick II in the mid-thirteenth century, it had degenerated into scuffles, sieges, and a pattern of capture and loss of small towns and cities throughout Northern Italy. The pope had enough support in the area to continue to harass pro-imperial holdings and attempt to regain various territories for the Papal States. For more on Frederick's Ghibelline supporters and his multiple papal adversaries, see Joseph Strayer, "The Political Crusades of the Thirteenth Century," in *A History of the Crusades*, v. 4, *The Later Crusades: 1189–1311*, ed. Kenneth Setton (Madison, Milwaukee, London: University of Wisconsin Press, 1969), pp. 355, 358; G.A. Loud, "The Case of the Missing Martyrs: Frederick II's War with the Church, 1239–1250," in *Martyrs and Martyrologies*, Papers read at the 1992 Summer Meeting and the 1993 Winter Meeting of the Ecclesiastical History Society, ed., Diana Wood, *Studies in Church History* 30 (Oxford: Blackwell Publishers, 1993),

States (off and on from ca. 774–1860) so that while it maintained its own civic structure and identity, it was overseen by a papal legate. In the mid-fourteenth century, Bologna was under the power of the leading family of Milan, the Visconti. In 1360, the Visconti lost Bologna to the papacy, a conquest initiated by Cardinal Gil Albornoz.[39] On March 19, 1376, however, the city of Bologna revolted when the leading families with the "unanimous" support of the people drove out the papal legate and reinstated an independent commune.[40]

The city took the opportunity given by the revolt in 1376 to establish legal control over the *studium* through statutory regulations recommended by new government committees whose job was to oversee the everyday running of the *studium*. Previously, much of this control was in the hands of the students, who were strongly supported in their domination by the papacy, even when Bologna was not under its jurisdiction. With the new city statutes written just after the revolt, the city appointed four men of different social strata to oversee the *studium*: a noble, a senator, a knight, and a merchant.[41] At this point, the new city statutes regarding medical professors began to augment the salary of doctors and lecturers of medicine "so that the *studium* may be

---

p. 143. For the relationship of political factionalism to this stage of student privileges, see Edward Pace, "Universities," *The Catholic Encyclopedia*, v. 15 (New York: Robert Appleton Company, 1912); available from http://www.newadvent.org/cathen/15188a.htm. Accessed June 30, 2011.

39   For 1360, see *Chronica Gestorum ac factorum memorabilium civitatis Bononie*, ed. Albano Sorbelli, Rerum Italicarum Scriptores (Città di Castello: Tipi della casa editrice S. Lapi, 1921), 23. 2, 49.2–3, 11.14; *Corpus chronicorum bononiensium*, 3 vols., ed. Albano Sorbellli, Rerum Italicarum Scriptores (Città di Castello: Tipi della casa editrice S. Lapi, 1906–1924), 18:1:3, 95–122.

40   For the revolt, see *Chronica Gestorum*, 23:2, 54.2–27. Unfortunately, no mention is made of the reception or treatment of various ambassadors who were at the papal court during this revolt or sent there afterwards. For further details on independence and the agreements between Bologna and the papacy, see Oreste Vancini, *La rivolta dei Bolognesi al governo dei vicari della chiesa (1376–1377): L'origine dei tribuni della plebe* (Bologna: N. Zanichelli, 1906). For more on Bologna's long-term struggles as a member of the Papal States in the late medieval and early modern periods, see Angela de Benedictis, "Quale 'corte' per quale 'signore'? A proposito di organizzazione e immagine del potere durante la preminenza di Giovanni II Bentivoglio," in *Bentivolorum magnificentia: principe e cultura a Bologna nel Rinascimento*, ed. Bruno Basile (Rome: Bulzoni, 1984), pp. 17–23; idem, *Repubblica per contratto: Bologna-una città europea nello Stato della Chiesa* (Bologna: il Mulino, 1995); idem, *Una guerra d'Italia, una resistenza di popolo: Bologna, 1506*, (Bologna: il Mulino, 2004).

41   Grendler, *Universities*, p. 10; Cecilia M. Ady, *The Bentivoglio of Bologna: a Study in Despotism* (Oxford: OUP, 1937), pp. 1–10.

transformed," presumably referring to its new role as a civic entity under a papal-free government.[42] The city also mandated that the annual appointment of the two faculty members in surgery as being under the control of the senior council of Bologna.[43]

Bologna did not maintain the severed ties with the papacy for very long, for in 1377 the city approached Pope Gregory XI regarding an agreement in which the city would recognize papal stewardship and would pay tribute to the pontiff in return for recognition of Bologna's new constitution.[44] This provided the best of both worlds: independence for the commune, combined with the protection of the holy pontiff, presumably to aid them in maintaining their constitutional freedom in the chaotic north of Italy. In 1378, the statutes of the College of Arts and Medicine closed with recognition of their reliance on the jurisdiction of the city and the approval of its officers and committees, as established in the new constitution of 1376 that was recognized by the 1377 papal treaty, which, of course, included the new relationship with the *podestà*.[45] Thus, in spite of the treaty with the pope, the city's control over the *studium* continued.

By 1381, the initial oversight group had expanded under the aegis of the council of senior Bolognese citizens into the *Riformatori dello Studio*. The *Riformatori* was a group of four to eight citizens who were appointed "for the preservation and increase of the *studium* of the commune of Bologna."[46] They claimed as their prerogatives the supervision of the formation of the faculty rolls, appointing and negotiating with the lecturers and professors at the *studium*, as well as how much the professors were paid and even the teaching schedule—although not the subjects taught, only when they were taught.[47] In the city statutes for the year 1389, rewritten a year after a major city council meeting and a redraft-

---

42   *Gli statuti del Comune di Bologna degli anni 1352, 1357; 1376, 1389 (Libri I–III)*, 2 vols., ed. Valeria Braidi (Bologna: Deputazione di storia patria per la province di Romagna, 2002), v. 2, pp. 1114–1115.

43   *Gli Statuti*, v. 2, pp. 1113–1115. This also included one professor of philosophy.

44   Ady, *The Bentivoglio*, pp. 5–6.

45   *Statuti delle Università*, p. 449. Interestingly, this closing expressly included the jurist colleges as part of this subordinate relationship.

46   *L'Archivio dei Riformatori dello Studio: inventario*, ed. Claudia Salterini (Bologna: Presso l'instituto per la storia dell'università, 1997), p. i, n. 1, line 10.

47   Grendler, *Universities*, 10; *L'Archivio*, iii. By tradition, the *Riformatori della Studio* goes by its Italian name over the Latin because the *Riformatori* itself was a group that continued, off and on, from 1381–1799. A parallel *Riformatori dello Studio* was also found in Padua, Ferrara, Parma, Turin, and Pavia; while a similar type of group (called variously the *Savi dello Studio* or *Ufficiali dello Studio* appeared in Siena and Florence, respectively). Grendler, *Universities*, 157. City appropriation of salaries happened slowly over course of

ing of the treaty with the papacy in the face of the Western Schism, an addition was made to the appointment of professors. The surgery faculty could also be appointed by "the elected reformers of the *studium*" as well as the senior council, as was the rule for 1376.[48] This shows continued control of the *studium* by the city, and the hold the *Riformatori* continued to exercise over the professors in spite of Bologna's tumultuous relationships with the popes.[49]

The response of the College of Arts and Medicine in the statutes to the continued presence of the pope in the city structure and the professors' continued relationship with the *Riformatori* was twofold. First, the language acknowledging their reliance on the city at the end of the statutes was missing from the 1395 iteration; instead, they referred consistently to the rules they had set up in 1378 and the constitution of 1376.[50] Second, they maintained the language of their relationship to the *podestà* and even added references to his role in collecting penalties, as seen above. The 1395 edition of laws came several years after Bologna's capitulation to the Roman Pope in 1392, and after the 1393 formation of a new civic committee, called the *Sedici Riformatori dello stato di libertà*, a council of nobles elected for life who would oversee the various other committees, including the annually elected *Riformatori*.[51] By referring to the letter of the law established post-independence, the professors were

---

the fourteenth century, for example, in the statutes of 1352–1357, the salaries for academic surgeons was set at 50 *lire* a year, *Gli Statuti*, v. 1, p. 280.

48   This was also found in reference to the yearly occurrence of the elections, *Gli Statuti*, v. 2, pp. 1114–1115. In later years, the *Riformatori* also controlled the way that classes were actually conducted, often sending a representative to the place and time the lecture was being held in order to "check up" on the professor and make sure all was going according to plan. The position was started in 1463 and called a *punctator*; De Coster, "Foreign and Citizen Teachers"; Grendler, *Universities*, 10, 14–15.

49   The Western Schism ran from 1378–1417, where several claimants to the papal throne existed. This followed close on the heels of the Avignon Papacy, where the French pope Clement V decided against moving to Rome in 1309 and set up the papal court in Avignon, France. After the return of the court to Rome in 1376, Urban VI was elected in 1378, but his personality and reputation declined rapidly, causing the cardinals to elect a rival pope at the end of that year. This, pope, Clement VII, returned to the palace at Avignon and ran counter to the popes in Rome. In 1409, the Council of Pisa renounced both popes as schismatic (among other things) and elected Alexander V, who became the third rival for the Holy See.

50   *Statuti delle Università*, pp. 477–80.

51   Grendler, *Universities*, p. 10; Ady, *The Bentivoglio*, pp. 4–5. For more on the formation of the new constitution, see *Chronica Gestorum*, 23:2, 175 and Vancini, *La rivolta dei Bolognesi*, *passim*.

attempting to maintain their autonomy under two new layers of oversight: a permanent committee of nobles and the overlordship of Rome.

A second phase of the *Riformatori* started in 1407, during struggles between the Milanese and the papacy, which were finally settled in 1410 in favor of the papacy when the reigning Visconti ceded Bologna to Antipope Alexander V.[52] Almost immediately, the CAM rewrote their statutes again under Alexander, but without the strongly worded material from previous editions, perhaps because of the proximity to the See at Pisa. Alexander died after ten months on the throne, and Bologna's care was passed to his successor, but soon lost again to Rome in 1412. In 1413, the Roman papal legate and three other men were appointed to the *Riformatori*, suggesting that immediately following Roman control the pope wanted a return of his influence in the running of the *studium*, by now long under control of Bologna directly.[53] It is evident that after the initial break with Rome in 1376, Bologna assumed jurisdiction over the *studium* and the rights that had formerly belonged to the papal-backed student body in such a way that the professors in the College of Arts and Medicine needed to reiterate their place within the administrative and legal context of the city at strategic moments in Bologna's relationship with Northern Italy on the whole.

It is apparent from the relationship between civic and educational statutory activity and the establishment of oversight committees that the city of Bologna was attempting to stabilize the *studium* and make it a part of the city's structure instead of its own entity. The generation of CAM statutes so closely

---

52   This "phase" of the *Riformatori* lasted until the 1520s, when a new committee was created, called the *Assunteria dello Studio*, whose job it became to appoint professors and name their salaries, while the *Riformatori* was in charge solely of class schedules. The *Assunteria* was then in contact with the pope when they needed help with large problems, or wanted to make an offer to a foreign scholar, Grendler, *Universities*, p. 20. As for the Pisan popes, Alexander V died in Bologna in May of 1410, and his replacement became John XXIII.

53   *Chartularium di Studii Bononiensis. Documenti per la storia dell'Università di Bologna dalla origine fino al secolo XV*, 11 vols. (Bologna: Instituto per la storia dell'Università di Bologna, 1909–1940), doc. *clxxxviii*, v. 2, p. 213. The settlement would not generate a lasting peace between Bologna and the papacy—the city would end up "capitulating" to the church seven times between 1392 and 1447, each capitulation followed by a revolt. In 1447, another formal relationship was arranged between the papacy (under Nicholas V, who had been a graduate of Bologna in both arts and law) and the commune, Ady, *The Bentivoglio*, pp. 5–6. The *Sedici* were themselves replaced by the Pope in 1513, at which point the pope had taken Bologna back into the Papal States and the city was then run by the pope's legate (in the name of the pontiff) and the Senate of the commune, as it had been in 1447, Grendler, *Universities*, p. 14.

after each link with the papacy shows that the professors wanted to maintain these ties with the city, as was also evidenced by their reliance on the support of the *podestà*. The pre-*Protomedicato* College of Arts and Medicine acknowledged their reliance on the city and its legal and governmental support through which they maintained their control over proper academic education of physicians. They used this backing to extend their influence over medical practitioners and surgeons in the city, whether or not they were formally tied to the *studium*. The legal relationships, especially, produced an educational environment that was more or less secure against student and papal interference and set the stage for the formal creation of the tribunal that would assume the responsibility of the *podestà* for prosecuting the violation of medical standards in the sixteenth century.

Overall, the relationship between the medical academy and the city of Bologna was a complex one. The medical professors threw their support behind the city, which began to establish oversight committees that reduced the role of the papacy in the government of the *studium*; a support evidenced by the changes in the CAM statures between 1378 and 1410. In addition, the physician professors established a close working relationship with the *podestà*, in which the latter was responsible for prosecuting medical crimes in the city. These crimes were defined by the statutes of the medical college and were aimed at controlling the non-academically trained medical practitioners in the city as a whole. On the one hand, these regulations acted as the precursor to the sixteenth-century *Protomedicato* tribunal in Bologna, but on the other hand, they also relied on a reiteration of a long-standing hierarchy of practitioners, in which the academically trained physicians were at the pinnacle and surgeons, barbers, apothecaries, and female practitioners made up the lower levels of the scale. In spite of the fact that many historians of medicine have described a medical marketplace in which this hierarchy did not exist, the recurrence of this hierarchy in the CAM statutes shows that the physician professors at Bologna were not above repeating a convenient and established idea to achieve their larger goals; in this case, a closer tie with the city.

CHAPTER 8

Medical Licensing in Late Medieval Portugal

Iona McCleery[1]

On 11 February 1338, Aires Vicente was licensed to practice surgery by the chief-examiner Master Afonso, Master Domingos, "expert in the art of coughs," and apothecary-surgeons Master Gil and Master Pero.[2] A few days later on 22 February, Master Domingos was himself licensed in surgery by chief-examiners Master Afonso and Master Gonçalo. This more detailed document explained that King Afonso IV (1325–57) mandated such examinations in order: "to remove harm from the people of my lands, seeing and considering how many make themselves physicians, and masters, surgeons and apothecaries practise these offices in my lands without having the knowledge or the skill to practise them."[3] Medical historians traditionally viewed such medical licenses as indicators of progress. They were methods of establishing orthodoxy based on knowledge and skill, embodying a keen sense of the "public good." The unlicensed were thus unorthodox in their practice and potentially harmful charlatans.[4] Recently, historians have developed a more nuanced view, with early-modernists especially putting forward the idea that charlatanism resulted more from competition amongst practitioners than from systems of licensing instituted to protect the sick. Where such systems existed they could reflect increasing state control for financial or political reasons as much

1   The research for this essay was funded by the Wellcome Trust (grant number 076812). A version was presented at the International Medieval Congress in Leeds in 2009 as part of two sessions I organized on medical orthodoxy. I would like to thank the other participants for their support and contributions: Alex Bamji, Monica Green, Clare Pilsworth, Chris Tuckley, Louise Wilson and Mary Yearl.
2   António Henrique de Oliveira Marques, ed., *Chancelarias Portuguesas: D. Afonso IV*, 3 vols (Lisbon: Instituto Nacional de Investigação Científica and Centro de Estudos Históricos da Universidade Nova, 1990–2), v. 2, pp. 170–1. All translations are mine.
3   Marques, *Chancelarias*, pp. 171–2.
4   An example of a teleological approach to licensing is Toby Gelfand, "The History of the Medical Profession," in *Companion Encyclopedia of the History of Medicine*, ed. W. F. Bynum and Roy Porter, 2 vols., (London and New York: Routledge, 1993), v. 2, pp. 1119–50. Even a sympathetic study of medieval unlicensed practitioners took it for granted that licensing was "in the public interest": Pearl Kibre, "The Faculty of Medicine at Paris: Charlatanism and Unlicensed Medical Practice in the Later Middle Ages," BHM 27 (1953): 20.

as altruism.[5] This essay offers an analysis of one licensing system: that of the expanding late-medieval state of Portugal, and argues that medical licenses were never straightforward regulators of behavior.

The documents referred to at the beginning of this essay are the earliest medical licenses to survive from Portugal. What survives for us to read are the royal chancery copies; the original charters presumably given to the licensee are no longer extant. There is nothing to suggest that licensing was a new innovation in the late 1330s, so it is plausible that it stemmed from a dynamic period of legislation carried during the reign of King Dinis (1279–1325).[6] This chronology would be in keeping with that established by Michael McVaugh and others for the Crown of Aragon where licensing developed in Catalonia and Valencia after 1329, based in Catalonia on legislation going back to 1289.[7] Unfortunately, in Portugal, most of the royal chancery records were re-edited in the fifteenth century, jettisoning much of interest to a medical historian.[8] Just six licensing letters survive from the reign of Afonso IV in the 1330s.[9] It is only from the 1430s that a continuous series survives (three hundred letters through until 1495), but they are also incomplete due to lost or damaged volumes. The only scholar to study these letters in detail, Iria Gonçalves, assumed without question that these letters represented all available practitioners throughout the

5   Alison Lingo, "Empirics and Charlatans in Early Modern France: the Genesis of the Classification of the "Other" in Medical Practice," *Journal of Social History* 19 (1986): 583–604; Roy Porter, *Quacks: Fakers and Charlatans in English Medicine* (Stroud: Tempus, 2001); David Gentilcore, *Medical Charlatanism in Early-Modern Italy* (Oxford: OUP, 2006); María Luz López Terrada, "Medical Pluralism in the Iberian Kingdoms: the Control of Extra-academic Practitioners in Valencia," *MH*, supplement 29 (2009): 7–25.

6   Maria Helena da Cruz Coelho and Armando Luís de Carvalho Homem, eds., *Portugal em Definição de Fronteiras: do Condado Portucalense à Crise do Século XIV*, Nova História de Portugal 3 (Lisbon: Editorial Presença, 1996), pp. 144–63.

7   Luis García Ballester, Michael R. McVaugh and Agustín Rubio Vela, *Medical Licensing and Learning in Fourteenth-century Valencia: Transactions of the American Philosophical Society* (Philadelphia: American Philosophical Society, 1989); Michael R. McVaugh, *Medicine before the Plague: Patients and Practitioners in the Medieval Crown of Aragon, 1285–1345* (Cambridge: CUP), pp. 95–103.

8   The royal chancery of Afonso V (1438–82) can be consulted online at http://digitarq.dgarq.gov.pt/details?id=3815943. Accessed February 15, 2013. For some guidance on the collection, see Judite Gonçalves de Freitas, "The Royal Chancellery at the End of the Portuguese Middle Ages: Diplomacy and Political Society (1970–2005)," *E-Journal of Portuguese History* 7 (2009), http://www.brown.edu/Departments/Portuguese_Brazilian_Studies/ejph/html/issue14/html/jfreitas.html Accessed 15 February 2013.

9   The sole study and first edition of these letters was Pedro de Azevedo, "Físicos e cirurgiões do tempo de D. Afonso IV," *Arquivos de História da Medicina Portuguesa*, n.s. 3 (1912): 3–11.

whole country for the whole of the fifteenth century.[10] Saul António Gomes later assumed that there was therefore little healthcare available and what there was virtually collapsed when the Jews were forced to convert or leave in 1497, since so many licensed physicians were Jewish. This collapse explained the licensing of uneducated healers in the early-sixteenth century, including bonesetters and pox specialists.[11] Few historians have considered instead how the wider bureaucratic reforms of King Manuel (1495–1521) might have led to the expansion of medical licensing at this time; nearly four hundred licenses survive from Manuel's reign alone.[12]

At first sight, these letters appear to be a valid method of assessing the level of medical practice available in late medieval Portugal. They perhaps imply that these medical practitioners had some kind of self-awareness as a group, used licensing as an institutional system of controlling membership of the group, and based membership on certain standards of academic knowledge and ethical practice, that is, they formed a medical profession according to the criteria put forward by modern historian Toby Gelfand.[13] Medievalists have been understandably reluctant to join in "professionalization" debates since the rules of engagement are always based on modern contexts. However, Michael McVaugh argued that the emphasis he saw in the Crown of Aragon on academic learning as a criterion for orthodox practice meant that medieval regulations "laid the foundations of future codes of professional licensing."[14] Exploring medical licensing in the same way as McVaugh, and also Danielle Jacquart, Katharine Park, Susan Edgington and others, allows comparison between Portuguese medicine and that of Aragon, Italy, France and Jerusalem.[15]

---

10   Iria Gonçalves, "Físicos e cirurgiões quatrocentistas—as cartas de exame," in *Imagens do Mundo Medieval*, ed. Iria Gonçalves (Lisbon: Livros Horizonte, 1988), pp. 9–52.

11   Saul António Gomes, "Higiene e saúde na Leiria medieval," in *III Colóquio Sobre a História de Leiria e da sua Região* (Leiria: Câmara Municipal de Leiria, 1999), pp. 41–2.

12   The sole study of these is Manuela Mendonça, "A reforma da saúde no reinado de D. Manuel," in *1as Jornadas de História do Direito Hispânico: Actas* (Lisbon: Academia Portuguesa da História, 2004), pp. 221–41.

13   Gelfand, "History of the Medical Profession." See also Ivan Waddington, *The Medical Profession in the Industrial Revolution* (Dublin: Gill and Macmillan, 1984); John C. Burnham, *How the Idea of Profession Changed the Writing of Medical History* (London: Wellcome Institute for the History of Medicine, 1998); Stephen Jacyna, "Medicine in Transformation, 1800–1849," in *The Western Medical Tradition, 1800–2000*, ed. W. F. Bynum *et al.* (Cambridge: CUP, 2006), pp. 11–101.

14   McVaugh, *Medicine before the Plague*, p. 103.

15   Katharine Park, *Doctors and Medicine in Early Renaissance Florence* (Princeton: Princeton University Press, 1985); Danielle Jacquart, *La Médécine Médiévale dans le Cadre Parisien*

Each of these regions saw the establishment of medical licensing between the twelfth and the fourteenth centuries, beginning with regulations instituted by King Roger of Sicily in 1140. In Mediterranean Europe, royal control of licensing seems common; in other regions it was towns, universities, bishops, guilds or colleges, or a combination of several of these. There does not seem to have been a full comparison of these systems, considering how they operated, why they differed and whose practice was encompassed.

A comparative study of medical licensing systems across Europe would shed light on the insight drawn from the Portuguese evidence that licensing was not a straightforward method of establishing medical orthodoxy. Iria Gonçalves's published list of licensed practitioners is fairly complete up to 1495, so the many unlicensed Portuguese practitioners that continue to be found defy easy explanation. Do they just *seem* not to have had a license because records are incomplete? Or, did they refuse to get one? Between c.1320 and c.1520 eleven hundred practitioners have so far been identified in a wide variety of occupational groups (physicians, barbers, surgeons, apothecaries and a group of healers that includes bonesetters, pox specialists and hernia repairers), most of which at some stage became subject to licensing.[16] Only 54% of Christian practitioners appear to have been licensed, in contrast to 85% of Jews. Surgeons were far more likely to be licensed than physicians. Barbers were always Christian and mostly unlicensed.

Another problem that could be addressed by a comparative study is the tendency of most studies of licensing systems to focus on regulatory systems from the perspective of law providers and practitioners. The "users" of medicine: that is the sick and their communities have usually been left out of the picture. Only a few historians have addressed the question of whether patients saw much difference between "orthodox" and "unorthodox" medicine. For example, studies of the trial of Jacoba Felicie, accused in 1322 of unlicensed practice by the medical faculty of the University of Paris, emphasize how her patients testified to her efficacy and skill, revealing how similar her practice

---

(Paris: Librairie Arthème Fayard, 1998); Laurent Garrigues, "Les professions médicales à Paris au début du XVᵉ siècle: practiciens en procès au parlement," *Bibliotheque de l'École des Chartes* 156 (1998): 317–67; Piers D. Mitchell, *Medicine in the Crusades: Warfare, Wounds and the Medieval Surgeon* (Cambridge: CUP, 2004), pp. 220–31; Susan B. Edgington, "Medicine and Surgery in the *Livre des Assises de la Cour des Bourgeois de Jérusalem*," *Al-Masāq: Islam and the Medieval Mediterranean* 17 (2005): 87–97.

16   This research will come out in Iona McCleery, *Medicine and Community in Late Medieval Portugal* (monograph in progress).

and clientele were to those of academically-trained physicians.[17] In the case of the Crown of Aragon, Michael McVaugh suggests that it was urban and royal patients who recognized the common identity of medical practitioners long before they themselves had any kind of group awareness. McVaugh argues that it was kings and communities who emphasized academic learning and its relationship to good practice, imposing concepts of medical professionalism on self-interested practitioners.[18]

McVaugh recognized the limitations of licensing—although it hardly features in his discussions of the patient-practitioner relationship—but as pointed out earlier, like many historians he also interpreted it teleologically as laying the "foundations" for the future.[19] In the UK, the lines of perspective of many historians interested in professionalization converge on the Medical Act of 1858, which sought to register all medical practitioners, and the General Medical Council (GMC) founded that same year, which still regulates medical education in Britain today. Despite the fact that the scope of the original Medical Act was limited, and that the GMC did not police the medical profession (which was supposed to regulate itself), they are sometimes set up as the pinnacles of progress in contrast to medieval attempts at regulation.[20] Yet rather than seeing medieval licensing as a step towards some kind of nonexistent ideal, it should be understood within the context of its own times. It should be possible to determine the role that licensing played in late medieval Portugal without resorting to retrospective judgments. The remainder of this chapter is inspired by a question posed by Sandra Cavallo in her monograph on barbers and other "artisans of the body" in early-modern Turin. Cavallo found that in a survey of practitioners done in 1695, 20% of surgeons in the city and 43% in the province had not felt it necessary to have a license. She therefore

---

17   Kibre, "Faculty of Medicine at Paris,"; Montserrat Cabré i Pairet and Fernando Salmón Muñiz, "Poder académico *versus* autoridad femenina: la Facultad de Medicina de París contra Jacoba Félicié (1322)," *Dynamis* 19 (1999): 55–78; Monica H. Green, "Getting to the Source: the Case of Jacoba Felicie and the Impact of the *Portable Medieval Reader* on the Canon of Medieval Women"s History," *Medieval Feminist Forum* 42 (2006): 50–63. For a similar case, see Faith Wallis and Geneviève Dumas, "Theory and Practice in the Trial of Jean Domrémi, 1423–27," *JHMAS* 54 (1999): 55–87.
18   McVaugh, *Medicine before the Plague*, p. 245.
19   McVaugh, *Medicine before the Plague*, pp. 166–89; McVaugh, "Bedside Manners in the Middle Ages," *BHM* 71 (1997): 201–23.
20   Michael J. D. Roberts, "The Politics of Professionalisation: MPs, Medical Men and the 1858 Medical Act," *MH* 53 (2009): 37–56; Mary Dixon-Woods, Karen Yeung and Charles L. Bosk, "Why is UK Medicine no Longer a Self-regulating Profession? The Role of Scandals involving "Bad Apple" Doctors," *Social Science and Medicine* 73 (2011): 1452–59.

questioned the purpose of the medical license. Her tentative answers were that licenses seemed to reflect the status and responsibility of practitioners rather than their competence; patients and their communities probably did not see much difference between a licensed and unlicensed practitioner since licenses do not seem to have formed the basis of interpersonal trust; and from the perspective of the licensing authorities, licenses had more to do with the balance of power in their territories than control of expertise.[21] The purpose of the license can also be questioned for late medieval Portugal, although the answers might not be the same.

In order to answer this question of the purpose of the license in the Portuguese context, it is necessary to focus on who was licensed in Portugal, by whom, and how. Unlike in other parts of Europe, licensing only applied to physicians and surgeons at quite a late date. Occasionally barbers and apothecaries were examined in medicine or surgery, but despite Afonso IV's wish to include them in the 1330s, apothecaries do not appear to have been regulated *as* apothecaries before the mid-fifteenth century and were not often licensed as such until after 1515. Barbers were not regulated until 1511, and even then only as shavers and sword specialists; Portuguese barbers were always linked to military men, not grocers as in other parts of Europe. It was only after 1511 (except in a couple of isolated cases) that bonesetters, pox specialists and hernia-repairers began to appear regularly as licensees, suggesting a possible early separation of shaving and minor surgery.[22] There appears to have been no licensing of midwives and only one (royal) midwife has so far been documented throughout the fifteenth century.[23] There is no evidence for episcopal licensing. There were also no medical guilds or indeed much in the way of occupational confraternities of any kind. There is some evidence that Portuguese towns had a system of licensing as they sometimes sent candidates to the royal court to have their practice confirmed. For example, in 1454 Isabel Martins, the only woman to be licensed during the fifteenth century, was licensed in surgery at the request of her town

---

21   Sandra Cavallo, *Artisans of the Body in Early Modern Italy: Identities, Families and Masculinities* (Manchester: Manchester University Press, 2007), pp. 224–31.

22   Normally, this separation is said to have occurred in the eighteenth century. See Cavallo, *Artisans of the Body*, pp. 38–57.

23   Caterina Afonso was the midwife of Leonor of Aragon (d.1445), wife of King Duarte (1433–38): ANTT, *Chancelaria de D. Afonso V*, bk. 19, fo. 91. As Leonor was a foreigner, it is possible that her midwife was also and therefore attracted attention as an imported professional. See Monica. H. Green, "Bodies, Gender, Health, Disease: Recent Work on Medieval Women's Medicine," *Studies in Medieval and Renaissance History*, 3rd ser., 2 (2005): 14–17.

Montemor-o-Velho.[24] However, there is very little information on the control of medical occupations in towns. The town council minutes for Oporto in 1392 include a letter from King João I (1385–1433) requiring all practitioners to be licensed, but there is no evidence that the council discussed it.[25] Nothing is known about how practitioners gained access to the itinerant Portuguese royal court or how they used their copies of the royal license.

It is clear that royal physicians or surgeons, referred to as "chiefs" of their occupation (*físico-mor* or *cirurgião-mor*), carried out the main system of licensing.[26] In the fifteenth century, some of these royal medics were university graduates: learned, well connected and occasionally in clerical orders. For example, Fernando Álvares Cardoso, Bachelor of Arts and Medicine (*fl.*1426–1452) was papal proto-notary and Dean of Évora (despite having four children later legitimized), both a royal physician and a royal confessor, briefly a medical examiner and holder of numerous other benefices.[27] The Portuguese case makes it clear that, although few in number (6%), clerical practitioners were often very high profile.[28] However, unlike in the Crown of Aragon and other places, possession of a medical degree was not a criterion for a license and it certainly did not replace royal examination. Only 10% of the total number of

---

24   ANTT, *Chancelaria de D. Afonso V*, bk. 15, fo. 99; Gonçalves, "Físicos e cirurgiões quatrocentistas," 20 and 37.

25   Artur de Magalhães Basto, ed., *Vereações: Anos de 1390–1395* (Oporto: Câmara Municipal, 1937), p. 226.

26   This system is very different to that of Castile and the United Spain. See María Luz López Terrada, "The Control of Medical Practice under the Spanish Monarchy during the Sixteenth and Seventeenth centuries," in *Beyond the Black Legend: Spain and the Scientific Revolution*, ed. Víctor Navarro Brotóns and William Eamon (Valencia: Universitat de Valencia and C.S.I.C., 2007), pp. 283–94.

27   António Domingues de Sousa Costa, ed., *Monumenta Portugaliae Vaticana*, 4 vols., (Rome: Livraria Editorial Franciscana, 1968–78), v. 4, pp. 187, 245–6, 259, 415–6, 460, 521–2, 559–61, 564–5, 572–3, 575, 594–5.

28   Clerics were not banned from practicing medicine, although those in higher orders (sub-deacon, deacon or priest) were supposed to seek dispensation first. See Darrel W. Amundsen, "Medieval Canon Law on Medical and Surgical Practice by the Clergy," BHM 52 (1978): 22–44. I have found hardly any monks or friars practicing medicine amongst the laity after the thirteenth century but members of the quasi-secular military orders certainly did so and so did João Vicente (d.1463), Master of Arts and Medicine, royal physician, bishop successively of Lamego and Viseu and founder of his own religious order known as the Blue Friars. His career is described in Francisco de Santa Maria, *O Ceu Aberto na Terra: História das Sagradas Congregações dos Conegos Seculares de. S. Jorge em Alga de Venesa e de S. João Evangelista em Portugal*, 4 vols. in 2 (Lisbon: Officina de Manoel Lopes Ferreyra, 1697), v. 2, pp. 551–611.

practitioners identified so far had degrees (111 people, of whom nineteen had licenses). Only in 1515 were graduates in medicine from the University of Lisbon exempted; those who had studied abroad still had to undergo examination.[29] The lack of a degree, however, did not imply that academic learning was unimportant. Examiners questioned candidates about their knowledge as well as observing their practice. For most examinations only a formulaic letter survives, but sometimes the academic questions were also preserved: Master Cohen was questioned in 1459 "on the care of putrid fevers in general," a reference to book four, fen one, treatise two of Avicenna's *Canon*, probably the most important university medical text of the period.[30] In the first surviving examination in 1338, that of Aires Vicente with whom this essay began, the examiner claimed that "he saw the cures he did, to whom he did them and in which parts of the body." Aires's patients then had to swear on the Holy Gospels that he had treated them "until he made them healthy."[31] In the fifteenth century, the candidate had to swear an oath on the Gospels or the Torah that they would practice on Christians, Muslims and Jews without deception or malice.[32]

In their analysis of licensing in fourteenth-century Valencia, McVaugh, García Ballester and Rubio Vela suggested four reasons why the King of Aragon might have sought greater control of medical and surgical practice: making medicine more Christian; genuine belief in the benefits of good practice based on academic knowledge; asserting royal power; and protecting economic interests.[33] This is a useful checklist for Portugal, although it should be remembered that most of the Portuguese documentation stems from the fifteenth rather than the fourteenth century, and is much more limited. To take the fourth reason first: economic interests, Portuguese examiners potentially had a financial incentive to identify the unlicensed as they could keep a large part of the fines: a complaint was made to the parliament held in Coimbra in 1472 that the chief-physician and chief-surgeon were fining any old woman or man who healed using herbs and words.[34] However, it is difficult to see how provincial herbalists could really have threatened the medical practice of elite practitioners at court or added much to their pockets. From the 1480s,

29 Mendonça, "Reforma da saúde," 239. Medical students and graduates are identified in archival documents by the terms *licenciado, estudante* or *escollar* in medicine, or they identify themselves as a *mestrado* or *doutorado* in Medicine.
30 Gonçalves, "Físicos e cirurgiões," p. 17.
31 Marques, ed., *Chancelarias Portuguesas: D. Afonso IV*, v. 2, pp. 170–1.
32 Gonçalves, "Físicos e cirurgiões," p. 18.
33 García Ballester, McVaugh and Rubio Vela, "Medical Licensing," pp. 41–50.
34 Gonçalves, "Físicos e cirurgiões," p. 14.

the numbers of licensed practitioners increased, but it is not clear whether this reflected more zealous, self-interested examiners, the expansion of royal power, or just better recording of the pluralistic medicine on offer.[35] It is particularly difficult to tell since only one example of somebody prosecuted for unlicensed practice has come to light; a royal pardon issued to José Contador, a Jew from Estremoz, denounced by a porter of Prince Henrique "the Navigator" for unlicensed practice of medicine and surgery.[36] Unfortunately, royal pardons are the only level of justice available, since all local levels have disappeared from the record; therefore, the existing documentation reveals most about probably atypical cases where the accused had access to the royal court.[37] It is possible that José fell out with Henrique's entourage for political and financial reasons. Henrique used his own medical practitioners as tax collectors, and they too sometimes ran into problems: in 1456 his physician and surgeon Master Isaac Franco got involved in a quarrel over tax and was denounced for denying God and the Virgin Mary.[38] Without the documentation available in other parts of Europe, it is not possible to say more about either of these cases, but it is difficult to see them as medical disputes.

What can be said about these cases is that rather than seeing them as signs of royal medics policing the kingdom out of their own interests, which seems to have been an impossible undertaking, practitioners may have increasingly chosen to present themselves for examination at court. Possibly this was for personal economic reasons. Sandra Cavallo suggests that many licensees in early-modern Turin came forward because they were going into business for themselves. The license represented their new financial and moral responsibilities but, in fact, they had already been practicing for years under a master of a shop.[39] Some of the Portuguese licenses are also suggestive of this: according to Gonçalves, 21.3% of licensees were described as sons, relatives or *criados* of established practitioners.[40] For example, Aires Vicente, whose license was

---

35   Afonso V (1438–82) averaged six licenses a year; João II (1482–95) averaged ten; Manuel
     (1495–1521) averaged sixteen: Mendonça, "Reforma da saúde," p. 229.

36   Manuel Lopes de Almeida, Idalino Ferreira da Costa Brochado and António Joaquim Dias
     Dinis, eds., *Monumenta Henricina*, 14 vols. (Coimbra: Executiva das Comemorações do
     V Centenário da Morte do Infante Dom Henrique, 1960–74), v. 9, pp. 174–5.

37   Luís Miguel Duarte, *Justiça e Criminalidade no Portugal Medievo (1459–1481)* (Lisbon:
     Fundação Calouste Gulbenkian and Fundação para a Ciência e a Tecnologia, 1999),
     pp. 20–22.

38   Almeida, Brochado and Dinis, eds., *Monumenta Henricina*, v. 12, pp. 160–1; v. 13, pp. 59–60.

39   Cavallo, *Artisans of the Body*, p. 227.

40   Gonçalves, "Físicos e cirurgiões," p. 15.

referred to at the very beginning of this chapter, was a *criado* of Master Gil, surgeon of Lisbon. A *criado* in modern Portuguese is a household servant; a reference to the once common practice of having a servant "raised" (*criado*) in one's household from childhood. In the Middle Ages, the status of *criado* operated at the crossroads between "ward," "pupil," "apprentice," and "client"; the most noble of aristocrats could be a royal *criado*, although he might not be a fatherless ward in the English legal sense. In a medical context, the word *criado* almost certainly refers to an apprentice, although we should not assume that this was always the case since medics could be *criados* of non-medics. Some of these *criados* acquired a royal license perhaps as a sign of new independence in their career.[41] This might suggest that as in Turin the license signified intra-occupational identity rather than competency.

One reason why these practitioners might have presented themselves for examination was because the royal license could have acted as a kind of insurance policy, offering some protection against legal proceedings, perhaps from competitors as much as patients. This theory might explain the dominance of surgeons amongst Christian licensees; surgery was sometimes more likely to incur malpractice suits due to the more visible workings of the practitioner on the body.[42] There is only one example of a malpractice case in Portugal, but it is the pardon of a royal surgeon, Master Dinis, who in 1443 was found guilty of causing the death of his patient after treating him for an injury.[43] There is no record that he had a license to practice or that it could have had any bearing on the case. The case for the license as a form of protection for Jews is easier

41   I belong to an international team funded by the National Endowment for the Humanities, which is translating into English three Portuguese chronicles by Fernão Lopes (d.c.1459), important sources for the Hundred Years' War (Woodbridge: Boydell, *forthcoming* in 2014). We decided to leave the word *criado* in the original language throughout as no single English word suffices.

42   McVaugh, *Medicine before the Plague*, p. 183; Monica H. Green and Daniel Lord Smail, "The Trial of Floreta d'Ays (1403): Jews, Christians, and Obstetrics in Later Medieval Marseille," *Journal of Medieval History* 34 (2008): 185–211; Franck Collard, "*Perfidus physicus* ou *inexpertus medicus*: le cas Jean de Grandville médecin du comte Amédée VII de Savoie," in *Mires, Physiciens, Barbiers et Charlatans: les Marges de la Médecine de l'Antiquité au XVIᵉ Siècle*, ed. Franck Collar and Évelyne Samama (Langres: Dominique Guéniot, 2004), pp. 133–49; Faye M. Getz, *Medicine in the English Middle Ages* (Princeton; Princeton University Press, 1998), pp. 72, 77; Carole Rawcliffe, "The Profits of Practice: the Wealth and Status of Medical Men in Later Medieval England," *SHM* 1 (1988): 76–77.

43   Pedro de Azevedo, ed., *Documentos das Chancelarias Reais Anteriores a 1531 Relativos a Marrocos*, 2 vols., (Lisbon: Academia das Ciências, 1915–34), v. 1, pp. 555–6.

to prove. García Ballester, McVaugh and Rubio Vela argued that licensing was a way of Christianizing medicine as well as a means of asserting royal power. Iberian kings generally had a policy of tolerating Jews and Muslims for economic and religious reasons, although what this policy—controversially known to historians as *convivencia* or "living together"—really meant at the time has long been debated.[44] It appears that Catalan or Valencian townspeople had a much less inclusive approach to Jews in the later Middle Ages, allowing kings to interfere in municipal concerns supposedly on the Jews' behalf.[45] García Ballester, McVaugh and Rubio Vela suggest that the municipal legislation for medical licensing instituted in Catalonia and Valencia in the 1330s may have implicitly targeted Jews or Muslims who practiced medicine amongst Christians. McVaugh goes further to suggest that when townspeople referred to the ignorance of practitioners they may have meant Jews, linking the control of practice to beliefs that Jews maliciously poisoned and deluded their patients. These historians also argue that emphasizing the importance of a university degree placed Jews in a position of dependency on royal favor—since only the king could grant them the privilege of a license without a degree—and linked licensing to the religious requirement that patients confess before treatment. These rules would have weakened the authority of Jewish practitioners.[46]

Negative stereotypes seem to have existed to a much lesser extent in Portugal, although Jews were still dependent on royal protection.[47] In 1426–7, there were complaints to the king that Jewish practitioners were capable of causing physical and spiritual harm if not prevented from treating Christian women, and that the king had too many Jewish practitioners in attendance

---

44   Maya Soifer, "Beyond *convivencia*: Critical Reflections on the Historiography of Interfaith Relations in Christian Spain," *Journal of Medieval Iberian Studies* 1 (2009): 19–35; Kenneth B. Wolf, "*Convivencia* in Medieval Spain: a Brief History of an Idea," *Religion Compass* 3 (2008): 72–85; Jonathan Ray, "Beyond Tolerance and Persecution: Reassessing our Approach to Medieval *convivencia*," *Jewish Social Studies* 11 (2006): 1–18.

45   García Ballester, McVaugh and Rubio Vela, "Medical Licensing," 48–50; Paola Tartakoff, "Christian Kings and Jewish Conversion in the Medieval Crown of Aragon," *Journal of Medieval Iberian Studies* 3 (2011): 27–39.

46   García Ballester, McVaugh and Rubio Vela, "Medical Licensing," 25–31, 42; McVaugh, *Medicine before the Plague*, pp. 95–102. See also Étienne Lepicard, "Medical Licensing and Practice in Medieval Spain: a Model of Interfaith Relationships?" in *Medicine and Medical Ethics in Medieval and Early Modern Spain: An Intercultural Approach*, ed. Samuel Kottek and Luis García Ballester (Jerusalem: Magnes Press, Hebrew University, 1996), pp. 50–60.

47   Maria José Ferro Tavares, *Os Judeus em Portugal no Século XV*, 2 vols (Lisbon: Universidade Nova, 1982–4).

on him.[48] In 1443 King Afonso V dispensed a number of Jewish practitioners attached to leading nobles from having to have their licenses renewed, stating nevertheless that Jews were particularly likely to be ignorant and harmful to their patients, which was why he had ordered all Jewish practitioners to seek confirmation of their licenses on pain of imprisonment.[49] In 1451, royal physician Master Afonso was granted a letter from the king confirming that he had received the degree of Doctor of Medicine from the University of Salamanca and quelling rumors that he was a Jew who had slept with Christian women, committed other excesses and been imprisoned.[50] These explicitly negative views seem to have been quite rare. There is some evidence of implicit hostility in Oporto: in 1391 the town council tried to get a Christian physician to come and settle in Oporto because they felt the lack of Christian practitioners.[51] As McVaugh suggests for Aragon, the inability of many practitioners on the grounds of their faith to participate in key civic institutions, such as town councils, that seem to have displayed outright hostility, may have prevented the development of medical guilds and delayed the appearance of a sense of occupational identity.[52]

The sheer numbers of Jewish practitioners in Portugal suggests, however, that Jewish medicine was far too important to be restricted too much and that historians may be overestimating the importance of guilds as an indicator of occupational identity. It is difficult to argue that the origins of licensing in Portugal relate to intercultural antagonism. None of the six letters to survive from the 1330s appears to have been issued to Jews. At the same time, these early letters, unlike most of the later ones, do not refer to the practitioners' religion. It is possible, therefore, that attitudes hardened in the later Middle Ages, perhaps as a result of the Black Death, although this is too convenient an explanation. After 1348, Jews continued to enjoy a peaceful existence in Portugal compared to Castile or Aragon (no massacres in 1391, for example), although it was not quite the haven that traditional historiography made out.

---

48 Margarida Garcez Ventura, *Igreja e Poder no Século XV: Dinastia de Avis e Liberdades Eclesiásticas (1383–1450)* (Lisbon: Edições Colibri, 1997), pp. 487–8.

49 António Dias Farinha, "Portugal e Marrocos no século XV," (Ph.D. Diss., 3 vols., University of Lisbon, 1990), v. 2, pp. 147–8.

50 Artur Moreira de Sá, *et al.*, eds., *Chartularium Universitatis Portugalensis (1288–1537)* (Lisbon: Centro de Estudos de Psicologia e de História da Filosofia anexo à Faculdade de Letras da Universidade de Lisboa, 1966), v. 5, p. 251. It is possible that this was the same individual as Dr Master Afonso Madeira, chief-physician and medical examiner from 1459 until his death in 1475, by which time he had become a knight of the royal household.

51 Basto, *Vereações*, pp. 76–77.

52 McVaugh, *Medicine before the Plague*, p. 245.

According to the chronicler Fernão Lopes, there was a bandit attack on a travelling Jewish spicer in the mid-fourteenth century, the Christian perpetrators of which were executed by Pedro I (1357–67); inappropriately so according to some.[53] There was an attack on the main Jewish quarter in Lisbon in 1449; interestingly barber Gonçalo Pires was one of many perpetrators of this riot later pardoned for his involvement.[54] In 1506, there was a terrible massacre of two thousand New Christians in Lisbon. This isolated massacre took place ten years after the Jewish community had been forced to convert due to wide-ranging changes in royal policy towards both Jews and Muslims. This episode forms a stark contrast to earlier tolerance and its causes are still a matter of debate.[55]

As far as Jewish medical practitioners were concerned, right up until the eve of the edict of expulsion in 1496, Portuguese kings had privileged many of them with exemptions from wearing identifying symbols (not instituted anyway until the end of the fourteenth century) and allowing them to associate with Christians as part of their job. Some were permitted to bear arms as a sign of prestige.[56] Many Jews probably did not bother to seek royal sanction for their commercial and professional activities amongst Christians since there are surprisingly few permits for such large communities.[57] There is little evidence for negative Jewish medical stereotypes in surviving literary works; certainly no

53   Fernão Lopes, *Crónica de D. Pedro*, ed., Giuliano Macchi and Teresa Amado, 2nd ed. (Lisbon: Imprensa Nacional/Casa da Moeda, 2007), pp. 28–30.

54   ANTT, *Chancelaria de Afonso V*, bk. 11, fo. 10.

55   François Soyer, "The Massacre of the New Christians of Lisbon in 1506: a New Eyewitness Account," *Cadernos de Estudos Sefarditas* 7 (2007): 221–43; François Soyer, *The Persecution of the Jews and Muslims of Portugal: King Manuel I and the End of Religious Tolerance (1496–7)* (Leiden: Brill, 2007).

56   Ventura, *Igreja e Poder*, pp. 481–90; François Soyer, "Living in Fear of Revenge: Religious Minorities and the Right to Bear Arms in Fifteenth-century Portugal," in *Vengeance in the Middle Ages: Emotion, Religion and Feud*, ed. Susanna Throop and Paul Hyams (Farnham: Ashgate, 2010), pp. 85–99. There are numerous examples of these privileges in the *Monumenta Henricina* and the *Chartularium Universitatis Portugalensis*.

57   As a case study, consider the ninety-five apothecaries and spicers, 13% of whom were Jews, who I have identified in the whole of Portugal between 1320 and 1520. This number seems remarkably low in comparison to other parts of Europe and can perhaps be explained by the types of documents available; mainly royal and municipal archives yielding cases likely to be atypical. It is possible that the majority of apothecaries and spicers were Jews who simply did not appear on the documentary radar. I have found only three licenses to trade with Christians amongst the Jewish spicers, but it is hard to believe that there was not more regular commercial activity.

fear of poison or other misdemeanor, although this does exist for Christian practitioners.[58] The fact that nobody needed a degree to practice medicine meant that there was no academic obstacle to Jewish practice, and they were thus less dependent on royal favor. It is possible that many Jewish practitioners operated within the large stable Jewish communities of Portuguese towns and never needed to come into contact with Christians (this might also explain the apparent absence of Jewish barbers). This means that it is almost impossible to reconstruct concepts of occupational identity from existing sources, since most records of the highly stratified Jewish communities have vanished. It may be the case that the lack of importance of a degree in the Portuguese licensing system may stem from the prominence of Jewish medical learning, although it was also due to the general weakness of the sole university. This prominence persisted. Although Jews were told to convert or leave Portugal in 1496–7, the king closed the ports to prevent them from leaving and established few methods of enforcing conversion; there was no Inquisition in Portugal until 1536 at which time many people did leave.[59] Medical practitioners were the only category of people allowed to continue to use books in Hebrew after 1497. In 1535, there was a complaint to the parliament in Évora that only New Christians were studying medicine.[60] It is possible that stereotypical stories of malicious practice by secret Jews began to appear after 1497, but the extensive literary and archival material of this period has not yet been studied with this topic in mind.[61] It might be significant that a great many practitioners sought confirmation of their licenses in 1498, sometimes after decades of practice. They may have been New Christians who suddenly felt more vulnerable.[62]

---

58   See Manuel Rodrigues Lapa, ed., *Cantigas de Escarnho e de Mal Dizer dos Cancioneiros Medievais Galego-Portugueses* (Lisbon: Galáxia, 1965), pp. 307–8, for a bloodletter who groped his female patients; and Lopes, *Crónica de D. Pedro*, p. 81, for a physician persuaded to poison a king's political opponent.

59   Soyer, *Persecution of the Jews and Muslims of Portugal*; Jon Arrizabalaga, "The World of Iberian *converso* Practitioners, from Lluís Alcanyís to Isaac Cardoso," in *Beyond the Black Legend*, ed. Brotóns and Eamon, pp. 307–22.

60   Tavares, *Judeus: Século XV*, p. 355.

61   For evidence of both positive and negative stereotypes of Jews in the plays of Gil Vicente, the most important playwright of sixteenth-century Portugal, see Márcio Ricardo Coelho Muniz, "1531: Gil Vicente, judeus e a instauração da Inquisição em Portugal," *Vitória* 7 (2000): 95–108.

62   Sixty licences were issued in 1498, four times the annual average: Mendonça, "Reforma da saúde," 229.

Royal promotion of medical licensing begs the question of why kings might have been interested in regulating healthcare. Medieval historians have argued that the interests of medieval towns in public health and healthcare provision were bound up in their understanding of their legal identities, perhaps based on the rediscovery of Roman law from the twelfth century. Officially appointed physicians and surgeons could be used to promote urban self-interest by uncovering crime, maintaining hygiene, accompanying armies into battle and identifying disease, thereby protecting persons and property and helping to make the town stronger and more secure.[63] It is possible to describe urban authorities (councilors, magistrates) as maintaining an active form of "security politics," since both military and hygiene measures protected the town.[64] Modern historians tend to agree that the enforcement of national public health policies was inspired more by the economic and political needs of the state than altruism, although they usually date these policies as having effect only from the eighteenth century.[65] Today, studies of state interventionism in modern healthcare and social welfare sometimes refer to "governmentality," a concept that originated in lectures given by Michel Foucault (d.1984) in the last decade of his life.

"Governmentality" refers to "mentalities" of government: how and why and by whom people are to be governed, and how people can be taught to govern themselves; that is, to behave in a prescribed manner as suggested or instituted by others, e.g. public health officials, doctors and nutritionists. When used to

---

63   McVaugh, *Medicine before the Plague*, pp. 190–91; Vivian Nutton, "Continuity or Rediscovery? The City Physician in Classical Antiquity and Medieval Italy," in *The Town and State Physician in Europe from the Middle Ages to the Enlightenment*, ed. Andrew W. Russell (Wolfenbüttel: Wolfenbüttler Forschungen 17, 1981), pp. 9–46.

64   For a discussion of the modern term "security politics," used in the field of International Relations to refer to national defence but also used in relationship to healthcare, see David Baldwin, "The Concept of Security," *Review of International Studies* 23 (1997): 2–26; Thomas Osborne, "Of Health and Statecraft," in *Foucault, Health and Medicine*, ed. Alan Petersen and Robin Bunton (London: Routledge, 1997), pp. 173–88; Andrew Price-Smith, ed., *Plagues and Politics: Infectious Disease and International Policy* (Basingstoke: Palgrave, 2001); Sara Davies, *Global Politics of Health* (Cambridge: Polity, 2010).

65   Deborah Dwork, *War is Good for Babies and Other Young Children: the History of the Infant and Child Welfare Movement in England, 1898–1918* (London: Tavistock, 1987); Nikolas Rose, "Medicine, History and the Present," in *Reassessing Foucault: Power, Medicine and the Body*, ed. Colin Jones and Roy Porter (London and New York: Routledge, 1998), pp. 47–72; Dorothy Porter, "The History of Public Health: Current Themes and Approaches," *Hygiea Internationalis* 1 (1999): 9–21; Patrick Carroll, "Medical Police and the History of Public Health," *MH* 46 (2002): 461–94.

explore the interface between biology, hygiene, medicine and politics, the approach is sometimes called "biopolitics."[66] This approach does not seem to have been applied to pre-modern states, which theorists, including Foucault, often viewed as decentralized and lacking in the will to impose discipline on "the people," even if they could imagine a national community of this kind. Yet, it is very likely that the kind of security politics, including medical licensing, practiced by many Mediterranean towns was eventually picked up by kings precisely because they *could* envisage a national population mobilized for economic and political benefit.[67] They saw benefit for themselves and their families, certainly. Yet in these licensing letters, government and sovereignty may have been separate enough for there to be a concept of national benefit, within the context probably, as shall be outlined, of international warfare and the immense taxation and exploitation of resources that it required. This separation between governmental practice and royal sovereignty is a crucial Foucauldian requirement for governmentality to exist and was already made possible because of expanding bureaucratic procedures in the late medieval state; the king did not issue all these letters personally.[68] Governmentality was an imaginative process that led to royal interventionism in daily life through the imposition of laws and the establishing of normative practices. It was also a two-way process; kings learned these biopolitical practices from their populace, especially from the townspeople who probably reached the zenith of their political power during the fourteenth and fifteenth centuries through military and parliamentary service, and in turn were influenced by royal and

---

66   Michel Foucault, "Governmentality," in *The Foucault Effect: Studies in Governmentality*, ed. Graham Burchill, Colin Gordon and Peter Miller (Chicago: University of Chicago Press, 1991), pp. 87–104; Alan Petersen and Robin Bunton, eds., *Foucault, Health and Medicine* (London: Routledge, 1997); Jane Buckingham, "Patient Welfare vs. the Health of the Nation: Governmentality and Sterilisation of Leprosy Sufferers in Early Post-colonial India," *SHM* 19 (2006): 483–99; Mitchell Dean, *Governmentality: Power and Rule in Modern Society*, 2nd ed. (London: Sage, 2010); Susanne Krasmann and Thomas Lemke, eds., *Governmentality: Current Issues and Future Challenges* (New York and London: Routledge, 2011).

67   Medievalists immediately engaged with the argument in Benedict Anderson, *Imagined Communities: Reflections on the Origin and Spread of Nationalism*, first published 1983 (rev. ed., London: Verso, 2006), especially pp. 9–37, that pre-modern people were unable to envisage a national community. See Simon Forde, Lesley Johnson and Alan Murray, eds., *Concepts of National Identity in the Middle Ages* (Leeds: Leeds Studies in English, 1995).

68   Although modern theorists tend to have a very simplistic understanding of pre-modern government, their general point that there has to be a sense of a "state" beyond the person of the king for governmental processes to operate seems to make sense. See Dean, *Governmentality*, pp. 98–111.

court policy.[69] Their implementation of royal policy and the ways in which the kings were influenced by urban policy is surely a form of "governmentality from below" worthy of study by medievalists.[70]

In the last section of this chapter, an attempt will be made to show how kings might have forged a biopolitical awareness that led them to implement systems of licensing. Many of the civil wars and rebellions that pockmarked Portugal's history during the thirteenth and fourteenth centuries can be explained by the antagonism of the old aristocracy to increasing royal centralization. From the mid-thirteenth century, kings surveyed and inventoried their territories, the boundaries of which were negotiated through treaties and wars with neighboring Castile. They subjected them to more regular taxation and heavier bureaucracy, which resulted from and led to close contacts with townspeople and an incipient parliamentary system (since medieval kings were not able to rule without a consensus, especially when they needed money). Kings employed university-trained lawyers and clerics to conduct royal business and they built prestigious castles and churches as instruments of power. The cost of wars and building projects and the desire to perform on the European royal stage encouraged the policies of centralization and taxation. During the fourteenth and fifteenth centuries, the Portuguese were regularly involved in foreign warfare, drawn into the Hundred Years' War on the side of the English. From 1415, Portugal suddenly expanded into North and West Africa and the Atlantic islands, extracting money, resources and troops from a land heavily affected by plague and famine.[71] There has been very little work on how the "fourteenth-century crisis" impacted on Portugal, but certainly persistent out-

---

69   Adelaide Millán da Costa, "State-building in Portugal during the Middle Ages: a Royal Endeavour in Partnership with the Local Powers?" in *Empowering Interactions: Political Cultures and the Emergence of the State in Europe, 1300–1900*, ed. William Blockmans, André Holenstein and Jon Mathieu with Daniel Schläppi (Aldershot: Ashgate, 2009), pp. 219–233.

70   For the concept of "governmentality from below," see Arjun Appadurai, "Deep Democracy: Urban Governmentality and the Horizon of Politics," *Public Culture* 14 (2002): 21–47. For medieval and early modern state-building "from below," see the essays in Blockmans, Holenstein, Mathieu and Schläppi, eds., *Empowering Interactions*.

71   Anthony Disney, *A History of Portugal and the Portuguese Empire*, 2 vols (Cambridge: CUP, 2009), v. 1, pp. 86–140; António dos Santos Pereira, "The Urgent Empire: Portugal between 1475 and 1525," *E-Journal of Portuguese History* 4 (2006), http://www.brown. edu/Departments/Portuguese_Brazilian_Studies/ejph/html/issue8/pdf/apereira.pdf (accessed 21 May 2012); António Henrique de Oliveira Marques, *Portugal na Crise dos Séculos XIV e XV*, Nova História de Portugal 4 (Lisbon: Editorial Presença, 1986); Coelho and Homem, eds., *Portugal em Definição de Fronteiras*; Costa, "State-building."

breaks of plague and food shortages in conjunction with warfare played a role in the shaping of urban and royal security politics.[72]

In all this activity, medicine played a role, perhaps as a means of marshalling healthy bodies in the interests of the state, but few medieval historians have considered early medical regulations from this perspective. In contrast, the welfare reforms of King Manuel and his successors in the sixteenth century have been seen as a form of imperial medicine: a method of maintaining the health of soldiers and sailors, imposing Portuguese values and practices on indigenous peoples and ensuring political control through institutional networks. For example, King Manuel quickly recognized the governmental potential of the *Misericórdias*, lay charitable confraternities founded in 1498 that established hospitals and welfare institutions from Brazil to Goa. If this can be argued for the sixteenth century, then it can perhaps also be argued for earlier periods of expansion.[73]

It would be absurd not to see the introduction of licensing, perhaps as early as the thirteenth century and its intensification in the fifteenth century, as unrelated to this centralizing activity. The licensing of people like Gracia Luís, permitted in 1511 to treat hernias, dislocations and bruises, does not imply the decline of healthcare provision, but the development of a more heavily regulated system similar to that of Italy in this same period.[74] David Gentilcore explains the increasing regulation of "charlatans" as more than a simple expansion of the system for economic reasons. He sees licensing as a result of anxieties about "the other," and categorizes the sixteenth century as a more repressive period due to the Reformation, urbanization, plague, and the proliferation of unsettling new knowledge about the world. Repression through

---

72   I organized a session on the fourteenth-century crisis in southern Europe (Portugal, Castile, southern France) at the International Medieval Congress in Leeds in 2013 as it seemed there was a lack of discussion about this topic. The only full study of plague in Portugal is Mário da Costa Roque, *As Pestes Medievais Europeias e o 'Regimento Proveitoso contra ha Pestenença* (Paris: Fundação Calouste Gulbenkian, Centro Cultural Portugûes, 1979).

73   Isabel dos Guimarães Sá, "Shaping Social Space in the Centre and Periphery of the Portuguese Empire: the Example of the Misericórdias from the Sixteenth to the Eighteenth centuries," *Portuguese Studies* 12 (1997): 210–21; Timothy Walker, "Acquisition and Circulation of Medical Knowledge within the Early-modern Portuguese Colonial Empire," in *Science in the Spanish and Portuguese Empires, 1500–1800*, ed. Daniela Bleichmar, Paula de Vos, Kristin Huffine and Kevin Sheehan (Stanford: Stanford University Press, 2009), pp. 247–70; Hugh Glenn Cagle, "Dead Reckonings: Disease and the Natural Sciences in Portuguese India and the Atlantic, 1450–1650", (Ph.D. Diss., Rutgers University, 2011).

74   ANTT, *Chancelaria de D. Manuel*, bk. 8, f. 69v.

legislation was a psychological method of seeming to control what could not really be controlled.[75] There is no doubt that Portugal did experience ruptures due to plague, although these have not yet been studied in the light of recent scholarship and cannot easily be tied to bursts in legislative activity. As pointed out earlier, the acceleration of licensing after 1497 may have reflected concern about mass conversions from Judaism. However, neither the Reformation nor the pressures of urbanization can easily be made relevant to Portugal; there were few Protestant sympathizers and there had been a tradition of densely populated towns for centuries.

Discussion of the influence of early-modern mentalities and stereotypes may be useful for understanding the expansion of licensing, but early-modern repressive tendencies or other socio-economic factors do not explain the initial regulations themselves. There are two further reasons for why medical licensing might originally have become a feature of medieval Portuguese communities: practices inherited from the Islamic past and genuine royal interest in healthcare. One of the reasons why Portugal already enjoyed a long urban tradition was because of its Islamic heritage. Studies that focus on urban medicine in northern Italy often forget that for parts of southern Europe there were alternative influences on communal identity other than Roman law. It has been argued that licensing in the Christian Mediterranean from the twelfth century might have been related to Islamic models of the state control of medical practice going back to the tenth century. Peter Pormann has urged caution, suggesting that there was no coherent model to be found across the Islamic world, and there is limited evidence of the application of regulations. However, there is some evidence that the Islamic model did influence the Christian kingdoms of the Iberian Peninsula due to the continuation of the office of the *muhtasib*: regulator of weights and measures, urban cleanliness and examiner of physicians, surgeons and drug sellers, long after the end of Islamic rule (after 1249 in Portugal).[76] McVaugh argues that in Valencia the similar position of *mustaçaf* "was as in Islam a regulator of hygiene and economic life," but that the Christian institution of medical licensing "expressed a very different regulatory

75   Gentilcore, *Medical Charlatanism*, pp. 100–101.
76   Peter Pormann, "The Physician and the Other: Images of the Charlatan in Medieval Islam," *BHM* 79 (2005): 189–227; Leonard C. Chiarelli, "A Preliminary Study on the Origins of Medical Licensing in the Medieval Mediterranean," *Al-Masāq: Islam and the Medieval Mediterranean* 10 (1998): 1–11; Ghada Khami, "State Control of the Physician in the Middle Ages: an Islamic Model," in *The Town and State Physician*, pp. 63–84; Edgington, "Medicine and Surgery," pp. 91–2. Note that there are hardly any Muslim practitioners recorded in late-medieval Portugal.

principle."[77] In Portugal, on the other hand, the *almotacé* had a similar regulatory role, but was a municipal office held at times by barbers, for example
in Vila do Conde, north of Oporto, in 1466 and twice in Oporto itself in 1512.[78]
Bearing in mind that little is known about how medical practice was regulated
in Portuguese towns, we should not be too hasty to assume that there was no
connection between economic life, public health and medical licensing. The
barbers of Vila do Conde, for example, were actively involved in identifying
a case of plague in 1466.[79] Barbers and apothecaries present at town council
meetings in Oporto and Funchal (on the island of Madeira) throughout the fifteenth century discussed everything from food provision and pricing through
to the relocation of a brothel and the state of the public latrines.[80] Since medical licensing in Portugal was sufficiently distinctive from the system McVaugh
describes in Aragon—no need for an academic degree, for example—it is possible that the origins of licensing in Portugal had a different trajectory. The
people first licensed by Afonso IV in the 1330s, although not obviously Jews or
converts, may have somehow fallen outside the purview of a pre-existing but
Christianizing urban system based on marketplace hygiene, allowing the king
to intervene in urban politics on behalf of well-connected practitioners. This
intervention may have allowed Afonso and perhaps also his father Dinis to see
the potential of urban security politics as part of their own governmentality.
They both spent a lot of time in the burgeoning city of Lisbon and its vicinity
and it may be no accident that they both broke with royal tradition to choose
burial in or near what had effectively become the capital city.[81]

77   McVaugh, *Medicine before the Plague*, p. 227.
78   José Marques, ed., "A administração municipal de Vila do Conde em 1466," *Bracara Augusta* 37 (1983): 64 and 66; Adelaide Millán da Costa, *Vereação e Vereadores: o Governo do Porto em Finais do Século XV* (Oporto: Câmara Municipal, 1993), pp. 123, 148.
79   J. Marques, "Administração municipal," 85–6, 97.
80   The latrines were discussed in Oporto in 1401: João Albino Pinto Ferreira, ed., *Vereaçoens, Anos de 1401–49: o Segundo Livro de Vereações do Municipio do Porto Existente no seu Arquivo* (Oporto: Câmara Muncipal/Gabinete de História da Cidade, 1980), p. 24, and the brothel in Funchal in 1492: José Pereira da Costa, ed., *Vereações da Câmara Municipal do Funchal*, 3 vols (Funchal: Secretaria Regional de Turismo e Cultura; Centro de estudos de história do Atlântico, 1995–2002), v. 1, p. 397. See also Maria José Ferro Tavares, "A política municipal de saúde pública (séculos XIV–XV)," *Revista de História Económica e Social* 19 (1987): 17–32.
81   Dinis was buried at Odivelas, his Cistercian foundation a few miles outside Lisbon, and Afonso IV was buried in Lisbon Cathedral at the heart of the city. Previously most kings had been buried in Alcobaça or Coimbra further north.

It is difficult to prove this argument. The urban records for Lisbon have not survived well, mainly due to the earthquake of 1755, and for a variety of reasons there are hardly any personal records, such as letters, which would help us understand royal policy. In most cases, it is not possible to reconstruct Portuguese royal health concerns and relate them to public health, as Michael McVaugh was able to do for the royal family of Aragon in the early-fourteenth century.[82] What we can do is to consider some fragments of evidence across several reigns. Several of the licensing letters referred to the need to protect the population from ignorant practitioners. In the words of the first document quoted in this essay, licensing functioned "to remove harm from the people of my lands." This may have been a real concern on the part of the king and his advisors. It is possible to demonstrate how some kings and their families were genuinely interested in healthcare. King Dinis's wife Isabel (d. 1336) was an active patron of welfare institutions in association with royal physician Bishop Martinho of Guarda (d.c.1322).[83] Dinis and Isabel's son Afonso IV, who issued the first surviving licensing documents in 1338, established a series of funerary chapels in Lisbon cathedral in the 1330s and 1340s, one of which was dedicated to saints Cosmas and Damian, the patron saints of medicine and surgery. Together with his wife Beatriz (d. 1359), Afonso founded a hospital attached to these chapels for twenty-four poor men and women and, unusually for an almshouse, made specific provision for their medical care should they fall ill.[84] A hundred years later King Duarte (1433–38) was acutely interested in his own melancholic illness and the potential impact of his ill health on his kingdom's well-being. He also provided Portugal's first surviving guide to plague management, probably based on observation of urban practice, and collected numerous recipes for a variety of health problems.[85] The first of the fifteenth-century licensing letters survives from his reign. Finally, King Manuel after 1495 whole-heartedly took on the completion of the highly medicalized hospital of All Saints in Lisbon, a project he had inherited from his predecessor João II. He is also associated with a Book of Hours that unusually depicts Cosmas and

82   McVaugh, *Medicine before the Plague*, chapter one.
83   Iona McCleery, "Isabel of Aragon (d.1336): Model Queen or Model Saint?" *Journal of Ecclesiastical History* 57 (2006): 668–92.
84   ANTT, *Gavetas*, Gaveta 1, maço 3, document 18, is the hospital"s foundation document from 1342.
85   Iona McCleery, "Both "illness and temptation of the Enemy": Melancholy, the Medieval Patient and the Writings of King Duarte of Portugal (r. 1433–38)," *Journal of Medieval Iberian Studies* 1 (2009): 163–78; Eadem, "Wine, Women and Song? Diet and Regimen for Royal Well-being (Duarte of Portugal, 1433–38)," in *Mental (Dis-)Order in the Middle Ages*, ed. Sari Katajala-Peltomaa and Susanna Niiranen (*forthcoming*, 2014).

Damian.[86] These examples suggest that we should not be too quick to see royal medical licensing in simple economic or power-broking terms. For some kings, further study of their understanding of kingship and its religious dimension (although Portugal does not conform to Northern European models of sacral monarchy) might help to explain why they considered medical licensing to be essential to their authority. It may truly have been something they did for the "public good," although this should not be understood in modern altruistic terms, but in relation to medieval concepts of the body politic *both* as they were understood by kings, and as they were understood by their officials and townspeople.[87] Exploring the latter has barely begun.

This chapter has explored some of the reasons why Portuguese kings may have initiated and expanded a system of medical licensing in their lands. It has been argued that kings did not issue licenses in a vacuum. Their ability to enforce a licensing system seems to have depended on local politics and occupational and religious identities, most of which are obscure, even if they incorporated it into their governmentality because it genuinely meant something to them. Kings may actually have learned its value from their own townspeople; medical licensing was perhaps originally a form of "governmentality from below."

Future histories of medical licensing thus have several avenues to explore. First, it is important to develop fully comparative studies of different licensing systems across Europe. This would seem to be a suitable topic for a large funding bid. Secondly, and as part of this larger project, it is important to determine in more detail just *how* kings were influenced by their townspeople and vice versa in matters of health and hygiene. Thirdly, but perhaps most crucially, this study of medical licensing has not addressed the issue of how the sick and their communities—in the main those same townspeople—perceived medical licenses. We do not know how licenses affected a practitioner's reputation or a patient's trust in him or her. A license might have encouraged initial confidence in the credentials of a practitioner, but it did not on its own necessarily

---

86   Abílio José Salgado and Anastásia Mestrinho Salgado, eds., *Regimento do Hospital de Todos-os-Santos (Edição Fac-Similada)*, (Lisbon: Comissão Organizadora do V Centenário da Fundação do Hospital de Todos-os-Santos, 1992); Dagoberto Markl, *Livro de Horas de D. Manuel* (Lisbon: Crédito Predial Português, 1983); *Oceanos* 26 (1996), special issue on manuscripts.

87   Takashi Shogimen, "'Head or Heart?' Revisited: Physiology and Political Thought in the Thirteenth and Fourteenth Centuries," *History of Political Thought* 28 (2007): 208–229.

engender and maintain trust in their person.[88] How a medical reputation was built up might depend on many factors: personal manners, family connections, wealth, local authority and neighborliness as much as successful cures. The historiography of the doctor-patient relationship says very little about the license and focuses instead on proper conduct at the bedside. Both doctor and patient seem to have learned to trust one another in this context, but the situation appears to have been fragile, as testified by contractual agreements and lawsuits taken out by both sides.[89] As an abstract concept, trust has not yet attracted much attention from medical historians, despite sociological studies on the current crisis of trust in modern healthcare.[90] How trust in medicine was historically built up, perhaps beyond the sickbed through non-medical social interactions, has not been studied much at all. If we are to understand the medieval medical license better, we should retreat from modern concepts

---

88   For this differentiation between "trust" and "confidence," see Dixon-Woods, Yeung and Bosk, "Why is UK medicine." "Trust" and good "reputation" are not quite the same thing either, although they are closely related. See Catherine Casson, "Reputation and Responsibility in Medieval English Towns: Civic Concerns with the Regulation of Trade," *Urban History* 39 (2012): 387–408. On the limited research that has been done on trust, see Geoffrey Hosking, "Trust and Distrust: a Suitable Theme for Historians?" *Transactions of the Royal Historical Society*, 6th ser., 16 (2006): 95–115; Dorothea Weltecke, "Trust: Some Methodological Reflections," in *Strategies of Writing: Studies on Text and Trust in the Middle Ages*, ed. Petra Schulte, Marco Mostert and Irene van Renswoud (Turnhout: Brepols, 2008), pp. 379–92. Useful for a future study on medical trust might be the idea of "thin" and "thick" forms of trust between immediate and wider members of a community, put to good effect in Edward Muir, "The Idea of Community in Renaissance Italy," *Renaissance Quarterly* 55 (2002): 1–18. Muir also explores how community use of institutions, spaces and policies of exclusion built up trust, something which might also be useful for understanding Portuguese medical practice. I will be exploring some of these ideas in my future book.

89   See the literature in footnotes 17 and 42 and also Joseph Shatzmiller, "Doctor's Fees and their Medical Responsibility," in *Sources of Social History: Private Acts of the Late Middle Ages*, ed. Paolo Brezzi and Egmund Lee (Toronto: Pontifical Institute of Medieval Studies, 1984), pp. 201–08; Andrew Wear, Johanna Geyer-Kordesch and Roger French, eds., *Doctors and Ethics: the Earlier Historical Setting of Professional Ethics* (Amsterdam: Rodopi, 1993); Rawcliffe, "Profits of Practice."

90   Mary Elston, "Remaking a Trustworthy Medical Profession in Twenty-first Century Britain," in *The New Sociology of the Health Service*, ed. Jonathan Gabe and Michael Calnan (Abingdon: Routledge, 2009), pp. 17–36; Michael Calnan and Rosemary Brown, "Trust Relations in a Changing Health Service," *Journal of Health Services Research and Policy* 13, supplement 3 (2008): 97–103; Dixon-Woods, Yeung and Bosk, "Why is UK medicine."

of it as a method of controlling charlatans, and try to pin it down within the commercial and legal contexts of the towns that implemented it and perhaps saw its effects most. In the end, it might be that the medical license meant most to competing medical practitioners who sought to construct a good reputation in the eyes of each other, despite social and religious differences. It may have meant relatively little to their patients.

CHAPTER 9

Dreaming of Valencia's Social Order in Jaume Roig's *Espill*

Jean Dangler

Jaume Roig was a physician and medical examiner from Valencia who wrote the *Espill* (*The Mirror*) in approximately 1460. Composed in five-syllable rhymed verse, the *Espill* is widely considered one of the most misogynist and misogamist works of medieval Iberian literature.[1] Framed in part as a journey, the work's first-person, fictional narrator recounts his perilous experiences with ordinary women, including his own mother, his three wives, a pastry chef and her daughters, nuns, abbesses, and women healers, such as physicians (*metgesses*) and midwives (*madrines*). Roig relies on numerous medieval discourses in the *Espill*, including misogynist literature, along with the sermon, the fabliaux, hagiography, and Marian writings.[2] The *Espill* consists of an introductory *Consulta* (Consultation) and *Perfaci* (Preface), along with four parts each divided into four sections from the narrator's life: his youth (*De sa joventut*); his married life (*De quan fon casat*); King Solomon's extensive sermon to the narrator in a dream, the longest section in the *Espill* (*De la lliçó de Salomó*); and, his widowhood and old age (*De enviudat*). In the preface, the narrator directs his discourse about women's supposedly innate evil to his nephew, Baltasar Bou, and to other impressionable men whom he seeks to edify so they will not suffer and make his same mistakes (vv. 240–291).[3] The *Espill*'s misogyny

---

1 Roig was probably born at the beginning of the fifteenth century, although the exact date is unknown. According to v. 681–682, he composed the *Espill* in *noves rimades: /comediades*, literally, "rhymed, measured news cut in half." All references to the Catalan text are from Jaume Roig, *Espill*, ed. Antònia Carré (Barcelona: Quaderns Crema, 2006). Unless otherwise noted, English translations are from The Mirror *of Jaume Roig: An Edition and an English Translation of MS. Vat. Lat. 4806*, ed. and trans. María Celeste Delgado-Librero (Tempe: Arizona Center for Medieval and Renaissance Studies, 2010).

2 For overviews and bibliographies on these topics, see Carré, *Espill*, pp. 39–46, and Delgado-Librero, *The Mirror*, pp. 13–59.

3 Carré maintains that Baltasar Bou was Roig's friend, and that Roig converted him into the narrator's nephew in the *Espill*, ingeniously playing with the symbolism and varied signification of Bou's first and last names, *Espill*, 608–09. Indeed, one such Baltasar Bou died in 1469 and was lord of Callosa, a town mentioned in the *Consulta*, although Delgado-Librero

depends on the repeated contrast between earthly and divine women, especially everyday women and the Virgin Mary, who is cast as the lily among
thorns: "*Sicut lilium inter spinas/sic amica mea inter fillias*" [As the lily is among
thorns, so is my friend among young ladies].[4] Roig often refers to ordinary
women as the daughters of Eve, signaling their sinful lineage and disposition,
along with their inevitable transmission of sin through childbirth.

One of the *Espill*'s main objectives is pedagogical, and Roig uses satire and
humor to teach bourgeois men in his professional and social milieu about how
ordinary women with their supposedly inborn defects possess an unquench-
able desire to jeopardize men's well-being.[5] But on a larger scale, Roig is pro-
foundly concerned about fifteenth-century Valencia's patriarchal social order,
which according to the *Espill* women consistently upend through their dealings
with men as wives, workers, and acquaintances. Marriage plays a fundamental
role in the *Espill* because it constitutes the basis of the entire medieval social
order, assuring society's continuation through a legal system that stabilized
wealth and power between individuals and groups.[6] Yet Roig's misogamy is less
a genuine appeal to men to reject marriage altogether and more a humorous,
satirical warning to them about women's threat. Marriage is the social relationship where Roig can achieve his gendered goal of warning men about women's
desire to harm their well-being. Medicine and law are essential in this effort
because they mould and shape marital relations, and thus Valencia's social
order, while contributing to the book's humorous reinforcement of misogyny,
misogamy, and gender concerns.

The focus on Valencia's social order is perhaps nowhere more evident than in
Solomon's dream-sermon that constitutes book three (vv. 6369–15295), where
the Israeli king's homily serves as the spiritual complement to Roig's secular,
naturalizing discourse. Solomon's corporeal and legal diatribes in the mystical dream realm corroborate Roig's worldly misogyny. The dream is ideal for
this dialectic between earthly and celestial authority because from the twelfth

---

emphasizes the lack of evidence showing familial relations between Bou and Roig, *The
Mirror*, p. 274n14.

4   These unnumbered Latin verses from the Song of Songs 2:2 are found after v. 46 at the end of
the opening *Consulta*. The English translation is my own.

5   Michael Solomon, *The Literature of Misogyny in Medieval Spain: The* Arcipreste de Talavera
and the Spill (Cambridge: CUP, 1997); Jean Dangler, *Mediating Fictions: Literature, Women
Healers, and the Go-Between in Medieval and Early Modern Iberia* (Lewisburg: Bucknell
University Press, 2001); and, Jean Dangler, "Motherhood and Pain in Villena's *Vita Christi* and
Roig's *Spill*," *La corónica* 27.1 (1998): 99–113.

6   Teresa Vinyoles Vidal, *Història de les dones a la Catalunya medieval*, Vic-Lleida: Eumo-Pagès,
2005, p. 169.

century on the interaction of the sacred and profane became increasingly
important in the dream space. With the introduction of Aristotelian and medical material into the Latin west in the twelfth century, dreams underwent what
Steven F. Kruger calls a "somatizing" shift that precipitated a greater focus on
the body.[7] The concentration on somatics produced a merging of naturalizing
and spiritualizing discourses, which differed from their separation in earlier
medieval dreams. The late medieval dream space readily accommodated medical and legal materials because they were so closely connected to the body.
Roig employs the dream space to demonstrate to his readers how medical
issues and legal concerns shape men's and women's bodies, their conjugal relations, and the urban arrangement, a strategy that coincided with the overt consolidation of medicine and law in fourteenth- and fifteenth-century Valencia.
He uses the dream to exemplify his lessons about men's and women's gender,
and to underscore the social need for people's disciplining and formation.

The *Espill* and Social Control

The *Espill's* connection to Valencia's fifteenth-century medical milieu is well
known by critics and evident from its opening *Consulta* or consultation, as if
the narrator is appealing to another person for his opinion or advice, as when
a patient visits a doctor. Roig supposedly wrote from the town of Callosa
d'En Sarrià in the province of Alacant (Alicante), where he settled after flee-
ing Valencia's plague (vv. 9–10).[8] Scholars such as Antònia Carré and Michael
Solomon emphasize the *Espill's* attention to illness, healing, and well-being
in pointing out the therapeutic value of literature and stories as theorized by
Glending Olson.[9] Additionally, the *Consulta* incorporates both medical discourse and religious ideals, as evidenced by references to the plague and the
Virgin. The first word of the *Consulta* before verse one seems to be an invocation to Jesus or the opening of a prayer, although the inclusion of the medically charged heading, *Consulta*, makes for complex semantic fields that both
contrast and parallel one another. Likewise, the narrator invokes a common
nonmodern trope as he entrusts the *Consulta* to a narratee, the gentleman Joan
Fabra, who is expected to correct and amend the *Espill* (vv. 1–2). This creates a

---

7   Steven F. Kruger, "Dream Space and Masculinity," *Word & Image* 14.1–2 (1998): 11.
8   This information may be biographical, since documentation supports an outbreak of the
    bubonic plague in Valencia from 1459 to 1467, as well as Roig's presence in Callosa d'En Sarrià
    at that approximate time, Carré, *Espill*, p. 604.
9   Carré, *Espill*, pp. 603–04; Solomon, *Literature of Misogyny*, p. 60.

further contrast and parallel to Jesus, even though Roig explicitly delivers his work to Fabra and not to Christ the spiritual authority.[10]

Scholars including Carré have analyzed medieval medicine as one of the *Espill*'s main sources, delving into topics such as lovesickness, women healers, and the reputation of men physicians in the fifteenth century.[11] Solomon offers a compelling explanation for the *Espill*'s intimate connection to medical topics, since he considers the book a manual with a pedagogical purpose to teach men about the evils of women and thereby preserve their sexual well-being. Solomon claims that medieval medical theory and misogynist discourse converged in the later Middle Ages due to anxiety about men's health, especially their sexual well-being, and that literature such as the *Espill* provided men readers and listeners with salutary information.[12] Relying on Olson's theory about medieval literature's therapeutic role, Solomon further contends that the *Espill*'s misogynist stories and anecdotes aimed to protect and cure men of excessive sexual desire, a "pestilence" that greatly concerned Roig and other late medieval writers, as exemplified by another work, the anonymous, fifteenth-century Catalan medical handbook, *Speculum al foderi* (*The Mirror of Coitus*). Solomon situates the Espill and Roig's concern about men's sexual health in fifteenth-century Valencia to argue more generally that "biomedical information" began to "play a significant role in political affairs" in a variety of ways.[13]

One of the most important medical-political developments in fifteenth-century Valencia was the rise of the professionalization of medicine, carried out in large part by legal means. The effort gained momentum in Iberia with the reception of Roman law and commentaries on Aristotle that promoted the responsibility of civic authorities for citizens' well-being. This legal and medical documentation brought about the production of contractual agreements between doctors and patients, which meant that authorities were increasingly charged with verifying physicians' credentials.[14] The professionalization of medicine in Iberia had two main goals, which were to dignify the male

---

10   Joan Fabra was a friend of the Roig family who gained prestige through diplomatic work and other social and political functions, as well as through his connection to important writers in Valencia during the fifteenth century, Carré, *Espill*, pp. 60, 603.

11   Carré, "La medicina com a rerefons cultural," in *Jaume Roig i Cristòfor Despuig. Dos assaigs sobre cultura i literatura dels segles XV i XVI*, ed. Antònia Carré and Josep Solervicens (Barcelona: Eumo, 1996).

12   Solomon, *Literature of Misogyny*, pp. 2–4, 11.

13   Solomon, *Literature of Misogyny*, pp. 4, 7, 60.

14   Luis García Ballester, "Ethical Problems in the Relationship between Doctors and Patients in Fourteenth-Century Spain," in *Medicine and Medical Ethics in Medieval and Early*

physician as society's preeminent healer and to elevate professional medicine as society's preferred healing method. During the fourteenth and fifteenth centuries, medical, royal, and municipal authorities developed legal mechanisms to achieve these goals, such as the creation of royal and municipal examination and licensing boards called *Protomedicatos*. Additionally, authorities enacted laws that excluded healers from traditional medical practice, such as Jews, Muslims, and women. Valencia adopted municipal statutes (*furs*) in 1329 that specifically marginalized women from medical practice and from dispensing "potions," although the laws permitted them to treat "little children" and other women.[15] Solomon demonstrates that the *Espill* bolstered this effort with its pejorative depictions of women healers, whose salutary interventions directly opposed those of the clinical healer, that is, the male physician.[16] I have examined in greater detail how the *Espill*'s reprobation of women healers reinforced the exclusionary goals of the professionalization of medicine. The marginalization of women, Muslims, and Jews from the licit practice of medicine was part of a broader phenomenon in Iberia from approximately the fourteenth century on, whereby society's governmental, religious, and cultural sectors were increasingly directed by homosocial groups of Christian men.[17] The *Espill* participated in this late medieval effort at professionalization and marginalization by tacitly dissuading men readers from seeking the services of women healers in their own society, and by promoting men's reliance on male medical professionals such as Roig himself.[18]

Roig was embroiled in the ideology and goals of the professionalization of medicine, since like his father he was a practicing physician and medical examiner in Valencia throughout his life. He served as royal physician to the German king and queen between 1446 and 1449, to Queen Maria of Castile in 1446, the wife of King Alfons el Magnànim (Alfons V), and in 1469 he treated the daughter of King Joan II for the plague. He practiced medicine at several local hospitals, including the Hospital d'en Clapers from 1450, the Hospital d'en Bou, and the Hospital dels Innocents for mental illnesses from 1452 to 1478, the year of his death. His recurring role as medical examiner of physicians,

---

      Modern Spain: An Intercultural Approach, ed. Samuel S. Kottek and Luis García Ballester (Jerusalem: Magnes Press, 1996), pp. 27–28.

15   Luis García Ballester, Michael McVaugh, and Agustín Rubio Vela, *Medical Licensing and Learning in Fourteenth-Century Valencia: Transactions of the American Philosophical Society* (Philadelphia: American Philosophical Society, 1989), pp. 60–61.

16   Solomon, *Literature of Misogyny*, p. 165.

17   Dangler, *Mediating Fictions*, pp. 13–14.

18   Dangler, *Mediating Fictions*, chapters one and two.

surgeons, and veterinarians between 1434 and 1477 made him a purveyor of the legal strategy of the professionalization of medicine, which was also demonstrated by restrictions against healers in Valencia's *furs*.[19]

Medicine and law converge in the professionalization of medicine and serve as the socio-historical impetus and backdrop for a variety of themes and episodes in the *Espill*, including admonitions against women healers and the concern about men's well-being. The rise of professional medicine as society's preeminent healing method coincided with the consolidation of legal statutes more generally in the Crown of Aragon and specifically in the Kingdom of Valencia during the thirteenth and fourteenth centuries. This was a crucial period for the integration of the *ius commune*, which was the combination of Roman law and canon law into Aragonese realms, and more importantly into the local codes of the *furs*. The Aragonese conqueror and king, Jaume I, was pivotal in Valencia's legal and political developments, since in 1240 he defied precedent for the incorporation of new territories into the Crown and effectively designated Valencia a new and independent kingdom by imposing its legal codes, the *Furs de València*, throughout the surrounding territory.[20] Although the kingdom still maintained a political connection to the Crown of Aragon, it was also a modern and mercantile society that contrasted Aragon's agricultural, seigniorial, and fishing structure. Greater consolidation of the kingdom through the enforcement of Valencia's *furs* took place in the fourteenth century (1329–1330), as discussed above in *furs* about healers.[21]

In the *Espill*, marriage serves as the nexus for medicine, law, and Roig's pedagogical goals about gender and the social organization. At the heart of marital relations is the misogynist notion that women seek to harm or disease men, as in the first part of the first book, *De sa joventut*, where the narrator insinuates that his mother made his father sick and eventually caused his death (vv. 820–29). After a loveless, miserable marriage, the narrator's father became ill with consumption, which eventually made him frenetic or crazy and killed him.

---

19   Carré, *Espill*, pp. 26–27; Carré, "La medicina com a rerefons cultural," 12–19; Delgado-Librero, *The Mirror*, pp. 3–5.

20   Josep Maria Font i Rius, "Valencia y Barcelona en los orígenes de su régimen municipal," in *Estudis sobre els drets i institucions locals en la Catalunya medieval* (Barcelona: Universitat de Barcelona, 1985), pp. 646–48; Pedro López Elum and Mateu Rodrigo Lizondo, "La mujer en el Código de Jaime I de los Furs de Valencia," in *Las mujeres medievales y su ámbito jurídico. Actas de las II Jornadas de investigación interdisciplinaria* (Madrid: Universidad Autónoma de Madrid, 1983), p. 126; and, Marie A. Kelleher, *The Measure of Woman: Law and Female Identity in the Crown of Aragon* (Philadelphia: University of Pennsylvania Press, 2010), pp. 20–22.

21   López Elum and Rodrigo Lizondo, "Mujer en el Código," p. 126.

The narrator obliquely refers to his father suffering "some illnesses," which he fails to specify because they have to do with his mother:

> Because of their miserable life or bad luck, certainly most unfairly, because of some illnesses (I do not want to say which ones, and I do not declare them because she was my mother) as a young man my father was consumptive and eventually he became frenetic, and so he died.[22]

The irony, of course, is that after refusing to name the illnesses the narrator immediately identifies them, drawing attention to his mother's possible involvement in their etiology. Roig generally depicts women as the source of disease in the *Espill*, indicating that wives are especially keen to subvert the patriarchal order by harming their husbands.[23] Medical and legal discourse converge in this scene when we learn that the narrator's mother is skilled not only in diseasing his father and causing his demise, but also in controlling the legal system of inheritance in her favor. Roig demonstrates extensive knowledge of legalities about wills and inheritances when the narrator claims his father wrote his testament according to his mother's wishes, making her his heiress and their son's guardian (vv. 830–49). Carola Duran i Tort argues that Roig was probably familiar with and correctly used legal terms because among other reasons his grandfather held a legal position as a notary.[24] María Luisa Cabanes Català shows that episodes describing testaments in the *Espill* correspond to one of three wills prescribed in Valencia's *furs*, the *testament obert* (open testament) written before a notary and three male witnesses.[25] Apparently the narrator's mother gained her advantage because she chose the notary without her husband's involvement ("Ella hí volgué/un seu notari" vv. 836–37), along with the vicar whom she knew personally beforehand as her confessor (vv. 838–39). She excluded her husband from these legal decisions and thus undermined patriarchal privilege and authority. The entire episode ended badly for her son the narrator as well, since he was left with a paltry inheritance of five sous and was thrown out of his house by his mother

22   Per llur mal viure/o mala sort,/cert, a gran tort,/per alguns mals/—no vull dir quals,/e no els declare/per ser ma mare—,/jove, fon hètic./En fi frenetic,/així morí (vv. 820–829).
23   Jean Dangler, "Marriage and Well-Being in Jaume Roig's *Spill*," *Catalan Review* 15.2 (2001): 35–47.
24   Carola Duran i Tort, "Aspectes jurídics en un fragment de *L'Espill* de Jaume Roig," *Llengua & Literatura* 4 (1990–1991): 428.
25   María Luisa Cabanes Català, "El *Spill* de Jaume Roig com a font per a la diplomàtica," *Revista de Filologia Valenciana* 3 (1996): 12–13.

(vv. 850–51, 862–64). Hence, his mother's actions fueled his mournful journey toward the Virgin, which was motivated by desire for a good woman and an heir. This scene is a telling example of how medicine and law work together in the *Espill* to transmit information and values to male readers about women, men, and the social order. It demonstrates that marriage is a salutary and legal concern because women use medical and legal knowledge against their husbands to subvert men's health and patriarchal authority.

Roig's interest in the connection between medicine, well-being, law, and social organization was fortified by his relationship to Valencia's central power brokers in the fifteenth century: the Catalan-Aragonese Crown, the municipality, and several of the city's most important religious institutions. Roig served as physician to royalty, but he was likely connected to city authorities through the local hospitals where he practiced medicine, since they probably depended on Valencia's municipality. He was also linked to leaders of Valencia's municipal power base in his role as medical examiner of physicians, surgeons, and veterinarians. Furthermore, Roig was firmly rooted in several focal religious groups. In addition to serving as physician at the Reial Convent de Predicadors in 1448, he was an active parishioner at the church of Sant Nicolau from 1455, and a benefactor of the convent of the Trinitat, where Isabel de Villena, another Valencian author, was abbess.[26] These undertakings demonstrate his involvement in institutional circles that were crucial to the establishment of Valencia's social order.

Roig also interacted professionally with the ranks of the city's bourgeoisie, since he participated in the literary salons or *tertulias* where writers gathered to discuss and read their works. He met with one such group organized around a canon of the Cathedral of Valencia and member of the bourgeoisie, Bernat Fenollar, which included Joan Moreno, Jaume Gassull, Narcís de Vinyoles, Baltasar Portell, and others. Unlike another, upper-class group formed around Berenguer Mercader, which focused on classical, learned literature and tropes, Fenollar and Roig's *tertulia* was known for its interest in satirical, comical works like the *Espill*.[27] The *tertulias* were crucial to Valencia's success as a

---

26   Carré, *Espill*, pp. 26–28; Carré, "La medicina com a rerefons cultural," pp. 12–19; Delgado-Librero, *The Mirror*, pp. 3–5.

27   For discussions of Roig's involvement with Valencia's burgeoning bourgeoisie, see David Wacks, *Framing Iberia: Māqamāt and Frametale Narratives in Medieval Spain* (Leiden: Brill, 2007), pp. 195–96; and, Martín de Riquer, *Història de la literatura catalana*, vol. 3, (Barcelona: Ariel, 1980), pp. 240–41. Delgado-Librero summarizes the importance of *tertulias* in Valencia in *The Mirror*, pp. 11–12, and discusses the patrician and bourgeois groups on p. 12n43.

wellspring of literary activity in the fifteenth century, which included poetry competitions known as the gay science or *gaya çiencia*, in which male poets competed for the prize as most skilled in praising the Virgin.[28] Perhaps the first printed literary work on the Iberian Peninsula was a collection of those praise poems to the Virgin, which included one by Roig, his only other literary composition besides the *Espill*.[29] Although *tertulias* in fifteenth-century Valencia were recreational gatherings for the enjoyment and advancement of literary composition and competition, they also have important political implications as exclusive homosocial domains for men from Valencia's powerful administrative, commercial elites.[30]

Dreaming of the Social Order in the *Espill*

The dream space is ideal for demonstrating the connection between medicine, law, and Valencia's social order in the *Espill*. Its late medieval focus on the body allows Roig to develop gender concerns about women's undermining of men's well-being, and to reinforce his interpretations through King Solomon's higher biblical authority. Roig's literary contacts certainly would have made him aware of changes in the late medieval literary dream space, especially since the dream figures prominently in two other Catalan works, Bernat Metge's late fourteenth-century *Lo somni* (The Dream) and Jaume Gassull's *Lo somni de Joan Joan* (Joan Joan's Dream), which was printed in Valencia in 1497. (As stated above, Gassull also belonged to Roig's literary *tertulia*). These writers likely would have been familiar with the historical trajectory of dreams in poetry and prose, which throughout antiquity and the early Middle Ages were mostly used to prefigure the future or as a mode of allegory to demonstrate

---

28   Roger Boase, *The Troubadour Revival: A Study of Social Change and Traditionalism in Late Medieval Spain* (London and Boston: Routledge and Kegan Paul, 1978), pp. 127–32.

29   *Les trobes en lahors de la Verge Maria*, Valencia, 1474. Roig's praise of the Virgin certainly may be taken at face value in *Les trobes*, although it is also crucial to his misogynist strategy in the *Espill*, where he highlights the Virgin's virtual inimitability in comparing her to evil earthly women.

30   Wacks discusses the large number of Jewish converts or *conversos* who comprised Valencia's urban elites in the fifteenth century, in *Framing Iberia*, chapter six, suggesting that their Christian faith might have been less authentic than it seemed. But their *converso* status does not make them apostates, nor does it necessarily contradict the importance of the Christian marker in the growing consolidation of power and influence in those homosocial spaces. Roig's seemingly unwavering devotion to Valencia's vital religious institutions is a case in point.

the symbolic makeup of an object or event. Early medieval dreams generally followed the guide established by Macrobius in the fifth century CE, who was renowned in the Middle Ages for his work, *Saturnalia*, and his commentary on Cicero's *Dream of Scipio* (*Somnium Scipionis*). Macrobius identified three kinds of dreams that either revealed a significant truth or foretold future events: the *somnium* was an enigmatic dream that demanded interpretation; the *visio* was a prophetic vision; and, the *oraculum* was a dream in which an authoritative figure offered advice.[31] Dreams were often difficult to categorize, which prompted an expanded typology during the Middle Ages that included dreams influenced by the devil. Jean-Claude Schmitt emphasizes the difficulty in distinguishing between diabolical dreams characterized by excessive food and drink, and spiritualizing, revelatory dreams.[32]

In the late Middle Ages, dream theory changed and the body became more prominent as writers such as Albertus Magnus and Vincent of Beauvais often linked dreaming to humoural complexion and bodily functions, including coolness, corporal heat, digestion, and the circulation of vapors and liquids in the body. Despite the fact that authors continued to have faith in the possibility of "*both* mundane and transcendent dreams," the introduction of medical material with its focus on psychosomatics made the dream space more complex.[33] The emphasis on the relationship between mind and body contributed to the idea that dreams operated according to a single process of mutual reinforcement of the transcendental and mundane, rather than their contrast. Kruger believes that "the new somatics of the dream" made possible a convergence of many kinds of dreams, such as the angelic, demonic, and human, which meant that the dream space became a realm where instead of "being played off against each other," "moral or spiritualizing" discourses joined "somatic or naturalizing" ones in mutual fortification.[34]

Solomon's dream-sermon in the *Espill* epitomizes these late medieval changes and relies on the mutual reinforcement of the corporal and the moral in the dream space.[35] King Solomon appears toward the beginning of the third

---

31   Tony Davenport, *Medieval Narrative: An Introduction* (Oxford: OUP, 2004), pp. 194, 196–97.

32   Jean-Claude Schmitt, "The Liminality and Centrality of Dreams in the Medieval West," in *Dream Cultures: Explorations in the Comparative History of Dreaming*, ed. David Shulman and Guy G. Stroumsa (New York: OUP, 1999), pp. 278–79.

33   *Ibid.*, p. 279; Kruger, "Dream Space," 11; Jacques Le Goff, *Pour un autre Moyen Age: temps, travail et culture en Occident* (Paris: Gallimard, 1977), p. 305.

34   Kruger, "Dream Space," 11.

35   The somatizing shift is patent as well in Metge's late-fourteenth-century *Lo somni*, which the *Espill* resembles in several ways, from its most basic organization in four parts to the discussion of women's perversity in part three and the arguments toward their defense

book while the narrator naps exhausted by women's deceits, which he experienced firsthand in books one and two when he recounted his life experiences
with women and searched in vain for a wife to bear him a boy or girl heir (vv.
6409–6419).[36] Solomon's dream-sermon begins as a strong condemnation of
the narrator's failure to follow Paul's advice to married and unmarried men
and women in I Corinthians 7:25–40, especially his recommendation that the
unmarried remain unattached and celibate (vv. 6494–6499):

> Oh, tired man! Old, tamed, and stupefied man! Old and aged! I believe
> you are already living your bad days, without strength and in the power of
> Eve's daughters.... Old hunted man! You brought it upon yourself
> because you didn't believe our Saul, now your great apostle Paul.[37]

The somatic and the spiritual coexist in book three as Solomon's moralizing
harangue parallels rather than contrasts Roig's misogynist and misogamist
messages in the previous two books. Solomon accuses the narrator of an
inability to escape women's grip, and he wonders why the pitiful man did not
renounce women after the absolution of his first marriage (vv. 6506–6512).
Solomon is the ideal religious and moral authority (*auctoritas*) to reinforce the
Espill's mundane, naturalizing narrative, since the Israeli king (ruled approximately 971–931 BCE) was well acquainted with women, having supposedly
married 700 wives and recruited 300 concubines (I Kings 11:3; vv. 7040–7045).
Additionally, two of the *Espill*'s most significant verses in the *Consulta* derive
from the Song of Songs 2:2, a work attributed to Solomon.

Carré observes that Solomon tries to dissuade the narrator from marriage
in the dream-sermon with biblical, medical, and legal examples.[38] Religious
discourse and medicine are firmly rooted in the late medieval dream space
as examples of the spiritual and somatic, while law also constitutes the natu-

---

in part four. Metge, whose surname means physician, was from a medical family in
Barcelona and also wrote a humorous, short work in verse on pharmacopoeia, entitled
Medicina apropiada a tot mal (Appropriate Medicine for Every Ill), Bernat Metge, *Lo
somni*, ed. Lola Badia (Barcelona: Quaderns Crema, 1999), p. 10.

36   The narrator refers to the desire for an heir with a popular, fifteenth-century expression
("e fos clavilla/del fust mateix," vv. 6418–6419; "a chip off the old block"), which also
appeared in Gassull's *Lo somni de Joan Joan*, in Carré, *Espill*, p. 676.

37   "Oh hom cansat,/vell amansat,/empagesit,/vell envellit/en tos mals dies!/Jo crec ja sies/
despoderat,/apoderat/per filles d'Eva! .... Vell acaçat,/tu t'ho volguist,/car no creguist/lo
Sau ans nostre,/ara gran vostre/apòstol Pau," (vv. 6469–6477; 6494–6499).

38   Carré, *Espill*, p. 679.

ralizing, somatic material that Kruger describes in late medieval shifts. Legal discourse is closely related to the body because it is usually gendered in the *Espill*, referring for instance to women adulterers or to women's dowries and trousseaus.

Roig incorporates medical theory in Solomon's dream-sermon similarly as he did in the scene with the narrator's mother, largely through the physical effects of contact with women on men in marriage and sex. For example, just before Solomon starts speaking, the narrator informs readers in a funny passage about his decision finally to marry a relative. The narrator claims their intimate kinship will double the chance for producing an heir, since not only would "natural" pleasure in coitus increase the possibilities for reproduction, but so would familial duty ("deute i natura," vv. 6433; 6426–6452). In his sermon, Solomon tries to dissuade the narrator from pursuing the relationship by describing a series of debilitating effects caused by coitus with a younger woman:

> Thoughtless man, if you think that with a young and fresh wife your crazy delight is going to increase and last a long time, I assure you that your bladder will soon and without delay be strangulated and ulcerous; that urination will come with great burning, pain, and itchiness; that your head, feet, and arms will tremble; and that at a fast pace you will soon die of apoplexy or lethargy.[39]

According to the Hippocratic-Galenic tradition on sex, evident throughout the Middle Ages in works such as Constantine the African's (d. 1065) *De coitu*, moderate coitus was considered essential for good health because it allowed people to expulse potentially dangerous semen or seed. It constituted one of the nonnaturals, which were elements external to the human body that could alter and re-establish its equilibrium, such as air, exercise and rest, food and drink, and sleep and wake, with corporeal evacuation considered as one of their most significant processes.[40] But immoderate or inappropriate coitus

---

39   "Si et tens per dit/ton foll delit/ab jove, fresca/muller, te cresca/e llong temps dure/jo t'assegure/d'estrangulada/e d'ulcerada,/molt prest—sens triga—/certa veixiga;/de gran ardor,/dolor, coissor/en l'orinar;/de tremolar/cap, peus e braços;/ab cuitats passos,/ d'apoplexia/o litargia/ben tost morir," (vv. 6811–6829).

40   Nancy Siraisi, *Medieval and Early Renaissance Medicine: An Introduction to Knowledge and Practice* (Chicago: University of Chicago Press, 1990), p. 101; Solomon, *Literature of Misogyny*, p. 43; Dangler, *Mediating Fictions*, pp. 101–02; Jean Dangler, *Making Difference*

could also result in serious illness, as Solomon maintains. These undesirable symptoms and illnesses were well known to medical healers from antiquity on. They were also common in medical literature in the fifteenth century as medical information on the human body was widely disseminated in vernacular handbooks and became more accessible to a non-specialist reading public.[41] King Solomon points out symptoms and illnesses that echo many of the dangers of excessive coitus described in medical literature, where theorists generally believed that immoderate sex depleted the body of moisture and caused it to heat up. These corporeal changes had damaging effects on the brain and on organs surrounding the cerebral cavity.[42] Hence, King Solomon cites two often fatal mental conditions when he mentions apoplexy, which caused paralysis, and lethargy, which caused profound fatigue and frequently death.[43] Excessive coitus also produced ulcers on the penis and testicles, flatulence in those who were so inclined, chest ailments, and kidney failure.[44]

In this passage, Solomon delivers information on the damaging effects of coitus within the *Espill*'s misogynist discursive realm, unlike the straightforward, ostensibly unbiased information available in medical handbooks and treatises. But he also centers on a common anxiety about elderly men's sexual well-being, who were directed to follow prescriptive medical information on the appropriate frequency of coitus depending on their physical makeup or complexion. This concern also appears in the anonymous, fifteenth-century Catalan manual on sexual well-being, *Speculum al foderi* (*The Mirror of Coitus*), which advises that all men with dry temperaments and thin bodies may become phthiscal or asthmatic when they engage in excessive sex. The *Speculum* especially warns older men who are thin to avoid coitus "as if it were a mortal enemy who attacks and kills" ["axí con de enemich mortal, cor fa lo caser e mata-lo"], since presumably their bodies would become too depleted

       in *Medieval and Early Modern Iberia* (Notre Dame, IN: University of Notre Dame Press, 2005), p. 84.

41   Solomon, *Literature of Misogyny*, p. 51.

42   *Ibid.*, pp. 55–56; Carré, *Espill*, p. 680.

43   Danielle Jacquart and Claude Thomasset, *Sexuality and Medicine in the Middle Ages* (Princeton: Princeton University Press, 1988), p. 165; Carré, *Espill*, pp. 679–80; María Teresa Herrera, *Diccionario español de textos médicos antiguos*, 2 vols. (Madrid: Arco Libros, 1996), v. 1, pp. 128–29; v. 2, pp. 930–31.

44   Solomon, *Literature of Misogyny*, p. 56; Jacquart and Thomasset, *Sexuality and Medicine*, pp. 177–88.

to survive.[45] In the *Espill* the narrator's advanced age is an impediment to his success in sex and marriage, since his spouses in book two and Solomon in book three often refer to him in a denigrating way as an old man (*vell*).

The narrator's denigration closely corresponds to Kruger's ideas about gender's key role in the late medieval and early modern dream space, namely about how dreams operated on the male body. Although Kruger focuses in particular on the male body, depictions of men and women form a clear dialectic in the *Espill* as mutually reinforcing and interdependent, and ought to be considered together. One of Kruger's central propositions is that the medieval dream space works to abase the male body,[46] which is clear in Solomon's sermon when he refers to the narrator as an old man whose body is unfit for sex and marriage. But Solomon's demeaning corporeal insults are constant, from the adjectives used at the beginning of the sermon and cited above, including tired (*cansat*), tamed (*amansat*), crude, unsophisticated, or uncouth (*empagesit*), aged (*envellit*), and hunted (*acaçat*), to the bodily effects of the narrator's insistence on choosing a wife. Incredulous, Solomon wonders why after being scorched (*socarrat*, v. 6598), skinned (*pelat*, v. 6599), and dried (*sec*, v. 6599) like an animal the narrator would return to married life. Solomon not only humiliates the man, but he physically demeans him by lowering him to the level of beasts and invoking the misogynist claim that women have cropped his nails and beak ("ungles e bec/t'han escatit," vv. 6600–6601). The narrator's animalization is further belittling because it lowers him to women's bestial level, which Solomon pronounces when he equates women with pests, snakes, foxes, monkeys, birds, moles, and rabid dogs among others (vv. 7688–7719).

Yet the denigration of the male body in and of itself is far from the dream space's final goal. Instead, Kruger considers its abasement as part of its very disciplining or construction:

> The abasement of male bodies in the dream vision landscape serves not so much to call into question cultural understandings of masculinity as to allow for an inculcation of those understandings—a disciplining of the male body that shapes it as culturally masculine and that works toward its full incorporation into male homosociality and heterosexuality.[47]

---

45   *The Mirror of Coitus: A Translation and Edition of the Fifteenth-Century* Speculum al foderi, ed. and trans. Michael Solomon (Madison, WI: Hispanic Seminary of Medieval Studies, 1990), v. 4, p. 48.

46   Kruger, "Dream Space," 12.

47   Kruger, "Dream Space," 13.

As Kruger suggests, Solomon's denigration of the narrator above is not intended to call into question the links between medical information, sex, women, and the man's body, but rather, to reinforce and incorporate them into a conventional paradigm of "male homosociality and heterosexuality." Kruger believes that the male body is molded as culturally masculine in the dream space through imagery such as landscapes, gardens, and architecture. Roig's reliance on such descriptions is evident as well in the dream-sermon, especially in Solomon's harangue about women's fault in the fall of cities, a common literary motif. Solomon refers to the Old Testament book of Isaiah 3 to warn the narrator about God's promise to inhabitants of cities where women are allowed to "crane their necks and dominate" ("collegen/e senyoregen," vv. 7127–7128). Solomon alludes to God's promise of abasement to Jerusalem's men in Isaiah 3, who as a result of tolerating women's haughtiness would receive their city's shame and die by the sword along with the city's warriors.

Solomon then sets a series of biblical and historical cities in chronological order, which were supposedly destroyed by women (vv. 7118–7649). From ancient, often biblical cities such as Nineveh, Rhodes, Sidon, Tyre, Sodom, Carthage, and Rome, to the Iberian towns of Sagunto, Cádiz, and Sigüenza, Solomon creates a conceptual landscape populated by good men, positive rulers, and malicious men. He reserves his most extensive description for Iberia's history, particularly Valencia's. First he extols Valencia's virtues, which consist mainly of its loyalty, but also its prudence (vv. 7196–7197), and later avers that Valencia deserved to burn in a fire in 1446 for tolerating women's vanity and allowing women to rule and order too much ("Bé ho mereixia/esta ciutat,/per vanitat/ells consentir/dones regir,/massa manar," vv. 7608–7613). One of the main purposes of this cityscape is to give biblical and historical figures, places, and events a measure of worth based on their gender. Since women cause cities to decay, Solomon suggests that as long as cities like Valencia permit women to give men orders, God will inflict punishment on people and places.

Kruger observes that many aspects of the dream landscape are often gendered, which characterizes Solomon's comments on cities as well, especially his references to Valencia as feminine throughout the sermon.[48] But in the dream space, the gendered female city must be controlled, which is why Solomon so often mentions legal codes, juridical entities, and punishment. For instance, when a consort of praetorian guards accompanied the Roman commander Quintus Sertorius to Valencia in the first century BCE, they declared the city exempt from taxes, an apparent reference to Valencia's independence

---

48   Kruger, "Dream Space," 13–14.

from Rome during Sertorius's eight-year rule (vv. 7158–7171).[49] Solomon does not depict Valencia's refusal to pay taxes to Rome as a rebellious avoidance of its legal obligation; instead, he underscores the importance of the city's loyalty to its Roman and later Goth rulers, and to those rulers' legal demands (vv. 7172–7185). The Catalonian and Aragonese king Peter the Ceremonious (1319–1387) also exempted Valencia from "all toll payments" ("de tot peatges," v. 7251) and from taxes previously established by the Almoravids (vv. 7251–7257). Examples such as these related to the legal realm throughout Valencia's history teach the *Espill*'s male readers about the city's worth as prudent and loyal, which are qualities demonstrated by the actions of its citizenry. These examples also instruct readers about Valencia as a gendered female entity in need of discipline and formation. The dream-sermon moulds and disciplines men by teaching them how to behave not only with women in marriage, but also in Valencia, instructing them on how to shape and dominate the gendered city from within by loyally obeying the rules and laws of political leaders.

The connection between the dream-sermon's legal discourse and the disciplining of bodies is even more patent in the dialectic with women in Valencia's history. Although Solomon occasionally mentions evil men, such as the Castilian king Peter I who laid siege to the city in 1364 (vv. 7226–7231), he reserves his most scathing critiques for women and the spaces they inhabit, such as markets and convents. In fact, Solomon avers that the best parts of the city had a rough start because of an atrocious countess who left her husband and became a prostitute, prompting the subsequent founding of a Magdalene convent for wayward women. After leaving her husband the count, the countess ended up selling fish for a sailor at a market where her husband recognized her. Perhaps because of his violent reaction toward his wife, the fish and meat sections rioted, and a mob carried the woman to jail where she was isolated and immured. The count donated her trousseau to the founding of a Magdalene convent for the enclosure of "fallen women" or prostitutes (vv. 7298–7382).

Besides reinforcing Solomon's contention about women's evil character and their damage to men through the demise of a marriage, the episode contributes to the disciplining of men's and women's bodies by teaching men how to behave and respond to women. Solomon relates that the count, upon seeing his wife selling fish at the market wanted to kill her and slit her throat ("la volc matar/e degollar," vv. 7354–7355). Despite the evident illegality of such a macabre act in the everyday world, in the *Espill*'s misogynist realm the count's emotionally violent reaction is part of the indoctrination of male readers about how to act and react as men. The violent reaction functions as a behavioral

---

49   Delgado-Librero, *The Mirror*, p. 334nn204–06.

model that teaches jilted husbands an appropriate emotional response to encountering their wayward wives. Solomon reinforces this masculine training when he relates that the punishments of immuring and isolation were no longer carried out in mid-fifteenth-century Valencia (vv. 7370–7372).[50] Although this remark neither sanctions nor critiques the loss of such practices, it resonates powerfully with other comments in the dream-sermon about punitive measures against women.

For instance, in a most direct statement about legal punishment, Solomon specifically mentions Valencia's municipal *furs* and emphasizes their impotence in disciplining women (vv. 6874–6895). He also contrasts the fecklessness of the *furs* to the resounding way that biblical law and legal codes from Castile and Aragon punish women more severely through stoning, decapitation, and hanging. Like the episode about the adulterous countess in the market, Valencia's legal penalties refer to an unfaithful woman:

> The one who commits fierce adultery, to her husband's outrage, loses her right to the dowry and the trousseau and must be sentenced to die, according to the ancient law, stoned. In Castile, her throat is slit. She is hanged high in Aragon. By law she does not die in Valencia: the fornicating whore, the strumpet, only receives a monetary penalty and passes with a simple punishment.[51]

Duran i Tort examines this passage within a broader discussion of Roig's accuracy in his treatment of legal issues related to marriage, that is, the dowry (*dot*), the trousseau (*eixovar*), and the increase (*creix*, vv. 6865, 6867), a fee a husband paid his wife when she married him as a virgin. She notes Solomon's obvious displeasure with the leniency of Valencia's penalty, since women adulterers only pay a monetary fine, compared to his envy about the severe punishments found in the "old law" (v. 6882, *llei vella*) of the Old Testament where women are stoned, or in Castile where they are decapitated or have their throats slit,

---

50   Immuring refers to walled enclosure as penalty, not as willful reclusion, as in anchoritic traditions.

51   "Dot, eixovar,/lo perd per dret/la qui comet/fer adulteri/a vituperi/del marit seu,/e morir deu/sentenciada:/apedregada/per la llei vella;/dins en Castella/mor degollada;/ alt enforcada/en Aragó;/per lo fur, no/mor en València: sols penitència/pecuniària/rep fornicària;/puta bagassa,/ab simple passa/punició!" (6874–6895).

or finally in Aragon where they are hanged.[52] Roig correctly cites what he interprets as lax punishment, at least for Christian women, since the *Furs de València* stipulate that adulterous Christian women be punished with a fine, while adultery involving a Jew or Muslim would be punishable by death.[53] Valencia's *furs* also opposed women's imprisonment, preferring instead to mandate corporal punishment and monetary fines. This passage and its larger context of the legal ramifications of women's adultery also respond in an exaggerated, misogynist way to a tendency in Valencia's *furs* to protect women's marital property, which Marie A. Kelleher recently confirms. Kelleher argues that although men's headship in marriage was tantamount in the *furs*, women's legal status as weak, incapable, and vulnerable could also be an advantage, since women were perceived as needing legal protection. The *furs* maintain that women's fragility should not be used to their disadvantage if a husband wished to encumber his wife's dowry, and are unequivocal in mandating "the need to protect women's marital property."[54] Women's dotal rights are precisely Roig's concern in the *Espill* when he focuses on women's deceit in adultery and their marriage as virgins, since the dream-sermon is an effort to warn men about women's duplicity and legal conjugal rights. Solomon repeats the disappointment about Valencia's inept civil law throughout the dream-sermon, suggesting that he laments the loss of women's punishment through isolation and immuring in the episode about the countess.[55]

These episodes aim to teach men how to treat, respond to, and imagine adulterous women (as hanged, stoned, dead, or with a slit throat) by abasing women's bodies similarly to men's so that gendered bodies acquire value through their mutual contrast and reinforcement. In the same way that men

---

52   Duran i Tort, "Aspectes jurídics," pp. 428–29, uses *decapitació* (decapitation) synonymously with *degollada* (v. 6885), while Delgado-Librero translates it as having her throat slit. Words derived from *degollar* carry both meanings.

53   *Furs de València*, ed. Germà Colón, v. 7 (Barcelona: Barcino, 1999), pp. 27–30.

54   Kelleher, *Measure of Woman*, p. 28.

55   Roig comments on adultery in the *furs* accurately, but his reference to no longer enclosing and isolating women is somewhat imprecise. Although the *furs* do not stipulate enclosure as a punishment for adultery, Magdalen houses were charged with confining and sequestering prostitutes in the fifteenth and sixteenth centuries as part of a larger project in Iberian cities to establish social and moral order through greater municipal control over prostitution, in Mary Elizabeth Perry, "Magdalens and Jezebels in Counter-Reformation Spain," in *Culture and Control in Counter-Reformation Spain*, ed. Anne J. Cruz and Mary Elizabeth Perry (Minneapolis: University of Minnesota Press, 1992), p. 125; Dangler, *Mediating Fictions*, pp. 74–75.

such as the count are denigrated through their wives' adultery (and prostitution in his case), so are adulterous women abased through Solomon's ghoul-
ish musings on their punishment, while the countess is further disparaged as
a prostitute. Solomon also maligns women prior to making his observations
about punishments in different realms when he describes their eagerness in
accepting their husbands' increase (*creix*, vv. 6865, 6867) despite cheating the
hapless men and marrying them as non-virgins. Whereas Solomon denigrates
men because of their ignorance and naiveté, women's faults are innate qualities of their gender, suggesting that men can be molded and changed, while
women's evil is immutable.

The references to legalities concerning marriage, such as adultery, dowries,
trousseaus, and the increase serve Solomon's abasement of men's and women's
bodies within an urban landscape focused on marriage and sex. But this denigration does not destabilize the authority of medical ideas about coitus, religious morality about sex, or the institution of marriage in the late Middle
Ages. Rather, it shapes men's and women's bodies as culturally masculine and
feminine and fortifies male homosociality and heterosexuality more specifically. The dream-sermon prepares its male readers for married life and sexual
relations with women by reinforcing a misogynist model of conjugal behavior based on women's deceit and men's victimization, paving the way through
Solomon's narrated historical landscape toward the only viable solution in
book four, which is to avoid women completely. Solomon highlights this point
when he declares that no reason for marrying a woman is good enough, since
none will allow men to avoid suffering:

> [M]arrying only to honor the sacrament, greatly fearing God? Or to have
> your own children and successors by a woman? Or to cool off your heat,
> or to avoid that most defamed sin (sodomy)? Or, if you don't want to live
> alone, to be served and maintained? On account of such considerations,
> you can get married with good arts. Or because of great dowries, because
> you are weak, or because of love.... For one pleasure you will certainly
> have as many sorrows as the man at arms has sweats and deadly exertions
> in his ventures.[56]

---

56   "...mas sols casar/per venerar/lo sagrament,/Déu molt tement,/per seus haver/de la
      muller/fills successors,/o per calors/refrigerar,/o per squivar/aquell pecat/pus difamat,/o,
      si no vols/habitar sols,/per ser servit/e costeït./Per tals esguards,/ab bones arts/casar-te
      pots,/o per grans dots,/per ser raixós,/o per amors.... /A un plaer/hauràs, certer,/tantes
      dolors,/quantes suors,/treballs de mort/a un deport/ha l'home d'armes," (vv. 10185–10206;
      10211–10217).

Many reasons fail to justify marriage to a woman, although Solomon's pessi-
mism does not undermine matrimony; rather, he links marriage to those very
objectives and values, and works toward inculcating the link in male readers.
The humor that results from this hyperbole about the supposed breakdown of
marriage accentuates rather than disrupts conventions of kinship and lineage,
medical ideas about moderate coitus, hetero- as opposed to homosexual activity, and the legal transfer of property in marriage.

In addition to how the dream space works to shape the male body through an
institutional landscape populated by legal and medical examples in marriage,
Kruger further avers that it disciplines the male body by depicting its indoctrination not as cultural and contingent, but as natural and divinely sanctioned:

> The disciplining of the male body, though it is cultural, works to obfus-
> cate that fact, calling on the resources of the dream—its simultaneous
> association with somatic process and divine transcendence—to allow
> the disciplining of the male body that occurs in the dreamscape to pres-
> ent itself not as cultural and contingent but rather as both natural and
> divinely sanctioned.[57]

In the *Espill* the entire book three serves as the authorizing, transcendent
reflection of the narrator's worldly discourse in books one, two, and four. In the
dream space, Solomon mediates between spiritual and worldly realms while
naturalizing the male body to make its shaping seem divinely authorized.
He invokes the omniscience and omnipotence of God himself to paraphrase
Sirach (Ecclesiasticus) 26:3 that only God can provide a man with a good wife.
But, Solomon claims, since no one other than Joseph, Mary's husband has been
so fortunate, everyday men must shun married life (vv. 6616–6627). Mundane
conjugal relations and even ecclesiastic legal remedies on earth pale in comparison to God's higher order; "The degree of affinity or kinship does not matter, nor do consulting the curia or getting a dispensation in cases of forbidden
degrees. That adds nothing to its goodness."[58] Solomon mentions legal remedies in reference to the narrator's statement at the beginning of book three
about needing to secure a papal dispensation from the ecclesiastic curia in
order to marry a relative (vv. 6442–6455). Clearly, however, even this papal dispensation will do him no good, since only God can confer a good wife on a
man. Hence, the narrator must align himself with God's higher order, which is

---

57   Kruger, "Dream Space," 14.
58   "No hi fa res grau/d'afinitat/ni parentat,/cort consultar/ni dispensar/en grau vedat:/a la
     bondat/no hi afig res," (vv. 6672–6679).

possible in the worldly realm through attention to the organization of cities, such as Valencia.

Kruger believes that literature that "works toward the inculcation of certain cultural, and specifically sexual-political, values" through dreams offers those values as "universal" because they are "natural to bodies" and part of a higher order.[59] Solomon naturalizes values related to marriage, such as choosing appropriate partners or wariness about women's innate deceit, through the abasement of the male body as we have seen. He also demonstrates that the male body is part of a divine order, which he carries out through the abasement of biblical figures or important men in history who were punished for tolerating uppity women. For instance, Samson was tied, blinded, and had his head shaved when Delilah betrayed him and the Philistines captured him (vv. 7924–7927), Hippocrates's wife apparently tried to kill him by preparing food he told her was deadly (vv. 7928–7929), and Virgil, whom Solomon calls "that poet" ("poeta aquell," v. 7930) was left hanging in a basket outside a building by a woman who wanted to humiliate him (vv. 7930–7932).[60] These men are only several of those who experienced corporeal denigration at the hands of women, just like the narrator in the *Espill*.

The effort to align the narrator with exemplary biblical men is patent in a later section of Solomon's sermon when the King impels him with commands such as, "Take John as your teacher also. Leave, like Matthew, the moneychanger's table."[61] Solomon leaves little doubt that the narrator can and must move toward a divine realm, when he declares, "Arrange everything towards God: your manners, your desires and your goals, all your paths, all your heart, will, and love, your actions and intentions, turning your back to the past."[62] Solomon's commands discipline and mould the narrator's natural functions, that is, his habits, desires, actions, intentions, and will toward

---

59   Kruger, "Dream Space," 14.
60   In the Old Testament book of Judges, Delilah famously cut Samson's locks of hair while he was sleeping, thereby stripping him of his power and allowing the Philistines to capture him. Delgado-Librero recounts a medieval story about Hippocrates in which he told his wife that eating the meat of a sow would kill a person in nine days, a dish she promptly prepared for him. The story of Virgil's public humiliation at the hands of a woman who invited him into a basket to hoist him up to her room was well known in the Middle Ages, *The Mirror*, p. 342nn245–47.
61   "També Joan/ .... pren-lo per mestre/Fuig, com Mateu,/del teloneu/de canviar," (vv. 12392, 12402–12405).
62   "A Déu venint/treballant sies:/les tues vies/desigs e fins/tots tos camins,/tot lo teu cor,/ voler, amor,/tes accions,/intencions,/a Déu ordena,/girant l'esquena/al ja passat," (vv. 12426–12437).

God, indicating not an incompatibility between the natural and the divine, but their correspondence. The human and the corporeal are not inherently corrupt here; rather, they must be molded to conform to a sacred order. Notably Solomon does not cast the alignment of the spiritual and the natural as ever complete; instead, with verbs such as *acostar* (approach), *venir* (come), and *treballar* (work, as in work toward with effort) it is a continual process, just like the making of gender. One of the reasons the dream space is so fitting for Roig's goals is because the process of aligning the mundane and divine parallels the process involved in molding men's gender, training them not in order to reach a final model of masculinity, but to constantly approach it.[63]

Roig and Solomon maintain that turning from women to approach the divine is the answer to women's inherent desire to damage men's well-being. But arranging the everyday social order is also highly important in the *Espill*, however perilous it might be for the construction of the male body. Solomon declares that trying to teach women causes men to lose their discipline: "He who teaches them loses his discipline, and his learning is for naught."[64] He cites a series of historical and biblical men who suffered at the hands of women, such as Socrates, who was humiliated when he tried to "correct and control his wife and daughter" ("volc esmenar/e ordenar/muller e filla," vv. 7981–7983). It is doubtful that Roig expected men readers to take Solomon's instructions at face value and leave their wives and daughters to pursue a perfect life with God, perhaps in a monastery. Instead, Solomon's misogynist advice is better understood as an endorsement of the social and gender orders, since through humor and hyperbole Roig creates what Kruger calls "particular gendered and sexualized understandings of 'humanness'" that are divinely sanctioned.[65] This divine endorsement occurs through women's very rejection in the *Espill*. Solomon's reiteration of the narrator's misogyny authorizes a social organization in which women pose a constant threat, and it promotes a gender order in which institutions including marriage, medicine, and law must be erected and shaped to control it.

It is difficult to capture the full meaning of this section with this short citation. Carré translates the first two verses here into modern Catalan as: "Treballa, doncs, per acostar-te a Déu," which indicates Solomon's command to the narrator to work toward approaching God, in *Espill*, p. 475.

63   Jeffrey Jerome Cohen and Bonnie Wheeler, "Becoming and Unbecoming," in *Becoming Male in the Middle Ages*, ed. Jeffrey Jerome Cohen and Bonnie Wheeler (New York: Garland, 1997), pp. *vii–xx*, discuss medieval gender and sexuality as a continual process.

64   "Qui les doctrina/perd disciplina,/en va té escola," (vv. 7951–7953).

65   Kruger, "Dream Space," 14.

The dream space is ideal for conveying this information in the *Espill* because it meshes the natural and the divine. The shaping of the male body into masculinity is supported not just by the worldly institutions of medicine, law, and marriage, but "by a divine and natural law that is in fact presented as the foundation of human institutions."[66] The disciplining of the male body and the rejection of the female body in the *Espill* occur in a historical landscape in which the biblical and ancient indeed serve as foundations of Valencia's history and institutions in the fifteenth century, with Solomon and Roig as their mediators and links.

---

66   Kruger, "Dream Space," 15.

CHAPTER 10

Portrait of a Surgeon in Fifteenth-Century England[1]

Sara M. Butler

The late medieval period witnessed a passionate struggle by physicians and surgeons for the professionalization of medicine. Endeavoring to distinguish themselves from medieval Europe's "broader set of healers" and thereby establish themselves "as the highest rung of a hierarchy of practitioners," physicians and surgeons went to great lengths to elevate their status in the public eye.[2] Their campaign for supremacy in the medical hierarchy played out in a number of different ways. Christian rhetoric, in particular, laid a strong foundation for the lofty status physicians and surgeons hoped to achieve. They were quick to exploit the spiritual facet of medicine to encourage an idealized conception of elite medical practitioners. Exemplified best in the figure of *Christus Medicus* (Christ the Physician), the powerful association between God and the medical profession in the Christian world extends back at least as far as St Augustine of Hippo, who declared: "[l]ike a skilled physician, the Lord knew better what was going on inside the patient than the patient himself. In the case of bodily infirmities, human physicians do what the Lord also is able to do in infirmities of the soul."[3] The passage of time and place only intensified this analogy. A fourteenth-century English preacher's manual underscores the strong bonds between medical practitioners and the divine:

> Christ comes as a good physician to heal us. Christ acts like a physician in the following way. A doctor investigates the condition of the sick person and the nature of his sickness by such methods as taking his pulse and inspecting his urine. Thus when Christ visits a sinner, he first enlightens him with his grace to understand himself and his own sin, so

---

1   This work was supported by a grant from the Loyola University New Orleans Committee on Grants and Research. For the purposes of this paper, all quotations from primary sources have been translated into modern English and punctuation has been inserted.

2   Katharine Park, "Medicine and Society in Medieval Europe, 500–1500," in *Medicine in Society: Historical Essays*, ed. Andrew Wear, *et al.* (Cambridge: CUP, 1992), p. 59; Faith Wallis, ed., *Medieval Medicine: A Reader* (Toronto: University of Toronto, 2010), p. 361.

3   As cited in R. Arbesmann, "The Concept of 'Christus Medicus' in St Augustine," *Traditio* 10 (1954): 19–20.

© KONINKLIJKE BRILL NV, LEIDEN, 2014 | DOI 10.1163/9789004269118_012

that he may repent of his sins and shun them. . . . Second, after diagnosing the sickness he gives the sick person a diet as he requires and prescribes what he should eat and what he should avoid; this means that Christ teaches us to avoid the occasions of sin and to seek the occasions for practising the virtues. Third, after he has prescribed and worked out a diet, he gives the sick person some syrup, an electuary, or some other medicine against the sickness to expel it; that is, Christ gives him contrition of his sins, which is made from bitter herbs . . . Fourth when the sick person is healed, he warns him against relapsing, and teaching him how to live, so that he fosters in him a good intention to lead a good life.[4]

Elite medical practitioners supported and encouraged this association. Bryon Grigsby argues that the celebrity of some medieval physicians was tied directly to their relationship with Christ: "[w]hile Christ was thought to be the perfect physician, his followers also gain acclaim as healers and curers."[5] Carole Rawcliffe makes a similar argument, saying "[f]ar from denigrating the skill of earthly practitioners, which to modern eyes seems all too fragile and limited, these ideas reinforced the image of the 'good physician', following in the steps of *Christus Medicus*."[6] Of course, God was also the ultimate scapegoat when medical treatment failed to produce results: there was a "clear awareness that, in the last resort, God, not man, would decide the outcome of so perilous an undertaking."[7]

Adoption and reinforcement of the ideology of *Christus Medicus* was just one way in which elite medical practitioners attempted to enhance their reputations. Nevertheless, it is critical to acknowledge that surgeons faced much

---

4   From *Fasciculus Morum: A Fourteenth-Century Preacher's Manual*, as cited in Carole Rawcliffe, *Medicine & Society in Later Medieval England* (London: Alan Sutton, 1995), p. 58.

5   Bryon Grigsby, "Medical Misconceptions," in *Misconceptions about the Middle Ages*, ed. Stephen J. Harris and Bryon Grigsby (New York: Routledge, 2008), p. 145. This attitude was not unique to the English. In his discussion of physicians who worked in Renaissance hospitals, John Henderson notes that "[p]ublic appreciation of their social role in looking after the bodies of the sick poor was matched by appreciation of their religious role in making available to their patients the spiritual medicine provided by Christus Medicus." John Henderson, *The Renaissance Hospital: Healing the Body and Healing the Soul* (New Haven: Yale University Press, 2006), p. 135.

6   Carole Rawcliffe, "More than a Bedside Manner: the Political Status of the Late Medieval Court Physician," in *St George's Chapel, Windsor, in the Late Middle Ages*, ed. C. Richmond and E. Scarff (Leeds: Maney Pub., 2001), p. 85.

7   Carole Rawcliffe, "Sickness and Health," in *Medieval Norwich*, ed. Rawcliffe and Richard Wilson (London: Hambledon, 2004), p. 302.

greater obstacles than did physicians.[8] For English physicians, the prestige of an Oxford degree and the social connections that came with it greatly facilitated this task. For English surgeons it was a much more difficult campaign. University education, which tended to be more theoretical than hands-on, was not part of a surgeon's training. Rather, like other craftsmen, surgeons were educated through an apprenticeship, being enfranchised only after five or six years working with an expert in the field. Surgery was a marginalized field, in large part, because it "was carried out with the hands and with instruments, and not with ideas, words, and books."[9] What is more, even in their own discipline, surgeons found it challenging to obtain recognition for their unique skills. The Company of Barbers was an amalgam of surgeons, barbers (those who made their careers clipping hair and shaving beards), and barber-surgeons (that is, those who practiced both). Yet, even in this mix, the kinds of surgery performed ranged quite dramatically from those who specialized in simple bloodletting to those who engaged in more complicated operations, such as the removal of cataracts and limb amputations.[10] At this time, continental Europe was embroiled in a heated battle for the professionalization of surgery, resulting in the discipline moving into the university environment, and prompting a proliferation of treatises in defense of surgery as an art as opposed to a craft (treatises by Henri de Mondeville and Guy de Chauliac are prime examples). England's remoteness and sparse population, however, shielded the kingdom from much of this conflict. As Robert Gottfried argues, throughout much of England, "there was less competition and strife between medical corporations because there were fewer kinds of practitioners."[11] London, however, remained the exception.

---

8   Robert S. Gottfried has argued that the most important factor in the "rise of surgery" in medieval England was the Hundred Years' War, which gave English surgeons a greater opportunity to dissect human bodies without interference (see his *Doctors and Medicine in Medieval England, 1340–1530*, Princeton: Princeton University Press, 1986). Gottfried's argument is mostly unfounded and has come under a lot of fire. See Martha Carlin's review of his book in *MH* 31.3 (1987): 360–62. Nonetheless, Bryon Grisby has made a similar argument about the importance of late medieval war to the professionalization of surgery; his argument, however, rests almost entirely on growing numbers of surgeons in a surgeon-physician ratio and thus provides a much more compelling argument. See Bryon Grigsby, "The Social Position of the Surgeon in London, 1350–1450," *Essays in Medieval Studies* 13 (1996): 74.

9   Wallis, *Medieval Medicine*, p. 288.

10   For a good sense of the scope of medieval surgery, see Tony Hunt, *The Medieval Surgery* (Woodbridge: Boydell, 1992).

11   Gottfried, *Doctors and Medicine*, p. 41.

In the city's cosmopolitan capital, surgeons worked hard to differentiate themselves from barbers, whom they considered "as little more than rude mechanicals."[12] Fifteenth-century London witnessed attempts to create a joint college of physicians and surgeons, "with absolute control over the licensing and practice of all forms of medicine in the capital."[13] The goal, naturally, was to avoid the dangers spelled out in a petition to Parliament by senior members of the universities of Oxford and Cambridge in 1421, who feared that "many uncunning and unapproved in the foresaid science practice and especially in physic . . . to great harm and slaughter of many men."[14] Social rank played a key role in all of this: the physicians and surgeons "clearly expected the Barbers to come to heal and take direction from their social and professional superiors."[15] The college's failure, undoubtedly, relates to the strength of the London barbers' guild, and the knowledge that the number of physicians and surgeons together was insufficient to attend to the medical needs of the kingdom's capital.[16] Nonetheless, the struggle of medicine's elite to gain social recognition for their endeavors met with some success: "[v]irtually all the physicians, most of the surgeons, and perhaps half the barber-surgeons in late medieval England were prosperous and bourgeois."[17]

---

12   Rawcliffe, *Medicine & Society*, p. 133. This approach speaks to the size of England's population of medical practitioners. Michael McVaugh argues that it was generally in smaller towns where physicians and surgeons "banded together for social and economic reinforcement, without much regard for status." See his *Medicine before the Plague: Practitioners and their Patients in the Crown of Aragon 1285–1345* (Cambridge: CUP, 1993), p. 108.

13   Rawcliffe, *Medicine & Society*, p. 121. For an interesting, layman's discussion of this rise to prominence, see Charles E. Bagwell, "Respectful Image," *Annals of Surgery* 241.6 (2005): 872–78.

14   *Rotuli Parliamentorum*, v. 4, p. 158. For a discussion of all legislation (royal, guild, municipal) resulting from the surgeons' bid for respectability, please see Sidney Young, *The Annals of the Barber Surgeons of London* (New York: Blades, East & Blades, 1890).

15   Rawcliffe, *Medicine & Society*, p. 134.

16   Grigsby has observed that in the decade 1420–30, there were twelve surgeons and nine physicians working in London: certainly, this small number of medical elites was insufficient to treat all of London's sick and dying. See Grigsby, "The Social Position of the Surgeon," 72. Robert Gottfried estimates that there were at least ten barbers for every surgeon working in London. See his *Doctors and Medicine*, p. 26.

17   Gottfried, *Doctors and Medicine*, p. 245. Carole Rawcliffe makes much the same argument, but she argues that their success was limited to the southeast of England. See her "The Profits of Practice: the Wealth and Status of Medical Men in Later Medieval England," *SHM* 1.1 (1988): 72.

Given the particular obstacles facing them, how did London's surgeons participate in this campaign for respectability? Medieval England's surgeons usually adopted one of two distinct methods of social advancement. First, many surgeons attempted to enhance their reputation through association. As Monica Green observes, "many of the new readers [of vernacularized medical literature] were male surgeons who, though not participating in Latinate university culture (or if so, only marginally), were nevertheless able to establish surgery as a respectable male profession because they could demonstrate their participation in a broader culture of learning."[18] Second, many others chose instead to exploit the more usual means of social advancement: office-holding. Margaret Pelling emphasizes the "civic orientation of surgeons," who saw a term as sheriff or alderman as a springboard for social advancement.[19] The career of Nicholas Wodehill, a fifteenth-century English surgeon living in London, offers us the opportunity to view yet another approach in the surgeon's war on status. Nicholas Wodehill turned to law and rhetoric as a means to transform himself into a gentleman, a social rank that he believed was most fitting of a surgeon. Nicholas Wodehill is an ideal candidate to examine how surgeons participated in the concerted effort to elevate the status of the profession. Not only was he an active proponent of the ideology of surgeons as instruments of God, but Wodehill was also a highly litigious man, who consciously manipulated his position as a surgeon to persuade others of his social value.

This study is important for a number of reasons. First, the extensive paper trail of Wodehill's court appearances open a window onto the life of a medieval surgeon during a pivotal era. The fifteenth century is critical not only because it was a key time for medical professionalization, but also the lack of surviving documentation from the medical profession of this period has led Vivian Nutton to label it "the missing century."[20] Second, the study of medical practitioners is restricted almost entirely to medical treatises: there exists almost no

18   Monica H. Green, "Integrative Medicine: Incorporating Medicine and Health into the Canon of Medieval European History," *History Compass* 7.4 (2009): 1224.

19   Margaret Pelling, "Politics, Medicine and Masculinity: Physicians and Office-Bearing in Early Modern England," in *The Practice of Reform in Health, Medicine and Science, 1500–2000: Essays for Charles Webster*, ed. Pelling and Scott Mandelbrote (Aldershot: Ashgate, 2005), p. 98.

20   Vivian Nutton explains that medical historians have universally ignored the fifteenth century because "it occupies an ambiguous position between the Middle Ages and the Renaissance, between an age of manuscript and one of print." Consequently, the century is overlooked because it falls between disciplines and skill sets. See Vivian Nutton, "Medieval Western Europe, 1000–1500," in *The Western Medical Traadition: 800 BC to AD 1800*, ed. Lawrence I. Contrad, *et al.* (Cambridge: CUP, 1995; repr. 2008), pp. 198–9.

record of their medical practice or their lives outside the medical profession.[21] Wodehill's exceptionally litigious nature resulted in an abundance of legal documentation, providing ample insight into the real world of medieval medicine. The records of his life help us to understand his sense of professional identity, how surgeons utilized that blurring between medicine and religion to deflect criticism and mould their public personas, and how they exploited the law to reinforce popular perceptions of surgeons as elite practitioners.

Nicholas Wodehill: The Early Years

The son of a goldsmith, Nicholas Wodehill began his career in the bustling northern capital of York. Presumably, he entered the medical profession in his teens; like most surgeons, his father would have arranged for him to pursue an apprenticeship with a local surgeon.[22] Even before he had attained his status as a freeman, however, Wodehill had already begun his battle for professional elitism by arranging a marriage with the daughter of Richard Russell, a successful vintner. This marriage promised to bring Wodehill great prosperity, not only through the property that would accrue to Wodehill as a result, but also through the connections to a man of such high standing in the Yorkshire community. However, as the legal record corroborates, Wodehill's plans fell short. He appeared before the chancellor sometime in the years 1432–34 to complain

---

21   The most celebrated example of a non-university trained medical practitioner who wrote about his daily practice was the fourteenth-century London surgeon John Arderne (c. 1307–70). Arderne's writing, though, makes it clear that he was not your ordinary medical practitioner. Not only was he determined to record his treatments, but his surgical practice tended to be highly specialized in a way that restricted his clientele. For example, he specialized in the treatment of *fistula in ano*, an exceptionally painful tubular ulcer that develops within the anus, generally associated with excessive horseback riding. Moreover, Arderne tells us little of his life beyond the operating table. See D'Arcy Power, ed., *Treatises of Fistula in Ano, Haemorrhoids, and Clysters by John Arderne* (London: Paul, Trench, Trübner, 1910). Arderne also wrote a short treatise on cures of the eye. See D'Arcy Power, ed., *The Lesser Writings of John Arderne* (London: Henry Frowde, 1913). Peter Jones has also written about a much less well-known medical practitioner of the fifteenth century, Thomas Fayreford, who compiled a list of 103 cures employed in his daily practice. The fascinating discovery of his manuscript has opened a window onto more general fifteenth-century medical practices; but once again, Fayreford fails to tell us much about his life beyond medical practice. See Peter Murray Jones, "Thomas Fayreford: an English Fifteenth-century Medical Practitioner," in *Medicine from the Black Death to the French Disease*, ed. Roger French, *et al.* (Aldershot: Ashgate, 1998), pp. 156–83.

22   Philip Stell, "Medical Practice in Medieval York," *Borthwick Paper* 90 (1996): 8–11.

about Isabel, widow of Richard Russell, his fiancée's stepmother.[23] Isabel was a woman with strong ties to York's urban elite. Her first husband, William de Lee, had been a bowyer; her second husband, Robert Gaunt, a merchant, had been sheriff of York in 1408–9; Richard Russell was actually her third husband; her fourth (and last) husband (married soon after this lawsuit) was Thomas Karre, draper, chamberlain of York in 1422 and sheriff in 1427–8.[24] Richard Russell died shortly before Wodehill's appearance in court; the prestigious engagement with Russell's daughter seems to have died with Russell. In an effort to hide Jane from Wodehill, Isabel sent her off to "strange places."[25] Aiding Isabel in her conspiracy against Wodehill were none other than John Marshall, canon of York minster;[26] Thomas Gare, reportedly one of the greatest merchants of the fifteenth century and mayor in 1420;[27] William Bowes, also a highly successful merchant, twice mayor of York (1417 and 1428) and Member of Parliament four times;[28] and finally, Robert Burlay, papal notary. With such a powerful contingent of both lay and ecclesiastical forces poised against him, one might think the most prudent path would be simply to "forget" that he had been affianced to Jane and try to find a more willing yet, still appropriate, bride.

It is a measure of Wodehill's dedication to employ this marriage as a stepping stone to greater communal standing that he chose instead to hunt down his fiancée and kidnap her in an attempt to force through the marriage. Rather

---

23 TNA: PRO C[hancery] 1/10/329 (*ca.* 1432–35). It is important to note that there were two vintners of York named Richard Russell operating at this time. One was a well known vintner and merchant of wool, who at one time was not only sheriff of the city of York, but also mayor twice (1421 and 1430). This Richard Russell was married to Petronella Russell and died in 1435. Our Richard Russell was married to Isabel Russell and died sometime before 1432. See James Raine, ed., *Testamenta Eboracensia, or wills registered at York* (Surtees Society, v. 30, 1885), pt, 2, pp. 52 and 57; see also Jenny Kermode, *Medieval Merchants: York, Beverley and Hull in the Later Middle Ages* (Cambridge: CUP, 2002), *passim*.

24 Robert H. Skaife, ed., *The Register of the Guild of Corpus Christi in the City of York* (Surtees Society, v. 62, 1872), pp. 18 and 23; Isabel's last will and testament can be found in *Testamenta Eboracensia*, pt. 2, p. 214.

25 TNA: PRO C 1/10/329 (*ca.* 1432–4). Wodehill undertook this lawsuit before he was finished his training, as in his bill he refers to himself simply as "Nicholas Wodehyll the younger" (in all later legal documentation he is very careful to draw attention to his status as surgeon).

26 J.A. Twemlow, ed., *Calendar of Papal Registers Relating to Great Britain and Ireland* 13 vols., (London: HMSO, 1915), v. 10, pp. 237–40: John Marshall appears among a group of canons excommunicated for their dispute of the election of Richard Andrew as dean of York.

27 P.M. Tillot, ed., *A History of the County of York: the City of York* (London: OUP, 1961), pp. 97–106.

28 Tillot, pp. 106–113.

than the marriage Wodehill hoped for, his actions led to Jane suing a felony indictment for rape and outlawry.[29] Unfortunately, the legal record obscures the severity of his crime. The term "rape" in the medieval context was highly ambiguous; it might mean either abduction on its own or abduction and forced coitus.[30] In the interests of compelling her into marriage, Wodehill may have coerced Jane into sexual intercourse, as the medieval church was content to interpret a betrothal followed by sexual relations as a valid marriage.[31] However, a marriage between Wodehill and Jane did not ensue, most likely because she was already married to John Caudell at that time.[32]

Astonishingly, none of this seems to have stood in the way of Wodehill's social success. Listed in the surviving register as "Nicholaus Wodhill, *medicus*," the guild enfranchised Wodehill as a full member in the year 1434–35.[33] A year or two later, by November of 1436, he was already a salaried employee, retained for life to serve Joan Beaufort, daughter of John of Gaunt and second wife of Ralph Neville, first earl of Westmoreland.[34] By all accounts, this was a relatively comfortable position; although the countess was in her final years, having survived the births of fourteen children, she would seem to have been in particularly good health.[35] It was also a lucrative position: Beaufort rewarded Wodehill with the rents from property in York worth five marks yearly.[36] Why did Beaufort select Wodehill as her personal practitioner? Carole Rawcliffe has observed that in York (the closest urban centre to the countess's residence at

---

29 CPR, Hen. VI, v. 3, p. 403. Like many other medieval men and women, Jane appears to have gone by several different names. The calendar refers to the victim as "Joan" rather than "Jane," but it is clear that it is the same person. Likewise, in her will, dated to August 31, 1479, she refers to herself as "Janett." See *Testamenta Eboracensia*, pt. 3, pp. 245–6.

30 Caroline Dunn, "The Language of Ravishment in Medieval England," *Speculum* 86 (2011): 79–116.

31 R.H. Helmholz, *Marriage Litigation in Medieval England* (Cambridge: CUP, 1974), pp. 26–27.

32 Her mother's last will and testament, dated to the year 1435, refers to Jane as the wife of John Caudell, and notes also the existence of their two children, William and Isabella. Although the will does not indicate the children's ages at the time of Isabel's death, it seems probable that in 1432 or 1433, likely dates for Jane's abduction, John Caudell was already a permanent fixture in Jane's life. *Testamenta Eboracensia*, pt. 2, p. 214.

33 Francis Collins, ed., *Register of the Freemen of the City of York*, v. 1 (Surtees Society, v. 96, 1897), p. 149.

34 CPR, Hen. VI, v. 6, 597.

35 C.H. Talbot and E.A. Hammond, *The Medical Practitioners of Medieval England: a Biographical Register* (London: Wellcome Institute Medical Library, 1965), p. 231.

36 This was a lucrative position for a surgeon; physicians generally garnered much more impressive salaries. See E.A. Hammond, "Incomes of Medieval English Doctors," *JHMAS* 15.2 (1960): 154–169.

the castle of Sheriff-Hutton, just twelve miles from the city of York), "physicians were relatively thin on the ground," and thus the countess likely had a small circle of individuals from which to choose.[37] All the same, Wodehill must have been well positioned socially and professionally to have stood out over older and more experienced medical men. Her death in 1440 brought an end to Wodehill's comfortable position, but not his annual income.

Soon after Beaufort's death, Wodehill relocated to the city of London. This is signalled in the general pardon issued to Wodehill in 1440 for the crime of rape and any subsequent outlawry, which refers to him (in an excessively long-winded fashion) as "Nicholas Wodhill alias Nicholas Leche, late of London, alias late of York, 'leche,' alias of York, surgeon." Why did Wodehill decide to make this move? Tensions over Jane's abduction might have escalated at this point, leading him to look for a fresh start in London where his foray into crime was not public knowledge. However, he quickly learned that it is not so easy to turn one's back on the past. Jane Russell and her stepfather (Thomas Karre, her mother's fourth and final husband) were unwilling to excuse Wodehill's transgressions, even after the king's pardon foiled the charges of felony. The patent rolls record that in January of the year 1445, the king's official scolded Wodehill for non-appearance in civil suits of trespass initiated by Jane and Karre.[38] The records of outlawries preserved in the court of Chancery document the precise nature of the accusations involved in these trespass suits, and help to clarify the brutality of Wodehill's crime. Thomas Karre's indictment focused on the kidnapping of Jane Russell. He implicated Nicholas Wodehill along with Robert Smythes of York, a barber, and John Neubald of York, a hosteller. Jane is listed here as servant to the said Thomas Karre, rather than his stepdaughter (the death of her mother ten years earlier presumably severed that connection at law). Thomas reports that, with force and arms,[39] the three men took and abducted Jane Russell and took her away from his service for a great time.[40] Jane's separate indictment of Wodehill declares that the abduction was also violent. She focused on Wodehill alone, claiming that "he assaulted her, beat her, wounded her and badly treated her so much so that her life was despaired of." She mentions nothing about the abduction, presumably because her stepfather was already suing for that crime, and neither mentions anything about

---

37   Rawcliffe, *Medicine & Society*, p. 134.
38   *CPR*, Hen. VI, v. 4, p. 304.
39   The phrase *vi et armis* (force and arms) is a standard inclusion that signals the nature of this trespass as being worthy of the king's judgment.
40   TNA: PRO C 88/128, m. 2.

sexual assault.[41] Both documents show that Wodehill had been exacted four times, then outlawed. Only after outlawry (and presumably after the scolding that appeared in the patent rolls) did he return to court in late January of 1445 to be convicted. He was sent to prison at the Fleet, although the records give no indication of how long he spent there until he was able to pay the fines associated with this civil suit.

What can this brush with the law tell us about the character of Nicholas Wodehill? The kidnapping and assault of Jane Russell-Caudell may have been simply the rash and impulsive actions of a young man jilted by his fiancée. In terms of the larger personality emerging from the legal record, this incident underscores Wodehill's strong sense of entitlement. Tossing morality and legal consequence to the wayside, Wodehill was determined to get what he felt he deserved by whatever means necessary. (Jane's mother must have recognized this personality trait; otherwise, she would not have gone to such great lengths to hide Jane from him). That Wodehill seems to have remained unmarried his entire life, is thus, most likely a boon for fifteenth-century Englishwomen. Wodehill's initial choice of courts also reflects his inability to play by the rules. The court of Chancery existed to supplement the shortcomings of the legal system. If a case was determinable at common law (or any other court of law), the chancellor did not need to waste his time hearing it. The chancellor expended his efforts on those cases that fell through the cracks of England's rigid legal system.[42] With respect to this lawsuit, Chancery was not the appropriate venue. The ecclesiastical courts were the obvious forum for a marital grievance. Wodehill chose Chancery in this instance (and as it will become apparent, in many other instances) because it was cheap, fast, effective, and did not rely on precedent. Rather, Chancery was a court of conscience: the chancellor simply listened to both sides of an argument and drew his conclusion based on a strong sense of Christian morality.[43] A man convinced of his own righteousness and respectability had good reason to be confident in taking his case to Chancery. And although the court's sentence has not survived, Wodehill's continued presence in the court of Chancery indicates that he probably experienced a measure of success. In fact, Wodehill may have believed he had the court's blessing in his pursuit of Jane Russell. Russell's tenacity and shrewdness in the courts did eventually outsmart Wodehill, landing him in prison for his

---

41   TNA: PRO C 88/128, m. 3.

42   Timothy S. Haskett, "The Medieval English Court of Chancery," *L&HR* 14 (1996): 245–313.

43   For a discussion of the effectiveness of the courts of Chancery, see Sara M. Butler, "The Law as a Weapon in Marital Disputes: Evidence from the Late Medieval Court of Chancery, 1424–1529," *Journal of British Studies* 43.3 (2004): 291–316.

transgressions; but with his connections and strong financial and social standing, it is likely that Wodehill's stay was short-lived.

Wodehill's repeated outlawries and time in prison did nothing to dampen his ambition; however, he did learn from his earlier experience that renegade lawlessness is less effective than a strong sense of righteousness and a continued presence in the courts. He may have also realized that marriage was not going to be his road to social success and thus determined to look elsewhere for the riches upon which to enter into the lifestyle of the gentry. A notarial instrument dated to October of 1454 and commissioned by Wodehill's father, "Nicholas Wodehille the elder, late of the city of London and now of Westminster, goldsmith," is the first written evidence of a fresh dispute. The document is a declaration concerning certain lands, rents and services in the parishes of Lyminge and Elmsted, located in the southeastern part of the county of Kent, which he had granted to his son, Nicholas the surgeon. Of course, there was a tiny hitch: one parcel of land, Petfeld, located in the parish of Lyminge, was not actually his land to give away. The declaration recounts how, orphaned at the age of ten, his father's illegitimate son, Edmond, became Nicholas the elder's guardian, an appointment that he used to further his own best interests. Edmond used the profits of Nicholas's inheritance to pay his debts, then he induced Nicholas to seal a deed of enfeoffement, putting Edmond in possession of Petfeld; he gave his ward a new doublet for his loss. Edmond arranged an apprenticeship for Nicholas with a goldsmith, and the two parted ways. Since that time, Petfeld had come into the hands of a man named William Swayn, although it is unclear whether Swayn bought or inherited the land from Edmond.[44]

Was Nicholas the elder telling the truth about Petfeld? Nicholas the elder undermines his own credibility, and he seems to do so deliberately. In his declaration, he notes specifically that "men of the same country" told him it was his father's will that Edmond be given that land; his mother, Agnes, who survived her husband a short time, was the only one who believed it should go to Nicholas. Why would Nicholas the elder even include this damning statement in his declaration at law? He immediately casts suspicion on his mother's claim as the jealous ramblings of an overprotective mother emboldened by her husband's death. Was Nicholas the elder trying to shake the foundation of his son's inheritance? Although his son's financial welfare was clearly the motivation behind this notarial instrument, Nicholas the elder also confesses that he had originally thrown his support behind William Swayn, rather than his own son. Admittedly, his backing came at a price: Swayn's lawyer, Richard Croft, had promised to help Nicholas the elder gain a general acquittance in an

---

44   CCR, Hen. VI, v. 6, p. 41.

unspecified lawsuit pending against him if he "should say no word that should avail his son in the plea." Nicholas the elder only reversed his stance when Croft failed to live up to his side of the bargain.[45]

Despite all this deception and embellishment, Nicholas the elder confidently swore that "he knew never nor yet knows anything for to bar him or his heirs from their right to Petfeld or any parcel of the foresaid lands, as he will answer at the day of Doom."[46] This bold declaration was enough to assure Wodehill that Petfeld rightly belonged to him. Once again, Wodehill turned to his preferred method of resolution: the court of Chancery. His first bill in Chancery concerning this matter, regrettably, has not weathered time as well as one might hope: grotty and tattered (most of the left side of the bill is missing), not much detail can be gleaned from it with great certainty. What is clear is that it was directed against a variety of people working together to prevent him from taking possession of Petfeld and attempting to chip away at his claim to the inheritance. Of particular interest, he targets two unexpected authorities: first, Robert Percy, clerk of the diocese of Norwich, notary public and registrar of the archdeaconry court of Westminster, and (specifically) the notary who certified Nicholas the elder's aforementioned declaration; second, Robert Coke, "ghostly father" (that is, confessor) to Nicholas the elder, and witness to the above declaration. Ostensibly, even his father's notary and confessor did not trust Wodehill's father.[47] A second bill in Chancery from the year 1456 follows up on this complaint, aimed this time at Richard Munden, a fellow surgeon of Canterbury,[48] and Thomas Glasier, a mason, both feoffees of Swayn's. Wodehill's story begins with his dispute against Swayn. "By the assent of both the parties," the "debate and controversy . . .upon the right title and possession of a certain piece of land called Petfield with the appurtenances" was put to arbitration. The award was in Wodehill's favor: Wodehill was ordered to

---

45   Notably, Nicholas the elder's behavior in this instance was not out of character. His checkered past indicates that he was not altogether trustworthy. The records of Chancery note at least two plaints of debt against Nicholas Wodehill, citizen and goldsmith of London, for significant sums of money. In October of 1418, Alice widow of John Langholme sued Nicholas for a debt of £40; in November of the same year, John Child the younger, citizen and barber of London, sued Nicholas for a debt of £80.The suit of Alice widow of John Langholme can be found in two files: TNA: PRO C 131/226/5 (1418) and C 241/212 (1418); the suit of John Child the younger appears in TNA: PRO C 131/226/7 (1418). TNA: PRO C[ourt of Common] P[leas] 40/825, r. 107 and r. 510 (1467) also includes a debt case involving Nicholas Wodehill the elder.

46   CCR, Hen. VI, v. 6, p. 41.

47   TNA: PRO C 1/16/223 (ca. 1454–56).

48   Talbot and Hammond, p. 281.

pay Swayn ten marks for the land, but stated that Wodehill "should have and hold to him, his heirs and assigns, forevermore the said piece of land with the appurtenances." William Swayn and any other person pertaining title or estate to the land was asked to deliver the evidences and muniments to Wodehill. Richard and Thomas "utterly refuse, unto great hurt" of Wodehill, landing him once more before the chancellor.[49] In the end, Wodehill was successful. A letter in the fine rolls dating to 10 November 1458 made a commitment by royal officials to enforce Wodehill's right to Petfeld (here described as "Prestfeld," but clearly the same place).[50] Later that month the death of his brother, Thomas Wodehill, cemented firmly Wodehill's claim with any title that he, too, had to the lands in Lyminge and Elmsted.[51]

The Business of Medicine

Only one of Wodehill's court appearances was related to his work as a medical professional. The surviving documentation, however, offers tremendous insight into both Wodehill's sense of identity as a surgeon, but also the business of medicine. A bill addressed to the chancellor, written sometime between the years 1467 and 1471, details the quarrel between Wodehill and his patient, William Chapman of London, gentleman. Wodehill's petition is shrewdly crafted to relate the pathetic story of a hard-working surgeon, devoted to his patient and his patient's family, repeatedly saving their lives, and yet thwarted at every turn by Chapman's tight-fisted ways. Some unspecified desperation led Wodehill to borrow £20 from his patient for a two-month period, with the plan to repay ten marks[52] on a certain day specified within the obligation, on the condition that if he did not make the repayment, Chapman would confiscate Wodehill's home in London. Despite Chapman's initial acceptance of the plan, he delivered only 40s. in hand to Wodehill and agreed to pay the rest when he had sealed the obligation for £20; naturally, once the obligation was sealed he failed to deliver the residual. Wodehill was not one to take no for an answer. With time and great labor, Wodehill eventually managed to cajole 100s. out of Chapman; but more importantly, with his medical services, he brought his patient back from death's door on at least three separate occasions. Because

---

49   TNA: PRO C 1/25/10 (1456).

50   CFR, v. 19, pp. 222–223.

51   CCR, Hen. VI, v. 6, pp. 343–346.

52   The medieval English mark was worth roughly 2/3 of a pound, or 13s. 4d. (that is, 13 shillings, 4 pence).

Chapman never paid him for his services, Wodehill believed that Chapman would apply the value against the debt. Nevertheless, Wodehill soon found himself on the verge of losing both his home and his reputation: "against all right and conscience," Chapman was suing Wodehill for recovery of the £20 specified in the obligation, but was not, apparently, taking into account that he had only ever given Wodehill 100s. and had not paid him for his labor. Fearing the loss of his home, Wodehill turned to the chancellor for assistance.[53]

Most cases in Chancery end there: only the bills are extant from the Middle Ages for the vast majority of litigation in Chancery.[54] Thankfully, Nicholas Wodehill's finely painted portrait of the struggling, high-minded surgeon victimized by his ungrateful patient is just one of a number of documents surviving from this case. The answer of William Chapman to Wodehill's bill is quite pointed. First, undoubtedly coached by his attorney, Chapman made sure to point out that the matter is indeed determinable at common law (the point of this formulaic inclusion, of course, is to signal to the chancellor that now is the ideal time to quash the case and send Wodehill away). Second, Wodehill's story was somewhat flawed. Actually, Wodehill was constantly borrowing money. At the outset, he was indebted to Chapman for only £4 18s. 4d, but the amount abruptly escalated to ten marks; in the end, they had an obligation for £20 drafted in which Wodehill agreed to deliver the sum of ten marks by a specified day, or lose his tenement in London to Chapman. As to Wodehill's medical services, Chapman claimed he had already paid Wodehill 10s., "which was more than he deserved and more than other surgeons would have taken of him to have healed him of the same for they were but small hurts," not the life-threatening injuries that Wodehill purported heroically to have cured. Chapman concluded with a curt and mechanical request that he hoped to see the case "dismissed out of this court with his reasonable costs and damages for his wrongful vexation."[55]

By attacking Wodehill's reputation as a medical practitioner and a businessman, Chapman had clearly struck a nerve. Wodehill's haughty replication

<hr/>

53   TNA: PRO C 1/1489/102 (ca. 1467–71).

54   Chancery bills were drafted by scribes in either English or French, and frequently lacked much of the formulaic language evident in other English court records, thus allowing the historian a clear understanding of the petitioner's perspective in his own words. For a fuller discussion of the Chancery courts, see Emma Hawkes, "'[S]he will ... protect and defend her rights boldly by law and reason ...']: Women's Knowledge of Common Law and Equity Courts in Late-Medieval England," in *Medieval Women and the Law*, ed. Noël James Menuge (Woodbridge: Boydell, 2000), pp. 145–61.

55   TNA: PRO C 1/1489/103 (ca. 1467–71).

dwelt on the extent of the injuries sustained by Chapman at various points over the last four years and affirmed that Chapman "paid never penny of reward" to Wodehill for his laudable medical achievements. To emphasize the gravity of his successes and his ingenuity as a surgeon, his replication included a detailed invoice of his services and their expenses. Because of the bountiful insight this financial statement offers into the day-to-day practice of a surgeon, it is included here in full:

These been the cures, costs and charges in the occupation and science of surgery done by Nicholas Wodehill unto William Chapman at diverse times and years in manner and form as follows:

First: in the fifth year of the reign of King Edward III, about Saint Nicholastide,[56] for a cure done unto the same William by the said Nicholas in curing and healing of wound which was struck with a dagger under the right breast by one John Cavend Bucheman, capper, at Aldrich Gate in the parish of Saint Anne in London, through which stroke the wind passed out at the wound to the great peril of the said William and in jeopardy of his life.—100s.

Item: for another cure done the fourth year of the reign of the said king to the said William where he was struck upon the right side of his head with a dagger within the Temple Bar by one Marmaduke Holme, gentleman of Lincolnshire, [one word unreadable here] through which stroke he was passed through the over table of his head and the bone so scaled where through he stood in right great peril of himself which stroke he had about the Ascension day in the year aforesaid.[57]—40s.

Item: the same third year about the Nativity of Our Lady,[58] for another cure done to the same William by the said Nicholas for edge of his nose which was hurt at the Pye in Smithfield with the edge of a great candlestick by one Peter Celler, where through his nose was almost smitten of which was likely to have been to him a great blemish and [one word unreadable here]—100s.

---

56 Approximately December 6, 1464.
57 Approximately a month and a half after Easter, 1464.
58 September 8, 1463.

Item: about the third year of the said king, for curing and healing of a puncture with a pin in the sinew of the first finger next the thumb of his right hand, which was hurt at Northampton as he said whereby he stood in jeopardy to have lost his hand or utterly to be maimed.—40s.

Item: about the said third year of the king aforesaid, for healing of an heat and fire, which determined from his body into the joint of the wrist of his right hand, which grew into a sore called *herisipila*[59] whereby he stood in jeopardy of his said joint and hand.—20s.

Item: about the same third year aforesaid, for curing and healing of a great aposteme[60] in the joint of a finger of his right hand, which determined into a sore called *panaricium*[61] whereby he stood in great jeopardy of his said finger and hand.—70s.

Item: at our Lady Day in Lent, the sixth year of the king aforesaid,[62] for a cure done unto Robert the son of the same William, which was cast against the edge of a stair by which cast the same Robert was grievously hurt so that the left hip was relaxed and all the leg sore bruised, wasted and consumed so that the said Robert might not stand, nor go, likely to have been maimed unto the time that he was helped by the might of God and the cure of the said Nicholas.—5 marks

Item: the month of November, the seventh year of the king aforesaid, about Martinmas tide,[63] for another cure done to the said William, whereas he was beaten grievously and sore upon head and jaws, whereby

---

59   *"Hericipula"* is the term used in the actual invoice; however, it seems likely that this is a mangled transcription of the term *herisipila*, which means "any disease involving inflammation of the skin (i.e. any aposteme) caused by excess or aberration of the humor choler." *Middle English Dictionary*, v. 10, p. 223. Juhani Norri suggests that the more usually transcription is *erisipela*, which Norri defines as an "aposteme caused by excess choler or by choleric blood." Juhani Norri, *Names of Sicknesses in English, 1400–1550: An Exploration of the Lexical Field* (Helsinki: Suomalainen Tiedeakatemia, 1992), p. 325.

60   *The Oxford English Dictionary* defines an aposteme as "a gathering of purulent matter in any part of the body; a large deep-seated abscess."

61   *"Pernaricius"* is the term used in the invoice, but the above spelling is the more likely one. A *panaricium* is a term that is still used in modern medicine to describe an inflammation of a digit.

62   March 25, 1466.

63   November 11, 1467.

the bones of his said jaws and teeth were loosened so that his throat and jaws were swollen that he might not eat, nor swallow, nor well drink, nor open his mouth to speak so that his wind was almost stopped right likely thereupon to be dead, which he took at the Tower Hill among thieves in the night, as he said.—100s.

Item: about Saint Thomas day in the month of December the year aforesaid[64] for a cure done unto the wife of said William of a sickness which was fallen out of her body into the calf of her left leg, where through she had so great pain that she might neither stand, nor go, nor sleep unto the time that she was cured by the same Nicholas.—3s. 4d.

Item: for another cure done to Richard, his sister's son, the same month and year. Where the said Richard had such [*hole in the page*]—ness that he might not hear. The same Nicholas, by the might of God and his cure, made him to hear and may hear right well at this day. Thanked be God.—20s.

Item: for taking away of a great wart from the same William of long time rooted and grown in the joint of his middle finger of his ring hand, which was to him a great annoyance and blemish.—10s.

Sum total—£26 10s.[65]

This account depicts a highly experienced professional accustomed to dealing with a wide variety of surgical and non-surgical ills. During the four short years Wodehill worked for Chapman, his patient was stabbed in the chest (a wound that apparently punctured his lungs), had his head hacked with a dagger, almost lost his nose, and was beaten so badly around the head that he could not eat or speak, scarcely breathe. Helped by the "might of God," Wodehill was consistently successful in his treatments. Wodehill's invoice also offers a look into the more mundane injuries and illnesses that surgeons treated. Although the invoice is plagued with a tendency to overstatement (conveniently placing Chapman or his family members on death's door or about to lose a limb whenever possible), it also suggests that he was called upon to treat a number of stubborn chronic conditions. The "heat and fire" issuing from Chapman's wrist and resulting in painful sores sounds uncannily like rheumatoid arthritis,

---

64   December 21, 1467.

65   TNA: PRO C 1/1489/104 (*ca.* 1467–71).

a condition that frequently leads to nodularity and the deformity of the hands (thus, the painful sores and inflammation referred to by the terms *herisipila* and *panaricium*). Chapman's wife suffered from a sickness which "was fallen out of her body into the calf of her left leg" producing a pain so intense that "she might neither stand, nor go, nor sleep." Anyone who has suffered from sciatica will instantly recognize the description of this bothersome condition. If Wodehill was actually capable of addressing this great diversity of ills, from life-threatening injuries to chronic diseases, even temporary deafness, then he was far more talented and versatile than are our surgeons today.[66] At a total of £26 10s., Wodehill's medical services may sound expensive; but if Wodehill's account provided a frank assessment of the seriousness of the injuries, £26 10s. is a small price to pay for life and good health.[67] More important still, his fees were more than adequate to pay off his debt to Chapman; in fact, if Wodehill's accounting was correct, this would leave Chapman indebted to our surgeon.

Wodehill's credibility, or lack thereof, formed the nucleus around which Chapman built his rejoinder, the final document in our Chancery case file. Referencing specifically the itemized wounds or illnesses spelled out in the invoice, Chapman repeatedly trivializes the nature of these injuries. Concerning the wound in his hand caused by the "puncture of a pin," "rehearsed in the fourth article," Chapman reports that his finger was merely "a little repelled" (a term drawn from humeral theory suggesting that an excess of fluid or humor was producing swelling) and the cure was worth no more than 3d. The sore called a "hircipula" was only a little blemish on his wrist, the healing of which was worth 1d. The "great appostem" on his finger was "a little boil," for which he paid Wodehill 4d. The story about his son Robert falling and injuring his leg was a fiction. Rather, he too, suffered from a "little boil upon the hip." Wodehill

---

66   Jeromy J. Citrome has argued that "Medieval surgeons were by no means limited to cutting and burning. Many surgeons employed medicinal baths in order to relieve pain and encourage the patient's body to sweat out its corruption, and nearly all acted as their own apothecaries in order to fashion soothing ointments for dermatological conditions." See his *The Surgeon in Medieval English Literature* (London: Palgrave, 2006), p. 15. Wodehill's experience indicates that some surgeons were even more expansive in their practice.

67   Ten pounds was a sufficient sum of money to support a gentleman for one year in later medieval England. Thus, £26 10s. represents roughly the wages needed to support William for two and a half years of his life. For a fuller discussion of normative costs in medieval medical expenses, see Robert Ralley, "Medical Economies in Fifteenth-century England," in *Medicine and the Market in England and its Colonies, c. 1450–c. 1850*, ed. Mark S.R. Jenner and Patrick Wallis (New York: Palgrave Macmillan, 2007), pp. 24–46. Ralley emphasizes that a medical practitioner who entered into a contract to heal generally devoted himself entirely to one patient at a time.

had only to lay a plaster on it, thus the healing was worth 1*d*. Where Wodehill alleges that Chapman was so beaten about the head that he could not eat or speak, Chapman claims he was only "a little repelled in the neck with the point of a custrell," (that is, he had a swelling in his neck caused by the sword of a knave), an injury worth only 5*d*. As to his wife's agony, all Wodehill did was make "a plaster of brown bread, vinegar and wormwood," labor William valued at 1*d*.[68] Chapman does at least suggest that Wodehill has a generous side: concerning the curing of his nephew's deafness, he says that "for truth, the said Wodehill out of his own free will helped the child," (and thus should not expect to get paid for it!). Finally, as to the cure in the first article, admittedly the most serious, in which Wodehill alleged Chapman was stabbed in the chest with a dagger, puncturing his lung, that incident apparently took place in the second year of the king's reign (1462–3), long before the obligation was even written and thus was not applicable. The only article that he did not deny was the removal of a wart on his hand, a service worth 2*d*. to Chapman. Given the petty nature of these injuries and Chapman's candid appraisal of their worth (a total value of 1*s*. 5*d*.), clearly Wodehill should be grateful for the generous 10*s*. Chapman purports to have paid him.[69]

On the surface, this disagreement is all about money and, as is predictably the case when disputes are aired in a courtroom setting, the truth is plainly absent from both accounts. Chapman plays down the nature of his wounds and poor health in an effort to diminish the worth of Wodehill's services; Wodehill, instead, describes the injuries as potentially fatal whenever possible to inflate the value of his treatments. The strong sense of dignity and righteousness pervading Wodehill's words, though, strongly suggest that ego was at the heart of his desire to bring this case to court. The modern reader of this invoice cannot help but wonder how William Chapman is still alive. Nicholas Wodehill might easily respond that he should not be. In a world described by an historian as "fraught with injury and disease but lacking many effective means to treat these problems," any man suffering the kinds of injuries that Chapman endured (even if they were only partly as serious as described) should be dead.[70] That he was still alive to answer Wodehill's complaint was due entirely

---

68   Plasters were not used exclusively to heal skin diseases, as one might expect. For internal disorders, "[a]ccording to their composition, they either encouraged or prevented the loss of heat and moisture, thus enabling the body to recover its humoral balance." Rawcliffe, *Medicine & Society*, p. 61.

69   TNA: PRO C 1/1489/105 (*ca.* 1467–71).

70   Michael D. Bailey, *Magic and Superstition in Europe: a Concise History from Antiquity to the Present* (Lanham, MI: Rowman & Littlefield, 2007), p. 80.

to the compact between God the physician and our earthly surgeon. Wodehill's accounting makes this abundantly clear. He does not hesitate to articulate how closely he works with God. When Chapman's son injured his left hip and leg falling down the stairs, God and Nicholas were there to attend him: Robert was "helped by the might of God and the cure of the said Nicholas." When Chapman's nephew experienced a bout of temporary deafness, who helped him to hear again? "The same Nicholas by the might of God and his cure made him to hear and may hear right well at this day. Thanked be God."[71] Only the final reference of gratitude to God alone suggests that Wodehill did, in fact, conceive of himself as the junior partner in this relationship.

Working with God

Wodehill's petition to the chancellor in 1467–71 clearly verbalizes his confidence in an integral connection with God as a surgeon; the legal record establishes that Wodehill lived out his conviction. Persuaded that his status as surgeon exempted him from the ordinary rules of mankind, he repeatedly broke the law, and then manipulated the law courts with his charisma and rhetoric. Records of other disputes between medical practitioners and their patients in the court of Chancery make it clear that Nicholas Wodehill was not the only medieval medical practitioner to have internalized the church's teachings on *Christus Medicus*. Other medical practitioners shared this perspective and endorsed it, confidently articulating the relationship between God and medicine to defend their reputations in court. Even university-trained physicians held firm to the belief that God might be both the cause of disease and the ultimate physician. For example, Piers de Seint Hillary, a London physician and Wodehill's contemporary, caught up in an argument with a disgruntled patient, openly voiced this perspective in his petition to the chancellor. His patient, William Gold of London, was suffering from divine punishment: "by the visitation of God, [Gold] was sore taken with great sickness." Nonetheless, Seint Hillary contracted with Gold to cure him of the disease for a sum of twenty marks (of which only five marks were delivered). As Seint Hillary brags in his petition, he achieved a good measure of success: Gold "was greatly relieved and well nigh healed and re-cured of his said sickness." Regrettably, Seint Hillary was called away on the king's business and was unable to complete the treatment. Furious, Gold "took diverse actions against" Seint Hillary, having him arrested six times "so that your said orator could in no way be in peace and rest" until

---

71   TNA: PRO C 1/1489/104 (*ca.* 1467–71).

he struck a deal with Gold. He gave Gold a ring of gold and other pieces of gold to the value of seven marks and more to quiet him; nonetheless, at the time of the petition, Gold had sued yet another plaint against Seint Hillary in the city of London for debt, and Seint Hillary was at his wit's end.[72] His bill makes it wholly apparent that Gold was precisely the kind of person God *should* strike down in illness.

Other medical practitioners touted their relationship with God in healing. William Parouns, a physician operating out of London who appeared before the chancellor sometime between 1486 and 1493, clearly saw himself as a vehicle of God's grace. His bill recounts that William Robynson of London, a haberdasher, was "sore sick of the infirmity of pestilence" when he approached Parouns for help.[73] Robynson hoped to covenant with Parouns for a cure, but Parouns refused (although he did not voice it, the tenor of his bill suggests that Parouns believed the man would die, an obvious reason for not entering into any sort of legal obligation to cure).[74] Robynson was persistent, promising Parouns that if he treated him with the "best of his cunning, [...] he would reward" Parouns "as well as ever he was rewarded for any cure." Parouns rose to the challenge, applying himself "diligently," administering medicines to the patient paid for from his own pocket. Within a month, "by the grace of God," Robynson, just like Lazarus before him, "returned to life," "made whole of his sickness." Miracles, unfortunately, do not come with a price tag. Since his astonishing recovery, Robyson had refused to reimburse Parouns for the cost of the medicines (20s.) or "to give unto him a competent reward for his labor and attendance upon the said William." Unwilling to be cheated out of his paycheck, Parouns turned to the chancellor for sympathy.[75] Hercules de Ferrariis, a clerk and medical practitioner called upon to help heal a London sheep shearer named William Bayly, voiced the same belief that he, too, worked with God's assistance. "Being sore sick and in jeopardy of his life," Bayly sent for

---

72   TNA: PRO C 1/46/55 (*ca.* 1467–72).

73   Although "pestilence" frequently meant bubonic plague, it was not reliably used in this manner. Without further description of the symptoms Robynson was suffering, it is not possible to determine if he meant bubonic plague, or if he was using the term to be synonymous with disease.

74   Throughout the antiquity and Middle Ages, fear that a patient might die was a frequent cause for refusing treatment. Some medieval cities attempted to quell medical practitioners' fears of a lawsuit by requiring that patients in danger of death must be shown to the masters of the guild. See Madeleine Pelner Cosman, "Medieval Medical Malpractice: the Dicta and the Dockets," *Bulletin of the New York Academy of Medicine* 49.1 (1973): 26.

75   TNA: PRO C 1/105/35 (*ca.* 1486–93).

de Ferrariis to help cure him. With the "help of God," de Ferrariis did just that. Portraying himself more as a saint than a businessman, de Ferrariis reports that he took nothing for his labor, asking only for the costs of the medicines that Bayly promised to pay (and of course, did not). In a pre-emptive move to avoid a plaint of debt, Bayly turned to the local courts. De Ferrariis found himself imprisoned by the sheriffs of London "for certain offences laid against him concerning his allegiance," brought against him by the now hearty and hale William Bayly.[76]

Admittedly, it is critical to acknowledge that the medical practitioners in question were all plaintiffs in their disputes, hoping to depict themselves as victims of exploitation in order to gain the compassion of the court. Thus, reading their petitions one experiences a kneejerk reaction of injustice and indignity that is not wholly representative of what actually happened. What is pertinent here is that each of these carefully crafted bills makes a conscious effort to remind the chancellor of their privileged and unique status as God's work force here on earth. How could the chancellor, God's man himself, not side with God?[77] While some of this was clearly rhetoric, the inflated sense of self perpetuated by men like Nicholas Wodehill strongly suggests that this message was not just popular analogy, but also internalized.

Conclusion

In the final years of his life, Wodehill managed mostly to avoid the legal record. He is mentioned once in the Patent Rolls for 1 April 1460. The rents from lands in York granted to him by his former employer had been confiscated to the king, although it is not explained why; in its place, the king granted Wodehill lordship of the manor of Clavering in Essex, valued also at five marks annually.[78] This grant was followed soon after by an order preserved in the close rolls for

---

76 TNA: PRO C 1/1501/4. The Public Record Office dates this case between 1386 and 1558; however, a man by the name of Hercules de Ferrariis (surely an unusual name) was responsible for writing a tomb inscription in 1510 for Cardinal Morone, thus this case probably belongs to the late fifteenth or early sixteenth century. See Nicola Bernabei, *Vita del Cardinale Giovanni Morone, Vescovo di Modena e biografie dei Cardinali Modenesi e di Casa d'Este, dei cardinali Vescovi di Modena e di quelli educati in questo Collegio di San Carlo* (Modena, 1885), p. 155.

77 Throughout the Middle Ages, the position of chancellor was normally occupied by members of the clergy, either a bishop or an archbishop. It was only during the period of the Wars of the Roses where we have a short-lived move away from this trend.

78 CPR, Hen. VI, v. 6, p. 597.

15 April 1460 to "the receivers, farmers, bailiffs or other occupiers for the time being of the manor of Clavering in Essex," to pay Nicholas Wodehill five marks a year for life.[79] He appeared once more in the court of Common Pleas in the year 1465 as surety for Richard Kneseworth of Cambridgeshire. Kneseworth was accused of failing to repay a debt. What is key about this particular court appearance is that it indicates Wodehill had accomplished his goal: the record describes him as "Nicholas Wodhill of London, gentleman."[80]

Wodehill's story has much to offer historians of medicine. First, records of medicine in practice, such as Nicholas Wodehill's remarkable invoice, offer a glimpse into the real life of a medieval practitioner during a century in which the evidence has generally been quite murky. Wodehill's account of his dealings with Chapman and Chapman's family demonstrate that surgeons were not, by far, restricted to the operating table.[81] While their expertise in cutting may have made them stand out from other empirics, patients expected surgeons to deal with more routine, non-surgical ills as well. Wodehill's invoice highlights also an astonishingly violent world. Here, we need to remember, that even if Wodehill's account does not represent the exact truth, it had to be crafted in a way that the chancellor would find it convincing. The world he illustrates is one in which a dispute with a neighbor might lead to a dagger through the chest.

Second, Wodehill's life, as recorded by the legal documentation, offers a distinct impression of his personality and sense of identity as a medical practitioner. Wodehill depicts himself as the consummate professional, loyal to his patients (even when they do not pay him), highly successful as a surgeon, but whose expertise and status is constantly underappreciated by those around him. To Wodehill, the ends were far more significant than the means. He allowed no one to stand in his way, and the fact that he was involved in a least one assault and abduction, and fought so hard to recover "an inheritance" that was seemingly not his to claim, hints strongly that he felt he was above the law. Wodehill was also exceptionally proud of his status as a surgeon. Crown or municipal records might refer to him as leech or *medicus*, but in his own documentation, he was always careful to highlight his position as a surgeon. Certainly, in York, this distinction does not seem to have been all that meaningful (thus, Wodehill's decision to team up with a mere barber to kidnap Jane Russell during his York days is entirely understandable). But in London, where Wodehill practiced for most of his career, this distinction was meaningful. As

---

79   CCR, Hen. VI, v. 6, pp. 414–17.

80   TNA: PRO CP 40/816, rot. 507*d*.

81   Philip Stell's study of medical practice in York draws the same conclusion. See Stell, 26–27.

Faye Getz argues, it was "in London that the medical profession established itself."[82] Assuredly, Wodehill's intense self-identification as a surgeon, as well as the heroic accounts of his practice were shaped by having witnessed the attempt to create a joint College of Physicians and Surgeons during his own lifetime. Wodehill, then, is a product of the fifteenth-century medical climate in London. Wodehill's life experiences demonstrate a historical reality to the firm social distinctions established between medical practitioners. His meteoric rise to success and close associations with elite society reveal that being a surgeon in late medieval England had serious financial and social perquisites. Whether Nicholas actually internalized popular perceptions of medical practitioners as an instrument of God is a question that remains to be answered; but his charmed life and repeated successes surely gave him reason to believe that God was on the side of medieval surgeons.

---

82   Faye Marie Getz, ed., *Healing and Society in Medieval England: a Middle English Translation of the Pharmaceutical Writings of Gilbertus Anglicus* (Madison, WI: University of Wisconsin Press, 1991), p. *xxiv*.

Medicine and the Law in Hagiography

∴

An Infirm Man: Reading Francis of Assisi's Retirement in the Context of Canon Law

Donna Trembinski

It is sometimes difficult to remember that St Francis of Assisi spent much of his life ill and incapacitated. In his relatively short life, perhaps forty-four years, Francis founded three new orders, renewed and deepened medieval notions of apostolic poverty and *imitatio christi*, dramatically changed the way preaching in towns was performed, travelled on a mission to the Middle East, and became an exemplar of medieval experiential Christianity. Given everything that Francis managed to accomplish, it is perhaps not surprising that scholars of Francis from Paul Sabatier[1] to Jacques Le Goff[2] have spent little time on Francis's disabilities, beyond his reception of the stigmata. Thus, when Joanne Schatzlein and Daniel Sulmasy wrote an article speculating that many of Francis's symptoms suggest he may have suffered from a type of leprosy commonly known today as Hansen's disease,[3] it was met with deafening silence from others working in the field. So invisible are Francis's disabilities within the scholarly literature that even scholars who work on the history of disability have thus far avoided discussing the implications of Francis's infirmities for his life and mission.

The most striking example of this can be found in Henry-Jacques Stiker's *A History of Disability*. While Stiker notes that Francis transformed medieval ideas about poverty, making individuals and groups previously marginalized newly deserving of admiration, he does not comment at all on Francis's own myriad disabilities. Unintentionally ironic, Stiker ends his discussion of Francis's influence on the acceptance of poverty as a positive virtue by stating "[i]t may be remarked that in the course of the inquiry into St Francis, I seem

---

1 Paul Sabatier, *The Life of Francis of Assisi*, trans. L.S. Houghton (London: Hodder and Stoughton, 1919).

2 Jacques LeGoff, *Saint Francis of Assisi*, trans. C. Rhone (London: Routledge, 2004).

3 See Joanne Schatzlein and Daniel O. Sulmasy, "The Diagnosis of St Francis: Evidence for Leprosy," *FS* 47 (1987): 181–217.

to have lost sight of the truly disabled."[4] Stiker certainly has, for from the very moment of his conversion, Francis was plagued by various infirmities.

The purpose of this chapter is to re-centre Francis's disabilities in the history of his life and Order. It elaborates on an argument that this author has made elsewhere; that while Francis's various infirmities granted him spiritual authority by virtue of his dedication to an ascetic lifestyle and his desire to imitate Christ, they were problematic for his role as the leader of a religious order.[5] Here, this chapter nuances the traditional narrative of Francis's decision to devolve the leadership of his Order onto others—that Francis disliked administering the Order and recognizing this, stepped down and that Francis's desire to lead a humble life of obedience led him to step away from the spotlight of leading an international order.[6] Instead, this chapter contends that in accordance with both monastic and ecclesiastical tradition and canon law, Francis stepped down and appointed a vicar or steward to act in his stead when he could no longer adequately perform his duties as leader. While Francis's desire for a simpler life no doubt played a role in his so-called retirement, Francis left the leadership of his order in the hands of others in the years after 1221 at least partially because his health failed him and canon law stipulated that he should.

It is always difficult to find the person behind the saint in hagiography. In many ways, hagiographies are intentionally formulaic, for their work is to demonstrate the sanctity of an individual.[7] However, by comparing early hagiogra-

---

4   Henri-Jacques Stiker, *A History of Disability*, trans. William Sayers (Ann Arbor, MI: University of Michigan Press, 2002), p. 83.

5   Donna C. Trembinski, "Illness and Authority: The Case of Francis of Assisi," in *Disability and the Law*, ed. C.J. Rushton (Newcastle: Cambridge Scholars Press, 2013, pp. 112–133.).

6   This is the most common reading of Francis' decision to step down from the order. Paul Sabatier's still justifiably famous biography of the saint argued that Francis could no longer remain Minister-General of an order that had become so different from the collective he had envisioned. See Paul Sabatier, *Life of Saint Francis*, ch. 14. Writing approximately 115 years later, Augustine Thompson argues in his new biography of Francis that Francis resigned from his leadership of the order in 1220, ostensibly to lead a life of humility. In reality, Thompson suggests, Francis "remained the de-facto leader" of the order. Augustine Thompson, *Francis of Assisi: A New Biography* (Ithaca, London: Cornell University Press, 2012), p. 80.

7   On the formulaic nature of hagiography and the work these mimetic texts accomplish, see the still relevant work by Hippolyte Delehaye, *Legends of the Saints: An Introduction to Hagiography*, trans. V.M. Crawford. (London: Longmans, Green and Co, 1907), pp. 22–39 and René Aigrain, *L'hagiographie: ses sources, ses méthods, son histoire*, Subsidia Hagiographica 80 (Brussels: Société des Bollandistes, 2000 (1953), pp. 206–222. The short introduction to

phies of Francis, and corroborating the evidence in the hagiographies with evidence from other sources such as chronicles and letters where feasible, it is possible to catch glimpses of the person who became St Francis. Such an effort is aided by the numerous early *lives* of Francis that still survive today, but this plethora of evidence is also problematic as historians have not yet absolutely determined which lives are the oldest and most reliable of the available early narratives.

The so-called "Franciscan Question" has vexed scholars for more than a century. Since Paul Sabatier recovered *The Mirror of Perfection* at the end of the nineteenth century, a text which he erroneously dated to 1228 and believed to be more reliable than any of the then known sources of Francis's life, historians have been trying to understand the relationship between the various early hagiographies of Francis and to determine which ones provide the most accurate insight into the saint's life.[8] Historians of Francis remain divided as to which sources are earliest and/or most reliable. These two qualities are not necessarily found in the same source for sources composed at a later date after Francis's death were sometimes written by closer companions of the saint than earlier hagiographies.

While the "Franciscan Question" still has no definitive resolution, there is some scholarly consensus concerning the relative dating and authority of the various texts.[9] The earliest known *vita* of Saint Francis was written by Thomas of Celano in 1228. It is important to note that this life was not written by a close companion of Francis. The life was written explicitly to foster the fledgling cult of Francis.[10] Thomas wrote a second life, the *Vita secunda* nearly twenty years

---

Benedicta Ward, *Signs and Wonders: Saints, Miracles and Prayers from the 4th to the 14th Century* (Aldershot, UK: Variorum, 1992), pp. *xi–xiv* is also quite useful.

8   On Sabatier as the originator of the Franciscan question see Michael Cusato, "Towards a Resolution of the Franciscan Question: Introduction to the Roundtable," in *FS* 66 (2008): 479–481; Jacques Dalarun, *The Misadventure of Francis of Assisi: Towards a Historical Use of the Franciscan Legends*, trans. Edward Hagman (St Bonaventure, NY: Franciscan Institute Publications, 2002), pp. 30–41; Luigi Pellegrini, "A Century of Reading the Sources for the Life of St Francis of Assisi," *Greyfriars Review* 7:3 (1993): 323–346.

9   Of course, scholarly consensus has been turned over many times, most recently by Jacques Dalarun, *Vers une résolution de la question franciscaine: La légende ombrienne de Thomas de Celano* (Paris: Fayard, 2007), which argues that the previously unknown author of the *Umbrian Choir Legend* was likely Thomas of Celano.

10   VP, in FF, pp. 273–424. On dating, see St *Francis of Assisi: Early Documents*, ed. Regis Armstrong, J.A. Wayne Hellmann and William Short, 3 vols., (New York, London, Santa Mesa: New City Press, 1999–2001), v. 1, p. 171.

after he completed his first *vita*, in 1247.[11] In between these two *lives* several other individuals wrote accounts of Francis's life. Henry d'Avranches's *Legenda versificata* was written just after Thomas of Celano completed the *Vita prima*, perhaps as early as 1230[12] and Julian of Speyer's *life*, which seems to be based on the *Vita prima*, was written by 1235.[13] The manuscript tradition of sources, already complicated, becomes far more so after 1244 when the Minister-General of the Franciscan Order, Crescentius of Iesi, asked all members of the Order who remembered Francis to record their accounts of his life and miracles. The *Umbrian Choir legend*, most recently attributed to Thomas of Celano as well, was written between 1237 and 1244.[14] Other texts, more clearly written as a direct response to Crescentius's call were compiled as well. The *Legend of Three Companions* is thought to have been composed by three of Francis's earliest companions, Leo, Angelo and Rufino. The majority of this text was completed between 1241 and 1247[15] but it appears to be based, in part, on the slightly earlier *Umbrian Choir Legend*.[16] A second collection of personal reminiscences about the saint was likely collected between 1244 and 1260. It is quite clear that portions of this collection, now called the *Assisi Compilation*, include very personal and very intimate recollections of the saint, in spite of the late date of composition. Hence, the *Assisi Compilation* is often regarded as amongst the most reliable sources for Francis's life.[17] By 1260, Francis's cult was flourishing. Likely in response to the need for a clear message about Francis, the new Minister-General of the Order, Bonaventure of Bagnoregio, wrote two official lives of the saint.[18] After his *lives*, the *Legenda maior* and *Legenda minor*,

---

11   VS, in FF, pp. 441–639. For dating, see *Francis of Assisi: Early Documents*, v. 2, p. 233.

12   HdeA, in FF., pp. 1131–1242. For dating, *Francis of Assisi: Early Documents*, v. 1, p. 423.

13   JS, in FF, pp. 1025–1095. On dating, *Francis of Assisi: Early Documents*, v. 1, p. 363.

14   *Francis of Assisi: Early Documents*, v. 2, p. 63.

15   LTS, in FF, 1373–1445. The first sixteen chapters of this text have been definitively dated to between 1241 and 1247. The date for the remainder of the text is more uncertain, but it was likely composed before 1260. *Francis of Assisi: Early Documents*, v. 2, p. 63. See also Jacques Dalarun's brief literature review about this source in *Misadventures*, pp. 189–190.

16   Dalarun, *Résolution*, pp. 136–142.

17   AC, in FF, pp. 1471–1690. The history and textual tradition of the so-called *Assisi Compilation* is quite complicated. The oldest manuscript dates from 1311, but parts of the manuscript, especially paragraphs 50–100 and 107–120 can be dated to as early as the 1240s. Much of the rest can be dated to between 1247 and 1260. See Dalarun, *Misadventures*, pp. 204–206.

18   On the possibility that the order wanted to control the "official" version of Francis's life, see Aviad Kleinberg, *Flesh Made Word: Saints' Stories and the Western Imagination*

were completed circa 1263,[19] they were adopted as the Order's official lives of Francis and in 1266, the Order asked that all other *lives* of Francis be removed from Franciscan houses, and if possible from the houses of other orders as well.[20] While Thomas of Celano's *vitae* of Francis are early and Bonaventure's are those the Order chose to adopt, most historians recognize that amongst the most important witnesses to the historical Francis are the recollections found in the *Legend of the Three Companions* and the older portions of the *Assisi Compilation.*

Almost all early Franciscan sources about Francis suggest that the saint was always subject to periods of illness, even in his twenties and thirties. Indeed, his conversion to religious life occurred when Francis had contracted a fever. Thus, Francis's earliest hagiographer, Thomas of Celano, writes that God struck Francis down with a bodily affliction that caused him to be worn out by a long illness.[21] To some extent, this inclusion may be a hagiographic trope,[22] but there exists at least some evidence that Francis suffered a variety of illnesses early in his life. Most notably, the *Vita prima* records that Francis was ill at Sant' Urbano, probably around 1213 and performed a miracle of turning water into wine for himself.[23] Both the *Vita prima* and Julian of Speyer's *life* record that Francis fell sick and ate chicken, but he confessed this act and did penance for it once his strength had returned.[24]

After his trip to Egypt in 1219, Francis began to experience much more severe infirmities. Plagued by regular fevers and bouts of weakness, some scholars have suggested that he contracted malaria in the East. So common is this assumption that Michael Cusato, a leading scholar of Francis can write that "[Francis] had indeed returned from the east with malaria and other related

---

(Cambridge, MA: Belknap Press, 2008), pp. 218–219. See also *Francis of Assisi: Early Documents*, v. 2, p. 495.

19   *Francis of Assisi: Early Documents*, v. 2, p. 503.

20   *Ibid.*

21   VP, b.1, c. 2, Most early hagiographies of St Francis include this incident. See HdA, c. 1 and JS, c. 1. English translations of all early hagiographies can be found in Francis of Assisi: Early Documents, trans. Regis J. Armstrong, J.A. Wayne Hellmann, and William J. Short. 3 vols. (Hyde Park, NY: New City Press, 1999–2001). References to passages in various *vitae* of Francis given below refer to book and chapter numbers while specific page numbers are given for the critical editions of the Latin *lives* found in the FF.

22   Donald Weinstein and Rudolph Bell, *Saints and Society: The Two Words of Western Christendom, 1000–1700* (Chicago: University of Chicago Press, 1982), p. 156.

23   VP, b. 1, c. 21, FF, p. 337.

24   VP, b. 1, c. 19, FF, p. 326; JS, b. 6, FF, p. 1054.

illnesses that would progressively worsen and lead to his death."[25] By 1220, Francis had developed a serious eye condition, which caused him constant pain and impaired his sight. Francis's eye pain and blindness have been attributed to impairments as diverse as glaucoma, iritus and corneal ulcers.[26] Though he sought medical attention for his eye condition, it never ceased to be a cause of great pain and distress. Anecdotal evidence from hagiographies and chronicles also suggest that at times, Francis was too infirm to walk. Julian of Speyer thus remarks in passing that [Francis] "caused his half-dead body to be carried around on an ass through towns and villages."[27] That Francis was, at times, too ill to walk and as a result sometimes travelled by donkey is less dramatically attested in the *Assisi Compilation*[28] and Thomas of Celano's *Vita secunda.*[29] The repeated references to Francis being so infirm he required transport by donkey in different early and reliable sources suggest that this anecdote has a solid kernel of truth to it.

In the last two years of his life, Francis suffered even more from his infirmities. Hagiographies (beginning with the first, Thomas of Celano's *Vita prima*) record that Francis received the stigmata sometime in the last two years before his death.[30] The wounds, especially the wound in his side, apparently caused the saint a great deal of pain. In recent years, there has been some debate about how the narrative of Francis' reception of the *stigmata* developed.[31] However, as Jacques Dalarun has recently argued, the presence of the stigmata is a theological judgment, but what cannot be denied is that Francis had wounds and was severely disabled in the last years of his life.[32] Thus, while the papal bull promulgating Francis's sanctification on July 19, 1228 (three days after Francis's

---

25   Michael Cusato, "Francis and the Franciscan Movement," in *The Cambridge Companion to Francis of Assisi*, ed. Michael J.P. Robson (Cambridge, CUP, 2012), p. 28. For a detailed discussion of possible diagnoses of Francis's symptoms, see Joanne Schatzlein and Daniel P. Sulmasy, pp. 183–184.

26   Several possible diagnoses of Francis's eye disease can be found in Rosario Zeppa, "San Francesco's Blindness," *The Journal of Paleopathology* 3.3 (1991): 133–135.

27   JS, c. 12; FF, p. 1082.

28   AC, c. 72; FF, p. 1575 and AC, c. 91; FF, p. 1615.

29   VS, b. 2, c. 17; FF, p. 487 and VS b. 2, c. 103; FF, p. 589.

30   VP, b. 2, c. 3; FF, pp. 369–373; JS, c. 12; FF, pp. 1077–1081; HdA, c. 12; FF, pp. 1199–1201.

31   Chiara Frugoni, *Francesco e l'invenzione della stimmate: Una storia per imagine fina Bonaventura e Giotto* (Turin: Einaudi, 1993). This work has caused quite a stir in the relatively small world of Franciscan Studies.

32   Jacques Dalarun, *The Stigmata of Francis of Assisi: New Studies, New Perspectives* (St Bonaventure, NY: Franciscan Institute Publications, 2006), p. 13.

inaugural feast day) does not mention the stigmata at all,[33] it does speak of Francis's suffering at the end of his life, stating that the saint "offered as a holocaust to the Lord his own flesh... mortifying his flesh by hunger, thirst, cold, nakedness, fasting, and countless nights of prayer." According to the bull, Francis thus "crucified his flesh with its passions and desires" and became one with Christ.[34]

No one who has read any of the early hagiographies of Francis is likely to deny that he suffered. It is a cornerstone of Francis's life as an imitator of Christ. However, this suffering is usually understood to provide Francis with an indirect type of spiritual authority that allowed him to found and lead the Franciscans at a time when the papacy had stated that it would not entertain the establishment of any new orders.[35] Yet, as this essay will demonstrate, in terms of the formal authority Francis needed to assert as the founder and leader of a new order, Francis's disabilities, if not his suffering *per se*, were an impediment.

While suffering was integral to medieval Christian identity,[36] there is a long tradition within the Catholic Church of assuring that its prelates and clerics

---

33   No papal bull or letter mentions Francis's stigmata until 1237. Dalarun, *Stigmata*, p. 19.

34   Gregory IX, *Mira circa nos*, in *Francis of Assisi: Early Documents*, trans. Regis J. Armstrong, J.A. Wayne Hellmann, and William J. Short (Hyde Park, NY: New City Press, 1999–2001), v. 1 p. 568. "... *Domino in holocaustum obtulit, igne supposito charitatis, illam fame, siti, frigore, ac nuditate, uigiliis multis, & jejuniis macerando; qua cum uitiis, & concupiscentiis crucifixa, dicere poterat cum Apostolo: Uiuo ego, jam non ego, uiuit autem in me Christus: quoniam jam non sibi uixerat, sed Christo potius* ..." Gregory IX, *Mira circa nos*, in *Bullarium Franciscanum, Romanorum Pontificum, Constitutiones, Epistolas ac Diplomata continens Tertibus Ordinis S.P.N. Francisci spectantia*, ed. H Sbaralea (Rome: Typis Sacrae Congregationis de Propaganda Fide, 1759), v. 1, p. 25.

35   On Francis's informal spiritual authority, see Caroline Walker Bynum, *Holy Feast, Holy Fast: The Religious Significance of Food to Medieval Women* (Berkeley: University of California Press, 1987), p. 255. Caroline Walker Bynum, "... And Woman his Humanity: Female Imagery in the Religious Writing in the Religious Writing of the Mater Middle Ages," in her *Fragmentation and Redemption: Essays on Gender and the Human Body in Medieval Religion* (New York: Zone Books, 1992), pp. 151–79. Jacques Dalarun has further suggested that the authority Francis projected due to his practice of *imitatio Christi* eventually allowed for greater opportunities for women in religious life by creating "a bridge between masculine religion and a new religion, feminized as the languishing body of Christ is feminized." Jacques Dalarun, *Francis and the Feminine*, trans. Paula Pierce and Mary Sutphin (St Bonaventure, NY: Franciscan Institute Press, 2006), p. 279.

36   Judith Perkins, *The Suffering Self: Pain and Narrative Representation in the Early Christian Era* (London and New York: Routledge, 1995).

are capable of fulfilling their duties. Thus, as early as the sixth century Pope Gregory noted that while a bishop could never be replaced no matter how ill or infirm he might be, if he were not able to perform his duties adequately, a steward should be appointed to act in his name.[37] In the twelfth century, Gratian quoted this letter in the *Decretum*, where he stipulates that an ill bishop or prelate should not be removed from his position or his benefice. Instead, a helper or *coadiutor* should be found who could take on the day to day administration of the order and who would, in all likelihood, become the next bishop upon the death of his predecessor.[38] This precept, found in writings of Gregory the Great in the sixth century and in Gratian's *Decretals* in the twelfth, is still found in the most recent of canon law collections, the *Codex of Canon Law*, promulgated in 1983.[39] Indeed, it is common practice in the Roman Catholic Church today for coadjutor bishops to be appointed as needed and to succeed to the role of diocesan bishop once that position becomes vacant.

Influential though Gratian's *Decretum* was, it was never officially adopted as a *summa* of canon law by the Catholic Church in the Middle Ages. Instead, Pope Gregory IX, who was Ugolino of Segni (Francis's appointed protector of the Order and the man who presided over his canonization in 1228), promulgated a new set of laws written by Raymond of Peñafort around 1231. Gregory insisted that Raymond's summary be regarded as the definitive legal position of the Church, and as a result Raymond's summary of canon law overshadowed Gratian's in popularity in the Middle Ages. Yet Gratian and Raymond dealt with the issue of infirm clerics in quite similar ways. Like Gratian's work, Raymond's *Decretals* insist that ailing clerics and bishops should keep their living, even if a steward must take over their duties. It was the Church's duty

---

37   Letter 11.29. See the *Patrologia Latina*, ed. J.P. Migne (Paris: Garnier fratres, 1866–1882), 77: 1141–1142. An English translation can be found in Gregory the Great, *The Letters of Gregory the Great*, trans. John R.C. Martyn, 3 vols. (Toronto: Pontifical Institute of Mediaeval Studies, 2004), pp. 774–775.

38   "*Et quod nusquam canones precipiunt, ut pro egritudine episcopi episcopus succedat, et ideo iniustum est, ut, si molestia corporis irruit, honore suo priuetur ergrotus. Sed suggerendum est, ut si quid, in regime, egrotat, dispensator illi talis requiratur, qui possit eius curam omnem agere et locum illius in regimine ecclesiae (ipso non deposito) conseruare, ut neque Deus omnipotens offendatur, neque ciuitas neglecta esse inueniatur.*" Gratian, *Decretum*, ed. A.L. Richter (Graz: Verlagsanstalt, 1959), 2.7.1.1, column 566. This is the particular topic of 2.7.1.3, column 567, a chapter that begins with the rubric "*infirmitatis causa loco suo quis priuare non debet*".

39   Canon 403, *Codex of Canon Law*. An English translation of this canon law collection can be found at www.vatican.va/archive/ENG1104/_INDEX.HTM. Accessed March 4, 2013.

to care for the sick.[40] However, the criteria given for when and why a person should be removed from his ecclesiastical duties are more clearly stated in Raymond. Quoting another letter of Gregory the Great, the *Decretals* states that churches ought not to be afraid of finding stewards to replace officials, since "if others were to be discouraged by the example of an individual's illness, it would perhaps not be possible to find [those] who are able to fight for the church."[41] To my knowledge, Raymond's decretal collection represents the first time such a statement is included as a reason for appointing stewards for those ill individuals in positions of leadership within the Church.

In the context of religious particularly, neither Gratian's *Decretum* nor Raymond's *Decretals* promulgated by Gregory IX included a discussion of the replacement of sick abbots, nor does the *Rule of St Benedict* or the *Rule of St Augustine* speak of what is to be done should an abbot take ill. Further, monastic customaries do not generally discuss the actions that should be taken should an abbot fall so ill or disabled he is unable to continue in his leadership role. Yet, there is evidence that a long tradition of using stewards or *coadiutores* in monastic and ecclesiastical settings existed in the Middle Ages. Thus, for instance, abbots of Cluny, would, at times, choose coadjutors who would aid them in the administration of the monastery and would, upon their death, become abbot. The clearest example of this occurred when Aymard, abbot of Cluny in the mid tenth century, became blind and could no longer continue to perform his duties. Upon his request, a *coadiutor*, the future St Mayeul of Cluny was appointed. Mayeul became the abbot of Cluny in his own right after Aymard resigned his post.[42] Such a practice ensured an infirm abbot would not negatively impact the abbey and also alleviated the inevitable period of confusion that accompanies an abrupt change in leadership. James King's recent work on the memoranda rolls of Oliver Sutton, Bishop of Lincoln from 1280–1299 also suggests that in Lincoln at least, the office of *coadiutor* was used

---

40   *"fraternitas tua diuini contemplatione iudicii praebeat aegrotanti."* Raymond of Peñafort, *Decretalium gregorii*, in *Decretalium collectiones*, ed. A.L. Richter (Graz: U. Verlagsanstalt, 1959), 3.6.1, column 481.

41   *"...quia, si alii eius essent exemplo deterriti, forte non posset qui militaret ecclesiae inueniri".* *Ibid.* The decretal is nearly word for word repeated from the register of Gregory's letters. *"quia diuersis in Ecclesia militantibus, uaria, sicut nosti, saepe contingit infirmitas. Et si hoc fuerunt exemplo deterriti, nullus de caetero qui Ecclesiae militet poterit inueniri..."* See the *Patrologia Latina*, 77:544–545. No recent translation of this letter into English exists.

42   See the *Vita sancti Maoili*, v. 2, p. 1 in the *Patrologia Latina*, 137: 733. I am grateful to Dr. Isabelle Cochelin for providing me with the above information.

regularly in cases where the primary holder of a benefice was incapacitated physically or mentally and could not perform his duties.[43]

In the Franciscan Order itself, the earliest extant legislation regarding the replacement of infirm people in leadership positions dates from a series of constitutional regulations promulgated at the general chapter of 1260. While the constitutions do not touch on the role of a steward for the Minister-General, they do instruct that a vicar may be appointed for a provincial-general when he travels to a chapter-general meeting, when he otherwise travels out of his province or when he is infirm.[44] The vicar retains his authority even if the minister is dissolved of his leadership role, or if the minister dies, until he is replaced at the next provincial chapter.[45] *Custodes*, who oversaw all friaries in a given territory, could similarly appoint a vicar when they left their provinces. Though not explicitly stated, the proximity of the note on the provincial ministers and the *custodes* along with the opening *"Custodes similiter"* would seem to suggest that in the case of *custodes* as well, a vicar could be appointed should a *custos* become too ill to carry out his duties effectively.[46] Thus, from the time of Bonaventure's generalship at the absolute latest, rules were in place within the Franciscan Order that specifically dealt with the replacement of ill individuals in positions of leadership. It is possible that these rules date from before 1260, possibly as early as 1239, given that the many *constitutiones* apparently given in that year are not extant today. However, none of the handful of the constitutions that do survive refers to the possibility of a custodial vicar for any position or reason.[47]

---

43 King sees a parallel between guardians for individuals determined to be of unsound mind who are appointed by the king and coadjutors appointed for the same reason by prelates of the English Church. James R. King, "The Mysterious Case of the 'Mad' Rector of Bletchingdon: The Treatment of Mentally Ill Clergy in Late Thirteenth-Century England," in *Madness in Medieval Law and Custom*, ed. W. Turner (Leiden, Boston: Brill, 2010), pp. 57–80. I am grateful to Dr. Turner for drawing this article to my attention.

44 *"Minister autem prouincialis, quando uadit ad capitulum generale uel alias extra suam prouinciam, uel sic infirmatur quod non possit prouinciali capitulo interesse, instituat uicarium de consilio decretorum."* Constitutiones generalis narbonensis (1260), in *Constitutiones generalis ordinis fratrum minorum* in Analecta Franciscana XIII, n. s. 1, ed. C. Cenci and R.G. Maillaux (Grottoferrata: Editiones Collegii S. Bonaventurae, 2007), 11.7, p. 99.

45 *"Uicarius uero, sic institutus a ministro, si minister in generali capitulo absolutus fuerit uel ipsum interim mori contingerit, remaneat uicarious auctoritate generalis ministri usquequo prouinciale capitulum congregetur."* Ibid., 11.8, p. 99.

46 *"Custodes similiter, cum ad generale uadit capitulum, instituat uicarium in custodia, de aliquorum suae custodiae consilio discretorum."* Ibid., 11.9, p. 99.

47 On the relatively few constitutions found from the meeting of 1239, see "Statua generalia ordinis edita in capitulis generalibus celebratis Narbonae an 1260, Assisii an. 1279 atque Parisiis ad. 1292," ed. M. Bihl, in *Achivum franciscanum historicum*, 36 (1941): 13–94 and

In spite of the lack of written regulations providing for the use of stewards or vicars before 1260, there is evidence from an early chronicle of the Order that such was the practice of the Franciscans from almost its earliest days. In Thomas of Eccleston's chronicle, composed (or perhaps collated) before 1258,[48] he records that Agnellus of Pisa, the first provincial minister of England, became ill with dysentery at Oxford (likely in 1236). Physicians treated him there, and the dysentery was cured; however, he then developed pain in his intestines and side. Believing himself about to die he received his last rites. With that done, Agnellus completed two final administrative tasks. He sent a representative to the Minister-General to ask for the appointment of his replacement, and he appointed a vicar who would act in his stead. With that done, he turned to prayer and died in peace.[49] This story is interesting for several reasons. In the first place, it demonstrates that even before the *Constitutions of Narbonne* of 1260, it was practice within the Order to name a vicar if a prelate within the Order was too ill to perform his duties. This may point to an earlier dating for that rule than 1260. Possibly it was included in the now fragmented collection of *constitutiones* of 1239, though, if Thomas can be trusted, Agnellus's decision to name a vicar predates even those regulations by three or more years. Certainly though, Thomas's story demonstrates that the canon law concerning the need to replace infirm prelates with stewards was taken seriously within the Order.

The practice of appointing vicars for infirm abbots, the canon law collections of Gratian and Raymond of Peñafort, and the early use of stewards within the

---

284–358, 338–339; Rosalind Brooke, *Early Franciscan Government: Elias to Bonaventure* (Cambridge: CUP 1959), p. 210. For the most recent edition of the Constitutions of 1239, see *Fragmenta Priscarum Constitutionum Praenarbonensium (1239)*, in *Constitutiones generalis ordinis fratrum minorum*, ed. C. Cenci and R.G. Mailleux (Grottaferrata: Editiones Collegii S. Bonaventurae, 2007), pp. 5–12; *Constitutionum praenarbonensium particulae (1239–1254)*, in *Constitutiones generalis ordinis fratrum minorum*, ed. C. Cenci and R.G. Mailleux (Grottaferrata: Editiones Collegii S. Bonaventurae, 2007), pp. 17–36, and *Vetigia constitutionum praenarbonensium (1239–1257)*, in *Constitutiones generalis ordinis fratrum minorum*, ed. C. Cenci and R.G. Mailleux (Grottaferrata: Editiones Collegii S. Bonaventurae, 2007), pp. 43–63.

48 On the date of Eccleston's chronicle, *De adventu fratrum minorum in Angliam*, see Bert Roest, *Reading the Book of History: Intellectual Contexts and Educational Functions of Franciscan Hagiography, 1226–ca 1350* (Ph.D. Diss., Groningen University, 1996), p. 40, and Brooke, *Early Franciscan Government*, p. 27. On the way in which the narrative was collected see Annette Kehnel, "The Narrative Tradition of the Medieval Franciscan Friars on the British Isles. Introduction to the Sources," *FS* 63 (2005): 477.

49 Thomas of Eccleston, *De adventu fratrum minorum in Angliam*, in *Analecta Franciscana I*, ed. Patres Collegii S. Bonaventurae, 217–256 (Quarrachi: Typographia Collegii S. Bonaventurae, 1885), 146. See the English translation in Jordan of Giano *et al.*, *Thirteenth Century Chronicles*, trans. P. Hermann (Chicago: Franciscan Herald Press, 1961), pp. 163–164.

Franciscan Order itself provide a new framework for understanding Francis's often fraught position as spiritual leader and worldly chief administrator of his Order. While Francis was not a bishop or a prelate of the Church, nor the abbot of a monastery, he was in a similar position of leadership with respect to his fledgling Order. This was increasingly the case as the Order became more structured and regularized in the years after it was formally recognized in 1209/1210. To be sure, Francis chafed against his role as an authority figure, wanting in the first instance for his brothers to be guided by the gospel and the gospel alone,[50] but other members of the Order recognized the need to regularize expectations and community life. In the years after 1210 and especially after 1217, it was the second group who won out. Formal organization became inevitable.

Francis was aided in the organization of his disparate Order by Ugolino of Segni, the future Pope Gregory IX. Francis and Ugolino met in Florence around 1217. It is at this first meeting that Francis likely asked Ugolino to become an informal advocate and protector of the Order, especially in dealings the Order had with the papal curia. Thompson argues that Ugolino agreed to become a protector of the Order because both he and Francis recognized the saint's shortcomings as an administrator,[51] while Moorman suggests that Ugolino wanted to help the Order because he believed that the dramatic novelty and seeming popularity of the new Franciscan Order would breathe new vitality into the Church.[52] Both of these positions are based on speculation rather than hard evidence. What can be determined is that Ugolino did become actively involved in the affairs of the Order after 1217. By 1218, Ugolino was taking greater control over many aspects of Franciscan organization.

Perhaps as a direct result of Ugolino's intervention and advice, when Francis departed for Egypt in 1219, he left the day-to-day administration of the Order in the hands of two vicars, Gregory of Narni and Matthew of Naples,[53] instead of simply leaving as he had done on his aborted trip to France two years earlier. In the time he was gone, Ugolino also instituted many changes within the Order. While not every change was to Francis's liking, from Ugolino's perspective, these changes were fundamental for a large and growing order. Thus, in the year of Francis's travels, Ugolino asked Pope Honorius to write letters

---

50   As evidenced in the *Regula non bullata*, which outlines Francis's expectations of his brothers by collecting verses of the gospels to create his rule. See the *Regula non Bullata* in FF, pp. 185–213 and, in English, *Francis of Assisi: Early Documents*, v. 1, pp. 63–86.

51   Thompson, *Francis of Assisi*, p. 60.

52   John Moorman, *A History of the Franciscan Order: From its Origins to the Year 1517* (Chicago: Franciscan Herald Press, 1968), p. 67.

53   Jordan of Giano, p. 4; Jordan of Giano *et al.*, trans. P. Hermann, p. 26.

ensuring that the friars would be welcomed wherever they preached.[54] Against Francis's wishes of absolute poverty, not just for the friars but also for the Order itself, Ugolino also began the process of providing convents for the friars, a step that angered Francis upon his return.[55]

By 1217 at the latest, Francis had taken on a clear leadership role in his Order, and had created the beginnings of an administration. He had appointed vicars who would function as leaders in his absence and advocates who represented the interests of the Order at the curia. He had also begun the process of formalizing the irregular meetings he called into formal yearly chapters[56] and the missions abroad, too, had become more professionalized.[57] In spite of his unwillingness to lead, Francis became the head of an order whose adherents numbered in the thousands.[58] Francis's leadership role, not wanted but taken on under duress, meant that Francis's increasing infirmities in the years after his return to Italy in 1219 posed a serious problem for the Franciscan Order.

The earliest *lives* of Francis and chronicles that discuss the saint and his behavior in the years around 1220 describe how his health deteriorated in the years after his return from Egypt, though the chronology of his increasing incapacity is not always clear.[59] The two earliest *lives* of Francis, the *Vita prima* of

---

54　Honorius III, *Cum delicti, Bullarium Franciscanum*, v. 1, p. 2. An English translation can be found in *Francis of Assisi: Early Documents*, v. 1, p. 558. See also Moorman, *History of the Franciscan Order*, p. 50.

55　Brooke, *Early Franciscan Government*, p. 64; Moorman, *History of the Franciscan Order*, p. 51.

56　Thompson, *Francis of Assisi*, p. 50.

57　Michael Robson, *The Franciscans in the Middle Ages* (Woodbridge: Boydell, 2006), p. 25.

58　Jordan of Giano states that 3000 Franciscans attended the Pentecost chapter of 1221, a number Thompson argues in high but not impossible. Jordan of Giano, p. 6; Jordan of Giano, trans. P. Hermann, p. 30; Thompson, *Francis of Assisi*, p. 88.

59　As I have argued elsewhere, Bonaventure's *Legenda maior* and *Legenda minor*, written circa 1263 and promulgated in 1266, present a fictionalized, sanitized version of Francis's life in which his infirmities are minimized. See Trembinski, "Illness and Authority." Thus, my exploration of the impact of Francis's disabilities will concentrate on lives written before Bonaventure's official *vita* and on chronicles that were written before 1263. A number of scholars have noted Bonaventure's return to conventionality in the *Legenda maior* and *Legenda minor*. See, for instance, Thomas Renna's discussion of a more conventional description of Francis's gift of prophecy in Bonaventure compared with Thomas of Celano's work in Thomas Renna, "Saint Francis as Prophet in Celano and Bonaventure," *Michigan Academician* 33.4 (2000): 321–332. See also Michael Cusato, "Talking about Ourselves: The Shift in Franciscan Writing from Hagiography to History (1235–1247)," *FS* 58 (2000): 37–75, in which he concludes by suggesting that Bonaventure's two *legendae* represented a return to more traditional modes of hagiography than had

Thomas of Celano and Julian of Speyer's *life*, both suggest Francis's eyes troubled him considerably towards the end of his life. Both state that the ailment was exacerbated by the saint's harsh ascetic practices.[60] So severe was Francis's eye condition that he began to experience the loss of his vision.[61]

Francis's increasing incapacity is affirmed by the eyewitness account of Jordan of Giano who attended the Order's Pentecost chapter of 1221. While there, Jordan saw that Francis was so weak that anything he wished to have communicated to the chapter was vocalized by Brother Elias. During the chapter Francis was "seated at the feet of brother Elias" and when he wished to make his thoughts known he would "tug at [Elias"] tunic" to attract his attention. Elias would bend down and listen, then report Francis's position to the crowd.[62] Thompson has recently argued that Francis's actions at this chapter were not a result of infirmity, but due to the saint's excessive humility;[63] however, there seems no good reason to doubt Jordan's eyewitness account and understanding of the events.

Francis's health continued to deteriorate in the final two years before his death. Regardless of one's position on the reality of Francis's stigmatization, the *lives* of Francis leave little doubt that he was severely incapacitated in the last two years of his life. By the time of his death in 1226, Francis was almost totally blind, unable to walk due to his various infirmities and suffering greatly from illnesses and the effects of carrying wounds that would later be classified as stigmata. As early as 1221 and certainly by 1223, Francis was in no condition to lead his large and quickly growing Order. Although Francis's decision to remove himself from the day to day administration of the Franciscan Order is most often described as voluntary, canonical legislation on the need to replace ill prelates and leaders, combined with the tension evident in the early hagiography between his stated withdrawal from leadership and his continued desire to shape the future of the Order suggests the possibility that Francis was encouraged to withdraw from an active role of leadership, perhaps against his own wishes.

---

been seen in the *Vita secunda* of Thomas of Celano, which tended to advocate for a return to radical apostolic poverty that many of the Spirituals believed Francis had embraced.

60   VP, b. 2, c. 4; FF, p. 373; JS, C. 12; FF, p. 1084.

61   HdA, c. 12; FF, p. 1199.

62   "*Et quia beatus Francisco tunc debilis erat, quidquid ex parte sui capitulo dicendum erat, frater Helias loquebatur. Et beatus Franciscus sedens ad pedes Heliae fratris, traxit eum per tunicam. Qui inclinatus est ad ipsum, quid uellet auseultauit et se erigens ait "Fratres, ita dicit Frater."* Jordan of Giano, p. 6; Jordan of Giano *et al.*, trans. P. Hermann, p. 33.

63   Thompson, *Francis of Assisi*, p. 89.

In the hagiography and chronicles of the Franciscan Order extant today, Francis voluntarily and spontaneously says he will no longer lead the Order at a chapter meeting.[64] He handed the onerous burden of leadership to Peter Catani, one of the earliest converts to Francis's new Order.[65] The date of that meeting is debated, but certainly his withdrawal took place before 1221.[66] When Peter died, not long after his appointment, Francis did not take up the reins of leadership again. Instead, he appointed another to lead the Order, Elias of Cortona.[67] The position of both Peter and Elias has been much debated within Franciscan scholarship; however, the fact that both were appointed by Francis rather than elected by the Franciscan brothers as later Minister-Generals would be after Francis's death suggests they led the Order at Francis's discretion.[68] Certainly, the papacy regarded both men as vicars rather than as leaders of the Order in their own right.[69] This lends credence to the possibility that Francis appointed individuals to lead the Order in his stead because the curia expected him to do so in accordance with tradition and canon law, rather than purely as an act of humility.[70]

That Francis resigned at least in part because he was so infirm that leading the Order had become an impossible hardship is attested in many early sources. Thus, the *Assisi Compilation*, and Thomas of Celano's *Vita secunda* both imply that Francis resigned his position because he could no longer care

---

64   Until quite recently, this has been called Francis's "resignation" as Minister-General, but as Jean François Godet-Calogeras has argued, Francis could not resign from the position of Minister-General of the Order because he never possessed such a title. The use of the term Minister-General began after Francis's death. Jean François Godet-Calogeras, "Francis of Assisi's Resignation: An Historical and Philological Probe," in *Charisma und religiöse Gemeinschaften in Mittelalter*, ed. G. Andenna, M. Breitensten and G. Melville (Berlin, Hamburg and Münster: LIT Verlag, 2005), pp. 281–300.

65   vs, b. 2, c. 111 and FF, pp. 577–578. On Francis's withdrawal in favor of Peter Catani, see Brooke, *Early Franciscan Government*, p. 76; Moorman, *History of Franciscan Order*, p. 51 and Thompson, *Francis of Assisi*, p. 80.

66   Rosalind Brooke suggests an early date of 1219, while most other biographers follow Moorman in placing the chapter in 1220. Brooke, *Early Franciscan Government*, pp. 77–81; Moorman, *History of Franciscan Order*, pp. 50–51, Thompson, *Francis of Assisi*, p. 80.

67   See Jordan of Giano, p. 16, which refers to Elias as the vicar (*vicarius*) of Francis. See also Brooke, *Early Franciscan Government*, p. 83; Moorman, *History of Franciscan Order*, p. 51 and Thompson, *Francis of Assisi*, p. 88.

68   Brooke, *Early Franciscan Government*, p. 113.

69   Brooke, *Early Franciscan Government*, p. 111.

70   This is a standard position on Francis's resignation and it dates from as early as Thomas of Celano's *Vita secunda* to as late as recently as Augustine Thompson's new biography. See the vs, b. 2, c. 111; FF, pp. 577–577, and Thompson, *Francis of Assisi*, p. 80.

for his brethren, entrusting his Order to the "ministers."[71] These texts also suggest that Francis was conflicted about that decision. Thus, *The Legend of the Three Companions* reports that Francis saw a vision of a black hen with a dove's feet and so many chicks that the hen was unable to keep them all under her wings. Francis interpreted this vision to mean that he would have so many followers that he would not "be able to protect them with his own strength."[72] The legend itself links this vision with Francis's decision to ask Ugolino of Segni to become the protector of the Order.[73]

That Francis's illness motivated him to step down as the leader of his Order is made even more explicit in the *Assisi Compilation*. In an anecdote that records a memory of Brother Leo, one of Francis's oldest and most trusted companions, Francis states that he resigned because his increasingly severe infirmities meant that he could no longer care for the brothers as their minister. Francis further laments that even before his resignation, members of his Order had begun to fall away from the ideals he expressed for the Order, and that if that had not already begun to happen he would have felt well enough to lead the Order in spite of his weakened state.[74] Here, clearly, Francis demonstrates that his resignation occurred because of his infirmities.

These anecdotes are most often taken to reflect the growing tension in the Order between those who believed that Francis advocated absolute poverty for the Order as well as individual friars and those who suggested that the vow of poverty only extended to friars within the Order, not the institution itself.

---

71   The two sources repeat the precise phrasing. "*Et nunc, propter infirmitates quas tu nosti, dulcissime Domine, curam eius habere non valens, ipsam recommend ministris.*" AC, c. 39; FF, p. 1512; VS, b. 2, c. 104; FF, p. 571.

72   "*Uiderat namque gallinam quamdam paruam et nigram, habentem crura pennata cum pedibus in modum columbae domesticae, quae tot pullos habebat quod non poterat eos sub alis propriis congregare, sed ibant in circuitu gallinae exterius remanentes. Euigilans autem a somno coepit cogitare de huiusmodi uisione, statimque per Spiritum sanctum cognouit se per illam gallinam figuraliter designari et ait 'Ego sum illa gallina, statura pusillus nigerque natura, qui debeo esse simplex ut columba et affectibus pennatis uirtutum uolare ad caelum. Mihi autem Dominus per misericordiam suam dedit et dabit filios multos quos protegere mea uirtute non potero, unde oportet ut eos sanctae Ecclesiae recommendem quae sub umbra alarum suarum eos protegat et gubernet.'*" LTS, c. 16; FF, p. 1436.

73   *Ibid.*

74   "*Quoniam licet tempore quo renuntiaui et dimisi officium fratrum, coram fratribus me excusarem in capitulo generali, quod propter infirmitatem meam de ipsis curam et sollicitudinem habere non possem, tamen modo, si secundum uoluntatem meam fratres ambularent et ambulassent, propter ipsorum consolationem nollem, quod alium ministrum haberent preter me, usque in diem mortis mee.*" AC, c. 106; FF, p. 1649.

They reflect the growing rupture between the Spirituals and the Conventuals within the Order.[75] However, such anecdotes might also reflect a second tension, between Francis and his vicars over control of the Order. If, as circumstantial evidence suggests, canon law argued for the necessity of replacing sick prelates with stewards and tradition demonstrates that abbots also had vicars who acted in their stead when they were incapacitated, it seems likely that Francis's resignation was spurred at least partially by his Order's desire to see a healthy substitute chosen to act in his place. Moreover, the tension between Francis and his vicars about the direction of the Order, especially in terms of apostolic poverty, suggest Francis was not always satisfied with the decision to allow others to lead his Order. If the anecdotes above reflect some truth about the saint's position on his withdrawal, Francis was conflicted about his removal. Perhaps his resignation from administration was not born wholly of his desire for humility, or from his recognition that he neither enjoyed nor excelled at administration, but because his increasingly disabled body forced that withdrawal upon him. Thus, a brother close to Francis could relate in the *Assisi Compilation* that the saint had once woken up during a bout of illness saying "who are those people who took my religion and my brothers from my hands. If I go to the general chapter, I will show them what I will."[76]

Upon his withdrawal from leadership, Francis asked for a guardian who would guide him in all things and to whom Francis would owe absolute obedience. Yet, the role of the guardian as described in the hagiography suggests he was responsible for the saint's physical well-being as well as his spiritual needs. The use of the word guardian, in Latin *guardianus*, is unusual in and of itself. The term, which Francis himself uses to describe his overseer,[77] seems to have been used only sparingly before its adoption into the Franciscan administrative language. In the Order today, as it meant soon after Francis's death, a guardian refers to a friar who is responsible for the spiritual care of a community of friars.[78] Its primary meaning until that point though, seems to have

75   On the discord between the Spirituals and the Conventuals, see David Burr, *The Spiritual Franciscans* (Philadelphia: University of Pennsylvania Press, 2001).

76   "*Et paulo post cum infirmitate nimia grauaretur, in uehementia spiritus in lectulo se direxit. 'Qui sunt isti, ait, qui religionem meam et fratrum de meis manibus rapuerunt? Si ad generale capitulum uenero, eis ostendam qualem habeam uoluntatem.'*" AC, c. 44; FF, p. 1517.

77   Francis of Assisi, *The Testament*, in *Francis of Assisi: Early Documents*, pp. 24–28; FF, pp. 227–232.

78   On the meaning of *guardianus* within the order, see *Francis of Assisi: Early Documents*, v. 1, p. 98, note a and Robson, *Franciscans in the Middle Ages*, p. xi.

been a person who provides protection,[79] a surprising link for Francis and his hagiographers to make if Francis merely wished to obey his guardian as an act of humility.[80] Yet, there is no doubt that at times Francis's guardian acted as a sort of protector, defending Francis's physical well-being from the saint's desire to destroy his already infirm body with severe ascetic practices.

Francis's guardian acts in Francis's self-interest even when his decisions do not accord with the saint's. For example, the *Assisi Compilation* includes a story of how Francis's pants caught fire when he was sitting too close to the hearth. Francis did not permit the fire to be extinguished by anyone until his guardian was called in and began to put out the flames "against Francis's wishes."[81] Francis was asked many times by his guardian and even the Vicar-General of the Order not to give away his tunic for doing so would endanger the saint's already fragile health.[82] In questions of his health, particularly, Francis seems to have had some difficulty with his promise of absolute obedience to his guardian. When asked to seek treatment for his eyes, early *vitae* record that Francis had to be ordered to do so, not only by his guardian, but also by his vicar, Elias of Cortona, and even the protector of the Order, Ugolino of Segni.[83] Francis's stated desire to obey his guardian thus seems not to have extended to matters of his own health, when even the chief administrators of the Order were forced to intervene. It is clear then, that at times, Francis's wishes conflicted with those to whom he submitted to obey. Yet, Francis could and did make his differences of opinion known. Even in an instance regarding his own health, though, Francis did not have the ultimate authority. Far from having authority over the whole Order, Francis did not even have bodily autonomy in the period after his withdrawal from leadership.

Reading the early *vitae* of St Francis with a critical lens and within the framework of canon law on prelates with disabilities has allowed me to open a space to nuance our understanding of Francis's withdrawal from the leadership of

---

79   « 5 guardianus » (par P. Carpentier, 1766), dans du Cange, *et al.*, *Glossarium mediae et infimae latinitatis*, éd. augm., Niort: L. Favre, 1883-1887, t. 4, col. 125a. http://ducange.enc. sorbonne.fr/GUARDIANUS5. Accessed March 3, 2013.

80   That Francis wants a guardian to obey is clearly outlined in *The Testament*. Francis wrote "And I so wish to be a captive in [my guardian's] hands that I cannot go anywhere or do anything beyond obedience and his will, for he is my master". *"Et ita uolo esse captus in manibus suis, ut non possim ire uel facere ultra obedientiam et uoluntatem suam, quia dominus meus est."* Francis of Assisi, *The Testament*, p. 28, FF, p. 231.

81   *"guardianus . . . illo [Francesco] nolente cepit extinguere ipsum."* AC, c. 86; FF, pp. 1607–1608.

82   AC, c. 89; FF, pp. 1613; AC, c. 91; FF, p. 1615.

83   VP, b. 2, cc. 4–5; FF, pp. 375–378; JS, c. 12; FF, pp. 1083–1084.

his Order. The traditional narrative of Francis resigning as a result of humility and desire to obey rather than to command need not be wholly abandoned to recognize that the saint's growing disabilities may have presented a problem for Francis's ability to lead his brothers. Certainly, the possibility that Francis stepped down as a direct result of his infirmities is attested in reliable accounts of the saint's life. Nonetheless, the circumstantial evidence of the early use of vicars within the Order described by Thomas of Eccleston, along with the role Francis's guardian in managing the saint's illnesses and disabilities suggest that illness may have played more of a role in Francis's retirement that has traditionally been recognized. His removal from leadership as a result of illness rather than absolute desire to leave his Order in the hands of others makes sense of Francis's visions and stories, which seem to indicate that he is at best ambivalent and at times outright hostile towards the direction the vicars have taken the Order Francis still clearly regarded as his own. Re-centering Francis's disabilities, then, allows readers to see a more complex portrait of the saint, or perhaps rather the man, behind the hagiography.

CHAPTER 12

Medicine and Miracle: Law Enforcement in the *Lives* of Irish Saints

Máire Johnson

Students of medieval Ireland are blessed with a substantial corpus of surviving written material from numerous genres. By far the largest portion of that corpus is filled with works that commemorate Ireland's saints. Although this category can include anecdotes, martyrologies, genealogies, eulogies and the like, of particular importance here are the biographies of Irish holy men and women. Extant in more than one hundred Latin *vitae* concerning some sixty individuals, and in roughly fifty vernacular *bethada* (sg. *betha, bethu*) that honor perhaps fifteen persons many of who also possess *vitae*, these *Lives* span the Irish Middle Ages from the seventh through the fourteenth century.[1]

Of equal importance to the hagiographical evidence and in a body nearly as significant in size is Ireland's collection of medieval legal texts. Comprising both Latin canon law and vernacular treatises of more secular emphasis, these works largely date to the earlier centuries of the period; ecclesiastical codes began to appear in the sixth and seventh centuries, while the Old Irish laws were codified especially in the seventh through ninth centuries.[2] Thus, the legal voices of church and state evolved nearly concurrently and, unsurprisingly, often parallel each other in focus and intent.[3]

---

1 Richard Sharpe, *Medieval Irish Saints' Lives: An Introduction to* Vitae Sanctorum Hiberniae (Oxford: Clarendon Press, 1991), pp. 5–6 and 347–63, and Pádraig Ó Riain, *A Dictionary of Irish Saints* (Dublin: Four Courts Press, 2011), pp. 39–42, especially 39–40. Note that from this point on, all Latin texts will consistently be referred to as *vitae*, largely or entirely vernacular works as *bethada*, and both groups together as *Lives*.

2 Fergus Kelly, *A Guide to Early Irish Law* (Dublin: DIAS, 1988), particularly pp. 40–41. See also Thomas Charles-Edwards, "Early Irish Law," in *A New History of Ireland I: Prehistoric and Early Ireland*, ed. Dáibhí Ó Cróinín (Oxford: OUP, 2005), pp. 342–3, and 368.

3 See, for instance, *Bretha Nemed Toísech*, a vernacular law code concerning the definitions of early Ireland's social hierarchy; §§13–14 equate the status and authority of bishops with that of kings, indicating the interpenetration of church and secular society by the writing of the code; edited and translated by Liam Breatnach, "The first third of the *Bretha Nemed Toísech*," *Ériu* 40 (1989): 14–15. Breatnach dates *Bretha Nemed* to between 721 and 742 CE in "Canon Law and Secular Law in Early Ireland: The Significance of *Bretha Nemed*," *Peritia* 3 (1984): 439–59.

It is not only the ecclesiastical and secular laws that are so intertwined, however. As Kim McCone has noted, the mass of written evidence surviving from the Irish Middle Ages "was undoubtedly produced either in monasteries or by people who had received an essentially monastic education."[4] Though McCone's emphasis was on the parallels between biblical models and the literary motifs and legal structures of early Ireland, a similar observation may also be made of the relationship between the *Lives* of Irish saints and the law codes of the society that produced them.[5] Indeed, Ireland's hagiographers sought to paint their sanctified subjects as ideal Irish Christians, leaders of the faith whose authority and prestige stemmed in part from the proper application of Irish law. As the saints navigate the Ireland envisioned in their *Lives*, they not only abide by, but also define and prosecute, the tenets of both canon and vernacular legal tracts.[6]

One of the many expressions of the interactions between hagiographical saint and historical Irish law can be found at the nexus provided by medicine, though here the concern is not with the diagnosis and treatment of health problems by physicians of the human body. Instead, it is through the miracles associated with a holy Irishperson that medical issues enter the story. Of particular importance are instances in which these miracles result in the imposition or alleviation of illness or injury, the granting or removal of senses like sight, and the affliction or relief of physical impediment. At this intersection of medicine, law, and miracle, the saint stands forth as a hagiographical law enforcer whose wonder-workings identify him or her as a doctor both of the individual soul and of the entire Irish body Christian. An analysis of this crossroads as it is embodied in the saint, then, illuminates aspects of all three elements of medieval Irish sanctity and society.

In this latter article, Breatnach also convincingly argues that *Bretha Nemed* is a translation of the largest medieval compilation of canon law, the *Collectio Canonum Hibernensis* of the early 700s. The *Collectio* was edited by Hermann Wasserschleben, *Die Irische Kanonensammlung* (Aalen: Scientia Verlag, 1966); dating is on p. *xiv*.

4   Kim McCone, *Pagan Past and Christian Present in Early Irish Literature* (Maynooth: An Sagart, 1991), p. 1.

5   McCone, *Pagan Past*, pp. 84–106.

6   For more information on the place of medieval law in Ireland's hagiography and its resulting influence on the image of Irish holiness, see: "'Vengeance is Mine': Saintly Retribution in Medieval Ireland," in *Vengeance in the Middle Ages: Emotion, Religion, and Feud*, ed. Susanna Throop and Paul Hyams (Burlington and Surrey: Ashgate, 2010), pp. 5–50; further work is also to be found in "Holy Body, Wholly Other: Sanctity and Society in the *Lives* of Irish Saints," (Ph.D. Diss., University of Toronto, 2010), currently under revision for publication.

Honor and Status in Irish Vernacular Law[7]

The nexus of law, medicine, and miracle lies at the heart of and serves to underline issues of status in the *Lives* of Ireland's saints. The Irish society visible in the vernacular law tracts of the seventh and eighth centuries is heavily stratified. These legal treatises not only define the grades of person, they also align the ranks of church and secular society. At the pinnacle of the hierarchy a bishop is equated with a king, and so on down the ranks.[8] Wreathing and defining this concept of status is the critical element of honor, or *enech*. Any insult or injury entitled the victim to compensation for having been dishonored. This compensation, or honor-price—termed variously as *lóg n-enech*, *díre*, or *eneclann*—was both based upon and to a degree determined the status of the individual to whom it applied: the laws accord higher value to those of superior social standing.[9] Honor-price and its exaction are prominent components of the juridical saint's portrait, as will be seen, but there are also more subtle expressions of status in the *Lives*.

The Place of Women

One of the signal elements of status about which the *Lives* offer a merging of medicine, law, and miracle involves the expectations placed on women. In the

---

7   Although there is a considerable amount of canon law to be found in the *Lives*, for the sake of space my emphasis here is upon the more secular tracts, with ecclesiastical works as *comparanda* where needed.

8   *Bretha Déin Chécht* §§1–2, ed. and trans. D.A. Binchy, *Ériu* 20 (1966): 22–3. For dating, see pp. 3–5. *Bretha Crólige* 1, 2, 4–5, ed. and trans. D.A. Binchy, *Ériu* 12 (1938): 6–9; for date see p. 1. *Críth Gablach*, ed. D.A. Binchy (Dublin: DIAS, 1970); see pp. *xiii–xv* for date. Though the entire tract addresses the definition of social grade (*grád*), see also Binchy's explanation of *grád*, pp. 98–9. *Críth Gablach* has been edited and translated by Eóin MacNeill (with some issues, noted by Binchy in his introduction to his own edition) in "Ancient Irish Law: The Law of Status or Franchise," *Proceedings of the Royal Irish Academy* 36C (1923): 281–306. Please note that while translations from Latin are wholly my own, translations from Old and Middle Irish lean heavily, though not exclusively, on the work of prior scholars.

9   *Críth Gablach*, pp. 84–5 (*enech*). For application of *enech*, *eneclann*, or *lóg n-enech* see for example §§6, 10–11, 18, 21, and 31–3 on pp. 1–2, 4–5, 9–10, 12, 18–19; for *díre* and its derivatives some instances are found in §§12, 13, 16, 18, 24 and 40 on pp. 5–7, 8–9, 13–14, and 21. In MacNeill, "Ancient Irish Law," see e.g. §§65, 66, 69, 72, 83, 84 on pp. 282–3, 284, 285, and 288–9.

Irish system of honor, status, and compensation women lacked independent standing. While a man's own social grade determined his honor-price, a woman was not legally her own person. Her status was derived from that of her male guardian, who was her father, her brother, the head of her kindred or, if she was married, her husband.[10] Generally, a girl was expected to either wed a husband or become a nun around the age of fourteen; unions were arranged by and at the will of the families of the intended and involved payment of the *coibche*, or bride-price, by the groom to his future father-in-law. If the girl became a nun, her family would not gain the *coibche*.[11]

In the *Lives*, female saints generally operate within the lines of these legal strictures, behaving according to the normal expectations of their gender. Sometimes, however, it is necessary for the hagiographical holy woman to force the issue of her sanctity with a reluctant family member. Saint Brigid of Kildare presents the clearest example of such a case, and her emphatic response weaves law with miracle and medicine. In her eighth-century *Vita I S Brigidae*, this premiere female saint of Ireland beseeches God for some sort of disfigurement to make her ineligible for marriage, as her resistant father has been sending a steady flow of suitors her way rather than simply permitting her to enter the religious life. In response to Brigid's prayer, God causes one of her eyes to burst (*crepuit et liquefactus est*). Her doubtless startled father is then compelled to recognize her true vocation and allows her to become a nun; Brigid's eye is subsequently healed at her consecration.[12]

In this Latin tale, blinding is afflicted upon the saint herself to protect her from an unwanted marital union. More than that, however, the dismaying spectacle of her liquefied eyeball also demonstrates in no uncertain terms that Brigid's earthly father was not really her true guardian. That honor belonged to none other than God himself. The spontaneous restoration of Brigid's eye and sight, just as she is declared a virgin of Christ, then erases any lingering doubts as to her sanctified identity.

---

10   Thomas Charles-Edwards, *Early Christian Ireland* (Cambridge: CUP, 2000), p. 129; also Kelly, *Early Irish Law*, pp. 70–72.

11   Kelly, *Early Irish Law*, pp. 70–72, 81–2; also Donnchadh Ó Corráin, "Women and the Law in Early Ireland," in *Chattel, Servant or Citizen: Women's Status in Church, State and Society*, ed. Mary O'Dowd and Sabine Wichert (Belfast: The Institute of Irish Studies, 1995), pp. 46–50.

12   *Vita I S Brigidae* 3.16, ed. and trans. Karina Hochegger, "Untersuchungen zu den Ältesten Vitae Sanctae Brigidae" (M.Phil. Diss., Universität Wien, 2009), p. 110. For a thorough discussion of the date, see pp. 89–98. Hochegger's dissertation is available online at othes. univie.ac.at/4797/1/2009-05-07_0000901.pdf. Accessed March 3, 2013.

Interestingly, though the *Vita I* does not explain the reason Brigid's father was so unwilling to permit her to enter the religious life, the later vernacular *bethada* are quite clear. In both the mid-ninth-century *Bethu Brigte* and the later medieval *Betha Bhrigdi* Brigid's human guardians (her brothers in the former and her father in the latter) express aggravation that Brigid's conse-cration would cause them to lose her *coibche*. In these *bethada*, however, it is not God who afflicts Brigid with partial blindness; it is Brigid herself. The saint plucks out her own eye and, at least in the ninth-century variant, offers it to her obstreperous brother. Brigid then also heals herself as soon as she receives the permission she seeks.[13] In these vernacular texts, the miraculous intersection of medicine and law is found in the agency of the female saint. Brigid's cause and cure of her own partial sightlessness highlights at one and the same time the hubris of her family for seeking payment for her hand, their metaphoric and spiritual blindness to her identity as sanctified, and the purity of that sanctity itself.

Sovereignty, Political Power, and the Perpetuation of Dynasty

Sovereignty is an issue on which the saints' acts frequently offer a miraculous and medical commentary. As with legal independence, political power was also generally the province of males. Although a candidate for kingship did need a strong lineage, blood alone was not a sufficient claim; not only did a leader have to prove superiority over all other males of his kindred (many of who were also lineally eligible), but he also had to show that he possessed *fír flathemon*, or "prince's truth."[14] *Fír flathemon* was demonstrated both by the individual's actions and by the responses of the natural world. A true ruler not only defended the kingdom's borders, provided for his people, and permitted ecclesiastical activity in his realm, but he also reigned over a bountiful land. Lost conflicts, actions taken against the church, or unproductive lands and ani-

---

13   *Bethu Brigte* 15, ed. and trans. Donncha Ó hAodha (Dublin: DIAS, 1978), pp. 5, 23, available online at the CELT. See also *Betha Bhrigdi* ll 1332–40, ed. and trans. Whitley Stokes, *Lives of the Saints from the Book of Lismore* (Oxford: The Clarendon Press, 1890), pp. 40, 188. A similar anecdote modeled on the Brigidine version is also found in the highly fragmentary *betha* of Saint Cranat, which is very late; see *Betha Cranatan* 4, ed. and trans. Charles Plummer, *Miscellanea Hagiographica Hibernica* (Brussels: Society of Bollandists, 1925), pp. 161–2, 165–6. The *Miscellanea* and the *Book of Lismore* texts are also available at CELT.

14   Kelly, *Early Irish Law*, pp. 18–21; Charles-Edwards, *Early Christian Ireland*, pp. 91–106; McCone, *Pagan Past*, p. 124.

mals disqualified a king from rule, at least in the legal codes, as these failures were seen as signs he lacked *fír flathemon*.[15]

A king could also lose his sovereignty in other ways. According to *Críth Gablach*, for instance, a ruler's honor, his ability to rule, and his noble status were all forfeit for such offenses as perjury, deceit, failing to honor his promises, or pronouncing a bad legal judgment. A king in such a position could find his grade reduced to that of a commoner—or below.[16] Additionally, in what seems an echo of the Old Testament statutes that priests should be physically perfect in order to sacrifice to God, deformities, imperfections, and ailments were also considered marks of dishonor and of missing *fír flathemon*.[17] It is also likely, of course, that these proscriptions against physiognomic or bodily blemish had practical considerations, as a king with a paralyzed arm or damaged hearing, for instance, would find ruling effectively much more difficult.[18]

Sometimes the nexus of law, medicine, and miracle occurs at the point of curing physiognomic and physical shortcomings in order to produce a perfected candidate for rule. Saint Patrick, for instance, facilitates the correction of the twisted, ugly features and stunted stature of one Eógan mac Néill. Eógan was said to be the scion of the legendary king of Tara, Niall Noígiallach, and was credited as the progenitor of the powerful Cenél nEógain dynasty; this

---

15   *Críth Gablach* 21, pp. 12–13; and "Ancient Irish Law," 100, p. 295. Also, consult McCone, *Pagan Past*, pp. 124, 141, 143–4, and Kelly, *Early Irish Law*, pp. 19–20. Kelly adds that "the annals provide no record of a king being deposed or suffering loss of rank as a result of defeat in battle." Instead, cowardice and flight from combat were cause for the demotion of honor-price and status.

16   §§21, 40–41, pp. 12–13, 21–2; also "Ancient Irish Law" 100, pp. 119–30, 295, 302–4. Note also the observations of McCone, *Pagan Past*, p. 124 and Kelly, *Early Irish Law*, p. 19.

17   Lev. 21:18–21. The interpenetration of Old Testament tenets and various literary and legal components of early Ireland has been explored by numerous scholars. See for example Charles-Edwards "Early Irish Law," pp. 358–60 and McCone, *Pagan Past*, pp. 24, 30–34, 66–72, 84–106. The most thorough study of the Mosaic underpinnings of Ireland's vernacular law, however, must be that of Donnchadh Ó Corráin, Liam Breatnach, and Aidan Breen, "The Laws of the Irish," *Peritia* 3 (1984): 382–438.

18   *Críth Gablach* 38–9, pp. 20–21 states that *fír flathemon* requires a proper king, in addition to being honest with his subjects, to be physically sound. See also "Ancient Irish Law" 124, p. 303. In the legal text *Bechbretha*, King Congall Cáech, or Congall "The Blind", is said to have lost the kingship of Tara as a result of being blinded in one eye by beestings; see §§31–2, ed. and trans. Thomas Charles-Edwards and Fergus Kelly (Dublin: DIAS, 1983), pp. 68–9. Kelly, *Early Irish Law*, p. 19 observes, though, that Congall held Tara and Ulster simultaneously; while he did apparently lose Tara when stung, Kelly reports that Congall continued to rule Ulster until he died in 637 CE. It would seem that the tenets of law and realities of life did not always agree. For another instance, see note 15 above.

dynasty provided kings of Ulster and Tara from the seventh through the eleventh centuries.[19] In the Patrician tale, Eógan's appearance is vastly improved after a single night spent sleeping in the same bed with a member of Patrick's retinue, the two lying under the blankets and with their arms around each other. Thereafter, the newly-attractive royal has only to reveal his desired height to the saint and his growth to that elevation is instantaneous (*protinus*).[20]

Another sovereign, King Domnall mac Aedo mac Ainmire of Tara, who ruled in the early seventh century, seeks aid from Saint Colmán mac Lúacháin for a rather more mundane medical problem. Like Androcles's lion, King Domnall steps on a thorn that festers in his foot, sickening him and threatening both his foot and his life. Saint Colmán prays over Domnall's foot, and then commands the royal patient to put his foot on a stone. When Domnall does so, the thorn enters the stone and his foot is instantly healed.[21] Colmán's hagiographical healing thus preserves Domnall's foot, his life, and his sovereignty all while demonstrating beyond doubt the potency of the sanctity with which Colmán is invested.

In both instances, the crossroads of medicine, law, and miracle is joined in the person of the king who receives the benefit of the saint's curative act. The legal importance of a man's physical health in the maintenance of his royal standing is rather obvious; not only would a lame, sick king have difficulty fulfilling the activities demanded of a ruler, but the infection would also weaken the king metaphorically, the festering thorn deemed a mark of lost *fír flathemon*. Similarly, physiognomic perfection and physical stature—while not as linked to survival or ability to rule in a literal sense—are also intimate com-

---

19   Francis J. Byrne, *Irish Kings and High-kings* (Dublin: Four Courts Press, 2001), p. 73. See also the entry for annal 465.2 reporting the obituary of Eógan mac Néill in AU.

20   *Vita IV S Patriciii* 71, ed. Ludwig Bieler, *Four Latin Lives of St Patrick: Colgan's* Vita Secunda, Quarta, Tertia, *and* Quinta (Dublin: DIAS, 1971), p. 104; the text is translated by F.J. Byrne and Pádraig Francis, "Two Lives of Saint Patrick: *Vita Secunda* and *Vita Quarta*," *JRSAI* 124 (1994): 56. The episode is carried forward into the later vernacular *Bethu Phátraic*; see the edition of Kathleen Mulchrone, *Bethu Phátraic: The Tripartite Life of Patrick, Text and Sources* (Dublin: Hodges Figgis & Co., 1939) ll 1755–72, pp. 92–9. For an earlier edition with translation turn to *The Tripartite Life of Patrick, with Other Documents Relating to that Saint Part I*, ed. and trans. Whitley Stokes (Stuttgart: Kraus Reprints, 1965), 150–153.

21   *Betha Colmáin maic Lúacháin* 44, ed. and trans. Kuno Meyer, *Betha Colmáin maic Lúacháin: The Life of Colmán Son of Lúachán* (Dublin: Hodges & Figgis, 1911), pp. 43–4. Domnall mac Aedo mac Ainmire is listed in the CS as ruling from 628–642. CS is edited and translated by Gearóid Mac Niocaill and William M. Hennessy and available in a unique CELT edition.

panions with Irish sovereignty. Patrick essentially unkinks both Eógan Mac Néill's back and his candidacy for the throne at the same time.

Sometimes, though, the saint's "patient" is not the king, but is instead the king's son, and thus the hagiographical healings are linked with preserving dynastic inheritance according to the tenets of Irish law. Saint Cronán of Roscrea blesses the mute and deaf son of King Fingén of Munster, for instance, and restores the lad's speech and hearing.[22] Another ruler's boy is so tortured by insanity that he must be kept chained; in an obvious echo of the spiritual revivification inherent in baptism, Saint Moling has the youth put into the saint's own bath, where he dies. Moling then has the cold body moved to the saint's own bed. He makes the sign of the cross over the corpse, and immediately (*statim*) the princeling awakens in pristine health.[23]

Even though these noble youths are not yet wearing crowns, the preservation of *fír flathemon* is still significant. Both as the likeliest candidates to inherit their fathers' rules and as signifiers of their fathers' fitness as kings, these royal sons must also demonstrate flawless physical and mental health. A king must have sons who could take his place, and if he does not it stains the image of his *fír flathemon*. Similarly, the lads themselves must also demonstrate their own *fír flathemon* if they hope to surpass all other potential claimants to their fathers' thrones. The marriage between laws concerning sovereignty and status, and the medical issue of sensory deprivation—whether physical or psychological—thus produces hagiographical healing as its miraculous child, a healing literally embodied in these royal sons.

The Saint as Law Enforcer

Not only do the marvelous deeds of the holy define and uphold the social standing and expectations of others, like kings, but they also serve to highlight the saint's own status, both with respect to his or her position in society and as an indicator of his or her identity as sanctified. This status, moreover, allows the saint to engage fully with the civil and criminal laws of early Ireland. By miraculously imposing upon or lifting medical penalties from wrongdoers,

22   *Vita S Cronani Abbatis de Ros Cre* 22, ed. W.W. Heist, *Vitae Sanctorum Hiberniae ex Codice olim Salmanticensi nunc Bruxellensi* (Brussels: Society of Bollandists, 1965), p. 279, and *Vita S Cronani Abbatis de Ros Cre* 25, ed. Plummer, *Vitae Sanctorum* v. 2, pp. 29–30.

23   *Vita S Dairchelli seu Moling Episcopi in Tech Moling* 8, ed. Heist, p. 355 and *Vita S Moling Episcopi de Tech Moling* 26, ed. Plummer, *Vitae Sanctorum* v. 2, p. 202.

who now become defendants, the saint emerges as plaintiff, prosecutor, judge, and enforcer of justice in the legal society of the *Lives*.

Territorial Disputes

Most cases in which the juridical saint is depicted involve issues of land tenure. Part and parcel of both secular and ecclesiastical status in early Ireland was the possession of landed property on which to live and graze cattle. Legal texts address many concerns surrounding property, including outlining the procedures by which a claim on a piece of land could be prosecuted. A claimant first had to undertake a formal, ritualized entry known as *tellach*. This process involved a series of steps each undertaken in the presence of witnesses, beginning with the grazing of horses on the disputed land. If the occupant promptly drove these horses off the pasturage, the claim was denied.[24]

Such land claims appear often in the *Lives*, universally depicted as instances in which someone attempts to displace a saint by initiating *tellach*. Saints subjected to such incursions include Patrick, Féchín of Fore, and Finnchúa Brí Gobunn, but the targets of hagiographical denial of *tellach* are always the hapless horses. In Patrick's and Féchín's *vitae* the horses die immediately upon grazing; in Finnchúa's *betha* they are turned into stones.[25] Though in every tale of this sort the demise of the horses certainly stands as a potent enactment of the saint's rejection of *tellach*, these episodes do not involve humans as "patients" who endure saintly "doctoring."

To find the joining of medicine and miracle with property law, it is necessary to turn to cases in which those slated for expulsion are not horses, but saints. Landowners could and did find themselves at odds with ecclesiastical personnel intent on founding a church or religious community in their territory. Physical removal of these settlers, even if they were monks, nuns, abbots, bish-

---

24   Thomas Charles-Edwards, "Boundaries in Irish law," in *Medieval Settlement: Continuity and Change*, ed. P.H. Sawyer (London: Edward Arnold Publishers, Ltd., 1976), pp. 83–7; also Fergus Kelly, *Early Irish Law*, pp. 109–10 ("usucaption") and 186–7 ("legal claim process"), as well as Kelly's *Early Irish Farming* (Dublin: DIAS, 1997), pp. 432–3.

25   Muirchú, *Vita S Patricii*, v. 1, p. 24, ed. and trans. Ludwig Bieler, *The Patrician Texts in the Book of Armagh* (Dublin: DIAS, 1979), pp. 108–111. The story is retained in the *Bethu Phátraic* ll 2706–20, ed. Mulchrone, 136–7 and ed. and trans. Stokes, pp. 228–31. Further see *Vita S Fechini Abbatis de Favoria* 6, ed. Plummer, *Vitae Sanctorum* v. 2, p. 177 and *Betha Finnchua Brí Gobunn* ll 2846–77, ed. and trans. Stokes, *Book of Lismore*, pp. 85–6 and 232–3.

ops, or saints, could occur whether the ground had yet to be broken or the buildings had been standing for years.

The legal term for removing a person by force was *gabáil lámae duine*, literally "seizing a person's hand," which carried into Latin as *trahere* or *tenere manum*.[26] The implication of physical violence or its potential is clear; *gabál lámae duine* meant that the unwanted persons were hauled bodily off the premises. Yet where the landowner had promised a plot to the church or its saintly agent and later changed his mind, the act of ejecting the ecclesiastic had its own consequences. Aside from charges of physical assault, which at a minimum entailed payment of the saint's full honor-price (and on which more will be said below), both canon and vernacular law declared that what was donated to the church was deemed to be God's and could not be taken back by its mortal donor.[27]

We certainly find fertile ground here. A man named Báeth ("fool") tells Saint Finnian of Clonard that the holy man cannot set up a monastic community in Eiscir Branainn and is immediately struck blind.[28] A man who lays hands on Saint Carthach in an attempt to expel him suffers the bursting of an eye and a curse of insanity.[29] The sight taken from these hagiographical man handlers serves to exact the saint's honor-price and to make manifest the assailant's inability or unwillingness to perceive the truth of both the saint's message and his sanctified identity. In favor of this interpretation is the assurance in the *Life* of Finnian of Clonard that once Báeth relents and does penance his vision—like the cleanliness of his soul—is fully restored.[30]

---

26 *Dictionary of the Irish Language Based Mainly on Old and Middle Irish Materials: Compact Edition* [*DIL*], "*gabál*" subsection (a).

27 *Canones Hibernenses* III.2, ed. and trans. Ludwig Bieler, *The Irish Penitentials* (Dublin: DIAS, 1975), pp. 166–7. This small collection of canons dates to the seventh century; see pp. 8–9. For a parallel example in vernacular law refer to *Bretha Nemed Toísech* 3, pp. 8–11.

28 *Vita S Finniani Abbatis de Cluain Iraird* 16, ed. Heist, 100 and *Betha Fhindein Clúana hEraird* ll 2624–27, ed. and trans. Stokes, *Book of Lismore*, 78, 225–6.

29 *Vita S Carthagi sive Mochutu Episcopi de Less Mor* 58, ed. Plummer, *Vitae Sanctorum* v. 1, p. 193. The example *par excellence* of a saint afflicting a defendant with insanity for (among other things) trying to expel him would have to be the tale of Saint Rónán Finn's malediction upon King Suibne. Suibne is so bereft of his senses because of the curse that he lives like a wild man, vacillating between madness and prophetic lucidity. *Buile Shuibne* (*The Frenzy of Suibne*), ed. and trans. Beatrix Färber and J.G. O'Keeffe (Cork: University College, 2001), CELT. As that tale falls outside the *Lives*, however, it is not considered further here.

30 *Vita S Finniani* 16, ed. Heist, 100 and *Betha Fhindein Clúana hEraird* ll 2624–27, ed. and trans. Stokes, *Book of Lismore*, pp. 78, 225–6.

Another group of would-be ejectors are halted in their movements before actual contact with the saint's person can occur. The noble who determines that his lands would be improved considerably by the expulsion of Saint Mochoemóg finds his feet stuck to the ground in a sort of paraplegia. The noble gains relief only when he commits himself to the saint's service. To wrap up the repentance, he then also offers the saint his monastic site in perpetuity.[31] A king's-man sent to eject Saint MacCarthinn also suffers paralysis; when the man attempts to extinguish MacCarthinn's sacred reviving fire as the first step toward eviction, his hands suddenly become rigid. As in Mochoemóg's *vita*, the king's-man does not gain release and restoration until he seeks humble pardon from MacCarthinn.[32] Similarly, the cruel Nechtan mac Oengussa and the retinue dispatched with him to cast Saint Finnian from his kindred's territories endure the paraplegia that adheres them to the earth and drops Nechtan dead. Submission to the saint restores life to limb, body, and soul.[33]

In each case, the saint's miracles impose a physical penalty upon those who would violate his land, his church, or his person. These *miracula* simultaneously exact a medical honor-price and demonstrate visibly the nature of the defendants' interior disconnect when confronted with the saint's potent holiness. The affliction of sensory loss isolates further those already internally separated from the community of believers, a separation they themselves revealed through their attempts to eject a saint violently from lands already legally and spiritually devoted to God.[34] Where penance and submission occur, the defendants' restoration to the body Christian and to their individual bodies occurs in parallel, signalling recognition of their insight and of their altered outlook. The tapestry here woven by medicine, miracle, and law delineates the boundaries both of exterior and interior worlds, and of geographical and

---

31   *Vita S Mochoemog Abbatis de Liath Mochoemog* 16, ed. Plummer, *Vitae Sanctorum* 2, pp. 171–2.

32   *Vita S MacCarthinni Episcopi Clocharensis* 3, ed. Heist, 345.

33   *Vita S Finniani* 31, ed. Heist, 105 and *Betha Fhindein Clúana hEraird* ll 2714–18, ed. and trans. Stokes, pp. 81, 228. It is remarkable how frequently this type of dispute appears in the *Life* of Finnian of Clonard.

34   In no hagiographical instance of which I am aware do female saints engage in this sort of property dispute. This may be a reflection of the legal limitations placed on a woman's ability to inherit property. According to vernacular law, a female could only inherit land if there were no eligible male claimants in her kindred, and then she only held it rather than owning it outright. Upon the heiress's decease, the territory reverted to her patrilineal family, excluding her husband and children. See Ó Corráin, "Women and the Law," 523 and Kelly, *Early Irish Law*, p. 76.

spiritual space, leaving the observer in no doubt about the truth of the saint's identity as God's favored.

In a couple of property disputes the *Lives* portray an additional legal component. Where an individual guilty of wronging another did not make some attempt at proper restitution, the victim—now a plaintiff—could seek to compel that restitution through a complicated formulaic procedure. The final stage of this process could entail the seizure, or distraint (*athgabál*), of the defendant's property. A plaintiff of superior social standing to that of the defendant could undertake distraint by simply appropriating a set amount of the defendant's moveable goods—usually livestock, but occasionally land—under the oversight of a legal professional.[35] If the defendant was of noble status, however, a different procedure was demanded, whether the plaintiff was of equal or lower grade.[36]

Indeed, where the defendant was either a king, a noble, a cleric, or a poet, the plaintiff was required to tender notice of his or her case. If no response was obtained, the plaintiff could then attempt to compel restitution by engaging in *troscud*, or legal fasting, against the defendant. To end the suit, the defendant had to make a pledge that he would provide proper concessions to the plaintiff. If the defendant denied the claims against him, he was expected to counterfast, abstaining from food and drink as long as the plaintiff did, or the defendant became liable for twice the original penalty. If, on the other hand, the defendant simply ignored the *troscud* against him entirely, he would lose all legal standing and could potentially even be slain with impunity. For the plaintiff's part, if the defendant made all the right gestures and pledges, the plaintiff had to cease his or her *troscud* immediately or the case lost all merit.[37]

---

35   Land was seldom the focus of distraint. Legally, plaintiffs could only seize land in two instances: either they had their own viable claim to the land's title, or they had a share in the land due to their familial ties. It is possible that some instances of landowners attempting to expel saints from their territories could be a form of distraint against the saint, but the hagiographers would be unlikely to frame their tales in a way that might tarnish their holy subjects. See D.A. Binchy, "Distraint in Irish Law," *Celtica* 10 (1973): 30.

36   Binchy, "Distraint," 20, 30–32; also Kelly, *Early Irish Law*, pp. 178–93.

37   Kelly, *Early Irish Law*, pp. 182–3. These procedures are outlined most fully in a subsection of *Di Cetharslicht Athgabála* 365.5–367.7, ed. Daniel Binchy, *Corpus Iuris Hibernici* (Dublin: DIAS, 1978). More accessible may be the German translation of Rudolf Thurneysen, "Das Fasten beim Pfändungsverfahren," *Zeitschrift für Celtische Philologie* 15 (1925): 260–275. Smaller vernacular treatises on the subject are "A Text on the Forms of Distraint," ed. and trans. D.A. Binchy, *Celtica* 10 (1973): 72–86, and *Bretha Nemed Toísech* 5, pp. 10–11. In the latter instance it is specified that *troscud* was not only the means of compelling an ecclesiastical defendant's restitution, it also was the proper course to take where the

Finnian of Clonard's *Life* frequently depicts this saint embroiled in some type of territorial flap, so it is little surprise that Finnian provides a clear example of the use of *troscud* to settle such a dispute. In the tale, an old man, Maine (Maneus), reputedly baptized by Saint Patrick himself, is denied a plot of land for building a church. Finnian travels to the fort of the king prohibiting Maine's plans, and engages in a one-night *troscud* against the ruler. In an obvious nod to Moses and the death of the firstborn, the king's dearest son dies that very night.[38] The next morning the king goes to answer the call of nature in another field, and is suddenly paralyzed in that pose (*in stacione sua*, literally "in his stance") until he does penance and offers the disputed plot to God and his saints. Finnian then releases the humbled—or perhaps humiliated—leader and revives his son.[39]

The medical penalty for denial of settlement in a property dispute, a refusal that already hagiographically declares the king to have rejected the legal and spiritual standing of Maine and of his baptizer, Saint Patrick, is again miraculous. The paralysis comes with a twist, however, as it is imposed in the form of physical and spiritual distraint against a defendant who is also guilty of ignoring *troscud*. The ruler's embarrassing posture during the paralytic penalty thus serves to strip away all shreds of social or legal standing the king might attempt to claim, forcing him to recognize the validity of the case against him at the same time that he also acknowledges the sanctity of Maine, Finnian, and Patrick.

Saints also weigh in on the issue of tribute or tax, which pertains to both property rights and distraint, and provides further examples of the nexus between law, medicine, and miracle. Those who entered into a reciprocal relationship with someone of superior standing were considered clients (*céili* or *aithig*) to the superior, or lord (*flaith*). Among the other duties of clients was the required annual payment of a food-rent or tribute, generally assessed based upon the client's amount of property and consequent ability to pay.[40] Churches and monasteries could become both clients and lords; as clients, they often sought exemption from the normal taxes a lord expected of a client.[41]

---

church or its agent was the plaintiff. Additionally, since *troscud* was inherently a means by which plaintiffs of lesser grade or standing could gain redress from a superior, many types of *athgabál* involving *troscud* could be undertaken by female plaintiffs; see Binchy, "Distraint," 51–7.

38   Exod. 12:29.
39   *Vita S Finniani* 30, ed. Heist, 105. Irish hagiographers were nothing if not wry.
40   Kelly, *Early Irish Law*, pp. 26–7, 30.
41   Kelly, *Early Irish Law*, pp. 33, 39–40.

One of the many hagiographical instances of attempts to gain tax forgiveness occurs in the *vita* of Saint Fínán of Kinnitty. Here Fínán asks Failbhe Flann to exempt the saint's community from taxation. Failbhe's tax collector (*proconsul*), however, declares to Fínán that even if the saint fasted for seven days he would not obtain tribute forgiveness. The tax collector's house is instantaneously immolated by lightning at Fínán's pronouncement while the *proconsul* himself is rendered mute. Not until King Failbhe himself performs penance to Fínán and forgives the tax is the "loquacious" (*locax*) tax collector relieved of his "tongue tied" (*lingua ligata*) state.[42]

Multiple legal issues are at play in this episode. There is the property-based matter of the monastic tribute first claimed and then forgiven by King Failbhe Flann. There is also the demonstrated verbal assault committed by the overly-talkative *proconsul*, whose incinerated home and subsequent muteness exact a medical honor-price from him on the saint's behalf.[43] But there is an additional component in action as well. Although it was possible to distrain a defendant of exalted status, technically kings were not to be distrained directly. To do so would tarnish the royal defendant's honor so severely that his social grade and all its privileges would be forfeit. One has only to recall the literal forfeiture imposed upon the king blocking Maine's church to see such debasement made manifest. To prevent this occurrence, distraint could be carried out against an intermediary of a status below that of the defendant himself. This intermediary, called the *aithech fortha* or "substitute commoner," would then be liable for all penalties assessed against the defendant in whose place he stood. Use of an *aithech fortha* thus allowed a plaintiff to pursue his or her case without tainting the defendant's honor.[44]

In the case of the tax collector's muteness, it appears that the *proconsul* is standing in for the king as *aithech fortha*. Because the *proconsul* does not regain his voice through his own actions, it seems the saint's honor-price for verbal assault is instead exacted through the destruction of the *proconsul*'s house. As *aithech fortha*, however, the *proconsul* suffers miraculous distraint of his speech until the defendant king makes proper restitution to the plaintiff saint. That restitution is accomplished only when the king whose place the *proconsul* occupies performs a proper submission and grants Fínán the desired tax exemption.

---

42   *Vita S Finani Abbatis de Cenn Etigh*, ed. Heist, 158; *Vita S Finani Abbatis de Cenn Etigh* 19, ed. Plummer, *Vitae Sanctorum* v. 2, p. 92.

43   More will be said presently on the issue of verbal assault.

44   "A Text on the Forms of Distraint," pp. 80–81; also see Kelly, *Early Irish Law*, pp. 25–6.

Verbal Assault

Thus far, mention of verbal assault has been only an aside to the ongoing analysis, but the issue of abusive speech occupied many episodes of the medico-legal miracles in the *Lives* of Irish saints. Medieval Irish society had a strong belief in the power of the spoken word. Properly—or improperly— pronounced, it was seen as capable of harming not only someone's reputation, honor, and status but also of causing physical injury and even death.[45] Consequently, vernacular law codes have much to say on the subject of verbal assault, or *áer*, "satirizing."

Satire, as an oral statement with the intent to criticize, mock, or insult, is the exact opposite of an act of verbal praise. Originally, satire was the sole province of the poetic class but, as Tomás Ó Cathasaigh has shown, the hagiographical saint also utilizes the same verbal structures in the formulation of a potent malediction.[46] If the satirist's target was guilty of the allegations leveled against him, the satire was legal and the target was expected to respond immediately either by promising recompense or by entering arbitration. The penalty for not responding was the loss of his full honor-price and the status it defined.[47] If the target was innocent, the satire was false and illegal. The individual satirized unjustly was considered a victim of verbal assault through defamation and it was the *satirist* who had to pay the victim's full honor-price.[48]

Legal satire certainly receives treatment in the *Lives* of Ireland's saints. In one such case, Saint Brigid is satirized by two blind Britons who come seeking healing from her. When she suggests that they refresh themselves in the guesthouse while she and her nuns pray for them, the Britons indignantly accuse her of reserving her miracles for her own people. Stung, Brigid sprinkles the

---

45   In the legal tract *Din Techtugad*, an excerpt of which is edited and translated by Fergus Kelly, *Early Irish Law*, 366, biased judgments raise blisters on the cheeks of the judge pronouncing them, while true judgments delivered upon this man by another judge heal the sores. See also p. 44, where Kelly lists several cases of injury or death said to be caused by satire, and p. 137, where he notes that the verbs for satirizing translate as "to strike" (*áerad*) and "to cut" (*rindad*).

46   "Curse and Satire," *Éigse* 21 (1986): 10–15. Also see Fergus Kelly's discussion of the professional poetic class, *Early Irish Law*, 49–50.

47   Binchy, *Críth Gablach*, 69 (*áer*); also Kelly, *Early Irish Law*, pp. 137–8.

48   *Críth Gablach* 6, 11, 12, pp. 1–2, 5–6, and 69 (*áer*); "Ancient Irish Law" 66, 83, 84, pp. 283, 288, 289. Church texts reserved particular censure for illegal satirists. See Kelly, *Early Irish Law*, pp. 49–50, and Charles-Edwards, *Early Christian Ireland*, p. 129.

blind men and their leprous servant with blessed water, instantly cleansing the leper and bringing sight to the blind.[49]

There are parallel elements here. First, the petitioners' criticism is made on spiritual grounds. The hagiographer has the Britons allege that Saint Brigid is not behaving in a properly Christ-like fashion by keeping her miracles for her Irish compatriots. "You heal the sick of your own people for Christ," they accuse her, "But we who are as strangers you neglect to cure."[50] The Britons thus charge Brigid *as a saint* with not living up to the standards set by the one in whose image she lives her life; Brigid is not following Jesus's injunction that to welcome strangers is to welcome Christ.[51] Indeed, nowhere in their challenge is Brigid's identity as sanctified part of the criticism. The Britons acknowledge that she *is* a saint who wields the curative grace marking her as holy. This point leads to the second element of the tale, namely that Brigid simply accepts the Britons' critique (*accepto opprobrio*) before moving to correct her error. In so doing, Brigid tacitly agrees that the satire is legal and just, and her swift provision thereafter of immediate health and wholeness stands as her act both of contrition before God and of restitution to those she has wronged. Brigid's response thus neatly avoids any tarnish to her honor, her church, or her God.

More common than cases of legal satire, however, are instances in which a hagiographical saint must respond to illegal satire directed at guiltless targets. In the vernacular law tracts, illegal satire encompasses multiple forms of verbal assault. These include mocking someone's appearance (e.g., hair color or nose shape) or a particular physical flaw (such as a hunched back, a clubfoot, or a skin condition), as well as coining a derogatory nickname (a *forainm* or *lesainm lenas*) that adheres to the identity of the intended victim and destroys his or her status.[52] The object of such mockery was entitled to receive restitution in the form of a full honor-price payment. A king who ignored a satire was deemed to have completely lost his honor and status; even if he did respond

---

49   *Vita I S Brigitae* 3.23, p. 114. The anecdote is retained in *Bethu Brigte* 27, pp. 9, 26 and *Betha Bhrigdi* ll 1372–6, pp. 41, 189.

50   *Infirmos generis tui sanas, nos autem quasi advenas neglegis pro Christo curare. Vita I S Brigitae* 3.23, p. 114.

51   Matt. 25:34–40.

52   Recall the prescriptions previously mentioned that demanded physical perfection particularly of rulers. Kelly, *Early Irish Law*, p. 137 and n. 91 suggests that *lesainm lenas* is possibly *lesainm lénas*, "a nickname that wounds." Charles-Edwards, *Early Christian Ireland*, pp. 25–6 discusses the *forainm*, the "extra name," as it is used to destroy the reputations of competitors for kingship in hagiography and elsewhere.

and received his full honor-price as compensation for illegal satire his standing could still be fatally tarnished, his *fír flathemon* gone.[53]

When, for instance, King Ailill of Munster angrily accosts Saint Ciarán of Saigir "with harsh words" (*asperis uerbis*), he is instantly (*ilico*) rendered mute for seven days. At the end of this silent week, Ailill submits to Ciarán and the saint blesses his tongue, restoring his speech.[54] Penitentials commonly decreed contrition periods in units of seven, such as seven years of penance for parricide, homicide, or adultery, or seven days for consuming food or drink contaminated by a dead mouse.[55] It seems that Ciarán of Saigir not only exacts a medical fee for having been verbally assaulted, but he also imposes a mandatory "time out" on King Ailill, compelling the ruler to both cease the attack and contemplate his wrongdoing. Ailill's submission to Ciarán simultaneously accepts the vocal honor-price and the remonstrance concerning the proper treatment of a saint. Ailill's restoration to speech then recognizes his completion of penitence and reintegrates him into the body Christian.

In other cases, saints confront individuals who defame someone else. When a priest in Saint Patrick's retinue laughs at a blind man, for example, the saint's pronouncement both renders the priest permanently sightless and grants vision to the man he mocked.[56] Saint Carthach, too, defends another, removing the debilitating arthritis from the foot of one of his monks and inflicting it upon the foot of the princeling who ridiculed the cleric's lameness. As with the priest's loss of sight in Patrick's tale, the arthritic agonies in Carthach's *vita* are a fixture of the princeling's life thereafter.[57] In both episodes, the pairing

---

53   *Críth Gablach* 21, pp. 12–13; "Ancient Irish Law," 100, pp. 295–6. Also Charles-Edwards, *Early Christian Ireland*, pp. 91–106 and McCone, *Pagan Past*, p. 124.

54   *Vita S Ciarani Episcopi de Saigir* 28, ed. Plummer, *Vitae Sanctorum* v. 1, pp. 228–9. A rather different version of the story is also in *Vita S Ciarani Episcopi de Saigir*, ed. Heist, p. 349.

55   Canons 1, 2, 3, 4, 5, 7, and 20 of the twenty-nine canons of *Canones Hibernenses* all involve periods involving the number seven; those specifically listed in the discussion above are Canons 1, 2, 3, 4, and 20, pp. 160–163.

56   *Vita IV S Patricii* 68, ed. Bieler, p. 104; trans. Byrne and Francis, p. 56. The tale is retained in *Bethu Phátraic* ll 1514–18, ed. Mulchrone, 82, and ed. and trans. Stokes, pp. 132–3.

57   *Vita S Carthagi sive Mochutu*, ed. Plummer, *Vitae Sanctorum* v. 1, p. 192. Notably, the princeling in question has led a host to the saint's foundation, Rahan, intent upon expelling Carthach and his monks. This event is reported both by *Chronicon Scotorum* and the *Annals of Ulster* as having occurred at Easter in 636 CE. In other words, the present tale is but a moment in a much larger property dispute that ultimately resulted in the expulsion of the saint and his community from their first home. The hagiographers who commemorate Carthach make certain to show the wake of miraculous penalties that fanned out behind this travesty of treatment.

of penalty for the defendant and cure for the victim can readily be seen as the miraculous levying of honor-price. The defendant's penalty exacts proper payment, while the victim's restored health is his due compensation for insult. Additionally, these two cases show verbal assault directed at persons under the saint's protection; as will be discussed in more detail below, the attackers are also paying the saints' honor-prices for violating that protection.

Physical Assault and Attempted Homicide

Irish saints in the *Lives* face more than just verbal assault. They also confront a fairly chronic problem with physical violence, including assault and attempted murder. Ireland's jurists tried to distinguish between "acceptable violence" such as warfare or self-defense, and the "unacceptable violence" of the melee and of assaults perpetrated upon non-combatants.[58] Under the tenets of both vernacular and ecclesiastical law, a non-combatant was anyone who did not ordinarily partake of violent combat or who lacked legal independence—in other words, women, children, slaves, and clerics.[59] In the late seventh century, the church weighed in on the matter through the promulgation of the *Cáin Adomnáin*, a legal treatise that designed a structure of hefty fines to enforce the immunity of non-combatants.[60] Multiple canons also testify to a perceived need to declare clerics of every grade off limits to attack.[61]

For its part, a significant subsection of Irish vernacular law is occupied with the issue of physical assault, most notably in the tract known as *Bretha Déin Chécht*. This text addresses the compensations due to an assault victim, categorizing the penalties according to the severity and location of the wounds and to the status of the victim. In most instances, the law decrees that the assailant should pay the victim's full honor-price.[62] If the injuries are particularly severe

---

58   Charles-Edwards, *Early Christian Ireland*, pp. 69–70.

59   Charles-Edwards, *Early Christian Ireland*, pp. 69–70. Also, see Kelly, *Early Irish Law*, pp. 43, 75, 79, 83–4, and 95 for discussion of the legal capacity of and the penalties for harming these protected classes of person.

60   Charles-Edwards, *Early Christian Ireland*, pp. 69–70. The *Cáin Adomnáin* has most recently been edited and translated by Gilbert Márkus, *Adomnán's Law of the Innocents— Cáin Adomnáin: A Seventh-Century Law for the Protection of Noncombatants* (Kilmartin: Kilmartin House Museum, 2008). Also, note Kelly, *Early Irish Law*, ppl. 79, 128, and 281 no. 74.

61   See for instance Book IV of the *Canones Hibernenses*, pp. 170–171.

62   See for example *Bretha Déin Chécht* 21, pp. 34–5 (including text and glosses), in which it is decreed that someone who lost either both feet and/or both hands, who was blinded in

or are on the head or face, they could additionally entail a penalty known as *íarmbrethemnas*, "after judgment," intended to compensate the victim for the public shaming the wound caused.[63]

In the *Lives* of the saints, cases of simple physical assault in which there is little other complicating issue and in which medicine, miracle, and law intertwine are relatively uncommon. As the evidence of property disputes reminds us, physical assault is much more often entwined with other legal violations. Saint Berach finds himself at the centre of one such occurrence when a band of youthful ruffians decides to throw stones at, slap, and insult him. The boys are suddenly stricken with total paralysis, turning them into living statues. In addition, Berach is turned away from the royal fortress while another man with whom the saint has been disputing his monastery's land enters with full honors. Berach does not release the boys until three conditions are met. First, the king himself offers Berach an honorable welcome. Second, the king seeks the saint's forgiveness. Finally, he asks Berach specifically to free the lads from their paralysis.[64]

Here the hagiographer has heaped several wrongs together and piled them all upon Saint Berach. He is assaulted physically by the stones thrown at him and the stinging slaps he receives. He endures verbal assault through the mockery cast his way. His honor is still further injured when his personal foe receives favors and he does not. That the king himself must do penance suggests that the youths rendered motionlessness may be legal dependents of the royal household; normally a minor's offense occasioned penalties to be paid by the legal guardian responsible, namely the father or foster-father. At the same time, though, a king was supposed to be exempt from this rule, raising the additional possibility that the king is being distrained and that the paralysis afflicting the troublemakers acts to both cease their onslaught and to mark them collectively as the king's *aithech fortha*.[65] The boys are thus literally held liable until the king himself performs penance.

---

both eyes, or had both ears injured or severed, was due full honor-price. Interestingly the reason given for such a penalty in the latter two instances is that "the head [is used] for the whole person" (*cenn arin duine uile*).

63   *Bretha Déin Chécht* 30, 31, 34, pp. 16, 18, 40–41, 44–5, and the notes on p. 63. In §34, for example, damage to the upper front teeth provokes the highest initial penalty, full honor-price for the shaming, and a hefty *íarmbrethemnas* for the disfigurement and dishonor; see pp. 44–5.

64   *Vita S Berachi Abbatis de Cluain Coirpthe* 14–15, ed. Plummer, *Vitae Sanctorum* v. 1, pp. 80–81.

65   Kelly, *Early Irish Law*, p. 83.

The tale is not just about varieties of assault, it also attends to the elite expectation of hospitality. Individuals of elevated status were entitled to *cóe*, "guesting", from their clients. *Cóe* required the provision of at least one night of hospitality and entertainment to both the noble seeking it and to his retinue—including nobles who also held ecclesiastical authority.[66] If the householder denied the request, penalties were expected. Whether the noble seeking *cóe* was merely refused, suffering the lesser *etech* ("rejection"), or was chased off with verbal and physical abuse through the more serious offense of *esáin* ("driving away"), he and his entire retinue were all due full honor-price. A landowner who habitually turned away superiors seeking *cóe* lost all legal status, including the right to his honor-price, making him an outlaw who could be hunted without penalty.[67]

There is no question that Saint Berach endures *etech* at the very least. The king treats Berach as though he were a vagabond in rags, denying the saint his due *cóe* while giving Berach's enemy high honors. That Berach does not lift the paralysis afflicting the troublemakers until three conditions are met, one of which is his welcome with due respect and status by the king, suggests that the lads' immobility is in no small part the miraculous exaction of Berach's honor-price for his dismissal and dishonor. Medicine, miracle, and law come together, both to uphold the saint's status and prestige and to demonstrate the saint's identity as God's agent.

Sometimes, though, the assailants who fall upon a hagiographical saint are intent upon more than mere injury. They never succeed, of course, nor do most whose goal is the death of the saint actually land a blow. In every instance in which a medical miracle halts the threat of murder, the would-be hagiocide is paralyzed completely; when the malefactors offer proper repentance, the saint invariably releases them. In one such instance, a monk angry at having been scolded by Saint Colmán Élo rises to kill Colmán, but finds himself "immobile like a statue" (*quasi statua immobilis*). He remains thus frozen "with his hands extended in the air" (*extensis in aere manibus*) until his penance provokes

---

66   See for example *Críth Gablach* 17, 27, pp. 9, 16 and p. 81 (*cóe*). §17 mentions *ráithe cue*, the "guesting season"; MacNeill translates this as "the winter quarter," losing some of the sense of why an additional penalty of half a host's *díre* should be added to the full honor-price mulct the section demands for breaking the host's furnishings. See "Ancient Irish Law," 90, 112, pp. 293, 299. The ecclesiastical codes also have much to say on the topic of hospitality; see the canons of Book V in *Canones Hibernenses*, 172–5 and Book LVI of *Collectio Canonum Hibernensis*, 221–2.

67   *Bretha Crólige* 43, pp. 34–5.

the saint's liberating prayers.[68] In another instance, a *laicus* tries to kill Saint Maedóc with an axe while the saint is still a boy, but the man's raised hand withers and he cannot lower it. The assailant confesses not only to his own wrongdoing, but also to his part in a murder plot instigated by the monastery's jealous steward. Naturally once the *laicus* has confessed, the youthful Maedóc's prayers free him from his enforced immobility.[69]

Importantly, in Ireland's hagiography a *laicus*—which means both "layman" and "warrior" in Hiberno-Latin—was generally a "grievously sinful" person relegated to the fringes of the faithful until he submitted to penitential correction. The most likely reasons for such persistent sin were plunder, bloodshed, violence, and sexual license, all activities associated with brigandage (on which more below).[70] Once committed fully to penitence, however, the *laicus* (*láech* in Irish) became "ex-lay" (*athláech*) and lived as a non-monk under the order and austerity of a monastic superior.[71] So, in addition to the clear messages concerning the inviolability of the holy person and the proper rendering of his honor-price for daring to assail him, this episode also highlights some of the church's concerns regarding the habitual occupations of the *laicus*.

In fact, some hagiographers go further still. Saint Cainnech of Aghaboe falls into the hands of twelve *latrones*, or brigands, who desire the holy man's demise. Cainnech tries to deter them with preaching, but they refuse to listen and raise their hands to slay him. Immediately (*statim*) their appendages wither "like twelve stones, not having the strength to move"; they then believe, do penance, and are liberated.[72] Saint Ciarán of Clonmacnoise is also targeted by *latrones* when the saint is but a lad; they are not only

---

68   *Vita S Colmani Abbatis de Land Elo* 19, ed. Heist, 215; *Vita S Colmani Abbatis de Land Elo* 14, ed. Plummer, *Vitae Sanctorum* v. 1, p. 264.

69   *Vita S Aidui sive Maedoc Episcopi ex Codice Cottoniano* 13, ed. Plummer, *Vitae Sanctorum* v. 2, pp. 298–9 and *Vita S Maedoc Episcopi de Ferna* 13, ed. Plummer, *Vitae Sanctorum* v. 2, pp. 145–6. In this latter case, it is not clear whether Maedóc is still a boy at the time of the hagiographical conspiracy.

70   Colmán Etchingham, *Church Organisation in Ireland A.D. 650 to 1000* (Maynooth: Laigin Publications, 2002), pp. 304–17.

71   Etchingham, *Church Organisation*, pp. 304–17. See also Richard Sharpe, "Hiberno-Latin *Laicus*, Irish *Láech* and the Devil's Men," *Ériu* 30 (1979): 75–92 and the discussion below on brigandage.

72   ... *quasi duodecim lapides ... non valentes se movere. Vita S Cainnechi Abbatis de Achad Bó Chainnich* 7, ed. Heist, 183 and *Vita S Cainnici Abbatis de Achad Bó Cainnech* 5, ed. Plummer, *Vitae Sanctorum* v. 1, pp. 153–4.

stricken with miraculous motionlessness but also become suddenly blind, at least until they do penance.[73]

Brigandage was an organized assault often perpetrated by bands of men living along the edges of Irish society. These bands, known as *fíanna* (sg. *fían*), filled a valuable social and economic niche; they often provided border defense, for example, or aided in the prosecution and enforcement of distraint cases. Sometimes they also served as roving warrior retinues in the service of a particular ruler. *Fían*-bands, however, tended to turn to settled Irish society to supplement their provisions. In some instances, their demands became onerous or resulted in violent raiding, and they crossed the line from *fían* to *díberga*, or brigands.[74] So where *fíannas*—the activity of the *fían*—was generally considered "acceptable violence" and viewed favorably, *díbergaig*—the work of the *díberga*—was not.

Indeed, *díbergaig* is the subject of considerable censure in Ireland's vernacular legal texts. The brigand is roundly condemned in codes like *Bretha Crólige*, which among other pronouncements declares that God himself would prefer to reject rather than exalt brigands.[75] Brigands are often associated with legal retribution that includes mandating the payment of the victim's full honor-price.[76] Importantly both *fían* and *díberg* became equated with the Hiberno-Latin *laicus* via the Irish *láech*, "warrior." *Laicus* and *díberg* were then also further collapsed into the meanings of *latro* (pl. *latrones*) and *latrunculus*

---

73   *Vita S Ciarani Abbatis Cluanensis* 7, ed. Heist, 79; *Vita S Ciarani Abbatis de Cluain mic Nois* 7, ed. Plummer, *Vitae Sanctorum* v. 1, p. 202. The same tale is retained in the much later vernacular work, *Betha Ciarain Clúana mac Nois* ll 4090–4094, ed. and trans. Stokes, *Book of Lismore*, pp. 122, 267.

74   Kim McCone, "Werewolves, Cyclopes, *Díberga* and *Fíanna*: Juvenile Delinquency in Early Ireland," *Cambridge Medieval Celtic Studies* 12 (Winter 1986): 1–22, especially 7–9. McCone reprises many of the arguments made here in *Pagan Past*, pp. 203–223.

75   *Bretha Crólige* 51, pp. 40–41.

76   See for example *Bechbretha* 39, pp. 74–5, where it is said that a raider who flees legal penalty, particularly if guilty of murder, lost all legal protection from either church or nobility until all the proper restitutions were made. It should be noted here that there are also numerous cases of simple thievery in the *Lives*, in which some medical miracle exacts the punishment the thieves deserve. These tales normally involve the thieves losing their sight (as in, e.g., *Vita S Comgalli Abbatis de Bennchor* 17, ed. Plummer, *Vitae Sanctorum* v. 2, p. 9) or become paralyzed and stick to their stolen booty (as in *Vita S Cainnechi* 55, ed. Heist, 196). For the sake of space, however, thievery is not separately analyzed in the current work.

(pl. *latrunculi*), "robbers, brigands," in Hiberno-Latin church texts—including the *vitae*.[77]

In essence, then, the hagiographical figures of Maedóc, Cainnech, and Ciarán of Clonmacnoise confront more than obstreperous monks or jealous stewards, they instead face brigands whom both vernacular laws and ecclesiastical texts like the *Lives* viewed with distinct disfavor. The punitive paraplegia that freezes these malefactors mid-attack not only affirms the sanctity of the saint's person and identity, but also pointedly highlights the inefficacy of *díbergaig* in the hagiographical Irish world. The assailants receive an object lesson in the status of the saint while simultaneously enduring a physical distraint that exacts the holy person's honor-price for the insult of assault. Where blindness is added to that penalty, the implication is clear; if they will not spiritually see their crime they must be stripped of their sight until their vision clears, first metaphorically then, after penance, literally through the saint's act of healing. Once again the saint's medical miracles both enforce the law and define the boundary between right and wrong, believer and unbeliever.

Homicide and the Issue of Sanctuary

When homicide does occur in the *Lives*, it does not usually involve the intersection of medicine, law, and miracle. A frequent component of the *vitae* and *bethada*, murder usually incurs consequences that are instantaneous and lethal.[78] Where a killing does entail a penalty taken through the infliction of illness or disability, the text focuses less on the murder and more on the identity of the victims in relation to the saint. In other words, medicine, law, and miracle meet not at the punishment of murder but at the enforcement of the saint's protection.

Medieval Ireland's vernacular law codes declare that an individual of sufficient social grade was entitled to offer persons of equal or lesser status safe conduct, physical asylum, and even immunity from legal process such as distraint. This protection or sanctuary, designated by *snádud, dítiu,* or *turtugud,*

---

77   This linguistic relationship was first explored by Sharpe, "*Laicus, Láech* and the Devil's Men." Sharpe also argued (and McCone, "Werewolves, Cyclopes, *Díberga* and *Fíanna*," 3–4 and *Pagan Past*, 202–23, agreed) that church condemnation of *díbergaig/fiannas* was particularly intense because of perceived associations between both of these and presumed pagan activities. This view has been upended, however, by Etchingham, *Church Organisation*, pp. 304–17.

78   See for example the miraculous capital punishment that befalls a man who kills Saint Patrick's charioteer in *Vita IV S Patricii* 77, ed. Bieler, 106, trans. Byrne and Francis, p. 58. The same story is also found in *Bethu Phátraic* ll 2574–85, ed. Mulchrone, pp. 129–30 and ed. and trans. Stokes, pp. 216–19.

could be extended for a period of time determined by the protector's rank; higher rank meant not only a longer duration but also that more persons could be under that individual's protection at the same time.[79] This protection was granted not only to members and guests of the household, but also to hostages, legal dependents, and even to anyone simply present within a specified zone around the protector's living quarters.[80]

Snádud could be transgressed, however, most notably through the harm or slaying of someone under another's protection. The laws frame such a violation, or *díguin*, as an attack upon the honor of the protector. *Díguin* mandates the payment not only of the proper penalties to the injured victim, or to the victim's kin in cases of homicide, but also of the full honor-price of the protector as recompense for the violent trespass of his *snádud*.[81] If the individual injured or murdered through *díguin* was a non-combatant, the fines could be much higher.[82]

There are a number of instances in which someone under the *snádud* of the saint commits murder, provoking the holy person's intervention when the killer is taken into custody. In such episodes, the hagiographer's subject does not punish the murderer. Instead, he exacts his own honor-price for the *díguin* that occurs when the guilty party is arrested. The most detailed case of this nature is found in the *vita* of Saint Rúadán of Lorrha. There Áed Guaire places himself under Rúadán's protection after slaying the herald of King Diarmait mac Cerbhaill; Rúadán's sanctuary could grant at least a temporary stay of legal action. Diarmait sends two retainers to retrieve Áed, but one is struck blind and the other punitively paralyzed. Áed is nevertheless seized and matters escalate to a mutual *troscud* between King Diarmait and Rúadán (along with a number of other saints and monks). The fasting is followed by a vehement curse war in which prophecies of blemishes, blinding, and limb loss feature

---

79 *Bechbretha* 39, pp. 74–5 and notes concerning §39 *cain dimet ind nemid*, p. 144, which discusses *dítiu*. Also *Críth Gablach* 5, 6, 7, 10, pp. 2, 5 and 106–7 (*snádud*), and "Ancient Irish Law," 65, 66, 69, 76, 82, pp. 282–5. See further *DIL* on snádud, dítiu, and turtugud.

80 Kelly, *Early Irish Law*, 141. See below for a brief discussion of hostages in early Ireland.

81 See *Críth Gablach*, 6, 8, 11, pp. 1, 3, 5; "Ancient Irish Law," 66, 70, 83, 283, 284, and 288 for examples. Also consult Binchy, *Críth Gablach*, 82–3 (*díguin*) and Kelly, *Early Irish Law*, p. 141. In addition to the standard penalty of a victim's honor-price, murder demanded an additional fine called the *éraic* or *cró*; both the honor-price and the *éraic* were payable to the dead person's kindred. See *Críth Gablach* 9, p. 5; also pp. 84–5 (*enech*) and 86 (*éraic*); "Ancient Irish Law" 75, p. 286; *Bretha Déin Chécht* 1–2, pp. 24–5.

82 *Bretha Crólige* 7, pp. 8–11; also the discussion of Charles-Edwards, *Early Christian Ireland*, pp. 69–70.

prominently. Diarmait eventually gives in, Áed Guaire is ransomed, and Saint Rúadán returns home in peace.[83]

Rúadán thus is painted capably besting a king whose secular jurisdiction in Áed Guaire's criminal case is actually just. Among those whom vernacular law labeled as forbidden from receiving sanctuary were fugitive murderers.[84] But Rúadán's claim is made superior, not because Diarmait has no standing but because Rúadán is a favored agent of God; as the hagiographer puts into King Diarmait's mouth, "God loves you more."[85] Notably, the saint's medical miracles do not directly impact the king himself. Instead, his retainers are afflicted. They each act as a type of *aithech fortha*, distrained in the king's place to exact Rúadán's honor-price and to compel submission to the saint. Diarmait eventually capitulates to Rúadán in clear acknowledgement both of the hagiographer's view of the proper relationship between church and state and of the advantage conferred by Rúadán's sanctity.

Much more common are episodes in which those under the saint's protection are the victims rather than the perpetrators of murder. In the *vita* of Saint Berach, for example, twelve men raid Berach's monastery at night, seizing considerable booty and decapitating the monk tasked with guarding those goods. The murdering brigands are stricken with miraculous paralysis and forced to stand immobile. Berach resuscitates the slain monk with a marvelous reattachment of the man's severed head, then goes to the brigands and releases them, whereupon they promptly commend themselves to Berach's rule thereafter.[86]

Again the focus is not on the punishment of the murderers, it is on proving the potency of the saint's *snádud*. The hagiographical miracles of the episode save the slain, erase the crime of homicide both physically and spiritually, and restore to health the monk, the souls of his slayers, and the entire body

---

83   *Vita S Ruadani Abbatis de Lothra* 12, ed. Heist, 163–5; *Vita S Ruadani Abbatis de Lothra* 15–18, ed. Plummer, *Vitae Sanctorum* v. 2, pp. 245–9.

84   Kelly, *Early Irish Law*, 141, 144. *Bechbretha* 39, 74–5 lists a man attempting to run from prosecution as a category of person denied sanctuary; see also note 79 above.

85   *Deus plus diligit uos. Vita S Ruadani Abbatis de Lothra* 12, ed. Heist, 165; *Vita S Ruadani Abbatis de Lothra* 18, ed. Plummer, *Vitae Sanctorum* v. 2, p. 249.

86   *Vita S Berachi Abbatis de Cluain Coirpthe* 24, ed. Plummer, *Vitae Sanctorum* v. 1, p. 85; also *Betha Beraigh* 29.85–6, *Bethada Náem nÉrenn: Lives of Irish Saints* (Oxford: The Clarendon Press, 1997), v. 1, pp. 41–2 and v. 2, p. 41. Such tales fall into a group I have elsewhere termed "recapitation" episodes. For a detailed exploration particularly of the clear critique of "unacceptable violence" and *díbergaig*, see Johnson, "Preserving the Body Christian: The Motif of 'Recapitation' in Ireland's Medieval Hagiography," *The Heroic Age: A Journal of Early Medieval Northwestern Europe* 10 (2007): [http://www.heroicage.org]. Accessed March 3, 2013.

Christian. The paralytic punishment that traps the brigands has the practical effect of halting their flight, but it also exacts the saint's honor-price for the *díguin* committed through the slaying of the monk, a man under Berach's protection both as a non-combatant and as a member of Berach's monastic community. Medicine, miracle, and law thus unite in the maintenance of a saint's *snádud*. The resurrection of the slain obviates the need to prosecute the murder and further demonstrates Berach's ability to maintain the integrity of, and to delineate the boundary around, the Irish community of Christ.

Not all hagiographical handling of the nature of sanctuary and protection necessarily involves murder, however. A slave-mistress who cruelly and violently hauls her female slave from the shelter of Saint Brigid's protection, refusing both Brigid's request for the slave's manumission and the recognition of Brigid's holiness, suffers the withering and paralysis of the hand that grabbed the girl and dragged her from the saint's side. Naturally Brigid heals the woman's appendage once she releases the slave.[87] The shriveled hand stands as both the medical levy miraculously exacting the saint's honor-price for the insult inflicted by the woman's act of *díguin* and as the fine for physical assault committed against the erstwhile slave; the slave also receives her liberty as part of that payment.

In another instance, a princeling incites a crowd against Saint Columba of Iona and his monks. In the ensuing melee twenty-seven of Columba's monks are wounded. In response, Columba rings his holy bell—an act of malediction—twenty-seven times within the princeling's hearing. The young noble promptly loses his senses, regaining lucidity thereafter only when he is defecating.[88] So debasing a miraculous punishment strips the princeling of his rank, his status, his mental health, and his *fír flathemon*. This string of penalties functions as the honor-prices of twenty-seven injured monks as well as the honor-price of Saint Columba himself. It seemingly even tops off the heap with the *íarmbrethemnas* due those clerics who had suffered considerable bodily harm; after all, Columba's curse could have simply rendered the noble insane with no opportunity for relief. Instead, the saint's retribution forces the princeling to experience clarity in a thoroughly humiliating pose, so that every time he relieves himself he must recall both the nature of his crime and the potency of the sanctity abiding in Saint Columba.

---

87 *Vita I S Brigitae* 12.74, p. 162.

88 *Betha Coluim Chille* Appendix §4, ed. and trans. Máire Herbert, "The Irish Life of Colum Chille," in *Iona, Kells and Derry: The History and Hagiography of the Monastic* Familia *of Columba* (Oxford: Clarendon Press, 1988), pp. 180–287. According to Herbert, this *betha* can be dated from internal references to the mid-twelfth century; see pp. 184–93.

Hostages also constituted a protected class both legally and in the *Lives*, where hostages are often under the *snádud* of saints. Far from our modern conceptualization of individuals kept bound and subjected to deprivation, hostages in medieval Ireland were usually elite members of a particular kindred or region taken by a chieftain or king to guarantee the obedience and loyalty of the hostages' people. If the hostages' home territory was to rise against the ruler holding them, he could legally declare the hostages' lives forfeit or, at the least, clap them in chains.[89] Most of the time, hostages were treated quite well, and lived as honored guests in the ruler's household. In fact, if the sovereign holding the hostages harmed them unjustly in any way, he would lose *fír flathemon* for having violated the contract of allegiance made at their taking, which could trigger insurrection. As with the attack upon or murder of any other protected person, the assault or homicide of hostages constituted *díguin* against the individual under whose protection they were held, adding that protector's honor-price to the other penalties for violence (including a possible war if the king was blamed!).[90]

Hostages and protection figure prominently in a number of *Lives* in which medicine, law, and miracle intertwine. A particularly apt and extraordinarily layered episode provides a fitting note on which to end this analysis. In this anecdote Failbhe Flann, a Munster ruler whom we have met before—and one against whom hagiographical saints are frequently arrayed—tries to claim some of Saint Mochoemóg's monastic lands by pasturing his horses in Mochoemóg's field.[91] Mochoemóg forcibly expels the horses, and his harsh treatment of the valuable animals angers Failbhe. The king orders that the hostages from Mochoemóg's region be killed unless that region's chieftain and the hostages' parents expel the saint from their territories. Infuriated in turn, the saint goes to confront the king, and the two engage in a loud argument that escalates into an all-out war of insult and malediction. The height of this astounding kerfuffle is reached when Failbhe calls Mochoemóg a "bald little man" (*calve parve*), whereupon the saint replies "If I am bald, then you will be one-eyed."[92] Immediately Failbhe is stricken with severe pain in his left eye,

---

89   *Críth Gablach* 32, 46, pp. 18, 23, and 95–6 (*gíall*); "Ancient Irish Law," 117, 134, pp. 300–301, 305. Also Kelly, *Early Irish Law*, 173–4.

90   *Críth Gablach*, pp. 95–6 (*gíall*); Kelly, *Early Irish Law*, pp. 173–4.

91   See, e.g., the story of Fínán of Kinnitty, Failbhe Flann, and Failbhe Flann's *proconsul* above.

92   *Si ego sum calvus, tu eris luscus.* The insult of "bald little man" may in part be a reflection of the story of Elisha and the boys who taunt the prophet, mocking his baldness; at Elisha's curse forty-two of the lads are torn to pieces by a pair of bears. 2 Kgs 2:23–4.

and its sight vanishes. Though Mochoemóg subsequently facilitates the easing of Failbhe's pain, he does not return vision to the king.[93]

The contentious issue is once again the definition of the saint's property and prerogative in the face of secular infringements. There is no actual *díguin* or expulsion, only the threats thereof; the infraction that finally results in a punitive medical miracle is the verbal assault Failbhe casts on Mochoemóg. But while Failbhe's words can only call attention to existing features of Mochoemóg's person—his height, his lack of hair—Mochoemóg's pronounce-ment makes an entirely new trait manifest itself on Failbhe's face.[94] King Failbhe's painful loss of vision in one eye exacts the saint's honor-price, marks outwardly Failbhe's internal near-blindness to Mochoemóg's rights, and inflicts a very public shaming upon the king that risks destroying his *fír flathemon* and stripping him of his sovereignty. In fact, to regain his honor and hold onto his right to rule, Failbhe ultimately obtains healing not from Mochoemóg but from another saint, Carthach of Lismore.[95] The crossroads of medicine, miracle, and law here thus makes clear the proper relationship between secular ruler and saint, and between the king and the church—particularly in Munster.

Medicine, Law, and Miracle

The saints of Ireland's medieval *vitae* and *bethada* move through a hagio-graphical society in which the tenets of vernacular law figure prominently. The present analysis has explored numerous cases in which saints inflicted medi-cal miracles upon members of their community in the service of upholding and defining the laws of early Ireland, with particular emphasis on the proper

---

93   *Vita S Mochoemog Abbatis de Liath Mochoemog* 19, ed. Plummer, *Vitae Sanctorum* v. 2, p. 174.

94   It is not clear whether Failbhe's words refer to the saint possessing male-pattern baldness or simply insult Mochoemóg's tonsure. In the former the satire would draw attention to a physical flaw and occasion payment of the saint's honor-price; in the latter, the king would verbally attack the symbol of Mochoemóg's commitment to God, and would again owe the saint his honor-price. It is always a bad idea, of course, to insult a saint, especially if anger propels one to ridicule the very sign of the saint's clerical status!

95   *Vita S Carthagi sive Mochutu Episcopi de Less Mor*, ed. Plummer, *Vitae Sanctorum* v. 1, pp. 194–5. The *vita* does not explain the source of Failbhe's shame-inducing wound, reporting only that he was too afraid to be seen publicly after his "eye had been broken by another occurrence" (*oculus ... aliquot eventu fractus est*). It does acknowledge, however, that the injury befell Failbhe after the king and his forces had devastated the neighboring kingdom of Leinster.

recognition of the saint's position. The saintly application of either ailment or cure, of sensory loss or physical restoration, or simply of erasing flaws that threaten the stability of a royal dynasty all demonstrate visibly (and sometimes painfully) the respect and prestige due a saint. The miracles that cause or cure health issues prove to the audience of the *Lives* that the status of a saint is superior to all other members of early Irish society, even the kings of major realms like Munster. By exacting penalties such as the saint's honor-price, these wonders make clear that the holy men and women of Ireland's *Lives* obtain their exalted status through the blessing of the sanctity conferred upon them as God's favored.

Yet, these episodes attend to more than just the status of the saint. The men and women commemorated in the *Lives* essentially prosecute legal cases by inflicting or relieving, healing or harming, reviving or depriving. Saints thus protect those in their charge, defend the innocent, chastise the wrongdoer, and punish the guilty through medical *miracula*. From property disputes to *díguin*, whether the saint is plaintiff, prosecutor, defense advocate, or judge, the intent is the same. The actions of the sanctified maintain the health of the body Christian both individually and collectively by applying relevant vernacular legal tenets. Ultimately, the intertwined strands of medicine, law, and miracle reveal a tension between the injured and the intact. The saints of medieval Ireland stalk this boundary as both metaphysical physicians and as hagiographical jurists, their steps defining the threshold between membership in and exclusion from the community of the faithful and tracing thereby the delicate line between the sacred and the profane.

Concluding Remarks

Katherine D. Watson

In drawing together the twelve contributions to this innovative volume on medicine and the law in the Middle Ages,[1] this conclusion will discuss some of the common themes that have emerged. In doing so, it will stress not only the links between the chapters but also some of the connections that can be made to related research on later periods of history, focusing especially on four topics: the sources that historians use to study the relationship between medicine and law; the importance of context (local or national) in understanding the development of that relationship; the notion of expertise as an analytical concept; and the gendered nature of the relationship between medicine and law which is exposed by the attribution of "expert" status. The chapter thus has two principal aims: to identify continuity and change in the interactions between medicine and law; and to highlight fruitful avenues for further study.

The relevance of the medieval period to later centuries, and vice versa, is unmistakable: the subjects comprising the first section of this book (compensation for injury, rape, wounding, mental incompetency, medical expertise) are all issues that continue today to concern and at times confound medical and legal professionals. So too is the question of professional identity raised by the

---

1 Very few edited collections have attempted to explore the interactions between medicine and law in a historical context. The influential volume edited by Michael Clark and Catherine Crawford, *Legal Medicine in History* (Cambridge: CUP, 1994) and the more recent collection edited by Imogen Goold and Catherine Kelly, *Lawyers' Medicine: The Legislature, the Courts and Medical Practice, 1760–2000* (Oxford: Hart Publishing, 2009) examine the ways in which the complex relationship between these two fields have acted to shape and reshape medical and legal theory and practice since the early modern period. Both concentrate largely on the Anglo-American perspective. John Woodward and Robert Jütte, eds., *Coping with Sickness: Medicine, Law and Human Rights—Historical Perspectives* (Sheffield: European Association for the History of Medicine and Health Publications, 2000) is more concerned with medicine than law. A more narrowly focused work, José Ramón Bertomeu-Sánchez and Agustí Nieto-Galan, eds., *Chemistry, Medicine and Crime: Mateu J.B. Orfila (1787–1853) and His Times* (Sagamore Beach, MA: Science History Publications, 2006) includes a European context, but with a greater stress on science than law. Alessandro Pastore and Giovanni Rossi, eds., *Paolo Zacchia: alle origini della medicina legale 1584–1659* (Milan: FrancoAngeli, 2008) is similar in its concentration on the career of a single influential individual. A much earlier book, Chester R. Burns, ed., *Legacies in Law and Medicine* (New York: Science History Publications, 1977) can be considered a pioneer in the study of the relationship between medicine and law, covering many of the themes that appear in the present volume.

© KONINKLIJKE BRILL NV, LEIDEN, 2014 | DOI 10.1163/9789004269118_015

four essays in Section II: who is an expert, under what conditions can they establish (and, indeed, defend) their claims to expertise? Only Section III considers a genre that might appear to be wholly medieval in scope and relevance: hagiography. Here, though, the revealing area of overlap between religious and legal sources provides a methodology which not only contributes to the history of disability,[2] but also, crucially, demonstrates how a lay understanding of medicine can shape legal outcomes. The papers in this collection, therefore, raise important historiographical, methodological and analytical points about the interactions between the disciplines and professions of medicine and law—in both theory and practice—that are pertinent to any period of post-Roman Western history.

The distinction between theory and practice is significant: as Turner and Butler point out in their introduction, legal sources allow us to see "medicine in action" at a time when most healthcare workers were unlikely to be literate, let alone authoring medical treatises. This is perhaps nowhere more evident than in the chapter by Fiona Harris-Stoertz: her use of law codes and *inquisitions post mortem*, among other sources, to argue for the twelfth-century re-emergence of midwifery as a distinct profession serves as a model for the ingenious ways in which legal sources can be read in combination with other forms of evidence to reach new conclusions about the past. The fact that such a broad range of sources informs the work included in this volume reinforces the notion that legal systems have been a "pervasive influence on medicine and its practice to this day,"[3] and that both law and medicine have long been strongly determining forces in society, acting (often in tandem) as drivers of change in relation to such issues as interpersonal violence and its relationship to honor and dispute resolution; the status of women, children and the disabled; and governance and regulation.

But my focus here is on legal sources and the ways in which they expose "medicine in action" from three unique, and uniquely informative, perspectives. Firstly, these documents can be used to investigate the life and career of

---

2 David M. Turner, *Disability in Eighteenth-Century England: Imagining Physical Impairment* (Abingdon: Routledge, 2012) explores the interactions between religious and medical models of disability, and uses criminal court records to access lived experience. The similarity between Turner's title and Irina Metzler, *Disability in Medieval Europe: Thinking about Physical Impairment in the High Middle Ages, c.1100–1400* (London and New York: Routledge, 2006) is striking.

3 Catherine Kelly and Imogen Goold, "Introduction: Lawyers' Medicine: The Interaction of the Medical Profession and the Law, 1760–2000," in *Lawyer's Medicine*, ed. Goold and Kelly, pp. 1–15, 2.

a single individual, as Sara Butler does in her study of the fearless and indefatigable Nicholas Wodehill, to identify the medico-legal activities of practitioners like Domenico Sanc in Carmel Ferragud's work on Cocentaina, or to build up a picture of a developing occupational identity such as that shared by Iona McCleery's Portuguese licensees. The access that legal sources give to the medical personalities of the past can be as or more revealing than the formal works produced for any other contemporary audience. Secondly, we can use legal sources to dig beneath the rhetoric employed in medical texts, to gain direct access to medico-legal testimony (medical evidence given to satisfy the needs of the civil or criminal law) and, by extension, the development of the types of ideas now associated with the discipline of forensic medicine. The remarkable perspicacity of a writer like Kampa Jeldric, outlined in Han Nijdam's chapter on Frisian compensation tariffs, seemed designed to systematize knowledge *and* to teach legal and medical practitioners how to work together to make medicine both useful and appropriate to the laws pertaining to wounding. This offered the kind of dual perspective which was to become a key attribute of the *consilia* and textbooks of much later periods.[4] Hiram Kümper warns us against assuming an unbroken continuity between medieval and early modern ideas about rape, yet his legal sources reveal the early origins of what has proved to be a long-lived and widespread forensic attentiveness to child and virginal victims of sexual assault.[5] Finally, legal sources shed light on the extensive

---

4   As, for example, the works of Paolo Zacchia or Alfred S. Taylor, two pioneering figures in legal medicine. See Silvia De Renzi, "Witnesses of the Body: Medico-legal Cases in Seventeenth-Century Rome," *Studies in History and Philosophy of Science* 33 (2002), 219–242 and Noel G. Coley, "Alfred Swaine Taylor, MD, FRS (1806–1880): Forensic Toxicologist," *MH* 35 (1991), 409–427.

5   Julie Gammon, "'A denial of innocence': Female Juvenile Victims of Rape and the English Legal System in the Eighteenth Century," in *Childhood in Question: Children, Parents and the State*, ed. Anthony Fletcher and Stephen Hussey (Manchester: Manchester University Press, 1999), pp. 74–95; Louise Jackson, *Child Sexual Abuse in Victorian England* (London and New York: Routledge, 2000), pp. 71–106; Roger Davidson, "'This Pernicious Delusion': Law, Medicine, and Child Sexual Abuse in Early-Twentieth-Century Scotland," *Journal of the History of Sexuality* 10 (2001): 62–77; Martin Ingram, "Child Sexual Abuse in Early Modern England," in *Negotiating Power in Early Modern Society: Order, Hierarchy and Subordination in Britain and Ireland*, ed. Michael J. Braddick and John Walter (Cambridge: CUP, 2001), pp. 63–84; Georges Vigarello, *A History of Rape: Sexual Violence in France from the 16th to the 20th Century*, trans. Jean Birrell (Cambridge: Polity Press, 2001), pp. 54–57; Stephen Robertson, *Crimes Against Children: Sexual Violence and Legal Culture in New York City, 1880–1960* (Chapel Hill and London: University of North Carolina Press, 2005), pp. 37–55; Sharon Block, *Rape and Sexual Power in Early America* (Chapel Hill and London: University of North Carolina Press, 2006), pp. 106–116; Cathy McClive, "Blood and Expertise: The Trials of the Female

role played by laymen in medico-legal matters. Joanna Carraway Vitiello's case studies reveal how important lay opinion could be to murder investigations in fourteenth-century Reggio Emilia, Wendy Turner shows that the triple test for mental competence (perception, cognition, memory) in medieval England was applied by lay escheators, neighbors and friends of the landholders in question,[6] while the annual rotation of judges in early medieval Frisia and the citizen judges of thirteenth-century Cocentaina remind us of the long history of local administration of the law in Europe.[7]

Whether all the interesting and important aspects of the relationship between medicine and the law can be studied to the same extent for all periods depends of course on primary sources, a consideration not unrelated to the development of modern states, their constituent institutions, and their record-keeping priorities, not to mention the vagaries of record survival. But as the chapters by Harris-Stoertz, Jean Dangler, Donna Trembinski and Máire Johnson show, we need not rely solely on legal or medical archival material to investigate the history of law and medicine, since many of the educated elites who produced the written records of the past did so with a fair degree of knowledge about both fields. Some of course were physicians, like Jaume Roig, whose religious beliefs underpin his understanding of how law and medicine work together in his *Espill* to "transmit information and values to male readers about women, men, and the social order." Others were clerics: manuscripts devoted to the cult of the Virgin Mary, miracle stories and *Lives* of St Francis and the Irish saints reveal the extent to which medical ideas and practices interacted with religious belief and canon law in the medieval world. As with the overtly legal sources that Butler relies upon, these documents too can serve as routes into the personalities of long-dead individuals such as the "wry" hagiographer who related the plight of the embarrassingly paralyzed Irish king in Johnson's chapter, the discomfited St Francis revealed by Trembinki's evaluation of his reaction to the direction that his Order began to take, Dangler's identification of Roig's misogyny as revealed by his use of the term "daughters

Medical Expert in the Ancien-Régime Courtroom," *BHM* 82 (2008): 86–108, pp. 96–100; Lynn Sacco, *Unspeakable: Father-Daughter Incest in American History* (Baltimore: Johns Hopkins University Press, 2009).

6   Compare the plight of Turner's mentally incompetent landholders to a much later but not dissimilar case: Emmeline Garnett, *John Marsden's Will: The Hornby Castle Dispute 1780–1840* (London: Hambledon, 1998).

7   This was perhaps most notable in the German states and England: see John H. Langbein, *Prosecuting Crime in the Renaissance: England, Germany, France* (1974), Clark, NJ: Lawbook Exchange, 2005.

of Eve," and the men who were present in the birthing chamber despite, as Harris-Stoertz notes, the supposed shame attached to such a practice. As she reiterates, learned texts "may have had little relation to actual practice," a truth which lies at the heart of this volume.

So what did influence "actual practice"? In addressing this question, we should consider the broader context in which medicine and law interacted. The prohibition against Christian midwives practicing on Jewish women in Sens is important not only for what it tells us about the professional status of midwives but for its timing: city counselors discussed and decided to legislate against this form of medical practice circa 1212 presumably because it was common enough to be of concern, a fact which provides the historian with at least three important pieces of information. A century later, temporal and geographical contexts were interlinked in Cocentaina when the court scribe Domingo Cepillo returned from Rome to introduce a new way of conducting examinations of injured persons into a border town particularly prone to violence and disorder. The professionalization of medicine that occurred in fifteenth-century Valencia evolved within an Iberian context of growing religious exclusion, supported by *furs* which regulated the city's medical practitioners. As a member of this increasingly exclusive community, Jaume Roig's civic activities and his *Espill* recount the effects of regional developments superimposed on local laws and values.

Local conditions are also the key to understanding the concessions that the government of Reggio Emilia made to its medical personnel: in addition to the more widely understood impact of the inquisitorial system on the introduction of investigatory techniques,[8] we must also consider the specific problems suffered by the city in the wake of the plague years of the mid fourteenth century. The groundwork for the later development of the *Protomedicato* in Bologna was laid during the late fourteenth century, as Kira Robison shows, for reasons specifically related to the needs of the city's government and medical faculty in relation to the papacy, which had been weakened by a schismatic crisis. The experiences of the Portuguese in the fourteenth and fifteenth centuries were similarly transformative, encouraging royal centralizing policies and the expansion of medical licensing. Although the precise reasons for this remain unclear, McCleery concludes that it may be most useful to try to locate the introduction of licensing policy "within the commercial and legal contexts of the towns that implemented it and perhaps saw its effects most." Medical professionalization was also proceeding quickly in fifteenth-century England,

---

8   Catherine Crawford, "Legalizing Medicine: Early Modern Legal Systems and the Growth of Medico-legal Knowledge," in *Legal Medicine in History*, ed. Clark and Crawford, pp. 89–116.

where Nicholas Wodehill's career, and tendency to go to law to advance his
professional aspirations, flourished within a context of idealizing Christian
rhetoric, a competitive London market, and a national penchant for litigation
as measured by the business of the principal common law courts, King's Bench
and Common Pleas.[9] Not only does Sara Butler's research on Wodehill provide us with an exceptional glimpse of the medical services that he offered,
but it suggests that his strategies owed much to the times, and the city, that
he lived in.

The concept of honor revealed by the relationship between medicine and
law speaks to a common cultural context which is explored by Nijdam and
Johnson, who show that Frisian and Irish compensation tariffs were designed
to acknowledge injury to body parts which were both functional and aesthetic,
corporeal and spiritual, external and internal; disfigurement injured a victim's
honor as well as his body.[10] Medical knowledge acted in such cases to support a
legal definition of injury at once physical and symbolic. But the importance of
status within the community was not confined to considerations of honor, as
the chapters throughout this book show that physicians and surgeons actively
sought to enhance their social status, often via legal measures and with the
support of civic authorities in mutual acknowledgment of the association
between professional and social status. In a sort of reversal of this process,
St Francis found himself eased out of his position of leadership because universal canon law and ecclesiastical tradition stipulated that he should appoint
a steward once he became too infirm to carry out his duties. The importance of
sound mental health, and the way in which the law could be used to support,
or undermine, those who did not possess it, offers an additional dimension
to our understanding of the ways in which medicine and law might meet in a
civil arena. The legal state of wardship and the virtual absence of formal medical involvement in matters of health further connect the chapters by Turner
and Trembinski, which offer welcome assessments of portions of medieval law
which did not centre on injury or death.

The fact remains, however, that physical violence lay at the heart of much
of what medieval people recognized as the most obvious and essential meeting point for medicine and law, making the business of the criminal courts

---

9   Christopher W. Brooks, *Lawyers, Litigation and English Society since 1450* (London:
     Hambledon, 1998), pp. 66–67, 75–84. There was a significant increase in the litigation
     conducted in these royal courts during the later fourteenth century, a trend more or less
     maintained until the resumption of civil war in the late 1460s.
10   Lisi Oliver, *The Body Legal in Barbarian Law* (Toronto: University of Toronto Press, 2011),
     pp. 102, 168, 171, 209, 240.

especially fascinating to scholars of legal or forensic medicine, as this form of boundary-crossing "medicine in action" is typically known. The introduction to this book briefly highlights some of the work which followed Guido Ruggiero's landmark study,[11] and several chapters refer explicitly to medico-legal matters, drawing on medical and legal texts and the records of the criminal courts. In doing so, the authors refer to experts, expert witnesses, and expertise. For instance, Nijdam observes that Frisian courts "summoned physicians as experts on various occasions: to establish the cause of death, assist the executioner, or act as an expert witness." Kümper offers a gendered analysis of the limits of the expertise of female practitioners in rape cases. Ferragud and Vitiello focus on the forms and functions that expert testimony took in the Kingdom of Valencia and late medieval Italy: written reports and *consilia* or oral testimony could be sought by judges or defendants in cases of assault or death—before, during or after a trial. In these instances the experts acquired their special status by virtue of their possession of specialist medical knowledge, attested by their education, experience and/or licensing. But what some of these findings also suggest—in common with work carried out on much later periods,[12] is that certain experts were more expert than others; Domenico Sanc being a case in point. While much of the historiography on the pre-modern period adopts a broad-brush approach to the types of medico-legal work undertaken and the range of practitioners who undertook it,[13] detailed study of a single city or region over time can reveal evidence that sheds light on contemporary notions of expertise and how it was acquired—even if, as Ferragud accepts, the acquisition of such status may have derived largely from the fact that there were limited numbers of medical personnel from which to choose.[14]

11   Guido Ruggiero, "The Cooperation of Physicians and the State in the Control of Violence in Renaissance Venice," *JHMAS* 33 (1978): 156–166.

12   Coley, "Alfred Swaine Taylor"; Pastore and Rossi, eds., *Paolo Zacchia*; Katherine D. Watson, "Medical and Chemical Expertise in English Trials for Criminal Poisoning, 1750–1914," *MH* 50 (2006): 373–390.

13   See for instance Alessandro Pastore, *Il medico in tribunale: La perizia medica nella procedura penale d'antico regime (secoli XVI–XVIII)* (Bellinzona: Edizioni Casagrande, 1998) and Joseph Shatzmiller, "The Jurisprudence of the Dead Body: Medical Practition at the Service of Civic and Legal Authorities," *Micrologus* 7 (1999): 223–230.

14   This reinforces a point made by Harris-Stoertz about the ability of a population to support midwives, and the availability of trained midwives. What these two historians suggest is that demographic factors have an impact on processes of medical professionalization. This being the case, quantitative studies of medical provision must be considered a key plank of many research agendas.

Medical expertise was not confined to the courtroom: Robison, McCleery, Dangler, Butler and Harris-Stoertz all deal with professionalization in ways which acknowledge that properly trained and accredited individuals possessed a recognized medical and/or surgical expertise, and that there was a growing standardization of what counted as appropriate qualifications. But although women were undoubtedly far less marginal members of the medieval medical community than it might once have been thought,[15] they appear here in only two roles: as the targets of Roig's distrust, and as midwives or women otherwise skilled in diagnosing the signs of rape. The editors have noted that much more work needs to be done on the role of ordinary women in medieval medicine, while the legal proscriptions against female agency are suggested by the use of marriage as a ruse to steal from mentally incompetent women and by the fact that female Irish saints did not appear to engage in property disputes, reflecting legal limitations placed on a woman's ability to inherit property. The gendered nature of the relationship between medicine and law thus serves as a final connecting theme, offering perhaps the foremost of the many avenues for further research identified by the contributors to this volume.

Criminal justice historians are keen to explore the ways in which socially constructed ideas about women have affected their participation in all stages of the legal process,[16] identifying rape and infanticide as particularly gendered forms of criminal behavior. These offences have also been examined from the perspective of the history of legal medicine;[17] but as Hiram Kümper notes in his

---

15   Lori Woods, "Mainstream or Marginal Medicine: The Case of a Parish Healer Named Gueraula Codines," in *Worth and Repute: Valuing Gender in Late Medieval and Early Modern Europe. Essays in Honour of Barbara Todd*, ed. Kim Kippen and Lori Woods (Toronto: Centre for Reformation and Renaissance Studies, 2011), pp. 93–121.

16   Key works for the British Isles include John Beattie, "The Criminality of Women in Eighteenth-Century England," *Journal of Social History* 8 (1975): 80–116; Barbara A. Hanawalt, *'Of Good and Ill Repute': Gender and Social Control in Medieval England* (Oxford: OUP, 1998); Garthine Walker, *Crime, Gender and Social Order in Early Modern England* (Cambridge: CUP, 2003); Karen Jones, *Gender and Petty Crime in Late Medieval England* (Woodbridge: Boydell, 2006); Anne-Marie Kilday, *Women and Violent Crime in Enlightenment Scotland* (Woodbridge: Boydell, 2007); Katherine D. Watson, "Women, Violent Crime and Criminal Justice in Georgian Wales," *Continuity and Change* 28 (2013): 245–272.

17   For works on the rape of children, see note 5 above. I have been unable to locate works which consider the historical medico-legal aspects of the rape of adult women in depth. There is a larger literature on the forensic aspects of infanticide: Robert Roth, "Juges et médecins face à l'infanticide à Genève au XIXᵉ siècle," *Gesnerus* 34 (1977): 113–128; Mark Jackson, "Suspicious Infant Deaths: the Statute of 1624 and Medical Evidence at Coroners' Inquests," in Clark and Crawford (eds), *Legal Medicine in History*, pp. 64–86; Mary Nagle

chapter, research on medieval rape seems to focus mainly on England, while infanticide in all periods is studied mainly from a socio-legal perspective.[18] Independent medieval women are infrequently visible in historical legal documents, so that the sources that do survive must be tackled creatively from an interdisciplinary perspective.[19] Given the importance of rape and infanticide in history respecting what they tell us about the impact of laymen on legal outcomes, the exercise of medico-legal arguments, social attitudes to women and, relative to rape, extraordinarily enduring anxieties about false allegations, these would seem to be topics worthy of wider international investigation in the medieval and early modern periods—appropriate source materials permitting. Gender history, women's history and crime history can combine to shed new light on the relationship between law and medicine, as a recent article on coerced medical examinations in cases of suspected infanticide shows.[20]

The importance of ordinary people in the practice of medicine dovetails with the role played by women in medicine. For example, female searchers of the dead played a key role in the system of processing and investigating death in early modern London but remained until quite recently largely hidden from view.[21] Like midwives, searchers were licensed, but few of these documents survive—a problem familiar to historians of medieval law and

---

Wessling, "Infanticide Trials and Forensic Medicine: Württemberg, 1757–93," in Clark and Crawford, pp. 117–144; Katherine D. Watson, *Forensic Medicine in Western Society: A History* (Abingdon: Routledge, 2011), pp. 105–111, 127–129; Willemijn Ruberg, "Travelling Knowledge and Forensic Medicine: Infanticide, Body and Mind in the Netherlands, 1811–1911," *MH* 57 (2013): 359–376.

18   The English-language historiography of infanticide is too large to cite here, but for a medieval example see Sara M. Butler, "A Case of Indifference? Child Murder in Later Medieval England," *Journal of Women's History* 19 (2007): 59–82. For later continental studies, see Alfred Soman, "Anatomy of an Infanticide Trial: The Case of Marie-Jeanne Bartonnet (1742)," in *Changing Identities in Early Modern France*, ed. Michael Wolfe (Durham, NC: Duke University Press, 1997), pp. 248–272 and Joanne M. Ferraro, *Nefarious Crimes, Contested Justice: Illicit Sex and Infanticide in the Republic of Venice, 1557–1789* (Baltimore: Johns Hopkins University Press, 2008).

19   P.J.P. Goldberg, "Introduction," in *Medieval Women and the Law*, ed. Noël James Menuge (Woodbridge: Boydell, 2000), pp. *ix–xiii*, on pp. *x–xi*.

20   Daniel J.R. Grey, "'What woman is safe…?': Coerced Medical Examinations, Suspected Infanticide, and the Response of the Women's Movement in Britain, 1871–1881," *Women's History Review* 22 (2013): 403–421.

21   Richelle Munkhoff, "Searchers of the Dead: Authority, Marginality, and the Interpretation of Plague in England, 1574–1665," *Gender and History* 11 (1999): 1–29; Kevin Siena, "Searchers of the Dead in Long Eighteenth-Century London," in *Worth and Repute*, ed. Kippen and Woods, pp. 123–152.

medicine. That does not mean that we cannot ask whether women played a similar role in earlier periods or in other countries, and, if they did, to what extent their duties overlapped with those of midwives, or came under pressure from male members of the medical profession. Legal proceedings are an obvious but not the only place to seek answers to such questions; one might also consider the records generated by, inter alia, poor relief, licensing, bequests, burials, hospitals, family correspondence, or city council minutes. The interdisciplinary methodology that medievalists must often adopt is well suited to such a project.

The comparative elements of the relationship between medicine and law are also in need of further study, both over time for a single location and across geographical regions. McCleery is most explicit about this: it is clear that there were regional distinctions in medical licensing (and thus the development of the medical profession) that should be studied in a European framework. Chapters in this book have done much to reveal the origins and impact of some of these local contexts, raising questions with which future researchers may wish to engage: the significance of demography and border (or indeed peripheral) locations; the effects of the movement of ideas via travelers, or of local customs and rivalries; or the influence of political, occupational and religious identities. The fact that, as Nijdam notes, some regional findings may be constructs related mainly to source survival further emphasizes the utility of comparative studies. Moreover, the religious orthodoxy of much of the medieval population and the vigor with which the church investigated miracle stories suggests that canonization processes may yet reveal more about medicine, law and lay understanding than they have so far tended to do.[22] Whilst the patient or lay perspective should thus be counted a desideratum for future projects, prospective research questions may in part be set by the discovery of new documents and new ways of interrogating, interpreting or comparing existing sources.

If the connection between law and medicine in the Middle Ages has been understudied, the essays in this volume serve as an important step towards rectifying that omission. Notable for their methodological and thematic cohesion, they offer fresh perspectives on matters of shared concern to both disciplines, including the cultivation of professional status, the provenance of expertise

---

22   Robert Bartlett, *The Hanged Man: A Story of Miracle, Memory, and Colonialism in the Middle Ages* (Princeton: Princeton University Press, 2004); Ronald C. Finucane, "The Toddler in the Ditch: A Case of Parental Neglect?," in *Voices from the Bench: The Narratives of Lesser Folk in Medieval Trials*, ed. Michael Goodich (Basingstoke: Palgrave, 2006), pp. 127–148. Neither considers the medical aspects of the witness testimony in detail.

and authority, the relationship between theory and practice, and the ways in which gender distinctions underscore these issues. In crossing disciplinary boundaries and defying historical periodization, the conclusions, questions and problems raised here provide a foundation on which to take forward the study of the "complex influences of law on medicine and medicine on law," and thus to further our understanding of how these two fields have come to hold such dominant positions in the modern western world.

Works Cited

Printed Primary

Akehurst, F.R.P., ed. *The Coutumes de Beauvaisis of Philippe de Beaumanoir*. Philadelphia: University of Pennsylvania Press, 1992.

Aldebrandin de Sienne. *Le Régime du Corps*. Ed. Louis Landouzy and Rober Pépin. Paris: Honoré Champion, 1911.

Almeida, Manuel Lopes de, Idalino Ferreira da Costa Brochado and António Joaquim Dias Dinis, eds. *Monumenta Henricina*, 14 vols. Coimbra: Executiva das Comemorações do V Centenário da Morte do Infante Dom Henrique, 1960–74.

Analecta Franciscana I. Ed. Patres Collegii S. Bonaventurae. Quarrachi: Typographia Collegii S. Bonaventurae, 1885.

Azevedo, Pedro de, ed. *Documentos das Chancelarias Reais Anteriores a 1531 Relativos a Marrocos*, 2 vols. Lisbon: Academia das Ciências, 1915–34.

Barnes, Jonathan, ed. *The Complete Works of Aristotle*, v. 1. Princeton: Princeton University Press, 1984.

Bartholomaeus Anglicus. *On the Properties of Things: John Trevisa's Translation of Bartholomaeus Anglicus De Proprietatibus Rerum, a Critical Text*. Oxford: Clarendon Press, 1975.

Bartlett, Robert, ed. and trans. *Miracles of Saint Aebbe of Coldingham and Saint Margaret of Scotland*. Oxford: Clarendon Press, 2003.

Basto, Artur de Magalhães, ed. *Vereações: Anos de 1390–1395*. Oporto: Câmara Municipal, 1937.

Bateson, Mary, ed. *Borough Customs*. Selden Society, vols. 18 and 21, 1904–6.

Bieler, Ludwig, ed. *Four Latin Lives of St Patrick: Colgan's* Vita Secunda, Quarta, Tertia, *and* Quinta. Dublin: DIAS, 1971.

———, ed. and trans. *The Irish Penitentials*. Dublin: DIAS, 1975.

———, ed. and trans. *The Patrician Texts in the Book of Armagh*. Dublin: DIAS, 1979.

Biggs, Frederick M., ed. *Sources of Anglo-Saxon Literary Culture: The Apocrypha*. Instrumenta Anglistica Mediaevalia 1. Kalamazoo: Medieval Institute Publications, 2007.

Bihl, M., ed. "Statua generalia ordinis edita in capitulis generalibus celebratis Narbonae an 1260, Assisii an. 1279 atque Parisiis ad. 1292." *Archivum franciscanum historicum* 36 (1941): 13–94 and 284–358, 338–339.

Binchy, D.A., ed. and trans. *"Bretha Crólige." Ériu* 12 (1938): 1–77.

———, ed. and trans. *"Bretha Déin Chécht." Ériu* 20 (1966): 1–66.

———, ed. *Críth Gablach*. Dublin: DIAS, 1970.

———, ed. and trans. "A Text on the Forms of Distraint." *Celtica* 10 (1973): 72–86.

————, ed. *Di Cetharslicht Athgabála* 365.5–367.7. *Corpus Iuris Hibernici*. Dublin: DIAS, 1978.

Bohn, Johannes. *De officio medici duplici clinici nimirum ac forensis*, 3rd ed. Leipzig: J.F. Gleditsch, 1704.

Braidi, Valeria, ed. *Gli statuti del Comune di Bologna degli anni 1352, 1357; 1376, 1389 (Libri I–III)*, 2 vols. Bologna: Deputazione di storia patria per la province di Romagna, 2002.

Breatnach, Liam, ed. and trans. "The First Third of the *Bretha Nemed Toísech*." *Ériu* 40 (1989): 1–40.

Brown, William, ed. *Yorkshire Inquisitions of the Reigns of Henry III and Edward I*. Yorkshire Archaeological and Topographical Association Record Series, vols. XII, XXIII, XXXI, XXXVII. York: J. Whitehead & Son, 1892–1906.

Buma, Wybren Jan, and Wilhelm Ebel, eds. *Westerlauwerssches Recht I. Jus Municipale Frisonum*. Altfriesische Rechtsquellen 6. 2 Vols. Göttingen: Vandenhoeck & Ruprecht, 1977.

————, eds. *Das Hunsingoer Recht*. Altfriesische Rechtsquellen 4. Göttingen: Vandenhoeck & Ruprecht, 1969.

————, eds. *Das Emsiger Recht*. Altfriesische Rechtsquellen 3. Göttingen: Vandenhoeck & Ruprecht, 1967.

————, eds. *Das Brokmer Recht*. Altfriesische Rechtsquellen 2. Göttingen: Vandenhoeck & Ruprecht, 1965.

————, eds. *Das Rüstringer Recht*. Altfriesische Rechtsquellen 1. Göttingen: Vandenhoeck & Ruprecht, 1963.

Burns, Robert I., and Samuel Parsons Scott, eds. *Las Siete Partidas*, v. 5. Philadelphia: University of Pennsylvania Press, 2001.

Buschmann, Arno. *Textbuch zur Strafrechtsgeschichte der Neuzeit: die klassischen Gesetze*. Munich: C.H. Beck, 1998.

Byrne, F.J. and Pádraig Francis, ed. and trans. "Two Lives of Saint Patrick: *Vita Secunda* and *Vita Quarta*." *JRSAI* 124 (1994): 5–117.

Cabanes, María D., ed. *Documentos de Jaime I de Aragón. 1258–1262*. Saragossa: Anúbar, 1982.

Calendar of Inquisitions Miscellaneous (Chancery), Henry III-Henry V. PRO, 7 vols. London: HMSO, 1916–1968.

Calendar of Inquisitions Post Mortem and other Analogous Documents Preserved in the Public Record Office. PRO, 20 vols. London: HMSO, 1904–1970.

Calendar of the Close Rolls Preserved in the Public Record Office, 1227–1485. PRO, 45 vols. London: HMSO, 1892–1954.

Calendar of the Fine Rolls. PRO, 22 vols. London: HMSO, 1911–62.

Calendar of the Patent Rolls, Preserved in the Public Record Office, 1216–1509. PRO, 52 vols. London: HMSO, 1907.

Cenci, C., and R.G. Maillaux, eds. "Constitutiones generalis ordinis fratrum minorum."
    Analecta Franciscana 13 (2007), n. s. 1: 69–104.

Chancelria de D. Afonso V. Lisbon: Direcção-Geral de Arquivos, 2008. http://digitarq.
    dgarq.gov.pt/details?id=3815943. Accessed February 15, 2013.

Charles-Edwards, Thomas, and Fergus Kelly, eds. and trans. *Bechbretha*. Dublin: DIAS,
    1983.

*Chartularium di Studia Bononiensis, Documenti per la storia dell'Università di Bologna
    dalla origine fino al secolo XV*, 11 vols. Bologna: Instituto per la storia dell'Università
    di Bologna, 1909–1940

Clanchy, M.T., ed. *The Roll and Writ File of the Berkshire Eyre of 1248*. Selden Society v. 90,
    1973.

Collins, Francis, ed. *Register of the Freemen of the City of York*. Surtees Society, v. 96,
    1897.

Colón, Germà, and Arcadi Garcia, eds. *Furs de València*. Barcelona: Barcino, 1983.

Costa, António Domingues de Sousa, ed. *Monumenta Portugaliae Vaticana*. 4 vols.
    Rome: Livraria Editorial Franciscana, 1968–78.

Costa, José Pereira, ed. *Vereações da Câmara Municipal do Funchal*, 3 vols. Funchal:
    Secretaria Regional de Turismo e Cultura; Centro de estudos de história do Atlântico,
    1995–2002.

da Saliceto, Guglielmo. *The Surgery of William of Saliceto: Written in* 1275. Trans. Leonard
    D. Rosenman. Philadelphia: Xlibris, 2002.

Dalby, Andrew, ed. *The Treatise: Le Tretiz of Walter of Bibbesworth*. Blackawton: Prospect
    Books, 2012.

Dias, João Alves, ed. *Portugal do Renacimento à Crise Dinástica*, Nova História de
    Portugal 5. Lisbon: Editorial Presença, 1998.

Dobozy, Maria, ed. *The Saxon Mirror: A "Sachsenspiegel" of the Fourteenth Century*.
    Philadelphia: University of Pennsylvania Press, 1999.

Eckhardt, Karl August, ed. *Die Gesetze des Karolingerreiches 714–911, vol. 2: Alemannen
    und Bayern*. Weimar: Böhlau, 1934.

Eckhardt, Karl August, and A. Eckhardt, eds. "Lex Frisionum." *Monumenta Germaniae
    Historica. Fontes iuris Germanici antiqui in usum scholarum separatim editi*, v. 12.
    Hannover, 1982.

Edius Stephanus. *The Life of Bishop Wilfred*. Ed. Bertram Colgrave. Cambridge: CUP, 1927.

Eudes of Rouen. *The Register of Eudes of Rouen*. Trans. Sydney M. Brown. Ed. Jeremiah F.
    O'Sullivan. New York and London: Columbia University Press, 1964.

Färber, Beatrix and J.G. O'Keeffe, ed. and trans. *Buile Shuibne (The Frenzy of Suibne)*.
    Cork: University College, 2001. CELT Edition http://www.ucc.ie/celt.

Felix. *Life of Saint Guthlac*. Ed. Bertram Colgrave. Cambridge: CUP, 1956.

Ferreira, João Albino Pinto, ed. *Vereaçoens, Anos de 1401–49: o Segundo Livro de Vereações
    do Municipio do Porto Existente no seu Arquivo*. Oporto: Câmara Muncipal and
    Gabinete de História da Cidade, 1980.

Fitzherbert, Anthony. *The New Natura Brevium*. London: W. Lee, M. Walbank, D. Pakeman, and G. Bedell, 1652.

Francis of Assisi. *Early Documents*. Trans. Regis J. Armstrong, J.A. Wayne Hellmann, and William J. Short. 3 vols. Hyde Park, NY: New City Press, 1999–2001.

Friedberg, Emil, ed. *Corpus iuris canonici*. Leipzig: Bernhard Tauchnitz, 1839.

Getz, Faye Marie, ed. *Healing and Society in Medieval England: a Middle English Translation of the Pharmaceutical Writings of Gilbertus Anglicus*. Madison, WI: University of Wisconsin Press, 1991.

Gijsel, Jan, ed. *Libri de Nativitate Mariae: Pseudo-Matthaei Evangelium*. Corpus Christianorum Series Apocryphorum 9. Turnhout: Brepols, 1997.

Given-Wilson, Chris, *et al.*, eds. *Parliamentary Rolls of Medieval England*. London: Scholarly Digital Edition, 2005.

Goerlitz, Theodor, ed. *Magdeburger Schöffensprüche für die Hansestadt Posen und andere Städte des Warthelandes*. Stuttgart and Berlin: Kohlhammer, 1944.

Gratian, *Decretum*. Ed. A.L. Richter. Graz: Verlagsanstalt, 1959.

Green, Monica H., ed. and trans. *The Trotula: A Medieval Compendium of Women's Medicine*. Philadelphia: University of Pennsylvania Press, 2001.

Gregory the Great. *The Letters of Gregory the Great*. Trans. John R.C. Martyn. 3 vols. Toronto: Pontifical Institute of Mediaeval Studies, 2004.

Guibert of Nogent. *Histoire de sa vie (1053–1124)*. Ed. Georges Bourgin. Paris: Alphonse Picard et fils, 1907.

Hale, Matthew. *History of the Pleas of the Crown*. London: A. Strahan, 1763.

Hall, George D.G., ed. *Ranulf of Glanvill, The Treatise on the Laws and Customs of the Realm of England commonly called Glanvill*. London: Clarendon, 1965.

Halliwell, James Orchard, ed. *The Chronicle of William de Rishanger of the Barons' War; The Miracles of Simon de Montfort*. Camden, o.s. v. 15. New York: Johnson Reprint Corporation, 1968, orig. 1860.

Hariulf Aldenburgensi. *Vita S. Arnulfi Confessoris*. AASS Boll. August, tome 3 (v. 37). Pp. 230–59.

Heist, W.W., ed. *Vitae Sanctorum Hiberniae ex Codice olim Salmanticensi nunc Bruxellensi*. Brussels: Society of Bollandists, 1965.

Hemingway, Samuel B., ed. *English Nativity Plays*. New York: Russell and Russell, 1964.

Herbert, Máire, ed. and trans. "The Irish *Life* of Colum Chille." *Iona, Kells and Derry: The History and Hagiography of the Monastic* Familia *of Columba*. Oxford: Clarendon Press, 1988. Pp. 180–287.

Herold, Johannes, ed. *Originum ac Germanicarum Antiquitatum libri*. Basel: Henricus Petri, 1557.

Heuckenkamp, Ferdinand, ed. *Le Chevalier du Papegau*. Halle: Max Niemeyer, 1896.

Homeyer, Carl Gustav, ed. *Des Sachsenspiegels erster Theil oder das Landrecht*. 3rd ed. Berlin: Dümmler, 1863.

Hrotswitha. *Historia Nativitatis Laudabilisque Conversationis Intactae Dei Genitricis Quam Scriptam Reperi Sub Nomine Sancti Jacobi Fratris Domini*. Ed. J.P. Migne. *Patrologia Latina*, v. 137. http://www.documentachatolicaomnia.eu/04z/z_0930–1002_Hrorshitha_Gandersheimensis_Historia_Nativitatis_Sub_Nomine_Jacobo_Fratris_Domini_MLT.pdf.html. Accessed Sept. 4, 2013.

————. *Historia Nativitatis*. In *Hrotsvithae Opera*. Ed. Paulus de Winterfeld. Monumenta Germania Scriptores rerum Germanicarum in usum scholarum separatism editi (ss rer. Germ.), v. 34, pp. 5–20.

Hunt, Tony. *Popular Medicine in Thirteenth-Century England: Introduction and Texts*. Cambridge: D.S. Brewer, 1990.

Jacobus de Voragine. *Legenda Aurea: Vulgo historia Lombardica dicta*. Ed. Thomas Graesse. Dresden and Leipzig: Libraria Arnoldiana, 1846.

Jansen, H.P.H., and Antheun Janse, eds. *Kroniek van het klooster Bloemhof te Wittewierum*. Hilversum: Verloren, 1991.

John of Joinville. "Life of Saint Louis." In *Joinville and Villehardouin: Chronicles of the Crusades*. Trans. Caroline Smith. London: Penguin, 2008. Pp. 137–336.

Johnston, Thomas S.B., ed. *Codex Hummercensis. Groningen, UB, PEIP 12. An Old Frisian Legal Manuscript in Low Saxon Guise*. Leeuwarden: Fryske Akademy, 1998.

Jordan of Giano. "Chronica." Ed. Patres Collegii S. Bonaventurae. *Analecta Franciscana* 1 (1885): 1–20.

Jordan of Giano *et al. Thirteenth Century Chronicles*. Trans. P. Hermann. Chicago: Franciscan Herald Press, 1961.

Kirby, Peter, ed. "Infancy Gospel of James." *Early Christian Writings*. (2001–2013). http://www.earlychristianwritings.com/infancyjames.html. Accessed Sept. 4, 2013.

Kisch, Guido, ed. *Leipziger Schöffenspruchsammlung*. Leipzig: Hirtzel, 1919.

Kölbing, Eugen, ed. *Romance of Beues of Hamtoun*. Early English Text Society, v. 46. London: Kegan Paul, Trench, Trübner & Co., 1885.

Lapa, Manuel Rodrigues, ed. *Cantigas de Escarnho e de Mal Dizer dos Cancioneiros Medievais Galego-Portugueses*. Lisbon: Galáxia, 1965.

Lopes, Fernão. *Crónica de D. Pedro*. Ed. Giuliano Macchi and Teresa Amado. 2nd ed. Lisbon: Imprensa Nacional/Casa da Moeda, 2007.

Luders, A., T.E. Tomlins, J. France, W.E. Taunton and J. Raithby, eds. *Statutes of the Realm*. London: Dawsons of Pall Mall, repr. 1963.

Mac Airt, Seán and Gearóid Mac Niocaill, eds. and trans. *The Annals of Ulster (to AD 1131)*. Dublin: DIAS, 1983.

MacNeill, Eóin, ed. and trans. "Ancient Irish Law: The Law of Status or Franchise." *Proceedings of the Royal Irish Academy* 36C (1923): 265–315.

Mac Niocaill, Gearóid and William M. Hennessy, eds. and trans. *Chronicon Scotorum*. Cork: Corpus of Electronic Texts, 2003. CELT Edition. http://www.ucc.ie/celt.

Malagola, Carlo, ed. *De pena doctorum non obedientium Rectori*, in *Statuti delle Università e dei collegi dello studio bolognese*. Bologna: N. Zanichelli, 1888.

Mannyng, Robert of Brunne. *Handlyng Synne*. Ed. Idelle Sullens. Binghamton: Medieval & Renaissance Texts & Studies, 1983.

Marie de France. *The Lais of Marie de France*. Trans. Robert Hanning and Joan Ferrante. Durham, NC: The Labyrinth Press, 1978; repr. 1982.

Márkus, Gilbert, ed. and trans. *Adomnán's* Law of the Innocents—Cáin Adomnáin*: A Seventh-Century Law for the Protection of Noncombatants*. Kilmartin: Kilmartin House Museum, 2008.

Marques, António Henrique de Oliveira, ed. *Chancelarias Portuguesas: D. Afonso IV*, 3 vols. Lisbon: Instituto Nacional de Investigação Científica and Centro de Estudos Históricos da Universidade Nova, 1990–2.

Marques, José, ed. "A administração municipal de Vila do Conde em 1466." *Bracara Augusta* 37 (1983): 5–116.

Menesto, E. and S. Brufani, eds. *Fontes Franciscani*. Assisi: Editizioni Porziuncula, 2005.

Meyer, Herbert, ed. *Das Mühlhäuser Reichsrechtsbuch aus dem Anfang des 13. Jahrhunderts, Deutschlands ältestes Rechtsbuch: Nach den altmitteldeutschen Handschriften herausgegeben, eingeleitet und übersetzt*. 3rd ed. Weimar: Böhlau, 1936.

Meyer, Kuno, ed. and trans. *Betha Colmáin maic Lúacháin: The Life of Colmán Son of Lúachán*. Dublin: Hodges & Figgis, 1911.

Migne, J.P., ed. *Patrologia Latina*. 221 vols. Paris: Garnier fratres, 1866–1882.

Miracula S. Vulfranni Episcopi. AASS Boll., March, tome 3, pp. 149–65.

Mommsen, Theodor, *et al.*, eds. *Corpus Iuris Civilis*. Berlin: Weidmanns, 1877.

Mulchrone, Kathleen, ed. *Bethu Phátraic: The Tripartite Life of Patrick, Text and Sources*. Dublin: Hodges Figgis & Co., 1939.

Muscio. "Gynaecia." In *Sorani Gynaeciorum vetus translatio Latina*. Ed. Valentin Rose. Leipzig: Teubner, 1882. Pp. 3–128.

Neckam, Alexander. *De Naturis Rerum*. Ed. Thomas Wright. Rolls Series, v. 34. London: Longman, Green, Longman, Roberts, and Green, 1863.

Nelson, Janet L., trans. *The Annals of St Bertin*. Manchester and New York: Manchester University Press, 1991.

Ó hAodha, Donncha, ed. and trans. *Bethu Brigte*. Dublin: DIAS, 1978. CELT Edition. http://www.ucc.ie/celt.

Paris, Gaston and Jacob Ulrich, eds. *Merlin: Roman en prose du XIIIe siècle*. Paris: Librairie de Firmin Didot et Cie, 1886.

Pierre de Fontaines. *Le Conseil de Pierre de Fontaines, ou Traité de l'ancienne jurisprudence Française*. Ed. M.A.J. Marnier. Paris: Joubert and Durand, 1846.

Plummer, Charles, ed. *Vita Sanctorum Hiberniae*. 2 vols. Dublin: Four Courts Press, 1997.

Plummer, Charles, ed. and trans. *Bethada Naem nÉrenn: Lives of Irish Saints*. 2 vols. Oxford: The Clarendon Press, 1997.

———. *Miscellanea Hagiographica Hibernica*. Brussels: Society of Bollandists, 1925.

Power, D'Arcy, ed. *The Lesser Writings of John Arderne*. London: Henry Frowde, 1913.

———. *Treatises of Fistula in Ano, Haemorrhoids, and Clysters by John Arderne*. London: Paul, Trench, Trübner, 1910.

Quinn, Ester C., ed. and trans. *The Penitence of Adam: A Study of the Andrius Ms.* Mississippi: University of Mississippi, 1980.

Radbertus, Paschasius. *De partu uirginis*. Ed. E. Ann Matter. Corpus Christianorum Continuatio Mediaevalis, v. 56. Turnhout: Brepols, 1985.

Raine, James. ed. *Testamenta Eboracensia, or Wills Registered at York*. Surtees Society, v. 30, 1885.

Raymond of Peñafort. *Decretalium gregorii*, in *Decretalium collectiones*. Ed. A.L. Richter. Graz: Universum Verlagsanstalt, 1959.

Rio, Alice, ed. *The Formularies of Angers and Marculf. Two Merovingian Legal Handbooks*. Liverpool: University of Liverpool Press, 2008.

Robert of Brunne. *Handlyng Synne, A.D. 1303, with those parts of the Anglo-French Treatise on which it was founded*. Ed. Frederick J. Furnivall. Early English Text Society, v. 119. London: Kegan Paul, Trench, Trübner, and Co., Ltd., 1901.

Robertson, James Craigie, ed. *Materials for the History of Thomas Becket*. 7 vols. Rolls Series, v. 67. London: Longman & Co., 1875–85.

Roche-Mahdi, Sarah, ed. and trans. *Silence: A Thirteenth-Century French Romance*. East Lansing, MI: Colleagues Press, 1992.

Roger de Hoveden. *Chronica*. Ed. William Stubbs. 4 vols. London: HMSO, 1868–71.

Roig, Jaume. The Mirror *of Jaume Roig: An Edition and an English Translation of MS. Vat. Lat. 4806*. Ed. and trans. María Celeste Delgado-Librero. Tempe: Arizona Center for Medieval and Renaissance Studies, 2010.

———. *Espill*. Ed. Antònia Carré. Barcelona: Quaderns Crema, 2006.

Ronca, Italo, ed. William of Conches, *Dragmaticon Philosophiae* (*Corpus Christianorum Continuatio Mediaevalis 152*). Turnhout: Brepols, 1997.

Ronca, Italo, and Matthew Curr, eds. William of Conches, *A Dialogue of Natural Philosophy* (*Dragmaticon Philosophiae*). Notre Dame, IN: University of Notre Dame Press, 1997.

Sá, Artur Moreira de., ed. *Chartularium Universitatis Portugalensis* (*1288–1537:* Lisbon: Centro de Estudos de Psicologia e de História da Filosofia anexo à Faculdade de Letras da Universidade de Lisboa, 1966.

Salgado, Abílio José, and Anastásia Mestrinho Salgado, eds. *Regimento do Hospital de Todos-os-Santos* (*Edição Fac-Similada*). Lisbon: Comissão Organizadora do V Centenário da Fundação do Hospital de Todos-os-Santos, 1992.

Salmon, Amédée M., ed. *Coutumes de Beauvaisis: Texte critique publié avec une introduction, un glossaire et une table analytique*, v. 1. Paris: A. Picard et fils, 1899.

Salterini, Claudia, ed. *L'Archivio dei Riformatori dello Studio: inventario.* Bologna: Presso l'instituto per la storia dell'Università, 1997.

Sayles, G.O. ed. *Selected Cases in the Court of King's Bench, Edward I.* Selden Society, v. 55, 1936.

Sbaralea, H., ed. *Bullarium franciscanum romanorum pontificium constitutiones, epistolas ac diplomata continens tribus Ordinibus minorum.* Rome: Typis Sacrae Congregationis de Propaganda Fide, 1759.

Shatzmiller, Joseph, ed. *Médecine et Justice en Provence Médiévale. Documents de Manosque, 1262–1348.* Aix-en-Provence: Publications de l'Université de Provence, 1989.

Skaife, Robert H. ed. *The Register of the Guild of Corpus Christi in the City of York.* Surtees Society, v. 62, 1872.

Skinner, Patricia and Elisabeth van Houts, trans. *Medieval Writings on Secular Women.* London: Penguin, 2011.

Solomon, Michael, ed. *The Mirror of Coitus: A Translation and Edition of the Fifteenth-Century* Speculum al foderi. Madison, WI: Hispanic Seminary of Medieval Studies, 1990.

Sorbelli, Albano, ed. *Chronica Gestorum ac factorum memorabilium civitatis Bononie.* Rerum Italicarum Scriptores. Città di Castello: Tipi della casa editrice S. Lapi, 1921.

———, ed. *Corpus chronicorum bononiensium,* 3 vols. Rerum Italicarum Scriptores. Città di Castello: Tipi della casa editrice S. Lapi, 1906–1924.

Stadler, Hermann, ed. *Albertus Magnus. De animalibus lbri XXVI: nach der Cölner Urschrift,* v. 2. Münster: Aschendorff, 1920.

Stokes, Whitley, ed. *The Tripartite Life of Patrick, with Other Documents Relating to that Saint Part I.* Stuttgart: Kraus Reprints, 1965.

———, ed. "Life of S. Féchín of Fore." *Revue Celtique* 12 (1891): 318–53.

———, ed. and trans. *Lives of the Saints from the Book of Lismore.* Oxford: Clarendon Press, 1890.

Strachey, J., ed. *Rotuli Parliamentorum, 1278–1503.* 6 vols. London: 1783–1832.

Stürner, Wolfgang, ed. *Monumenta Germaniae Historica: Constitutiones et acta publica imperatorum et regum…, Supplementum: Die Konstitutionen Friedrichs II. für das Königreich Sizilien.* Hannover: Hahn'sche Buchhandlung, 1996.

Tardif, Ernest-Joseph, ed. *Coutumiers de Normandie,* v. 1. Rouen: Espérance Cagniard, 1881.

Thomas de Cantimpre. *Liber de natura rerum.* Ed. H. Boase. Berlin and New York: Walter de Gruyter, 1973.

Thomas, S.E., and J.H. Baker, eds. *Readings and Moots at the Inns of Court in the Fifteenth Century,* v. 2. Selden Society, v. 105, 1989.

Thurneysen, Rudolf, ed. and trans. "Das Fasten beim Pfändungsverfahren." *Zeitschrift für Celtische Philologie* 15 (1925): 260–275.

Twemlow, J.A., *et al.* eds. *Calendar of Papal Registers Relating to Great Britain and Ireland.* 13 vols. London: HMSO, 1915.

Wallis, Faith, ed. *Medieval Medicine: A Reader.* Toronto: University of Toronto Press, 2010.

Walter de Bibbesworth. *Le Tretiz.* Ed. William Rothwell. Aberystwyth: The Anglo-Norman Online Hub, 200. http://www.anglo-norman.net/texts/bibb-gt.pdf. Accessed Sept. 3, 2013.

Wasserschleben, Hermann, ed. *Die Irische Kanonensammlung.* Aalen: Scientia Verlag, 1966.

Woodbine, George E. and Samuel E. Thorne, eds. *Bracton on the Laws and Customs of England.* 4 vols. Cambridge, MA: Belknap Press, 1968.

Wright, T. *A Volume of Vocabularies, A Library of National Antiquities.* Liverpool: Joseph Mayer, 1882.

Zacchia, Paulus. *Quaestiones medico-legales . . . Editio tertia, correctior, auctiorque, non solum variis passim locis, verum & subjunctis, quae nun recens prodeunt.* Amsterdam: Joannis Piot, 1651.

Secondary Sources

Ackerknecht, Erwin H. "Midwives as Experts in Court." *Bulletin of the New York Academy of Medicine* 52.10 (1976): 1224–28.

Ady, Cecilia M. *The Bentivoglio of Bologna: a Study in Despotism.* Oxford: OUP, 1937.

Agrimi, Jole, and Chiara Crisciani. *Les 'Consilia' Médicaux.* Trans. Caroline Viola. Turnhout: Brepols, 1994.

———. *"Medici e "vetulae" dal Duecento al Quattrocento: problemi di una ricerca."* In *Cultura popolare e cultura dotta nel Seicento.* Ed. Paolo Rossi. Milan: Franco Angeli, 1983. Pp. 144–59.

———. "The Science and Practice of Medicine in the Thirteenth Century According to Guglielmo da Saliceto, Italian Surgeon." In *Practical Medicine from Salerno to the Black Death.* Ed. Luis García Ballester, *et al.* Cambridge: CUP, 1994. Pp. 60–87.

Amundsen, Darrel W. "Medieval Canon Law on Medical and Surgical Practice by the Clergy." *BHM* 52 (1978): 22–44.

Anderson, Benedict. *Imagined Communities: Reflections on the Origin and Spread of Nationalism.* London: Verso, 2006.

Appadurai, Arjun. "Deep Democracy: Urban Governmentality and the Horizon of Politics." *Public Culture* 14 (2002): 21–47.

Arbesmann, R. "The Concept of 'Christus Medicus' in St Augustine." *Traditio* 10 (1954): 1–28.

Arrizabalaga, Jon. "The World of Iberian *converso* Practitioners, from Lluís Alcanyís to Isaac Cardoso." In *Beyond the Black Legend: Spain and the Scientific Revolution.*

Ed. V. Navarro Brotóns and W. Eamon. Valencia: Instituto de Historia de la Cienscia Y Documentacíon, 2007. Pp. 307–22.

Ascheri, Mario. "'*Consilium sapientis*,' perizia medica e '*res iudicata*': Diritto dei '*dottori*' e istituzioni comunali." In *Proceedings of the Fifth International Congress of Medieval Canon law. Monumenta Iuris Canonici*, ser. C, v. 6. Ed. Stephen Kuttner and Kenneth Pennington. Vatican City: Biblioteca Apostolica Vaticana, 1980. Pp. 533–579.

Azevedo, Pedro de. "Físicos e cirurgiões do tempo de D. Afonso IV." *Arquivos de História da Medicina Portuguesa*, n.s. 3 (1912): 3–11.

Baader, G. "die Bibliothek des Giovanni di Marco da Rimini. Eine Quelle der med-izinischen Bildung im Humanismus." *Studia codicologica* 124 (1977): 43–97.

Bagwell, Charles E. "Respectful Image." *Annals of Surgery* 241.6 (2005): 872–78.

Bailey, Michael D. *Magic and Superstition in Europe: a Concise History from Antiquity to the Present*. Lanham, MI: Rowman & Littfield, 2007.

Baldwin, David. "The Concept of Security." *Review of International Studies* 23 (1997): 2–26.

Bartlett, Robert. *The Hanged Man: A Story of Miracle, Memory, and Colonialism in the Middle Ages*. Princeton: Princeton University Press, 2004.

Beattie, John. "The Criminality of Women in Eighteenth-Century England." *Journal of Social History* 8 (1975): 80–116.

Bertomeu-Sánchez, José Ramón, and Agustí Nieto-Galan, eds. *Chemistry, Medicine and Crime: Mateu J.B. Orfila (1787–1853) and His Times*. Sagamore Beach, MA: Science History Publications, 2006.

Bedell, John. "Memory and Proof of Age in England 1272–1327." *Past and Present* 162 (1999): 3–27.

Bell, H.E. *An Introduction to the History and Records of the Court of Wards and Liveries*. Cambridge: CUP, 1953.

Benedek, Thomas G. "The Changing Relationship between Midwives and Physicians during the Renaissance." *BHM* 51 (1977): 550–64

Biggar, Raymond G. Review of Robert Mannyng of Brunne, *Handlyng Synne*, ed. Idelle Sullens. *Speculum* 62.4 (1987): 969–73.

Biller, Peter. *The Measure of Multitude: Population in Medieval Thought*. Oxford: OUP, 2000.

———. "Childbirth in the Middle Ages." *History Today* 36 (Aug., 1986): 42–49.

Binchy, D.A. "Distraint in Irish Law." *Celtica* 10 (1973): 22–71.

Bitel, Lisa. *Women in Early Medieval Europe, 400–1100*. Cambridge: CUP, 2002.

Blanshei, Sarah Rubin. *Politics and Justice in Late Medieval Bologna*. Leiden: Brill, 2010.

———. "Criminal Justice in Medieval Perugia and Bologna." *L&HR* 1:2 (1983): 251–75.

Block, Sharon. *Rape and Sexual Power in Early America*. Chapel Hill and London: University of North Carolina Press, 2006.

Blumenfeld-Kosinski, Renate. "Gautier de Coinci and Medieval Childbirth Miracles." In *Gautier de Coinci: Miracles, Music, and Manuscripts*. Ed. Kathy M. Krause and Alison Stones. Turnhout: Brepols, 2006. Pp. 197–214.

———. *Not of Women Born: Representations of Caesarean Birth in Medieval and Renaissance Culture*. Ithaca and London: Cornell University Press, 1990.

Boase, Roger. *The Troubadour Revival: A Study of Social Change and Traditionalism in Late Medieval Spain*. London and Boston: Routledge and Kegan Paul, 1978.

Boehm, Christopher. "The Natural History of Blood Revenge." In *Feud in Medieval and Early Modern Europe*. Ed. Jeppe Büchert Netterström and Birte Poulsen. Aarhus: Orhus University Press, 2007. Pp. 189–203.

Bonnet-Cahilhac, Christine. "Si l'enfant se trouve dans une présentation contre nature, que doit faire la sage-femme?" In *Naissance et petite enfance dans l'Antiquité*. Ed. Véronique Dasen. Fribourg: Academic Press, 2004. Pp. 199–208.

Botta, Fabio. *"Per vim inferre": Studi su stuprum violento e raptus nel diritto romano e bizantino*. Cagliari: Edizioni AV, 2004.

Branco, Maria João. "A procissão na cidade: reflexões em torno da festa do Corpo de Deus na Idade Média." In *A Cidade: Jornadas Inter e Pluridisciplinares, Actas*. Ed. Maria José Pimenta Ferro Tavares. 2 vols. Lisbon: Universidade Aberta, 1993.

Breatnach, Liam. "Canon Law and Secular Law in Early Ireland: The Significance of *Bretha Nemed*." *Peritia* 3 (1984): 439–59.

Bremmer, Rolf H. *Hir is eskriven. Lezen en schrijven in de Friese landen rond 1300*. Hilversum: Uitgeverij Verloren, 2004.

Brittain, Robert Peter. "Origins of Legal Medicine: The Origin of Legal Medicine in France." *Medico-Legal Journal* 34 (1966): 168–74.

Brooke, Rosalind. *Early Franciscan Government: Elias to Bonaventure*. Cambridge: CUP 1959.

Brooks, Christopher W. *Lawyers, Litigation and English Society since 1450*. London: Hambledon, 1998.

Brownmiller, Susan. *Against Our Will: Men, Women, and Rape*. New York: Simon and Schuster, 1975.

Brundage, James A. *Law, Sex, and Christian Society in Medieval Europe*. Chicago: Chicago University Press, 1987.

Buckingham, Jane. "Patient Welfare vs. the Health of the Nation: Governmentality and Sterilisation of Leprosy Sufferers in Early Post-colonial India." *SHM* 19 (2006): 483–99.

Bullough, Vern. *The Development of Medicine as a Profession: the Contribution of the Medieval University to Modern Medicine*. New York: Hafner Publishing Company, 1966.

Burnham, John C. *How the Idea of Profession Changed the Writing of Medical History*. London: Wellcome Institute for the History of Medicine, 1998.

Burns, Chester R., ed. *Legacies in Law and Medicine*. New York: Science History Publications, 1977.

Burr, David. *The Spiritual Franciscans: From Protest to Persecution in the Century After Saint Francis*. Philadelphia: University of Pennsylvania Press, 2001.

Butler, Sara M. "A Case of Indifference? Child Murder in Later Medieval England." *Journal of Women's History* 19 (2007): 59–82.

———. "The Law as a Weapon in Marital Disputes: Evidence from the Late Medieval Court of Chancery, 1424–1529." *Journal of British Studies* 43.3 (2004): 291–316.

Bynum, Caroline Walker. ". . . And Woman his Humanity: Female Imagery in the Religious Writing of the Later Middle Ages." In *Fragmentation and Redemption: Essays on Gender and the Human Body in Medieval Religion*. Ed. Bynum. New York: Zone Books, 1992. Pp. 151–179.

———. *Holy Feast, Holy Fast: The Religious Significance of Food to Medieval Women*. Berkeley: University of California Press, 1987.

Byrne, Francis J. *Irish Kings and High-Kings*. Dublin: Four Courts Press, 2001.

Cabanes Català, María Luisa. "El *Spill* de Jaume Roig com a font per a la diplomática." *Revista de Filologia Valenciana* 3 (1996): 7–23.

Cabré, Montserrat. "Women or Healers? Household Practices and the Categories of Health Care in Late Medieval Iberia." *BHM* 82 (2008): 18–51.

Cabré i Pairet, Montserrat, and Fernando Salmón Muñiz. "Poder académico *versus* autoridad femenina: la Facultad de Medicina de París contra Jacoba Félicié (1322)." *DYNAMIS* 19 (1999): 55–78.

Cadden, Joan. *Meanings of Sex Differences in the Middle Ages: Medicine, Science, and Culture*. Cambridge: CUP, 1993.

Cagle, Hugh Glenn. "Dead Reckonings: Disease and the Natural Sciences in Portuguese India and the Atlantic, 1450–1650." Ph.D. Diss., Rutgers University, 2011.

Calnan, Michael, and Rosemary Brown. "Trust Relations in a Changing Health Service." *Journal of Health Services Research and Policy* 13, supp. 3 (2008): 97–103.

Cannon, Christopher. "*Raptus* in the Chaumpaigne Release and Newly Discovered Document Concerning the Life of Geoffrey Chaucer." *Speculum* 68 (1993): 74–94.

Cardoner, Francesc. *Història de la medicina a la Corona d'Aragó (1162–1479)*. Barcelona: Scientia, 1973.

Carlin, Martha. Review of *Doctors and Medicine in Medieval England, 1340–1530*, *MH* 31.3 (1987): 360–62.

Carraway, Joanna. "Contumacy, Defense Strategy, and Criminal Law in Late Medieval Italy." *L&HR* 29.1 (2011): 99–132.

Carré, Antònia. "La medicina com a rerefons cultural a l'*Espill* de Jaume Roig." In *Jaume Roig i Cristòfor Despuig. Dos assaigs sobre cultura i literatura dels segles XV i XVI*. Ed. Antònia Carré and Josep Solervicens. Barcelona: Eumo, 1996.

Carroll, Patrick. "Medical Police and the History of Public Health." *MH* 46 (2002): 461–94.

Casson, Catherine. "Reputation and Responsibility in Medieval English Towns: Civic Concerns with the Regulation of Trade." *Urban History* 39 (2012): 387–408.

Cavalca, Desiderio. *Il bando nella prassi e nella dottrina giuridica medievale*. Milan: Giuffrè, 1978.

Cavallo, Sandra. *Artisans of the Body in Early Modern Italy: Identities, Families and Masculinities*. Manchester: Manchester University Press, 2007.

Caviness, Madeline H., and Charles Nelson, "Silent Witness, Absent Women and the Law Courts in Medieval Germany." In *Fama: The Politics of Talk and Reputation in Medieval Europe*. Ed. Thelma Fenster and Daniel Lord Smail. Ithaca and New York: Cornell University Press, 2003. Pp. 47–72.

Charles-Edwards, Thomas. "Early Irish Law." In *A New History of Ireland I: Prehistoric and Early Ireland*. Ed. Dáibhí Ó Cróinín. Oxford: OUP, 2005. Pp. 331–70.

———. *Early Christian Ireland*. Cambridge: CUP, 2000.

———. "Boundaries in Irish Law." In *Medieval Settlement: Continuity and Change*. Ed. P.H. Sawyer. London: Edward Arnold Publishers, Ltd., 1976. Pp. 83–7.

Chiarelli, Leonard C. "A Preliminary Study on the Origins of Medical Licensing in the Medieval Mediterranean." *Al-Masāq: Islam and the Medieval Mediterranean* 10 (1998): 1–11.

Chittolini, Giorgio. "A Geography of the 'Contadi' in Communal Italy." Trans. Shona Kelly Wray. In *Portraits of Medieval and Renaissance Living: Essays in Memory of David Herlihy*. Ed. Samuel K. Cohn, Jr. and Steven A. Epstein. Ann Arbor, MI: University of Michigan Press, 1996. Pp. 417–438.

Cifuentes, Lluís. "La literatura quirúrgica baixmedieval en romanç a la Corona d'Arago: escola, pont i mercat." In *Literatura i cultura a la Corona d'Aragó (s. XIII–XV): actes del III Col·loqui internacional "Problemes i mètodes de literatura catalana antiga"* (Girona, 5–8 de juliol de 2000). Ed. Lola Badia, Miriam Cabré and Sadurní Martí. Barcelona: Curial—Publicacions de l'Abadia de Montserrat, 2002. Pp. 321–335.

———. "Vernacularization as an Intellectual and Social Bridge: the Catalan Translations of Teodorico's Chirurgia and of Arnau de Vilanova's Regimen sanitatis." *Early Science and Medicine* 4 (1999):127–148.

Citrome, Jeremy J. *The Surgeon in Medieval English Literature*. New York: Palgrave Macmillan, 2006.

Clanchy, Michael. *From Memory to Written Record: England 1066 to 1307*. 2nd ed. Oxford: Blackwell, 1993.

Clark, Elaine. "Social Welfare and Mutual Aid in the Medieval Countryside." *Journal of British Studies* 33 (1994): 381–406

Clark, Michael, and Catherine Crawford, eds. *Legal Medicine in History*. Cambridge: CUP, 1994.

Clayton, Mary. *The Apocryphal Gospels of Mary in Anglo-Saxon England*. Cambridge: CUP, 2006.

———. *Cult of the Virgin Mary in Anglo-Saxon England*. Cambridge: CUP, 2003.

Coelho, Maria Helena da Cruz, and Armando Luís de Carvalho Homem, eds. *Portugal em Definição de Fronteiras: do Condado Portucalense à Crise do Século XIV*. Nova História de Portugal v. 3. Lisbon: Editorial Presença, 1996.

Cohen, Jeffrey Jerome, and Bonnie Wheeler. "Becoming and Unbecoming." In *Becoming Male in the Middle Ages*. Ed. Jeffrey Jerome Cohen and Bonnie Wheeler. New York: Garland, 1997.

Coisar, Roisin. "*In Memoriam*: Shona Kelly Wray." In *The Medieval Review* 12.06.22 https://scholarworks.iu.edu/dspace/handle/2022/3631.

Coley, Noel G. "Alfred Swaine Taylor, MD, FRS (1806–1880): Forensic Toxicologist." *MH* 35 (1991): 409–427.

Collard, Franck. "*Perfidus physicus* ou *inexpertus medicus*: le cas Jean de Grandville médecin du comte Amédée VII de Savoie." In *Mires, Physiciens, Barbiers et Charlatans: les Marges de la Médecine de l'Antiquité au XVIᵉ Siècle*. Ed. Franck Collard and Évelyne Samama. Langres: Dominique Guéniot, 2004. Pp. 133–49.

Cook, Harold. *The Decline of the Old Medical Regime in Stuart London*. Ithaca: Cornell University Press, 1986.

Cosman, Madeleine Pelner. "Medieval Medical Malpractice: the Dicta and the Dockets." *Bulletin of the New York Academy of Medicine* 49.1 (1973): 22–47.

Crawford, Catherine. "Legalizing Medicine: Early Modern Legal Systems and the Growth of Medico-legal Knowledge." In *Legal Medicine in History*. Ed. Michael Clark and Catherine Crawford. Cambridge: CUP, 1994. Pp. 89–116.

Crawford, Sally. *Childhood in Anglo-Saxon England*. Stroud: Sutton Publishing Ltd., 1999.

Crisciani, Chiara. "*Consilia*, responsi, consulti: I pareri del medico tra insegnamento e professione." In *Consilium: Teori e pratiche del consigliare nella cultura medieval*. Ed. Crisciani, Carla Casagrande, and Silvana Vecchio. Florence: SISMEL, Edizioni del Galuzzo, 2004. Pp. 259–79.

———. "Artefici *sensati*: *experentia* e sensi in alchimia e cirurgia (secc. XIII–XIV)." In *Alchimia e medicina del Medioevo*. Ed. Chiara Crisciani and Agostino Paravacini-Bagliani. Florence: SISMEL, Edizioni del Galuzzo, 2003. Pp. 135–59.

Cullman, O. "Infancy Gospels." In *New Testament Apocrypha*, v. 1. Rev. and ed. W. Schneemelcher. Trans. R. McL. Wilson. Louisville and London: Westminster John Knox Press, 1991. Pp. 414–20.

Cusato, Michael. "Francis and the Franciscan Movement." In *The Cambridge Companion to Francis of Assisi*. Ed. Michael. J.P. Robson. Cambridge: CUP, 2012. Pp. 17–33

———. "Towards a Resolution of the Franciscan Question: Introduction to the Roundtable." *FS* 66 (2008): 479–481.

———. "Talking about Ourselves: The Shift in Franciscan Writing from Hagiography to History (1235–1247)." *FS* 58 (2000): 37–75.

da Costa, Adelaide Millán. "State-building in Portugal during the Middle Ages: a Royal Endeavour in Partnership with the Local Powers?" In *Empowering Interactions:*

Political Cultures and the Emergence of the State in Europe, 1300–1900. Ed. William Blockmans, André Holenstein and Jon Mathieu with Daniel Schläppi. Aldershot: Ashgate, 2009. Pp. 219–233

———. *Vereação e Vereadores: o Governo do Porto em Finais do Século XV*. Oporto: Câmara Municipal, 1993.

Dahm, Georg. *Das Strafrecht Italiens im ausgehenden Mittelalter: Untersuchungen über die Beziehung zwischen Theorie und Praxis im Strafrecht des Spätmittelalters, namentlich im XIV. Jahrhundert*. Berlin and Leipzig: Walter de Gruyter, 1931.

Dalarun, Jacques. "The Great Secret of Francis." In *The Stigmata of Francis of Assisi: New Studies, New Perspectives*. Ed. Jacques Dalarun; Michael F. Cusato; Carla Salvati. St Bonaventure, NY: Franciscan Institute Publications, 2006. Pp. 9–28.

———. *Francis and the Feminine*. Trans. Paula Pierce and Mary Sutphin. St Bonaventure, NY: Franciscan Institute Press, 2006.

———. *The Misadventure of Francis of Assisi: Towards a Historical Use of the Franciscan Legends*. Trans. Edward Hagman. St Bonaventure, NY: Franciscan Institute Publications, 2002. Pp. 30–41.

Dall'Osso, Eugenio. *L'organizzazione medico-legale a Bologna e a Venezia nei secoli XII–XIV*. Cesena: Università di Bolonia, 1956.

Dangler, Jean. *Making Difference in Medieval and Early Modern Iberia*. Notre Dame, IN: University of Notre Dame Press, 2005.

———. *Mediating Fictions: Literature, Women Healers, and the Go-Between in Medieval and Early Modern Iberia*. Lewisburg: Bucknell University Press, 2001.

———. "Marriage and Well-Being in Jaume Roig's *Spill*." *Catalan Review* 15.2 (2001): 35–47.

———. "Motherhood and Pain in Villena's *Vita Christi* and Roig's *Spill*." *La corónica* 27.1 (1998): 99–113.

Davenport, Tony. *Medieval Narrative: An Introduction*. Oxford: OUP, 2004.

Davidson, Roger. " 'This Pernicious Delusion': Law, Medicine, and Child Sexual Abuse in Early-Twentieth-Century Scotland." *Journal of the History of Sexuality* 10 (2001): 62–77.

Davies, Sara. *Global Politics of Health*. Cambridge: Polity, 2010.

De Coster, Anuschka. "Foreign and Citizen Teachers at Bologna in the Fifteenth and Sixteenth Centuries: Statutes, Statistics, and Student Teachers." *Annali di Storia delle Università italiane* 12 (2007): http://www.cisui.unibo.it/annali/12/testi/19DeCostner_testo.htm. Accessed May 24, 2010.

de Meyer, Isaac Joseph. *Recherches historiques sur la pratique de l'art des accouchements, a Bruges depuis le XIV Siècle jusqu'à nos jours*. Bruges: Felix de Pachtere, 1843.

de Renzi, Silvia. "Medical Expertise, Bodies and the Law in Early Modern Courts." *Isis* 98.2 (2007): 318–19.

———. "Witnesses of the Body: Medico-legal Cases in Seventeenth-century Rome." *Studies in History and Philosophy of Science* 33 (2002): 219–242.

de Vegvar, Carol Neuman. "Images of Women in Anglo-Saxon Art II: Midwifery in Harley 603." *Old English Newsletter* 25.1 (1991): 54–56.

Deacy, Susan, and Karen F. Pierce, eds. *Rape in Antiquity: Sexual Violence in the Greek and Roman World.* London: Duckworth, 2002.

Dean, Mitchell. *Governmentality: Power and Rule in Modern Society*, 2nd ed. London: Sage, 2010.

Dean, Trevor. *Crime and Justice in Late Medieval Italy.* Cambridge: CUP, 2007.

Deegan, Marilyn. "Pregnancy and Childbirth in the Anglo-Saxon Medical Texts: A Preliminary Survey." In *Medicine in Early Medieval England.* Ed. Marilyn Deegan and D.G. Scragg. Manchester: Center for Anglo-Saxon Studies, University of Manchester, 1989. Pp. 17–26.

Demaitre, Luke. *Leprosy in Premodern Medicine: A Malady of the Whole Body.* Baltimore: Johns Hopkins University Press, 2007.

———. "Medical Practice and Practitioners." In *Medieval France: and Encyclopedia.* Ed. William Kibler. New York: Psychology Press, 1995.

Dendle, Peter, and Alain Touwaide, eds. *Health and Healing from the Medieval Garden.* Woodbridge: Boydell, 2008.

Desmaze, Charles. *Histoire de la médecine légale en France d'après les lois, registres et arrêtes criminels.* Paris: Charpentier, 1880.

Diepgen, Paul. *Frau und Frauenheilkunde in der Kultur des Mittelalters.* Stuttgart: Thieme, 1963.

Dilcher, Gerhard and Eva-Marie Distler, eds. *Leges—Gentes—Regna. Zur Rolle von germanischen Rechtsgewohnheiten und lateinischer Schrifttradition bei der Ausbildung der frühmittelalterlichen Rechtskultur.* Berlin: Erich Schmidt Verlag, 2006.

Dilcher, Hermann. *Die sizilische Gesetzgebung Kaiser Friedrichs des Zweiten. Quellen der Constitutionen von Melfi und ihrer Novellen.* Cologne: Böhlau, 1975.

Dillard, Heath. "Women in Reconquest Castile: The Fueros of Sepúlveda and Cuenca." In *Women in Medieval Society.* Ed. Susan Mosher Stuard. Philadelphia: University of Pennsylvania Press, 1976. Pp. 71–94

Disney, Anthony. *A History of Portugal and the Portuguese Empire.* 2 vols. Cambridge: CUP, 2009.

Dixon-Woods, Mary, Karen Yeung and Charles L. Bosk. "Why is UK Medicine no longer a Self-regulating Profession? The Role of Scandals involving 'Bad Apple' Doctors." *Social Science and Medicine* 73 (2011): 1452–59.

Donnison, Jean. *Midwives and Medical Men: A History of Inter-Professional Rivalries and Women's Rights.* London: Heinemann, 1977.

Duarte, Luís Miguel. *Justiça e Criminalidade no Portugal Medievo (1459–1481)*. Lisbon: Fundação Calouste Gulbenkian/Fundação para a Ciência e a Tecnologia, 1999.

Dunn, Caroline. *Stolen Women in Medieval England: Rape, Abduction, and Adultery, 1100–1500*. Cambridge: CUP, 2013.

———. "The Language of Ravishment in Medieval England." *Speculum* 86 (2011): 79–116.

Duran i Tort, Carola. "Aspectes jurídics en un fragment de *L'Espill* de Jaume Roig." *Llengua & Literatura* 4 (1990–1991): 423–32.

Dursteller, Eric. Review of Jutta G. Sperling and Shona Kelly Wray, eds. *Across the Religious Divide: Women, Property, and Law in the Wider Mediterranean (ca. 1300–1800)*. In *Renaissance Quarterly* 63.4 (2010): 1325–27.

Dwork, Deborah. *War is Good for Babies and Other Young Children: the History of the Infant and Child Welfare Movement in England, 1898–1918*. London: Tavistock, 1987.

Eccles, Audrey. *Obstretrics and Gynaecology in Tudor and Stuart England*. London and Canberra: Croom Helm, 1982.

Edgington, Susan B. "Medicine and Surgery in the *Livre des Assises de la Cour des Bourgeois de Jérusalem*." *Al-Masāq: Islam and the Medieval Mediterranean* 17 (2005): 87–97.

Elston, Mary. "Remaking a Trustworthy Medical Profession in Twenty-first Century Britain." In *The New Sociology of the Health Service*. Ed. Jonathan Gabe and Michael Calnan. Abingdon: Routledge, 2009. Pp. 17–36.

Escrig, José Antonio Llibrer. "La formacion de compañías para el tintado de paños. El caso de Cocentaina en el siglo XV." *Anuario de Estudios Medievales* 41.2 (2011): 59–72.

———. "Industria textil y crecimiento regional: la Vall d'Albaida y el Comtat en el siglo XV." 2 vols. Ph.D. Diss., Universitat de València, 2010.

———. *Los orígenes de la industria de la lana en la Baja Edad Media: el Comtat en el siglo XV*. Valencia: Consell Valencià de Cultura, 2007.

Etchingham, Colmán. *Church Organisation in Ireland A.D. 650 to 1000*. Maynooth: Laigin Publications, 2002.

Farinha, António Dias. "Portugal e Marrocos no século XV." 3 vols. Ph.D. Diss., University of Lisbon, 1990.

Fellows, Jennifer. "Mothers in Middle English Romance." In *Women and Literature in Britain, 1150–1500*. Ed. Carol M. Meale. Cambridge: CUP, 1993. Pp. 41–60.

Ferragud, Carmel. "El metge sota sospita. Actuacio mèdica en els testimonis pericials a ferits devant la cort del justícia criminal de València (1396)." *Recerques* 62 (2011): 69–94.

———. "Els barbers de la ciutat de València durant el segle XV a través dels llibres del justícia criminal." *Anuario de Estudios Medievales* 41.1 (2011): 31–57.

———. *Medicina per a un nou regne*. Alzira: Bromera, 2008.

————. "Organització social i atenció mèdica a la Cocentaina baixmedieval: el procés a Abrahim Abengalell (1318)." *Asclepio* 57.2 (2005): 3–24

————. *Medicina i promoció social a la Baixa Edat Mitjana (Corona d'Aragó, 1360–1410)*. Madrid: CSIC, 2005.

————. "La sociabilitat i el treball dels jueus a Cocentaina abans de la pesta negra." *Alberri* 15 (2002): 151–178.

————. *El naixement d'una vila rural valenciana. Cocentaina, 1245–1304*. Valencia: Publicacions de la Universitat de València, 1998.

Ferraro, Joanne M. *Nefarious Crimes, Contested Justice: Illicit Sex and Infanticide in the Republic of Venice, 1557–1789*. Baltimore: Johns Hopkins University Press, 2008.

Ferrer i Mallol, Maria Teresa. "La incursió de l'exèrcit de Granada de 1304 pel regne de València i l'atac a Cocentaina." *Alberri* 15 (2002): 53–149.

Findlen, Paula. *Possessing Nature: Museums, Collecting, and Scientific Culture in Early Modern Italy*. Los Angeles: University of California Press, 1994.

Finucane, R.C. "The Toddler in the Ditch: A Case of Parental Neglect?" In *Voices from the Bench: The Narratives of Lesser Folk in Medieval Trials*. Ed. Michael Goodich. Basingstoke: Palgrave, 2006. Pp. 127–148.

————. *The Rescue of the Innocents: Endangered Children in Medieval Miracles*. New York: St Martin's Press, 1997.

————. *Miracles and Pilgrims: Popular Beliefs in Medieval England*. Totowa: Rowan and Littlefield, 1977.

Fischer-Homberger, Esther. *Medizin vor Gericht: Gerichtsmedizin von der Renaissance bis zur Aufklärung*. Berne, Stuttgart, and Vienna: Hans Huber, 1983.

Fleming, Rebecca. *Medicine and the Making of Roman Women: Gender, Nature, and Authority from Celsus to Galen*. Oxford: OUP, 2000.

Font i Rius, Josep Maria. "Valencia y Barcelona en los orígenes de su régimen municipal." In *Estudis sobre els drets i institucions locals en la Catalunya medieval*. Ed. Jose María Font Rius. Barcelona: Universitat de Barcelona, 1985. Pp. 639–57.

Forbes, Thomas R. "A Jury of Matrons." *MH* 32 (1988): 23–33.

————. *Surgeons at the Bailey: English Forensic Medicine to 1878*. New Haven: Yale University Press, 1985.

————. "The Regulation of English Midwives in the Sixteenth and Seventeenth Centuries." *MH* 8.3 (1964): 235–44.

Forde, Simon, Lesley Johnson and Alan Murray, eds. *Concepts of National Identity in the Middle Ages*. Leeds: Leeds Studies in English, 1995.

Foucault, Michel. "Governmentality." In *The Foucault Effect: Studies in Governmentality*. Ed. Graham Burchill, Colin Gordon and Peter Miller. Chicago: Chicago University Press, 1991. Pp. 87–104.

Fraher, Richard. "Conviction According to Conscience: The Medieval Jurists' Debate Concerning Judicial Discretion and the Law of Proof." *L&HR* 7.1 (1989): 23–88.

———. "The Theoretical Justification for the New Criminal Law of the High Middle Ages: 'Rei publicae interest, ne crimina remaneant impunita.'" *University of Illinois Law Review* (1984): 577–595,

Freitas, Judite Gonçalves de. "The Royal Chancellery at the End of the Portuguese Middle Ages: Diplomacy and Political Society (1970–2005)." *E-Journal of Portuguese History* 7 (2009): http://www.brown.edu/Departments/Portuguese_Brazilian_Studies/ejph/html/issue14/html/jfreitas.html. Accessed March 16, 2012.

French, Roger. *Medicine before Science: the Business of Medicine from the Middle Ages to the Enlightenment.* Cambridge: CUP, 2003.

———. *Canonical Medicine: Gentile de Foligno and Scholasticism.* Leiden: Brill, 2001.

French, V. "Midwives and Maternity Care in the Roman World." *Helios*, n.s. 13.2 (1986): 69–84.

Frijda, Nico H. *De wetten der emoties.* Amsterdam: Bakker, 2008.

Frugoni, Chiara. *Francesco e l'invenzione della stimmate: Una storia per imagine fina Bonaventura e Giotto.* Turin: Einaudi, 1993.

Fukuyama, Francis. *Trust: the Social Virtues and the Creation of Prosperity.* London: Hamish Hamilton, 1995.

Fullana, Luis. *Historia de la villa y condado de Cocentaina.*Valencia: Imprenta Huici, 1920.

Furió, Antoni, and Ferran Garcia-Oliver. "Rural Mobility in a Frontier Land (the Valencian Country, 1250–1350)." In *La mobilità sociale nel medioevo.* Ed. Sandro Carocci. Rome: École française de Rome, 2010. Pp. 513–554.

Gallent, Mercedes. "Precedentes medievales de la medicina legal: la *dessospitació* en el Reino de Valencia." *Saitabi* 50 (2000): 11–28.

Gamberini, Andrea. *La città assediata: poteri e identità politiche a Reggio in età viscontea.* Rome: Viella, 2003.

Gammon, Julie. "'A denial of innocence': Female Juvenile Victims of Rape and the English Legal System in the Eighteenth Century." In *Childhood in Question: Children, Parents and the State.* Ed. Anthony Fletcher and Stephen Hussey. Manchester: Manchester University Press, 1999. Pp. 74–95

García Ballester, Luis. *La búsqueda de la salud. Sanadores y enfermos en la España medieval.* Barcelona: Península, 2001.

———. "The New Galen: a Challenge to Latin Galenism in Thirteenth-century Montpellier." In *Text and Tradition: Studies in Ancient Medicine and its Transmission, presented to Jutta Kollesch.* Ed. Klaus-Dietrich Fischer, Diethard Nickel, and Paul Potter. Leiden: Brill, 1998. Pp. 55–83.

———. "Ethical Problems in the Relationship between Doctors and Patients in Fourteenth-Century Spain." In *Medicine and Medical Ethics in Medieval and Early Modern Spain: An Intercultural Approach.* Ed. Samuel S. Kottek and Luis García Ballester. Jerusalem: Magnes Press, 1996. Pp. 11–32.

————. *La medicina a la València medieval: medicine i societat en un país medieval mediterrani*. Valencia: Institució Valenciana d'Estudis i Investigació, Edicions Alfons el Magnànim, 1988.

————. "Academicism versus Empiricism in Practical Medicine in Sixteenth–Century Spain with Regard to Morisco Practitioners." In *The Medical Renaissance of the Sixteenth Century*. Ed. Andrew Wear *et al.* Cambridge: CUP, 1985. Pp. 246–70.

————. *Historia social de la medician en la España de los siglos XIII al XVI*, [v. 1, *La minoría musulmana y morisca*]. Madrid: Akal, 1976.

García Ballester, Luis, Michael McVaugh, and Agustín Rubio Vela. *Medical Licensing and Learning in Fourteenth-Century Valencia: Transactions of the American Philosophical Society*. Philadelphia: American Philosophical Society, 1989.

García Ballester, Luis, and Michael R. McVaugh. "Nota sobre el control de la actividad médica y quirúrgica de los barberos (barbers, barbitonsores) en los Furs de Valencia de 1329." In *Homenatge al doctor Sebastià Garcia Martínez*. Valencia: Conselleria de Cultura, Educació i Ciència: Universitat de València, 1988. Pp. 73–88.

Garnett, Emmeline. *John Marsden's Will: The Hornby Castle Dispute 1780–1840*. London: Hambledon, 1998.

Garrigues, Laurent. "Les professions médicales à Paris au début du XVe siècle: practiciens en procès au parlement." *Bibliotheque de l'École des Chartes* 156 (1998): 317–67.

Garver, Valerie. "Childbearing and Infancy in the Carolingian World." *Journal of the History of Sexuality* 21.2 (2012): 208–44.

————. *Women and Aristocratic Culture in the Carolingian World*. Ithaca and London: Cornell University Press, 2009.

Geis, Gilbert. "Lord Hale, Witches, and Rape." *British Journal of Law and Society* 5 (1978): 26–44.

Gelfand, Toby. "The History of the Medical Profession." In *Companion Encyclopedia of the History of Medicine*, 2 vols. Ed. W.F. Bynum and Roy Porter. London and New York: Routledge, 1993. V. 2, pp. 1119–50.

Gentilcore, David. *Medical Charlatanism in Early-Modern Italy*. Oxford: OUP, 2006.

————. *Healers and Healing in Early Modern Italy*. Manchester: Manchester University Press, 1998.

————. "'All that Pertains to Medicine': *Protomedici* and *Protomedicati* in Early Modern Italy." *MH* 38 (1994): 121–142.

Getz, Faye Marie. *Medicine in the English Middle Ages*. Princeton: Princeton University Press, 1998.

Gibson, Gail McMurray. "Scene and Obscene: Seeing and Performing Late Medieval Childbirth." *Journal of Medieval and Early Modern Studies* 29.1 (1999): 7–24.

Godet-Calogeras, Jean François. "Francis of Assisi's Resignation: An Historical and Philological Probe." In *Charisma und religiöse Gemeinschaften in Mittelalter*. Ed.

G. Andenna, M. Breitensten and G. Melville. Berlin, Hamburg and Münster: LIT Verlag, 2005. Pp. 281–300

Goldberg, P.J.P. "Introduction." In *Medieval Women and the Law*. Ed. Noël James Menuge. Woodbridge: Boydell, 2000. Pp. *ix-xiii*.

Gomes, Saul António. "Higiene e saúde na Leiria medieval." In *III Colóquio Sobre a História de Leiria e da sua Região*. Leiria: Câmara Municipal de Leiria, 1999. Pp. 9–43.

Gonçalves, Iria. "As festas do "Corpus Christi" do Porto na segunda metade do século XV: a participação do concelho." In *Um Olhar Sobre a Cidade Medieval*. Ed. Iria Gonçalves. Cascais: Patrimonia Histórica, 1996. Pp. 153–76.

———. "Físicos e cirurgiões quatrocentistas—as cartas de exame." In *Imagens do Mundo Medieval*. Ed. Iria Gonçalves. Lisbon: Livros Horizonte, 1988. Pp. 9–52.

Gonthier, Nicole. "Les victimes de viol devant les tribunaux à la fin du Moyen Âge d'après les sources dijonnaises et lyonnaises." *Criminologie* 27.2 (1994): 9–32.

Goodey, C.F. *A History of Intelligence and 'Intellectual Disability': The Shaping of Psychology in Early Modern Europe*. Farnham, Surrey & Burlington, VT: Ashgate, 2011.

Goold, Imogen, and Catherine Kelly, eds. *Lawyers' Medicine: The Legislature, the Courts and Medical Practice, 1760–2000*. Oxford: Hart Publishing, 2009.

Gottfried, Robert S. *Doctors and Medicine in Medieval England, 1340–1530*. Princeton: Princeton University Press, 1986.

Gravdal, Kathryn. *Ravishing Maidens: Writing Rape in Medieval French Literature and Law*. Philadelphia: University of Pennsylvania Press, 1991.

Greci, Roberto. *Mercanti, politica e cultura nella società Bolognese del basso medioevo*. Bologna: CLUEB, 2004.

Green, Monica H. "Integrative Medicine: Incorporating Medicine and Health into the Canon of Medieval European History." *History Compass* 7.4 (2009): 1218–45.

———. *Making Women's Medicine Masculine: The Rise of Male Authority in Pre-Modern Gynaecology*. Oxford: OUP, 2008.

———. "Gendering the History of Women's Health Care." *Gender and History* 20 (2008): 487–518.

———. "Getting to the Source: The Case of Jacoba Felicie and the Impact of the *Portable Medieval Reader* on the Canon of Medieval Women's History." *Medieval Feminist Forum* 42 (2006): 50–63.

———. "Bodies, Gender, Health, Disease: Recent Work on Medieval Women's Medicine." *Studies in Medieval and Renaissance History* 2 (2005): 1–46.

———. "Books as a Source of Medical Education for Women in the Middle Ages." *Dynamis* 20 (2000): 331–69.

———. "The Possibilities of Literacy and the Limits of Reading: Women and the Gendering of Medical Literacy." In *Women's Healthcare in the Medieval West: Texts and Context*. Ed. Monica H. Green. Aldershot: Ashgate Variorum, 2000. Section VII. PP. 1–76.

————. "Medieval Gynecological Texts: A Handlist." In *Women's Healthcare in the Medieval West: Texts and Contexts*. Ed. Monica H. Green. Aldershot: Ashgate Variorum, 2000. Section VIII. Pp. 1–36.

————. "Documenting Medieval Women's Medical Practice." In *Practical Medicine from Salerno to the Black Death*. Ed. Luis García Ballester, Roger French, Jon Arrizabalaga, and Andrew Cunningham. Cambridge: CUP, 1994. Pp. 322–52.

————. "Women's Medical Practice and Health Care in Medieval Europe." *Signs* 14 (1989): 434–73.

Green, Monica H., and Daniel Lord Smail. "The Trial of Floreta d'Ays (1403): Jews, Christians, and Obstetrics in Later Medieval Marseille." *Journal of Medieval History* 34 (2008): 185–211.

Green, Rosalie. "The Missing Midwife." In *Romanesque and Gothic: Essays for George Zarnecki*. Ed. Neil Stratford. Woodbridge: Boydell, 1987. Pp. 103–105.

Greilsammer, Myriam. "The Midwife, the Priest and the Physician: The Subjugation of Midwives in the Low Countries at the End of the Middle Ages." *Journal of Medieval and Renaissance Studies* 21.2 (1991): 285–329.

Grendler, Paul F. *The Universities of the Italian Renaissance*. Baltimore: Johns Hopkins University Press, 2002.

Grey, Daniel J.R. "'What woman is safe...?': Coerced Medical Examinations, Suspected Infanticide, and the Response of the Women's Movement in Britain, 1871–1881." *Women's History Review* 22 (2013): 403–421.

Grigsby, Bryon. "Medical Misconceptions." In *Misconceptions about the Middle Ages*. Ed. Stephen J. Harris and Bryon Grigsby. New York: Routledge, 2008.

————. "The Social Position of the Surgeon in London, 1350–1450." *Essays in Medieval Studies* 13 (1996): 71–80.

Grimaldi, Natale. *La signoria di Barnabò Visconti e Regina della Scala in Reggio, 1371–1385*. Reggio Emilia: Cooperativa fra lavoranti tipografi, 1921.

Grimm, Jacob. "Über die Notnunft an Frauen." *Zeitschrift für deutsches Recht- und deutsche Rechtswissenschaft* 5 (1841): 1–29.

Guardiola, Ginger Lee. "Within and Without: The Social and Medical Worlds of the Medieval Midwife, 1000–1500." Ph.D. Diss. University of Colorado, 2002.

Guy, John R. "The Episcopal Licensing of Physicians, Surgeons, and Midwives." *BHM* 56 (1982): 528–42.

Hagemann, Hans-Rudolf. "Vom Verbrechenskatalog des altdeutschen Strafrechts." *Zeitschrift der Savigny-Stiftung für Rechtsgeschichte, Germanistische Abteilung* 91 (1974): 1–72.

Hammond, E.A. "Incomes of Medieval English Doctors." *JHMAS* 15.2 (1960): 154–169.

Hanawalt, Barbara A. *'Of Good and Ill Repute': Gender and Social Control in Medieval England*. Oxford: OUP, 1998.

————. "Violent Death in Fourteenth and Early Fifteenth-Century England." *Comparative Studies in Society and History* 18.3 (1976): 297–320.

Hanson, Ann Ellis. "A Division of Labor: Roles for Men in Greek and Roman Births." *Thamyris* 1.2 (1994): 157–202.

Harper, Stephen. *Insanity, Individuals, and Society in Late-Medieval English Literature: The Subject of Madness.* Lewiston, Queenston, Lampeter: The Edwin Mellen Press, 2003.

Harris-Stoertz, Fiona. "Pregnancy and Childbirth in Twelfth- and Thirteenth-Century French and English Law." *Journal of the History of Sexuality* 21.2 (2012): 263–81.

———. "Pregnancy and Childbirth in Chivalric Literature." *Mediaevalia: An Interdisciplinary Journal of Medieval Studies Worldwide* 29.1 (2008): 27–36.

———. "Suffering and Survival in Medieval English Childbirth." In *Medieval Family Roles.* Ed. Cathy Jorgensen Itnyre. New York: Garland Press, 1996. Pp. 101–20.

Haskett, Timothy S. "The Medieval English Court of Chancery." *L&HR* 14 (1996): 245–313.

Hawkes, Emma. "[S]he will … protect and defend her rights boldly by law and reason …": Women's Knowledge of Common Law and Equity Courts in Late-Medieval England." In *Medieval Women and the Law.* Ed. Noël James Menuge. Woodbridge: Boydell, 2000. Pp. 145–61.

———. "She was ravished against her will, what so ever she say": Female Consent in Rape and Ravishment in Late-medieval England." *Limina* 1 (1995): 47–54.

Helmholz, R.H. *Canon Law and the Law of England.* London and Ronceverte: The Hambledon Press, 1987.

———. *Marriage Litigation in Medieval England.* Cambridge: CUP, 1974.

Henderson, John. *The Renaissance Hospital: Healing the Body and Healing the Soul.* New Haven: Yale University Press, 2006.

Henstra, Dirk Jan. "De eerste optekening van de algemeen-Friese keuren." *It Beaken* 64 (2002): 99–128.

———. *The Evolution of the Money Standard in Medieval Frisia. A Treatise on the History of the Systems of Money of Account in the Former Frisia (c. 600–c. 1500).* Groningen: D.J. Henstra, 2000.

Herbert, Máire, ed. and trans. *Iona, Kells and Derry: The History and Hagiography of the Monastic Familia of Columba.* Oxford: Clarendon Press, 1988.

Herrera, María Teresa. *Diccionario español de textos médicos antiguos.* 2 vols. Madrid: Arco Libros, 1996.

Hewson, M. Anthony. *Giles of Rome and the Medieval Theory of Conception: a Study of the 'De formatione corporis humani in utero.'* London: The Athlone Press, 1975.

His, Rudolf. "Die Körperverletzungen im Strafrecht des deutschen Mittelalters." *Zeitschrift der Savigny–Stiftung für Rechtsgeschichte. Germanistische Abteilung* 41 (1920): 75–126.

Histed, Elise Bennett. "Medieval Rape: A Conceivable Defence." *The Cambridge Law Journal* 63 (2004): 743–69.

Hosking, Geoffrey. "Trust and Distrust: a Suitable Theme for Historians?" *Transactions of the Royal Historical Society*, 6th ser., 16 (2006): 95–115.

Hudson, John. *Land, Law, and Lordship in Anglo-Norman England*. Oxford: Clarendon Press, 1994.

Hughes, Muriel Joy. *Women Healers in Medieval Life and Literature*. Freeport: Books for Libraries Press, 1943.

Huizenga, Erwin. *Tussen autoriteit en empirie. De Middelnederlandse chirurgieën in de veertiende en vijftiende eeuw en hun maatschappelijke context*. Hilversum: Verloren, 2003.

Huneycutt, Lois L. *Matilda of Scotland: A Study in Medieval Queenship*. Woodbridge: Boydell Press, 2003.

Hunt, R.W. *The Schools and the Cloister: The Life and Writings of Alexander Nequam*. Ed. and rev. Margaret Gibson. Oxford: Clarendon Press, 1984.

Hunt, Tony. *The Medieval Surgery*. Woodbridge: Boydell, 1992.

Huot, Sylvia. *Madness in Medieval French Literature: Identities Found and Lost*. Oxford: OUP, 2003.

Hurd-Mead, Kate Campbell. *History of Women in Medicine from the Earliest Times to the Beginning of the Nineteenth Century*. Haddam: The Haddam Press, 1938.

Hurl, Jennine. "'She being bigg with child is likely to miscarry.' Pregnant Victims Prosecuting Assault in Westminster, 1685–1720." *London Journal* 24 (1999): 18–33.

Ingram, Martin. "Child Sexual Abuse in Early Modern England." In *Negotiating Power in Early Modern Society: Order, Hierarchy and Subordination in Britain and Ireland*. Ed. Michael J. Braddick and John Walter. Cambridge: CUP, 2001. Pp. 63–84.

Jackson, Louise. *Child Sexual Abuse in Victorian England*. London and New York: Routledge, 2000.

Jackson, Mark. "Suspicious Infant Deaths: the Statute of 1624 and Medical Evidence at Coroners' Inquests." In *Legal Medicine in History*. Ed. Michael Clark and Catherine Crawford. Cambridge: CUP, 1994. Pp. 64–86.

Jacquart, Danielle. *La médecine médiévale dans le cadre parisien. XIVe–XVe siècle*. Paris: Fayard, 1998.

———. "Comienzos de la enseñanza médica en Montpellier: una puesta a punto." In *Granada 1492–1992. Del Reino de Granada al futuro del mundo mediterráneo*. Ed. Manuel Barrios and Bernard Vincent. Granada: Universidad de Granada, Diputación Provincial de Granada, 1995. Pp. 323–335.

———. "Medical Practice in Paris in the First Half of the Fourteenth Century." In *Practical Medicine from Salerno to the Black Death*. Ed. Luis García Ballester, *et al.* Cambridge: CUP, 1994. Pp. 186–211.

———. *Le milieu medical en France du XIIe au XVe siècle*. Geneva: Librairie Droz, 1981.

Jacquart, Danielle, and Claude Thomasset. *Sexuality and Medicine in the Middle Ages*. Trans. Matthew Adamson. Princeton: Princeton University Press, 1985.

352
WORKS CITED

Jacyna, Stephen. "Medicine in Transformation, 1800–1849." In *The Western Medical Tradition, 1800–2000*. Ed. W.F. Bynum *et al.* Cambridge: CUP, 2006. Pp. 11–101.

Jambeck, Karen K. "The *Tretiz* of Walter of Bibbesworth: Cultivating the Vernacular." In *Childhood in the Middle Ages and Renaissance: The Results of a Paradigm Shift in the History of Mentality*. Ed. Albrecht Classen. Berlin and New York: Walter de Gruyter, 2005. Pp. 159–83.

Jenner, Mark S.R., and Patrick Wallis, eds. *Medicine and the Market in England and its Colonies, c.1450- c.1850*. New York: Palgrave Macmillan, 2007.

Johnson, Máire. "'Vengeance is Mine': Saintly Retribution in Medieval Ireland." In *Vengeance in the Middle Ages: Emotion, Religion, and Feud*. Ed. Susanna Throop and Paul Hyams. Burlington and Surrey: Ashgate, 2010. Pp. 5–50.

———. "Holy Body, Wholly Other: Sanctity and Society in the *Lives* of Irish Saints." Ph.D. Diss., University of Toronto, 2010.

———. "Preserving the Body Christian: The Motif of 'Recapitation' in Ireland's Medieval Hagiography." *The Heroic Age: A Journal of Early Medieval Northwestern Europe* 10 (2007): http://www.heroicage.org.

Jones, Karen. *Gender and Petty Crime in Late Medieval England: The Local Courts in Kent, 1460–1560*. Woodbridge: Boydell, 2006.

Jones, Peter Murray. "Thomas Fayreford: an English Fifteenth-century Medical Practitioner." In *Medicine from the Black Death to the French Disease*. Ed. Roger French, *et al.* Aldershot: Ashgate, 1998. Pp. 156–83.

Kealey, Edward J. *Medieval Medicus: A Social History of Anglo-Norman Medicine*. Baltimore and London: Johns Hopkins University Press, 1981.

Kehnel, Annette. "The Narrative Tradition of the Medieval Franciscan Friars on the British Isles. Introduction to the Sources." *FS* 63 (2005): 461–530.

Kelleher, Marie A. *The Measure of Woman: Law and Female Identity in the Crown of Aragon*. Philadelphia: University of Pennsylvania Press, 2010.

Kelly, Fergus. *Early Irish Farming*. Dublin: DIAS, 1997.

———. *A Guide to Early Irish Law*. Dublin: DIAS, 1988.

Kelly, Henry Ansgar. "Statutes of Rape and Alleged Ravishers of Wives: A Context for the Charges against Thomas Malory, Knight." *Viator* 28 (1997): 361–419.

Kemp, Eric W. *Canonization and Authority in the Western Church*. New York: AMS Press, 1980.

Kenney, James F. *The Sources for the Early History of Ireland (Ecclesiastical): An Introduction and Guide*. Dublin: Pádraic Ó Táilliúir, 1979.

Kermode, Jenny. *Medieval Merchants: York, Beverley and Hull in the Later Middle Ages*. Cambridge: CUP, 2002.

Khami, Ghada. "State Control of the Physician in the Middle Ages: an Islamic Model." In *The Town and State Physician*. Ed. Andrew W. Russell. Wolfenbüttler: Herzog August Bibliothek, 1981. Pp. 63–84.

Kibre, Pearl. "The Faculty of Medicine at Paris, Charlatanism and Unlicensed Medical Practices in the Middle Ages." *BHM* 27 (1953): 1–20.

Kilday, Anne-Marie. *Women and Violent Crime in Enlightenment Scotland.* Woodbridge: Boydell, 2007.

King, Helen. *Hippocrates' Woman: Reading the Female Body in Ancient Greece.* London: Routledge, 1998.

Klestinec, Cynthia. *Theaters of Anatomy: Students, Teachers and Traditions of Dissection in Renaissance Venice.* Maryland: Johns Hopkins University Press, 2011.

Koopmans, Rachel. *Wonderful to Relate: Miracle Stories and Miracle Collecting in High Medieval England.* Philadelphia: University of Pennsylvania Press, 2011.

Krasmann, Susanne, and Thomas Lemke, eds. *Governmentality: Current Issues and Future Challenges.* New York and London: Routledge, 2011.

Kruger, Steven F. "Dream Space and Masculinity." *Word & Image* 14.1–2 (1998): 11–16.

Kümper, Hiram. "Did Medieval Canon Law Invent Our Modern Notion of Rape? Revisiting the Idea of Consent Before and After 1200." In *Law and Marriage in Medieval and Early Modern Times.* Ed. Per Andersen, Kiris Salonen, Helle Møller Sigh, and Helle Vogt. Copenhagen: DJØF, 2012. Pp. 127–38.

Langbein, John H. (1974). *Prosecuting Crime in the Renaissance: England, Germany, France.* Clark, NJ: Lawbook Exchange, repr. 2005.

Lanning, John Tate, and John Jay TePaske. *The Royal Protomedicato: The Regulation of the Medical Profession in the Spanish Empire.* Durham, NC: Duke University Press, 1985.

Laqueur, Thomas. *Making Sex: Body and Gender from the Greeks to Freud.* Cambridge, MA: Harvard University Press, 1990.

Laurent, Sylvie. *Naître au moyen âge: de la conception à la naissance: la grossesse et l'accouchement (XIIe–XVe siècle).* Paris: Léopard d'Or, 1989.

Le Goff, Jacques. *Saint Francis of Assisi.* Trans. C. Rhone. London: Routledge, 2004.

———. *Pour un autre Moyen Age: temps, travail et culture en Occident.* Paris: Gallimard, 1977.

Lee, Becky R. "A Company of Women and Men: Men's Recollections of Childbirth in Medieval England." *Journal of Family History* 27.2 (2002): 92–100.

———. "Men's Recollections of a Women's Rite: Medieval English Men's Recollections Regarding the Rite of the Purification of Women after Childbirth." *Gender & History* 14.2 (2002): 224–41.

Lemay, Helen Rodnite. "William of Saliceto on Human Sexuality." *Viator* 12 (1981): 165–81.

Lepicard, Étienne. "Medical Licensing and Practice in Medieval Spain: a Model of Interfaith Relationships?" In *Medicine and Medical Ethics in Medieval and Early Modern Spain: An Intercultural Approach.* Ed. Samuel Kottek and Luis García Ballester. Jerusalem: Magnes Press, Hebrew University, 1996. Pp. 50–60.

Lett, Didier. *L'enfant des miracles: Enfance et société au Moyen Âge (XIIe–XIIIe siècle)*. Paris: Aubier, 1997.

Lingo, Alison. "Empirics and Charlatans in Early Modern France: the Genesis of the Classification of the 'Other' in Medical Practice." *Journal of Social History* 19 (1986): 583–604.

Lockwood, Dean Putnam. *Ugo Benzi: Medieval Philosopher and Physician, 1376–1439*. Chicago: University of Chicago Press, 1951.

López Elum, Pedro and Mateu Rodrigo Lizondo. "La mujer en el Código de Jaime I de los Furs de Valencia." In *Las mujeres medievales y su ámbito jurídico. Actas de las II Jornadas de investigación interdisciplinaria*. Madrid: Universidad Autónoma de Madrid, 1983. Pp. 125–35.

López Terrada, María Luz. "Medical Pluralism in the Iberian Kingdoms: the Control of Extra-Academic Practitioners in Valencia." *MH*, supp. 29 (2009): 7–25.

———. "The Control of Medical Practice under the Spanish Monarchy during the Sixteenth and Seventeenth Centuries." In *Beyond the Black Legend: Spain and the Scientific Revolution*. Ed. Víctor Navarro Brotóns and William Eamon. Valencia: Universitat de Valencia and C.S.I.C., 2007. Pp. 283–94.

Loud, G.A. "The Case of the Missing Martyrs: Frederick II's War with the Church, 1239–1250." In *Martyrs and Martyrologies*. Ed. Diana Wood. *Studies in Church History* v. 30. Oxford: Blackwell Publishers, 1993. Pp. 141–52.

MacKinney, L.C. "Childbirth in the Middle Ages as Seen in Manuscript Illustrations." *Ciba Symposium* 8.5/6 (1960): 230–36.

Magnus, Ulrich. "Compensation for Personal Injuries in a Comparative Perspective." *Washburn Law Journal* 39 (2000): 347–362.

Maitland, F.W., and F. Pollock. *The History of English Law before the Time of Edward I*. 2 vols. London: C.J. Clay & Sons, 1899.

Markl, Dagoberto. *Livro de Horas de D. Manuel*. Lisbon: Crédito Predial Português, 1983.

Marques, António Henrique de Oliveira. *Portugal na Crise dos Séculos XIV e XV*, Nova História de Portugal v. 4. Lisbon: Editorial Presença, 1986.

McCarthy, Caley. "Midwives, Medicine, and the Reproductive Female Body in Manosque, 1289–1500." M.A. Diss, University of Waterloo, 2011.

McCleery, Iona. "Both 'Illness and Temptation of the Enemy': Melancholy, the Medieval Patient and the Writings of King Duarte of Portugal (r. 1433–38)." *Journal of Medieval Iberian Studies* 1 (2009): 163–78.

———. "Isabel of Aragon (d.1336): Model Queen or Model Saint?" *Journal of Ecclesiastical History* 57 (2006): 668–92.

McClive, Cathy. "Blood and Expertise: The Trials of the Female Medical Expert in the Ancien-Régime Courtroom." *BHM* 82 (2008): 86–108.

McCone, Kim. "Werewolves, Cyclopes, *Díberga* and *Fíanna*: Juvenile Delinquency in Early Ireland." *Cambridge Medieval Celtic Studies* 12 (1986): 1–22.

———. *Pagan Past and Christian Present in Early Irish Literature*. Maynooth: An Sagart, 1991.

McGlynn, Margaret. "Idiots, Lunatics, and the Royal Prerogative in Early Tudor England." *The Journal of Legal History* 26.1 (2005): 1–20

McVaugh, Michael R. *The Rational Surgery of the Middle Ages*. Florence: SISMEL, Edizione del Galluzzo, 2006.

———. "Surgery in the Fourteenth-century Faculty of Montpellier." In *L'Université de médicine de Montpellier et son rayonnement (XIIIᵉ–XIᵉ siècles)*. Ed. Daniel Le Blévec. Turnhout: Brepols, 2004. Pp. 39–49.

———. "Surgical Education in the Middle Ages." *DYNAMIS* 20 (2000): 249–81.

———. "Therapeutic Strategies: Surgery." In *Western Medical Thought from Antiquity to the Middle Ages*. Ed. Mirko Grmek, *et al.* Cambridge, MA: Harvard University Press, 1998. Pp. 273–90.

———. "Bedside Manners in the Middle Ages." *BHM* 71 (1997): 201–23.

———. *Medicine before the Plague: Practitioners and their Patients in the Crown of Aragon, 1285–1345*. Cambridge: CUP, 1993.

Mendonça, Manuela. "A reforma da saúde no reinado de D. Manuel." In *Iᵃˢ Jornadas de História do Direito Hispânico: Actas*. Lisbon: Academia Portuguesa da História, 2004. Pp. 221–41.

Metge, Bernat. *Lo somni*. Ed. Lola Badia. Barcelona: Quaderns Crema, 1999.

Metzler, Irina. *A Social History of Disability in the Middle Ages: Cultural Considerations of Physical Impairment*. New York: Routledge, 2013.

———. *Disability in Medieval Europe: Thinking about Physical Impairment in the High Middle Ages, c.1100-c.1400*. New York: Routledge, 2005.

Miller, William I. *Eye for an Eye*. Cambridge: CUP, 2006.

———. *Bloodtaking and Peacemaking. Feud, Law, and Society in Saga Iceland*. Chicago and London: University of Chicago Press, 1990.

Mitchell, Piers D. *Medicine in the Crusades: Warfare, Wounds and the Medieval Surgeon*. Cambridge: CUP, 2004.

Mommsen, Theodor. *Römisches Strafrecht*. Leipzig: Duncker & Humblot, 1899.

Moore, R.I. "Between Sanctity and Superstition: Saints and their Miracles in the Age of Revolution." In *The Work of Jacques le Goff and the Challenges of Medieval History*. Ed. Miri Rubin. Woodbridge: Boydell, 1997. Pp. 55–67.

Moorman, John. *A History of the Franciscan Order: From its Origins to the Year 1517*. Chicago: Franciscan Herald Press, 1968.

Morejón, Don Antonio Hernández. *Historia bibliográfica de la medicina española*. London: Johnson Reprints, 1967.

Moreno, Anibal Ruiz. *La Medicina en la legislación medieval española*. Alcalá la Real: Formación Alcalá, 2009.

Muir, Edward. "The Idea of Community in Renaissance Italy." *Renaissance Quarterly* 55 (2002): 1–18.

Muniz, Márcio Ricardo Coelho. "1531: Gil Vicente, judeus e a instauração da Inquisição em Portugal." *Vitória* 7 (2000): 95–108.

Munkhoff, Richelle. "Searchers of the Dead: Authority, Marginality, and the Interpretation of Plague in England, 1574–1665." *Gender and History* 11 (1999): 1–29.

Munro, Vanessa, and Clare McGlynn, eds. *Rethinking Rape Law: International and Comparative Perspectives*. Milton Park: Routledge, 2010.

Munske, Horst Haider. *Der germanische Rechtswortschatz im Bereich der Missetaten. Philologische und sprachgeografische Untersuchungen. I. Die Terminologie der älteren westgermanischen Rechtsquellen*. Berlin and New York: de Gruyter, 1973.

Münster, L. "La medicina legale in Bologna dai suoi albori alla fine del secolo XIV." *Bollettino dell'accademia medica pistoiese Filippo Pacini*, 26 (1955): 257–71.

Musacchio, Jacqueline. *The Art and Ritual of Childbirth in Renaissance Italy*. New Haven: Yale University Press, 1999.

Naessens, Mariann. "Sexuality in Court: Emotional Perpetrators and Victims versus a Rational Judicial System?" In *Emotions in the Heart of the City: 14th–16th Century*. Ed. Elodie Lecuppre-Desjardin and Anne-Laure Van Bruaene. Turnhout: Brepols, 2005. Pp. 119–56.

Narbona, Rafael. *Malhechores, violencia y justicia ciudadana en la Valencia bajomedieval (1360–1399)*. Valencia: Ayuntamiento de Valencia, 1990.

Nicoud, Marilyn. "Formes et enjeux d'une medicalisation médiévale: réflexions sur les cités italiennes (XIIIe–XVe siècles)." *Genéses* 82 (2011): 7–30.

Niederhellmann, Annette. *Arzt und Heilkunde in den frühmittelalterlichen Leges. Eine wort- und sachkundige Untersuchung*. Berlin and New York: de Gruyter, 1983.

Nijdam, Han. "Belichaamde eer, wraak en vete. Een historisch- en cognitief-antropologische benadering." *Tijdschrift voor Geschiedenis* 123 (2010): 192–207.

———. "Klinkende munten en klinkende botsplinters in de Oudfriese rechtsteksten: continuïteit, discontinuïteit, intertekstualiteit." *De Vrije Fries* 89 (2009): 45–66.

———. *Lichaam, eer en recht in middeleeuws Friesland. Een studie naar de Oudfriese boeteregisters*. Hilversum: Verloren, 2008.

———. "Measuring Wounds in the *Lex Frisionum* and the Old Frisian Registers of Fines." In *Philologia Frisica Anno 1999. Lêzingen fan it fyftjinde Frysk filologekongres 8, 9 en 10 desimber 1999*. Ed. Piter Boersma, *et al*. Leeuwarden: Fryske Akademy, 2000. Pp. 180–203.

Norri, Juhani. *Names of Sicknesses in English, 1400–1550: An Exploration of the Lexical Field*. Helsinki: Suomalainen Tiedeakatemia, 1992.

Nutton, Vivian. "Medieval in Medieval Western Europe, 1000–1500." In *The Western Medical Tradition: 800 BC to AD 1800*. Ed. Lawrence I. Contrad, *et al*. Cambridge: CUP, 1995. Pp. 139–206.

———. "Healers in the Medical Market Place: Towards a Social History of Graeco-Roman Medicine." In *Medicine in Society*. Ed. Andrew Wear. Cambridge: CUP, 1992. Pp. 15–58.

———. "Continuity or Rediscovery? The City Physician in Classical Antiquity and Medieval Italy." In *The Town and State Physician in Europe from the Middle Ages to the Enlightenment*. Ed. Andrew W. Russell. Wolfenbüttel: Wolfenbüttler Forschungen 17, 1981. Pp. 9–46.

O'Boyle, Cornelius. *The Art of Medicine: Medical Teaching at the University of Paris 1250–1400*. Leiden: Brill, 1998.

———. "Surgical Texts and Social Contexts: Physicians and Surgeons in Paris c. 1270–1430." In *Practical Medicine from Salerno to the Black Death*. Ed. Luis García Ballester, *et al*. Cambridge: CUP, 1994. Pp. 156–185.

Ó Cathasaig, Tomás. "Curse and Satire." *Éigse* 21 (1986): 10–15.

Ó Corráin, Donnchadh. "Women and the Law in Early Ireland." In *Chattel, Servant or Citizen: Women's Status in Church, State and Society*. Ed. Mary O'Dowd and Sabine Wichert. Belfast: The Institute of Irish Studies, 1995. Pp. 45–57.

Ó Corráin, Donnchadh, Liam Breatnach and Aidan Breen. "The Laws of the Irish." *Peritia* 3 (1984): 382–438.

Ó Riain, Pádraig. *A Dictionary of Irish Saints*. Dublin: Four Courts Press, 2011.

Oldham, James C. "On Pleading the Belly: A History of The Jury of Matrons." *Criminal Justice* 6 (1985): 1–64.

Oliver, Lisi. *The Body Legal in Barbarian Law*. Toronto: University of Toronto Press, 2011.

Orr, Patricia. "Men's Theory and Women's Reality. Rape Prosecutions in the English Royal Courts of Justice, 1194–1222." In *The Rusted Hauberk. Feudal Ideas of Order and their Decline*. Ed. Liam O. Purdon and Cindy L. Vitto. Gainesville: University Press of Florida, 1994. Pp. 121–59.

Ortalli, Gerardo. "La perizia medica a Bologna nei secoli XIII e XIV." *Deputazione di storia patria per la provincia di Romagna. Atti e memorie*, n.s., 17–19 (1969): 223–259.

Osborne, Thomas. "Of Health and Statecraft." In *Foucault, Health and Medicine*. Ed. Alan Petersen and Robin Bunton. London: Routledge, 1997. Pp. 173–88.

Park, Katharine. "Holy Autopsies: Saintly Bodies and Medical Expertise, 1300–1600." In *The Body in Early Modern Italy*. Ed. Julia L. Hairston and Walter Stephens. Maryland: Johns Hopkins University Press, 2010. Pp. 61–73.

———. "Birth and Death." In *A Cultural History of the Human Body in the Medieval Age*. Ed. Linda Kalof. Oxford and New York: Berg, 2010. Pp. 17–38.

———. *The Secrets of Women: Gender, Generation, and the Origins of Human Dissection.* New York: Zone Books, 2006.

———. "Relics of a Fertile Heart: The 'Autopsy' of Clare of Montefalco." In *The Material Culture of Sex, Procreation and Marriage in Premodern Europe.* Ed. Anne L. McClanan and Karen Rosoff Encarnaciòn. New York: Palgrave McMillian, 2002. Pp. 115–34.

———. "The Criminal and the Saintly Body: Autopsy and Dissection in Renaissance Italy." *Renaissance Quarterly* 47.1 (1994): 1–33.

———. "Medicine and Society in Medieval Europe, 500–1500." In *Medicine in Society: Historical Essays.* Ed. Andrew Wear. Cambridge: CUP, 1992. Pp. 59–90.

———. *Doctors and Medicine in Early Renaissance Florence.* Princeton: Princeton University Press, 1985.

Parsons, John Carmi. "Mothers, Daughters, Marriage, Power." In *Medieval Queenship.* Ed. John Carmi Parsons. New York: St Martin's Press, 1993. Pp. 63–78.

Pastore, Alessandro. *Il medico in tribunale: La perizia medica nella procedura penale d'antico regime (secoli XVI–XVIII).* Bellinzona: Edizioni Casagrande, 1998.

Pastore, Alessandro, and Giovanni Rossi, eds. *Paolo Zacchia: alle origini della medicina legale 1584–1659.* Milan: FrancoAngeli, 2008.

Pazzaglini, Peter Raymond. *The Criminal Ban of the Sienese Commune, 1225–1310.* Milan: Giuffrè, 1979.

Pelligrini, Luigi. "A Century of Reading the Sources for the Life of St Francis of Assisi." *Greyfriars Review* 7.3 (1993): 323–346.

Pelling, Margaret. "Politics, Medicine and Masculinity: Physicians and Office-Bearing in Early Modern England." In *The Practice of Reform in Health, Medicine and Science, 1500–2000: Essays for Charles Webster.* Ed. Margaret Pelling and Scott Mandelbrote. Aldershot: Ashgate, 2005. Pp. 81–106.

———. *Medical Conflicts in Early Modern London: Patronage, Physicians, and Irregular Practitioners, 1550–1640.* Oxford: OUP, 2003.

Pennington, Kenneth. "Innocent III and the *ius commune*." In *Grundlagen des Rechts: Festschrift für Peter Landau zum 65. Geburtstag.* Ed. R.H. Helmholz, Paul Mikat, Jörg Müller, Michael Stolleis. Rechts- und Staatswissenschaftliche Veröffentlichungen der Görres-Gesell-schaft, NF 91; Paderborn: Verlag Ferdinand Schöningh, 2000. Pp. 349–366.

Pereira, António dos Santos. "The Urgent Empire: Portugal between 1475 and 1525." *e-Journal of Portuguese History* 4 (2006): http://www.brown.edu/Departments/Portuguese_Brazilian_Studies/ejph/html/issue8/pdf/apereira.pdf. Accessed May 21, 2012.

Perkins, Judith. *The Suffering Self: Pain and Narrative Representation in the Early Christian Era.* London and New York: Routledge, 1995.

Perry, Mary Elizabeth. "Magdalens and Jezebels in Counter Reformation Spain." In *Culture and Control in Counter-Reformation Spain.* Ed. Anne J. Cruz and Mary Elizabeth Perry. Minneapolis: University of Minnesota Press, 1992. Pp. 124–44.

Petersen, Alan, and Robin Bunton, eds. *Foucault, Health and Medicine*. London: Routledge, 1997.

Petrelli, Richard L. "The Regulation of French Midwifery during the *Ancien Régime*." *JHMAS* 26.3 (1971): 276–92.

Phillips, Kim M. "Written on the Body: Reading Rape from the Twelfth to the Fifteenth Century." In *Medieval Women and the Law*. Ed. Noël James Menuge. Woodbridge: Boydell, 2003. Pp. 125–44.

Pinker, Steven. *The Better Angels of our Nature. Why Violence has Declined*. New York: Viking, 2011.

Pollock, Frederick and Frederic W. Maitland. *The History of English Law before the Time of Edward I*. 2nd ed. Two vols. London: CUP, 1968.

Pomata, Giana. "Practicing between Earth and Heaven: Women Healers in Seventeenth-Century Bologna." *DYNAMIS* 19 (1999): 121–2.

———. *Contracting a Cure: Patients, Healers, and the Law in Early Modern Bologna*. Baltimore: Johns Hopkins University Press, 1998.

Poni, Carlo. "Local Market Rules and Practices: Three Guilds in the Same Line of Production in Early Modern Bologna." In *Domestic Strategies: Work and Family in France and Italy, 1600–1800*. Ed. Stuart Woolf. Cambridge: CUP, 1991. Pp. 69–101.

Pormann, Peter. "The Physician and the Other: Images of the Charlatan in Medieval Islam." *BHM* 79 (2005): 189–227.

Porteau-Bitker, Annik. "La justice laïque et le viol au Moyen Âge." *Revue historique de droit français et étranger* 66 (1988): 491–526.

Porter, Dorothy. "The History of Public Health: Current Themes and Approaches." *Hygiea Internationalis* 1 (1999): 9–21.

Porter, Roy. *Quacks: Fakers and Charlatans in English Medicine*. Stroud: Tempus, 2001.

———. "The Patient's View: Doing Medical History from Below." *Theory and Society* 14 (1985): 167–74.

Post, Gaines. *Masters' Salaries and Student-Fees in Mediaeval Universities*. Cambridge, MA: Medieval Academy of America, 1932.

Postan, Michael M. *The Cambridge Economic History of Europe: Trade and Industry in the Middle Ages*. Cambridge: CUP, 1987.

Powell, Hilary. "The 'Miracle of Childbirth': The Portrayal of Parturient Women in Medieval Miracle Narratives." *SHM* 25.4 (2012): 795–811.

Power, Eileen. *Medieval Women*. Cambridge: CUP, 1975.

Price-Smith, Andrew, ed. *Plagues and Politics: Infectious Disease and International Policy*. Basingstoke: Palgrave, 2001.

Prior, Lindsay. *The Social Organization of Death: Medical Discourse and Social Practices in Belfast*. New York: St Martin's, 1989.

Ralley, Robert. "Medical Economies in Fifteenth-century England." In *Medicine and the Market in England and its Colonies, c. 1450–c. 1850*. Ed. Mark S.R. Jenner and Patrick Wallis. New York: Palgrave Macmillan, 2007. Pp. 24–46.

Rashdall, Hastings. *The Universities of Europe in the Middle Ages*. Oxford: Clarendon Press, 1895.

Rawcliffe, Carole. "Sickness and Health." In *Medieval Norwich*. Ed. Carole Rawcliffe and Richard Wilson. London: Hambledon, 2004. Pp. 301–26.

———. "More than a Bedside Manner: the Political Status of the Late Medieval Court Physician." In *St George's Chapel, Windsor, in the Late Middle Ages*. Ed. C. Richmond and E. Scarff. Leeds: Maney Pub., 2001. Pp. 71–91.

———. *Medicine & Society in Later Medieval England*. London: Alan Sutton, Pub., 1995.

———. "The Profits of Practice: the Wealth and Status of Medical Men in Later Medieval England." *SHM* 1.1 (1988): 61–78.

Ray, Jonathan. "Beyond Tolerance and Persecution: Reassessing our Approach to Medieval *convivencia*." *Jewish Social Studies* 11 (2006): 1–18.

Reames, Sherry L. *The Legenda Aurea: A Reexamination of its Paradoxical History*. Madison, WI: University of Wisconsin Press, 1985.

Renna, Thomas. "Saint Francis as Prophet in Celano and Bonaventure." *Michigan Academician* 33. 4 (2000): 321–332.

Riquer, Martín de. *Història de la literatura catalana*. V. 3. Barcelona: Ariel, 1980.

Rizelli, Giunio. *Lex Iulia de adulteriis. Studi sulla disciplina di adulterium, lenocinium, stuprum*. Lecce: Edizioni del Grifo, 1997.

Roberts, Michael J.D. "The Politics of Professionalisation: MPs, Medical Men and the 1858 Medical Act." *MH* 53 (2009): 37–56.

Robertson, Stephen. *Crimes Against Children: Sexual Violence and Legal Culture in New York City, 1880–1960*. Chapel Hill and London: University of North Carolina Press, 2005.

Robinson, Olivia F. "Unpardonable Crimes: Fourth Century Attitudes." In *Critical Studies in Ancient Law, Comparative Law and Legal History*. Ed. John W. Cairns. Oxford: OUP, 2001. Pp. 117–126.

Robson, Michael. *The Franciscans in the Middle Ages*. Woodbridge: Boydell, 2006.

Roest, Bert. "Reading the Book of History: Intellectual Contexts and Educational Functions of Franciscan Hagiography, 1226–ca 1350." Ph.D. Diss., Groningen University, 1996.

Roffe, David, and Christine Roffe. "Madness and Care in the Community: A Medieval Perspective." *British Medical Journal* 311. 7021 (1995): 1708–1712.

Roque, Mário da Costa. *As Pestes Medievais Europeias e o "Regimento Proveitoso Contra ha Pestenença."* Paris: Fundação Calouste Gulbenkian, Centro Cultural Português, 1979.

Rose, Nikolas. "Medicine, History and the Present." In *Reassessing Foucault: Power, Medicine and the Body*. Ed. Colin Jones and Roy Porter. London and New York: Routledge, 1998. Pp. 47–72.

Roth, Robert. "Juges et médecins face à l'infanticide à Genève au XIXᵉ siècle." *Gesnerus* 34 (1977): 113–128.

Rothwell, W. "A Mis-Judged Author and a Mis-Used Text: Walter de Bibbesworth and His 'Tretiz.'" *The Modern Language Review* 77.2 (1982): 282–93.

Ruberg, Willemijn. "Travelling Knowledge and Forensic Medicine: Infanticide, Body and Mind in the Netherlands, 1811–1911." *MH* 57 (2013): 359–376.

Rubin, Miri. *Mother of God: A History of the Virgin Mary*. New Haven and London: Yale University Press, 2009.

———. *Charity and Community in Medieval Cambridge*. London and New York: CUP, 1987.

Rubin, S. "The *bot*, or Compensation in Anglo-Saxon Law: A Reassesment." *Journal of Legal History* 17.1 (1996): 144–54.

Ruggiero, Guido. "The Cooperation of Physicians and the State in the Control of Violence in Renaissance Venice." *JHMAS* 33 (1978): 156–66.

Rushton, Cory James, ed. *Disability and Medieval Law: History, Literature, Society*. Newcastle upon Tyne, England: Cambridge Scholars Publishing, 2013.

Sá, Isabel dos Guimarães. "Shaping Social Space in the Centre and Periphery of the Portuguese Empire: the Example of the Misericórdias from the Sixteenth to the Eighteenth Centuries." *Portuguese Studies* 12 (1997): 210–21.

Sabatier, Paul. *The Life of Francis of Assisi*. Trans. L.S. Houghton. London: Hodder and Stoughton, 1919.

Sacco, Lynn. *Unspeakable Father-Daughter Incest in American History*. Baltimore: Johns Hopkins University Press, 2009.

Salvat, Michel. "L'accouchement dans la literature scientifique medievale." In *L'enfant au Moyen Age*. Senefiance, v. 9. Paris: Cuerma, 1980. Pp. 89–106.

Santa Maria, Francisco de. *O Ceu Aberto na Terra: História das Sagradas Congregações dos Conegos Seculares de. S. Jorge em Alga de Venesa e de S. João Evangelista em Portugal*. 4 vols. in 2. Lisbon: Officina de Manoel Lopes Ferreyra, 1697.

Sarti, Mauro, and Mauro Fattorini. *De Claris Archigymnasii Bononiensis professoribus: a saeculo XI usque ad saeculum XIV*. Bologna: Ex officina regia fratrum Merlani, 1896.

Saunier, Annie. "Le visiteur, les femmes et les 'obstetrices' des paroisses de l'archdiaconé de Josas de 1458 à 1470." In *Santé, Médecine et Assistance au Moyen Âge*. Paris: Comité des travaux historiques et scientifiques, 1987. Pp. 43–62.

Schatzlein, Joanne, and Daniel O. Sulmasy. "The Diagnosis of St Francis: Evidence for Leprosy." *FS* 47 (1987): 181–217.

Schmitt, Jean-Claude. "The Liminality and Centrality of Dreams in the Medieval West." In *Dream Cultures: Explorations in the Comparative History of Dreaming*. Ed. David Shulman and Guy G. Stroumsa. New York: OUP, 1999. Pp. 274–87.

Schulenburg, Jane Tibbetts. "Saints and Sex, ca. 500–1100: Striding Down the Nettled Path of Life." In *Sex in the Middle Ages: A Book of Essays*. Ed. Joyce E. Salisbury. New York and London: Garland Publishing, 1991. Pp. 203–31.

Seymour, M.C. *et al.*, ed. *Bartholomaeus Anglicus and his Encyclopedia*. London: Variorum, 1992.

Shahar, Shulamith. *Childhood in the Middle Ages*. London and New York: Routledge, 1990.

Sharpe, Richard. *Medieval Irish Saints' Lives: An Introduction to* Vitae sanctorum Hiberniae. Oxford: Clarendon Press, 1991.

———. "Hiberno-Latin *Laicus*, Irish *Láech* and the Devil's Men." *Ériu* 30 (1979): 75–92.

Shatzmiller, Joseph. "The Jurisprudence of the Dead Body: Medical Practition at the Service of Civic and Legal Authorities." *Micrologus* 7 (1999): 223–230.

———. *Jews, Medicine, and Medieval Society*. Berkeley: University of California Press, 1994.

———. "Doctor's Fees and their Medical Responsibility." In *Sources of Social History: Private Acts of the Late Middle Ages*. Ed. Paolo Brezzi and Egmund Lee. Toronto: Pontifical Institute of Mediaeval Studies, 1984. Pp. 201–08.

Shogimen, Takashi. "'Head or Heart?' Revisited: Physiology and Political Thought in the Thirteenth and Fourteenth Centuries." *History of Political Thought* 28 (2007): 208–229.

Siems, Harald. *Studien zur Lex Frisionum*. Ebelsbach: Gremer, 1980.

Siena, Kevin. "Searchers of the Dead in Long Eighteenth-Century London." In *Worth and Repute: Valuing Gender in Late Medieval and Early Modern Europe*. Ed. Kim Kippen and Lori Woods. Toronto: Centre for Reformation and Renaissance Studies, 2011. Pp. 123–152.

Sigal, Pierre André. "La Grossesse, l'accouchement et l'attitude envers l'enfant mort-né à la fin du moyen âge d'après les récits de miracles." In *Santé, Médecine et Assistance au Moyen Age*. Paris: Comité des travaux historiques et scientifiques, 1987.

———. *L'homme et le miracle dans la France médiévale*. Paris: CERF, 1985.

Simili, Alessandro. "The Beginnings of Forensic Medicine in Bologna." In *International Symposium on Society, Medicine, and Law: Jerusalem 1972*. Ed. Heinrich Karplus. Amsterdam and London: Elsevier, 1973. Pp. 91–100

———. "Sui primordi e sulla procedura della medicina legale in Bologna." *Atti e Memorie dell'Accademia di Storia dell'Arte Sanitaria*, Serie II, Any IX (1943): 41–56.

Singer, Charles. "Thirteenth Century Miniatures Illustrating Medical Practice." *Proceedings of the Royal Society of Medicine* 9 (1915): 29–47

Siraisi, Nancy G. *History, Medicine, and the Traditions of Renaissance Learning*. Ann Arbor, MI: University of Michigan Press, 2007.

———. *Medicine and the Italian Universities, 1250–1600*. Leiden: Brill, 2001.

―――. "How to Write a Latin Book on Surgery: Organizing Principles and Authorial Devices in Guglielmo da Saliceto and Dino del Garbo." In *Practical Medicine from Salerno to the Black Death*. Ed. Luis García Ballester, *et al.* Cambridge: CUP, 1994. Pp. 88–109.

―――. "Girolamo Cardano and the Art of Medical Narrative." *Journal of the History of Ideas* 52.4 (1991): 581–602.

―――. *Medieval and Early Renaissance Medicine: An Introduction to Knowledge and Practice*. Chicago: University of Chicago Press, 1990.

―――. *Taddeo Alderotti and his Pupils*. Princeton: Princeton University Press, 1981.

Sixto, Ricardo. *La contratación laboral en la Valencia medieval. Aprendizaje y servicio doméstico (1458–1462)*. Ph.D. Diss., Universitat de València, 1993.

Smoak, Ginger L. "Midwives as Agents of Social Control: Ecclesiastical and Municipal Regulation of Midwifery in the Late Middle Ages." *Quidditas: On-line Journal of the Rocky Mountain Medieval and Renaissance Association* 33 (2012): 79–96.

Soifer, Maya. "Beyond *Convivencia*: Critical Reflections on the Historiography of Interfaith Relations in Christian Spain." *Journal of Medieval Iberian Studies* 1 (2009): 19–35.

Solomon, Michael. *The Literature of Misogyny in Medieval Spain: The* Arcipreste de Talavera *and the* Spill. Cambridge: CUP, 1997.

Soman, Alfred. "Anatomy of an Infanticide Trial: The Case of Marie-Jeanne Bartonnet (1742)." In *Changing Identities in Early Modern France*. Ed. Michael Wolfe. Durham, NC: Duke University Press, 1997. Pp. 248–272.

Sorbelli, Albano. *Storia della Università di Bologna*, 2 vols. Bologna: N. Zanichelli, 1944.

Soyer, Francois. "Living in Fear of Revenge: Religious Minorities and the Right to Bear Arms in Fifteenth-Century Portugal." In *Vengeance in the Middle Ages: Emotion, Religion and Feud*. Ed. Susanna Throop and Paul Hyams. Farnham: Ashgate, 2010. Pp. 85–99.

―――. "The Massacre of the New Christians of Lisbon in 1506: a New Eyewitness Account." *Cadernos de Estudos Sefarditas* 7 (2007): 221–43.

―――. *The Persecution of the Jews and Muslims of Portugal: King Manuel I and the End of Religious Tolerance (1496–7)*. Leiden: Brill, 2007.

Spufford, Peter. *Money and its Use in Medieval Europe*. Cambridge: CUP, 1989, repr. 1993.

Stell, Philip. "Medical Practice in Medieval York." *Borthwick Paper* 90 (1996): 1–35.

Stewart, Frank H. *Honor*. Chicago: Chicago University Press, 1994.

Stiker, Henri-Jacques. *A History of Disability*. Trans. William Sayers. Ann Arbor, MI: University of Michigan Press, 2002.

Strayer, Joseph. "The Political Crusades of the Thirteenth Century." In *A History of the Crusades*, v. 4. Ed. Kenneth Setton. Madison, Milwaukee, London: University of Wisconsin Press, 1969. Pp. 343–75.

Stout, Debra. "Medieval German Women and the Power of Healing." In *Women Healers and Physicians: Climbing a Long Hill*. Ed. Lilian R. Furst. Lexington: University Press of Kentucky, 1997. Pp. 13–42.

Sutherland, Donald W. "Peytevin v. La Lynde." *Law Quarterly Review* 83 (1967): 527–546.

Taglia, Kathryn. "Delivering a Christian Identity: Midwives in Northern French Synodal Legislation, c. 1200–1500." In *Religion and Medicine in the Middle Ages*. Ed. Peter Biller and Joseph Ziegler. York: Boydell, 2001. Pp. 77–90.

Talbot, C.H. and E.A. Hammond. *The Medical Practitioners of Medieval England: a Biographical Register*. London: Wellcome Institute Medical Library, 1965.

Tartakoff, Paola. "Christian Kings and Jewish Conversion in the Medieval Crown of Aragon." *Journal of Medieval Iberian Studies* 3 (2011): 27–39.

Tavares, Maria José Ferro. "A política municipal de saúde pública (séculos XIV–XV)." *Revista de História Económica e Social* 19 (1987): 17–32.

———. *Os Judeus em Portugal no Século XV*, 2 vols. Lisbon: Universidade Nova, 1982–4.

Theilmann, J.M. "The Regulation of Public Health in Late Medieval England." In *The Age of Richard II*. Ed. J.L. Gillespie. Stroud: Sutton, 1997. Pp. 205–24.

Tillot, P.M. *A History of the County of York: the City of York*. London: OUP, 1961.

Toner, Barbara. *The Facts of Rape*. London: Hutchinson, 1977.

Toubert, Hélène. "La vierge et les deux sage-femmes: L'iconographie entre les Evangiles apocryphes et le drame liturgique." In *Georges Duby, l'ecriture de l'histoire*. Ed. Claudie Duhamel-Amado and Guy Lobrichon. Brussels: De Boeck Universite, 1996. Pp. 401–32.

Traver, Francisco Roca. *El justicia de Valencia (1283–1321)*. Valencia: Ayuntamiento de Valencia, 1970.

Trenchard-Smith, Margaret. "Perceptions of Unreason in the Byzantine Empire to the End of the First Millennium." Ph.D. Diss, University of California Los Angeles, 2006.

Turner, David M. *Disability in Eighteenth-Century England: Imagining Physical Impairment*. Abingdon: Routledge, 2012.

Turner, W.J. "Town and Country: A Comparison of the Treatment of the Mentally Disabled in Late Medieval English Common Law and Chartered Boroughs." In *Madness in Medieval Law and Custom*. Ed. W.J. Turner. Leiden and Boston: Brill, 2010. Pp. 17–38.

———. "Defining Mental Afflictions in Medieval English Administrative Records." In *Disability and Medieval Law: History, Literature, Society*. Ed. C.J. Rushton. Newcastle upon Tyne, England: Cambridge Scholars Publishing, 2013.

———. "Mental Incapacity and Financing War in Medieval England." In *The Hundred Years War, Part II: Different Vistas*. Ed. Andrew J. Villalon and Donald Kagay. Leiden and Boston: Brill, 2008. Pp. 387–402.

Turner, Wendy J., and Tory Vanderventer Pearson, eds. *The Treatment of Disabled Persons in Medieval Europe: Examining Disability in the Historical, Legal, Literary, Medical, and Religious Discourse of the Middle Ages*. Lampeter, Wales: Edwin Mellen Press, 2010.

Tuttle, Leslie. *Conceiving the Old Regime: Pronatalism and the Politics of Reproduction in Early Modern France*. Oxford: OUP, 2010.

Vallerani, Massimo. *The Medieval Public Trial*. Trans. Sarah Rubin Blanshei. Washington, D.C.: Catholic University Press, 2012.

van der Dennen, J. "Waarom wraak zoet is." http://www.nvmp.org/030304.htm.

van der Lugt, Maaike. *Le ver, le démon et la Vierge: Les théories médiévales de la génération extraordinaire. Une étude sur les rapports entre théologie, philosophie naturelle et médecine*. Paris: Les Belles Lettres, 2004.

van Oosten, M.S. "Inleidende beschouwingen over het oudere Friese bewijsrecht." *Tijdschrift voor Rechtsgeschiedenis* 18 (1950): 440–76.

van Renswoude, Irene. "'The word once sent forth can never come back': Trust in Writing and the Dangers of Publication." In *Strategies of Writing: Studies on Text and Trust in the Middle Ages*. Ed. Petra Schulte, Marco Mostert and Irene van Renswoude. Turnhout: Brepols, 2008. Pp. 393–413.

van Uytven, Raymond. *De zinnelijke middeleeuwen*. Louvain: Davidsfonds, cop., 1998.

Vann Sprecher, Tiffany D. and Ruth Mazo Karras. "The Midwife and the Church: Ecclesiastical Regulation of Midwives in Brie, 1499–1504." *BHM* 85.2 (2011): 171–92.

Vauchez, André. *Sainthood in the Later Middle Ages*. Trans. Jean Birrell. Cambridge: CUP, 1997.

Vela, Carles. *Especiers i candelers a Barcelona a la Baixa Edat Mitjana. Testaments, família i sociabilitat*. Barcelona: Fundacio Noguera, 2007.

Ventura, Margarida Garcez. *Igreja e Poder no Século XV: Dinastia de Avis e Liberdades Eclesiásticas (1383–1450)*. Lisbon: Edições Colibri, 1997.

Vercauteren, Fernand. "Les médecins dans les principautés de la Belgique et du nord de la France, du VIIIᵉ au XIIIᵉ siècle." *Le Moyen Age* 6 (1951): 61–92.

Vigarello, Georges. *A History of Rape: Sexual Violence in France from the 16th to the 20th Century*. Trans. Jean Birrell. Cambridge: Polity Press, 2001.

Vincent-Cassy, Mireille. "Viol des jeunes filles et propagande politique en France à la fin du Moyen Âge." In *Le corps des jeunes filles de l'antiquité a nos jours*. Ed. Louise Bruit Zaidman. Paris: Perrin, 2001. Pp. 117–40.

Vinyoles Vidal, Teresa. *Història de les dones a la Catalunya medieval*. Vic-Lleida: Eumo-Pagès, 2005.

Vries, Oebele. "*Her Bendix is wrbeck fonden*. De altfriesische Terminologie im Bereich des Zivilrechts." In Oebele Vries, *De taal van recht en vrijheid*. Eds. Anna Popkema, Han Nijdam and Goffe Jensma. *Studies over middeleeuws Friesland*. Gorredijk: Bornmeer, 2012. Pp. 308–345.

———. *"Toe aer heer ende aegh syoen* ("Zu Ohrenhör und Augensicht") Eine altfriesische alliterierende Paarformel im Sinnbereich des Zeugenbeweises." In Oebele Vries, *De taal van recht en vrijheid*. Eds. Anna Popkema, Han Nijdam and Goffe Jensma. *Studies over middeleeuws Friesland*. Gorredijk: Bornmeer, 2012. Pp. 371–382.

———. *"Seka mit brande and mit breke*. Oudfriese terminologie met betrekking tot het rechtsinstituut 'woesting.'" In Oebele Vries, *De taal van recht en vrijheid*. Eds. Anna Popkema, Han Nijdam and Goffe Jensma. *Studies over middeleeuws Friesland*. Gorredijk: Bornmeer, 2012. Pp. 284–307.

———. "Geschichte der Friesen im Mittelalter: West- und Ostfriesland." In *Handbuch des Friesischen. Handbook of Frisian Studies*. Ed. Horst Haider Munske *et al.* Tübingen: Niemeyer, 2001. Pp. 538–550.

Wacks, David. *Framing Iberia: Māqamāt and Frametale Narratives in Medieval Spain*. Leiden: Brill, 2007.

Waddington, Ivan. *The Medical Profession in the Industrial Revolution*. Dublin: Gill and Macmillan, 1984.

Walker, Garthine. *Crime, Gender and Social Order in Early Modern England*. Cambridge: CUP, 2003.

Walker, Sue Sheridan. "Proof of Age of Feudal Heirs in Medieval England." *Mediaeval Studies* 35 (1973): 306–23.

Walker, Timothy. "Acquisition and Circulation of Medical Knowledge within the Early-modern Portuguese Colonial Empire." In *Science in the Spanish and Portuguese Empires, 1500–1800*. Ed. Daniela Bleichmar, Paula de Vos, Kristin Huffine and Kevin Sheehan. Stanford: Stanford University Press, 2009. Pp. 247–70.

Wallis, Faith, and Geneviève Dumas. "Theory and Practice in the Trial of Jean Domrémi, 1423–27." *Journal of the History of Medicine and Allied Sciences* 54 (1999): 55–87.

Ward, Benedicta. *Miracles and the Medieval Mind: Theory, Record, and Event, 1000–1215*. Philadelphia: University of Pennsylvania Press, 1982; rev. 1987.

Watson, Katherine D. "Women, Violent Crime and Criminal Justice in Georgian Wales." *Continuity and Change* 28 (2013): 245–272.

———. *Forensic Medicine in Western Society*. London: Routledge, 2011.

———. "Medical and Chemical Expertise in English Trials for Criminal Poisoning, 1750–1914." *MH* 50 (2006): 373–390.

———. *Poisoned Lives: English Poisoners and their Victims*. London: Hambledon, 2004.

Wear, Andrew, Johanna Geyer-Kordesch and Roger French, eds. *Doctors and Ethics: the Earlier Historical Setting of Professional Ethics*. Amsterdam: Rodopi, 1993.

Weijers, Olga. *Terminologie des universités au xiiie siècle*. Rome: Edizione dell'Ateneo, 1987.

Weinstein, Donald, and Rudolph Bell. *Saints and Society: The Two Words of Western Christendom, 1000–1700*. Chicago: University of Chicago Press, 1982.

Weltecke, Dorothea. "Trust: Some Methodological Reflections." In *Strategies of Writing: Studies on Text and Trust in the Middle Ages*. Ed. Petra Schulte, Marco Mostert and Irene van Renswoude. Turnhout: Brepols, 2008. Pp. 379–92

Wemple, Suzanne F. "Consent and Dissent to Sexual Intercourse in Germanic Societies from the Fifth to the Tenth Century." In *Consent and Coercion to Sex and Marriage in Ancient and Medieval Societies*. Ed. Angeliki E. Laiou. Washington, D.C.: Dumbarton Oaks Research Library and Collection, 1993. Pp. 227–43.

Wessling, Mary Nagle. "Infanticide Trials and Forensic Medicine: Württemberg, 1757–93." In *Legal Medicine in History*. Ed. Michael Clark and Catherine Crawford. Cambridge: CUP, 1994. Pp. 117–144.

Whaley, Leigh. *Women and the Practice of Medical Care in Early Modern Europe, 1400–1800*. New York: Palgrave Macmillan, 2011.

Wheatley, Edward. *Stumbling Blocks before the Blind: Medieval Constructions of a Disability*. Ann Arbor, MI: University of Michigan Press, 2010.

Wiesner, Merry E. "Early Modern Midwifery: A Case Study." In *Women and Work in Preindustrial Europe*. Ed. Barbara A. Hanawalt. Bloomington: Indiana University Press, 1986. Pp. 94–113.

Wilson, Adrian. *The Making of Man-Midwifery: Childbirth in England, 1660–1770*. Cambridge, MA: Harvard University Press, 1995.

Winer, Rebecca Lynn. "Defining Rape in Medieval Perpignan: Women Plaintiffs before the Law." *Viator* 31 (2000): 166–82.

Witowski, Gustave-Joseph Alphonse. *Histoire des accouchements chez tous les peuples*. Paris: G. Steinheil, 1887.

Wolf, Kenneth B. "*Convivencia* in Medieval Spain: a Brief History of an Idea." *Religion Compass* 3 (2008): 72–85.

Woods, Lori. "Mainstream or Marginal Medicine: The Case of a Parish Healer Named Gueraula Codines." In *Worth and Repute: Valuing Gender in Late Medieval and Early Modern Europe. Essays in Honour of Barbara Todd*. Ed. Kim Kippen and Lori Woods. Toronto: Centre for Reformation and Renaissance Studies, 2011. Pp. 93–121.

Woodward, John, and Robert Jütte, eds. *Coping with Sickness: Medicine, Law and Human Rights—Historical Perspectives*. Sheffield: European Association for the History of Medicine and Health Publications, 2000.

Wray, Shona Kelly. "Women, Testaments, and Notarial Culture in Bologna's Contado (1348)." In *Across the Religious Divide: Women, Property, and Law in the Wider Mediterranean (ca. 1300–1800)*. Ed. Shona Kelly Wray and Jutta Sperling. Routledge Research in Gender and History 11. New York and London: Routledge, 2010. Pp. 81–94.

———. *Communities and Crisis: Bologna during the Black Death*. Leiden: Brill, 2009.

————. "Instruments of Concord: Making Peace and Settling Disputes through a Notary in the City and *Contado* of Late Medieval Bologna." *Journal of Social History* 42 (2009): 733–760.

————. "Tracking Family and Flight in Bologna during the Black Death." *Journal of Medieval Prosopography* 25 (2004): 145–160.

————. "Boccaccio and the Doctors: Medicine and Compassion in the Face of Plague." *Journal of Medieval History* 30 (2004): 301–322.

————. "Women, Family, and Inheritance in Bologna during the Black Death." In *Love, Marriage, and Family Ties in the Middle Ages*. Ed. Isabel Davis; Miriam Müller; Sarah Rees Jones. Turnhout: Brepols, 2003. Pp. 205–215.

————. *"Speculum et Exemplar*: The Notaries of Bologna during the Black Death." *Quellen und Forschungen aus italienischen Archiven und Bibliotheken* 81 (2001): 200–227.

————. "The Experience of the Black Death in Bologna as Revealed by the Notarial Records." *Journal of the Rocky Mountain Medieval and Renaissance Association* 14 (1993): 44–64.

Wray, Shona Kelly, and Dennis Dutschke. "Un ritrovato laudario italiano." *Italianistica* 14 (1985): 155–183.

Wray, Shona Kelly, and Jutta Sperling, eds. *Across the Religious Divide: Women, Property, and Law in the Wider Mediterranean (ca. 1300–1800)*. Routledge Research in Gender and History 11. New York and London: Routledge, 2010.

Wright, Michael J.W. "Anglo-Saxon Midwives." *ANQ: A Quarterly Journal of Short Articles, Notes, and Reviews* 11.1 (1998): 3–5.

Young, Sidney. *The Annals of the Barber Surgeons of London*. New York: Blades, East & Blades, 1890.

Zaccagini, Guido. *La vita dei maestri e degli scolari nello Studio di Bologna nei secoli xiii e xiv*. Geneva: Leo S. Olschki, 1926.

Zeppa, Rosario. "San Francesco's Blindness." *Journal of Paleopathology*, 3.3 (1991): 133–35.

Index

378 · INDEX

Visconti family 136, 140n, 146, 191, 194
  Barnabò Visconti 136, 146
  Regina della Scala 136, 146

Wallis, Faith 6
Walter de Bibbesworth 84
waste 9, 14, 159, 166, 172
wergeld (man-price) 19, 26–29, 40–41, 46, 50–51, 54
Western schism 193, 321
William Durandus 133, 147–48
William of Saliceto 97, 178, 180n
wills (*also* testaments, executors) 4, 160, 166–67, 226
witness testimony (*also* deposition) 3–4, 7–12, 22, 51–53, 61, 70–71, 80, 88, 94, 109–11, 115, 119–20, 127, 131–33, 136, 139, 142, 147–48, 150–51, 154–56, 163–64, 172, 226, 319, 323, 326n
Wodehill, Nicholas 18, 21, 247–66, 319, 322
women 6, 10–12, 17, 21, 58, 60–64, 68, 71–79, 81, 83, 86–87, 89–91, 94–101, 103–7,

146, 150, 153–54, 173, 206–7, 216, 220–28, 230–31, 233–38, 240–41, 250n, 252, 275n, 288, 290–91, 305, 316, 318, 320–21, 324–26
healers (*also* midwives) 10–11, 13n, 17, 20, 58–87, 96–110, 129, 177n, 179n, 187, 198–99, 201, 220, 223–25, 318, 321, 323n, 324–26
wounding (*also* assault) 3, 9–12, 19, 34, 95, 105–6, 114, 119, 123–24, 126, 132, 144–45, 251–52, 265, 297, 301–10, 313–15, 317, 319, 323
wound, assessment of 3, 9, 33–34, 40, 42–51, 53–56, 94, 105, 109–56, 259, 274, 282, 305–06, 313, 317, 319
  man 54–55
  treatment of 23, 42, 44, 46–48, 51, 56–57, 257, 259–61
Wray, Shona Kelly 1–7, 15, 18
Wright, Michael J.W. 65

York 74, 102, 168, 248–51, 264–65

zodiac man 54

Printed in the United States
By Bookmasters